INDIES STEAMSHIP LINES

| PORTO RICO LINE |
| WARD LINE |

Tons—*Operating 21,906 Miles*

d all Principal Ports on the South Atlantic, Gulf of Mexico and Carribean Sea, Mexico, Cuba, San Domingo, Porto Rico

PORTO RICO LINE

12 Steamers, aggregating 32,620 tons, operating 5,900 miles

DIRECT SERVICE
Between
NEW YORK, NEW ORLEANS, GALVESTON
PORT ARTHUR and points on the Island
of PORTO RICO

DIRECT SAILINGS
Between
NEW YORK, SAN JUAN, PONCE, MAYAGUEZ
Weekly

NEW ORLEANS, SAN JUAN, PONCE
MAYAGUEZ
Three Sailings Monthly

GALVESTON, PORT ARTHUR, PORTO RICO
Monthly Service

PORTO RICO ISLAND SERVICE
Frequent Service

Through Bills of Lading issued to Aguadilla,
Arecibo, Arroyo, Humacao and Fajardo.

New York & Porto Rico Steamship Co.
12 Broadway
NEW YORK

WARD LINE

20 Steamers aggregating 78,383 tons, operating 6,823 miles

DIRECT SAILINGS
Between
NEW YORK, HAVANA, CUBA
Tri-Weekly

NEW YORK, CIENFUEGOS
Weekly

NEW YORK, GUANTANAMO, SANTIAGO AND
MANZANILLO
Bi-Weekly

NEW YORK, TAMPICO, MEXICO
Weekly

NEW YORK, PROGRESO, YUCATAN
Weekly

NEW YORK, VERA CRUZ, MEXICO
Weekly

NEW YORK, NASSAU, BAHAMAS
Fortnightly

New York & Cuba Mail Steamship Co.
Pier 14, East River
NEW YORK

SCHEDULES, RATES AND DETAILED INFORMATION PROMPTLY UPON APPLICATION

LLS OF LADING TO ALL POINTS

RLD THROUGH THE AGWI LINES' CHARTERING DEPARTMENT, 12 BROADWAY

St. Wharf	MOBILE, ALA., Mallory Line Wharf	PHILADELPHIA, PA., 701 Chestnut St.
Strand	NORFOLK, VA., Clyde Line Wharf	TAMPA, FLA., 509 Franklin St.
West Bay St.	NEW YORK, 290 Broadway	WILMINGTON, N. C., Clyde Line Wharf

full description of the various ports and countries to which the AGWI Lines operate

THE AMERICAN MARITIME LIBRARY: VOLUME IV

The Mallorys of Mystic

Packet ship *Eliza Mallory*, launched by the Mallory yards in 1851. Ran in intercoastal and transoceanic service until lost on the Florida coast in 1859. Courtesy Mystic Seaport.

The Mallorys of Mystic

SIX GENERATIONS IN AMERICAN

MARITIME ENTERPRISE

By

JAMES P. BAUGHMAN

Published for

THE MARINE HISTORICAL ASSOCIATION, INCORPORATED, MYSTIC SEAPORT

by

WESLEYAN UNIVERSITY PRESS

Middletown, Connecticut

ISBN: 0-8195-4048-x

Library of Congress Catalog Card Number: 70-184363
Manufactured in the United States of America
First edition

For Susan

CONTENTS

LIST OF ILLUSTRATIONS

xi

LIST OF ILLUSTRATIONS

LIST OF TABLES AND FIGURES

ACKNOWLEDGEMENTS

THE author's special thanks go to the following individuals who graciously allowed him to interview them in person or by mail concerning the Mallory family enterprises: F. Willard Bergen, David M. Brush, W. Lyle Bull, Frank M. Bynum, Frank A. Dwyer, George J. Farrell, J. Ellis Knowles, Huntington T. Morse, Maitland Smith, and William N. Westerlund. These interviews and this correspondence have been made a part of the Mallory Family Papers at the Marine Historical Association, Inc.

Particular thanks also go to the following individuals, who patiently guided the author through the manuscript collections, corporate records, or libraries for which they are responsible: Gerald E. Morris and Charles R. Schultz of the G. W. Blunt White Library of the Marine Historical Association, Inc.; Robert W. Lovett of the Baker Library, Harvard University Graduate School of Business Administration; C. Y. Chen and James C. Clark of Marine Transport Lines Inc.; Cecille McDonald of Cadwalader, Wickersham & Taft; and John L. Lochead of the Mariners Museum. In addition, I wish to express appreciation to Robert G. Albion, Robert Evans, Jr., Thomas F. Godfrey, Ralph W. Hidy, Arthur M. Johnson, John H. Kemble, Henrietta M. Larson, Josephine M. Peck, Fritz Redlich, and Leonard A. Swan, Jr., who shared valuable research notes and ideas freely in the best traditions of scholarship.

My thanks also to the Editorial Advisory Board of the American Maritime Library, Marion V. Brewington, Robert E. Farlow, Benjamin W. Labaree, and Willard M. Wallace, who offered valuable criticisms; to Helen Grey, coordinator of publications for the Marine Historical Association, Inc.; and to

Barbara Kovitz, Joanne Haire, Toni Robbins, Christine Fursten-berg, and Meredith Barker who typed numerous drafts and handled assorted research and editorial chores.

My deepest gratitude is reserved for the three men most responsible for this book. Charles W. David, former assistant to the president and director of library development for the Marine Historical Association, Inc., conceived of the project, enlisted the author's original interest, and was a source of unfailing encouragement throughout. Philip R. Mallory was similarly supportive and most generous in sharing his recollections of his family's past. Clifford D. Mallory, Jr., a true friend, was a mine of valuable information and in all respects the catalyst for the project during its research and writing stages. To each of these men I owe special thanks.

Portions of the research for this book were supported by a research fellowship from the Marine Historical Association, Inc. Small incidental expenses were also covered by funds from the Division of Research of the Harvard University Graduate School of Business Administration. For this support I am most appreciative.

Throughout the research and writing of this book, I have interacted with dozens of individuals, corporations, and academic institutions. As a precondition of these interactions, I requested and in all cases received freedom of access to and interpretation of the information I sought. Thus, it is I who bear full burden for the facts and opinions presented herein.

James P. Baughman

The Mallorys of Mystic

Introduction:

〜〜〜〜〜〜〜〜〜〜〜〜〜〜〜〜〜〜〜〜〜〜〜〜〜〜〜〜〜

A BUSINESS, A FAMILY, AND A TRADITION,

1760–1941

"... death only will make me pull down the flag of Mallory."
—Henry R. Mallory to E. M. Bulkley, December 7, 1906

THE United States is bordered by three seas, and its maritime industries have always been considered "in the national interest." Native American by law in ownership, equipment, and personnel, the United States merchant marine and its attendant enterprises have provided livelihoods for millions of individuals and thousands of firms. Yet few American industries have suffered such severe challenges to business success. There have been the episodic and romanticized dangers of pirates, press gangs, blockades, and storms; and the less colorful but more chronic rivalries of sail and steam, of ships and railroads, and of aggressively nationalistic shipping policies.

In view of these hazards, many Americans have approached the sea with only short-run interest: as an adventurous lark; as a physical toughener; as a windfall of profits because of a war, a gold rush, or a nation's taste for tea. Even men of longer commitment have ultimately forsaken the sea to recast their energy and capital into ventures ashore. Some moved unwillingly, as did whalers beached by kerosene and steel corset stays; others knowingly, as did Rowland Macy from whaling to retailing or the Browns of Providence and Commodore Vanderbilt, who saw more profitable employment in factories and railroads for fortunes born at sea.

But other businessmen never "came ashore." They stuck by the sea, accepting its hazards and its declining position in

America as supplier of food and carrier of commerce. Some diversified their risk by adding nonmaritime investments to their portfolios. Others remained maritime specialists, bearing risks and pursuing profits within the limitations set by their preoccupation.

Because of its inherent drama and its obvious economic and political importance, the American merchant marine has received considerable attention from historians. There are the fine studies of ports, trade routes, and ships by Samuel E. Morison, Robert G. Albion, Carl C. Cutler, David B. Tyler, and Howard I. Chapelle. There is the comprehensive industry history by John G. B. Hutchins.

Curiously, however, there have been very few studies of individual American maritime entrepreneurs from which industry-level studies may draw the flesh and bones of life. With only a few exceptions, those that have appeared deal with the late colonial and early national periods and focus on men or firms to whom maritime enterprise was a means rather than an end. These works typically deal with merchants who, because of uncertainties in market information and water transport, vertically integrated their trading enterprises so as to own or control the vessels that carried their goods: Byron Fairchild's *Messrs. William Pepperrell,* Kenneth W. Porter's *John Jacob Astor* and *The Jacksons and the Lees,* Stuart Buchey's *Robert Oliver,* Robert A. Davison's *Isaac Hicks,* and Elva Tooker's *Nathan Trotter* come immediately to mind.

These works are welcome and important, but they do not meet the need for more and better studies of American maritime specialists—those individuals and firms to whom maritime enterprise was an end in itself. A few such studies have been published, such as Wheaton J. Lane's *Commodore Vanderbilt,* Leonard A. Swann's *John Roach,* and my own *Charles Morgan.* More are welcome.

It is in this context that the book has been written. For the Mallory family of Mystic, Connecticut and New York City provides a remarkably continuous example of American maritime entrepreneurship in action. Since 1760, six consecutive generations of Mallorys have gone down to the sea to harvest its produce and carry its trade. Their commitment to seafaring under the American flag has been unswerving—often in the face of more profitable opportunities elsewhere—and encompasses sailmaking, sealing, whaling, salvage, brokerage, shipbuilding, and coastal and transoceanic carriage in everything from clipper ships to oil tankers. They have sustained a place in the forefront of their industry despite changing transport technologies, obsolescences in traditional cargoes and trade routes, and vacillations in public policies toward shipping.

Using the Mallorys as subjects, this study is offered as a business biography of an important and representative set of American maritime specialists: important in the diversity, longevity, and scale of their enterprises; representative because their experience approximates something between a normative and optimal competitive solution of the prospects and problems of their industry. This book is plainly and simply a case study intended to complement more aggregative industry studies of the sort mentioned above. It is as much personal history as it is institutional history and vulnerable to criticisms leveled at those approaches to understanding of the past. It is most emphatically not intended to be the economic analogue of a campaign biography of the Mallorys.

The "inside-out" perspective that permeates this book was not idly chosen. It was consciously selected as the best way of bringing to center stage the perceptions and behavior of men engaged in the day-to-day competitive struggle. These men were doers, not theorists or conceptualizers. They acted more often than they reflected. They were self-styled, with self-styled definitions of utility, propriety, progress, and success. They interacted both creatively and destructively with their environment. Their history is important because it illuminates the untidy, intensely human, and microscopic processes of economic life that underlie tidier, more impersonal, and macroscopic measurements and evaluations of economic change.

But there is far more to the Mallorys' history than pursuit of profit. What follows is business history in its analysis of the interaction of private, profit-seeking, economic decision-makers and their environment. It is equally the social and economic history of a family's intensely personal character and tradition—elements as important as profits in plotting and steering the courses laid.

For the Mallorys, a sense of family and tradition has been ever and acutely present in business life. The forming of tradition is, of course, seldom conscious. Rather, it consists of an accretion of principles, precedents, and symbols which comes to affect the actions of men. Those so affected need not realize the source or strength of their persuasion; nor will they always admit to traditionalistic elements in their decisions. Yet even the most "modern" or "forward-looking" man may still be guided into the future by what has gone before, frequently not questioning those traditions, always acting in a manner consistent with them. Such was the case with the Mallorys. Family and tradition affected their setting of business priorities and goals, organization, management succession, and competitive practices. In both strategic and tactical situations precedent could override profit. Thus, to understand their business, one must also comprehend what was "given" as a result of their heritage.

The family has been intensely American, Protestant, and Republican. And the custodian of its tradition and its spiritual and material arbiter has been "Father." For the period of greatest business activity this meant, successively: Charles (1796–1882); Charles Henry (1818–1890); Henry Rogers (1848–1919); and Clifford Day (1881–1941). They were in each case (save Henry Rogers) the eldest son of their generation, and all held their position by law (as executors and trustees under their fathers' estates) and by seniority in family and firm.

While personalities differed and could clash, family solidarity remained firm. Intimacy of fathers and sons in life meant continuity at death. Thus Charles Henry administered his father's estate and its bequests to himself and his brothers. Henry Rogers and Clifford Day performed similar services for their sires. The problem of one family member became the problem of all: employment or venture capital could be supplied through the firm; personal financial wants could be lessened by family-wide assessments levied by the current family head. Each generation looked not only to its own affairs but also to the care and comfort of the next, with the major share

6

of each estate invested in testamentary trusts for those surviving. Philanthropy was generous, but never took precedence over or exceeded the provisions for loved ones.

Interwoven with these traditions of religious principle, family precedence, and trust was a tradition of the sea. Part of this maritime heritage was born of geography. Charles Mallory lived and raised his family close to the wharves of Mystic. His sons grew up in the sail loft and shipyard, prowled the waterfront, and fished and sailed the waters of Long Island Sound. Charles Henry Mallory moved his home to Brooklyn in 1865, and for his sons and theirs the teeming waters of the Port of New York were ever near at hand. Young Mallorys were trained to sail as soon as they could grasp a tiller, and seafaring for pleasure was both result and reinforcement of the family's business. Home life, education, and recreation combined into a tradition of family interdependence and succession and dedication to the sea. This heritage was transmitted through employment and equity in the firm with appropriate ritual and symbol: the house flag became the family coat of arms.

What emerged was a commitment to the family enterprise and to seafaring that rose far above the economics of the market place: the business existed to make profits but also to be improved and passed on to succeeding generations; and, the sea was not to be abandoned for the farm, factory, or forum. To violate these precepts was unspeakable.

The Mallorys' moral code and commitment to the sea set the bounds of their business environment. While decisions within their maritime frame of reference were primarily economically motivated and "businesslike," decisions involving the framework itself were most often swayed by tradition. While they were ubiquitous in the breadth and range of their maritime activities, they remained maritime specialists, nevertheless.

Thus, the Mallorys form a valuable case study in American maritime history: a family of businessmen who chose not to abandon the sea but, rather, to dedicate their lives to mastery of its natural and man-made currents. Their experiences in this quest illustrate some of the individual, profit-oriented responses induced by broader patterns of American economic development. Similarly, their problems in mobilizing goods, services, and ideas are reflections of broader imperfections in those markets. Yet it is precisely this interaction of men and environment which is the essence of business history. In short, the Mallory story is essentially how a declining industry could still be profitably rationalized by businessmen of prideful heritage, specialized skill, and energetic adaptability.

Chapter 1

〜〜〜〜〜〜〜〜〜〜〜〜〜〜〜〜〜〜〜〜〜〜〜〜〜〜〜〜〜〜〜

CHARLES MALLORY, SAILMAKER,

1816–1853

" 'Ships? There would always be ships.' And what were ships
without sails?"—Carl C. Cutler, *Greyhounds of the Sea*

THE visitor to Mystic Seaport in Connecticut sooner or later
stands before an imposing three-story wooden building appropriately placed between the Greenman shipyard and
the square-riggers at the water's edge. As his eye inevitably
ascends to a splendid weather vane in the shape of a sperm
whale, it passes a simple sign, "Charles Mallory, Sailmaker."
Curiosity aroused, our visitor may venture in and climb the
massive wooden steps to the sail loft itself. He notices the
purposeful clutter of tools and the pot-bellied stove suspended
above the floor so that work might be safely spread beneath.
But his overwhelming sensation is one of smell: of canvas,
cordage, leather, tallow, beeswax, tar, and sweat soaked into the
walls and floors that surround him. If he wrinkles his nose and
draws away, he is a lubber born and lubber he will die. If he
breathes deeper so as to savor the fragrances of ships and the
sea, he cannot but ask: What sort of life was this? What sort of
men were these?
To these questions we answer: Come about. Bear toward
the Mallory Building farther along the cobbled water-front
street. Here beneath its owner's piercing gaze, but often over-
looked by visitors amidst more eye-catching portraits, ship
models, and memorabilia, lies Charles Mallory's sailmaker's
palm. Few tools are as simple; few are so functional; yet few are
so intensely personal. Sweat-soaked and stained by the push-
pull of uncalculable stitches, it molded itself to its master's

hand—measuring his grasp, manifesting his strength. To touch it is to touch a man, a family, and a beginning.

Mallory had deep roots in Connecticut. He was a fifth-generation American and a sixth-generation New Englander. His principal forebear, Peter Mallory, had come from England to New Haven before 1644 and had sired the next in line, another Peter, in 1653. The family moved to Stratford, where Charles's great-grandfather Stephen was born in 1694, and later to Milford, where were born his grandfather Moses in 1724 and his father David in 1760.

The family was Protestant and of ordinary station. Peter Sr. was variously a chimney sweep, a small planter, and a speculator in tobacco and lands. His son was a shoemaker, although married in 1678 to Elizabeth Trowbridge, who was descended from two prominent New Haven merchant families, the Trowbridges and the Lambertons. Stephen was a ferryman, and Moses is remembered only for his impressed service as a private in Peck's Company of Connecticut troops during the Revolutionary War.[1]

But Charles grew up in a remarkable household. Born in Waterford on February 24, 1796, he was the eighth of the ten children of David and Amy Crocker Malary (as they spelled the name). His mother, as recalled by her eldest grandson, "was a jovial, jolly woman, quick-witted and fond of fun—never a sick day in her life—never had a headache, and died of old age at the age of 96." David Malary "was a big, raw-boned, horny-handed man," who "had a greater share of Faith than most men. He was deeply religious, but not bigoted, and belonged to the Baptist Church."[2] But his mature sobriety masked a daring youth. When his father had been drafted into the Continental Army, sixteen-year-old David volunteered as his substitute. After six months, he re-enlisted, served three years with Pond's Company, Meigs's Connecticut Regiment, and saw action in the Sag Harbor and Compo expeditions. In 1779, he "resigned" from the army and shipped out under an assumed name aboard the New London privateer *Oliver Cromwell.*

The vessel already had an enviable prize record under the dashing Captain Seth Harding. Sailing now under Captain Timothy Parker, she took four prizes in Long Island Sound before being captured by three British frigates in June 1779. Young Malary and the rest of her crew were confined to the infamous prison ship Jersey until their exchange in August. Malary immediately sailed again as a privateersman, was again captured, confined in Jersey, and exchanged. He shipped out a third time, only to be recaptured. He escaped, returned to privateering, but was again taken prisoner after a "battle with a British gunboat." Malary escaped again, however, in the confusion of General Benedict Arnold's occupation of New London. He led one of his Hessian guards "to a case of gin, secured his gun while he was drinking, made him his prisoner, and marched him to the American line and surrendered him." A fifth cruise as a privateer cut short Malary's seagoing career when he fell between his ship and its wharf and was seriously injured. His resulting disability forced him ashore, where he settled in Waterford as a farmer and butcher.[3]

With so salty a parent, small wonder several of David Malary's children followed seafaring occupations: daughter Amy married John Rogers, a caulker and sometime seaman of New London; son Richard became a ship's cooper; daughter Sally married a sailmaker, Nathan Beebe of Bank Street, New London; and both Charles and his brother Nathan were apprenticed to Beebe's craft.

Thus young Charles was no stranger to the water front or to hard work and discipline. He lived at home during his common-school years, but at twelve was "put out" in New London with a Mr. Christopher, a neighbor of the Beebes on Bank Street. "I done the chores about the house and helped him over at the mill," Charles recalled, earning $3.40 to $4.00 per month and keep until apprenticed for seven years to his brother-in-law Beebe in 1810.[4]

Beebe was "an excellent workman and a man of pleasing parts, when in his normal mind," but apparently liked his rum, and his "overruling vice caused him to neglect his business." He "often said that Charles Malary was the likeliest apprentice he had ever had," but he was far from the kindest of masters himself. Twice Charles ran away but voluntarily returned. And between August 16 and 22, 1814, he was mustered as a militia private in the aftermath of the British attack on nearby Stonington. But his dislike for his brother-in-law and his restlessness did not deter him from learning and perfecting his craft. At eighteen, he became Beebe's foreman, an unusual honor for an apprentice, and his indenture was commuted to six years (one senses a family compromise and Beebe's realization of Charles's worth to an otherwise slovenly shop). He remained beyond his contractual obligation for six months at $1.25 per day and board (25 cents above the going wage for journeymen), but soon he and Beebe quarreled again, over the latter's refusal to repay a 75 cent loan, and the employment terminated.[5]

Thus on Christmas Day 1816, a twenty-year-old Charles Malary (he spelled it thus until 1826) counted his cash on hand of $1.25, slung his tools and single change of clothes on his back, crossed the Groton ferry, and swung off on foot to pursue his craft on his own account. His arguments with Beebe had lessened his chances of employment in New London, and he had already tried to find work in Essex to no avail. Now he was on his way to Boston, where sailmakers were reputedly in demand. His tale of what followed was told so often that it became the foundation of his family's subsequent tradition of maritime enterprise. Fifty-four years later, his eldest son could still recite "Father's Christmas Story" almost verbatim and recall the pleasure with which it was annually recounted to the assembled Mallory clan:

> . . . At this time the Government was doing a large business in building ships on Lake Erie and his object was to stop on the way, earn money enough to pay his expenses, and finally reach the Lakes. Mr. Beebe had been doing work for the fishermen in Mystic, a small hamlet on the Mystic River about seven miles east of New London, and my father was acquainted with many of the fishermen. He arrived there on Christmas Day and found some of his old acquaintances playing ball in what was called Randalls Orchard.
>
> Here he picked up his first job in repairing a suit of sails for a fishing smack. After this was done another offered, and he continued to work expecting when his last job was done to pack up and start on his way to the Lakes via Boston. In the course of a short time his acquaintances extended to Stonington and Westerly. After working about six months he concluded to settle.,. . .[6]

When Mallory arrived in 1816, the Mystic River Valley already counted some two hundred years of history. A battleground for the Pequots and Narragansets even before English settlement in 1650, the area was jointly claimed by Connecticut and Rhode Island until early in the eighteenth century. In 1664 the Connecticut town of Stonington set its boundaries eastward at the Pawcatuck River and westward at the Mystic. In 1703 the Connecticut-Rhode Island line was fixed at the Pawcatuck, and in 1705 the town of Groton separated from New London and established its western boundary at the Thames River and its eastern limit at the Mystic.

These developments placed each bank of the Mystic in a different Connecticut town and raised jurisdictional peculiarities which survive even today: residents of the west bank must look to Groton for government and public services, while those on the east bank are similarly tied to Stonington. This political artificiality interfered little with settlement, however. Near the mouth of the river, on its Groton side, arose the village of Noank. Farther upriver, at the best ford, grew Portersville, later known as Mystic Bridge, which has become today's Mystic. Some three miles farther inland lay Head of the River, today known as Old Mystic.

The Mystic area was much more an economic than a political entity. The valley's land was arable, but its fine stands of timber, several protected anchorages, and shelving river banks were more conducive to maritime pursuits. From its earliest settlement, Mystic men and ships roamed the fishing grounds and coasting trades from Nova Scotia to Hatteras and were well represented on the sea lanes of the Atlantic, the Caribbean, and the Pacific.

Young Mallory soaked up his new home's maritime heritage. His first lodging was with Captain Jeremiah Holmes. In younger days, Holmes had been impressed by a British man-of-war for three years but escaped—some said with a knife in each hand. His excellent gun laying, learned in the Royal Navy, had ironically driven off the British attack on Stonington in 1814.

At the Holmes fireside the tales were frequent and long about other Mystic men such as Captain Jeremiah Haley, who had fought off a Royal Marine landing party near Noank in 1813; or the Fannings: John, who had served with Jones in *Bonhomme Richard*; and Edmund, who by 1799 had twice circumnavigated the globe (the first American-flag captain, vessel, and crew to do so), discovered Fanning and Palmyra islands, and in *Volunteer* and *Sea Fox* during 1815-1817 was exploring the sealing grounds off the Falklands.

But much more than tales of derring-do fascinated the young sailmaker. Always practical, he was more interested in the shipyards which lined the Mystic River as these were directly related to the demand for his skill. As early as the 1680's, boats, sloops, shallops, and smacks were abuilding in the area and by 1816 several yards capable of larger vessels were in operation. The twisting five-mile river, which was characterized by shelving bends and points, was an ideal shipbuilding site. At Noank were the Lathams and the Morgans. Near Portersville was the Packers' yards, and Benjamin Morrell was active at the Narrows (between Portersville and Head of the River). At Head of the River were the Burrowses (on the Groton side) and the Leedses (on the Stonington side), and master carpenters and launching sites for smaller vessels were available at numerous other points along the river.[7]

Mallory opened for business on the Stonington side of the river near Portersville.[8] For his first loft, he hired a section of "the Old Red Store owned by Asa Fish," an "old weather-beaten building" that suited his needs and produced the second installment of his "Christmas story":

> The shop was a cold place to work. Some of the clapboards were off and the icy air from the river numbed his fingers, no matter how fast he plied the needle or stirred about. He heard that a man named Denison who lived at the head of the river had a sheet iron stove to sell. After his day's work he walked to Denison's, saw the stove, but balked at the price. Not that he thought $2.50 was too big a sum, but he did not have so much money with him. "How are you going to get the stove down to your place," asked Denison. "I shall carry it on my back," answered Mallory. Denison looked at the powerful young man and said, "If that is the case, you take the stove and I will call and collect for it." With the stove on his back, Mallory walked three miles through the frosty night with the snow six inches deep and never stopped till he reached his sailloft.[9]

As a sailmaker, Mallory's expertise related to all shipboard fabrics. These included the myriad sails as well as canvas hose, tarpaulins, awnings, "coats" (covers), hammocks, and sacking—and associated ropes, twines, metal fitting, and leatherwork. Occasionally, he might stitch up a set of colors for a ship, as well. He worked closely with the rigger, whose responsibility encompassed the running and standing lines and tackle which supported the masts and manipulated the yards, booms, gaffs, and sails. Both had to be masters of "marlinspike seamanship," but the crafts were separate.

Mallory's tools were simple and his capital investment small. There were dividers, protractors, and squares to lay off sail plans on paper and then to transfer them to the loft floor as full-size patterns. There was a folio-size plan book in which he recorded scale drawings of popular or successful designs and which facilitated reorders by the same vessel even from miles away. There was a cashbook to enter orders, record payments, and keep inventories. Most important, of course, there were his bench and its contents: palms and needles; fids, spikes, prickers, and stabbers for splicing line, forming grommets, and working cloth; serving mallets and boards to tighten stitches and reinforce ropes; knives and shears for cloth, rope, and twine; rubbers to flatten stitches and seams. Nearby were sail hooks, fid blocks, tackle, and jigs to hold sails and boltropes taut for working, and, of course, a stencil, inkpot, and brush to trademark his finished products.

His raw materials were even simpler: duck; twine; beeswax to lubricate and preserve the twine; tallow to lubricate splices; cordage for boltropes; leather for sheathing and jackets; and such miscellaneous hardware as clew irons, thimbles, eyes, and grommets. [10] Wax, tallow, leather, and some hardware he obtained locally. Cordage and most hardware, the former by the pound and the latter by the piece, he bought from various New York houses. Duck and twine came from the factory of John Colt & Co. of Paterson, New Jersey.

Mallory's preference for Colt's products marks him as a progressive sailmaker indeed. Colt and Seth Bemis of Watertown, Massachusetts, had been the leaders in developing American substitutes for European linen duck (called "Russian" regardless of origin). Under the pressure of shortages during the Napoleonic Wars, and as part of the general development of domestic textile production, Bemis had begun the handloom manufacture of American *cotton* duck in 1809 and introduced the power loom to that line in 1816. Colt opened his famous Passaic Mill No. 1 in 1814 to manufacture yarns and twine from American flax, added linen duck in 1817, converted to cotton products in 1822, and added power looms in 1824. "Colt's Duck Mill" brand canvas and twines dominated the American market by 1825 because of their strength and because they contained none of the starching and dressing which made earlier ducks less pliable and more likely to mildew.[11]

Mallory was using Colt's duck and twine exclusively by the 1820's, and he derived a large share of his income as a sailmaker from the perquisites and sales commissions allowed him by the manufacturer. He placed his orders and made his remittances by mail and received his goods by coastwise shipment. Colt paid all freight, but Mallory absorbed inventory costs. Ownership of the goods remained with Colt until they were sold by the sailmaker. Mallory received a 5 per cent commission on his gross sales of duck and twine, and an additional 5 per cent on those sales made for cash. He also received a flat "sailmakers' perquisite" of 25 cents per bolt of duck sold.

In his dealings with Colt, Mallory was a middleman, not a consumer. His relationship to the factory was as agent, not as purchaser. He was responsible for finding a market and setting the price for the goods which he ordered. But he received commissions for his services rather than profits from any markup between the factory and the selling price (see Table 1.1).

This system was usual in the trade and encouraged the sailmaker to sell at the highest possible prices, and preferably for cash, since commissions were based on gross value of sales. It placed great trust in his integrity, too, as he was on his honor to report the true price and volume of his sales to a manufacturer many miles away. Mallory kept this faith with Colt throughout his sailmaking years.[12]

Mallory's second source of income as a sailmaker was his labor charges. These were based on his craft skill (unlike his middleman's income, which was managerial in origin) and repre-

sented the value he added to duck, twine, rope, and hardware by manufacturing them into sails. His tasks and their attendant charges were remarkably standardized (see Table 1.2) and, when compared in form and amount with those of his contemporaries in New London, Cape Cod, and New York, they suggest the existence of an upper-Atlantic-coast standard as well. But standard practice could still be internally complex and contradictory. Mallory mixed piecework and timework and, prior to 1829, calculated rates in shillings and pence as often as in dollars and cents; yet his sums were always totaled in the latter. His cashbooks also record payments in labor, flour, "old canvass," lobsters, and other "kind" in the settlement of accounts.

Reading between the lines of these cashbooks, one sees Mallory grow as an active and successful craftsman-capitalist. His first set of books was opened on January 1, 1818, and record only three sailmaking jobs in his first six weeks of enterprise. These are interspersed with wages earned "skowing" wood downriver and "farming" to supplement his income. By the 1820's, however, the young sailmaker had come into his own.

Mallory's daybooks for the periods January 20, 1826–January 18, 1830, and October 8, 1832–August 13, 1835, have survived. Although ledger accounts and profit-and-loss accounts for these periods are not available, the daybooks give a rough idea of the scope and volume of the Mallory sail loft. They record 2,582 separate jobs, an average of just over one per possible working day. In all, during these accounting periods, Mallory worked on 228 different vessels: 13 ships, 2 barks, 17 brigs, 61 schooners, 29 sloops, and 106 smacks. He also handled all of his own correspondence and bookkeeping and the foremanship of a growing work force.

As his business grew, and in periods of heavy work, Mallory employed local or itinerant seamen who could turn a fair stitch at 1 cent to 1¼ cents per yard sewn. He preferred, however, to hire journeymen sailmakers on a more regular basis. He arranged for the latters' housing and sustenance and carried them on account in his books. They were debited with cash and supplies advanced to them, with days lost, with bills and notes paid off for them, and with rent, board, and provisions. They were

17

credited with labor performed at 92 cents per diem (ten hours) and with variable allowances for "night work." Balances were struck irregularly between master and journeymen to settle these accounts.

Mallory's earliest known journeymen were his brother Nathan and William Gibson, who worked for him in the early 1820's. Between 1825 and 1835, his most regular employees were Grover C. King, Jeremiah Beebe, Thornton Paillon (or Paillou), and William N. Grant. All worked more than half of that period; Beebe stayed the longest; but Grant was evidently the most able. On June 25, 1833, Grant was given an extra stipend of $30 per year "for clothing and washing," and on April 1, 1838, he was admitted as Mallory's partner. The loft's name then became "Mallory & Grant, Sailmakers."

A different perspective on Mallory's volume of business and income is gleaned from his accounts with John Colt & Co. (see Table 1.3). Again the accounts are only partial and suggestive. Mallory's gross income from sales of Colt's duck and twine is calculated by adding his commissions and perquisites: $4,075 or 12 per cent of gross sales of $35,297—roughly $679 per year. These figures represent, of course, only Mallory's income as sales agent for materials and would have to be combined with his labor charges to total his gross sailmaking income. This is not possible because of lack of business records.[13]

Mallory quickly established himself as the most skillful and busiest sailmaker between New London and Providence. He was always to be seen wherever ships were building, outfitting, or refitting—if not on business, at least to listen and learn. Though quiet, modest, and unostentatiously formal, his lanky, raw-boned frame, mutton-chop whiskers, and deep-set, almost hypnotic eyes gave him a commanding presence. As a personal friend was to recall, "throughout the world-wide range of his acquaintances there will be nowhere found a tongue to whisper aught against his integrity or his broad Christian charity. It is the universal expression of all who know him that 'Charles Mallory is an honest man.' "[14]

Mallory's rise in business was matched by added responsibilities at home and increasing prominence in community affairs. He had joined the First Congregational Church upon

settling in Mystic in 1817 and became its staunchest supporter. There he married Eliza Rogers of New London on February 22, 1818, and there was christened their first child, Charles Henry, who was born prematurely on September 30 in the "chamber" the young couple had "hired" from Captain Jerry Holmes. Like his father, Charles Mallory certainly "had a greater share of faith than most men." He had no interest in politics and proudly claimed throughout his life that he had never attended a picnic or had a lawsuit. God, family, and business in that order were his life. He regularly attended the Presbyterian and Congregational sermons at the Road Meeting House and the Baptist revivals at Groton Schoolhouse. He helped found the nonsectarian Mariners Free Church of Mystic and sang in its choir. He would ride miles on horseback for a camp meeting or to hear a new itinerant preacher. No wonder his eldest son's earliest recollections (except for "visiting the sail loft") were "the music and exhortations" of the Sabbath and learning "to 'intone' as well as the best of them." [15]

Reflection upon Mallory's character and early success, however, must not obscure some of the realities of his business prospects. Both shipping and cotton textiles were still growth industries in the 1820's, and Mallory benefitted from the prosperity of both. In his own particular circumstances as a sailmaker, however, there were barriers to continued growth along old lines and beckonings to diversify along new.

While the demand for sails in the United States in general and the Mystic area in particular was still increasing in the 1820's, the consignment-selling policies of duck and twine manufacturers limited the sailmaker's share in gross sales of materials to 10 to 12 per cent. Further, we can see in retrospect that prices for cotton sailcloth and twine were almost constant over the years 1815-1861. This retrospective view confirms the perceptive sailmakers' intuitive understanding that to increase his sales volume was the only way to raise his chances of profit. He knew that to expect any large increase in the value he received per unit on sales of materials was foolish unless the commission and perquisite system was abandoned; and that was not likely.

Second, he knew that the bulk of his income and profits

came from his labor charges. His wage level was twice that of a common laborer, but he was severely limited in potential earnings by the low productivity of handwork and the ease by which marginal competitors could appear and undercut his prices—in a pinch, almost any sailor could "rough stitch" a sail. Again, retrospective knowledge confirms the intelligent sailmaker's view. Sailmakers' money wages did increase about 60 per cent between 1820 and 1850, but their real wages increased only about half of that amount. Not until the innovation of the sewing machine (which was accomplished between 1870 and 1890) were these interrelationships to be altered and the productivity of individual sail lofts substantially increased. Thus, while a sailmaker of the 1820's could certainly expect steady employment in his lifetime, as far as the ambitious young Mallory could see it would be employment at only gradually increasing profit levels. There would be few chances of innovational profits or windfalls and little likelihood of large returns on investment from sailmaking itself.[16]

Mallory might have been content to remain a sailmaker under these conditions, but he obviously aspired to more. He realized that his craft placed him in daily contact with both business information and entrepreneurial possibilities. His ability and his integrity were widely known, and his business horizons steadily lengthened and broadened under the dual stimuli of environmental opportunities and his own desires.

There is no doubt that Mallory's own talent and drive found a ready market. Before 1850, and indeed throughout the nineteenth century, the United States suffered persistent irregularities and limitations of supply in some of its most basic resources, goods, and services. Coupled with the social mobility of the American work force, these circumstances reduced some chances of labor specialization, but spawned a generation of "men, whose flexibility equalled their energy" and who "flourished in a social order that permitted them freely to shift from task to task, wherever the opportunity of gain appeared."[17] In the triangle of eastern Connecticut bounded by New London, Norwich, and Pawcatuck—just as in countless other economic regions in the United States—these general inducements for men of energy and purpose to multiply their enterprises were reinforced by visible opportunities for gain. But because of the immaturity of both the national and the regional economies, capital markets were small, financial intermediaries lacking, and the difficulties of mobilizing savings for productive investment great. [18] In overcoming these difficulties, men like Mallory came to play important economic roles far transcending their particular entrepreneurial activities.

There were few formal financial intermediaries in Mallory's section of Connecticut prior to 1848. Norwich (with four commercial banks, a mutual savings bank, and a marine insurance company) and New London (with three commercial banks, a mutual savings bank, and a marine insurance company) were Mallory's nearest large financial centers. Closer to home were the Stonington Bank, opened in that village in May 1822 by Mallory's long-time friend and sometime associate Charles P. Williams, and the Mystic Bank, incorporated at Head of the River in May 1833, by his neighbors, the Noyeses. Even so, the services offered by these institutions were restricted to the facilitation of day-to-day trading, and their long-term commitments were small and specific. The savings banks paid interest on deposits and dividends on their capital stock, and they invested their funds solely in first mortgages on real estate and in government securities. The commercial banks accepted demand and time deposits (both noninterest-bearing; the former drawable by check), made loans on collateral security, and discounted promissory notes, bills of exchange, and out-of-town bank notes. Their portfolios were also predominantly composed of fixed-income obligations: mortgage loans, government bonds, and the securities of manufacturing and financial corporations.

For a sailmaker like Mallory, these banks had uses, but rather particular ones. He used them as depositories for his cash and valuables and to facilitate his commercial transactions with short-term credits and a greater variety of liquidity combinations. It was often convenient for him to be able to settle accounts by check rather than by cash, and he regularly "sold" his own promissory notes, bills of exchange, and out-of-town bank notes (or those of others which he had received in the course of business) to the banks at a discount and received local bank notes or cash in return. But all that these transactions represented was the conversion of inferior financial obligations into better ones in the normal course of trade—"inferior" and "better" in relation to the local market or Mallory's own liquidity preferences at the moment.

It was not typical of Mallory or of business practice in the maritime industries of Connecticut prior to 1848 to depend on either savings banks or commercial banks for long-term credit except in the form of loans on real-estate collateral. Loans on personal or security collateral were rare. Most of the credit operations of the banks were associated with the short-term financing of trade: with the discounting of bills of exchange and 30-, 60-, 90-, and 120-day promissory notes secured by bills of lading and warehouse receipts representing merchandise. It is true that so-called "accommodations" were sometimes made and what was originally drawn as short-term paper was redis-counted again and again so as to become, *de facto* if not *de jure,* long-term credit. Nevertheless, it seems clear that in his first three decades of business life, Mallory (like most Mystic enter-prisers) did not consider commercial paper as an important means of long-term or large credit.

For his sizable and long-term capital needs, Mallory (like his peers) depended on an older and more personal system of credit and exchange. This so-called "open-account" system was typical of the Mystic Valley until well into the 1850's. Mer-chants, artisans, and laborers simply incurred or discharged debts by reciprocal entries on the books of the parties to the transaction. Accounts lay open, sometimes for years, on the premise that amounts payable and amounts receivable—if they were between neighbors or regular business associates—would tend to cancel over time. If not, balances could be "reckoned & settled" upon mutual consent: sometimes by the opening of a new account; sometimes by exchanges of cash, goods, or real estate; sometimes by the giving or receiving of promissory notes; sometimes by the assignment of accounts or notes receiv-able; or, not uncommonly, by the pledge or performance of labor or services.

In such an economy, an individual's assets comprised his cash and property on hand, his notes and accounts receivable, and the services due him. His liabilities were his notes and accounts payable and any services owed by him. Net working capital would then represent the excess of assets over liabilities. But it should be obvious that a businessman's standing and liquidity depended not only on his bank account or property but also on his ability to "draw" and his liability to be drawn against for cash or credit on book account; and his possibilities for selling notes and bills payable or receivable (at a discount, of course) to raise cash.

This system of trading was typical of early nineteenth-century America, and in small, inbred towns like those of the Mystic Valley it was quite pervasive. In part, it reflected a society in which as late as 1850, some 70 per cent of the labor force were *not* employees but farmers, mechanics, small trades-men, or slaves. It also reflected the widespread payment of wages in kind, which often made laborers "involuntary trades-men" to convert kind to cash. It frequently arose in the defer-ment of meeting payrolls to hedge against inventory and accounts-receivable risks. It was also useful in ventures which required large amounts of capital and/or presupposed a slow return on investment. It proved especially suitable in whaling, for example. Many of the capital outlays for outfitting vessels and crews were merely bookkeeping transfers within a circle of investors, agents, crew, and suppliers. Settlement of these accounts was postponed until voyage's end. Only then were significant amounts of cash likely to change hands in the balanc-ing of supply, wage, commission, and profit-and-loss accounts.

This so-called "open-account" system also characteris-tically interlocked the constituents of an economic community into a web of mutual interests. Some were merely the common-place relationships of buyer-seller, debtor-creditor, employer-employee. But the system operated in other ways, as well, with important economic effects: it made creditors prime allocaters of economic resources; it could serve as a rudimentary sort of debt financing for new enterprises; it could distribute large capital outlays and risks over numerous individuals; and it could spread the benefits of profit or the disaster of loss widely. As long as profits lubricated the system, which otherwise tended to become one of frozen assets, all was well. But losses to creditors or illiquidity of debtors impeded the mechanism. In Mystic prior to 1850, the system worked well as it was semiclosed, local, and relatively insensitive to cycles in New York or Boston. It also meant that men with marketable goods or skills or with cash or credit on their books inevitably found themselves financially involved in many enterprises besides their own.[19]

Charles Mallory was no exception. As a sailmaker, he did regular business with numerous shipowners, seamen, and storekeepers. He was often drawn into their affairs. He might accept a share in a vessel in payment for work on her sails. Affinity with a chandler, storekeeper, or ship captain might lead to a venture on joint account. Typical was a Mallory speculation with his neighbors Joseph Cottrell and Benjamin F. Hoxie: on April 2, 1839, the three bought a cargo of spars at $550, "from Captain Woodburn of the Schooner *Clarissa*"; these they sold off at $700, with Mallory receiving 50 per cent of the profit upon closing of the book account on June 19, 1840.[20] Scores of similar ventures in domestic and foreign exchange, real estate, duck, sugar, oars, cordage, marine hardware, and lumber with Cottrell, Hoxie, and other Mystic, Stonington, and New London friends and relatives became increasingly commonplace on the books of the Mallory sail loft after 1820. But any balance sheet of the profits of these activities is impossible because of gaps in the Mallory daybooks and the absence of any surviving ledger accounts.[21]

The incidence of such ventures, their diversity, and their multiplication as the 1820's and 1830's progressed suggest that Mallory was increasingly the capitalist rather than the craftsman. His admission of Grant as a partner in 1838 was further indication of his diluted interest in his original occupation and confirms Charles Henry Mallory's later recollection that by 1830, "father did not confine himself so exclusively to his trade as formerly . . . although sail making (for which he had now large orders and employed a number of men) gave him a start in the world." The firm of Mallory & Grant lasted until October 15, 1843, when Grant withdrew. As late as January 1849, a credit agency could still report Mallory as "lgely. engagd. in sailmakg.," but the responsibility of the loft (except for the drawing of sail plans, which he obviously enjoyed and continued to do until the 1860's) had long since been delegated by

Mallory to his journeymen. In 1853, he leased the loft to his foreman and kinsman I. D. Clift (whom he had trained from apprenticeship), and Clift operated the loft under his own name until 1877.[22]

An appraisal of Mallory's earnings as a sailmaker is impossible because of gaps in the financial record. But what is vastly more important than calculations of profits and losses is the realization that it was a craft skill, rather than inherited wealth, technological innovation, or managerial expertise, that earned Charles Mallory his first business experience, prestige, profits and opportunities. Yet in less than a decade, he was well on his way toward becoming a capitalist rather than merely a craftsman. His craft placed him at the informational and operational centers of his economic environment, and his nascent entrepreneurial talents were aroused and found equal to the challenge.

Others in the same position might never have gazed beyond the security of their craft skill and might well have ignored the other opportunities posed by their surroundings. But, in the words of his eldest son, Mallory was constantly looking beyond the sail loft and "gradually working into business that proved in the end to be more profitable."[23] The result was that between 1822 and the early 1860's, under the elder Mallory's guidance but with the increasingly significant participation of his sons, the Mallory family broadened and diversified its investments and applied its capital and managerial talents along three lines: the ownership and operation of American-flag sailing vessels in whaling and the carrying trades; shipbuilding; and commercial banking. All these activities were interrelated and all coexisted for varying periods of time, but not until the decade of the Civil War were these lines of endeavor reappraised and reshuffled.

It was during these four decades that, individually and as a family, the Mallorys came to consider themselves "American shipmen," first and foremost. Hindsight permits us to summarize this commitment and to evaluate the Mallorys' pragmatic perceptions of opportunities and the ways in which they sought to achieve compatibility of various investments within their over-all entrepreneurial goals. It also sharpens our historical appreciation of the successes and disappointments of men to whom all was not so clear.

Chapter 2

WHALING INVESTORS AND AGENTS,

1822–1860

"... a succession of 'full ships,' returning season after season to the same firm, indicated a keen business sense in the selection of masters and mates, in the formulation of shrewd and far-sighted policies, and in the successful adaptation of means to ends."—Elmo P. Hohman, *The American Whaleman*

IT is ironic that Charles Mallory's two earliest business preferences—sailmaking and whaling—scarcely survived his own lifetime as viable large-scale economic activities among Americans. Yet in the uncertain years after the Peace of Ghent, when steamboats were still the playthings of tinkering mechanics and kerosene, petroleum, gaslight, and electricity were almost five decades in the future, sails for propulsion and whale oil for illumination, lubrication, and its organic qualities were staple products. And for New Englanders like Mallory, they and the sea were a livelihood as natural as life itself.

Investment in whaling vessels and the assumption of the duties and risks of their management for self and others were the Mallory family's earliest large-scale business diversifications. In a sense, given Charles Mallory's ambition, his domicile, and his times, his move into whaling was almost inevitable. Whaling satisfied his appetite for greater managerial challenge and contained the possibility of substantial profits, both of which had been lacking in sailmaking. Yet success was in no sense certain or infinite. While the full colorful history of American whaling is beyond the scope of this study, it *is* germane to discuss Mallory's attraction to that industry, his expectations, and his experience. For in the history of the Mallorys of Mystic, whal-

ing formed the first crucial bridge between small-business anonymity and large-scale notoriety and success.

From the perspective of the present, it is easy to dismiss
the nineteenth-century New England whaling industry as a
relatively short-term response to an expanding, urbanizing, and
mechanizing nations's demands for illuminants and lubricants
and milady's penchant for combs and flexible corsets. In the
macroeconomic sense, whaling was not America's most important antebellum industry by any means. From almost nothing in
1815, the annual value of whale products climbed steadily to
about $3,000,000 in 1830. From 1830 to 1876, the mature
years of the industry, the annual value of products stayed above
$3,000,000 and in the period 1835–1865 was in the
$6,000,000 to $9,000,000 range per year. At its peak, about
1853–1854, the value of whale products was nearly
$11,000,000 per annum, or about 1 per cent of the total value
added by manufacture.

These broad-gauge data, however, obscure the fact that
from at least 1842 to 1861 there were never less than 500
American-flag vessels engaged in the whale fishery (the peak
year being 1845–1846: 730 vessels, 233,000 tons) and that for
that entire period, whaling was encouraged by the federal government as in the national interest. Thus, while it is easy to
point to other sectors of the economy as more productive,
whaling was for many a viable and sometimes lucrative business.[1]

What was the attraction of whaling for a young Connecticut sailmaker whose prime economic indicators were the numbers of masts and barrels he saw daily on the water front?
Although commercial whaling in America dated from earliest
colonial times, it had been the speciality of Massachusetts, not
Connecticut. The latter counted only occasional whaling clearances before 1810, and from 1811 to 1820 cleared none at all.
The next three decades, however, saw a steady increase in her
participation in both whaling and the associated sealing industry. Why the change?

Connecticut maritime entrepreneurs were both pushed and
pulled toward whaling. As Hutchins has shown, the opportunities for American-flag vessels to earn "large profits" in the

foreign carrying trades were "considerably diminished" after 1815. The "cessation of war, the reappearance of a large amount of foreign-flag tonnage on the primary world trade routes, the lessened demand for American exports, and the increased order and rationalization in trade" were responsible. Not that there was "any substantial weakening of the competitive position of American vessels in the direct foreign trades"; rather, American vessels were merely experiencing their fair share of a decline in total demand.[2]

Part and parcel of this decline in demand was a drastic fall in the level of ocean freight rates—60 percent during the period 1815-1823. In some quarters of New England, particularly in Massachusetts and Rhode Island, this decline in the profitability of the oceanic trades renewed shifts of capital from shipping into manufacturing begun before or during the War of 1812. In other quarters, such as in eastern Connecticut and New York City, there were merely shifts of capital from less profitable into more profitable *but still maritime* markets: namely, from transoceanic carriage into the North American coasting trades and the American-flag whale fishery. Significantly, in 1820 the coasting and the fishing fleet exceeded that employed in foreign trade for the first time.[3]

There were also pulls toward coasting and whaling. Leaving the attractions of the coastal market to the next chapter, what was increasingly appealing about whaling? The major attraction was the discovery between 1818 and 1821 of new whaling grounds of great promise. The traditional whaling grounds had been those of the Atlantic and an area of the Pacific south of the equator and within 100 leagues of the western coast of South America. In 1818, however, the so-called "off shore grounds" were discovered in the zone from 5° to 10° south latitude and from 105° to 125° west longitude. So productive were these grounds that over fifty vessels were cruising them annually by 1820, and more soon followed. Between 1819 and 1820 equally productive grounds were found off the coast of Japan. By 1822 over thirty American whalers per year were making the long transpacific haul. Both old and new entrepreneurs could be counted in this van.

Predictably, as vessels were shifted from the carrying trades to sealing and whaling, there was some market dilution. Prices for sperm oil, whale oil, and bone declined between 1815 to 1823, but no faster than the rate of decline in the general wholesale price index. Actually, during the period 1816–1820, prices for whale products in the American market remained higher than they had been since before 1800 or would be for any five-year period until 1846–1850. There were definitely profits to be made.

Sealing and whaling also had their propagandists, and a significant number clustered in Mallory's portion of Connecticut. Edmund Fanning of Stonington had taken seals on voyages of 1797–1799, 1799, 1813, and 1815–1817. His exploits were followed closely in eastern Connecticut and kindled enthusiasm among his neighbors for the commercial possibilities of sealing and whaling. In 1817, Fanning and another Stonington captain, Benjamin F. Pendleton, initiated a series of annual sealing expeditions from eastern Connecticut ports.

While Fanning and Pendleton were busy promoting sealing voyages, others were exploring the commercial possibilities of whaling. The first Connecticut whalers in ten years cleared New London and Stonington in 1820 for the newly discovered Pacific grounds. The vessels returned the following summer with good cargoes of oil and bone. In 1821, eight vessels cleared New London for the new whaling grounds, among them *Mary Ann,* which shipped Charles Mallory's eighteen-year-old nephew, Alvin. These vessels' landings in 1822–1823 seemed to confirm all reports of the industry's profitability.[4]

Connecticut's rekindling of interest in sealing and whaling thus coincided with Charles Mallory's second decade as a sailmaker. The coincidence of man and times proved mutually fortuitous. The sailmaker found his craft in demand by the many vessels building and outfitting between the Thames and the Pawcatuck rivers; and the fledgling capitalist soon found ready opportunities for reinvestment of his loft's increased earnings. The earliest of these investments were in sealers, whalers, and fishing smacks. They soon gave him the profits and products which led him to invest in merchantmen as well.

There is little doubt that sealing and whaling had become a mania in the Mystic River Valley by 1822. The successes of the fleets of 1817–1821, and the energetic promotion of the idea by the Fannings, the Sheffields, the Pendletons, the Williamses, and the Palmers, nourished further investment. Charles Mallory was caught up in the general excitement. Between August 1822 and June 1828, he acquired shares in three whalers and three sealers. He was a latecomer as an investor, and his initial equity was passive and small. Yet these were his first ventures into shipowning.

Mallory's initial shares were in the whalers *Hydaspe* and *Hersilia II,* which were completed in August and December 1822 in the Mystic River yard of David Leeds and departed almost immediately for the Pacific whaling grounds. These vessels were almost civic projects under the guidance of Benjamin Pendleton, each vessel having over thirty local shareholders. Mallory's equity of 1/64 was probably only the usual share offered a ship's sailmaker in lieu of cash payment for his services. The vessels returned in 1824 and found the price for sperm oil only 70 per cent of what it had been in the year of their departure (prices for whale oil and bone had held steady). Nevertheless, they reportedly made such good catches that their profits remained high.

Thus while Mallory's share was small, his first venture into shipowning was probably profitable. He sold out his interest in *Hersilia II* in December 1824 and in *Hydaspe* in February 1826, but he was busily acquiring new shares: he was one of seventeen investors in the five-year-old sloop *Only Son,* between September 1823 and early 1825; one of eight in the older brig *Huntress* between June and September 1825; and one of twenty-one in the new Mystic-built sloop *Eliza Ann,* between October 1825 and August 1827. All three were sealers and, thus, continued his pattern of passive, small, and brief ventures into the current shipowning fad.[5]

While these investments were typical for their time and place, they were major decisions for Mallory. He was popular and busy, but certainly not rich. He probably still had little surplus capital. Indeed, as he told the story in later years, the fulfillment of a childhood pledge in 1824 taxed his resources to the limit. He had sworn as a boy to purchase the house and six acres in Waterford which his parents had rented for so many years. When finally offered the house at a reasonable price and the land at $30 an acre, one-half down, he accepted and set a day to sign the mortgage in New London. As the appointment neared, he grew nervous, sure he "could never pay for the place in the world." His wife encouraged him to go ahead, saying (as he always told the story), "You are smart, and I can do a great deal of work myself to help you." Even so, Mallory set out on foot to cancel the agreement, but on his way resolved to consummate what he later considered "the best investment I ever made." His parents lived out their lives on this homestead, David reaching the age of seventy-nine and his widow ninety-six. In their later years, their neighbors would look forward to and long remember "the fine coach bearing Charles and his wife that often stopped on Mallory Hill and the quantities of good things that the coachmen would bring in." [6]

But things were not so flush in the 1820's, and Charles's decision and Eliza's pledge of 1824 were all the more remarkable, given their own circumstances at home. They lived in Captain Holmes's chamber until Charles Henry was three, and there Eliza bore her second and third children, Ann, born in August 1820, and David, born in October 1821. By then, crowded for space for themselves and wishing additional rooms wherein they might board Charles's apprentices, they rented a large house from the famous Captain Jerry Haley.

In the Haley house began an incredible chain of personal joys and tragedies that speaks for itself. In July 1823 a third son, John, was born, but in December, Ann died at only three years, four months, and fourteen days. A fourth son, George, was born early in 1824, but in July, John died eleven days after his first birthday. With the loss of two infants in less than eight months and the financial burdens of caring for aging parents and three healthy, strapping boys, small wonder Charles and Eliza Mallory felt stretched to their spiritual and financial limits.

But the worst was not over. Another boy, William, was born in April 1826, but he, too, died in infancy, six months after his first birthday. A sixth and healthy boy followed,

Franklin, born early in 1828. To celebrate, Charles Mallory bought a large, two-story house from Captain Thomas Potter, which became the family's Mystic homestead and stands today. Here five more children were born, of which only two survived infancy. Robert, born in September 1829, died one year, one month, and fifteen days later. Benjamin, born in April 1831, died one year, one month, and fifteen days later. A second Benjamin, born in early 1833, and a daughter Annie, born in June 1835, were healthy enough to survive. But Fanny, born in December 1836, died nine months after her first birthday.[7]

The emotional stress of bearing twelve children in eighteen years to see only six live past the age of four is almost inconceivable. But Eliza and Charles persevered and found solace in their religion, their five sons' and one daughter's health, and Charles's new business interests which began in June 1828 when he joined seven neighbors in purchasing the New York whaler *Acasta* and bringing her to Stonington. The syndicate was headed by Charles P. Williams, the leading shipowner and banker of Stonington, and under his management, *Acasta* made six profitable voyages until her loss in the South Seas in September 1840.[8]

There is no evidence that Mallory was any more than a passive investor in the three whalers and three sealers with which he was associated before 1830. This made him liable for a share of their prevoyage outfitting costs in proportion to his equity, and he participated in their profits or losses to the same extent. But he had no managerial responsibilities or authority. This pattern changed abruptly in June 1830, when Mallory formed a syndicate of seventeen for the purchase of the Massachusetts whaler *Aeronaut* and became her managing agent and principal shareholder.

To understand the new responsibilities Mallory thus assumed, it is useful to review the business side of whaling. Vessels, exclusive of outfit, were built, purchased, or chartered by groups of investors (normally ten to twenty, each individual thus acquiring fractional equity proportional to his share of the total capital outlay. "Outfit"—being equipment and stores necessary for one voyage—was similarly financed but separately accounted for. These shares in "vessel" and "outfit"—usually

32

multiples of 1/8—became the basis for compulsory division of maintenance and repair costs and for apportioning profits. Each shareholder, at his own option, might also insure his percentage of vessel, outfit, and cargo. The system limited the liability of each investor to his proportion of the whole and thus differed from contemporaneous mercantile partnerships and anticipated the limited liability of the corporation.[9]

Return on investment came in a variety of forms. First, of course, were profits realized on the sale of sperm oil, whale oil, and bone. Upon a ship's return, the "gross value" of her cargo was computed at current market prices for the various quantities and qualities of product, regardless of whether actually sold then or held for later sale. "Net proceeds" were then calculated by subtracting from this gross value such charges incurred by the ship as pilotage, wharfage, gauging, cooperage, watchmen's fees, and commissions and guarantees paid for handling and sale of cargo. Approximately 70 per cent of these net proceeds then were allocated to owners and some 30 per cent to captain, mates, and crew.

From the owners' 70 per cent might still be deducted depreciation of vessel and outfit (say, 5 to 10 per cent per annum), interest on capital invested (say, 6 per cent per annum), and insurance (say, 4 to 7 per cent per voyage), although only the last two were normally reckoned in the first half of the nineteenth century. The remainder, depending on the accounting procedures employed, represented net profit to equity on cargo.

There were other sources of owners' profits, however—at the expense of their work force. Crews were compensated on the "lay" system, which comprised various fractional shares of the net proceeds of cargo. Captains, mates, boat steerers, and coopers received "short lays" from 1/8 to 1/100; able and ordinary seamen, stewards, cooks, and shipsmiths received from 1/100 to 1/160; green hands and boys received "long lays" from 1/160 to 1/200, and which might range down to 1/250 and 1/350. Bounties and rewards for good performance might be added, and the seaman's meals were furnished free, but the lay constituted his wage.

Lay proportions were agreed to at "signing on" and represented the seaman's *gross* share of net proceeds. Take-home pay was another question. The *net* value of the lay was computed only at voyage's end. It varied inversely with two groups of charges regularly debited against the gross lay. "Owners' list" began with each man's outfitter's bill. These bills were paid in full by the ship's agent (usually in 30- to 180-day notes) upon commencement of the voyage and represented the costs of hiring and outfitting the man. The agent then debited the seaman's lay account and charged him interest at about 25 per cent per voyage until settlement at voyage's end. Seamen were also charged $10 to $20 per head by the agent to defray costs of hiring stevedores to load and unload the vessel and $1 to $3 each to stock the ship's medicine chest. The agent further debited lay accounts with any advance made to third parties, such as to a seaman's creditors of family.

"Captain's list" was the second group of charges against the gross lay. It included the man's slop-chest account and any cash advances made at sea (the latter at 25 per cent interest per voyage). The slop chest was stocked as an investment at owners' expense, and profits on sales to the crew were expected to average 100 per cent. To make the system work at sea, the captain usually received an incentive percentage on sales of slops.

Coordination of these factors and systems of production was the task of the whaling agent, who was usually, but not necessarily, a shareholder in vessel and outfit. His managerial responsibilities included procurement of vessel, outfit, and crew, maintenance and repair of ship and equipment, inport ship-servicing, marketing of cargo, computation and distribution of profits and lays, and associated legwork, correspondence, and records-keeping. He was compensated through commissions: usually 2 1/2 per cent on gross costs of outfit and crew procurement and up to 15 per cent of gross value for guarantees and sales or cargo. He might also profit on markups of outfit and slops if they came from his own shelves; and, of course, if he was an owner, he received his share of net proceeds.

While these were the institutions and practices of whalemen, profit depended on their amalgamation. In his unsurpassed study of the risks and organization of American whaling, Elmo

P. Hohman identifies luck, possession of capital, and connections as ingredients of success. He speaks of financial results ranging between "ruinous losses and magnificent profits"; of the need for adequate funds to tide over long voyages or successive setbacks; and of "the aristocracy of oil and bone" who considered whaling their mare clausum. Yet he concludes: "Over a long period large earnings were due primarily to sound judgment, good management, and that real, if indefinable, combination of qualities called business ability."[10]

Since Charles Mallory's contemporary reputation was that of a successful whaling agent and owner, his career can test some of Hohman's generalizations. Mallory was hardly an innovator; many of his policies were commonplace for his trade; and he made mistakes. Yet he was a thorough and responsible businessman who was able to blend a profitable enterprise.

By New Bedford or Nantucket standards, Mallory's whaling investments were small. But by Connecticut standards, he was an important individual entreprenuer. Between 1828 and 1849, he was a passive investor in twelve whalers managed by others. Between 1830 and 1862, he was principal owner and managing agent for sixteen whalers under his own red, white, and blue house flag. All these vessels hailed from New London, Stonington, Groton, or Mystic.[11] From 1830 through 1862, an annual average of 9 per cent of Connecticut's whaling fleet sailed under Mallory's flag; and in the peak period for 1834 through 1845, Mallory accounted for an annual average of 15 per cent of Connecticut's whalers. In Mystic, Mallory's influence was even more pervasive. Mallory-flag vessels annually averaged 75 per cent of the Mystic whaling fleet; and in eleven of these thirty years, he sent out 100 per cent of Mystic's whalers (see Tables 2.1 and 2.6).[12]

These admittedly rough measures of market shares suggest that Mallory probably exerted irregular, short-term influences over prices for vessels, outfits, and products in the Mystic Valley, but that state and national price levels were insensitive to his individual activities. On the other hand, *he* was sensitive to price-level changes and geared some of his investment decisions to visible demand as reflected in local landings and prices. For example, his speculative investments in the vessels of others cluster during the depression years 1836-1841, when ship costs were down, crews and outfits were cheaply available, and prices for whale products were at their antebellum height.

In the absence of any real power over prices and possessed of no innovative technology, Mallory was pitting his local cost curve, his own acceptable profit levels, and his personal managerial acumen against national price movements for his capital goods and the products of their employment and the economies of scale enjoyed by large operators in Massachusetts. In order to prosper in such circumstances, a marginal area like Mystic had to aspire to moderate goals and astutely manage its limited resources and position. This was Mallory's entrepreneurial challenge in whaling, and he proved equal to the task.

Part of Mallory's success derived from his understanding of and adherence to the tried and true methods of minimizing the risks of whaling. To lessen the physical risk of losing his capital goods or his cargoes—which represented about 1.5 per cent of all losses in the industry—he took advantage of the increasing availability of low-cost marine insurance (at rates averaging 2 1/2 per cent per annum). [13] He also fully appreciated the inherent advantages of fractional-share, limited-liability ship-owning and spread his investment in portions over numerous vessels. Of course, as previous and subsequent chapters indicate, he did not have all of his earning assets in whaling by any means.

In hedging against possible losses on sums advanced his crews, which was his prime labor risk (although accounting for only about 1.5 per cent of all industry losses), Mallory was again typical. The lay system, high interest rates on cash advances to crews, profits on slop sales, and confiscation of effects and balances due deserters were his and his fellow agents' normal insurance of a return on their investment in labor.

The lay was also an important means of shifting the burden of some of the risks associated with irregular financial returns due to fluctuations in quantity, quality, and price of cargoes. The lay system proportioned wages to profits, thus reducing labor costs in direct proportion to losses and canceling them completely in cases of total loss.

If all went well, the lay functioned as a rudimentary

profit-sharing plan. But little enough was left the seamen after their debits were totaled. Witness the pitiful account of Daniel Wheeler, who spent the last two-and-one-half years of his life on 1/150 lay on board Mallory's *Robin Hood*:

Daniel Wheeler (Decd.)

	To Owns & Agt. Ship Robin Hood	Dr
1854 Oct. 5	To Cash advancd. you before sailing	$18.00
	To Bill Slops for outfit	99.12
Dec. 6	To Cash for your Mother	2.00
1855 Sept. 11	To Cash for Do	4.00
1856 May 7	To Cash for Do	3.00
Sept. 2	To Cash for Do	3.00
Oct. 6	To Cash for Do	3.00
Oct. 29	To Cash for Do	5.00
1857 March 31	To Cash for Do	2.00
May 23	To Paid D. D. Mallory & Co.'s Bill, Goods for Do	3.12
	To Bill Slops from Slop Chest on Voyage	91.33
	To Cash & Coms. of Capt. McGinley for Do	87.00
	To Bill Clothing from Wm. Burns' Chest	33.12
	To Interest & Ins. on Cash & Slops advanced	36.64
	To Lay Days, Medicine & Gauging	13.00
	To Cash & Goods for your Mother	15.40
		$418.73
By your Share 1/150th part Sales Oil & Bone		Cr
Cargo, Ship Robin Hood @ $63,570.00		$423.80

Thus, for 1,032 days at sea, Wheeler received net wages of $63.59 of which $40.52 had been drawn out by his mother while he was away. He had been charged $223.57 for his "slops" and a total of $136.64 for interest, insurance, lay days, medicine, and gauging. At the other end of the wage scale, Wheeler's captain (estimating his lay at 1/10th part) probably received gross wages of $6,357 plus the items credited to "captain's list." [14]

From the management point of view, the purpose of the lay, however exploitative of the seamen, was to shift some of the business risks of whaling ventures from equity to labor. The inequalities of the system were ignored by all whaling agents (Mallory included) as irrelevant. But they certainly enjoyed an advantage unavailable to other businessmen: "Instead of the usual situation in which the entrepreneur contracted to pay a definite rate of wages to his workmen and assumed the risks of an industry, a special condition was created under which the whaling merchant materially lightened his financial burdens by proportioning his wages bill to the amount of his profits." [15]

In addition to adhering to these normal industry practices, Mallory pursued some distinctly successful business policies of his own. The first of these related to the cost and quality of his vessels. Related was the matter of control.

While Mallory spread his whaling investment over twenty-eight vessels, he obviously preferred personal management of his long-term funds. Many of his "speculations," however, he trusted to the management of others. Twelve times he invested in the vessels and ventures of others, but none of these commitments of funds exceeded twelve years in duration, and the average was five. In contrast, for his sixteen own-flag vessels, his average financial commitment was for ten years, with seven exceeding that figure and one lasting twenty-five years.

As stewards for his outside investments he favored only a few close friends: he took shares in four of the numerous vessels managed by Charles P. Williams (whose son later married a Mallory daughter) and in four of those operated by his brother-in-law Benjamin Brown of New London (Mrs. Brown was Mrs. Mallory's sister), who sent out forty-five voyages between 1827 and 1859; the remaining four were managed by such close Mystic neighbors and fellow church parishioners as the Pendletons, the Randalls, and the Ashbeys. [16]

As for cost and quality, Mallory made it a practice to invest only in secondhand whalers. His sixteen own-flag whalers averaged fourteen years of age at the time of his first equity; five were over fourteen, two were twenty, and one was thirty! His twelve passive speculations were also in ships averaging fourteen years of age. These preferences reflect environmental circumstances in part: a marginal whaling area like Connecticut would likely add capacity from the used-ship market rather than from new construction as did Massachusetts; and Mystic was physically unable to build vessels in the range of 250 to 450 tons until late in the whaling era. [17]

Used vessels were also only a fraction of the cost of a new ship, a fact well appreciated in Mystic. Even though costs for new sailing ships declined steadily between 1820 and 1860, good used ships could be the better buy. [18] Reliance on old vessels obviously took a good eye for a bargain, proper management, knowledgeable maintenance, and luck. Mallory apparently had these in abundance. One measure of his ability is the duration of his investment in his own-flag vessels, which included some remarkable ship husbandry: he worked *Coriolanus,* which was seventeen years old when he bought her, for seventeen more years; he got sixteen years out of the twenty-year-old *Robin Hood*; and he worked the thirty-year-old *Bingham* fourteen years. An alternative indication of the quality of Mallory's ship management is gained when the ratio of his vessels' time at sea to time in port is computed. This is done for seven Mallory own-flag whalers in Table 2.2, where their performance is compared to that of the pride of New Bedford's fleet.

From Table 2.2 we can see that despite the age of his vessels (which presumably meant higher-cost and longer maintenance periods), Mallory was able to turn them around at a very respectable rate. Of course, any vessel could have difficulties at any given moment; witness the 323 days required to turn *Aeronaut* around in 1848–1849; the 347 days consumed by *Leander* in 1857–1858; the 369 days and 408 days consumed by *Romulus* in 1857–1858 and 1859–1860; and the 409 days consumed by *Bingham* in 1839–1840. Conversely, however, *Aeronaut* was turned around in an amazing 13 days in 1834 between voyages lasting 362 and 655 days respectively! The best turn-around times for the other vessels were: *Bingham,* 59 days; *Blackstone,* 55 days; *Coriolanus,* 61 days; *Leander,* 46 days; *Robin Hood,* 102 days; and *Romulus,* 58 days.

If we consider turn-around time as a rough indicator of the whaling agent's ability to keep his assets at sea and earning (rather than in port and wasting), we must conclude that over the long haul Mallory and his old ships were good performers. Taking the two brand-new Morgan vessels which were managed by the best agent in New Bedford as a comparison (see Table 2.2), we can see that Mallory got more shorter voyages out of his old vessels and at a turn-around rate 67 per cent of that achieved by the brand-new ships.

These data, fragmentary as they are, suggest that some of Mallory's profit margin sprang from his lower capital investment and successful ship maintenance and not from any technological advantage or lower outfitting or labor costs. Outfitting costs, since they did not include capital improvement or replacement charges, were roughly the same for all vessels of similar tonnage, regardless of age or area. For example, an outfit for the brand-new *Charles W. Morgan* cost $16,287.77 in New Bedford in 1841, while an outfit for the twelve-year-old *Romulus* cost $17,416.18 in Mystic in 1842 (both were of comparable tonnage); or, an outfit for the sixteen-year-old *Leander* cost $11,000 in Mystic in 1841, while the forty-year-old *Bingham* (of comparable tonnage) cost $11,135.27 to outfit there in 1844. Since labor costs were solely a function of profits, there were no comparative advantages of one area over another in terms of wages. Indeed, the lays granted by Mallory to his crews conform nicely to the industry norms estimated by Hohman. [19]

Another distinct Mallory policy was to function simultaneously as owner, agent, and supplier of whaling vessels and thus to reap the profits (or losses) of each role. In part, this was typical of small whaling ports like Mystic, which could not sustain the degree of business specialization common in larger towns such as New London and New Bedford. It was also Mallory's persuasion.

As agent, he received commissions on vessel management, on cargo sales, on slop-chest sales, and the "interest and insurance" charges against the crew's lays. Using the Wheeler account again as our example, the items designated "Interest & Ins. on Cash & Slops advanced" and "Lay Days, Medicine & Gauging" would have accrued to Mallory in his capacity as agent. He would also have received approximately 15 per cent commission on the sales of the ship's cargo; that is, 15 per cent of the item "Sales Oil & Bone Cargo, Ship Robin Hood @ $63,570.00." As an owner of the vessel and outfit, he also received profits (or losses) on these cargo sales. And as a supplier, he profited on sales of outfit and slops to other owners or agents or from the markup on these items when supplied to his own vessels. [20]

Sailmaking provided Mallory's earliest, longest, and probably most regular role as a supplier. But he soon added others. In the mid-1830's, he formed a 50–50 partnership with his Mystic neighbor Joseph C. Cottrell for both speculative investments, as previously described, and ships' outfitting. Cottrell was Mystic's largest lumber and hardware dealer, and his expertise and capital complemented Mallory's. In May 1837, Cottrell formed a separate partnership with a young Mystic general-store keeper, Benjamin F. Hoxie, and in 1839 Mallory joined them as a silent partner in a wholesale-retail merchandising firm styled "B. F. Hoxie & Co." He had similar silent affiliations with Ira H. Clift's store, and in 1842 Mallory set up his twenty-one-year-old second son and Isaac W. Denison in a general store styled "David D. Mallory & Co." Time and again, it was these tradesmen who supplied outfit and slops for Mallory-flag whalers—at discounted prices and on liberal credit. [21]

Mallory's simultaneous investments in sailmaking and coasting, his integration of the functions of supplier, agent, and owner, and gaps in the accounting record preclude computation of Mallory's incremental profits from whaling. His experience conforms to Hohman's conclusions as to the sources and irregularities of earnings. Further analysis can also suggest his profit levels in comparison with those of his contemporaries.

To a large extent, profits in whaling depended on timing. If ships could be speedily outfitted at low rates and could return to high market prices for their catch, voyages were profitable. First and foremost, however, one's ship had to survive its cruise and return with its cargo. As to the question of his ships' surviving, Mallory had good luck. Only three vessels operated by others were lost during a period of Mallory equity. *Charles Adams,* managed by B. and F. Pendleton of Stonington, burned in the Falkland Islands in 1837 after two voyages in which Mallory participated. *Atlas,* which Charles P. Williams, Joseph Lawrence, and Mallory bought in 1836, was lost at sea in 1839 on her maiden voyage under the Lawrence flag (she had previ-

ously been managed by Williams). *Acasta* completed six successful voyages under Williams' flag, 1828–1839, before foundering
at sea in September 1840 with an on-board catch valued at
$26,350.

Among his own-flag whalers, Mallory lost *Uxor* in the
Crozet Islands (Indian Ocean) on October 28, 1841, after six
successful sealing voyages which had landed 2,300 barrels of
seal oil. *Vermont* was lost on Saint Paul Island (Indian Ocean)
on August 11, 1847, on her second voyage under the Mallory
flag. Also on her second voyage, *Atlantic* was "captured" (presumably by pirates) off Fayal Island in the Azores. On March
22, 1854, while acting as tender to several larger vessels, *Lion*
was wrecked on English Bank near Montevideo. *Frank,* while
acting as tender to *Romulus,* struck an iceberg off Desolation
Island in the Straits of Magellan and sank on February 14,
1859. *Lion* was on her second Mallory voyage; *Frank* on her
first.

While shipwreck always meant hardship and possible injury
or death for crews and disappointment for owners, these particular losses involved no great financial debit and probably caused
only slight managerial inconvenience. The five own-flag whalers
that Mallory lost were spread over thirty-two years of operations; three were small auxiliary vessels; and all were insured to
the full value of outfit and vessel. Further, under the lay
system, all lays were canceled if a vessel was lost, thus relieving
management of any obligation to pay out labor costs on the
unsuccessful venture. The only real loss was the loss of any
catch that might have been on board.

If all went well and the ship returned safely, however,
things were quite different. One fairly complete set of accounts
has survived for Mallory's whaler *Bingham* on a voyage to "the
N.W. coast," May 23, 1844, to March 12, 1846. These charac-
terize the typical settlement of voyage accounts and distribution of profits. [22]

In his capacity as managing agent, Mallory first totaled the
cost of *Bingham's* outfit for this voyage at $12,174.97. Sales of
used copper, rigging, and boats from the vessel reduced this to
$11,135.27, which was debited against 23 owners as follows: 12
at 1/32; 6 at 2/32; 1 at 3/32; 1 at 5/64; 2 at 1/64; and Mallory

himself at 3/64. Upon the vessel's return, its gross value of cargo was reckoned at $32,066.32 and its net proceeds at $21,244.61.

The gross value (rather than the net proceeds, which would have been more common) of $32,077.32 was used to compute the lays. The amount of each lay was determined by the job which one performed on the ship. For instance, the captain's share of the profit was 1/17 and the first mate's 1/25, while the lowliest "green hand" received 1/225. But the system also differentiated varying degrees of skill among the men. [23] Against these lays were debited outfitters' and slop-chest bills, advances, flat charges (e.g., $12 for "lay days," $1 for "medicine"), and interest on advances computed on a scale from 20 per cent per voyage on amounts of $5 to 15 per cent per voyage on amounts of $15.

The difference of $10,821.72 between gross value and net proceeds accrued to Mallory as agent and represented his gross income in that capacity. From this he balanced the lay accounts, paid charges against ship and cargo, and retained the rest to cover his commissions, guarantees, interest, and prerequisites as agent for owners, ship, crew, and cargo.

Net proceeds of $21,244.61 represent a return of 175 per cent on outfitting costs of $12,174.97. From the former amount, owners would still deduct any insurance premiums they might have paid on their share of ship, outfit, and cargo and charge interest and depreciation on capital invested (not typically done) and any other capital expenditures they might have incurred. It can be readily seen that the 175 per cent return on cost of outfit left a wide margin from which to absorb other outlays. Further, since *Bingham* was forty years old and had been in Mallory's fleet for nine years when she began this voyage, interest and depreciation charges against capital employed in the ship herself must have been nil. The likelihood of a handsome net profit on investment in ship and outfit should be clear.

But how typical a voyage was this one? Or, more important, how profitable were Mallory's ships against those of his peers? Voyage profits depended on the extent of the catch, its quality, its nature (e.g., sperm oil brought more than whale oil), and the market price the ship found upon her return. A very large catch did not automatically mean higher profits, because if the market was low, the profits were low as well. Timing was crucial and beyond the control of the manager (unless he deliberately withheld his vessel's return, which was difficult to do in the absence of regular communication with vessels at sea). For example, if *Robin Hood* had been able to secure the average annual prices for oil and bone upon her return from her fifth Mallory voyage in 1857, her catch would have been valued at $84,965. As it was, her actual gross value of catch when she returned on August 2 was $63,570. In contrast, *Bingham* came much closer to average in the example cited above. Her gross value of catch of $32,066.32 compared well with a hypothetical value of $33,807 based on the average annual prices for oil and bone during 1846. [24]

By computing hypothetical values for the catch of Mallory whalers, we can at least *suggest* the range and norms of his vessels' profitability. We can also *suggest* which voyages were probably the most profitable and compare his ships' earning power with those of his contemporaries.

If we multiply the reported quantities of sperm oil, whale oil, and bone landed by Mallory whalers by the average national prices of those products during the year of landing, we derive a rough rank order of voyage profits and the comparative earning power of the various vessels involved. [25] This has been possible for a total of fifty-four of the known sixty-two voyages made by Mallory-flag whalers, 1830–1862 (89 per cent). The results of these computations are presented in Tables 2.3 through 2.5.

Turning first to Table 2.3, we see the estimated highest and lowest voyages (by value) for each of eleven ships as well as the average per ship. We see that the most lucrative voyage ever made by a Mallory whaler was probably that of *Robin Hood* from October 4, 1854, to August 2, 1857. Close behind were her two previous voyages, both of which topped $60,000 (estimated), and those of *Romulus*, October 4, 1854, to May 30, 1857, and *Aeronaut*, June 23, 1849, to May 31, 1852. We can also see that the actual voyage of *Bingham* used in the example above was probably a slightly above average voyage.

In Table 2.4 the total estimated gross value of these fifty-four voyages is computed as $1,698,986, and the earning power of individual vessels and the fleet as a whole is suggested. If the time at sea is considered the earning time of the assets in question, the gross income each ton of shipping generated per each month it was at sea is a rough estimate of the earning power of the vessels individually and collectively. More important, however, is the comparison made in Table 2.5. Here the estimated gross income and estimated earning power of Mallory and his vessels are compared with contemporaries in nearby New London.

New London was Mallory's closest metropolis, and her whaling agents set the standard for Connecticut. Table 2.5 presents the estimated gross income and estimated earning power of all New London whaling agents managing thirty or more voyages, as these would be considered Mallory's peers. From the table, we can see that Mallory's brother-in-law, with whom the former had made some of his earliest whaling investments (notably in the bark *Friends* and the ship *Mentor,* 1836–1841), was well qualified to tutor his kinsman and that Charles Mallory himself was an apt pupil. Against the top eight New London firms—and thus against the best in Connecticut—Mallory ranked sixth in estimated gross value of catch and his ships ranked seventh in earning power per month-ton at sea. Rough as they are, these comparisons substantiate Mallory's contemporary reputation as a successful whaling agent and a leader of the industry in his state.

As for the Mallory whalers, the tables presented in this chapter put them in perspective, too. Comparing the vessels that made more than two Mallory-flag voyages, we can combine three measures of performance into a ranking of "best." If the turn-around ratio (a measure of the ship's record of staying at sea and earning, column 7, Table 2.2), the average gross value per voyage (a measure of the ship's luck at finding high market prices upon her return, column 5, Table 2.3), and the estimated gross income earned per month-ton at sea (a leavening measure to equilibrate the earning power of ships of various sizes, column 4, Table 2.4) are weighed equally, the vessels rank as follows: *Aeronaut, Coriolanus, Robin Hood, Leander, Bingham,*

Blackstone, and *Romulus.* Since four of the top five were also the oldest in age, the ranking reaffirms Mallory's ability to work old ships profitably.

Despite this competence and obvious success in whaling, Mallory had left the industry by 1862. It remains then to account for his decision in the context of industry economics and to summarize the part whaling played in the growth of the man and his family.

The incidence and duration of Mallory's own-flag investments in whaling provide the best index of his decisions to enter, to remain in, and to leave the whaling industry. These investments fall into three groups: those of 1831–1835; those of 1841–1845; and those of 1858. The timing and liquidation of each of these groups of investments reveal the waxing and waning of Mallory's interest.

During 1831–1835, Mallory purchased five of his total of sixteen own-flag sealers and whalers. More important, as a measure of his commitment to whaling as profitable employment for his capital, *none* of these vessels was withdrawn because of conditions of supply or demand in the industry. Two were removed involuntarily (*Uxor,* shipwrecked in 1841; *Bingham,* abandoned in San Francisco when her crew jumped ship to join the Gold Rush in 1849); three were voluntarily scrapped because of unseaworthiness (*Tampico,* 1841; *Blackstone,* 1846; and *Aeronaut,* 1855). Since this first group of vessels was replaced during 1840–1846 by a second group, totaling seven vessels, we can assume that Mallory's first decade in whaling was satisfactorily profitable and his commitment to the industry was as strong in 1846 as in 1831.

The second group of Mallory-flag whalers reaped the rich harvests of whaling's golden age. Godfrey has estimated that net annual profits (on capital invested) for voyages by New London whalers ran 9 per cent, 1847–1851, and 19 per cent, 1852–1856. [26] Mallory's returns were presumably in the same ranges. As for the seven vessels of his second group of whalers, three were involuntarily removed from service (*Vermont,* shipwrecked in 1846; *Atlantic,* "captured" in 1847; and *Trescott,* abandoned by her crew in San Francisco during the Gold Rush in 1849); four were voluntarily removed (*Leander* and *Corio-*

lanus, scrapped in 1860 and 1861; *Romulus* and *Robin Hood,* sold in 1860 and 1861).

From these data it can be seen that Mallory voluntarily removed only one ship from his whaling fleet from 1841 to 1860 (the thirty-four-year-old *Aeronaut*), again demonstrating his satisfaction with and commitment to the industry. Further, he added four more vessels to his fleet in the 1850's: the small tenders *Lion* (1852), *Wilmington* (1853), and *Frank* (1858), and the whaler *Cornelia* (1858). Looked at another way, however, his decision to phase out of the industry is also apparent: he added no significant new tonnage from 1845 to 1857 and none after 1858. Also, between 1860 and 1862, he voluntarily liquidated his remaining investment in whaling. Why?

The answer rests on a mixture of industry economics and personal preferences. First, of course, profit levels in the whaling industry were declining. Price inflation following the Panic of 1857 raised prices for oil and bone, but those for vessels and outfit rose faster. Whalemen also uniformly reported longer voyages for smaller catches during the latter 1850's, further raising the risk of no return at all on higher outfitting costs. And from the demand side, lard oil and coal gas were encroaching on whale oil's share of the market for illuminants, and after 1856 kerosene and other petroleum products had begun to appear in the illuminant and lubricant markets. The major impact of these new products was to come in the late 1860's, but their challenge was clear by the beginning of the decade.

These factors all depressed profit levels in whaling. Godfrey ascribes to them prime cause for the decline in net annual profits (on capital invested) for voyages by New London whalers to a rate of -7 per cent (1857–1861).[27]

Mallory evaluated these industry trends against his own circumstances and interests. On January 1, 1860, he had five whalers in service: *Leander* and *Robin Hood,* both thirty-five years old and both at sea; *Coriolanus* and *Romulus,* the former thirty-three and outfitting at Mystic for sea, the latter thirty years old and at sea; and the nineteen-year-old *Cornelia,* outfitting at Mystic. By January 1, 1862, only *Cornelia* remained under his flag, and by the following New Year's Day she, too, was gone. How did he liquidate this fleet?

Leander was sold for salvage at Pernambuco, Brazil, on January 3, 1860. *Romulus* returned from sea on May 9, 1860, and was sold to parties in Cold Spring Harbor, New York. *Robin Hood* returned from sea on September 17, 1861, and was sold to the federal government as one of the famous "Stone Fleet" which was sunk to blockade the Confederate port of Charleston. [28] *Coriolanus,* which put to sea on July 10, 1860, was sold for salvage at Mauritius in November 1861. *Cornelia,* which put to sea on June 16, 1860, returned on June 17, 1862, and was sold to parties in New London.

More important than how the last Mallory whalers were liquidated is why? The age of the vessels involved and the declining profit levels of the industry are part of the answer. Also, the threat of civil war and the possibility of Confederate and/or English harassment of American-flag vessels on the high seas were factors considered. More important, however, were the Mallorys' growing preferences for other sorts of maritime activities. Since 1826, Mallory capital had been invested in merchantmen, since 1849 in shipbuilding. By 1860, the profits and prospects of these investments far outweighed those of whaling.

If Mallory's success as a sailmaker and his transition from craftsman to capitalist represent the first two stages in his family's evolution as maritime entrepreneurs, his transition from whaling to tramp and common carriage and to shipbuilding constitutes the third.

~~~~~~

Chapter 3

SAILING TRAMPS AND SAILING PACKETS,

1826–1860

"No ship can always have a flood tide and a fair wind."
—Charles Mallory

O N November 4, 1826, four years after his first investment in whaling, Charles Mallory purchased a share in the 46-ton sloop *Connecticut.* From that date through December 31, 1861, the elder Mallory and his sons invested (for varying lengths of time) in at least twenty-six sloops, thirty-five schooners, eight brigs, eight barks, and fifteen ships employed in the domestic and foreign commerce of the United States. Thus while whaling was Mallory's first investment and managerial diversification, he almost simultaneously allocated an additional share of his resources to the ownership and operation of merchantmen. And, as time passed, success in the carrying trades induced him to phase out sailmaking and whaling, to commence shipbuilding, to convert to steam, and to expand radically the financial, managerial, and geographical scale of his family's maritime enterprises.

The timing and long-run significance of Mallory's initial involvement with merchant vessels can best be understood in the broader contexts of shipping economics and the American situation between 1815 and 1861. Further, some terminology and concepts defined now will facilitate understanding of later chapters in the business history of the Mallory family. Several questions are particularly relevant: How was the world maritime freight market structured in Mallory's day; what segments of that market attracted his money and attention; when and why?

In what business functions did Mallory specialize in those market segments; how successful was he in achieving his intentions?

Functionally, Mallory was more often a "carrier" and not a "shipper"; that is, he possessed vessel capacity for which he sought cargoes rather than cargoes for which he sought vessels. Thus, like most carriers, he rarely owned the goods he transported, and he sought maximum freight rates in the market place rather than the minimization of rates to which shippers characteristically aspire. As do all carriers, Mallory specialized in the procurement, manning, maintenance, deployment, and replacement of vessels (skills transferable from and to whaling); in the gathering and handling of passengers and freight; in related disbursements, collections, and accounting; and, of course, in the formulation and implementation of business policy intended to maximize the employment and minimize the expense of his fleet.[1]

In making managerial decisions, Mallory relied on his own criteria and judgment and on that of his sons, his partners, and his captains, but their access to information and their ability to decide among alternatives was facilitated by the existence of an organized maritime freight market centered in New York.[2] In that market, the capacities, types, deployment, and desires of available vessels were matched—at a price—with the volume, type, distribution, and destinations of available cargoes. Offerings of vessels and cargoes were brought into reciprocal cognizance and mutual advantage by middlemen who earned their living by compromising the needs of carriers and shippers.

For the Mallorys, in the years between 1826 and 1861, strategies and tactics in the carrying trades most often involved decisions as to whether a vessel should "tramp" or should be placed in a "line," and which "branch markets" best suited her technology and her owners' goals.

The word "tramp" implies a pragmatic vessel employed in a perfectly mobile, world-wide maritime freight market: "A deep-sea tramp ship is prepared to carry any cargo between any ports at any time, always provided that the venture is both legal and safe."[3] In reality, however, the maritime freight market is less than perfectly mobile; it is actually a set of "branch markets" each of which tends toward *some* specialization of ships, cargoes, and harbor services. The degree and/or kind of specialization characteristic of each branch market is a function of the interaction of the technology, capacity, and desires of carriers; the nature and volume of cargoes and the desires of shippers; the supply of harbor services; and the policies of whatever government controls the marketplace.

For example, a regular supply of passengers, who value service above price, and/or a high-volume supply of goods whose transport requires special and recurrent mixtures of consignment size, speed, voyage frequency, and care (*besides requiring an economical freight rate*), usually induce a branch market characterized by "liners" rather than by tramps: "A liner is usually defined as a ship plying a fixed route, sailing according to a predetermined timetable, and offering cargo space at fixed rates to all those who wish to engage such space."[4] Or, to suggest other possibilities: a distinct branch market might be technologically created by peculiar geographical and climatic conditions; or, one might be politically created by a national policy of cabotage.

Branch markets are created by all sorts of geographic, technological, political, economic, and social interactions. They are not necessarily permanent, and they are not mutually exclusive. For example, overcapacity on liner routes drives marginal vessels into tramping, just as undercapacity on liner routes attracts vessels never intended to run as liners. In any branch market, however, there is some tendency toward standardization of price, service, and technology. Branch markets dominated by tramps are merely those in which shippers and their goods are more sensitive to transport price than to transport service and in which less standardization of carrier technology, service, and price is, therefore, demanded.

For the carrier, mobility within and between branch markets is crucial to survival. Mobility is possible within rather broad limits but is never perfect; for, as Thomas Thorburn has proven: "vessels in one branch market can . . . (theoretically) replace vessels in other branch markets, but (practically) the difference between costs and freight rates per ton cargo increases and causes greater losses to the owners of the ship the farther the vessel is employed from the branch market to which it economically belongs."[5]

Thorburn's axiom and the concepts of "tramps," "liners," and "branch markets" facilitate understanding of the technology, deployment, and profitability of Mallory-flag merchantmen, even though data on "costs and freight rates per ton cargo" are lacking.[6] The patterns of investment and management are clear: between 1826 and 1861, the Mallorys specialized as carriers in two well-defined branch markets: one "coastal," the other "intercoastal." They achieved excellent mobility within, and partial mobility between, these markets by blending foreign and domestic carriage, tramp and liner services, and their own managerial skills with those of specialized middlemen.

The coastal branch freight market was at least ten years old when it attracted a portion of Charles Mallory's capital in 1826. He and his descendants operated cargo vessels in the coastal market continuously from that date until 1941, but their first two stages of involvement are all that require analysis at present: the years 1826 to 1848 mark a first era; the years 1849 to 1861 mark a second; later stages will be considered in subsequent chapters.

Geographically, the coastal market in Charles Mallory's day encompassed the mainland and offshore islands between Canada and northern Latin America. Economically, this market was partially a product of declining profits in American-flag, transatlantic carriage; but, more importantly, it was a function of domestic regional specialization and the persistent inadequacy of interregional land transport. Politically, the coastal market was also the result of certain maritime policies adopted by the United States.

Between the year Mallory became a sailmaker and the year he decided to invest in water-borne commerce, the annual volume of American foreign trade increased. At the same time, however, the prices received by importers and exporters and the freight rates commanded by foreign-trade carriers decreased. These changes in the volume and value of exports and imports reinforced a shift in the employment of American-flag tonnage:

out of transatlantic commerce and into inshore foreign commerce, coasting, whaling, and fishing. Mallory was well aware of this shift and had invested in its whaling component beginning in 1822.

More important than declining transatlantic freight rates in fostering this redistribution of the American merchant marine, however, was a rising demand for domestic water carriage being generated by regional economic specialization. Water carriers provided the first mass, cheap, and expeditious means of north-south interregional trade. They also provided a sizable segment of north-west trade, via southern seaports. The railroad was a later and better answer to interregional trade, but there was not one mile of track in the United States before 1830, and only 633 miles as late as December 31, 1834. Not until the 1850's was there any significant competition between railroads and coastal water carriers.

Besides being a part of American regional economic specialization, the coastal branch freight market drew some of its definition from policies of the federal government. The domestic coastline was extended by the acquisition of Louisiana (1803), Florida (1819), and Texas (1845), and a series of cabotage acts commencing in 1817 made coastal waters a mare clausum for American-flag vessels. In order to load goods or passengers in one United States port bound for another, vessels had to be 100 per cent American-built, 100 per cent American-owned and officered, and have crews which numbered at least 75 per cent American citizens. Thus, American vessels could comfortably avoid foreign competition in the coasting market; and, yet, with no change in technology or in capital requirements, they could foray out of their protected domestic trade into foreign trade with Canada, Bermuda, the Bahamas, the West Indies, Cuba, Mexico, Central America, and northern South America.[7]

Between November 4, 1826, and December 31, 1848, all the cargo vessels in which the Mallorys invested operated in this coastal branch market: twenty-three sloops, seventeen schooners, eight brigs, three barks, and two ships.[8] All were sailing vessels; none were Mallory-built; most mixed domestic and foreign carriage. Prior to 1835, all Mallory-flag merchantmen sailed as tramps; after 1835, some sailed as liners; prior to 1848, none were interchanged with other branch markets, but a few were rotated between the coastal freight market and whaling, fishing, and wrecking.

The trick to tramping was to keep one's vessel continually employed at profitable rates. "*You lay in port too long to make any money,*" the Mallorys wrote one of their captains in 1861. "It never will do to lay one day idle without some object .... Do not fail to *work fast*. Write oftener."[9] Tramp voyages were chain affairs, moving goods wherever available and always looking beyond the current cargo to the chances for a return or continuing shipment. "Your ship is wearing out every day and I should wish her to do as good a business as possible while she lasts.... I should not come home in the ship as long as I could do a fair business away," were another captain's instructions in 1858.[10]

Tramp cargoes were procured in several ways. One method was for the captain or ship's agent to advertise the vessel "on berth" and willing to receive such passengers and freight as presented themselves for a designated port or itinerary. If and when filled to captain's or agent's satisfaction, the vessel would sail.

"Berth service," using the assistance of an agent, was usually considered a last resort by the Mallorys and most carriers. Agents' commissions for procuring freights were 5 per cent, and even if the captain did his own cargo solicitation, port charges tended to cumulate. By far the preferred method of procuring tramp cargoes was to string together a series of government or private charters. In such agreements, the charterer typically contracted for exclusive use of the vessel for a voyage (either one-way or "round") or for a specified period of time.

"Time charters" were riskier than "voyage charters," but could be more profitable. The opportunity costs of time charters were high if freight rates rose in the general charter market; of course, if rates fell, time charters were a hedge against loss. The more popular voyage charter permitted finer adjustments to market fluctuations and was more flexible in terms of vessel deployment. The need for renegotiation of a series of voyage charters, however, was an added managerial burden. The carrier received either a lump sum or a rate per measure of freight; the charterer assumed costs of freight procurement, cargo handling, and all vessel expenses except insurance, wages, and provisions. If a third party negotiated the charter, as was common, he was paid a brokerage fee of 2½ per cent of the amount of the charter. The Mallorys' goal was always charters "on a fixed rate of freight" with "all expenses paid, say wharfage, stevedore, clerk hire, etc. free of commissions."

Actually, the usual tramp voyage in the coastal market combined berth and charter service. The itinerary of the maiden voyage of the schooner *Francis Amy,* which Mallory owned with her captain Henry Ashbey of Mystic and Charles P. Williams of Stonington, is illustrative of tramping's pragmatism:

10-6-37 to 10-17-37	— Stonington to New York with whale oil.
11-15-37 to 4-6-38	— New York to New Orleans to Matagorda, Texas, to New Orleans with freight and passengers.
5-25-38 to 6-9-38	— New Orleans to St. Marks, Fla., to New Orleans on U.S. government voyage charter.
6-25-38 to 10-27-38	— New Orleans to Havana to New Orleans to Matanzas to New Orleans to Matanzas to Havana with freight and passengers.
11-20-38 to 4-1-39	— Havana to Logona and Tabasco to Havana to Tampico with freight and passengers.
4-8-39 to 4-29-39	— Tampico to New Orleans on Mexican government voyage charter.
5-26-39 to 6-19-39	— New Orleans to Charleston to Mystic with lumber, freight, and passengers.
6-19-39 to 10-8-39	— Refitting at Mystic.
10-8-39 to 10-12-39	— Mystic to New London to New York in ballast.
11-27-39	— New York to Gulf of Mexico ports with freight and passengers. [11]

This voyage is typical in its long in-port periods awaiting charter, berth-freight, and passengers and in its duration away from Mystic. It is also representative of the mixture of domestic and foreign carriage to be found in the coastal market. Between 1826 and 1848, the Mallorys' cargo fleet spent approximately 40 per cent of its ton-days in foreign trade with Western Atlantic, Caribbean, and Gulf of Mexico ports and about 60 per cent in domestic coasting. [12]

Long absences from home and the need to keep a vessel continually employed made captains the key to success in tramping. A clue to the qualities desired in a shipmaster is found in a letter of recommendation penned by Charles Henry Mallory in 1859: "He is an upright, honest man, very economical and I think a good sailor. His judgment is as good as most masters possess, and as to business matters he will follow your instructions to the letter." [13]

All Mallory shipmasters in the domestic and foreign carrying trades were given procurations appointing them "our lawful and proper attorney" fully empowered "in all matters and things" relating to their vessel. [14] In short, they had responsibility *and* authority. Since they were also usually co-owners in their vessels, to the extent of 1/16 to 1/4 part, they were expected to be discreet, and correspondence from home often concluded: "whatever is for the benefit of yourself will be for the benefit of the balance of the owners"; or, "as long as you can make a saving business your judgment will dictate what to do." [15]

The master, by virtue of his procuration, was authorized to "bind" the ship at all times; that is, to "make" the best berth or charter arrangement possible or to sell the ship itself, if desirable. Authority to sell his vessel "in any port and at any time" went out to sea with each master; acceptable minimum prices were included in his instructions and were reiterated or revised in letters which typically ended, "get more if you can!" [16]

The correspondence between the Mallorys in Mystic and their captains at sea concentrated on updating their mutual knowledge of the freight market. The process of acquiring and using market data was constant and was roughly comparable to the collection, evaluation, and dissemination of military intelli-

Charles Mallory in his prime as a shipbuilder and manager, *ca.* 1850.
Courtesy Mystic Seaport.

Charles Henry Mallory while he was his father's right-hand man in Mystic,
ca. 1850. Courtesy Mystic Seaport.

gence. The interrelationship of the major sources of information and advice are depicted in Figure 3.1. The captain on the scene made the final decision, however, as to the proper employment of his vessel. Those who did well were always commended, even if it was merely to be told that they had "done the best thing under the circumstances." Those who erred, in the owners' judgment, were quickly reprimanded: "Your charter is very low and it is very difficult to get insurance for that place," wrote Charles Henry Mallory to Captain J. W. Holmes in 1858, for example.[17]

The major problem in the acquisition of market information, during the period 1826–1848, was the fact that communication throughout the coastal market was no faster than the fastest means of transportation. This meant that decisions often had to be made on the basis of stale data. For example, a minimum of 7 days was required for an exchange of messages between New York and Charleston; 14 to 16 days between New York and New Orleans; and 22 days between New York and Galveston. Obviously, then, the captain and/or the agent on the scene had to have discretion to act and be trusted to act responsibly.[18]

Between 1826 and 1835, then, all the Mallory-flag cargo vessels operated as tramps in the coastal freight market; this was a basic managerial decision. Flexibility within that choice, however, was achieved by intermixing berth and charter service and domestic and foreign carriage. Additional flexibility was also achieved by temporarily shifting excess capacity out of the coastal market and into fishing and wrecking. Only one Mallory-flag vessel was ever shifted between coasting and whaling: the brig *Tampico,* which Charles Henry Mallory commanded in tramp coasting between 1831 and 1838, finished out her life with three sealing voyages between 1838 and 1840.

Vessels were more often shifted between coasting and fishing and coasting and wrecking. The sloops *Relief, Francis Park,* and *Richard H. Watson* and the schooners *Coasting Trader* and *Empire* are known to have completed cod-fishing as well as coasting voyages between 1833 and 1848. More interesting, however, is the Mallorys' connection with wrecking. This activity grew out of their particular interest in Florida.

Connecticut men were always to be found in the large ports of the coastal market: Charleston, Savannah, Havana, Mobile, New Orleans, Galveston, Tampico, and Vera Cruz. But they were especially involved in the establishment of Florida ports during that area's transition from Spanish to American rule.

Mystic fishermen and coastal tramps had used Key West as a stopover as early as 1819; and between the change of flags in 1821 and the establishment of a United States customs district and port of entry in 1822, Key West became a commercial outpost of Connecticut and New York. Benjamin Sawyer, Mason R. Packer, Amos Tift, Sr., and his sons Amos, Jr., Asa F., and Charles came out from the Mystic-Stonington area to establish general stores and ships'-service enterprises. Even a branch of the Mallorys relocated in Key West, including the future United States Senator and Confederate States Secretary of the Navy, Stephen Russell Mallory. In Apalachicola, the story was the same, with expatriate members of such Mystic families as the Ashbeys and the Clifts becoming prominent settlers.[19]

Florida was a good market for northern products, especially for the types of sloops, schooners, and associated gear (such as cordage and sails) which Mystic produced. In return came "logwood and cochineal from Campeche, pimiento, coffee, and rum from Jamaica, molasses and sugar from Cardenas and Matanzas, and a steady stream of cotton from the American gulf ports"—all either passed by or through Key West.[20]

It was the location of Key West that added wrecking to its commercial life. The navigational perils of the Florida Strait cast many a rich-laden prize ashore to be salvaged for profit. Both criminal and legitimate salvagers had operated along the Strait for generations, but by the 1820's several highly organized, legal wrecking stations were in existence: especially those of John W. Simonton of New Jersey, established at Key West in 1822, and of Jacob Housman of New York, established on Indian Key in 1825. The establishment of a Federal Superior Court at Key West in 1828, possessing admiralty jurisdiction and the sole power to license wreckers, centralized legitimate commercial wrecking there.

Owners of wreckers, once licensed by the Superior Court, were free to seek salvage where they found it. While ancient sea law recognized the first salvor to arrive at a disaster as wreck master, most jobs required the services of several sloops or schooners and their crews of seamen and divers. Cargo thus salvaged was consigned on commission to merchants in Key West, who shepherded it through the salvage court and subsequent auction. One-half of total salvage awarded by court and auction went to the owners of the wreckers involved; one-half to their crews.[21]

Mystic men were prominent among the crews and owners of wrecking vessels and among the salvage merchants of Key West. There were profits to be made all along the line: salvage awards themselves; commissions as agents for wrecking vessels and their salvage; resale of salvaged property purchased at auction. And the chain of profit stretched northward to New York and Connecticut. James D. Fish, a Mystic-born New York merchant, recalled of his Florida correspondents: "We gave them credit and bought their supplies. They took advantage of these [salvage] auctions and consigned their purchases to us to sell for their account, often at a very large profit."[22]

Charles Mallory was an integral part of this trade. His daybooks of the 1820's and 1830's record instances of sails, cordage, and lumber shipped to Florida ports on his own account, and several vessels in which he owned an interest were licensed wreckers. The sloop *George Eldredge* (in which Mallory owned 1/16, the Ashbeys 2/16, and the remainder was held by Eldredges and Packers), for example, shared salvage on two ships, five brigs, and two barks during the wrecking season of 1838. In at least a dozen instances, Mallory also bought salvaged ships' gear at auction through the Tifts in Florida for resale in New York by James D. Fish.[23]

Wrecking and fishing were ancillary to commerce, however; and, significantly, Mallory shifted no coastal cargo vessels into other branch *freight* markets prior to 1848. This fact would seem to suggest some economic and technological specialization among even Mallory's tramp fleet; it echoes Thorburn's caution against assumptions of complete tramp mobility. What is cer-

tain, however, is that, after 1835, Mallory increasingly inter-
mixed liner and tramp service in the coastal market—a mixture
which increased his ability to keep his merchantmen employed.

Sailing packet lines were New York City's innovation and
specialty. They sailed on schedule, as advertised, regardless of
their fullness, and were more specialized common carriers than
either pure tramp or semitramp berth vessels. They appeared on
the New York–Liverpool route in 1817; New York–New Orleans in 1818; New York–Charleston, New York–Savannah, and
New York–Mobile in 1819. In all, between 1817 and 1861, at
least 105 coastal sailing packet lines operated for various
periods of time between New York and ports south of Baltimore, and at least 51 translantic lines between New York and
Europe. Boston, Philadelphia, and Baltimore were not far behind, with a combined total of 102 southern lines and 23
European lines known to have operated for various periods
between 1818 and 1861.[24]

The sailing packet "lines" were entities only in their public
face and management. There was no corporation or partnership
that owned all or even most of the vessels on any line. Rather,
vessels as needed were procured by voyage or time charter
(usually the former) in the general market. The key entrepreneur was the line manager who chose a route with trade sufficient to sustain packet service; who provided a regular supply of
carriage to evoke further shipments; who promoted shipments
to fill or increase his supply of carriage; and who "placed"
vessel capacity on and off the line to conform to normal and
abnormal freight movements. His task was to fulfill his commitments to shippers and carriers at a profit to both and a profitable commission or fee to himself. His selling point to shippers
was sufficient and dependable capacity to move their goods on
schedule. To carriers, he offered more regular employment for
their vessels than they could find in the tramp or berth charter
markets.[25]

Profits from the packet-line system accrued to line managers and their associated agents in the form of fees and commissions and to shipowners as net proceeds from charter parties.
Vessel owners agreed to provide vessel, crew, and provisions and
to pay clerk hire, stevedores' bills, and port charges. The line

manager agreed to "use his best exertions and all his influence to load the said ship to the best advantage and give her quick dispatch," to furnish "a full cargo of lawful merchandise (or sufficient for ballast)," and to pay "all outside brokerage and commissions which he may have to pay for securing freight, and for all cards, placards, and advertising."

The line manager received a commission "on the whole amount of the freight list due and payable when the ship is laden," which was 5 per cent in the coastal market and 7½ to 10 per cent in overseas foreign trades. The manager's regular agent at the other end of his line received 2½ per cent for collecting freight and on any advances made to the vessel. The shipowners received the proceeds (less this pair of commissions) from "freight, at current rates, charges on all goods or merchandise going on board said ship, exception ship's stores." [26]

A large share of the management and capital of the New York-based sailing-packet lines stemmed from Connecticut men who had relocated in Manhattan to represent their fellows at home. Charles Mallory was introduced to the packet business by two of these Connecticut-New Yorkers: Samuel B. Ashbey and Elisha D. Hurlbut.

Ashbey was a well-connected Mystic merchant who moved to New York in the 1830's and opened a chandlery near the Fulton Fish Market. He was soon joined by another Mystic man, James D. Fish, who was the son of Mallory's first business landlord. Ashbey & Fish, 136 Beekman Street, opened in May 1841. From 1842 to 1846, with the addition of Captain Charles D. Pool of New London, the firm operated at 105 South Street as Ashbey, Pool & Co. and after 1853 at the same location as James D. Fish & Co. [27]

Ashbey and Fish specialized in facilitating coastal trade on a Mystic-New York-southern axis, and the firm's role was recalled by Fish:

> Our new store became a sort of Exchange where New London and Mystic people met to transact business with us or with one another, and to get letters sent there for them. Captains returning from sea came directly to us for news from home.
>
> . . . our customers often left their money with us subject to their

order. . . . These deposits amounted in the aggregate to thousands of dollars. . . .

Captains of the packet sloops that did most of the freighting business between Mystic and New York, had their letters sent to our office, and purchased of us such goods as they required in our line. . . .

To add to the social comforts of our friends and customers, we had in the lofts of our store, cots and hammocks, and could accommodate as many as twenty-five at once of those who might be in the city for a few days. . . .

Obviously, 105 South Street was an important place at which to call in New York, and Charles Mallory was a frequent and honored guest. Fish recalled that Mallory "dealt with us exclusively for their supplies, and intrusted to us the placing of his marine insurance, which he always effected for both vessels and freights. His patronage was a considerable portion of our business." [28]

Elisha D. Hurlbut & Co., located at 84 South Street, was Mallory's other major contact in New York. The Hurlbuts had begun as general New York representatives for New London, Stonington, Essex, and Deep River venture capital. They soon specialized as packet-line managers and carried their principals along. In October 1825 they opened their first line, New York–Mobile, and by 1831 offered a year-round schedule between those ports. In 1827, they extended their Mobile line to New Orleans and had established a separate schedule to the Crescent City by 1849. In 1836, a third "Hurlbut Line" opened, New York–Apalachicola, and between 1841 and 1848 the firm opened additional lines between New York and Bremen, Le Havre, Antwerp, and Rotterdam.

The Hurlbut lines were Mallory's first exposure to large-scale packet operations. Between April 23, 1835, and the end of 1848, six vessels in which he owned an interest were regularly placed on Hurlbut lines to Mobile, Apalachicola, and New Orleans: the ship *Charles P. Williams,* the bark *Montauk,* and the brigs *Ann Eliza, Republic, Metamora,* and *Francis Ashbey.* [29]

Their experience with the Hurlbut lines encouraged Mallory and his co-owners to place these and similar vessels in other southern packet lines. Between October 14, 1840, and the end of 1848: the bark *Mazeppa* served variously in Scott & Morell's "Orleans Line" and John Elwell's "Merchant's Line," both New York–New Orleans; *Francis Ashbey* also served in Elwell's line; *Republic* sailed in Price & Morgan's "New Orleans Packet Line," Philadelphia–New Orleans, and Mailler & Lord's "Mutual Line," New York–Mobile; and the ship *John Minturn* sailed in John Laidlaw's "Third Line" and Stanton & Frost's "Union Line," both New York–New Orleans.[30]

Charles Mallory's purchase of a share in the sloop *Connecticut,* in 1826, thus introduced him to a well-defined and expanding branch of world maritime trade. He followed up with investments in fifty-three more cargo vessels over the next twenty-two years and, in the process, became thoroughly conversant with the commodities, ports, technology, and business organization of the coastal market. By 1848, Mallory-flag merchantmen were as common in the ports of the Western Atlantic, the Gulf of Mexico, and the Caribbean as Mallory-flag whalers were on the high seas. The sailmaker and whaling agent had now further diversified his maritime enterprises and was competently and profitably managing a fleet of commercial water carriers.

During these same years, Charles Mallory had also successfully launched his eldest son on a career that complemented his own. Called "Henry" by his family, Charles Henry Mallory was a chubby but strong boy whose cherubic features favored his mother and reflected a more genial and outgoing personality than that of his reserved and austere father. But he was very much his father's son. His "earliest recollections were of visiting the sail loft, where my father would place me on a pile of sails and I would go to sleep. My mother had to work hard to bring up a large family of children, who came along every eighteen months, and by taking me to the sail loft for my nap would relieve my mother of care. Here I used to be much amused by the noise, and the apprentice boys took much notice of me."

Henry started his education at Miss Harris' "school for the small fry over the Palmer Store near the bridge." The next year (1824), he was "promoted to the District School, about one mile from the Bridge." His recollections of the next ten years display his own whimsical streak and the pleasures and pains of Connecticut schoolboys of over a century ago:

> The school house was about eighteen feet square, and about nine foot posts, with a small wing or porch where the water pail, wood, and hats and overcoats, when there were any, were kept. The writing desks were carried around the wall on three sides, and a rude bench with legs sticking through the top sides sometimes an inch or two, comprised the first seats for older scholars. When they were seated their backs were to the center of the room. Another tier of smaller benches were placed inside these for the smaller children. A stove was placed in the center of the room, and the Teacher's desk, elevated about two feet above the others, was placed on the west side of the room, where the smaller seats would have been if there had been room. All ages and all classes and colors attended this school, as it was the only school house within a radius of one mile. Stalwart boys and girls of twenty and even older and little snips not over three years of age, made up the school. In the summer when only the smaller portion attended, a female teacher was hired. The teacher boarded around, and the pay was about $20. per month in the winter, and $10. to $12. in the summer. In general more tyrannical persons never breathed on the face of the earth. The little ones suffered to the tune of three or four floggings a day, while the larger boys, of whom the Master was afraid, did pretty much as they pleased. The neighboring woods furnished switches of large dimensions which are always kept in order, and the order, "Take off your jacket Sir" was often repeated. They were a cruel set, but on the other hand there was a great deal of mischief done. The boys large and small were often in scrapes. . . . There were a number of ponds near by where the boys did their skating, and the girls their sliding, and a nice field for ball playing. Orchards were very near, and as a consequence not much fruit was harvested. The fact was the school house was a nuisance to the farmer nearest by.[31]

As for most New England boys of his generation, and particularly amongst the Mallorys, keeping of the Sabbath was the natural, spiritual complement to common schooling. For Charles Henry it was no different, but his recollections of "goin'-to-meetin' " again reflect his own chuckling and infectious sense of humor:

There was no church nearer than what was called the Road Meeting House, about three miles from our house. This church my father and mother attended (Presbyterian or Congregationalist). They used to ride and I usually walked with the other boys in the neighborhood. The meeting House was an ancient structure, square with doors on the East South and West, square pews with high benches and seats on the four sides. The pulpit was an elevated cage with a large sounding board overhead, and galleries on three sides. The music of the Choir was not modern, and the tune was set by the leader who handled a tuning fork with much "gusto." There was no stove or other means of heating in the building, it being considered wicked to heat a building of that kind, "it would be too comfortable." Here I used to sleep over the sermons of the worthy old minister who was long winded, and never preached unless he took a good strong gin or brandy swig, at a tavern near by. But he was considered a great man. "A prophet among the people."

There were occasionally meetings held in a school house in Groton (across the river), where an occasional sermon was delivered by Elders Burrows and Wighter, two old Baptist preachers. These meetings were usually well attended, and many good men were always ready to exhort and pray and sing. Among them I recollect as most prominent were Black Quart Beacon Fish (father of Asa Fish) and Mr. Packer. These were good men and their influence is still felt in the community, although they have been long since departed. My father attended these meetings often, and took me with him where I listened to the music and exhortations and soon learned to "intone" as well as the best of them, when I got out among the boys. There was a great deal of laughing and fun making among the boys and girls at the meetings, as these and an occasional singing school were the only places of amusement.

About 1830 a subscription was got up and a church edifice was built on the site of the Union Baptist Church. It was called the Mariners Free Church, and services were held by all sects (Orthodox). No communion services were held in this church for many years, but finally the Baptists, who were very numerous, swallowed up the property, and it was said by many that it was obtained by them in not a very Christian manner. The choir in this Church were composed of the leading men and women of the village. Asa Fish was a long time the leader. Jas. Gallup, Simon Gallup, Simeon Fish, Daniel D. Edgecomb, George Eldridge and others. My father also sang in this Church. The seats were few and for the most part the boys and girls sat in the galleries. Here I attended Church, and the mischevious boys were kept as straight as possible by Simeon Gallup, who was a terror to Evil doers. From the window in the gallery of this Church we had an extended view of the ocean. This was my favorite window.[31]

By this time who can doubt Charles Henry's own evaluation: "I was always full of mischief. In fact, a leader among the boys of my own age. An oracle in the making and sailing of small boats in the ponds." When he reached eleven, however, his father began to tighten the reins. "My father was determined that all of his sons should learn the sail making trade," Charles Henry recalled, and until he was fifteen he alternated the winter quarter of the year in boarding school in Stonington with spring, summer, and fall quarters in the loft: "I acquired great proficiency in sewing. I could do my 100 yards a day with ease, and spend some of the time in play. In fact, about all the time my father was away I was in some mischief with the other boys. . . . We wrestled, pitched pennies, etc."

About some things, however, the young Mallory never teased. "I was very fond of the water, and was always from my first rememberance crazy for a Boat. Many is the time my father's voice (when I thought he was far away), 'Henry come ashore,' has thrilled the blood in my veins. I always came ashore knowing what I should get when I landed, but somehow I was never broken of the great fondness I had for the water." No ship could tie up to the town wharf or lay alongside the Mallory sail loft for very long before Charles Henry "had examined every part of her from the keel to the truck." He badgered his parents "to embark a whaling voyage" but they would not consent. His father did permit him to go along on a coasting voyage when he was thirteen. He sailed as cabin boy on the schooner *Whale* to and from Bangor to load a cargo of 60,000 board feet of lumber. "My principal business on this cruise," he recalled, "was to load the pipes for the Captain and his crew." But he also stood a few tricks at the helm, tried his hand at trimming lumber with an adz (nearly amputating a toe in the process), saw whales and seals, "was very sea sick," "picked up a great deal of Geography," and got a thoroughgoing, refreshing, and lifelong "taste of the sea." He was hooked.

Charles Henry's fourteenth year was pure agony; his fifteenth (1833) was pure bliss:

> I worked steadily during the Summer (except stealing off whenever there was an opportunity), and every opportunity teased my mother to let me go to sea. I stood too much in awe of father and let my mother do the business. My father owned an interest in a new Brig, about six months old, called the *Apalachicola.* She was at this time a very handsome vessel, and a fast sailer. She was built for the Southern Coasting trade between New Orleans and Apalachicola. This vessel was anchored opposite the sail loft, and was undergoing a Summer overhaul, being painted, etc. She was constantly before me. In the day time I could look out of the open door and there she was, and in my sleep she was constantly before me in my dreams.
>
> I was determined if possible to get my father's consent to go in her. She would leave in September and return in June.
>
> In July my father agreed to let me go. I was overjoyed and restless, and it appeared that the time for sailing would never come. My mother was busy fitting me out with (of course) many things which I did not require, and never did a young sailor start off from home with a better or more generous outfit than I had.[31]

For the next thirteen years, Charles Henry Mallory's "life was passed continually on the water." He continued to ship out as a seaman on *Apalachicola* (at $13 per month) during the years 1833–1838. In 1839, on his twenty-first birthday, he became her captain. Later, he commanded the brigs *Tampico* and *Ann Eliza* and the ship *Charles P. Williams* and became thoroughly familiar with the ports, cargoes, and practices of the coastal market. On July 25, 1841, he married Eunice Denison Clift of Mystic in the Road Church, and they spent their honeymoon and most of the first four years of their married life at sea. Late in 1844, however, Charles Henry built her a house in Mystic across the street from his parents', and here their first child, Charles Rogers, was born on January 18, 1845. Eunice came from two of Mystic's best families and fitted right into the Mallory circle. She was "a 'strict tea totaler' so far as taking anything from a glass was concerned, but a fork or spoon made it another matter and her mince pies, plum puddings, and brandied peaches were a delight."[31]

In 1846 Charles Mallory's familiar hail of "Henry, come ashore" was heard again. But now it was a plea rather than a command. Deeply involved in whaling, the elder Mallory needed his son's knowledge and experience to supervise the family's rapidly expanding cargo business. The younger man complied and never went to sea again. He became his father's right hand and business heir. It was he who expanded the family's investment in water-borne commerce after 1848 and had to cope with new business conditions in the coastal market and elsewhere.[32]

The characteristics which had defined the coastal market since 1815 increasingly changed after 1848, some only slightly, but others quite radically. There was no further territorial extension of the eastern domestic coastline of the United States, no change in the federal cabotage policy, and little change in the nature of cargoes or in the market's proportions of tramp and liner service. The major changes were in the market's proportions of foreign and domestic trade, in the speed of interport communication, in the technology of water carriers, and in the availability of competitive land transport. There were also important transactions between the coastal market and an entirely new branch market, the intercoastal. All these environmental pressures challenged the Mallorys' desire to sustain and enlarge their investment in American-flag merchant vessels.

The functional relationship which the Mallorys bore to the maritime freight market did not change between 1848 and the Civil War. They continued to be carriers and not shippers or middlemen, and they continued to mix tramp and liner service. What changed was the degree of their specialization in cargo vessels and the number of branch markets which occupied their attention.

As noted in preceding chapters, Charles Mallory retired from active sailmaking and leased his loft in 1853. Also, he added no significant new whaling tonnage between 1845 and 1857 and none after 1858, and he liquidated his whaling fleet entirely after 1860. In contrast, between January 1, 1849, and December 31, 1861, the Mallorys added (for various lengths of time) thirty-eight more cargo vessels to their merchant sailing fleet: three sloops, eighteen schooners, five barks, and twelve ships. [33] All these vessels mixed domestic and foreign commerce; the sloops and smaller schooners specialized in the tramp trades of the coastal market and interchanged between carriage and fishing; the ships specialized in the line trades of the new intercoastal market and in transoceanic tramping, but occasionally interchanged with the line trades of the coastal market; the barks and larger schooners specialized in the line trades of the coastal market, but occasionally were to be found in intercoastal and transoceanic trade.

Tramping in the coastal market was not much different after 1848 from what it had been before. As late as November 25, 1861, for example, Charles Henry Mallory contracted to furnish his schooner *Zouave* to Captain James Packer, the latter "to take charge of said schooner *Zouave* and employ her in legal and legitimate trade in Southern waters of the United States and foreign fruit ports," to victual and man her, with "any expense to keep her in good condition to be charged to owners of said schooner." Gross earnings from freights were to be divided 50–50, after deducting expenses. Packer also received a procuration to sell the ship for $6,000 or more, he to get 5 per cent on any such sale. [34] These terms were almost identical with those made between the elder Mallory and his Florida captains in the 1820's and 1830's.

Mallory coasting vessels were larger, though, after 1848, and they were more likely to be schooners than sloops. Also market information was improved by the establishment of interport telegraphy east of New Orleans in 1848. Apparently, well-managed tramp schooners could still profitably overcome steadily declining freight rates, and the Mallorys continued to invest in such vessels.

The larger schooners and all the barks were designed specially for packet service in the coastal market, which the Mallorys still found attractive. The usual deployment pattern was to consign a vessel to one of the regular lines as long as rates held high, but take her off if something better offered in transoceanic tramp markets (see Table 3.2). [35] But competition was exceedingly close: 25 per cent of the 196 known lines initiated between eastern and southern ports prior to the Civil War opened after 1848, and steamships and railroads were increasingly factors to be reckoned with.

Steamship lines appeared briefly on the New York–Charleston run between 1832 and 1839 and were regular participants after 1846. One New York–Savannah line opened in 1848 and a second in 1858; three opened from New York to Havana, Mobile, and New Orleans between 1848 and 1850, but only one survived until the Civil War. These lines, with their superior speed, were quite effective in taking passengers, mails, short-haul cotton, and long-haul package freight away from the sailing packets.[36]

Railroads were less effective competitors on both the long and the short hauls of the coastal market prior to the Civil War. The railroads built by the southern port cities were perpendicular to the coastline and fed rather than paralleled water carriers. While coastal ports north of Savannah were circuitously interconnected by rail by the 1850's, ports south and west of Savannah were not interconnected by rail until after the Civil War. Those railroads which penetrated the southern backland from the North and the Northwest did divert some freight away from the seaboard, but their effect was only beginning in the mid-1850's and their speed gave them, as yet, no great comparative advantage.[37] The major rail threat to water carriers in the coastal market was indirect: from east-west roads which were beginning to channel west-south trade away from its traditional Mississippi Valley course.

Despite the appearance of steamships and railroads, the Mallorys still found the coastal market a viable and profitable trade for sailing vessels, and they continued to add capacity until 1865. But specific data on earnings from either tramps or packets in the coastal trades are lacking. What is certain, however, is that the coastal market was the Mallorys' first and longest-standing investment area as water carriers. We will return to it again as they convert their technology to steam and become middlemen as well as carriers, but for now we must turn to their other major interest of the period between 1848 and 1861: the intercoastal market. This market was precipitated suddenly by the discovery of gold in California and the consequent escalation in demand for transportation and communication between the Atlantic and Pacific coasts of the United States. While it lasted, it was heady wine, indeed.

On January 28, 1848, gold was discovered on the American River in California. Reports of the strike had reached San Francisco by February; by June, Salt Lake City; by August, New York. Official notice was received in Washington on September 16 and confirmed by President Polk in a message to Congress on December 5—and the Gold Rush was on. Since news of the discoveries reached the eastern seaboard just as overland routes westward were being closed by winter storms, a sea voyage to California was the quickest alternative for the anxious prospector.

Yet the natural passage from New York to San Francisco stretched 14,194 nautical miles around Cape Horn; from New Orleans, the distance of 14,314 nautical miles was even greater. The alternate route, involving an overland segment, crossed the Isthmus of Panama, 4,992 nautical miles, New York to San Francisco. The longer routes, though fiercely demanding, were more reliable, for the whole voyage could be made in one ship; Panama was quicker if proper connections could be made. But the hazards and costs of California travel were ignored by gold seekers in their clamor for passage. Ninety vessels cleared Atlantic ports for California during the first month of 1849, and seventy more advertised departures. Watercraft of all types were pressed into service, yet could not meet the demand. In all, 775 vessels cleared eastern ports for California, during 1849. [38]

Mystic and Mallory were smitten like the rest of America. Within two months of the first news of gold, six schooners and two ships were "up for California" at Mystic—including the venerable, twenty-three-year-old Mallory whaler *Trescott*. The spirit of the times was reported by the New London *Chronicle* of December 29, 1848:

> The ship *Trescott* is fitting out at Mystic with the utmost dispatch by Mr. Mallory, whose business character is sufficient guarantee of the energy with which the enterprise will be conducted. The ship will be commanded by a man of experience, and if the adventurers of the *Trescott* do not bring home their full share of the golden fleece, we have overestimated the qualities of the Argonauts.

The "man of experience" was Mallory's nephew Alvin who made a 194-day passage via Rio de Janeiro and Valparaiso, January 1–August 7, 1849. Other Mallory vessels soon followed, including the whalers *Bingham* (diverted from Honolulu) and *Eleanor* (sent out from Mystic), the sloop *J. A. Burr,* and the schooners *Bay State* and *California.*

The Mallorys, like most other water carriers, thus entered the intercoastal market by shifting vessels from whaling and the coasting market. By 1850, packet lines, on the model of those in the coastal and the transatlantic markets, had taken over the intercoastal market as well. And there was a firm demand for large sailing vessels, capable of the Cape Horn passage, but which could be built in four to six months and break 110 days, New York to San Francisco.[39]

Mallory's infatuation with California commerce is clear: of the thirty-eight merchant sailing vessels in which he and his sons invested between January 1, 1849, and December 31, 1861, twelve were ships expressly designed for the intercoastal market. Equally important, ten of these twelve were Mallory-built in Mallory shipyards. Reserving a discussion of these vessels' design and of the output of the Mallory yards until the next chapter, it is germane here to evaluate the family's success in intercoastal trade.

The most profitable segment of the intercoastal market was the New York to San Francisco run; and that run was dominated by packet lines similar in organization and function to those in the coastal and transatlantic markets. Shipowners could consign their vessels to a line manager in two ways: if the line had sufficient freight on hand to fill the ship, a lump-sum voyage charter was negotiated ("all expenses paid, say wharfage, stevedore, clerk hire, etc. free of commissions"); if the line had insufficient freight on hand, the manager contracted to load the ship at an agreed-upon freight rate per cubic foot of "measurement goods" and was paid a 7½ percent commission on the amount of the final freight list.

The most obvious shipowners' risk in such ventures was getting stuck with an agent who could not deliver goods sufficient for a profitable voyage: "The *Sutton* has now been on the berth six weeks to day and has not taken over 500 tons in

Aeronaut, shown here as a packet ship, was purchased by Charles Mallory in 1832 and converted to a whaler. Over the next twenty-two years she made eleven voyages under the Mallory flag and landed $238,562 worth of whale products. Courtesy Mystic Seaport.

Clipper ship *Charles Mallory*, built for the Mallorys by Irons & Grinnell of Mystic in 1851. Made one New York–San Francisco voyage of 106 days. Lost off Brazil in 1853. Courtesy Mystic Seaport.

Clipper ship *Twilight,* launched by the Mallory yards in 1857 and called "one of the best ships ever built" by the New York *Herald's* maritime editor. Her maiden run of 100 days, 20 hours from New York to San Francisco was one of the fastest ever and her six-voyage average on that route was an outstanding 116 days. Also note Charles Henry Mallory's yacht *Richmond* in left foreground. Courtesy Mystic Seaport.

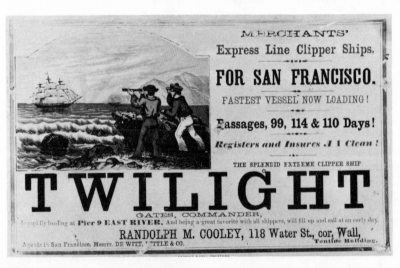

Advertisement for Mallory clipper *Twilight,* 1860. Courtesy Baker Library, Harvard Graduate School of Business Administration.

that time—whereas she should have been at sea! The owners tell me I must get her off," Charles Henry Mallory angrily wrote an agent in 1859; "shippers cannot be induced to ship on her to any extent unless they are guaranteed dispatch."[40] But these problems were reduced by dealing only with the largest New York houses: Sutton & Co.'s "Dispatch Line," Randolph M. Cooley's "Merchants' Express Line," William T. Coleman & Co.'s "California Line," Cornelius Comstock & Co.'s "Clipper Line," and Wells and Emanuel's "Empire Line."

The California representatives of these lines performed reciprocal services in procuring return freights from San Francisco to New York. The great difficulty, however, was that there were always far more ships than eastbound cargoes. Consequently, the Mallorys always made it the captain's responsibility to decide what to do, once he had reached the Golden Gate. The flavor of the trialogue among owners, captains, and agents is suggested by a letter from Charles Henry Mallory in Mystic to William T. Coleman & Co.'s San Francisco representative:

> The ship *Twilight* to your address ought to be in your port about the 1st day of May and I am anxious that she should obtain a return charter, either direct or otherwise, either to the United States or some port in Europe. You will please if you hear of any thing in the market which you consider a fair business, for a ship of her tonnage and capacity, to give such encouragement to the parties having it as will induce them if necessary to wait a few days for the arrival of the ship and to consult with captain, as I do not wish to bind the ship in the absence of the captain, who has the sole control in matters of that kind when away from home. . . .[41]

Mallory captains were authorized to keep their ships in the Pacific as long as they could find profitable employment—defined as net income of $1,000 to $2,000 per month after all ship's operating expenses were paid but before allowances for insurance, depreciation, and cost of capital. In seeking such business, the captains had several choices. To remain in the Pacific meant shuttling between California and China (via Hawaii), coasting among Chinese, Australian, and Philippine ports, the lumber trade between the Pacific Northwest and San Francisco, or various combinations of the three. These options, however, were always evaluated against the various options of "coming home": a San Francisco–New York cargo (perhaps with stops en route at Callao and/or Rio de Janeiro); carrying oil off-loaded by American whalers in Honolulu to New Bedford and New London; carrying guano from the Chincha Islands or Callao to Hampton Roads; carrying indentured coolie laborers from China to Cuban sugar plantations; or carrying tea and silks from the Orient to New York, Philadelphia, or Boston. [42] Coming home, however, involved the additional risk of finding less than profitable freight rates on the New York–San Francisco outbound leg. Coming home "in ballast" was the ultimate disgrace and coming home to a "bad market" only slightly less so. Indeed, all Mallory shipmasters were authorized to sell their vessels (at specified minimum prices, of course) if no profitable trades could be found.

The sequencing of a succession of profitable voyages from this array of conflicting possibilities obviously required intelligent and trustworthy shipmasters: men who could figure profit margins as well as they could navigate; men who could calculate their vessel's break-even point regardless of the type of cargo, length of voyage, or freight rate involved; men who could look beyond today's market to tomorrow's or next month's. [43] Their problems were compounded, however, by the slowness of communications between them and their owners: as late as 1860, an average exchange of letters between New York and San Francisco took two months and a New York–Hong Kong exchange twice that. [44] Even then, owners' instructions could do little more than provide guidelines for the captain. Witness this example from the dull, pragmatic, do-the-best-you-can days of the late 1850's:

Mystic Bridge, 16th June, 1859

Captain J. D. Gates
San Francisco
Ship E. F. Willets

Dear Sir:

By the newspapers I saw you reported 15 days from New York on 12th, and if you have kept up this rate of sailing will probably be in San Francisco on recept. of this mail. You have a power of attorney to sell the ship, and the price I believe I did not name to you. The Willets ought to bring 36,000 dolls., but I do not wish you to refuse 28,000 dolls., without in your judgement a prospect of making a very handsome freight should offer. I do not anticipate a sale, as there are a very few purchases for ships at present, but there might possibly be an opportunity to dispose of her.

As to business, I do not know what to write. Moore and Folger have written about returning to New York, but I am afraid they will not be willing to pay anything like a fair charter. Mr. Rollinson of the firm of Wm. T. Coleman & Co. proposes to load you home (lay on) also Crosby & Dibble proposed the same thing. You can call on them all, but I am fearful that they will not hold our inducements sufficient.

They are offering charters for guano from Christmas Island to New York at 15 dolls. per ton, and I should have taken one for your ship, but did not know about the quality of the guano or safety of the harbour. You will probably have some offers of that kind and must be governed by your own judgement as to accepting or refusing.

I had some conversation with Mr. Rollinson about lading your ship for China and he promised to do all he could for you. If you could get a freight over say, 2, 3, or 4,000 dolls., I think it would be the best thing you could do, as your ship is small and would command a fast passage from China home.

As to oil freights from the Sandwich Islands, I am fearful that the prospect is poor. Still, you can form an opinion in San Francisco, as probably there will be persons over from the Islands to charter ships to bring oil. An oil freight from the Islands would bring you about 12,000 to 13,000 dolls. at 7¢ per gallon—which in my opinion is no better than 15 dolls. per ton from Christmas Island or Jarvis Islands allowing the expenses to be the same, and I think that they would be from 1 to 1,500 dolls. more with oil than guano. And 8,000 dolls. from San Francisco to New York would be 1,000 dolls. better than either, allowing the expenses to be paid by charterers as customary.

If Coleman & Co. or Crosby & Dibble would lay you on and give you 25¢ per foot, and you could get your wharfage and other expenses reasonable with good dispatch, I do not think I should leave it for any other business without something should offer more than I can at present think of. If a full freight and passengers should offer for China, say 6,000 or 8,000 dolls., why of course that would in all probability be better.

I have endeavored to give an idea of what my views are, and you will be governed by your own judgement in the selection of business for the ship; as she is small and desirable that will have to enter into your calculations. If you come home with say 7,000 dolls. to 8,000 dolls. the ship will leave something. If you go to China seeking, you will have to take your chances. My experience is, in these matters, never to leave a certainty for an uncertainty.

Your family are well. Yours truly.

C. H. Mallory [45]

As these instructions imply, the Mallorys regularly calculated rule-of-thumb transfer rates for each vessel on each route for each possible type of cargo; that is, the "rate which, if it continues, will more or less enable the owner to break even but will leave him wondering whether he would be better using his capital and his entrepreneurial skills in another direction which will yield him a proper profit." [46] Table 3.1 gives some examples of these rates and Table 3.2 suggests how the captains' decisions were translated into voyage itineraries. In general, Mallory vessels spent six to eight months in the Pacific or elsewhere for every month spent on the run between New York and San Francisco.

But what of earnings? Unfortunately, evidence is sparse, but that which is available suggests that Mallory barks and ships were above average in their earning power. Table 3.3 compares the actual profitability of three Mallory vessels with hypothetical industry averages for clipper ships as estimated by Evans. These data suggest that the Mallorys' vessels earned 20 to 30 per cent on the actual value of their capital even during the lean years following the Panic of 1857. This rate of return was just over twice what they would have earned on railroad stocks or in the short-term money market for the same years. [47]

Actually, the Mallorys were probably even closer to the upper end of Evans' estimates. Evans' model and the Mallory data in Table 3.4 consider earnings on vessel equity only. The Mallorys, however, functioned simultaneously as builders, outfitters, and agents and took markups and commissions in those capacities *before* dividends were paid to their equity investment. As it was in whaling, so it was in clipper ships. Further, the Mallorys seem to have enjoyed slight comparative cost advantages and better (or more fortuitous) freight rates than their industry's average.

All the Mallory barks and ships were of the size (800–1,500 register tons) considered best "earners" by Evans. The Mallorys were fully aware that these "medium clippers" carried more cargo per register ton and could be loaded and turned around faster than their more "extreme" competitors. Their advertising pounded this home: "No delay in Loading. Smallest Clipper Up" (*Elizabeth F. Willets*); "Small, Sharp, and Popular . . . Being of Very Small Capacity Will Fill Quick" (*Haze*). [48] The Mallorys could build these ships for $10 per register ton less than the industry average, and their costs of insurance, outfitting, and maintenance were proportionately lower. Figure 3.2 translates profitability into income and expenditures and graphically portrays wherein the Mallorys' competitive advantages lay. [49]

There is no doubt that the Mallorys' slight cost advantages had disappeared by 1860 and that the general depression of the late 1850's reduced their earnings; witness Charles Henry Mallory's comments on September 19, 1859: ". . . It is really discouraging to have any thing to do with ship property at the present time. Although most people in the business are prophesying better times, I would rather see them come, than to be constantly anticipating them. . . ." But these complaints have to be taken with a lump of salt. As Evans has shown, "poor" earnings meant 10 to 20 per cent returns on capital rather than the 30 to 50 per cent of "average" times. [50]

Unquestionably, then, the Mallorys profited handsomely from their investments in the carrying trades. Their primary growth was through the reinvestment of earnings, but it remains to examine some of their techniques of mobilizing dollars and physical capital during the 1840's and 1850's.

77

Chapter 4

SHIPBUILDERS AND BANKERS,

1849–1860

"It took a hundred years to build the clippers. It took a generation of undiluted hell to develop the men to sail them."
—Carl C. Cutler, *Greyhounds of the Sea*

"Capital invested in banking is now paying larger dividends than that invested in any of the ordinary productive pursuits."—*Report of the Connecticut Bank Commissioners,* 1851

A shipyard and a commercial bank were the capstones of the first generation of Mallory business enterprise. No two institutions could better capture the blend of craftsmanship and capitalism which the family had come to represent. Both were created primarily to serve Mallory needs, but each served its community and industry as well. Curiously, one used local means to enter national markets; the other used its access to national markets to improve local means. The shipyard was possible and successful primarily because of plentiful supplies of materials, technology, and labor in the Mystic Valley; the bank was predicated on the fact that local pools of cash and credit had grown too small for the needs of the Mallorys and their associates.

Through their activities in sailmaking, whaling, and the carrying trades, the Mallorys had always been intimately involved with the numerous shipbuilders of Connecticut and New York, but always as customers or suppliers, never as investors or competitors. Yet their opinions on vessel capacity, speed, economy, endurance, and beauty were widely sought—particularly the views of Charles Mallory. His sailmaker's eyes dissected every vessel they beheld, and his broad experience in maritime enterprise could translate economics into sail plans and half models. His recognition of quality had been a distinct business asset in the period 1822–1848, when he had ventured his capital in vessels built by others. After 1848, he capitalized further on his knowledge and love of fine ships by turning his own craftsman's hands and his family's business skills to their construction.

Mallory's decision to diversify into shipbuilding and the types of ships he built were logical outgrowths of his own success and sense of entrepreneurial purpose, but they were also functions of his time and place. His decision and the clippers he chose to build were his individual responses to a generally rising demand for American-flag sailing vessels, particularly a demand for ocean-going ships and barks. Each year between 1830 and 1861, the American merchant marine added net capacity to its coastal and transatlantic markets. And to these older and steadier demands were added the euphoria and the rapid expansion of capacity characteristic of the intercoastal and transpacific markets after 1849.

As both a cause and an effect of this growth of American-flag carriage, the American shipbuilding industry underwent "a boom of . . . extraordinary proportions between 1847 and 1857 . . . which marked the peak in the construction of wooden ships" in the United States. The average annual output of sailing vessels, which had stood at 88,200 tons for the period 1815–1830, reached 99,700 tons for the period 1831–1846 and 308,000 tons during 1847–1857. And, as Hutchins has shown, shipbuilding activity "was mainly centered in the construction of ships and barks, many of them over 1,000 tons in size, which were now the primary units of the ocean-going marine." He estimates that 1,480 such vessels were built in the period 1831–1846, while 2,858 were launched during 1847–1857.

Hutchins has also described the process by which this remarkable increase in output came about:

> The industry was still basically a highly competitive, handicraft one in which few economies of large-scale operations developed. The expansion took place, therefore, primarily through an increase in the number of yards. In nearly every town whose waterway could float a large ship the construction of freighters or clippers was under-

taken. . . . The older and better-known yards were expanded . . .
[and] the number of yards multiplied as foremen, journeymen, and
even apprentices who could secure a little capital set up establish-
ments and began construction, sometimes on order, but more often
on speculation. . . . [1]

Shipbuilding in the Mystic Valley expanded at the pace and
in the ways described by Hutchins. Long-established small-craft
builders—such as the Lathams, the Morgans, and the Palmers of
Noank—continued to supply the steady demand for whaling
tenders, fishing smacks, and coasting sloops and schooners.
Long-established large yards—such as Geo. Greenman & Co. at
Adams Point and Irons & Grinnell at Pistol Point—became larger
still and increased the size of the vessels which they built. And
new builders of large vessels appeared, such as Maxson, Fish &
Co. at West Mystic (1852) and the Mallorys. Long aware of his
neighbors' success, it required only the generally rising demand
for vessels and the exciting prospects of the California trade to
trigger Charles Mallory's decision.

Between 1848 and 1854, Mallory and his sons commenced
shipbuilding at two sites on the Mystic River: the "old yard,"
which Charles had acquired as fallow land in 1838, lay on the
east bank just north of town; the "new yard," located across
the river on Appleman's Point, was purchased between 1853
and 1854 in a series of transactions by Mallory's sons. From
these yards, between 1858 and 1861, the family launched ten
ships, five barks, and three schooners. They also developed a
lucrative yacht-building business and, in 1859, built the first of
the series of wooden coastal steamers which ultimately became
their hallmark.

The Mallorys were able to start up their yards so rapidly
because of their own capital accumulation, but also because
they benefited from the Mystic Valley's previously well-estab-
lished pools of raw materials, labor, and technology.[2] Despite
increased competition for the resources necessary for shipbuilding, however, all the yards, both old and new, seem to have
remained community-centered. They often built on joint
account when individual business lagged or scale demanded, and
they regularly subcontracted among each other. For example,

prior to the Civil War, Mallory took shares in three sloops, six schooners, and three ships built by the Greenmans—including the famous clipper ship *Prima Donna* which completed fourteen New York–San Francisco round voyages, 1858–1877.[3] At Irons & Grinnell, the Mallorys invested in one sloop, three schooners, one bark, and one ship—including two namesake vessels, the schooner *D. D. Mallory* and the clipper ship *Charles Mallory.* Although differing in design, the latter was a sort of "sister" to the ship *Eliza Mallory* built in the Mallory yard.[4]

The Mallory yards were also interlocked with a web of ships' suppliers and outfitters along the Mystic–New York axis. These support activities had grown up in the service of whaling and coasting, but they could also serve shipbuilders—and did. In Mystic, the Mallory yards dealt most often with Joseph Cottrell & Co., Isaac W. Denison & Co., I. D. Clift & Co., Chapman, Randall & Co., Leonard Mallory & Co., and David D. Mallory & Co. In New York, it was J. D. Conkling, Terry & Della Torre, Fox & Polhemus, Willets & Co., and James D. Fish & Co. Cottrell was Mallory's closest friend and oldest partner, who by the 1850's was operating a lumber yard and planing mill with Irons & Grinnell and the Mallorys as silent equity. Clift had taken over the Mallory sail loft and catered to Mallory needs. Isaac W. Denison & Co., (including Cottrell, George W. Ashbey, Benjamin F. Hoxie, and Daniel W. Denison as silent partners) was the 1850 successor to the several Cottrell-Hoxie-Mallory general merchandise partnerships of the 1820's and 1830's. Chapman, Randall & Co. was a foundry and machine shop, operated by Isaac Randall with various partners after 1847.

The Mallory names among these firms are also significant and serve to introduce several younger family members who were maturing as businessmen. Leonard Mallory, Charles's nephew, opened a tinware business with his uncle's support about 1851. By the 1860's, a credit report noted that "he furnishes all the vessels built at the yard of Charles Mallory and controls much of the trade on his side of the river through family connections." David D. Mallory & Co. was a provisioning firm and general store opened in 1842 by Mallory's twenty-one-year-old second son. His third son, George W., joined the firm at twenty-one (in 1845), and it was well known that "thr.

father throws bus. into thr. hands." and that "they fit out their fathers vessels." [5]

In New York, Conkling, along with William Smith & Co., Benn & Dean, and W. A. Ellis, were the Mallorys' prime lumber agents. From Terry & Della Torre and E. H. Barstow they bought rope, chain, cable, and hardware; from Fox & Polhemus it was sailcloth and canvas; from Willets & Co. it was copper. James D. Fish & Co. were, of course, outfitters, provisioners, and fiscal and insurance agents. All these firms were leaders in their trades, and some, like Willets and Fish, were investors in the Mallory ships they supplied.

The key figure in the management of the shipyards, however, was Charles Henry Mallory.[6] Just as he did for merchant vessels at sea and for outport agents, he handled all correspondence and business affairs for the yards. He commuted weekly, if not oftener, between Mystic and New York to coordinate family interests, and he was particularly concerned with the purchasing of materials and the outfitting and marketing of vessels. His Mystic office and his rooms at the United States Hotel in New York were the command posts for tactical execution of strategy conceived at home with "Father." Foremanship of the yards' work force, however, was delegated to a group of Mystic-bred master carpenters, including Peter and John A. Forsyth, Mason Crary Hill, D. O. Richmond, and Daniel Edgecomb, who worked either by the job or under time contract. Hill's specialties were ships and barks, while Richmond was more inclined toward sloops, schooners, and sailing yachts. Edgecomb supervised interior cabinet and joiner work and helped keep the books. But all worked closely with Charles Henry Mallory, who was a good rule-of-thumb ship designer himself.

Reflecting the demands of the 1850's, the Mallory yards prior to the Civil War produced only medium-sized "clipper" ships, barks, large schooners, and sailing yachts. Most were built for their own-flag employment and management, but several were built on order for outside parties. By 1858, the yard was building some vessels for stock and was actively advertising its wares in New York through James D. Fish & Co., who were allowed a 5 per cent commission on any sales they negotiated.

How good were these Mallory-built vessels? Were they technically and economically competitive? Were any exceptional? Obviously, to answer one must examine the interrelationships of cargo capacity, speed, and operating costs.

The schooners and the first three barks were no different from hundreds of their peers.[7] Their figureheads and rig affected some of the sharpness popularized in the clipper design, but their tonnage, commodious holds, and shallow drafts revealed them as packet-type vessels intended for the domestic cotton trade of the coastal market. Similarly, the first Mallory-built ship was a run-of-the-mill packet designed for the transatlantic cotton triangle. *Eliza Mallory* made one undistinguished New York–San Francisco passage of 158 days and a better-than-average San Francisco–Honolulu passage of 12 days; but she was certainly no clipper. By contrast, her so-called "sister ship" *Charles Mallory,* built by Irons & Grinnell, was of the "extreme" clipper design—"trim yacht-like vessels, with short, full midship bodies, and very long, sharp ends." She made her maiden run, New York–San Francisco, in the outstanding time of 106 days.[8]

Alboni (1852) and *Pampero* (1853) were the first two Mallory-built clippers. They were constructed on contract for James Bishop & Co. of New York and were managed throughout their careers by that house, the Mallorys retaining only a token equity. Both vessels were of extreme clipper design, and *Alboni's* maiden appearance was described by the New York *Herald* in October 1852:

> This is a new eastern built vessel lately arrived at this port. She is a noble looking vessel of 917 tons measurement. Her appearance at once attracts and impresses the beholder with the conviction that he is looking on a veritable clipper. She is a very sharp vessel: and, head on, has a wedge-like appearance. Her lines are concave, and her timbers being carried very forward, and having neither billet-head nor head-board, her out water, in preserving its uniformity, describes an arc, the extremity—and as though supporting the bow sprit—being ornamented with a carved representation of the American Eagle preparing for a swoop.
>
> From her bow her lines run an easy sheer, terminating in a clean sharp run. From stem to stern, her lines are as regular as though she

were cast in a mould. Her stern is of a square form—light and plain. She has a topgallant forecastle, and a house abaft the foremast, containing the kitchen, etc. She has a lengthy cunk poop, and a cabin well fitted and furnished.

Her between decks are striking, her timbers being heavy and fastened in a most substantial manner, having more bolts in her than any clipper of her size before constructed. Her bottom is of oak, with cedar top—the ceiling and deck frame of yellow pine. Her keelsons are copper bolted, and measure as follows: keelsons and keel through 5, 8/12. feet, side keelsons 12 by 14 inches; bilge streaks 9 by 15. In the lower hold she has 12 inch hanging knees, and 9 inch ones between decks.

The dimensions of the vessel are: length, 170 feet; breadth, 36 feet; depth 20 feet—being 7, 1/2 feet between decks and 12, 1/2 feet in lower hold.

Her spars are made of the best materials, and well proportioned to her hull. Their dimensions are: foremast 74 feet, main 78, misen, 70: topmast 40; topgallant 24; royal 18; skysail, 13; main and fore yards, 68; topsail yards, 56; topgallant, 44; royal 31; skysail, 24; bowsprit, 22; jib boom, 22; flying, 12.

While a fine vessel and a good earner, *Alboni* never achieved early predictions of her speed. She seemed always to strike bad weather, and her best run on the New York–San Francisco route—the standard by which clipper speed was judged—was her maiden voyage, a mediocre 129 days (1852–1853). Her four-voyage average (1852–1858) was 148 days—slow for a ship of her design. *Pampero,* however, fully deserved her reputation for speed. She made a 108-day New York–San Francisco run in 1853–1854 and, for four passages on the route (1853–1860), averaged 119 days. She also set the all-time San Francisco–Hong Kong sailing record of 31 days (1854).[9]

When they built for themselves, however, the Mallorys favored that species called by Cutler "half or medium clippers," that is, "fine, sharp, fast ships, but cleverly designed to carry very heavy cargoes." While the average capacity for a clipper in the California trades was about 60 per cent over registered tonnage, this could be increased 10 to 15 per cent by lengthening, broadening, and flattening midship sections. All the six ships and two barks built between 1853 and 1861 for Mallory own-flag management incorporated these refinements. And all were designed for a fair turn of speed.

At no time were the Mallorys seduced by speed at the expense of cargo capacity or economy. They always strove to build vessels that could interchange among various markets and always sought the general as opposed to the specialty cargo. Nevertheless, they knew the facts of competitive life: "a reputation for being very fast brought cargo and passengers to a ship; fame for her captain and owner, but Hell for the crew." [10] And reputations were made on the New York to San Francisco run. "You will proceed from New York to San Francisco with all possible despatch," were typical instructions to their captains. "You will be very careful not to touch at any intermediate port except in case of *extreme necessity,* as such a course would ruin your voyage and injure the reputation of the ship to a very great degree." [11] Mallory sailing cards always included the times of previous fast passages (usually with one or two days knocked off for good measure). [12]

With full acknowledgment that so-called record passages and day's runs are not the best measure of speed under sail, the performance in these terms of the Mallory-built fleet is still worthy of note. [13] One should keep in mind that clipper-ship passages from the East Coast to the West Coast normally exceeded 120 days; 110 days was regarded as excellent time; and the all-time records made by *Flying Cloud* and *Andrew Jackson* of a few hours over 89 days were only three in number. For full-built craft, 150 days or more was the average run. [14]

Samuel Willets (1854) and *Elizabeth F. Willets* (1854) were owned in association with members of the copper, hardware, and trading firm of Willets & Co., New York. *Samuel Willets* made one passage New York to San Francisco in 120 days (1855) and might have become one of the best clippers had she not been lost off New Jersey in July 1857.

Elizabeth F. Willets was a gem. Small for a clipper, she was, nevertheless, a very consistent performer. Her best run to San Francisco was 111 days (1859), and she had a five-voyage average (1855–1860) of 129 days. She was similar to the Mallory-built *Hound* (1853), which made known San Francisco voyages of 115 days (1856–1857) and 131 days (1858). *Eliza-*

beth F. Willets was also the victor in a famous four-ship match. On September 1, 1858, she, *Raduga,* and *Skylark* cleared San Francisco in consort for Honolulu with *West Wind* close behind. Racing across the Pacific, *Elizabeth F. Willets* showed her wake to the other clippers and rounded Diamond Head at 2:00 P.M. on September 16. The other vessels followed at one-hour intervals in as impressive a procession of American-flag ships as the Sandwich Islands had ever seen. After loading in Honolulu, she again showed her speed in establishing an antebellum record of 89 days from Hawaii to New Bedford.[15]

Mary L. Sutton (1855) was built by Hill at the new yard and owned and managed by the Mallorys until her loss at Baker Island in November 1864. She was a good earner and a fine sailer; she made San Francisco passages of 103 (1860) and 110 days (twice, 1856 and 1860–1861) and averaged 115 days for eight California runs (1856–1864). Her two passages in fifteen months (1860–1861), New York–San Francisco, averaging 107 days were outstanding achievements.[16]

Haze (1859) and *Twilight* (1857) were as beautiful as their names. The former was a smallish California clipper owned by the Mallorys, J. D. Fish & Co., and Terry & Della Torre. Her two known voyages were not impressive for speed, averaging 167 days (1865–1866) on the San Francisco run. *Twilight* was something else again. "She is . . . considered one of the best ships ever built," raved the New York *Herald.* "Her model—for stability, capacity, and sailing qualities—is all that could be desired, combining strength and beauty, and looks to perfection the bold and dashing clipper."[17] Her maiden run of 100 days, 20 hours, to San Francisco (1858) was one of the best, and she followed it with runs of 114 (1859) and 109 (1861) days. Her six-voyage average (1858–1864) was 116 days.[18]

By the standards of speed and endurance of their day, then, *Mary L. Sutton, Twilight,* and *Pampero* were exceptionally stylish and consistent clipper ships. *Alboni, Elizabeth F. Willets, Hound,* and *Haze* were slower, but durable and profitable.[19] *Lapwing* (1859) and *Tycoon* (1860) were compact versions of their big sisters: "clipper-barks" designed and rigged for transoceanic passages on the Atlantic cotton triangle. *Lapwing* was built in the new yard by Hill with three-fourths of her

Clipper ship *Haze,* launched by the Mallory yards in 1859. Ran in inter-coastal and transoceanic service until sold in 1865. Courtesy Mystic Seaport.

Advertisement for Mallory clipper *Haze*, 1862. Courtesy Baker Library, Harvard Graduate School of Business Administration.

Yacht *Richmond*, launched by the Mallory yards in 1855. The first and most famous product of the Charles Henry Mallory–D. O. Richmond designing and building partnership. Sold to William West in 1857 after a long string of regatta victories with Mallory himself at the helm. Courtesy Mystic Seaport.

Yacht *Haswell*, launched as *Sylphide* by the Mallory yards in 1858. The second product of the Charles Henry Mallory–D. O. Richmond designing and building partnership. Sold to Henry Butler in 1858. Courtesy Mystic Seaport.

ownership remaining with the Mallorys throughout her career. The remainder was taken by James D. Fish & Co. and Terry & Della Torre of New York. *Tycoon* was built and owned under the same circumstances and was described by Charles Henry Mallory in a letter to a prospective buyer, May 1, 1860:

> ... she is in length 150 feet, in breadth 35 feet and 17 feet depth of hold—10 feet lower hold & 7 feet between decks, about 800 tons Register—can be registered at Custom House about 700 tons She is calculated for the Galveston & European trade. Will carry a large cargo, sail well, and be a sightly vessel, being sharp above water, round stern, and every thing to give her a Clipper appearance.
>
> Is of heavy frame of oak and chestnut, heavily fastened, and in every respect a first class vessel & I think will carry more cargo on the same draft than any other vessel in the States. Will be finished with a full roof to mainmast with capacity for say 300 bales of cotton & room in deck house for 40 bales of cotton. As to tobacco, I do not know, but suppose she would be a good ship for that trade as she would require no ballast & I think would not draw more than 11 ft. 6 in. with a full cargo of Virginia tobacco. I place her as not less than 2,200 bales compressed cotton on 10 feet of water.
>
> The price will be completed with one suit of every thing excepting copper and cabin furniture, 34,000 dollars, if finished with full roof. If person purchasing should not want full roof, price would be something less.[20]

The earning power of these Mallory ships and barks has been considered in the previous chapter and a slight comparative advantage discovered in their costs of construction. It is now appropriate to ask: How *do* Mallory prices compare? How competitive *were* they as shipbuilders?

It is clear that the Mallorys could build barks in the 600-ton range for about $42 per ton and ships in the 1,000-ton range for about $60 per ton. These prices were for vessels "completed with one suit of everything" *except* "coppering" of the hull, interior "joiner work," and "cabin furniture." Coppering added $3 per ton. The prices for joiner work and furniture were too variable to be included in the "ready-for-sea" price and were always accounted for separately.

Evans, working only with clipper ships in the period 1851–1860, estimates that a figure between $60 and $75 a ton "would be a good measure" for the "at-sea cost" of new vessels. One infers, then, that the Mallorys' ready-for-sea prices of $45 to $63 per ton were quite attractive even in the depressed markets after the Panic of 1857. Their advantages sprang mainly from the low labor costs that prevailed in the Mystic River Valley. As late as February 1862, even though materials were at a "very high price," the Mallory yards were offering to deliver barks at $42.50 per ton for "everything . . . with exception of coppering & joiner work." They were indeed competitive as shipbuilders—in price as well as design.[21]

Interestingly, at the very time the Mallory yards were establishing their clippers' reputations for quality and economy, they were also engaged in an unusual side line: the commercial construction of sailing yachts. While not as lucrative as the building of merchantmen, yacht building was aesthetically of equal (if not superior) rank.

While all Charles Mallory's sons were sailing enthusiasts, it was Charles Henry who first distinguished his family's name in yachting. He was an ardent yachtsman, a founding member of the New York Yacht Club, and was frequently asked to sail other men's boats in important races. His reputation as a builder and sailer of fast yachts extended throughout New York and New England, and he was the intimate of such other enthusiasts as Charles H. Haswell, the noted naval architect and marine engineer. Something of Charles Henry's yachting philosophy is captured in his response to a challenge by the yacht *Edgar* in July 1858:

> . . . I am not in the habit of betting money and although the temptation in this case is great I must decline. But if the *Edgar* really wants to sail, I will sail with her singly when she comes East. . . . I do not expect to have a fast boat and, being from the country [do not expect], that our city friends will be pleased at being beaten without a good deal of feeling, but I propose to sail in all regattas when convenient, and if I beat or am beaten I do not mean to stir up bad blood on my part, as I build and sail boats for the pleasure and if I am beaten bad, will try again. . . .[22]

Actually, Mallory combined business with his pleasure. With D. O. Richmond, he regularly built yachts for sale: "I wish to build one each season [for myself] and cannot afford to build unless I sell," he noted on November 9, 1858. Apparently, smaller yachts were built at sites of Richmond's choosing, while others were built in the Mallory yards themselves: "Mr. Richmond has built for me a great many boats and is now building one for me. But all [our] large boats like the *Richmond,* I have built by the day under Mr. Richmond's superintendence in ship yards, as he has not the room," Mallory explained.[23]

Whatever the exact division of labor between Mallory and Richmond, the former probably supplied most of the capital and some of the designing skill. The team's expertise attracted inquiries from all along Long Island Sound and as far away as New Bedford and Boston. Mallory's confidence in his designs is reflected in his correspondence with prospective customers:

> *7-19-58*: "I should much prefer to build a boat of the same size as the *Richmond,* with what alterations I might choose to make in model and finish her complete (with exception of cabin) and sail her myself against the *Richmond,* and if beaten forfeit a very handsome sum, if we could agree on the price."

> * * *

> *8-24-58*: Offers to build a 40-foot keel yacht for Henry Butler of Pawtuxet, Rhode Island, "guaranteed to beat the *North Star*" for $2,500; "in case she should not beat the N.S. will forfeit 250 dolls., myself to sail her or choose my boatmen in the race."

> * * *

> *7-1-59*: Offers to build a yacht for Charles H. Haswell of New York and sail her against the *Julia* in the first New York Yacht Club regatta of the season. If she beats *Julia,* the price will be $7,000. If she is beaten, Haswell may subtract 20 per cent—"with first price I should make something, with last lose."

> * * *

> *6-11-60*: Offers to build Haswell another yacht of 125 tons "complete without cabin or brass work" for $6,750. "Should like your order and for 1,000 dolls. will guarantee to beat any boat of her class of the same rig, or furnish the boat for $5,750 if beaten after a fair trial."

> * * *

> *4-27-64*: "Your enquiring if I would furnish model for yacht to be built by other parties is rec'd. I should be happy to oblige you but

I think it is asking too much, as for instance if the yacht should prove dull the fault would be placed to the maker of model and if very fast the builder would get the benefit besides having the lines to refer to in future." [24]

As implied above, the Mallory-Richmond yachts were built from half models (as were all the Mallory vessels) and furnished "complete with one coat of paint and furnish everything with exception of ropes, sails, anchors and clews, and cabin and fixtures." What quoted prices survive are obviously job rates, are unrelated to tonnage, and vary from $1,650 to $7,000 in the 25-to-125-ton range. Construction usually took four months with payment "as yacht advances." [25] By May 1859, Mallory was raising prices because of a "20 per cent" increase in labor costs since March "and I would rather you would not order at that price as I have more business than I wish unless it is more remunerative." [26]

The exact number or the names of all the Mallory-Richmond yachts built before the Civil War are unknown, but the famous ones were famous indeed. *Richmond* was the first and the prize testimonial to her designers' skill. A sloop-rigged "sandbagger," she was built in twenty-six days so that Charles Henry could sail her in the Newport regatta of 1855, which he won. She won again in New Bedford the following summer, as the New Bedford *Mercury* of August 9, 1856, described: "That saucy little *Richmond,* with her immense sails, and the defiant air of audacity she possessed, in dashing before some of her great competitors extorted much admiration. She is indeed a living model of a yacht and has not an atom of dead wood in her composition." Mallory sailed her to four firsts and a fourth in New York Yacht Club regattas for "3rd class boats," during 1855–1857, before selling her to William West of New Bedford.

Sylphide, renamed *Haswell,* was launched on May 27, 1858, and took one first (second class) before her sale to Henry Butler of Pawtucket for $2,500. With Charles Henry Mallory at the helm, she also won the New York regatta off Sandy Hook on June 2, 1859. *Bonita* was designed by another Mallory associate, W. H. Brainard, launched by Charles Henry in April

1859, and sold to George Huested of New Bedford. *Mallory,* another sloop, was launched on August 1, 1859, and took at least one second (third class) before her sale to James T. Bache of New York. The schooner *Zouave,* launched in August 1860, doubled as a yacht owned jointly by Charles Henry and David D. Mallory and as a coasting sloop.[27]

If the Mallory clippers were one index of both American and family economic and social prosperity, the Mallory yachts were another gauge of rising affluence. But granting the antebellum demand for commercial and pleasure vessels, and granting that the output of the Mallory yards was competitive in price and quality, it remains to appraise their industrial, regional, and national importance as shipbuilders.

All told, during the years 1850–1859, American shipbuilders launched 2,466 ships and barks.[28] Of this total, the Mallory yards accounted for only 0.6 per cent. With such a small market share, where, then, is their significance as builders of large sailing vessels?

Their significance lies in their share of the market for the particular types of vessels in which they chose to specialize. Cutler and Hutchins have estimated that of the total number of ships and barks built in the United States during 1850–1859, only 445 (18 per cent) could lay any claim to the title of "clipper." What importance did the Mallorys have in the construction of these vessels which were their specialty?[29]

Table 4.1 summarizes the geographic distribution of the builders of the 445 vessels acknowledged to have been clippers. From the table, it is clear that Connecticut contributed only a small share of national output, which, by some standards, might be written off as marginal. Interestingly, however, 91 per cent of Connecticut's clippers (93 per cent by tonnage) were built in Mystic. Thus it was actually a single town and not the state as a whole which had 5 per cent of the national market. Further, while Mystic produced about 5 per cent of all American clippers, "her ships made more than 10 per cent of the fast voyages around Cape Horn to San Francisco, taking 110 days or less as the criterion of a fast clipper run."[30]

Quality was, thus, the hallmark of the Mystic yards, and the Mallorys were leaders among fast company. In terms of speed, the most glamorous Mystic clippers—*David Crockett* (1853) and *Andrew Jackson* (1855)—were products of the Greenmans and Irons & Grinnell, respectively. As described above, however, the Mallorys had their share of swift sailers. As Table 4.2 indicates, the Mallory yards were also the largest among the Mystic clipper builders in terms of output: 43 per cent by number and 39 per cent by tonnage.

The Mallorys thus accounted for 39 per cent of all clippers built in Connecticut, 1850–1859 (36 per cent by tonnage). Ranked on a national scale, they launched 2 per cent of both the number and tonnage of clippers built in the United States prior to the Civil War. In addition, they launched the five clipperlike barks previously described.

Table 4.3 puts the Mallorys' national market share in clear perspective. Only four builders exceeded them in individual output, and no single firm commanded very much more of the market than they did. These data reinforce Hutchins' conclusions about the atomistic nature of competition among clippership builders and reveal the Mallorys' notable rank among their peers.

Once again, then, the needs of the Mallory enterprises had caused their proprietors to broaden their investment with both personal and community success. Unlike the move from sailmaking into whaling and the carrying trades, which had been the forward integration of suppliers into the realm of their customers, the move into shipbuilding was a backward integration by consumers into production of capital goods. Both moves were well timed and made business sense for the Mallorys and economic sense for their region. Both were typical of the pragmatic process by which the family's basic commitment to American-flag shipping was sustained prior to the Civil War.

Amidst this very success and coincident with some of their most dramatic maritime accomplishments, the Mallorys also chose to become bankers. On August 5, 1851, they and several associates met in the general store of Tift & Russell in Portersville and opened stock subscription books for a new commercial bank. Before sundown, the entire capital offering of 2,000 shares had been taken at $50 per share, $12.50 down, and the stock ledger of this new "Mystic River Bank" left little doubt as to its initiatory and presiding equity. Among the ten largest stockholders were:

Charles Mallory	60 shares
Charles H. Mallory	20 shares
David D. Mallory	20 shares
Joseph Cottrell	60 shares
Benjamin F. Hoxie	50 shares
Geo. Greenman & Co.	72 shares
Nathan G. Fish	60 shares
George W. Ashbey	60 shares

This was the same group so long associated in whaling and commerce and, more recently, in shipbuilding. They now affiliated themselves once again in the ownership and operation of a financial institution. Charles Mallory served as the bank's president from its opening on August 1, 1851, to August 7, 1860, and as a director from the start until its conversion into a national bank on December 1, 1864.[31]

For men apparently up to their ears in maritime enterprise, why should the Mallorys become bankers, too? The creation of the Mystic River Bank was well within their broader entrepreneurial purposes, and it highlights their subtle but continuous importance as regional and sectoral financial intermediaries. Charles Mallory had begun the process in his transition from craftsman to capitalist, and it continued throughout his family's antebellum years. In profitably capitalizing on his craft skill, Mallory had done more than merely add to the American output of manufactured cotton goods. Because he had consistently earned greater returns than he felt his sail loft could or should absorb, he had increasingly acquired the means and the inclination to shift surplus funds away from the business that earned them and into other enterprises. And each of his diversifications, in turn, had generated sufficient profits to permit both their sustenance and further diversification.

The patterns of Mallory's choices caused dollars earned in sailmaking to purchase shares in whalers and coasters, and the profits of whalers and coasters to underwrite clippers. In making these business choices, however, Mallory and his sons were also performing an economic function, both for their industry and for their region. They were taking the trouble and bearing the risks of accumulating capital, and they were making decisions as to where and when it should be employed. They were, thus, serving as intermediaries between savings and investments—initially only for themselves but increasingly for their neighbors and for their business peers.

They had originally performed this function of financial intermediation in a very personal and community-centered way through the venture and open-account systems characteristic of the Mystic Valley's business adolescence. By the 1850's, however, the scale and diversity of the Mallory enterprises were demanding and generating a volume of funds that far exceeded both the capacity of the older systems of capital accumulation and the local opportunities for profitable investment. As the family increased the range and size of its business activities, it required access to larger-than-local pools of savings and a broader-than-Mystic investment spectrum. The Mystic River Bank was the means to those ends, and it served both the family and its community.

The Mallorys' choice to transform their long-standing but personal role as financial intermediaries into the formal bricks and mortar of an incorporated commercial bank was possible because of the growth and sophistication of banking practices in the upper Atlantic states after 1840. But the *reasons* for their decision to become bankers were twofold: first, they wished to earn transactional profits from a more systematic serving of the short-term credit and liquidity needs of Mystic businessmen and to earn additional profits on the bank's investment portfolio; second, and more important, they wished to use the bank as a means of access to cash and credit in amounts and for time periods beyond the capacity of local resources and on especially favorable terms. They were successful in both endeavors, and, as in shipbuilding, they served their community while they served themselves.

As an investment, banks were a good possibility by the 1850's. With the end of the 1837–1843 depression and with a rash of state legislation permitting banking under general incorporation laws, new banks seemed everywhere. Not one commercial bank and only six savings banks had been incorporated in Connecticut from 1843 to 1848; the next ten years counted the charter of forty-seven new commercial banks and twenty-six savings banks. [32] And in spite of such rapid expansion, dividends on bank stock stayed high until the Panic of 1857: "Capital invested in banking is now paying larger dividends than that invested in any of the ordinary productive pursuits," the Bank Commissioners of Connecticut stated in 1851, although they hastened to add that this was "a state of things which cannot be considered healthy or desirable." [33] To the Mallorys, only the first half of the statement appealed. They could look around them at their two closest commercial banks and see the Mystic and the Stonington Bank averaging dividends of 7.8 per cent and 7.3 per cent per annum, respectively, for the six years, 1847–1852; they could see the Mystic Bank even paying a 10 per cent dividend in 1850. [34]

Such high dividends were partially the result of a greater volume of transactional profits from traditional commercial banking activities, but they were also symptomatic of wider investment opportunities. In Connecticut, banks were particularly benefiting from New York City's need for funds. As elements of the largest and most active money market in America, New York banks and brokers had more investment opportunities than funds—particularly in the commercial-paper and call-loan markets. As one method of attracting investment capital to the metropolis, by 1844 some New York banks and brokers were paying interest ranging from 3 to 6 per cent on balances left with them by country banks. These balances were then invested at higher rates, usually in the brokers' call-loan market.

Previously, country-bank balances left with city banks had not drawn interest and had been for the dual purpose of redeeming country bank notes when they appeared in the city and of enabling country banks to sell exchange on New York when the rate was favorable. Now, country-bank funds were migrating to the cities irrespective of redemption needs and were evermore involving country bankers profitably in the growth of a national capital market. One result was the upswing in country-bank investment, With the dark days of the Panic of 1857 yet unborn, commentators extolled the prospects rather than the risks: "for the past few years investments in bank stocks have been so profitable as to induce almost every capitalist to purchase such stocks at large premiums." [35]

Thus, the Mallorys' Mystic River Bank was not unusual for its time and place, and its proprietors made its political and economic loyalties as clear as the designs on its bank notes. Its nearest competitors—the Mystic Bank (1833), the Stonington Bank (1822), and the Ocean Bank of Stonington (1851)—used pictures of Archimedes, Washington, and Franklin on their bank notes. The Mallorys' bank also used Franklin and Washington, but featured the great Whig politicians Clay, Cass, Webster, Taylor, and Fillmore. These were intertwined with scenes of shipbuilding, whaling, cooperage, wharves, and sailing ships. In its public context, then, the Mallorys and their associates intended their new bank as a profitable mechanism for resolving the financial needs of the particular economic community in which it was located.

In offering short-term credit and liquidity to Mystic businessmen, the Mystic River Bank functioned as a typically American bank of deposit, issue, and discount. By accepting demand deposits drawable by check, the bank helped to replace the town's older, open-account system with a more liquid and more-than-local circulating medium and method of settlement. It extended short-term credits by discounting promissory notes and bills of exchange,—issuing its own bank notes to the borrower in amounts less than the face values of his notes and bills. And, since the volume of bank notes issued in the discounting process was backed by only fractional specie reserves, the bank was further augmenting the circulating medium while it was enlarging the supply of credit.

The services of the bank also provided the residents of Mystic with more formal and regular access to wider capital markets. The bank maintained balances with correspondent banks in New York and Boston both for the redemption of its bank notes in those centers (besides redemption at its own counters) and to maintain its capacity to sell exchange on those points. Of course, it performed reciprocal services for its correspondents, and it bought and sold the bank notes of other banks and commercial paper at discount—all to the benefit of

Mystic businessmen desiring a means of easily exchanging financial obligations as their liquidity preferences varied.

From its discounting and exchange business, from its portfolio of loans on real property, and from interest received on its New York balances, the bank generated profits for its investors (the Mallorys included). Dividends of 8 per cent per annum were paid on the capital stock in 1853 through 1857; 4 per cent in the depression year of 1858; and 6 per cent per annum in 1859, 1860, and 1861. The Mystic River Bank thus performed a community role in serving the credit and liquidity needs of its customers and earned a good rate of return for its investors. Its operations were those of a sound, conservatively managed institution with ample reserves (by the standards of the 1850's) to meet its obligations.[36]

The bank's most significant role, however, is not apparent in its balance sheets. In several senses, the Mystic River Bank also functioned as part of an arrangement for channeling cash and credit back and forth along the Mystic–New York axis according to the specific needs of the Mallorys, their associates, their suppliers, and their customers.

The other corporate parties to the entente were the Market, the American Exchange, and the Marine banks of New York City. The Market Bank was closely associated with merchants and packet-line managers operating in the coastal and intercoastal markets. The American Exchange Bank was also well connected in maritime circles, particularly among such important shipping investors and outfitters as the Mallorys' friends the Willetses. Samuel Willets, for whom a Mallory clipper was named, had been an incorporator of the bank in 1838 and served a two-year term as its president in 1854–1855. Among the incorporators of the Marine Bank in 1853 was the Mallorys' prime New York agent and widely related former Mystic resident, James D. Fish; and Fish was to become his bank's vice president in 1860 and its president in 1861.

These banks and the Mystic River Bank bought each others' stock; moved deposits amongst themselves in response to their individual and collective needs; maintained balances with each other for bank-note redemption, short-term investment, and exchange; cosigned each other's notes; and discounted and rediscounted each other's paper. There was nothing illegal in this arrangement, but its extent and dynamics were not publicly known. In short, an arrangement tied by blood and by business created a joint pool of cash and credit far greater than the individual resources of its members. It was from this pool that the Mallorys (and their fellow insiders) served their large and long-term credit needs—on preferential terms.[37]

The prime means by which they obtained their long-term credit was through "accommodation" loans. Unlike promissory notes originating in short-term transactions between merchants (which were endorsed by their maker and by the merchant who received the note in payment for the goods which secured it), accommodation notes required no collateral other than the "personal security" of their maker and any cosigners he was able to include.[38] As the saying went at the time, business "produced real paper" while accommodation paper "produced business." The former was supposed to be nonrenewable and short-term; the latter was expected to be renewed as long as the credit was needed and the personal security of the borrower remained sound. "Such loans were given for the development of capital resources and [were] slowly repaid, if ever, in installments over a period of several years."[39]

The volume of accommodation loans obtained by the Mallorys through their banking connections was considerable. Both Connecticut and New York banking laws severely restricted the amounts directors could borrow from their own banks. But banking arrangements such as that to which the Mystic River Bank was a party sidestepped the restriction: the city and country banks, although associated, carefully refrained from interlocking their directorates so that the New York banks could accommodate the needs of the Mystic directors and the Mystic banks (along with the other country banks) could accommodate the needs of the New York directors. In the process, all had sufficient borrowing power even through the depression years of 1858–1859.

Thus, by the 1850's the immaturity of financial institutions which had made the capital-mobilizing initiative of entrepreneurs like the Mallorys so crucial was rapidly being replaced by more formal financial intermediaries and by more national capital markets. For Connecticut businessmen seeking funds as well as for those seeking investments, two new truths were oft repeated:

> . . . [there] has [been] a tendency to concentrate the most of the surplus capital of our citizens at those points where banks are located, and thus to compel those who are under the necessity of borrowing money to carry on their business, to resort to those points for that purpose. . . .
>
> *　*　*
>
> Every businessman is at the present time compelled to borrow of banks, when formerly loans were obtained from individuals.[40]

The Mallorys had reacted to these environmental trends and to their increasing needs for funds in their characteristically direct way: they capitalized on change and became bankers themselves. The Mystic River Bank was at one and the same time an institution of high utility to its community, a profitable investment for its stockholders, and the financial arm of the Mallory family enterprises.

By 1861, then, the Mallory maritime interests encompassed the financing, construction, and operation of sailing vessels in three major freight markets and in whaling. The sail loft was there to remind the family of its beginnings, but the transition from craftsmen to capitalists was complete.

~~~~~~

Chapter 5

THE ERA OF THE CIVIL WAR,

1861–1865

"... our men are leaving every day & we have more work than can be done."—Diary of Charles Henry Mallory, 1864

AS the decade of the 1860's dawned, there was no doubt along the coasts of the United States or on the high seas that the intelligence, integrity and initiative of Charles Mallory and his sons had earned them the roles they enjoyed as economic and social leaders. The twenty-year-old sailmaker who had hiked into the Mystic Valley on Christmas Day 1816, with his tools on his back and $1.25 in his pocket, was now in his sixties and listed by Dun & Bradstreet as "the wealthiest man in Mystic—the richest man in the vicinity—worth $300,000, credit A-1—a sound substantial man." [1]

Mallory's sons were also his pride. The eldest, Charles Henry, who had worked in the sail loft at eleven, gone to sea at fifteen, and come ashore to manage his father's interests, was now in the full vigor of his forties with a devoted wife, three fine sons, and net assets of $50,000 himself. David, George, and Franklin Mallory, who had worked in the loft and invested in their father's and brother's ships and shipyards, were by the 1860's busily rebuilding their general store, which had burned in 1858, and hoping to regain the $100,000 per annum gross on $20,000 stock in trade that they had earned before the fire. Benjamin Mallory, who had sailed before the mast at fourteen and had become a schooner captain at nineteen, was now employed in the Mallory whaling fleet. [2]

The economic strength and social position of the family was thus secure well before the first business generation had passed. Collectively, on January 1, 1861, the Mallorys held managing equity in an impressive variety of enterprises: three whalers and outfits on the high seas jointly valued at $75,000; thirteen sloops and schooners operating in the coastal market valued at $40,000; three barks operating in the coastal market valued at $74,000; five clipper ships operating in the inter-coastal and transoceanic markets valued at $260,000; a sail loft and two shipyards with a joint book value of over $15,000; a commercial bank whose assets totaled $214,000; extensive real-estate holdings in their home town and a host of shares in such local public-service associations as the Mystic Bridge Fire Company, the Elm Grove Cemetery, and the Mystic Academy.

In most respects, these assets reflected their traditional lines, with one new and promising addition:—the construction of steamboats. David and George Mallory had taken a small flier in steam as early as 1852, when they had supplied 1/24 of the capital required by William Miller of New London to launch *Mystic* for the Long Island Sound excursion trade.[3] By 1859, they had persuaded their father and their older brother to lay down a steamer in the Mallory yards. One can imagine the mixed emotions of the old sailmaker and his clipper- and yacht-designing son in consenting to do so.

To successful sailing entrepreneurs like the Mallorys, steam was not considered a competitive threat until the mid-nineteenth century. They could consult their own ledgers to assure themselves of sail's profitability and could see only a slight intrusion of steam into their markets. In 1817, the year Charles Mallory first stitched a sail on his own account, steam tonnage accounted for only 0.6 per cent of the American merchant marine. By 1822, when he first ventured his capital in vessels, steam's share was only 1.7 per cent. By 1849, however, the year of the first Mallory-built vessel, steam's share had risen to 13.8 per cent.

By 1859, the year the Mallorys launched their first steam-er, 14.9 per cent of American tonnage was steam-propelled, and the new technology could not be ignored by even the mossiest old shellback sailor.[4] What is remarkable is that the builders of the Mystic Valley resisted as long as they did. Through early 1858, the various Mystic yards had launched only four steam vessels: three by the Greenmans, in 1842, 1855, and 1858; and one by an unknown builder in 1850. Things rapidly changed.

The impetus for change came from outside of Mystic, but involved the Mallorys and all their shipbuilding neighbors. The Commercial Steamboat Co., which had been operating screw steamers between Providence and New York since 1851, decided in late 1857 to escalate its competition with Cornelius Vanderbilt's and Daniel Drew's New York–Stonington line. To do so, the Providence line placed a series of orders for wooden "propellors" with the three major Mystic yards. Over the next six years, the Greenmans delivered *Albatross* (1858); Maxson, Fish & Co. delivered *Kingfisher* (1863) and *Sea Gull* (1863); and the Mallory yards delivered *Penguin* (1859), *Falcon* (1861), and *Eagle* (1861).[5]

For Mystic, the Commercial Steamboat Co. contracts were a fortuitous shot in the arm just when the demand for clipper ships was slacking due to overcapacity in the intercoastal market and foreign-flag competition on the transoceanic routes. For the Mallorys, the contracts were these things, too, but the three vessels they built for the Providence line during 1859–1861 also introduced the family into the age of steam in a rapid, intensive, but manageable way. Luckily, the pool of shipbuilding capacity and expertise that Mystic enjoyed by the 1850's complemented their own considerable skills: they shared problems and solutions with the Greenmans, the Randalls, and Cottrell's recently opened Mystic Machine Company; also, they benefited from the advice of a yachting chum of Charles Henry Mallory, Cornelius H. Delamater of the Delamater Iron Works of New York. The results were encouraging enough to induce them to seek steamer construction contracts on their own.[6]

Varuna and *Stars and Stripes* were the first steamers built on speculation by the Mallorys. They were laid down in 1860, and their specifications were rapidly disseminated to prospective buyers. As early as January 30, Charles Henry described the family's plans:

> . . . a line of steamers between New York & Galveston. They will be propellors of sufficient power to make the passage in about 8 days or one trip per month. Of 4,000 tons and capacity for 60 first class

passengers. I have no doubt that they will pay & am going into it as soon as the stock is taken—3/4 of one boat is now taken & I have no doubt but the balance will be taken this week and the steamer ready to leave New York by the 1st of August. She will cost ready for sea about 75,000 dols., not more, capacity about 1,600 bales cotton.

By May 9, he reported *Varuna* on the stocks, "ready for covering," with a projected completion date of September 15 and a price tag of $75,000 to $80,000. "There are parties, one in particular, who want her for the trade between New York and New Orleans but nothing definite has yet been done. Also one concern who . . . propose to take quite an interest in her and run her wherever the ownership can be taken and the business looks like a remuneration." [7]

Stars and Stripes was a smaller, slower, and cheaper propellor "commenced for the Texas business from New York." Her slower speed and lesser draft would be adequate in the Texas trade where passenger and mail business was slight and harbors shallower; the swifter, deeper *Varuna* was better suited for New Orleans, where conditions were reversed. In price, *Stars and Stripes* was advertised at $40,000. [8]

Thus, it was business as usual for the whole of 1860 with prospects for an exciting new line. The whalers *Leander* and *Romulus* were sold in January and May, *Robin Hood* was at sea, and *Cornelia* and *Coriolanus* shoved off on voyages in June and July. The clippers *Hound, Elizabeth F. Willets, Mary L. Sutton, Twilight,* and *Haze* were all at sea and employed in intercoastal and transoceanic trade. The sloops and schooners were tramping about the coastal market, and the barks *Mustang, Lapwing,* and *Tycoon* were deployed on the transatlantic cotton triangle. The indications of profit in coastal steamships were promising. Yet the onrush of civil war soon destroyed this complacency and transformed the organization, technology, scale, and purposes of the Mallory business.

Although the Mallorys were profoundly affected by the Civil War, it took them completely by surprise. They were not closely enough tuned to politics to have predicted secession or its aftermath, and they show no evidence of contingency planning against the possibility of interstate war. The reason for this political naiveté was simple: for forty years and with singular fixation of purpose the family had pursued personal and community aggrandizement to the neglect of regional or national consciousness. The problems of Mallorys and of Mystic came first, and these rarely encompassed the controversies over territorial expansion, slavery, and protectionism that were aggravating other regions and the nation in general.

It was not that the Mallorys were unaware of or unresponsive to the sectional controversies of the day; it was, rather, that they concerned themselves with these issues *only* when their personal or community interests were involved. Even then, their response was usually pragmatic and seldom doctrinaire. They had opposed the Mexican War when it threatened to disrupt trade in the coastal market; but they were happy to secure government charters hauling men and supplies for the armies of Taylor and Scott. They had favored the annexations of Texas and California because statehood for those regions extended the coastal market protected by American cabotage and created the new, but equally protected, intercoastal market. They morally opposed slavery, but were, at best, only passive fellow travelers of abolitionism. They were, of course, concerned lest the southern trade deteriorate, and they were meeting increasing foreign-flag competition on the high seas, but their reactions had been those of maritime businessmen, not of politicians: diversify your markets; reduce your costs; redeploy and rotate your vessels to best advantage; sell out when you can. And, since they were carriers and not exporters or importers, they were free traders more interested in freight rates than in customs duties and were usually bored by the whole protectionist debate. When forced by circumstances to take stock of their politics, they found themselves to be unionist, old-line Whigs, slightly skeptical of the newfangled "Republican" party and slightly puzzled as to why compromising liberalism of the Clay and Webster variety no longer worked to level intersectional controversy.

With the election of Abraham Lincoln as President on November 6, 1860, the Mallorys' political apathy became untenable. By February 1, 1861, South Carolina, Mississippi, Florida, Alabama, Georgia, Louisiana, and Texas had all adopted ordinances of secession. On February 4, 1861, a constitutional convention convened at Montgomery, Alabama, and two weeks later elected Jefferson Davis as Provisional President of the Confederate States of America. Since the status of the ports of the coastal market was thus cast in doubt, the Mallorys finally began to take notice. On February 11, Charles Henry issued the first of a series of letters to their homeward-bound captains at sea: "Owing to the unsettled state of the country I think you had better go to some port in the West Indies . . . or come direct to New York or some Northern port as there is no knowing what may be the result of our present troubles." By March 9, he was quizzing his Galveston agent; "Is there any fear in your opinion of seizure of Northern shipping at ports in your state?"

The crisis came solidly home in a very personal way, in the form of a letter from the family's cousin, Stephen Russell Mallory, postmarked Montgomery, Alabama, and dated March 15. They had not heard from him since his branch of the family had located in Florida in the 1830's, but they had followed his career as an attorney and influential United States senator with familial affection. He now addressed them, however, as prospective Secretary of the Navy of the Confederate States! [9]

Secretary-to-be Mallory inquired into the details of steamship construction in general and the vessels of his cousins in particular. They readily described both *Varuna* and *Stars and Stripes,* giving specifications, capabilities, and prices, and estimated it would take four months to build comparable vessels. They carefully parried other requests, however, professing ignorance of "any light draft strong fast ship of this class for sale" or of "a first rate ship carpenter" who might be at leisure. They also declined what for the date was an incredible suggestion: "You also ask me," wrote Charles Henry, "if I would like to try my hand at building a very fast light draft screw ship." Yes, "but in the present unsettled state of the nation I should not wish to enter into any arrangement unless it was strictly legitimate and above board. I trust that all may be peaceably settled as I look forward with horror to a collision between the two sections of my beloved country." [10]

If their cousin's inquiry did not convince them of the

probability of war, there was no doubt after the Confederate shelling of Fort Sumter on April 12. On April 19, President Lincoln ordered the blockade of all southern ports from South Carolina to Texas (extended to North Carolina and Texas on April 27). On April 22, the family addressed both Governor William A. Buckingham and Secretary of the Navy Gideon Welles, offering their schooner *Zouave "free of compensation"* for the protection of the Connecticut coast and to intercept any southbound vessels or cargoes: "The *Zouave* is as fleet as the winds, and would answer until something better could be procured which could be done in shape of steam gun boat in about 60 days." [11]

The offer was refused, but from this point on, the family's wartime business strategy rapidly jelled: whaling was to be liquidated as soon as possible; sloops and schooners were to forgo the coastal market south of Philadelphia and were to be laid up if necessary or sold if feasible; barks and clippers were to be kept at sea, changing flags if necessary, and sold if possible; construction of sailing vessels was to be frozen in deference to an escalation of steamship building; steamers were to be built for sale to private parties, for sale to the government, and/or for own-flag operation in private and public carriage; and every effort was to be made to obtain contracts for the construction of naval vessels. To pursue such goals in a situation of crisis and scarcity obviously called for conservation of the family's financial, technological, and human resources and prudent management of their expenditure.

The whalers were easily eliminated. The thirty-seven-year-old *Robin Hood,* which returned from her sixth profitable Mallory-flag voyage on September 17, 1861, was sold to the government on October 16 for $4,000, less 2½ per cent commission. She became one of the famous "Stone Fleet" sunk by the federal navy in an attempt to blockade the Confederate port of Charleston. The thirty-five-year-old *Coriolanus,* then on her seventh Mallory-flag voyage, was condemned and sold in Mauritius in November 1861. The twenty-one-year-old *Cornelia,* often called "the last of the Mystic whalers," was sold to New London parties shortly after her return from her third Mallory-flag voyage, on June 17, 1862.[12]

It is impossible to document the Civil War histories of the thirteen Mallory-flag sloops and schooners except to say that they were sold off as profitably as possible, and most of them had disappeared from the family's books by 1865. The barks and ships, however, can be accounted for, as they were important assets which Charles Henry Mallory conscientiously tried to maintain as economically and as safely as he could.

Hound, which was valued at $24,000 on January 1, 1861, was advised on December 23: "If you can find no business under the flag and cannot sell the ship, you put her under the Danish flag as I consider that the best." She did find some American-flag business on the New York–London–Shanghai route and paid dividends of $3,600 (January 1, 1862) and $8,000 (November 12, 1862). By September 14, 1863, Charles Henry Mallory was advertising the ship "for sale freight or charter. I shall be very happy to sell for a great deal less than she is worth." On October 12, he succeeded in selling her for $17,500—"which is cheap, but she is . . . not a desirable ship for Business." [13]

Haze, which was valued at $48,000 on January 1, 1861, and insured for $50,000, was run on the New York–San Francisco route and paid at least two dividends: $8,000 on January 1, 1862, and $16,000 on March 23, 1863. By October 27, 1863, she was advertised for sale at $62,500; by September 22, 1864, at $80,000; but was still under the Mallory flag at war's end. [14] *Mary L. Sutton,* valued at $72,000 on January 1, 1861, was also kept on the New York–San Francisco run and paid dividends of at least $20,000 (April 26, 1861) and $9,600 (January 1, 1862). The Mallorys were hoping to sell her for "$70,000 at least after paying all expenses" when she was lost off Baker Island in November 1864 (fully insured). [15] *Twilight,* valued at $80,000 on January 1, 1861, ran primarily in the intercoastal and transatlantic markets, paying dividends of at least $1,500 (September 22, 1862). She was priced for sale on August 23, 1864, at $100,000 and was considered "as good property as could be had probably . . . will earn as much as a new one, whereas a new ship would cost $150,000 to build." Nevertheless, she was still in Mallory hands when peace came. [16]

The case of the *Elizabeth F. Willets* is the best illustration of the problems and process of Mallory management of a clipper during the war. *Willets* was valued at $37,328 on January 1, 1861, and was in Shanghai when the war began. On June 10, her captain was advised: "You will stay in the East as long as you can find anything to do. If American ships can find no business you will have to sell the ship. If you cannot sell at a fair price and can put the ship under Dutch colors and find a good business, do so. Use your judgment but be careful and guard against being taken 'in' in change of papers." [17]

On November 6, 1861, however, the Mallorys learned of Captain E. Williams' sudden death in Shanghai. They immediately dispatched letters to their agents there, Bower, Hamburg & Co., to take charge of the vessel, discharge the first mate (who was a known drunkard) if necessary, and hold it for the arrival of Captain A. K. Williams (then first mate of *Hound*), who would take command. The ship was to be sold at $25,000 to $30,000 (Mexican), if possible. No takers were found, but the ship did find employment sufficient to remit dividends of $12,800 (October 6, 1862), $4,000 (November 14, 1862), and $3,600 (April 6, 1863). [18] By May 14, 1863, the *Willets* was still in Chinese waters, and her captain was told to keep her there as long as he could earn $1,500 per month "after paying your expenses." By October 10, he was advised, "Do not fail to sell the ship if you can get anything like a fair price for her. You will recollect that the ship, if she sells for $20,000 [silver] in Shanghai will net almost double the amount here [in currency]. Do not bring her home if you can possibly sell her." A follow-up letter of October 30 was even more explicit on the choices available and on Mallory preferences:

> Yours of the 19th. of August is recd. I am sorry to hear that you find the market for freight so poor. I do not know what to advise. It would be ruinous to come home in ballast. But if business should be better even for foreign flags the chances for selling the *Willets* would be better. I have sold the *Hound* for 17,500 dolls. which is cheap, but she is like the *Willets* not a desirable ship for Business. I can not impress it too strongly on your mind that the *Willets* should be sold. Certainly she will bring 10,000 dolls. & upwards. If you can earn your expenses and send home 500 dolls. per month it will be much better than to come home in ballast or if you can keep the ship in

good order & at the same time keep out of debt it would be much better than to return in ballast.

I think business must be better before long. Business for ships here is good for nothing. My advice is to keep the ship there as long as possible—and if you can get no business under the American Flag & *cannot sell,* and if by putting her under the Belgian Flag you can get business you have my permission to do so. But I would rather the ship should be sold for 12,000 dolls. even than that. If you have anything like an offer close up the matter at once. . . .

You must do the best that you can but I shall rely upon your disposing of the ship away from home. I shall not get any more insurance on her probably, as the earning will not afford it. . . .

Captain Williams was able to remit $16,000 in December 1863, but he again hit slim pickings. By February 1, 1864, he was instructed: "As long as you can earn $4,000 in each two months you will continue to do so that is much better than you can do with the ship at home. You will use your utmost endeavors to sell the ship as it would be ruinous to bring her home." The captain was able to comply, fortunately, and *Elizabeth F. Willets* was sold in Shanghai shortly thereafter for $15,500. [19]

The three Mallory-flag barks had less prosperous but more colorful wartime careers. *Mustang,* which was valued at $10,400 on January 1, 1861, continued to run on the upper portion of the coastal market, paying dividends of $400 (January 1, 1862), $1,280 (May 13, 1862), $9,600 (November 24, 1862), $1,600 (December 1, 1862), and $227 (April 23, 1863), before disappearing from the Mallory books. [20] *Lapwing,* valued at $27,200, ran in the transoceanic trades and paid at least one dividend, $3,200 (January 1, 1862). On March 28, 1863, while bound from Boston to Batavia with a cargo of coal, she was captured at lat. 31° N., long. 33° 35′ W., by the C.S.S. *Florida.* Three Confederate officers, fifteen men, and a twelve-pound howitzer were put aboard, and *Lapwing* sailed for a short time as tender to the *Florida.* She actually took one prize herself before being burned at sea. [21] *Tycoon,* valued at $32,000 on January 1, 1862, also ran in the transoceanic market, except for two government charters: a $5,000 voyage from New York to Key West in February 1862 and miscellaneous voyages at $206 per day from August 26 to September 11, 1863. From these, she paid at least $5,600 (January 1, 1862) and $20,000 (October 21, 1862) in dividends. She was captured and burned, at lat. 10° 55' S., long. 31° 25' W. (thirty-six days from New York bound for San Francisco), on April 27, 1864, by the C.S.S. *Alabama*—"*Alabama's* sixty-fourth and last prize, her fifty-fourth bonfire at sea." [22]

With some travail, then, the Mallorys were able to extricate themselves from the ownership and management of most of their deepwater sailing vessels over the course of the war, and not wholly at a loss. This extrication was conscious and was dictated both by their discouragement with profit levels in the intercoastal and transoceanic markets and by the very lucrative wartime opportunities in steam. These were the opportunities that transformed their business during 1861-1865.

Cornelius S. Bushnell of New Haven was the catalyst who introduced the Mallorys to the possibilities offered by the wartime demand for steamships, and under Charles Henry's urgings, the head of the family agreed. Bushnell was a former sea captain and a yachting associate of the Mallory brothers. More important, he was president of both the Shore Line Railroad and the New Haven Propellor Company and had been one of those interested in *Varuna* and *Stars and Stripes.* As war came, Bushnell persuaded the Mallorys to sell those vessels to the government rather than continue to seek civilian buyers. As a demonstration of his point, he bought *Stars and Stripes* from her builders for $35,000, ran her under government charter for some two months (netting $15,000), and then sold her to the United States Navy on July 29, 1861, for $55,000. She was armed with four eight-inch guns and a twenty-pound Parrott rifle and assigned to the blockade of the Carolina ports.

Bushnell also offered the Mallorys $135,000 to sell him *Varuna* and "to fit the vessel for the merchant service, with all her joiner work, cooking apparatus, copper, boats, and everything complete for the merchant service, and to cut the ports (if they wanted her for government use) to fit her for the armament so far as it related to the ports." After some family debate, Charles Mallory accepted $110,000, as the vessel lay, "without the joiner work, the coppering, the ports, or any of these matters." Bushnell had *Varuna* fitted out at the Delamater Iron Works and at the Westervelt shipyard in New York and on December 31,1861, sold her to the United States Navy for $135,000. [23]

The navy armed *Varuna* with eight-inch cannons and two thirty-pound Parrott rifles and assigned her to accompany the U.S.S. *Monitor* to Hampton Roads, Virginia. Later, she was assigned to the Gulf of Mexico and, on the night of April 24, 1862, became the heroine of the river battle for New Orleans, sinking four Confederate vessels before being rammed and sunk by the *Governor Moore* (ex- *Charles Morgan*) of the Louisiana State Navy.[24]

Bushnell unsuccessfully tried to involve the Mallorys in another of his plans in mid-1861. Except for John Ericsson, he was the most persistent and persuasive among the numerous individuals urging the Union Navy to construct ironclad warships. In April and May, the Navy Department had advertised for bids to construct twenty-three 507-ton, heavily armed screw gunboats "which could be used for close, inshore work and for supporting amphibious operations." This was not the type of vessel Ericsson, Bushnell, and the other ironclad proponents had in mind, and they continued to press their proposals.[25]

In June, as part of his ironclad campaign, Bushnell asked Charles Mallory to quote a delivered price for hulls for one or more "Iron cased gun boats" to his order. Mallory responded that he would be willing to supply one hull "exclusive of all iron work other than is specified in the specifications for Gun Boats issued by the Navy Department and to be fitted and completed the same as those in every particular—for the sum of Eighty-Thousand Dollars." Apparently, he misunderstood Bushnell's desire to build a unique, new-style ironclad and thought Bushnell sought vessels as specified by the navy in April and May.[26]

Meanwhile, Bushnell and sixteen other aspirants had submitted their ironclad proposals to a special naval evaluation board. On September 16, 1861, the board approved contracts for three of the seventeen proposals: John Ericsson's *Monitor* at $275,000; Cornelius S. Bushnell's *Galena* at $235,000; and unnamed vessels to be built by Merrick & Sons of Philadelphia at

$780,000. Regrettably for the Mallorys, Bushnell decided to build *Galena* at Maxson, Fish & Co.'s yard, where he had found a better price and sensed a clearer understanding of his design. She was launched in April 1862, only one month after *Monitor,* but was totally eclipsed in notoriety by the dramatic success of the Ericsson vessel. The Merrick & Sons ships were never completed.

Although they missed their chance to build Mystic's first and the nation's second ironclad, the Mallorys did get some benefit from the twenty-three gunboat contracts let in July 1861. All these vessels were to be built by private shipyards and engine works, and contracts were let separately on "hulls" and "machinery." Six of the hull contracts went to New York yards, five to yards in Maine, four to Massachusetts, three each to Connecticut and Pennsylvania, and one each to Maryland and Delaware. New York firms secured thirteen of the machinery contracts, Pennsylvania five, Massachusetts three, and Connecticut two.

Charles Mallory bid unsuccessfully for two of the hull contracts, but his neighbors, Maxson, Fish & Co., obtained one: $53,000 to build the hull of U.S.S. *Owasco.* They promptly subcontracted the vessel to the Mallory yard at $50,000. By September 14, Mallory had over a hundred men at work on the gunboat under the supervision of "Wm. Brainard, boss carpenter, Crary Hill, Government inspector." As the Mystic *Pioneer* described her:

> The bully boat is of a navy pattern, and not so beautiful on the water line as the Mystic models. The Government would have done better to have submitted her mould to Mystic hands, but 'Uncle Samuel's' are tied by red tape. The boat will be 170 feet extreme length; 158 feet on the water line, 28 feet overall in width, and 12 feet deep, to be pierced for 12 thirty-two pound guns, six on a side, and will carry a heavy pivot gun, probably a ten inch Columbiad, midships. I suppose she will gauge about 500 tons. The keel was laid in the middle of July and she will be afloat, I think, early in September. Her heavy oak frame is strapped within, diagonally, but a net work of bars, each bar being 3-1/2 inches in width by 1/2 inch thick. This boat thoroughly built and fitted, exclusive of machinery, ordinance, fuel and provision, will cost $53,000, a sum that will

scarcely cover her cost to the builders. She will move by a fixed four-bladed screw of the best pattern.

As launched on October 5, 1861, U.S.S. *Owasco* was schooner-rigged and registered 507 tons. She was towed to the Novelty Iron Works of New York for installation of her machinery and armament and saw extensive service in the Gulf of Mexico.[27]

Owasco and her attendant "red tape" apparently soured the Mallorys on trying to build naval vessels.[28] They decided to capitalize on their own strengths as designers and builders, to concentrate on the public and private demand for merchantmen and transports, and to forgo the complex bidding and compliance procedures, the narrow profit margins, and the lengthy collection periods involved in warship construction. They continued to lay down one steamship after another, but none was for the navy: some were job orders for specific private parties; most were built on own account and were intended (in descending order of preference) for government sale, private sale, or own-flag operation in the public and private charter markets: *Delamater* and *Haze II* were launched in late 1861; *Thorn, Creole, Union, Augusta Dinsmore,* and *Mary Sanford* in 1862.

Delamater was a tug ordered by the Delamater Iron Works of New York. *Haze II* and *Thorn* were offered for sale to the government, then chartered to the United States Quartermaster General on the Mallorys' own account (see Table 5.1), and in May 1863 were both sold to the Forbes family of Boston through the latter's agent, C. B. Fessenden. *Creole* was sold to the New York & Virginia Steamship Co. on October 20, 1862. *Union* was built for Louis L. Hargous & Co. of New York for approximately $75,000 and sold by that firm to the navy on January 6, 1863, for $90,000. *Augusta Dinsmore* and *Mary Sanford* were built for A. M. Smith & W. D. Dinsmore of New York and were sold by that firm to the navy on July 13, 1863, for $114,777.45 and $100,000, respectively.[29]

The Mallory yards launched five more steamers in 1863. *Governor Buckingham* was intended for government charter on the family's own account, but was sold to the navy on July 29 for $110,000. *Montaines,* the only iron vessel ever built in

Mystic, was a project of David D. Mallory and Joseph Cottrell's son, Joseph Oscar, which they sold for river service in Cuba to Thomas F. Youngs of New York. *Yazoo* was offered for sale or charter to the government, but was then sold to the New York & Virginia Steamship Co. *Varuna II* cost $97,890.80 to build and was "put up . . . expressly for an armed ship, it being thought . . . that privateers would be in demand." She was first offered for sale to the navy, and then was chartered, on the Mallorys' own account, to the Quartermaster General. *Victor*, which cost $107,013.92, was also chartered to the army following her fitting out (see Table 5.1). [30]

By mid-1863, the Mallorys were offering to build additional vessels for sale to the government at $175,000 (guaranteeing a speed of 12 knots); $150,000 (guaranteeing 11 knots); "or diminishing price *'pro rata'* as to speed." But the government purchase market had dried up, at least for the type of wooden propellors the Mallorys favored. Not one of the ten steamers which they launched during 1864 and 1865 was purchased by federal authorities: *Aphrodite* and *Ulysses* were built by David D. Mallory and Joseph O. Cottrell, operated briefly under government charter, and were then sold to private parties: *Ariadne, Atlanta, Euterpe, General Sedgwick, Ella, Loyalist,* and *Twilight II* were run on the family's own account. [31] Thus, the market had definitely shifted: own-flag operation was a last resort in 1861–1862; it was a first choice during 1863–1865.

Most of the Mallory steamers which operated on own account did so under War Department charters. These were voyage or time charters made directly with quartermaster officers or negotiated (at 5 to 10 per cent commission) through New York ship brokers. Voyage charters were for a fixed price per job; time charters were paid for through a more elaborate system of calculations. The government took vessels on time charter at a per diem rate and assumed the costs of "all pilotage and port charges," of "all fuel," and of war-risk insurance. The owners "manned, victualled, tackled, apparelled, and ballasted" their vessels, "furnished [them] in every respect fit for merchant service," and assumed the costs of "running and keeping in repair." If and when the owners' cumulative "net profit per annum" reached 66 2/3 per cent of the vessel's appraised value, the government could take over the vessel and assume its expenses without further payment to the owners.[32]

New York was the command post for the Mallory-flag steamers operating under government charter (see Table 5.1); Charles Henry Mallory was the key manager. As early as February 10, 1862, he notified the trade to contact him "at United States Hotel where I can be seen any day in the week with exception of Mondays & Saturdays." By April 22, he testified under oath that "my business is entirely in the city; I go home sometimes once a week, sometimes once a fortnight . . . [and] all the business in New York is done in my name." His prime business was liaison with ship brokers like J. D. Fish & Co., N. L. MacReady & Co., and Bishop, Son & Co.—all of whom placed Mallory vessels on commission—and the Delamater Iron Works, which supplied the engines and machinery for most of the Mallory-built hulls.[33]

Other family members and trusted employees were also on call to assist. On May 15, 1862, for example, Captain Benjamin E. Mallory was dispatched by his brother to find and join *Thorn,* then under charter near Fortress Monroe, Virginia. The younger Mallory's instructions were clear:

> If in your opinion every thing is going on properly you will abstain from any direct interference with the duties of the vessel except to advise and consult with the Captain. But if in your opinion things are not properly conducted, you will write me at once stating particulars & I shall advise you as to further action. You will if possible have the steamer kept in the employment of the United States Government.

Captain William Morgan of *Thorn* was merely told that Mallory had been "sent down to assist you in the shore business of the Boat and also on board. . . . You will please confer and advise with my brother as to management of Boat both on board and on shore as he has full power to act."[34]

After the loss of his ship *Mary L. Sutton,* Captain Elihu Spicer, Jr., joined the New York office as co-agent and chief trouble shooter. The problems were always the same: expenses accumulating more rapidly than government payments and merchant captains stiff-necked at military red tape or just generally untrustworthy. Captain Morgan of *Thorn* had to be reminded, for instance, "always be prepared to say *'yes'* to *any order* given" by the army. Captain F. W. Cooley of *General Sedgwick* and Captain E. Whitehurst of *Varuna II* were similarly chastised: "You will do me the favour by writing me as often as convenient as I have not recd. a letter from you since you had the command. . . . Whenever you write Captain Spicer at New York send copy of the same to my address, so that in the absence of Capt. Spicer I may be able to see what is to be done. I shall expect to hear from you as often as twice a week, where you are and where there is communication by mail or otherwise. Write me the particulars, etc."

Spicer himself was sent into the field in July 1865 to investigate reports that the captain and the purser of *Varuna II* had their wives on board, and he had orders, if so, to fire the culprits. "I wish you to impress it on the minds of the masters & all others that if they persist in going contrary to their orders they will be discharged, without notice." [35]

With Spicer to bear part of the load in New York, Charles Henry Mallory could turn some of his attention to pressing problems in Mystic, particularly to rising costs in the shipyard. In 1861, for example, *Eagle, Stars and Stripes,* and *Varuna I* had been priced "ready for sea" between $45 and $50 per ton. As late as February 1862, although apologizing for "the very high price of materials," the Mallory yards were still quoting delivered prices in these ranges. By September–October, 1863, however, they were advising prospective customers, "It is very expensive building at present, at least double what it was thirty months since. . . . It is hardly worth while to expect to get anything in the shape of floating craft at this time at anything like a reasonable price. . . . The price would not be less than 90 to 100 Dolls. per Ton." In August, 1864, Charles Henry quoted the *minimum* cost of "a new ship & fit her ready for sea, every thing to be of the best quality, $100 per ton-register."

These increases in delivered prices reflected increases in construction costs. *Varuna II* and *Victor,* the last two Mallory steamers launched in 1863, had cost $97.21 and $80.64 per ton, respectively. Costs per ton for five of the ten steamers launched in 1864–1865 are known: *Ariadne* ($94.27), *Atlanta*

($123.22), *Euterpe* ($100.18), *General Sedgwick* ($93.55), and *Ella* ($125.56). By fall 1864, the Mallorys were asking $150 to $190 for these ships, *used,* and by December 19, they were quoting *new* delivered prices at "$190 per ton complete with iron stern work & no condensers. . . . brass stern work & condensers [at] an extra charge of at least $12,000." [36]

Only part of these rising costs could be traced to shortages in materials: chestnut and pine were used in lieu of oak; blocks, spars, cordage, cable, chain, anchors, and propellors were either locally made or purchasable in New York and Boston. Troublesome shortages and work stoppages did occur, however, in the manufacture and installation of engines, boilers, and shafts and such important items as pumps, winches, and lifeboats. Charles Henry had to expedite each situation as it developed.

For machinery, the Mallory yards depended primarily on the Delamater Iron Works of New York, the Reliance Machine Company, and the Mystic Iron Works. Delamater's, of course, was the third largest marine-engine builder in the United States by the 1860's, and its proprietor was more than a business associate of the Mallorys; he was a long-time and trusted friend. While Delamater filled the bulk of the Mallorys's orders for engines, boilers, shafts, pumps, and winches and most of their vessels fitted out at his New York wharf, they still found it desirable to form the Reliance and Mystic Iron companies to fill out the rest of their needs. [37]

Reliance was one of the numerous partnerships of the Randall, Smith, and Chapman families. A cotton-gin and tool producer before the war, the company was incorporated on March 1, 1862, and thereafter concentrated on marine engine-building, boilermaking, and general foundry and machine-shop work. Reliance supplied the machinery for a number of Mystic-built steamers, including several launched by the Mallorys, but it was a debt-financed company that went under in July 1864 as business slacked. Charles and Charles Henry Mallory had to rescue it as receivers and salvage twenty cents on the dollar for its stockholders. [38]

The Mystic Iron Works was more intimately involved with Mallory shipbuilding activities. It was incorporated on October 11, 1862, by Joseph O. Cottrell and David D. Mallory and "backed by their fathers who [are] among the wealthiest men in the Village." At its peak, the works employed 150 men in Mystic and at subsidiary locations in Stonington and New London and made the machinery for *Thorn, Montaines, Aphrodite, Ulysses, Yazoo,* and *Twilight II,* built at the Mallory yards, for the U.S.S. *Spuyten Duyvil* and for *Cleopatra,* built by Samuel H. Pook of New Haven, and probably made engines, boilers, and subassemblies for other vessels as well.[39]

Charles Henry Mallory solved the problem of obtaining lifeboats by reactivating his yacht-building partnership with D. O. Richmond and including the Mystic block and spar makers J. & W. Batty. They supplied boats to all the Mystic shipbuilders at competitive prices: $3.50 per foot for boats 13 to 17 feet in length; $4.00 per foot for boats 18 to 21 feet in length; $4.50 to $5.50 per foot for boats 22 feet or over. Also, in the midst of a war, the partners (along with John A. Forsyth at the main yard) continued to build yachts: the small sailboats *Kate* and *Fanny* for the Mallory "fry"; a 16-foot sailboat for Cornelius H. Delamater; a 13-foot sailboat for James D. Fish; the sloop-yacht *Kate,* launched June 5, 1864, for Charles Henry Mallory's own use; and the schooner-yacht *Josephine,* completed on August 6, 1864, for Richard F. Loper of Philadelphia and Stonington.[40]

The major problem in Mystic was, thus, not materiel but men—particularly after national conscription began on March 3, 1863. All men twenty to forty years of age were liable for induction unless they could hire a substitute to take their place or could purchase "commutation" exemptions at $300 each. During 1863, Connecticut drafted 11,539 men, but only 248 of those drafted actually served: 8,000 of the remainder purchased exemptions or obtained medical or religious commutation; the other 2,248 hired substitutes. By 1864, with the commutation exemptions repealed and draft quotas increasing, the manpower squeeze was on.[41]

In Mystic the pinch was felt. The *Pioneer* of February 21, 1863, had crowed: "If any more strangers contemplate settling among us, we advise them to bring their tents with them, for at present we cannot build fast enough to accommodate the newcomers." By April 16, 1864, Charles Henry Mallory noted dourly, "Our men are leaving every day & we have more work than can be done." By June, he was using "contrabands" (i.e., escaped slaves) sent north by Captain Spicer. By July and August, he was willing to pay as high as $850 for substitutes to enter the Union forces instead of key employees. Apparently, though, he was generally successful in protecting his work force, and the pressure eased as the supply of ships and wartime demands equalized.[42]

The boom was over by mid-1864, as costs for labor and materials began to rise faster than the prices for finished vessels. By August 22, Charles Henry Mallory communicated a new decision to his agents and captains: "We have concluded to stop building altogether . . . the steamers on hand are paid for with trifling exceptions . . . why we should [build to] sell for less than cost when it will take one year to replace them & say nothing about the care & trouble is a question." The emphasis was now to be returned to the operation rather than the construction of vessels.[43]

Even by the end of 1864, the Mallorys could see that the war had caused or, when peace came, would cause major redirections of their scale, organization, technology, and business intentions. They had benefited from the rapid escalation of demand during 1861–1863 and had managed to master the cost-price squeezes of 1864–1865. Their success was reflected in the credit reports for "Charles Mallory & Sons": " 'C.M.' is our most successful bus. man. co. a. 1. wor. from $750,000 to $1,000,000. paid income tax year before last on $185,000. nett income at present time about $2,000 per day" (January 25, 1865); "A. No. 1. wor. $1,500,000 or more. the richest firm in town" (August 12, 1865).[44]

But in the process of this rapid capital accumulation, whalers, sailing packets, and coasting tramps had gone the way of sailmaking, and the Mallorys' deepwater clipper fleet had all but disappeared. The need they felt to be active commercial bankers also dwindled as the capital resources grew and their access to formal financial intermediaries increased. Charles Mallory had retired as president of the Mystic River Bank in August 1860 and served as an officer of that institution only once more (a directorship in 1863–1864). And when the bank reorganized itself on December 1, 1864, as the Mystic River National Bank, the Mallorys remained large shareholders, but not managers.

In place of the activities which had characterized its antebellum years, the family now faced a large commitment to the construction and operation of steamships (see Table 5.2). Their location of doing business had also changed. It was now as much New York as Mystic; and key decision-makers were as often of the second generation as of the first. As peace came it was Charles Henry Mallory and his brothers who assumed the difficult tasks of converting the family's steamship investments to a civilian market and of managing the decline of sail.

Chapter 6

C. H. MALLORY & CO.,

1865–1875

"Have about concluded very reluctantly to open a commission house in New York, Captain Spicer to be one third interested and to be guaranteed $30,000 for the first year. Have engaged a small office of J. D. Fish & Co., 153 Maiden Lane. It will depend very much on the views of my Father and brothers whether I follow out my present ideas or give up all thought of the matter."

—Diary of Charles Henry Mallory, January 11, 1866

GENERAL LEE'S surrender at Appomattox on April 9, 1865, triggered the swiftest and least-planned demobilization in American postwar history. On April 14, Charles Henry Mallory received notice that "Secretary Stanton has issued an order to stop all drafting and recruiting, and that the Quarter masters are to cut down the expenses in their department up to lowest possible amount. Also the Navy department are to lay up a portion of the Navy, and ships purchased are to be sold."

The full impact of such a summary reconversion of the economy from war to peace was delayed, however, as a horrified nation mourned its President's assassination—the very day of Stanton's announcement. Charles Henry Mallory's thoughts were those of legions:

Thus one of the most barbarous tragedies has been enacted in our capital and our lamented chief magistrate, one of the purest men that the sun ever shone upon, been taken from us by the hand of an agent of that accursed system of slavery and state rights. We cannot believe that God in his Providence has kept the President in safety through four years of responsibility and anxiety, such as few men in this world are called on to suffer, has permitted him to be taken from us at this time but for some wise purpose. The nation mourns his loss. I as an individual had set him up as an idol almost in my heart. He was eminently a merciful man—he had a kind heart—he could not see his greatest enemy suffer and to his nation's enemy he was inclined to exercise mercy towards. He has fulfilled his mission and God grant that a man may be raised up in his stead to complete what he in all probability had so nearly brought to an end.

Amidst the ceremony of the state funeral and the inauguration of President Johnson and amidst the hair-raising reports of the pursuit of the assassins, demobilization continued. By April 28, blanket orders had been issued by the President "to discharge transports and cut down expenses in all the departments," and he followed, on May 1, with a "proclamation opening the avenues of trade." However glad Americans were that peaceful commerce could be resumed, for shipowners the cruel facts remained that several hundred thousand tons of shipping had been summarily dumped on a civilian market far too small to support them all. The result was competitive chaos, until those businessmen with sufficient experience, resources, and fortitude survived.[1]

Like most American-flag shipowners, the Mallorys' enterprises had been inseparable from the Union war effort for four years. At the cessation of hostilities, they still had all their remaining eight steamships under federal charter; a ninth was on the stocks in Mystic. Their two clippers, *Haze* and *Twilight*, were still under the American flag and were en route New York to San Francisco. Swift decision-making was the order of the day: *Twilight* arrived in San Francisco on April 22 and awaited orders; on June 17, the steamship *Twilight II* was launched from the Mallory yard and began fitting out at the Mystic Iron Works; on August 28, *Haze* arrived at San Francisco; and between April 29 and October 3, *Varuna II*, *Ariadne*, *Atlanta*, *Victor*, *General Sedgwick*, *Ella*, *Loyalist*, and *Euturpe* were successively released to civilian service.

Charles Henry Mallory took charge, as he had done throughout the Civil War. He was hindered by having been elected a Republican state senator from Connecticut's Seventh

District on April 3; and, from May 2 through July 21, he had to attend the legislative session in Hartford as well as look after business in Mystic and New York. Nevertheless, with Captain Spicer's assistance, he managed the family's transition from war to peace. On May 8, he "gave directions to . . . run all of our steamers on southern routes and try and develop the business."

The Mallory steamers found the demand they expected in the trade-starved South, but they found a depressing over-capacity of carriers, too. Charles Henry summed up the family's first six months' postwar experience on October 13, 1865:

> . . . Have been very much engaged trying to induce consignes to advance the rate of freight. While the market for all kinds of goods is very high, the freight market never was so low by steamers. The Southern market is being supplied by immense quantities of goods at a very low rate and the owners of steamers are suffering. Many green hands are purchasing steamers and forming new lines from the South and cutting down the rate of freight. I prophesy that they will wake up before long and find that they have made a mistake and that their money is gone. We have 2 steamships running to New Orleans, 3 to Savannah, and 2 to Wilmington [N.C.] and their expenses are larger than their receipts. While the depreciation and the wear of machinery and boilers is frightful, I do not feel as though I could or ought to be willing to stand such business a great while. . . .

Two months later, things were hardly brighter. On October 15, *Atlanta* foundered at lat. 36° 3′ N., long, 72° 30′ W. with forty-eight fatalities. Six days later, *Victor* broke her steering gear and beached on Cape Hatteras, necessitating expensive towing to Norfolk and New York for repairs. On November 4, *Varuna II* grounded in New York harbor and went into drydock for two weeks. On November 14, the brand-new *Twilight II* was wrecked by the pilot at Wilmington, North Carolina, while attempting a night entrance into the Cape Fear River: "This is the third steamer in trouble in less than one month, two a total loss and one in a very bad state, all of them not over three-fourths covered by insurance. It does appear that the savings of years is wasting away rapidly. I trust that these mishaps will soon come to an end. I must try and see if it is not possible to stop some of the leaks. If things go on as they are now doing we had better lay the boats up."

123

Things got worse before they improved. On December 13, *Ariadne* rammed and sank the brig *William Edward.* "Here is a chance for an expensive law suit," noted Charles Henry. "We have had a constant succession of disasters for the last two months and I trust that they may cease before long, for if they do not we shall all be ruined as far as this world's goods are concerned." [2]

But he persevered and he learned: "We are living in exciting times, a man has ten years experience in one in these days." Particularly, he perceived the need for more system in the family's business activities and for faster and more coordinated decision-making. His father's age was beginning to show, and Mystic was much too far from the center of things, anyway, to remain finely tuned to the market. Commuting back and forth to New York was exhausting, and the alternative of consigning vessel management to others had grown too expensive.

By December 21, 1865, Charles Henry was seriously "contemplating hiring an office in New York and going into the commission business" himself. While reluctant to "confine" himself to the city, he increasingly saw that postwar competition could not be handled by prewar organization and at the leisurely antebellum pace. "We are now paying out large sums of money for commissions and receiving no benefit but rather to the contrary," he complained. "I think we must do our own business to protect ourselves."

Long discussions ensued within the Mallory family, with Cornelius H. Delamater (whom Charles Henry considered "a model man"), and with Captain Elihu Spicer, Jr. (who had borne so much of the managerial burden during the war). Brother David was not particularly interested in Charles Henry's proposal, then being deep in plans to convert the assets and plant of the Mystic Iron Works into the Mystic Woolen Company and the Lantern Hill Silex Company; brother George preferred to work with his father in the shipyard; and brother Benjamin had gone back to sea. Nevertheless, the family gave its blessing, and by January 11, 1866, the decision had been made "reluctantly to open a commission house in New York." On February 1, "C. H. Mallory & Co." opened for business at 153 Maiden Lane in an office rented from J. D. Fish & Co. Charles

Henry Mallory comprised two-thirds of the partnership and Captain Spicer one-third, with Spicer guaranteed a $30,000 income for the first year.

This was the beginning of a new generation of Mallory business, but it was a wrench with the past. Charles Henry valiantly tried to live in Mystic and work in New York, but by November 11, 1866, he commented, "This is the first Sunday with few exceptions that I have spent away from my home in Mystic for years. I miss my visit to Fathers Sunday night very much and have no doubt but that I am missed also. . . . I cannot bear the idea of leaving my old home for the winter although I know that it is for health and I believe for my interest to spend the winter where my business is."

By February 9, 1868, after two more years of commuting, he finally concluded "that my duties and cares are getting so numerous here that I may become so involved in business as to finally be obliged from the very nature of the case to become a resident in the city and to leave my old home." On October 8, he rented a furnished home at 150 Henry Street at $3,500 per annum, and on November 23, Mrs. Mallory and his sons joined him there. Daughter Fanny had just married Charles P. Williams of Stonington on October 28, and daughter Kate was away at school. But Charles (who had been working for Captain Spicer in New York since September 19, 1865), Henry (who had joined his brother on January 7, 1867), and young Robert (who would enter the firm on October 10, 1873) lived with their parents.

As late as April 1870, Charles Henry Mallory kept his domicile in Connecticut, but was stung when some of his neighbors "objected to my voting in my native town." Perhaps that resolved the question at last, for on April 15, he purchased a home at 9 Grace Court, Brooklyn, for $29,500 "including parlour carpets, gas fixtures and parlour mirror," and on May 24 his family moved into its lifelong home. Business and home life were once again inexorably intertwined—in the Mallory tradition.[3]

The partnership styled "C. H. Mallory & Co." was capitalized at $60,000. But this investment was only nominal, for throughout its five decades of life, the firm existed to manage and not to own maritime properties. To the public, the firm was a typical New York commission house, albeit one that specialized in maritime affairs. It offered the agent's usual, ubiquitous services on commission: buying, selling, receiving, and forwarding of goods; drawing, endorsing, collecting, and disbursing of moneys. For the family, however, the firm became the central and coordinated managerial agency for Mallory maritime assets.

In addition to a general commission business on its own account, C. H. Mallory & Co. directed four major family endeavors for varying periods of time between 1865 and 1875: (1) disposal of the output of Charles Mallory's shipyard, either by sales or own-flag employment;[4] (2) management of Mallory-flag sailing tramps in the intercoastal and transoceanic markets; (3) management of a berth-sail service in the coastal market; and (4) management of coastal steamship lines.

These activities and the decisions which interstitched them were evolutionary and sometimes contradictory. They were, however, logical extensions of the family's antebellum experience tempered by the postwar situation. They reflect vestiges of Charles Mallory's preferences, but they also exhibit Charles Henry Mallory's new perceptions of traditional markets and his determination to segment them profitably in new ways over the common denominator of the technological shift from sail to steam.

Nowhere were old ways and new conditions more in conflict than in the family's attitudes toward the future of deepwater sail. Charles Mallory's faith that well-built, American-flag, wooden clippers would always find a ready market died hard, despite his son's dissent and mounting deficits on voyage accounts. Charles Henry had jumped at the chance to sell *Twilight* for $46,500 gold in mid-1865 and had hoped to sell *Haze* as well. His hopes of extricating the family's clipper investment were dashed, however. Twice more, the elder Mallory overruled Charles Henry's better judgment and built vessels whose clipper design limited their prospects for full employment—leaving the frustrating task of managing them to C. H. Mallory & Co.

Haze, Twilight III, and *Annie M. Smull* were the ships owned by the family and operated by the firm in the period 1865-1875. All were of clipper design and suited for only certain trades. They were, thus, employable as "tramps," but only in rather narrowly defined markets and not in the theoretically ubiquitous sense of that term. All were Mallory-built and all were operated on the New York–San Francisco–Shanghai–Liverpool circuit. This basic route had variations, of course, such as substitutions of Amoy, Hong Kong, Manila, Singapore, Penang, Rangoon, or Calcutta for Shanghai; or of Bristol, Dublin, Hamburg, Le Havre, or Amsterdam for Liverpool (see Table 6.1). The vessels were usually chartered "out" to San Francisco in one of the clipper lines and, once in California, cabled offers found on the market there to C. H. Mallory & Co. for decision. From San Francisco they might then be ordered to Europe, direct with wheat, via Manila for sugar, or via China, Malaysia, Burma, or India for tea and oriental goods. From Europe, it was usually home to New York with coal or iron, or, all too often, in ballast.

Technologically, these ships were good performers. All were capable of what the Mallorys called "a good solid passage." They also made several well-paying individual voyages, but, for the period 1865 to 1875, they were not outstanding investments.

Haze, which the family considered "a remarkably good ship and an excellent sea boat," was the work horse, but even she had her difficulties, being laid up for fifteen months in 1870–1871 because of "not being able to find any paying business for her." *Twilight III* was launched by Charles Mallory on October 25, 1866, despite Charles Henry's misgivings: "There is no inducement as the times now are of laying out any money on ships. They are a complete drug in the markets." She was not rigged until April 1867, but was then able to sustain steady employment, although at declining rates. *Annie M. Smull,* which Charles Mallory built against his eldest son's advice, was launched on September 16, 1868. Named for a beloved and recently deceased daughter, she was a triumph of design but a losing business. The ship cost $115,000 and "if not sold . . . [was] intended for the California and China trade. . . . I fear," however, Charles Henry confided to his diary, that "she will not be a very profitable investment."

He was right. *Smull* was offered for sale in the New York

market at cost-plus, then at cost, then as low as $92,500, with no takers. Reluctantly, C. H. Mallory & Co. accepted her management: by April 26, 1870, "she has been 3 months loading and not freight enough to pay her expenses"; by March 17, 1871, "for the last 18 months she has been a ruinous piece of property."[5]

Even so, none of the Mallory clippers was permanently laid up between 1865 and 1875, indicating that some profits were accruing. As Sturmey has suggested, owners of tramp vessels (consciously or unconsciously) conceive of three alternative market prices for their ships' services: a "continuation rate," which would keep the vessel at full employment at fully satisfactory profit levels; a "transfer rate," which might employ the vessel regularly but at a profit level marginal enough to suggest transfer to some other employment; and a "layup rate," that is the "rock bottom rate which the owner will ever accept." From the evidence available, it appears that the Mallorys were usually able to find transfer rates for their clippers prior to 1875.[6]

They had better success with their barks. *Caleb Haley, Galveston, Sabine,* and *Brazos* were designed for the New York–Galveston–Liverpool tramp circuit (see Table 6.1). Here the European-bound cargo was cotton, and the returns were iron, coal, or package freight. Again, there were variations of the basic route which might include in-transit stops at Havana for sugar and cigars or might substitute Falmouth, Le Havre, or Antwerp for Liverpool, and New Haven or Boston for New York. *Galveston* also did a stretch of "China coasting" among such ports as Shanghai, Amoy, Hong Kong, Singapore, Penang, Rangoon, Manila, and Yokohama.

Charles Henry Mallory championed barks against his father's preference for ships. They were less expensive to build and to operate and could find employment in the protected coastal market as well as in the intercoastal and transoceanic trades. The family had enjoyed brief success with *Lapwing* and *Tycoon* between 1859 and 1864, and they tried barks again following the war. *Caleb Haley,* built by Maxson, Fish & Co. in 1866, was their venture. Charles Henry looked her over "with the idea of purchasing an interest" on February 12 and "found her to be a first class vessel in every particular." She cleared

New York for the Gulf in early April, but was lost off Mexico in September.

Galveston, designed by Charles Henry and launched from the Mallory yard on September 18, 1866, was "intended for the Southern trade," too. She picked up where *Haley* had failed and was kept busy at continuation rates (save for one transfer to China coasting) through 1875. *Sabine,* purchased for $59,000 from her builder George Gildersleeve of Portland, Connecticut, on October 21, 1868, followed. Her purpose was revealed by Charles Henry Mallory: "intended for the Galveston and Liverpool trade. We take an interest in her and are to act as her agents. . . . will I think prove to be a good property."

By May 31, 1869, he reported that *Sabine* "has made a very good voyage . . . has coppered herself and made a dividend of 20% in 8 months." The Mallorys were so pleased that they purchased her sister ship *Brazos* when Gildersleeve launched her in 1870. C. H. Mallory & Co. managed her in "the Galveston and Liverpool trade" through 1875. [7]

Because of their long periods at sea and the limited number of employment options open to them, the Mallory-flag sailing tramps actually consumed little managerial time. There would be a flurry of decision-making in the New York office when a cable requesting orders arrived or when a vessel called at New York. On the whole, however, C. H. Mallory & Co. was much more occupied in the constant attention demanded by its berth-sail service and coastal steamship lines and, briefly, by the almost comic-opera interlude of the "Spanish gunboats."

On May 5, 1869, Cornelius H. Delamater approached his friend Charles Henry Mallory to subcontract an agreement his ironworks had made to build thirty wooden gunboats for the Spanish Navy. "I am offered 20 of them to build if they can be done in 90 days and if the price is made right," Charles Henry noted. "It can be done with a little energy, but I fear it will appear to be a mountain to my brother George who has much influence with Father so far as the ship building is concerned. I hope to hear the result to-morrow."

The next day, having heard from Mystic, he "went up to Delamater's Ironworks . . . and agreed for Father to build 15 gun boats. . . . They are to be built in 90 days, the size is 145 feet long, 22 feet beam, and 8 feet hold." Charles Mallory was to build eight of the steamers himself and had subcontracted two to Geo. Greenman & Co. and five to Hill & Grinnell. Spain's price to Delamater was $50,000 each, complete with engines, sails, and a 100-pound swivel gun; Mallory's price to Delamater was about half that, without engines and armament; Greenman & Co.'s and Hill & Grinnell's price to Mallory was about $10,000 each.

By July 24, the first gunboat was launched. On August 4, however, Charles Henry reported that "the 30 Spanish gunboats building here and at Mystic were seized by the U.S. Marshall on information from the Peruvian Minister that they were to be engaged in making reprisals on the Peruvian Government." Two federal marshals appeared in Mystic with orders to "seize and detain" the vessels there, and a United States revenue cutter took station off Noank Lighthouse to enforce their authority.

Charles Mallory reportedly took the whole episode as a joke, remarking, "To Peru and to sea! Why, bless me, the thought is absurd . . . they haven't got any engines or boilers, no copper, no sails, no cables, and won't have for some time. To Peru! . . . Ha, Ha!!" Charles Henry noted, "I don't think that anything serious to the contractors will come out of it," and was proven right. By September 16, he recorded, "The 15 gun boats are all completed and lie at the wharf waiting orders to be towed to New York." Five were delivered to Delamater's on October 21, five more on October 30, and the last five on November 11. By December 10, the federal authorities had officially released the vessels to Spain; seventeen of them sailed for Cuba on December 19 and the remainder on January 7, 1870. Accounts were settled among the builders by April 1, and the Mallorys had another good story to tell. [8]

They were much more concerned, anyway, with postwar developments in the coastal market. Here they perceived a viable business opportunity, but responded not with sailing packets or sailing tramps but with a combination of steam liners and berth sailers. This curious, but complementary, pattern grew from the nature of the coasting trades between 1865 and 1875. And these trades became the Mallorys' specialty.

The technology of the coastal market had abruptly

"Spanish Gun Boat No. 1," one of fifteen launched by the Mallory yards in 1869. Courtesy Mystic Seaport.

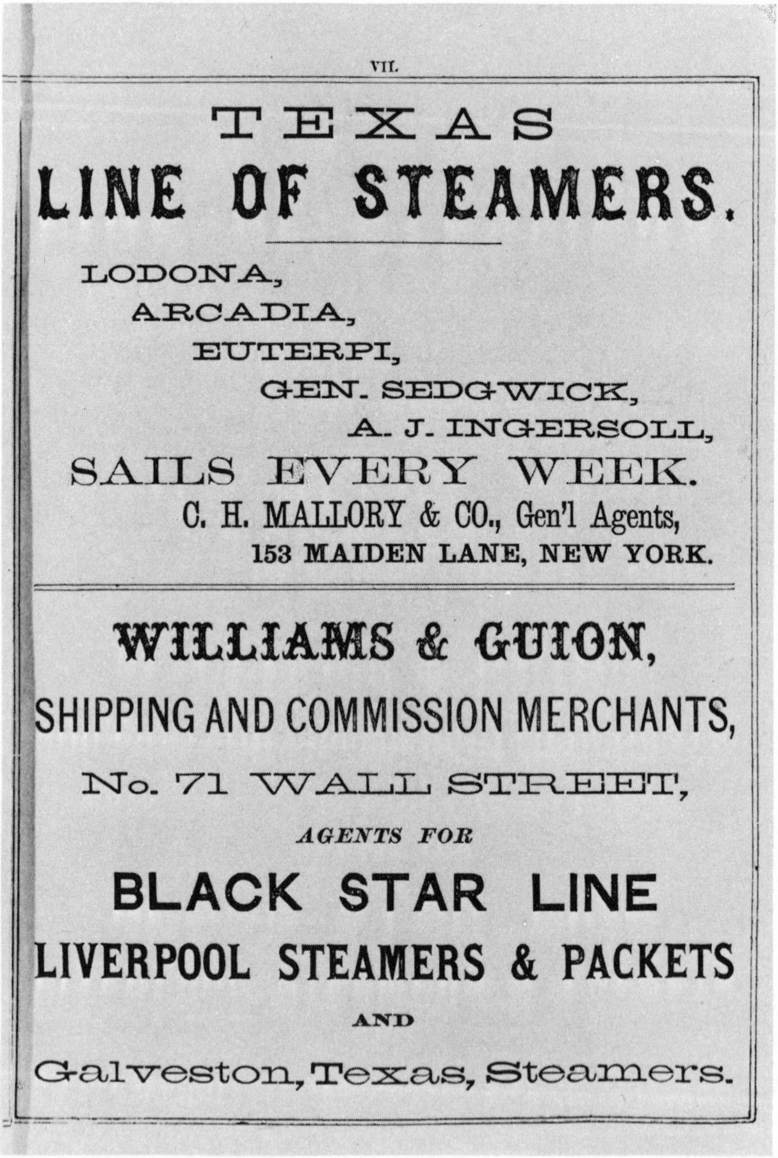

TEXAS
LINE OF STEAMERS.

LODONA,

ARCADIA,

EUTERPI,

GEN. SEDGWICK,

A. J. INGERSOLL,

SAILS EVERY WEEK.

C. H. MALLORY & CO., Gen'l Agents,

153 MAIDEN LANE, NEW YORK.

WILLIAMS & GUION,

SHIPPING AND COMMISSION MERCHANTS,

No. 71 WALL STREET,

AGENTS FOR

BLACK STAR LINE

LIVERPOOL STEAMERS & PACKETS

AND

Galveston, Texas, Steamers.

First known advertisement for C. H. Mallory & Co., *W. Alvin Lloyd's Rail Road Guide* (New York: W. Alvin Lloyd & Co., 1867), p. vii.

changed. The sudden and massive construction of steamships during the Civil War had not only improved that breed but was providing stiff competition for sailing packets, now that the war had passed. Yet there were two crucial characteristics of the coasting·trade that carried over from antebellum years: cabotage and a high volume of goods demanding liner, not tramp, service. Cabotage still meant that all coastal water carriers were constrained by roughly the same cost curve. The quantity of liner goods and the comparative advantages of steam over sail determined the profits available within the market protected by cabotage.

The Civil War had also retarded the growth of land-transport alternatives, and the slowness by which reconstruction and integration of southern railroads progressed prolonged the comparative advantages of water carriers. For the entire period 1865–1875, tramp shipping and not railroads was the most feasible transport alternative to liners in the coastal market.[9] Then, as always, with tramps the best substitute, shippers of liner goods were willing to pay freight rates above the theoretical tramp alternative to obtain desired mixtures of transport cost and transport service. In addition, as Thorburn has shown:

> ... many decisions regarding the water transport of goods are made without consideration to alternative means of transport. The freight rate offered by the shipowner is then accepted without further inquiry. Most likely an investigation of possible alternative transports is made now and then, however. The outcome of such an investigation usually decides the means of transport for some time onward. [10]

It was to this combination of shippers' needs and inertia that line operators like the Mallorys responded with capacity and handling facilities more appropriate and a schedule more convenient than were those of the cheaper tramp alternatives. And, since their success depended on maintaining a regular volume of such a mixed trade (like any line carrier), they worked constantly to attract and hold permanent customers and to concentrate traffic at ports most convenient to themselves and to a majority of shippers.

Tactically, any line operator's major problems are to maintain schedules at as close to capacity as possible according to regular, seasonal, or unanticipated demands through constant attention to vessel deployment and to construct and administer a complex system of commodity rates based on what the traffic will bear. His rates must be high enough in the aggregate to cover the long-term costs of his line and still earn him a profit, but not high enough to attract new liner competition or drive shippers back to tramps.

Rate competition is, then, anathema to line operators—unlike the tramp market, where the lowest rates usually get the job. By definition, the line's harbor costs are high because of the frequency of its service, the mixed nature of its cargoes, and the expenses of holding regular customers. It usually under-utilizes the capacity of its vessels for the same reasons, and its administrative costs are high in maintaining a home office and outport agents. Thus, in some measure, its higher rates are necessary.

The Mallorys understood and accepted these economic facts of life in their decisions to initiate and sustain steam-liner and berth-sail service between New York and southern ports during 1865–1875. Their purposes and managerial maneuvering form an excellent case study of the requirements for survival and profit in those trades.

While phasing its vessels out of military service during 1865 and early 1866, C. H. Mallory & Co. had sampled the trade of all the significant southern ports from North Carolina to Texas. By mid-1866, however, the firm had decided to concentrate its efforts on the two most active: New Orleans and Galveston. These harbors and their cargoes seemed most compatible with the Mallorys' desires to operate steam liners. Of course, other maritime entrepreneurs had precisely the same idea.

New Orleans was a competitive jungle. The city had fallen on April 25, 1862, and, by June, a steady stream of American-flag vessels was serving the "back door" to the Confederacy. With the coming of peace, however, many vessels transferred to other routes, and the New York segment of the New Orleans trade had shaken down to three weekly steamship lines: the Atlantic Mail Steamship Co.; the New York Mail Steamship Co. (the "Star Line"); and Cromwell's New York and New Orleans

Steamship Line.[11] All were superior in equipment and capital resources to the Mallory fleet.

Consequently, Charles Henry originally contented himself with bits and pieces of the New Orleans trade. Mallory-flag steamers made three round voyages to the Crescent City during 1866, but only on voyage charters or as substitute vessels in the other lines. His major initial effort to share in New Orleans business was actually his purchase of the steam tug *Bigonia* for $22,500 (gold) on July 12, 1865. He changed her name to *Balize*, in honor of the pilots' settlement at the mouth of the Mississippi River, and on September 19 dispatched her "to New Orleans for the purposes of towing ships from sea to the town." Since the Port of New Orleans lies 110 river miles from the open sea, steam tugs had always found a ready business towing sailing vessels across the treacherous bars and upstream against the powerful current. They often shared the salvage profits of wrecking, as well.

Balize's captain was instructed "to lay the boat up," if "he could not pay his expenses," or, hopefully, "there might be a purchase found for her in New Orleans." By March 1866, however, he had run the boat $7,085 into debt, and Charles Henry "immediately ordered him home." By May 6, when *Balize* arrived in New York, it was clear that "she has made one of the most ruinous voyages that I have ever been interested in, all owing to the inefficiency of the Captain. I have not seen him," Charles Henry confided to his diary, "but expect to do so in the morning and hope that I shall be able to control myself." By April 12, 1867, the "unpleasant business" was settled and *Balize* was sold for $8,000—"a great sacrifice." [12]

In the meantime, however, C. H. Mallory & Co. had been able to pry its way into the heart of New Orleans commerce. In early 1866, the Atlantic Mail Steamship Co. had withdrawn from the New Orleans trade, to be followed in 1867 by the Star Line. The Mallory steamers immediately increased their sailings, completing twenty-one round voyages to New Orleans during 1867. By the first quarter 1868, the Mallorys' "Southern Line" was sharing the route with the Cromwell Line and the newly formed "Merchants' Steamship Line"—all offering weekly steamers between New York and New Orleans.

The "season" for the New Orleans trade was mid-August to mid-March, and it took two agencies and four to six steamers to maintain weekly service. In New York, C. H. Mallory & Co. handled freight procurement and vessel turn-around, supervised accounts, and secured, manned, maintained, and deployed vessels. The New Orleans end was handled by George A. Fosdick & Co. Since the minimum voyage time, dock to dock, was six days and usually took seven or eight, two steamers were always in port loading, respectively, at New York and New Orleans; two were always in transit, one each way; and others were kept available or on call to be laid on the line in emergencies or during flush times.

Carrier undercapacity never lasted long, however; and, actually, the Mallorys *first* full cargo New York–New Orleans did not come until January 1869! The more chronic problems of the New Orleans trade, which were only aggravated by the number of competitors, were its off-season slump from April to August and the perennial lack of northbound liner goods. Through constant managerial attention, however, C. H. Mallory & Co. combated these circumstances in a variety of ways.

First, as line carriers always seek to do, the three main competitors standardized rates and schedules staggered among themselves to the disadvantage of "outsiders." While no formal pool or freight conference was arranged, the result was virtually the same. With rates standardized, however, one's profits depended even more on one's efficiency. The Mallorys were no exception, and they used several means to maximize the employment of their New Orleans steamers at minimum costs: summer lay-ups of vessels and semiweekly schedules; shifting vessels to other routes on voyage or time charter; filling vessels with cargoes "on ship's account"—usually potatoes and hay southbound and fruits and sugar northbound.

Most often, however, the New Orleans steamers "came home" via Havana. This option was particularly feasible after completion of a submarine cable between Key West and Havana on September 10, 1867, made it possible to sample the Cuban market without leaving New York or New Orleans. The stop at Havana regularly added $2,000 to $4,000 to the value of a steamer's northbound cargo. Sometimes Mobile, Vera Cruz,

Tampico, or Port-au-Prince substituted for Havana. Also on occasion, rather than return in the line at unprofitable rates or in ballast, steamers were put on berth in New Orleans for other northern ports not enjoying liner service to the South: New Haven, Providence, Fall River, New Bedford, and Portland, for example. [13]

C. H. Mallory & Co. used all these tactics to hedge against loss, and its partners were able to sustain profits on the New Orleans line through 1873 (see Table 6.2). But their bread and butter was their line between New York and Galveston.

Galveston had been the last major Confederate port to surrender (on June 2, 1865, two months after Appomattox and thirty-eight months after New Orleans!), and her availability to American-flag carriers was, consequently, slower to materialize. Nevertheless, two weekly steamship lines from New York were running to the Island City by the end of 1865: one operated by the experienced New York–Charleston packet firm of Spofford & Tileston; the other a joint venture of the firms of Williams & Guion of New York and the Clyde family of Philadelphia. The Mallorys, in the meantime, were busily experimenting with New Orleans, Wilmington, Savannah, Charleston, Mobile, and Apalachicola.

By December 1865, however, Charles Henry Mallory had decided to sample the Galveston trade: *General Sedgwick* was put on berth for that port and sailed on January 4, 1866, "not more than five eighths full of freight and but a very small complement of passengers." She returned to New York on February 6, "grossing about $15,000" for the round voyage and was instantly chartered "for Galveston and back to New York at 27 and a half cents per foot and 2 cents per pound for cotton home, full cargo both ways."

The rates and volume of cargo in the Galveston trade were better than anything else in the steam segment of the coastal market, and by February 20, C. H. Mallory & Co. had concluded to open its own line of propellors between Galveston and New York. Twenty-one round voyages were completed during 1866, thirty-five in 1867; and the Mallorys' "Texas Line" soon emerged as the dominant carrier on the route.

Success of the Texas Line sprang from a carefully planned

competitive strategy and careful attention to its implementation. Charles Henry Mallory and Captain Spicer were the strategists; their plans were simple but effective. Banking on their quantity of vessels and the quality of their equipment and management, the Mallorys made their schedules and services as competitive as possible with those of Spofford & Tileston and Williams & Guion. Weekly, year-round voyages were guaranteed insofar as humanly possible and whether full or not; steam lighters manned by special crews were stationed at the tricky Galveston bar to anticipate navigational delays and expedite cargo handling and vessel turn-around; and the largest and most respected commission house in Galveston, William Hendly & Co., was retained as agents.

Mallory rates were structured to match those of the established lines, regardless of cost, and the possibility of rates' falling low enough to attract tramps to the route was neatly eliminated. On August 10, 1866, C. H. Mallory & Co. opened a fortnightly berth-sail service between New York and Galveston. Their purpose was to earn a profit, of course, but more importantly they used their berth sailers to skim the cream of any nonliner freight which might enter the Galveston–New York market. Thus, the possibility of tramp competition was nullified and the contest restricted to a battle among steamship operators which the Mallorys felt sure they could win.

The Galveston trip took a minimum of eight to nine days one way prior to 1875. This meant that four to six steamers were necessary to maintain the weekly service desired. As a further competitive edge, however, the Mallorys maintained enough steamers to schedule both northbound and southbound stops at Key West. This added $500 to $2,000 to the value of their northbound voyages per trip and won them a United States mail contract paying $200 per round mail voyage between New York and Key West.

Unlike their entrance into the New Orleans trade, which began and remained vastly subordinate to two other lines, the Mallorys intended to win the Galveston trade, and they did. As early as June 21, 1866, Williams & Guion approached Charles Henry Mallory to negotiate a reduction of the competition between their lines, and by December 20 they had reached an

Yazoo, wooden steamship built by Mallory yards in 1863 for the New York & Virginia Steam Ship Co. A sister ship, *Creole*, was also Mallory-built in 1862. Note "clipper bow" and double square rig characteristic of early Mallory-built steamers. Courtesy Mariners Museum.

Ariadne, wooden steamship built in the Mallory yards in 1864 and run in the Gulf trade by C. H. Mallory & Co. until her loss in 1873. Courtesy Mystic Seaport.

Clipper ship *Annie M. Smull*, built by Charles Mallory in 1868 over his eldest son's vigorous protests. Sold in 1885 after a transoceanic tramp career that Charles Henry Mallory could only describe as "ruinous." Shown at rigging wharf of Mallory yards *ca.* 1869. Courtesy Mystic Seaport.

entente: the two steamers managed by Williams & Guion, *Virginia* and *Wilmington,* were consigned to the Mallorys' Texas Line in return for a percentage share of joint profits; rates, schedules, and services were arranged to compete with those of Spofford & Tileston.

The pool was short-lived, as Charles Henry noted with disappointment on February 8, 1867: "The arrangement which we had with Messrs. Williams & Guion was broken off to-day. They wanted us to do all the work for nothing and they to have the credit of it. It is to be after this a square stand up fight and nobody benefited but the shippers of goods. The trade will not support three lines and some of us must go to the wall. It is a bad business for the owners of the ships."

But the "square stand up fight," which all line carriers abhor, lasted only until August 12, 1869: "Business very good," recorded Charles Henry:

> I was never more busy in my life. . . . We have made one arrangement for a consolidation of the steam lines between this port and Galveston to-day. Spofford & Tileston agree to haul off their steamers for the consideration of $135 for each steamer sailing in the line being paid to them. Williams & Guion give us the *Virginia* and *Wilmington* to run in our line with the understanding that they have the privilege of putting in 1/3rd of steamers employed in the line. We to have the agency of the line at this end, and Messrs. T. H. McMahan & Co. the agency in Galveston. Our old agents in Galveston, Wm. Hendly & Co., will feel reluctant at giving up the business, and no doubt they will get up in opposition and do us all the harm possible. I think we cannot be placed in a much worse position than we were before, and if opposition comes up we must do all that is possible to defeat it. Time will determine whether we have made a mistake. I think not.

No opposition appeared, and the Mallorys actually bettered the arrangement. Within a year, Williams & Guion had sold its share in the pool to its previously silent partners, the Clydes, and the latter significantly improved the quality of the vessels comprising their portion of the line: on November 26, 1870, the brand-new iron steamship *Clyde* replaced the Clydes' nineteen-year-old wooden steamer *Virginia*: on March 16, 1872,

George W. Clyde, another new steamer owned by the Clydes, replaced Williams & Guion's older and smaller *Wilmington.*

The success of the Texas steamship line and of its complementary berth-sail service is mirrored in their number of voyages and their gross earnings (see Table 6.2). Most of the sailers employed were either voyage-chartered or "loaded on commission," but Charles Henry and Captain Spicer took as much as 1/32 each in several of the larger vessels, notably the schooners *Abbie E. Campbell, Eliza S. Potter, Louisa W. Birdsall, Louise P. Mallory, Robert Palmer,* and *Ruth Robinson,* and the brigs *Florence* and *William Mallory, Jr.* The barks *Galveston, Sabine,* and *Brazos* also were employed in the service on the southbound leg of their New York–Galveston–Liverpool triangle. On balance, the berth-sail service seems to have been profitable as well as successfully performing its basic function of forestalling serious tramp competition on the route.[14]

Having bested their competition at sea between New York and Galveston, the partners of C. H. Mallory & Co. concentrated on improving their position in the port of Galveston and in her hinterland. Their ambitions, of course, were to reduce their in-port costs and to induce more shippers to patronize their line; and these goals quickly involved them with the Galveston, Houston & Henderson Railroad and the Galveston Wharf Co. The former was the Island City's sole railroad prior to 1875; the latter was a quasi-public firm that was rapidly monopolizing the Galveston water front.

All the New York steamship lines had patronized Bean's Wharf in Galveston before 1870, but none had enjoyed shipside rail transfer facilities. Inland cargoes were exchanged with shallow-draft steamers of the Houston Direct Navigation Co., which plied Buffalo Bayou, or catered to the railroad, which ran inland to Harrisburg and a connection with Houston's growing inland rail network. By 1873, however, C. H. Mallory & Co., the railroad, and the wharf company had significantly improved matters by constructing a joint water-rail terminal, by negotiating cooperative and expeditious through-freight handling and rates, and by bettering quality and capacity of the Texas Line.

The catalysts in these developments were Texas' most energetic and affluent private bankers, cotton factors, and commission agents, Ball, Hutchings & Co. Founded in 1854 by four dry-goods merchants, George Ball, John H. Hutchings, and John and George Sealy, the firm was vigorously dedicated to the expansion of Galveston's commerce. Its members had helped found the Galveston, Houston & Henderson in 1853 and the corporate predecessor of the Galveston Wharf Co. in 1854. Following the Civil War, with Hutchings as president of the wharf company and John Sealy a director, and with Sealy as vice president and Hutchings a director of the railroad, their firm acted to integrate Galveston's rail-water facilities.[15]

In late 1869, Hutchings negotiated the first of several agreements to interconnect the wharves and the railroad; on June 2, 1870, he chaired a wharf company committee appointed to "correspond with Steamship owners, and make the best arrangement possible to get a line of [New York] steamers to land and discharge freight at the wharves of this company." On its own account, however, Ball, Hutchings & Co. simultaneously contacted the Mallorys and the Clydes and purchased one-quarter interest in *Clyde* (then fitting out in Philadelphia), *City of Galveston* (a previously unnamed steamer which had been building in the Mallory yard since February), and a new Mallory-flag steamer to be built and named *City of Houston.* On June 17, 1870, Ball, Hutchings & Co.'s interest in these three vessels was purchased by the wharf company for $20,000, as an overture of good will toward the steamship line.

Hutchings' committee reported on July 2 "that C. H. Mallory & Co. of New York offer the best terms for the interest of this company," and its recommendation was so voted: "that the Galveston Wharf Company and its friends will take one quarter interest in each of the four steamships in contemplation of construction by C. H. Mallory & Co. for the New York and Galveston trades," these to be in addition to the company's interest in *Clyde, City of Galveston,* and *City of Houston.* [16]

The inducements offered the Mallorys by Ball, Hutchings & Co. and the Galveston Wharf Co. underscore the tasks of vessel procurement, rotation, and replacement which were then (and now) so crucial to successful line management. They also triggered new preferences for C. H. Mallory & Co. Prior to 1870, the Mallorys had considered the spot-charter and used-ship markets and the capacity of their family's shipyard as adequate sources of vessel supply. After 1870, they increasingly abandoned both as insufficient for their needs.

To maintain the liner schedules which it set for itself during 1866–1870, C. H. Mallory & Co. drew on four sources for vessels: there were the seven wooden propellors which remained in 1866 from the twenty-three launched by the Mallory yard before and during the Civil War; vessels were also "engaged" as needed on either time or voyage charters; there were the steamships consigned to Mallory management by the Williams & Guion–Clyde agreements; and there were new vessels built in the Mallory yard.

The seven Civil War propellors gave fairly good postwar service, but all were off the books by 1873: *Varuna II* was sold to J. M. Forbes & Co. of Boston for $92,500 on February 27, 1866; *Loyalist,* after running as a Mystic–New York packet during 1865–1866, was sent out to Galveston as a lighter in 1867 and served there until foundering on May 7, 1869; *Euterpe* ran New York–Galveston until burned at Galveston on October 1, 1870, with an uninsured loss of $4,000; *Ella* ran in the Gulf lines and as a summer excursion steamer on Long Island Sound until sold to Palmer Smith of Norwich for $10,125 on April 10, 1872; *Victor* ran in the New Orleans and Havana trades until lost off Jupiter Light, Florida, on October 20, 1872; *Ariadne* and *General Sedgwick* were the backbone of the Galveston line until the former foundered at Oregon Inlet, North Carolina, on February 7, 1873, and the latter was retired on April 15.

Prior to 1873, C. H. Mallory & Co. also chartered a number of steamers, as needed, to increase the capacity of its lines. Most of these were voyage charters, but six vessels steamed for rather long-time charters under the Mallory flag: *Lodona,* an iron-hulled propellor engaged for the Galveston line on February 20, 1866, and run until her loss off Saint Augustine, Florida, on August 22, 1871; *Charles W. Lord,* also chartered for the Texas trade between December 20, 1866, and November 4, 1872; *Gulf City,* under charter to New Orleans and Mobile from February 16, 1867, until her loss off Cape Lookout, North Carolina, on January 11, 1869, was the Mallorys' old *Augusta*

Dinsmore under a new name; *Tillie,* chartered for the Galveston line on March 2, 1867, purchased for $36,500 to keep her in service (September 9, 1870), and sold on April 10, 1872, to the New London & Northern Railroad; *Gulf Stream,* another iron steamer, and *Weybosset,* an old Greenman-built propellor, run on the New Orleans line, October 26, 1867–September 8, 1871, and March 6, 1869–May 24, 1872, respectively.

The Mallorys' Mystic shipyard, in the meantime, had launched the Spanish gunboats and five other wooden propellors: *A. J. Ingersoll,* in March 1866, for W. L. Lincoln & Co. of Boston and Andrew J. Ingersoll of Mobile, and managed on two voyages by C. H. Mallory & Co. prior to her sale to J. M. Forbes & Co. for $105,000 on December 14; *Fanny* and *Kate* (later *Mystic*), two steam yachts designed, built, and sold by C. H. Mallory as a lark during 1867–1868; *Varuna III,* launched on June 23, 1869, "for the Galveston trade," placed in the line on September 11, but lost in the Gulf hurricane of October 20, 1870 (her captain and fifty-five others perished and $38,400 of her $80,000 value was uninsured); and *Bolivar,* launched December 23, 1869, as a Galveston lighter, sent out on January 29, 1870, and sold April 10, 1872, with *Tillie* for $70,000.

Small, mostly wooden propellors were, thus, sufficiently available to sustain the Mallory lines for half a decade after the Civil War, with careful and constant management. But the agreements signed with Ball, Hutchings & Co. and the Galveston Wharf Co. in 1870 crystalized Charles Henry Mallory's own yen for bigger and better vessels and supplied the demand and the marginal capital to achieve his desire.

City of Galveston, City of Houston, and *City of Austin* were the transitional vessels. *City of Galveston,* a wooden propellor twice as large as any of her Mallory-built predecessors, was already on the ways in Mystic when Ball, Hutchings & Co. bought into her. Charles Mallory launched her on August 27, 1870, and after taking on her machinery at the Delamater Iron Works, she entered the Galveston line on November 12. *City of Austin,* almost a carbon copy, was launched on September 6, 1871, and entered the line on December 16.

Although Charles Henry considered *City of Austin* "a fine steamer," he had serious reservations about the type of vessel his father could produce. "I find that for light draft, Iron ships are much to be prefered," he had noted in his diary on October 1, 1870. "In a few years it will be considered folly to build wooden steamers and I think wooden sail vessels also." And he was busily putting his preference into practice. He had already carved the model for the iron steamship *City of Houston* and contracted her for $150,000—not to his father's yard in Mystic, but to Reaney, Son & Archbold of Chester, Pennsylvania. She was launched on April 15, 1871, and sailed on her maiden voyage to Galveston on August 12.

C. H. Mallory & Co.'s need for iron steamers in the Galveston trade only widened the disagreements between the first and second generations begun over the future of sail and the superiority of barks to ships. Of the next four vessels financed by the Mallory-Ball-Hutchings-Sealy collaboration, three were iron, one was iron-strapped, and none was built by Charles Mallory. Almost as insulting to the elder's pride, *City of Galveston's* excessive draft forced her redeployment to the New Orleans line in 1872!

John Roach of Chester, Pennsylvania, and the Gildersleeve yard of Portland, Connecticut (which had built the barks *Brazos* and *Sabine*), supplied the next four Galveston liners. Captain Spicer had met Roach on the train during the construction period of *City of Austin* and renewed their friendship when Roach purchased the Reaney yard in June 1871. On August 4, C. H. Mallory & Co. contracted with him for *City of San Antonio*; the $163,750 iron steamship was launched on April 10, 1872, and joined the Texas Line on July 6. The Gildersleeves sold Spicer a partially built iron-strapped steamer which was completed to his specifications, named *City of Dallas,* and added to the line on November 23. Again with Roach: *City of Waco* was contracted for $200,000 on September 4, launched on May 7, 1873, and joined the line on November 29; *State of Texas,* contracted for $200,000 on December 12, 1872, launched on December 20, 1873 (almost five months late because of the depression), made her maiden voyage to Galveston on March 21, 1874.

Ball, Hutchings & Co. had an interest in all these vessels. *City of Austin, City of San Antonio, City of Waco,* and *State of*

City of Austin, third of the so-called "City" ships; she was launched by the Mallory yards in 1871. Typical of the wooden steamships preferred by Charles Mallory. Shown unloading at Fernandina, Florida, *ca.* 1875. Courtesy Mariners Museum.

State of Texas, iron steamship by John Roach delivered to New York & Texas Steamship Co. in 1874. Typical of those vessels which were preferred by Charles Henry Mallory and which formed the backbone of the Mallory Line 1875–1885. Courtesy Mariners Museum.

City of Rio de Janeiro, pioneer of John Roach's unsuccessful United States & Brazil Mail Steamship Line, which operated under the management of C. H. Mallory & Co., 1878–1881. Courtesy Mariners Museum.

Texas were the four steamers financed under the Galveston Wharf Co. resolution of July 2: "Mr. George Ball made this enterprise a success," President Hutchings' annual report of January 6, 1873, noted, "by taking $10,000 of the stock in each ship—and against much opposition and reluctance the remainder of the one quarter of the stock guaranteed by the Wharf Company was taken by private parties here." The firm also provided one-quarter of the financing for *City of Dallas,* for *Ariadne* (after August 19, 1871), and for the steam lighter *Samuel F. Maddox* purchased in 1871; repurchased the wharf company's shares in *Clyde, City of Galveston,* and *City of Houston* on May 23, 1873; and, with Cornelius H. Delamater, helped finance the iron-strapped steamer *Carondelet* which Charles Mallory launched for the New Orleans trade on October 7. [17]

By April 1, 1874, though the sailing fleet so long identified by Charles Mallory's house flag was dwindling, no one doubted that C. H. Mallory & Co. had become the very model of successful steamship enterprise. Its partners had purged their two lines of small, old-fashioned vessels and now owned three-fourths of nine large steamships totaling 10,208 tons, none more than five years old. Their minority stockholders were the richest and best-connected bankers in Texas, and they managed two more fine steamships, totaling 2,214 tons, for the wealthy Clyde family. As owners and operators of American-flag steamships they ranked third behind the gigantic Pacific Mail Steamship Co. and Charles Morgan of New York.

More important, Charles Henry Mallory and Captain Spicer now obviously grasped the economics of line carriage (in their own context of time and place, of course) and the maneuvering room available to the knowledgeable manager. They had learned that it was beyond any agent's ability, under normal market conditions, to increase the cargo per ship or decrease the time per voyage more or less than 5 per cent; and that the prime short-run means of varying the supply of cargo space they offered were to spot-charter, lay up, or reactivate their own steamers and to lay on or lay off "outside" vessels. They now knew that the lead time to build vessels was eight to twelve months and the cost upward of $200,000—twice the time and the price of the 1860's. And they had learned that significant economies in vessel performance only gradually evolved, however vigorous and well financed might be their construction and replacement program.

On the demand side, the partners had learned to concentrate on those markets and ports with a naturally high volume of liner goods; to woo shippers with good service, good will, quantity discounts, and rebates; to try to extend their influence over port authorities and lines of inland transport. They had learned to forestall price competition at sea by staggering schedules and equalizing rates with other lines and to drive off tramps with a complementary berth-sail service. They knew how to hedge against fluctuations in demand by varying their capacity in the manner previously described, and they knew that supplementary income could be earned from brokerage and commission; from spot charters; from shipments on own or vessel's account; from lighterage, towing, and salvage; and from carrying the mails.

C. H. Mallory & Co.'s skill was reflected in its reputation. As early as May 2, 1867, Dun & Bradstreet's credit reporters expressed confidence "that there is no better or safer shipping house in N.Y." By December 12, 1873, the superlatives had only increased: "A first class house in high standing as to character, responsibility, and business ability. They are doing a large and increasing business. Have met with but few losses and are perfectly sound in every way." The senior partner's rapid capital accumulation was also evidence of success. From July 1, 1870, to February 1, 1873, Charles Henry's net worth rose from $182,915 to $565,342: personal and real property valued at $205,000; $179,793 to his credit on profit and loss account with C. H. Mallory & Co.; and $9,500 in life insurance. His father, in the meantime, was still reported by Dun & Bradstreet as "A-1. Worth $1,000,000 & upward." [18]

The Mallorys thus had the resources to weather the financial panic triggered by the failures of Jay Cooke & Co. and Henry Clews & Co. in September 1873; but they were affected. Credit tightened, and the southern market, in particular, contracted. New Orleans was more affected than Galveston. As early as November 18, Charles Henry observed, "Business has been poorer today for New Orleans than any day for the past 5 years," and the depression carried over into 1874.

C. H. Mallory & Co.'s partners stayed close to the changing times. Captain Spicer, whom the influential New York *Nautical Gazette* had just commended for his "more than usual good taste and judgment in all matters pertaining to the construction and outfit of the fleet . . . a thorough executive officer," went out to New Orleans in January to drum up trade and collect accounts. Charles Henry followed him in April. By July 28, they had "displaced" George A. Fosdick & Co. as their New Orleans agents "and sent a young man from our office, Mr. Cameron, to take their place." The real problem was clear enough by September 30: "I have about concluded that this business will never pay until the number of lines is reduced." Rising costs of larger vessels and more frequent voyages had finally caught up with falling freight rates. "With measurement goods at ten cents per foot," observed the New Orleans *Republican* (one-third of what they had been in 1866), "Mr. Mallory claims that ships must be more economical than his are to make money."

Riots in New Orleans in early 1875 and no improvement in freight rates made up Charles Henry's mind. By January 8, he observed that "the Louisiana troubles put a stop to everything in that direction"; and, on January 20, he pulled out for good: "We send no New Orleans steamer this week and it is very doubtful if we can send another steamer in that direction. The business has been very disastrous for the past year and our losses for the line, reckoning insurance & repairs, cannot fall short of $100,000."

In fact, he had already begun to experiment with other routes as a possible replacement for New Orleans. At the invitation of merchants of Morehead City, North Carolina, *City of Dallas* had begun a weekly service from New York on November 25, 1874. After fifteen round voyages, however, her receipts proved disappointing enough to justify closure of the line on April 21, 1875 (see Table 6.2). To employ more of the excess capacity caused by termination of the New Orleans line, C. H. Mallory & Co., on March 10, had chartered *City of San Antonio* at $225 per day to run one month in the Old Dominion

Steamship Co.'s New York–Baltimore line; on March 31, *City of Houston* was chartered to run New York–Bermuda until July 1 at $100 per day and one-half of net profits.

These were stopgaps, however, and left only Galveston as the backbone of the business; there, trade was also depressed, but the Mallory position was strong. The Southern Line had always been the smallest among the three New Orleans competitors. In contrast, the Texas Line had faced no serious competition since 1869 and had successfully allied itself with powerful local interests. The investments by Ball, Hutchings, the Sealys, Henry Rosenberg, and others in Mallory vessels made the Mallorys partners with the Island City's most substantial and influential economic group.

On July 31, 1875, however, the complacency of the Mallory-Galveston entente was dramatically shattered—not by further depression, but by the appearance of a formidable competitor: "Business is very poor," Charles Henry recorded, "and Chas. Morgan a millionaire of 80 years old comes on with a new line in opposition to ours with intention of driving us out of the business & I fear he will succeed finally as he has too much money for us." [19]

Morgan was no newcomer to the steamship segment of the coastal market. Indeed, he had been its pioneer, opening a New York–Charleston line in 1832 and a New Orleans–Galveston line in 1837. He had always preferred the short-haul, intra-Gulf routes and was their monopolizer. In 1869, he had purchased an eighty-mile railroad between New Orleans and Brashear, Louisiana; he had dredged a seaway from Brashear to the Gulf via Atchafalaya River and Bay; and by April 1, 1874, had fifteen steamships totaling 14,544 tons on intra-Gulf routes: three to six per week between Brashear and Galveston; two to three per week between Galveston and Indianola; two per month between Brashear and Brazos St. Iago; one to two per week between Brashear, Rockport, and Havana; and various schedules to Florida, Cuba, and Mexico.

In mid-1874, Morgan had decided to open a Brashear–New York line and had placed orders with Harlan & Hollingsworth of Wilmington, Delaware, for four iron steamships totaling 9,527 tons. From Brashear he expected to tap New Orleans via his railroad, serve the rich Teche sugar country, and interconnect with his steamers to Texas ports. His New York steamers were to be twice the size of any under the Mallory flag, and it was the first of these, *Brashear*, which opened his line in July 1875. *New York, Lone Star,* and *Algiers* soon joined their sister.[20]

The Mallorys' Texas Line immediately felt the pinch: "Chas. Morgan is determined to ruin us if possible," Charles Henry noted on August 28. "Our recpts., with the same amount of freight as compared with last year, cannot be less than $40,000 per month on the wrong side, while our expenses are not lessened a fraction. Had we an ordinary man against us we should hope to see the end of it soon, but now we cannot expect it. We must work for much less than our living for some time to come, I fear." By September, he was almost despondent: "I am fretted and worried very much and hardly know what I am about, my business is in such miserable condition and no good prospects for the future. I have a large number of good steamers on hand and nothing for them to do and they lay rotting at the dock under expenses. . . . There is a good deal of freight moving but we get nothing for carrying it. . . . Business is in a sad condition and I hope it will not drive me crazy. Every thing appears to go wrong."

He was not passive, however. During September and October he laid up *City of Houston,* time-chartered *City of San Antonio* to the Savannah Line for one month at $150 per day, and voyage-chartered *Carondelet* New York–Port-au-Prince–Venezuela and return. He also decided to terminate his firm's berth-sail service so as to concentrate on meeting Morgan's rate war. Early in November, he again voyage-chartered *Carondelet* out and back to Venezuela via Saint Thomas and *City of Galveston* out and back to Port-au-Prince.

Then disaster struck. On November 9, *City of Waco* burned to the waterline in Galveston harbor with cargo, crew, and passengers all lost. At the worst possible time the Mallorys had lost one of their newest and finest Galveston steamships and suffered a hard blow to their line's prestige—besides the horror of the human tragedy. The year closed in gloom, and Charles Henry spoke for all the Mallorys: "We are having very bad success with our line after running along smoothly for a number of years. . . . Our business is in a sad state and I cannot see any prospect of a fair business from any quarter. . . . Our competitor Morgan is ruining our trade & how long he will continue to is hard to say. . . . This has been so far as business goes a ruinous year." Yet his skill and fortitude were to be further tested. [21]

Chapter 7

C. H. MALLORY & CO.,

1876–1885

"Saturday August 26th. A very sad day for me. Before I left the house I received a telegram informing me that my father died this morning. . . . The last remaining link is broken. I left for Mystic at 1 p.m., arrived at 5:30 and found sorrow enough."—Diary of Charles Henry Mallory, 1882

IN the decade following 1875, the second generation of Mallory management came into its own. The inevitability of old age and death made final the transition begun in the 1860's. Through the medium of C. H. Mallory & Co., it was Charles Henry and Captain Spicer who increasingly, and then solely, defined the family's business goals, formulated appropriate strategies, and implemented their decisions, come what may.

It was a decade of simplification, consolidation, and improvement of the Mallory enterprises; an era in which marginal trades and equipment inherited from the past were eliminated as humanely, expeditiously, and economically as possible; in which only the most profitable of the old lines and the most promising of new ventures were sustained. The Galveston line, of course, received the most immediate and continuing attention, for it was the major commitment. Viable new lines to South Carolina, Georgia, and Florida ports were also developed, and a spectacularly unprofitable line to Brazil was born and died. It was also an era in which important new relationships were established with railroads.

In the Galveston trade, the immediate problem was the competition of the Morgan Line, a threat of ever-increasing dimensions. Not only was Charles Morgan now operating a rival service to New York; he was also busy with plans to cut Galveston off from its hinterland. Piqued at the preferential treatment accorded the Mallorys by the Galveston Wharf Co., and irritated by Island City quarantines that always seemed to detain his Brashear line as the Mallorys' New York liners steamed by, Morgan had decided to move his prime Texas port of call inland from Galveston to Houston.

Houston was further up Buffalo Bayou than Galveston, commanded precisely the same hinterland, and already had superior lines of inland transport. While Galveston had only one railroad (and that one for all practical purposes ran only to Houston via Harrisburg!), Houston was the intersection for four important roads.

Running westward via Harrisburg was Thomas W. Peirce's Galveston, Harrisburg & San Antonio Railway, which crossed the Brazos River at Richmond, the Colorado at Columbus, and was pushing on toward San Antonio and the Rio Grande. Eastward from Houston via Liberty ran the Texas & New Orleans Railroad, which would reach the Sabine River at Orange on August 1, 1876, and was the target of Charles Morgan's railroad then building westward from New Orleans via Brashear.

Northward from Houston ran the Houston & Texas Central Railway and the International & Great Northern Railroad. The H. & T. C. connected with the Missouri, Kansas & Texas Railway at Denison, via Hempstead, Hearne, Bremond, Dallas, and Sherman. Its two branches probed equally inviting hinterlands: Hempstead to Austin and beyond; Bremond to Waco and beyond. The I. & G. N. was a consolidation of several lines which operated trackage from a junction with the G. H. & S. A. at Peirce, via Houston, to Palestine; from Palestine westward to Hearne and eastward to Troup and Longview; and from Troup to Mineola. Cutting across the H. & T. C. and the I. & G. N. was the Texas & Pacific Railway, running Shreveport-Marshall-Longview-Dallas and Texarkana-Paris-Sherman.[1]

Morgan hoped to tap this rail network at Houston and shunt its New Orleans and New York freight around Galveston and the Mallorys. His strategy was grand: bypass Galveston with an exclusive seaway from Houston to the Gulf and buy into as many of the Houston railroads as he was financially able to control. On July 1, 1874, he had signed the first of several contracts with the Buffalo Bayou Ship Channel Co. to bring deepwater to Houston. By April 21, 1876, the Morgan-dug channel opened to a Morgan water-rail terminal at Clinton, and by September 11 a Morgan-built railroad had covered the 7.4 miles between Clinton and Houston. By May 7, 1877, Morgan had also purchased a controlling interest in the largest of the Texas railroads, the Houston & Texas Central.[2]

Galveston's businessmen, of course, could not and did not ignore the Morgan-Houston attempt to tap their hinterland and bypass their port. And since the Mallorys' friends and partners, Ball, Hutchings & Co., were the leading strategists of Galveston's reaction to Morgan, the Mallory Line was involved on land as well as sea.

The Ball, Hutchings & Co.-Galveston strategy comprised four major elements. First, the physical facilities of the wharf company and of the Galveston, Houston & Henderson were to be further improved—particularly those of the railroad—so as to expedite rail-water interchange with Mallory Line steamships. Second, traffic and financial ties between the G. H. & H. and the two Houston railroads in most direct opposition to Morgan were to be strengthened and through freights increased. Third, continuing financial support, privileged rates, and rebates were to be accorded the Mallory Line to help offset its losses from price competition at sea. Fourth, a new Mallory-flag, intra-Gulf line between Galveston, Corpus Christi, and Brazos St. Iago was to challenge the Morgan Line's long-time monopoly of the ports of South Texas.

Under the prodding of John Sealy, who moved up from vice president to president in 1876, and Hutchings, who became treasurer, the Galveston, Houston & Henderson rapidly bettered itself. Its antiquated gauge of 5 feet 6 inches was reduced to 4 feet 8½ inches, permitting interchange of cars with other Texas roads, and its rate structure was thoroughly overhauled to reduce the handling costs borne by shippers. Joint freight arrangements with the Gulf, Harrisburg & San Antonio and the International & Great Northern were also improved so as to combat Morgan's increasing influence over the Houston & Texas Central and the Texas & New Orleans.

The partners of Ball, Hutchings & Co. and of C. H. Mallory & Co. had no difficulty in improving relations with the G. H. & S. A., for it was owned and operated by the same group that controlled the G. H. & H. and connected with that road at Harrisburg. Thomas W. Peirce of Boston and John Sealy were the links: Peirce serving as president of the G. H. & S. A. (after 1870) and as president of the G. H. & H. (1871–1876); Sealy serving as vice president (1871–1876) and president (after 1876) of the G. H. & H. The link with the International & Great Northern was H. M. Hoxie, a cousin of the Mystic Hoxies, who served simultaneously as general superintendent of the I. & G. N. and director and vice president of the G. H. & H.

The community of interest between the Mallory Line and these non-Morgan railroads extended C. H. Mallory & Co.'s influence farther inland in Texas than ever before. Significantly, when the G. H. & S. A. reached San Antonio on February 5, 1877, Charles Henry Mallory was there, "at the invitation of Mr. Peirce," enjoying the "great event" but not neglecting to call "at the principal stores and banks" in search of trade. Northeast of Houston, along the route of the I. & G. N., the story was the same—water carriers previously content to load and unload cargoes "at end of ship's tackle" now competing vigorously for freight at inland points and locked in a rate war at sea.[3]

The Clydes were the first to cut and run. On March 16, 1876, they terminated their pool with the Mallory Line and removed *Clyde* and *George W. Clyde* from the Galveston trade. Although he had lost *City of Galveston* on February 5, off Key West, Charles Henry still had sufficient excess capacity left over from the New Orleans line to fill the gap. But for longer-run protection, on May 9 he contracted for a new iron steamship. *Rio Grande* was launched by Roach on October 22 and joined the Galveston line on December 16. Evidencing C. H. Mallory & Co.'s new alliance, *Rio Grande's* shareholders were Charles Henry Mallory, Elihu Spicer, Jr., John Roach, George Ball, John Hutchings, John Sealy, A. P. Lufkin, and Henry Rosenberg (both prominent Galveston merchants), and Jeremiah N. Sawyer (the Mallory Line's salaried manager in Galveston).

This group also financed a Galveston–Corpus Christi–Brazos

St. Iago Line to increase competitive pressure on the Morgan Line. Brazos St. Iago, at the mouth of the Rio Grande, had been a Morgan port of call since 1847 and Corpus Christi, at the mouth of the Nueces River, since 1866. Both ports lacked inland railroads and were, consequently, quite dependent on water carriers for access to primary markets. The volume of their trade and the chance to undercut Morgan induced the Galveston-Mallory response.

On December 14, 1876, Charles Henry contracted with Roach for a $120,000 iron steamship expressly for the South Texas trade. *Western Texas* was launched June 23, 1877, and sailed for Galveston on August 26. She was five feet shallower than any of her Mallory-flag sisters and could easily negotiate the bars and bays leading to Corpus Christi and Brazos St. Iago. She met Morgan's steamers from Brashear, Louisiana (now Morgan City), to those points in head-on price competition.[4]

The Mallory-Morgan rate war was in full swing throughout 1877. "Our business is in a sad state," Charles Henry commented on August 2; "the great competition is demoralising and unless there is a change soon I cannot see any way to continue at a profit. We are just about paying expenses, keeping the ships in good condition, & paying insurance . . . and all this comes from Mr. Chas. Morgan, an old man of 82 years who, although reputed to be worth $20,000,000, is using every effort to crush me and drive me out of a business which I have built up after a close confinement of 12 years." By September 4, he was still pessimistic and echoes the age-old dilemma of the line operator who must maintain service no matter how far prices may plunge: "We are having plenty of business, but at very poor rates of freight, and I see but little hope of anything brilliant for a long time to come."

The change came unexpectedly on March 26, 1878: "There appears to be a little light shining on our Galveston line to-day. Mr. Whitney (Mr. Morgan's son-in-law) called and expressed a wish to fix the matter up in some way that would be satisfactory to both and wished us to make an appointment and meet him and see if we could not come together. It is a hard matter to do, but I shall try my best to make some arrangement," Mallory resolved.

153

The reason for the Morgan Line's change of heart was simple: "Mr. Morgan is very ill and has given his business up to his son-in-law who appears anxious to make a fair arrangement with us." Whitney and his partner Alexander C. Hutchinson were more interested in completing their railroad between New Orleans and Houston than in further development of the ship channel and were content to leave the New York–Texas water route to the Mallorys.

Five meetings were held between Charles Henry Mallory and Charles A. Whitney, and John Sealy came north "on a flying trip" at Charles Henry's request "to advise about settlement." Morgan's death on May 8 turned the tide: "Mr. Chas. Morgan died at noon to-day. He was 83 years of ago. He was a very clever, smart man," Mallory recorded in his diary, "but for the past 3 years he has used his best endeavours to ruin me, and has kept me in hot water most of the time. He failed to accomplish his ends after spending at least $3,000,000 in the attempt. . . . I have been hoping to arrange matters with him for the past 2 or 3 months as he had virtually given up the test and expressed a wish to make up and settle matters with me." Even so, the matter dragged on. As late as May 29, Mallory felt "sorely tired about an arrangement for harmonising our business with the Morgan Line. I feel that they are trifling with me or in other words are playing a huge game of bluff. I want advice & don't really know which way to turn or how to decide." But as head of the business he *had* to decide, and he did so on June 10: "Signed an agreement with the Morgan Line . . . which I hope will prove in the end to have been the right thing to do. . . . The business has become so demoralized that it will be a long time before it can be brought up to a healthy standard again. But we must work along by degrees and try to make it pay finally." [5]

While precise details of the agreement have not survived, its intent and effects are clear. The Morgan Line restricted itself to a New York–New Orleans service with connections to Texas points via its subsidiary railroads and intra-Gulf steamers. It promised to refrain from direct New York–Texas sailings and to set no rates or schedules directly competitive with the Mallory's New York–Galveston line. The Mallory Line canceled its Galveston–Corpus Christi–Brazos St. Iago service, agreed not to reenter the New York–New Orleans trade (which was still a remote possibility), and consented to the establishment of a fixed differential on water rates between New York and Texas' two leading ports: henceforth, regardless of the amounts involved, the New York–Galveston all-water rate was to be maintained 10 cents per cwt. below the New York–Houston all-water rate.[6]

The agreement of June 10, 1878, meant that the Morgan Line could charge 10 cents per cwt. more, f.a.s. (free alongside ship) its Clinton terminal, than the Mallory Line could charge f.a.s. its Galveston wharves. This difference, however, soon became academic. The Texas railroads, acting in consort, nullified the water-rate differential from the shippers' point of view. Railroad rates from the port cities to "Texas Common Points" were standardized and a reverse differential was applied: it cost 10 cents more per cwt. by rail from Galveston to Texas Common Points than from Houston. Thus, on through shipments, the higher water rate to Houston was canceled by the higher land rate to Galveston:

New York–Galveston water rate via Mallory Line:	$ .65		New York–Houston water rate via Morgan Line:	$ .75
Galveston–Texas Common Points rail rate:	$ .85		Houston–Texas Common Points rail rate:	$ .75
New York–Texas Common Points via Galveston:	$1.50		New York–Texas Common Points via Houston	$1.50

The Morgan Line made the water-rate differential academic from the carriers' point of view. On September 28, 1880, the Morgan system completed the first all-rail line between New Orleans and Houston; in October, Morgan Line sailings to Clinton were terminated, and the water-borne threat they had posed to the Mallorys' Galveston line expired. By the end of 1880, long-haul steamship service between New York and ports of the Western Gulf of Mexico had acquired the pattern it held for the next twenty years: the Morgan Line and the Cromwell Line divided the New Orleans trade; the Mallory Line had Galveston to itself.

Although once again victorious on the New York–Texas water route, the Mallory Line had still to face competition from all-rail lines between the Southwest and the East. The Texas railroads, which had previously merely extended the Mallorys' influence inland, were now linking up with eastern lines and threatening to serve the Southwest without crossing the coast-line at all. By hard work, however, Charles Henry Mallory, Captain Spicer, and their Galveston partners hammered out an entente with the railroads' traffic associations during 1880–1885.

Using a $1.20 all-rail rate from St. Louis to the Texas Common Points as their base, the railroad associations established differential all-rail rates between the Texas Common Points and other eastern and northern cities. These rates were fixed proportions of the St. Louis base rate: for example, by 1885, the rate between New Orleans and the Texas Common Points was "St. Louis minus 10"; the Louisville rate was "St. Louis plus 16"; the Cincinnati rate was "St. Louis plus 25"; and the Chicago, Cleveland, and Pittsburgh rates were "St. Louis plus 30."

The water-rail rate from New York to the Texas Common Points was *not* a differential of the St. Louis all-rail base rate. Rather, it was the Mallory Line rate between New York and Galveston plus the intrastate all-rail rate from Galveston to the Texas Common Points. A competitive dividing line between the "St. Louis plus" rates and the "Mallory plus" rate was possible, however, and it was codified by 1885: "north and south through Buffalo, Pittsburgh, Wheeling, Bristol and south from Bristol to the southern boundary of North Carolina, thence east along the southern boundary of North Carolina to the Coast, and including all Atlantic Seaboard cities south of that line." [7]

At all points east of this dividing line, the "Mallory plus" water-rail rate commanded the market to and from the Texas Common Points. At all points west of this dividing line, the "St. Louis plus" all-rail rates were the more economical to the Texas Common Points. And parity was maintained between the two systems quite easily:

> . . . a change at one point would cause a horizontal and equal change in the rates from all other points and territories. If the steamship lines would announce a reduction of ten cents, the rail lines would immediately counter by lowering the St. Louis rate ten

Mallory Line

—— OF ——

STEAMERS.

Galveston to New York.

Shippers and Consignees will find this route the most
advantageous in point of

Low Rates, Dispatch and Few Transfers.

Freight Reaches New York

AS QUICKLY AS IF CARRIED BY RAIL.

The Traveling Public may be assured of commodious and well appointed
State-rooms, an excellent table—the more enjoyable with an appetite whetted by
invigorating sea air.   Courteous treatment to passengers has always characterized
the officers and employees of this line.

The benefits arising from a sea voyage, particularly to those long resident in
the interior, are too well known to be stated here.

J. N. SAWYER, Agent,

GALVESTON.

Mallory Line advertisement, *Texas Business Directory for 1878–9* (Galveston: Shaw & Blaylock, 1878), p. 108.

Mallory Line advertisement, *Appleton's Illustrated Railway and Steam Navigation Guide* (New York: D. Appleton & Co., 1877), p. 35.

cents, and with it would fall the rates from all other interstate points and also within Texas. The changing of a rate by the rail lines would have the same effect. The whole level of rates fluctuated as a single unit, all rates changing to correspond with the change of a single key rate.[8]

The result of the Mallory Line's entente with the railroads was quite simple: "from all the points of origin east of the Buffalo-Pittsburgh line, practically all the traffic to Texas . . . did move via the water route." Table 7.1 indicates the volume and sources of profit as of 1882–1883 and is representative for 1880–1885. As it had been since 1869, the Galveston trade thus remained the backbone of the Mallory Line.[8]

A weekly "Florida Line," which opened on January 22, 1876, became the other prime moneymaker for C. H. Mallory & Co. The line actually ran between New York City, Port Royal, South Carolina, Brunswick, Georgia, and Fernandina, Florida— with Jacksonville often substituted for Fernandina—and, as in Texas, railroads were part of its reason for being. The Mallory steamers connected with the Port Royal Railway, which ran 111 miles inland to Augusta, Georgia, and crossed the railroad between Charleston and Savannah at Yemassee; with the 171-mile Brunswick & Albany Railroad; with the 186-mile Macon & Brunswick Railroad; and with the Atlantic, Gulf & West India Transit Railway, which connected the Atlantic port of Fernandina with the Gulf port of Cedar Key, 155 miles across northern Florida. Connections were also made with local steamers serving "all points on the St. John's River."[9]

At sea, the Mallorys' Florida Line threaded its way among the vessels of six other steamship lines which jammed the middle and southern segments of the Atlantic coastal market: the Clyde Line, running New York–Wilmington, Philadelphia–Charleston, Philadelphia–Norfolk–Portsmouth–Richmond; the Old Dominion Steamship Co., running New York–Norfolk–Portsmouth and New York–West Point; the New York & Charleston Steamship Co. and the New York & South Carolina Steamship Co., both running New York–Charleston; the Ocean Steamship Co. (owned by the Central Railroad of Georgia), running Boston–Savannah, New York–Savannah, and Philadelphia–Savannah; and the Merchants & Miners Transportation

Co., running Boston–Norfolk–Portsmouth–Baltimore, Providence–Norfolk–Portsmouth–Baltimore, Boston–West Point, Providence–West Point, and Baltimore–Savannah.[10]

What seemed like a maze of competition, however, was actually quite carefully structured to reduce the number of competitive points. The regulating agency was the Southern Railway & Steamship Association, which had been organized on October 13, 1875, and which, by 1880, comprised "40 railroad companies and 29 coastwise steamship lines," the Mallorys included. The relationship of the association to the Florida Line was simple:

> The business of the Southern Railway and Steamship Association does not . . . directly embrace steamer traffic between Northern and Southern seaports; but the influence of the association is sufficient to regulate and maintain all these . . . rates, and to prevent any combination in conflict with the rates determined through the operations of the organization.

This meant that the Mallorys and other water carriers were not required to pool their earnings with those of railroad members, but that the water rates that could be charged and the traffic patterns available were closely controlled by decisions of the association:

> . . . To all the Southern seaports and to certain of the interior competing points nearer the coast, the coastwise steamer lines are allowed to make rates in connection with the great trunklines extending from the centers of trade of the Western and Northwestern States to Boston, New York, Philadelphia, and Baltimore; which rates shall be less by fixed differences than the direct rail rates which may prevail between such Southern seaports and the centers of trade of the Western and Northwestern States. On the other hand, the rail rates between the interior points embraced in the operations of the association and the centers of trade of the Western and Northwestern States, and of the States of Tennessee and Kentucky, are so graded as to favor direct shipments on the interior rail lines rather than by the way of the trunklines from the West to the Northern seaports, thence by steamer to Southern ports, and thence by rail to the interior points above referred to.

In plain language, these agreements meant that the Mallorys' Florida Line dominated all-water shipments between New York and its allocated southern ports; carried a large volume of northbound rail-water through shipments; and carried a lesser volume of southbound water-rail through freights. In dollars, earnings from the New York–Port Royal–Brunswick–Fernandina service probably ran about 30 per cent of those of the New York–Key West–Galveston line (see Table 7.1). [11]

To maintain their two weekly lines, and with the financial assistance of the Ball, Hutchings & Co. group, the partners of C. H. Mallory & Co. continued to employ and perfect their system of vessel procurement, deployment, maintenance, and replacement. Vessels built before 1875 were used primarily on the shorter Florida line: *City of Galveston,* until her loss off Key West on February 5, 1876; *City of Houston,* lengthened fifty feet by Roach in 1876, but sunk near Fernandina on October 23, 1878; *City of Austin,* until sunk off Fernandina on April 25, 1878; *City of Dallas,* until sold for $50,000 on August 19, 1881. *City of San Antonio* and *State of Texas,* both altered by Roach in 1882, were the only "City-class" steamships remaining in the Mallory fleet by the end of 1885. Charles Mallory's large wooden steamship *Carondelet* also survived.

The Roach-built *Rio Grande* and *Western Texas* were added during the Morgan competition of 1876–1877, but during 1878–1885 Roach supplied six more iron steamships to C. H. Mallory & Co. for use on the Texas and Florida lines: *Colorado,* contracted September 4, 1878, launched April 14, 1879, and costing $279,357; *Guadeloupe,* contracted July 28, 1880, sold January 5, 1881, "for a small advance," recontracted, launched August 27, and costing $290,000; *San Marcos,* contracted January 5, 1881, launched November 13, and costing $315,780; *Lampasas,* contracted September 5, 1882, launched May 12, 1883, and costing $401,258; *Alamo,* contracted September 5, 1882, launched June 16, 1883, and costing $401,258; and *Comal,* contracted December 15, 1884, launched June 16, 1885, and costing $301,574. In each case, approximately one-fourth of the cost of these vessels was borne by the Ball, Hutchings & Co. group.

To cope with the transshipment problems still characteristic of Texas, South Carolina, Georgia, and Florida ports, C. H.

Mallory & Co. also built a fleet of six steam lighters at the Gildersleeve yard, Portland, Connecticut: *C. F. Deering* (1880), *C. E. Goin* (1880), *P. C. Golder* (1881), *S. A. Walker* (1881), *O. M. Hitchcock* (1881), and *S. B. Baker* (1883). All were named after long-time customers or friends.

Neither were the names of the new large steamships idly chosen. Charles Henry Mallory wanted them to avoid intercity hostility and yet to define his line's prime market. He consciously chose neutral but descriptive names: *Rio Grande, Colorado, Guadeloupe, San Marcos, Lampasas,* and *Comal* all commemorated Texas rivers or creeks; *Alamo,* of course, was Texan to the core; and *Western Texas* was suggestive but impersonal. Significantly, not one of the new vessels commemorated a particular city (as had so many of their predecessors); not one commemorated a Louisiana subject (such as *Carondelet*); not one commemorated a South Carolina, Georgia, or Florida subject, although most ran in that line at one time or another. Charles Henry also increasingly allowed use of the term "Mallory Line" in advertisements. He found this a useful marketing ploy during competition with the Morgan Line, and he allowed its consumer acceptance to override his personal feelings that the term was pretentious.

Most of the vessels added to the Mallory fleet between 1875 and 1886 were satisfactory; only one was lost prior to 1886: *Guadeloupe,* stranded on Barnegat Shoals on November 19, 1884. *Rio Grande* was the swiftest, being the first steamship to break six days on the Galveston run (5 days, 19 hours, 30 minutes in June 1880). *Western Texas* was the problem child. Specifically designed for Texas coastal service, but denied that trade because of the Morgan compromise, she was found too shallow and too small for either of the New York lines. She was voyage- and time-chartered, as the market permitted, to Nassau, Havana, Vera Cruz, and between Venezuelan ports. But Charles Henry Mallory's relief was evident when he sold her to the Oregon & Pacific Railroad Co. on February 7, 1884, for $120,000 (her contract price eight years before!).

The real problems in vessel management faced by C. H. Mallory & Co. during 1876–1885, however, were not on the Texas and Florida lines. They sprang from Charles Mallory's

Alamo, iron steamship by John Roach delivered to the New York & Texas Steamship Co. in 1883. Typical of those vessels which formed the backbone of the Mallory Line in the late 1880's. Courtesy Mariners Museum.

Dining saloon, steamship *Alamo.* Courtesy Mystic Seaport.

San Marcos, built 1881, side-loading cotton in a southern port. Courtesy Mariners Museum.

legacy of large wooden steamers and sailing ships and from a folly conceived by John Roach.

Old age took care of most of the Mallory-built wooden propellors, but not *Carondelet* or *Aurora.* The former was kept in service on the lines as a backup vessel or chartered to southern, West Indian, and Latin American ports, if possible. The expenses of running her old-fashioned engines and maintaining her wooden hull were great, however, and she was frequently laid up. Not until April 4, 1889, was Charles Henry able to sell her, for $40,000, and "glad that we are rid of her." *Aurora,* launched on September 1, 1874, was the last steamer built by Charles Mallory, but her career was pitiful. Charles Henry wrote her epitaph on January 2, 1878: "George came down from Mystic this morning and tells me that he has made a sale of the new boat which has been lying at Mystic for 3 years [*sic*], price about $46,000, which is at least $30,000 less than her cost."

The marrow-deep Mallory belief in the profitability of Connecticut-built clippers died even harder than the family's dedication to wooden steamers. Despite his growing doubts concerning *Haze, Twilight III,* and *Annie M. Smull,* even Charles Henry could still be seduced by upswings in ocean freight rates and the availability of a venerable Mystic-built ship. A flurry of San Francisco business prompted him to buy a controlling interest in *Prima Donna* for $40,000 on June 22, 1875, with "the hope she may prove a good purchase." She did not, despite C. H. Mallory & Co.'s best managerial efforts: in 1877 she was laid up for nine months "for want of remunerative business"; again, in 1878–1879, for eleven months ("there is nothing for her to do . . . and I do not know what to do with her"). Finally, on June 15, 1883, after a series of lay-ups, she was sold for $19,000, less 5 per cent, "and glad to get rid of her."

Haze, Twilight III, and *Annie M. Smull* went the way of *Prima Donna.* The story was always the same: heavy expenses against transfer or lay-up rates, no matter how far-ranging the voyage (see Table 7.2). *Haze* was retired by 1885. Charles Henry's last mention of *Twilight III,* on November 15, 1884, was that "she has been absent over 2 years and has grossed in the whole time only $27,000:" Her "ruinous" career ended in her sale in 1885. *Annie M. Smull's* sale, for $21,725 on May 24, 1883, recouped only a fraction of her cost and persistent deficits on voyage account.

Natural calamity, the end of the Mallory berth-sail service to Texas, and a proliferation of British and American steamers on the sea lanes between Europe and the Gulf of Mexico killed off the Mallory-flag barks. *Galveston* was stranded on Duck Key, Florida, on October 19, 1876, and sold for $1,980 salvage on July 5, 1877. *Sabine* was sold for $16,000 on October 14, 1879; *Brazos* for $22,150 on October 10, 1882—"and glad of it."

The explanation of Charles Henry's disgust with ocean sail, of course, was the increasing loss in comparative advantage which the American merchant marine suffered on the high seas after the Civil War. Just as good management could not make wooden steamers profitable by 1885, good management could not overcome the market conditions facing ships and barks. World freight rates were declining, and the cost curves of American-flag sailing ships relative to those of other-flag ships were rising. In the world tramp market, where cabotage could not protect them and price, not service, was decisive, the result was that American-flag ships of the sort the Mallorys favored found only lay-up rates or less. Mallory-flag sail died gallantly; but it died.[12]

The disadvantages faced by American-flag shipping in world markets were underscored even more clearly for the Mallorys because of their role in John Roach's United States and Brazil Mail Steamship Line. Here friendship and euphoria overcame skepticism, but led to fiasco.[13]

In addition to his shipbuilding enterprises, Roach had long dreamed of operating steamships from New York and Philadelphia to Europe and Latin America. The American visit of the Brazilian Emperor Dom Pedro in late 1876 included extensive discussions with Roach and his representatives, and the result was an Imperial Decree of November 10, 1877: Roach was to establish steamship service between Rio de Janeiro, Bahia, Pernambuco, Pará, Saint Thomas, and New York by May 10, 1878; a twenty-four-day schedule New York–Rio de Janeiro was to be maintained and twenty-three days northbound. In return,

Roach was to receive a ten-year mail subsidy of 200,000 milreis per annum (about $100,000).

Roach had laid the keels of two steamships intended for the line five days before the decree was signed. On March 6, 1878, *City of Rio de Janeiro* was launched with Charles Henry Mallory and Captain Spicer among the dignitaries present. They returned to Chester on April 6 to see *City of Para* slide down the ways—with the blessings of President Rutherford B. Hayes.

Mallory and Spicer were more than casually interested in Roach's plans, for in December their firm had been offered the general agency of the proposed Brazilian line. They were impressed by the opulence of the Roach steamships, but not by their design; they thought them too narrow, too deep, and too top-heavy and were proven correct when 390 tons of ballast were found necessary to stabilize the vessels. Nevertheless, as a favor to Roach and as an opportunity whose prospects seemed to outweigh its flaws, they agreed to invest a token 1/10 in the steamships and undertake their management. Then deep in the demoralizing competition with Morgan, the partners welcomed the euphoric beginnings of such a glamorous new venture.

City of Rio de Janeiro, under the management of C. H. Mallory & Co., inaugurated the United States and Brazil Mail Steamship Line on May 4, 1878—six days short of Dom Pedro's deadline—and was followed by *City of Para* on June 6. [14] Roach's dreams for his line were grand: "his chance to demonstrate to potential investors and ship operators that steamships under the United States flag could successfully compete for the foreign carrying trade. . . . Deliberately and with loud fanfare, he presented his company as the significant test case to show what a line, not blighted by parasitic speculators or bungling greenhorns, could accomplish." [15] A classic cost-price squeeze, however, turned Roach's dreams to nightmares.

The costs of operating Roach's large steamships and of maintaining the lavish passenger accommodations and service he felt necessary to publicize the line steadily mounted. Bunkerage and coal in Brazil were controlled by British interests, which openly discriminated against the American-flag vessels. In New York, stevedores struck the line for higher wages. And the crews of the two vessels added to the upset: *City of Rio de Janeiro* rammed three other vessels on three successive voyages during the first half of 1879, necessitating expensive repairs and law-suits; *City of Para's* boilers were so neglected by her black gang as to require their complete overhaul after only eight months' service, and no sooner had she left her repair berth than her captain ran her aground and put her right back. "The results of these mishaps were additional expenditures of $97,000 for repairs and maintenance, claims for damages not altogether covered by insurance, loss of time to make the repairs, and a charter fee of $250 a day for [C. H. Mallory & Co.'s] . . . *Colorado*" as a substitute vessel in the line.[16]

Roach was also absorbing the heavy costs of trade promotion and of unsuccessfully lobbying for a United States mail contract. Against these outlays, he found little relief. His steamships faced vicious rate competition from heavily subsidized British lines between New York and Brazil and from German and British tramps; furthermore, collection of his Brazilian subsidy lagged—and when paid, was in Brazilian funds that had depreciated 30 per cent since Dom Pedro's decree.

Roach and C. H. Mallory & Co. hung on for thirty-seven round voyages between New York and Rio de Janeiro, but at less than lay-up rates: "While the break-even point, including interest, maintenance, and depreciation (calculated on the basis of a 20-year life for the vessel), was $48,789.00 per voyage, the average revenue amounted to only $41,210.00." Charles Henry was discouraged by May 8, 1880: "I can see nothing here—a dead loss of the whole investment. . . . The quicker the ships are sold the better for all concerned." By July 2, he was fed up: "I wish I had never had anything to do with it. And I must in some legitimate way get out."

But Roach persisted, and Charles Henry stuck with him until mid-1881. Then, as *City of Para* sailed on the last voyage from New York on May 5, Mallory struck the balance: "There has been a great deal of hard work and much anxiety for nothing. I trust that I shall profit by experience and not engage in another matter of the same kind." [17] The two Roach liners were sold to the Pacific Mail Steamship Co. and the partners totaled their losses: Roach set his at almost $1,000,000; Mallory set his "individual loss" at $40,000.

Success of the Texas and Florida lines was, thus, tempered by failures in ocean sail and in Brazilian steamships; and both profits and losses were clouded by growing difficulties with labor.

The particular problems of the Mallory Line were, of course, only symptomatic of the numerous labor-management confrontations which characterized American industry during the 1870's and 1880's. The "national" railway strike of 1877 and rising membership in the militant Knights of Labor (from 9,000 in 1879 to a claimed 703,000 in 1886) were indexes of the same trend. Tensions in the maritime industries were more sporadic than those in railroading and manufacturing, but smoldering resentments increasingly burst into flame. The nineteenth-century disputes centered on the wages of longshoremen in the Atlantic and Gulf ports, and the problem became more and more volatile as the Knights of Labor challenged shipowners determined to maintain their ancient "right" to set the conditions of work on their vessels, piers, and wharves.

Trouble had first flashed in New York in 1874. Steamship operators (the Mallorys included) set city-wide longshoremen's wages at 30 cents per hour for day work, 45 cents at night, and announced, effective November 16: "Those not agreeable to working at the stated rate need not apply at the piers." The Longshoremen's Protective Union responded by striking all piers in New York, Brooklyn, Jersey City, and Hoboken; and, at its peak, the dispute involved 8,000 to 10,000 men. The steamship owners countered with a lockout of union men, and a ready supply of scabs broke the strike in thirty days.[18]

At first glance, the longshoremen's wage rates seem high *for the time*: common laborers, in contrast, earned 14 to 15 cents per hour; railway roustabouts 17 to 18 cents. The dock workers argued, however, that the uncertainties they faced in employment merited their hourly premium over comparable classes of workers: a longshoreman had to be prepared to work whenever and wherever a ship was loading and continuously until the job was done; yet, to work at all, he had to be chosen by a hiring boss at each morning's "shape-up"; if he was not chosen, he could not work. Under these conditions, management's labor policies had always been to hire only those men who would work for an arbitrary wage and to rely on the oversupply of dock workers and the power of the hiring bosses to keep that wage low. Management-labor relations had been simple: pay only what daily situations demanded and work for whatever wages were available.

By the late 1870's and early 1880's, under the organizational prodding of both local leaders and the national Knights of Labor, things were changing on the water front:

> . . . A cargo gang would secretly decide at the last minute not to report, . . . a fast-operating "jungle telegraph" would spread word to other longshoremen living in the area not to be available. . . .
>
> It was a maddeningly difficult campaign for the employers to fight. One night there would be plenty of dockers, but the next day, or the following one perhaps, every longshoreman . . . would suddenly vanish with the sun. It did little good to fire the men involved . . . for a new gang would prove no more dependable than the old one. Strikebreakers were ineffective. . . . By the time a cargo officer realized what was happening and managed to round up scabs from pier-side taverns or from the billiard parlors, the damage had already been done. [19]

The Mallory Line's Pier 20 was first hit by one of these wildcat strikes in late 1879. The longshoremen demanded a 10-cent wage increase and the hiring of only union men. Trouble dragged on into 1880, as Charles Henry Mallory noted on February 9:

> . . . For the past number of months our longshoremen have been very arbitrary, striking for higher wages without any notice and demanding that we should employ no men but such as they wished, and also demanding exorbitant wages (40¢ an hour) that it became necessary that we should take some steps toward independence. Accordingly this morning, we notified them that we did not require their service and put 70 strange men at work who did not belong to the "Trade Union." We had plenty of Policemen to protect them but, nevertheless, a number were injured by having stones thrown by the out men who congregated by hundreds near the wharf. . . .

Thus, the Mallory Line adopted the stance toward the longshoremen chosen by every other shipping line in the United States: "We have commenced and must if possible carry it through at all hazards. I know of no good reason why I should not have the privilege of employing whomever I wish, and hardly think it right that I should be compelled to discharge men at their dictation." [20]

The united front of shipping operators held the line at 40 cents or less against the New York longshoremen through the first half of the 1880's. In Galveston, however, similar disputes flared which the Mallory Line had to face alone; and, in Texas, the labor problem had unfortunate racial overtones which only clouded the issues further. A brief flurry occurred November 4–6, 1883, when 150 white longshoremen struck against the Mallory Line's employment of nonunion Negroes. Ten of the strikers were fired, no adjustments in wages or hours were made, and matters stewed for almost two years.

On October 15, 1885, however, real labor problems began for the Mallory's Texas Line. White longshoremen affiliated with the Knights of Labor struck the line for a 10-cent hourly increase and union recognition. Captain Sawyer, the Mallory agent, locked out the 134 union men and hired Negro scabs at the old rates. By November 8, the strike was broken with no wage increase, no reemployment of the strikers, and no union contract. On January 28, 1886, however, it broke again over the same issues. Again, Negro strikebreakers were used, but the Knights of Labor were more successful in interfering with Mallory service: "shippers are very sensitive & wish to be sure that their goods may not be stopped by the Strikers," Charles Henry commented. He estimated that Galveston business went down as much as 40 per cent as a result.

Amidst bitterness and public recriminations, the strike in Galveston dragged on. No Mallory Line sailings were canceled, but very little freight moved. The line won the test of wills, however, and on April 27, Charles Henry recorded:

> . . . Our agents at Galveston telegraphed this afternoon that the boycott against our line was removed to-day. I am glad of it, as it was entirely unprovoked and did us a great damage. We would submit to no conditions and gave them to understand that no matter how long they kept it on, it would have no effect, as we could not afford to have an ignorant set of men control our business. I trust we shall have no further trouble, but as strikes & boycotts are epidemic no one knows what tomorrow will bring forth.

Actually, the strikers had weakened their own position by dividing their attention between boycotting the Mallory Line and the "Great Southwest Strike" against the Gould railroads which had begun on February 18 and lasted through May 4. Mallory was adamant and openly condoned violence firm in his belief that the strike was unprovoked by management. The Mallory Line was then paying 40 cents for daywork and 60 cents for nightwork, rates equal to if not 10 to 20 cents higher than those paid by other steamship lines in the coastal market. Nevertheless, similar flare-ups among the Galveston longshoremen would be a fact of life for the next three decades.[21]

C. H. Mallory & Co.'s labor relations with its longshoreman were violent and unenlightened during 1876–1885 and would become more so. But like most nineteenth-century businessmen, the Mallorys carried none of the suspicion and hostility they directed against blue-collar organized workers over to their clerical and professional workforce. Indeed, they continued to strengthen their officer corps, their office force, and the internal organization and administration of their firm.

The partnership had begun its business life in the loft above J. D. Fish & Co. at 153 Maiden Lane. By March 1872, it had leased an adjoining building and added space for freight wagons and draft horses in 1876. Pier 20, East River, was leased from the city in five-year increments and, on April 29, 1878, C. H. Mallory & Co.'s offices were moved to the covered pier itself. From Pier 20, the Mallory sailing time was always 3:00 P.M.: the Southern Line every Wednesday; the Texas Line every Saturday; the berth-sailers every other Saturday; the Florida Line every Friday; and the Brazil Line monthly. When no Mallory-flag vessels were in port, other steamers and sailers were loaded or unloaded on commission for the account of the firm, or the firm's wagons and teams worked other piers by the job or by the day.

On the pier and in the office, Charles Henry Mallory was decisively in charge. Except on the issue of organized labor, he was a genial, jovial man whose quick smile and ready wit could temper even the most sober matter of business with good humor; an approachable and affectionate man with time to gossip and whose pockets could always produce "peanuts, hoar hound, lemmon or peppermint drops" for the "small-fry." He arose at dawn, so as to catch the earliest morning ferry to Manhattan, and spent the day "around and about" the water front. Evenings were for family affairs at Grace Court or weekly excursions to the latest play, musicale, or lecture in town. The Sabbath was rigorously observed at home and in attendance at Henry Ward Beecher's thundering sermons at Plymouth Church. Summers and Christmas were for Mystic—to sail, to honor the family's elders, and to renew the familial traditions and heritage. Every day was meticulously recorded in a diary, the entries beginning with the weather, passing on through the business and social events of the moment, the health of family and friends, prayers for self and others, and concluding with the current price of gold on the New York exchange. Each day ended with a mariner's snack: "a little raw salt cod-fish and some pilot bread, or 'hardtack.' " [22]

As competent and self-possessed as he was, however, Charles Henry Mallory still leaned heavily on the exceptional abilities of his partner and alter ego, Elihu Spicer, Jr. Eight years younger, Spicer was Mystic-born and the son of Charles Mallory's most trusted shipmaster (under whom Charles Henry had first put to sea in *Apalachicola*). The younger Spicer had also been a Mallory mariner: at sixteen sailing as cabin boy on the packet ship *John Minturn*; at twenty-four becoming master of the bark *Fanny* in the coastal trade; between 1850 and 1862 commanding a series of Mallory clippers in the California and China trades; during 1863–1865 supervising in the field all Mallory-flag government transportation contracts. Tragically, Spicer lost two of his three children in the 1860's, his wife in 1871, and his only son, Uriah, in 1877. He consequently submerged himself in the affairs of C. H. Mallory & Co. and became so dedicated to that mission that he often had to be forced into rest and recreation by his friend and partner. Spicer and William Mason, a New Zealander hired as head bookkeeper on February 20, 1869 (and later a partner), were primarily responsible for the smooth staff work that became C. H. Mallory & Co.'s hallmark. [23]

It also fell to Captain Spicer to induct Charles Henry's three sons into the firm and to oversee their commercial education. The eldest was Charles Rogers, a bright, robust, and thoroughly charming fellow, who drove his father to prayer. As a boy in Mystic, "Charley's" passions were sailing, fishing, swimming, and carpentry in that order. Yet he dutifully attended the Mystic Bridge School until he was fourteen, made top marks, and earned local notoriety for his histrionic declamations on such predictable subjects as "The Yankee Privateer" and "A Sea Voyage." He also passed the more rigorous tests of his father's Sunday School class, but broke his parents' hearts by not formally joining the congregation.

To introduce him to the firm, Charles and Charles Henry gave young Charley the ritualistic task of sorting, binding, numbering, and indexing their business correspondence. This he did adequately but unenthusiastically, and as a teenager he was more often to be found puttering around the Mystic shipyard, badgering the shipwrights and carpenters for wood scraps, old tools, used fittings, and chances to use the saw, the plane, the lathe, and the forge for projects of his own (usually boats or wagons for himself and his brothers).

Hoping still to enforce more regular habits upon the eldest of the third generation, the family shipped Charley off (at fifteen) to West Cornwall, Connecticut, and Dr. Henry Gold's famous preparatory school on Cream Hill. Although contemptuous of Gold's austere discipline, the young Mallory beat the system and graduated first in his class in 1863. Later that year he entered Yale and successfully completed his freshman and sophomore years before his academic interest expired. Bored stiff at nineteen, on September 3, 1865, he "concluded that he would like to work in the ship yard." His father consented with misgivings, confiding to his diary: "[I]t is very hard to decide what to do with boys, when so much depends upon their choice of business in life. I do not know what to advise in the matter but am well satisfied that it is very necessary for their future welfare that they should be taught to be industrious."

Eight days and a pair of blistered hands cured Charles of his notion of becoming a shipbuilder. On September 19, his father recorded: "Charles left on the 2 p.m. train for New York . . . to commence a business life. He goes on the wharf at pier No. 36 North River where there are steamers loading and discharging daily. His business will be to attend to the delivery and receipt of cargoes and to make himself generally useful under the superintendence of Captain E. Spicer, Jr. It is a good place to learn the rudiments of a commercial life." The combination of New York, Captain Spicer, and responsible outdoor work finally turned the tide. By October 3 his father could note, "Charles is quite well, he is busy on the dock receiving and delivering cargoes—learning to work—it comes hard but I trust it is for his good." [24]

Eighteen-year-old Henry Rogers Mallory, who joined his brother on Pier 36 on January 7, 1867, was another case entirely. Where Charles Henry often despaired of his eldest boy's redemption, he stood almost in awe of the "curious mixture" of his second son. It was not a question of nerve or brains. Where Charley was a sailor, Henry was a horseman and well earned his boyhood nickname of "Buster." He followed Charley through Mystic Bridge School and Dr. Gold's, always equaling and often surpassing his elder brother's excellent marks. The difference was temperament. Where Charley was gregarious, spendthrift, careless, and irreverent, Henry was aloof, miserly, meticulous, and pious. They were, in short, very much their father's sons: Charley the behavioral extreme of that puckish strain in Charles Henry's character; Henry the logical extension of his father's deep commitment to family, business, and God. And as time passed, it was Henry, not Charley, who emerged as the familial leader of the third generation. [25]

Charley and Henry remained under Captain Spicer's tutelage and on salary until 1870—the former raised from $1,000 to $1,500 per year on April 22, 1868; the latter $520 to $800 on the same date. After January 1, 1870, however, each received 10 per cent of the C. H. Mallory & Co.'s "net profits" (on profit-and-loss account) besides a nominal salary. The boys' 10 per cent always came out of Charles Henry Mallory's two-thirds share so that Captain Spicer would receive his full one-third of net profits. Charley lived with his parents at home until his marriage in 1872, and then commuted to work from a house at 153 Columbia Street, Brooklyn, which his father bought him as a wedding present. Henry also lived at home until his marriage in 1873, when he moved into his father's wedding-gift home at 105 Columbia Street.

On January 1, 1873, the two older boys were admitted to the firm as junior partners and their annual compensation raised to $2,000 plus 10 per cent of net profits. Their younger brother Robert entered the firm on October 10, just after his seventeenth birthday. "Bob" was his own man, more like his grandfather than his father and brothers. He was kept on straight salary throughout the 1870's and 1880's and found a comfortable niche as Henry's understudy.[26] "He impressed me as of rougher material than Henry, bordering on gruffness," Henry's office boy recalled. "He was not as immaculate in his dress as was Henry R., who arrived at the office each morning with a fresh flower in his lapel."[27]

Thus was the third generation launched. On April 24, 1882, Dun & Bradstreet summarized the personnel, division of responsibilities, and reputation of the enterprise:

C. H. Mallory & Co., Steamships. Pier 20, E. R. Firm composed of C. H. Mallory, Henry R. Mallory, Chas. Mallory 2nd, Elihu Spicer, Jr. Chas. H. is considered the principal capitalist but has little to do with the details of the business. H. R. is the cashier and manager of the business finances, Chas. appears to attend to the details of portions of the bus., and Spicer is general business manager. The concern has been reputed to be wealthy for years, are doing a large business, and must derive a good income from their commissions. The partners own their residences in Brooklyn, some of which are quite valuable, and have also a large interest in vessel property. We do not hear their credit or safety in any way questioned.

The firm's books testified to the accuracy of the credit reporter's opinion. Net profits for the year 1878 were twice what they had been in 1868. By the end of 1881, they had increased another third per annum, and the gain between 1881 and 1882 was 20 per cent. Table 7.3 summarizes the firm's profit-and-loss accounts for 1882 and 1883 as representative of the firm's mature experience. It should be emphasized that these were only the profits earned by the ship-operating arm of the Mallory enterprises. Each of the Mallorys also earned dividends on his share in the steamships and sailing vessels and from whatever personal investments he had. In Charles Henry Mallory's case these ran about four times his earnings from C. H. Mallory & Co.; for the older boys, these were about twice their earnings from the operating firm.[28]

Notably absent from among either the partners in C. H. Mallory & Co. or the investors in the steamships of the years 1876–1885 were Charles Henry's father and brothers—mute testimony that the New York–Mystic breach was widening. The older Mallory had retired from shipbuilding in 1876 to look after his real estate, his bank stock, and his investments in sailing vessels. David, with his father's financial assistance, had converted the Mystic Iron Works into the Mystic Woolen Co. in 1866, the Norwood Manufacturing Co. in 1871, and the Oceanic Woolen Co. in 1872, but had liquidated that line by the end of 1875. More successful was David's management of the Lantern Hill Silex Co., which he organized with the backing of Charles Mallory and Charles P. Williams in September 1870. The silex mine remained David's prime business through the first half of the 1880's, but he and his older brother had little in common: "Saw brother David in the street this morning," Charles Henry noted wistfully on February 6, 1877; "he never comes to see us when he is in the city." [29]

Charles Henry remained closer to brother George. George stayed with his father until the Mallory shipyard closed down, even building three steam fishing vessels there on his own account in 1875. He then established his own consulting firm at 55 Broadway, New York, specializing in "Plans, Specifications, Estimates, Contracts and Superintendence for all kinds of work connected with Iron Vessels, Mills, Grain Elevators, Dry Docks, Simple or Compound Engines, for Mines, Mills, or Steam Vessels. Steam Boilers of every kind, Hydraulic Apparatus and all kinds of Engineering Apparatus and Structures." He died at fifty-nine, February 15, 1883. Brothers Franklin and Benjamin seemed to go from one failure to another, only to be bailed out by their father and Charles Henry.[30]

Thus, through his own abilities, desires, and actions, because of his father's age, and because of his brothers' other interests and indifferent success, Charles Henry Mallory had become the head of the family's maritime business in 1880. He soon became head of the family, as well. Eliza Rogers Mallory, who shared her husband's faith, who had boarded his apprentices, who had borne him twelve children and buried seven in infancy, and who was still in mourning for her beloved daughter Annie who had died in 1864, passed peaceably to rest on September 4, 1881. On August 26, 1882, in his eighty-seventh year, Charles Mallory followed his wife to peace—"the last remaining link is broken," Charles Henry mourned, "... sorrow enough." [31]

Chapter 8

THE NEW YORK & TEXAS STEAMSHIP CO.,

1886–1906

"Thursday June 24th. . . . Captain Spicer and myself went to Jersey to-day and signed Articles of Incorporation of the New York & Texas Steamship Co. in conformity with the laws of the State of New Jersey. The Co. takes in all the steamers of the lines to Galveston and Florida, all the owners being in favour."—Diary of Charles Henry Mallory, 1886

CHARLES HENRY MALLORY closed the diary of his sixty-third year optimistically: "I have enjoyed fairly good health, my business has not been all that I could wish or expect, but I have no cause for complaint. My dear family have all been spared and are all in good health." [1] But the first half of the 1880's left him acutely aware of generational change. His mother, his father, and brother George were gone and remembrances of things past were clouded by his remaining brothers' bickerings over settlement of the Mystic estate. [2] His three oldest children were married, he was already several times a grandfather, and his sons were well launched in the family firm. Yet many of the businessmen involved in the birth and growth of C. H. Mallory & Co. were passing: Charles A. Whitney in 1882; George Ball and John Sealy in 1884; Thomas W. Peirce in 1885. And his dear friends and frequent associates, James D. Fish and John Roach, had passed, not to death, but to humiliatingly public failure: Fish sentenced to ten years in prison for his role in the Marine Bank failure of 1884–1885; Roach into receivership in mid-1885.

Perhaps it was the painful litigation over his father's estate; surely it was a realization that he and Spicer were aging;

certainly it was a desire to smooth the transition from the second to the third generation that prompted Charles Henry Mallory to reorganize and incorporate the family's maritime enterprises in 1886. A closely held corporation could consolidate ownership of the Mallorys' maritime assets and form a natural counterpart to the partnership of C. H. Mallory & Co., which had already centralized family management. By the mid-1880's, these seemed the best means for perpetuating the family's still unswerving commitment to American-flag common carriage.

On June 24, 1886, Charles Henry Mallory, Elihu Spicer, Jr., Cornelius H. Delamater, Charles Rogers Mallory, Henry Rogers Mallory, and their attorney, Joseph W. Spencer, drafted and signed a certificate of organization for the "New York and Texas Steamship Company." Capitalized at $3,000,000, the company was to be incorporated for fifty years under the New Jersey Corporations Act of April 7, 1875 (as amended); its domicile was set at 21 Montgomery Street, Jersey City, but its "objects" were far-ranging:

> The Transportation of Goods, Merchandise, and Passengers upon water, between the Ports and Cities of New York, Jersey City, Fernandina, and Galveston . . . and also a General Transportation Business, of Goods, Merchandise, and passengers upon water, between any ports and places domestic or foreign, as such General Transportation Business upon water may require including the purchasing, leasing, owning, equipping, and managing of such vessels, lighters, wharves, real estate, and other property as may be necessary or incidental to the conduct of such business.

The corporate plan was approved by New Jersey's secretary of state on June 29, and on July 1 the company opened for business with an organizational meeting to adopt bylaws. The incorporators voted to establish a five-man board of directors, elected annually by and from the stockholders; a president and a vice president, elected annually by and from the board; a secretary and a treasurer, elected annually by the board; and, of these officers, only the secretary and the treasurer were to be salaried. Annual and special meetings of stockholders and monthly, annual, and special meetings of directors were scheduled at Jersey City. All books of the company, except stock and transfer ledgers (which had to remain in Jersey City), were to be kept at Pier 20, East River, New York City.

To obtain the capital equipment necessary for their company's purposes, the incorporators issued $2,500,000 of its authorized capital stock in exchange for full title to thirteen vessels, controlling shares in three more, and C. H. Mallory & Co.'s "engines and all stevedore's materials for loading & unloading wherever held." [3]

These exchanges determined the ownership of the new company. The various shareholders in the steamships of the Mallory Line were transformed into the common stockholders of the New York & Texas Steamship Co.; the equity they received in the corporation was equal to their former holdings of ship shares; and no money changed hands.

The distribution of the 25,000 $100 shares neatly summarizes the sources of Mallory-flag steamship finance between 1871 and 1886 and identifies the presiding equity in the new corporation. First, of course, were the partners and employees of C. H. Mallory & Co.[4] Second were the Mallorys' long-time friends and prime ship and engine builders.[5] Third, the Galveston group.[6] The New Jersey attorney for the new company and trusted captains and relatives held the remainder.[7] With the composition of the equity what it was, the election of officers was routine: Charles Henry Mallory, president and director; Elihu Spicer, Jr., vice president and director; Cornelius H. Delamater, Charles Rogers Mallory, and John H. Hutchings, directors; Henry Rogers Mallory, treasurer; and William Mason, secretary.[8]

As incorporated, the New York & Texas Steamship Co. consolidated all the maritime assets previously held as personal property by the Mallorys and their associates. It was only an owner, however. It was not intended to be and never functioned as an operating company. The key to this functional divorcement of property and management was contained in Article 15 of the company's bylaws:

> The Board of Directors may, if they shall see fit, contract with a responsible person or firm for the general management, supplying, and running of the vessels of the Company, by such person or firm,

as the agent or agents of the Company, and may, in such contract, fix the compensation of such person or firm at a sum equal to a percentage of the gross earnings of said vessels, or otherwise, as they shall deem best. The term of such contract shall not exceed ten years from the date thereof.

The next step was to appoint the agents provided for in the bylaws.[9] By December 14, 1886, the board of directors had approved an agreement with C. H. Mallory & Co.; it was signed and dated on December 30 and became effective January 1, 1887.

C. H. Mallory & Co. consented to be the "sole agent" of the New York & Texas Steamship Co. "for the general conduct and management of the business of transportation . . . and for the general management, supplying, equipping, running, and managing of the Steamships, vessels, lighters, wharves, and other property now owned, chartered, leased, or employed or hereafter to be owned, chartered, leased, or employed" by the steamship company, ". . . wheresoever said business may be conducted or said vessels or other property may be." Also, "subject to confirmation" by the steamship company, the agents were authorized to contract for "the constructing, buying, and selling of all vessels and lighters" which the company might "use or sell," "to superintend the construction of any and all vessels and lighters built by or for" the company, and "to act as its brokers in selling any and all vessels and lighters."

The agents were authorized to appoint and discharge subagents in outports, as required, and to fix their compensation. Such subagents were to be paid by and be responsible to C. H. Mallory & Co. The agents were also authorized to hire, fire, supervise, and fix wages of all officers, crews, and wharf gangs, but these persons were to be paid by and considered employees of the New York & Texas Steamship Co.

For its services, C. H. Mallory & Co. was to receive 5 per cent of the gross "outward" freight and passage receipts earned by vessels of the steamship company from New York to any port; 2 1/2 per cent of the gross "homeward" freight and passage receipts earned by vessels of the steamship company from any port to New York (a matching 2 1/2 per cent to be

Stock certificate Number 1, New York & Texas Steamship Co., 1886. Issued to Charles Henry Mallory and signed by himself as president and by his son Henry Rogers Mallory as treasurer. Courtesy Mystic Seaport.

(Left) Elihu Spicer, Jr., while senior partner in C. H. Mallory & Co. and president of the New York & Texas Steamship Co. Courtesy Mystic Seaport. (Right) Henry Rogers Mallory, while senior partner in C. H. Mallory & Co. and president of the New York & Texas Steamship Co. From Moses King, *Notable New Yorkers of 1896–1899* (New York: Moses King, 1899), p. 259.

(Left) Charles Mallory, while partner in C. H. Mallory & Co. and officer of the New York & Texas Steamship Co. From Moses King, *Notable New Yorkers of 1896–1899* (New York: Moses King, 1899), p. 259. (Right) Robert Mallory, while partner in C. H. Mallory & Co. and officer of the New York & Texas Steamship Co. Courtesy Mystic Seaport.

paid to the outport subagent); 5 per cent of the gross earnings of company lighters; 1 1/2 per cent commission on the cost of construction and equipment when superintending the building of vessels for the company; and 1 per cent of the gross amount of any vessel sales it made as the company's broker. The agency could also conduct a stevedoring business on its own account, and both it and the company could make investments in securities and real property irrespective of each other's holdings.

The original agreement between the New York Texas Steamship Co. and C. H. Mallory & Co. was for five years, but subsequent renewals perpetuated the arrangement. Actually, the basic legal and managerial divisions of labor established in 1886 remained the organizational framework for the family's enterprises until 1906. In reality, they meant little more than business as usual for the Mallory Line. Rather than acting as agent on commission for various groups of individual steamship owners, as it had done from 1866 to 1886, the partnership now operated all the capital equipment of a single corporation. And since the agency partners and the corporate executives were the same persons, family control and continuity of purpose were insured.[10]

Mallory purposes changed little in the three decades after 1886. The basic business commitment to specialization as American-flag line carriers in the coastal market never wavered; the technological dedication to iron steamships held firm; and the preferences for connecting New York City with Texas and the South Atlantic states remained. These policies were sustained by constant attention to the conditions of competition and the maintenance of cooperative agreements with the land and other water carriers concerned.

In Texas, the Mallory Line was able to continue all its basic policies: its community of interest with the Galveston Wharf Co.; cooperation with any railroads that could reach tidewater at Galveston; and maintenance of its offshore pact with the Morgan Line. As the patterns of railroad construction and ownership solidified during the 1880's and 1890's, however, the New York Texas Steamship Co. found itself primarily the associate of three of the major southwestern rail systems, while the Morgan Line became the subsidiary of the fourth.

The Mallory Line's connection with the Galveston, Houston & Henderson, which had been arranged by the wharf company and the Ball, Hutchings & Co. group in 1870–1871, evolved as the steamships' link with the Missouri, Kansas & Texas system and with Jay Gould's Missouri Pacific group. The Missouri Pacific had leased the M. K. & T. on December 1, 1880; the M. K. & T. had leased the International & Great Northern on June 1, 1881; and on March 6, 1883, the I. & G. N. had leased the G. H. & H. While not parties to the railroad maneuverings, the Mallorys still benefited by the resultant interconnection of their steamships with such an extensive rail system.

Although the M. P.–M. K. & T. leases were canceled on March 2, 1888, and the Katy's right of passage over the I. & G. N. and the G. H. & H. was thrown into the courts for seven years, the Mallory steamers continued to connect with those roads patronizing the G. H. & H.; and, on December 23, 1895, official connections were reestablished with both the M. P. and the now independent M. K. & T. On that date, the I. & G. N. and the M. K. & T. agreed to 50–50 ownership of the G. H. & H., so that both systems would have equal access to Gulf tidewater.[11]

Another Ball, Hutchings & Co. project gave the Mallory Line its link with the third of the great southwestern systems. On May 23, 1873, the Gulf, Colorado & Santa Fe Railroad had been chartered by Galveston merchants to build inland *around* Houston. No construction had begun until May 1, 1875, and as late as March 1879, the road was no farther along than Richmond. On April 15, however, John Sealy and his partners had purchased the road and kicked its construction program into high gear. By the end of 1885, the road was complete from Galveston to Temple, with branches from Alvin to Houston and from Somerville to Conroe; from Temple, a western branch ran to Lampasas and Brownwood and a northern branch to Cleburne and Fort Worth; from Cleburne, another branch ran to Dallas.

In 1886, Sealy sold the road to the Atchison, Topeka & Santa Fe, which was seeking a Gulf outlet. By 1888, the Fort

Worth branch of the G. C. & S. F. had been joined to the Santa Fe tracks at Purcell, Oklahoma; the western branch had been extended to San Angelo; and the Dallas branch had reached Paris. In Galveston, shipside transfer facilities were established with the Mallory Line on property owned by the Galveston Wharf Co.[12]

By cooperating with Galveston's oldest and youngest railroads during the 1880's and 1890's, the Mallory steamships were firmly tied into the Missouri Pacific, the Katy, and the Santa Fe. The steamship line held no equity in the railroads, and vice versa, but the corporate and executive portfolios of each were well stocked with bonds of the others. Cordial relations were also maintained with the Galveston, Harrisburg & San Antonio, but never to the same degree. The reason was simple: in the mid-1880's, the G. H. & S. A. had become the key railroad in the expansion of Collis P. Huntington's Southern Pacific group east of El Paso and, as such, was much more involved with the Morgan than with the Mallory lines.

The Southern Pacific had reached El Paso on May 19, 1881. Within two months, Huntington had begun to buy into Texas and Louisiana railroads, and by February 10, 1885, he had consolidated his holdings as the Atlantic Division of Southern Pacific: the G. H. & S. A., the T. & N. O., the Louisiana Western, Morgan's Louisiana & Texas Railroad and Steamship Co., the H. & T. C., and the Direct Navigation Co. These roads gave him all-rail lines from San Francisco to New Orleans, via El Paso, San Antonio, and Houston; from Houston southwestward to Victoria and Beeville and northward to Dallas and Denison; and from Houston northeastward to Shreveport.

Huntington's acquisition of the Direct Navigation Co. and the Morgan companies also gave him the potential to compete with the Mallory Line at either Houston or Galveston. But the Mallory-Morgan truce of 1879 was honored and was continued until 1902. Mallory Line steamships had Galveston to themselves and connected with the entire Southern Pacific system via the Galveston, Harrisburg & San Antonio and the barges of the Direct Navigation Co. The Southern Pacific ran no New York steamers to or from Texas ports, but continued to run the triweekly Morgan Line against the weekly Cromwell Line from New Orleans to New York and a weekly service between New Orleans and Havana.[13]

Throughout the 1880's and 1890's, the two New York–New Orleans lines and the Mallorys' New York–Key West–Galveston line remained competitive to Texas points. For example, in 1888, C. H. Mallory & Co. found it necessary to open a branch of its New York agency at 381 Broadway, "compelled to do so by the fact that branch offices of the Morgan and Cromwell Lines had been opened on that thoroughfare, and it was found that many shippers who would otherwise patronize the line, objected to coming so far from their places of business to ascertain freight rates, etc."

The Morgan Line, because of its superior equipment and transcontinental connections, always had the capacity to challenge the Mallorys' monopoly of the New York–Galveston sea lane, but did not do so prior to 1902. It did use its power occasionally, however, to keep things as agreed. In 1889, for instance, M. C. Hawley, the Morgan Line's freight agent, objected to the Mallorys' special passenger rates to large shippers. Hawley's threat to "cut the rates to every point to which we carry freight" set the board of the New York & Texas Steamship Co. scurrying to correct matters within seven days.[14]

On balance, however, the Morgan-Mallory agreements were more important in protecting the Mallorys' New York–Galveston service against "outside" competition. Only once between 1879 and 1902 was an opposition line mounted, and that attempt was promptly crushed by the combined power of the Mallory Line, the Morgan Line, the Cromwell Line, and their respective railroad allies.

On July 14, 1897, T. Hogan & Sons of 11 Broadway, New York, as agents for the Miami Steamship Co., opened the "Lone Star Line" between New York and Galveston. The New York *Maritime Reporter* of July 28 reflected the general astonishment among transportation men that anyone should challenge the *status quo* in the Southwest: the Lone Star Line was

> acting quite independently of any combination with any of the railroads tributary to Galveston. . . . Either . . . in starting the line its managers did not give the matter sufficiently serious consideration

and being unfamiliar with the trade entered it recklessly; or, . . . it may have been entered upon as a neat little piece of speculation with the object in view of being ultimately bought off by the older line.

The Mallory Line had no intention of buying out its new competitors. Price cuts matched price cuts until the water rate per cwt., New York–Galveston, fell from 80 cents to 1 cent. On September 14, the board of the New York & Texas Steamship Co. "discussed very fully the situation" and "the decision was unanimous that there must be no compromise or admission of that line to the Galveston Trade and that its opposition must be met and fought to the end." [15]

What followed is best told in the words of the representatives of the Interstate Commerce Commission who investigated and approved the final solution:

> . . . At the outset the various railroads leading from the port of Galveston seem to have accorded to the Miami Company the same rates and privileges in substance which were given the Mallory Line. The Miami Company, however, found it to its advantage to somewhat reduce the rates between New York and Galveston, and this operated to effect a reduction in rates throughout the territory . . . the shrinkage being in all cases in the ocean transportation from New York to Galveston. This created more or less dissatisfaction since these ocean and rail rates from New York are fixed with reference to the all-rail rates from the same points to the same destinations, and in the early part of 1898, the railroad lines leading from Galveston, the Mallory Line, and the two steamship lines leading from New York to New Orleans entered into an arrangement by which it was, among other things, agreed that the railroad lines should break off all connections with the Miami Steamship Company.

From February 1898 to May 1898, and again from October 1898 to May 1899, the battle was joined:

> Traffic between interior points and the Atlantic seaboard was handled by [the Mallory, the Morgan, and the Cromwell] . . . steamship lines in connection with the rail lines upon through bills of lading in both directions, and the through rate was divided between the water and the rail lines upon a basis which allowed to the rail line less than its local tariff from Galveston to point of destination. . . .

By these actions, the railroads voluntarily accepted less than their usual share of through freights in order to compensate the Mallory, Morgan, and Cromwell lines for losses caused by falling water rates. As far as the Lone Star Line was concerned, however:

> The railroad companies then declined to honor [its] through bills of lading and also declined to form through routes [with it] upon the basis of the divisions hitherto in force. The Miami Steamship Company could, of course, transport the freight from New York to Galveston and there tender it to the railroad companies for transportation to destination, but the railroad companies exacted in all cases their local tariff and required the Miami company to prepay the freight charges. In case of traffic going in the opposite direction, the railroad companies declined to issue any through bill of lading and required the shipper to prepay the transportation charge to Galveston, if the traffic was to go by the Miami Company.
>
> The Interstate Commerce Commission investigators concluded that under these conditions the Miami Company could not hope to participate in that traffic; for not only did it receive much less for the same service than its competitors, but the handling of the business by that line was so hedged about with difficulties as to make it almost impossible for the shipper to patronize its route.

The proprietors of the Lone Star Line took the situation into the federal courts, alleging violations of the Interstate Commerce Act and the Sherman Antitrust Act. The courts found for the Mallory Line and its associates:

> the Miami Company was entitled to no relief; that the railway companies might require the prepayment of their freight charges; that they were not compelled to enter into joint arrangements with one steamship company because they did with another; and that even if the anti-trust act was violated, only the United States Government could maintain an injunction suit.[16]

Following the decision of the courts, the Lone Star Line withdrew its four steamers from the New York–Galveston route, and by June 1, 1899, water-rail competition in the Southwest resumed its classic pattern: the Mallory Line and the Missouri Pacific, the Katy, and the Santa Fe versus the Morgan Line, the Cromwell Line, and the Southern Pacific. Freight rates

Mallory Line New York Pier No. 21, *ca.* 1890, with iron steamship *San Marcos* alongside. Courtesy Mystic Seaport.

Mallory Line longshoremen on lunch break, New York, *ca.* 1890. Courtesy Mystic Seaport.

Mallory Line New York Piers No. 20 and 21, *ca.* 1890, with iron steamships *Nueces* (l.) and *Alamo* (r.) alongside. Courtesy Mystic Seaport.

Mallory Line stevedores unloading tomatoes from iron steamship *Lampasas*, New York, *ca.* 1890. Courtesy Mystic Seaport.

to Texas Common Points continued to be set on the dual basing point system: "St. Louis-plus" for all-rail rates; "Mallory-plus" for water-rail rates via Galveston. On the Mallory Line, the New York–Galveston water rate on first-class shipments was restored to 80 cents, the Galveston-Houston differential of 10 cents was retained, and intrastate rates were charged from Houston to Texas Common Points. Water-rail shipments to or from regions beyond the common points were divided according to the mileage carried by each line, and the Mallorys' sea segment was equilibrated with 350 railroad miles.

Of course, rate-making by railroad traffic associations was declared illegal by the United States Supreme Court in the *Trans-Missouri Freight Association* decision of March 1897 (166 U.S. 290) and the *Joint Traffic Association* decision of October 1898 (171 U.S. 505); and the rail and water carriers of the Southwest dutifully disbanded their "Administrative Board" in 1898. Yet the common points system of rate-making persisted in the Southwest for another two decades, more or less under the supervision of the Texas Railroad Commission and the Interstate Commerce Commission. Not until the *Shreveport* decision of 1914 (234 U.S. 342) were matters comprehensively reviewed and changed.[17]

The Southern Pacific actually made the final pre-1914 adjustment in the conditions of water carriage to and from Texas during 1899–1902. Huntington had decided to reopen a Galveston–New York service, but on terms reasonably competitive with the Mallory Line. Perhaps the Lone Star Line's brief excursion into the Western Gulf had convinced him that there was now enough business for two steamship lines to Texas. In any case, between February 4 and May 1, 1899, he had obtained city and state grants of land in Galveston and wharfage rights separate from those of the Galveston Wharf Co.

The disastrous Galveston storm and Huntington's death, both in 1900, delayed matters; but on July 6, 1901, the Southern Pacific Terminal was incorporated to complete the project and connect it with the G. H. & S. A. On August 2, 1902, the Morgan Line inaugurated steamship sailings between New York and Galveston. As a conciliatory gesture to the Mallory Line, the Morgan vessels carried freight only and left the passenger trade via Galveston exclusively to the New York & Texas Steamship Co. Of course, the Mallorys would have preferred no Morgan Line at all, but they could do nothing now but compete to the best of their ability. And so the situation remained until 1906.[18]

While it devoted its major attention in the 1880's and 1890's to its Texas arrangements, the Mallory Line still had to hold its chosen place amongst the water and rail carriers serving the South Atlantic states. Between 1886 and 1896, the New York & Texas Steamship Co. and C. H. Mallory & Co. merely continued policies begun by the latter in the 1870's: connect New York and Key West weekly as part of the Galveston line; provide a separate, weekly line between New York, Port Royal, Brunswick, and Fernandina; connect with any railroads or local water carriers having access to Mallory-served ports; and abide by the rates and traffic allocations set by the Southern Railway & Steamship Association. After 1896–1897, as the association was disbanded, bilateral arrangements with specific railroad systems increased and a Mallory-flag New York–Mobile Line was inaugurated.

There was little change in the informal agreements among water carriers to allocate the South Atlantic ports. The situation in 1906 was about what it had been in 1886. The New York and Charleston and the New York and South Carolina steamship companies were gone by 1890, but the other major lines remained. The Clyde Line still served Wilmington, Georgetown, Charleston, and Jacksonville from New York and Philadelphia and had added Boston to its ports of call in 1897. The Ocean Steamship Co. still connected Savannah with New York and Philadelphia and had added Boston in 1898. The Merchants & Miners Transportation Co. still ran between Savannah and Baltimore, Providence, and Boston and had added Philadelphia in 1901. The Mallory Line still ran between New York and Brunswick; it had dropped Port Royal and Fernandina in 1896 and added Mobile in 1902.

The patterns of rail-water carriage in the South Atlantic states between 1886 and 1906 were much more the result of railroad consolidations than of the activites of steamship lines. Yet the Mallory Line was affected by the process. Its connection with the Brunswick & Albany, which dated from 1875, tied it into Henry B. Plant's growing rail system in 1885 and into the Atlantic Coast Line on May 13, 1902, when that line absorbed the Plant roads. By tapping the Atlantic Coast Line at Brunswick, the Mallory Line reached inland points east of a line from Richmond, Raleigh, Charlotte, Atlanta, and Montgomery, as well as points east of Tallahassee and Tampa.

Cooperation with the Macon & Brunswick, which also dated from 1875, linked the Mallory steamships with the Richmond & Danville and East Tennessee, Virginia & Georgia railroads in the 1880's. The E. T., V. & G. operated trains Brunswick-Macon-Atlanta-Chattanooga; Chattanooga-Selma-Meridian; Chattanooga-Selma-Mobile; Chattanooga-Memphis; and Chattanooga-Bristol (where it met the Norfolk & Western). The R. & D. operated Washington-Danville-Greensboro-Salisbury-Charlotte-Spartanburg-Atlanta- Birmingham-Greenville; Danville-Richmond–West Point; Greensboro-Raleigh-Goldsboro; Salisbury-Asheville-Morristown; Charlotte-Columbia-Augusta; and Asheville-Spartanburg-Columbia. Between July 1, 1894 (when the E. T. V. & G. and the R. & D. became nuclei of the new Southern Railway) and 1906, additional construction and acquisitions incorporated Danville-Norfolk, Columbia-Savannah-Jacksonville, Charleston-Augusta, Chattanooga-Louisville–St. Louis, and Birmingham–New Orleans lines into the system. It was also the Southern Railway that persuaded the Mallory Line to stop sailings to Port Royal and Fernandina and to concentrate on serving Brunswick. In return, the railroad guaranteed the steamships a small subsidy per voyage in addition to their normal share of through freights.[19]

Thus, from its wharves at Brunswick, the Mallory Line gained the capacity to reach the heartland of the South, just as it had come to serve the Southwest from Galveston. And when it added Mobile as a port of call, its connections there with the Southern, the Louisville & Nashville, and the Gulf, Mobile & Ohio gave access to the Mississippi Valley as well.

The decision to serve Mobile was made in the summer of 1902, and the line opened in September. There had been no direct New York–Mobile steamship service since the 1870's, except for a weekly "Hollander Line" which operated during

1900. The formidable New York–New Orleans lines maintained by Morgan and Cromwell had always been too close for comfort. But "after due allowance for the bad odor left behind by the Hollander Line," the directors of the New York & Texas Steamship Co. decided to try their hand. Their justification of the Mobile line is quite revealing of their intentions, of the systematic appraisal of opportunities so typical of the Mallory enterprises, and of the interrelationship of those enterprises by 1902:

> *1st,* Because it covers the port against competitors, who were ready to establish a similar service, which if it had been done by any other than Morgan or Mallory Line, was sure to work injury to the revenue of our Texas Service, as traffic destined for points in the interior, can be handled via Mobile, New Orleans, or Galveston, under practically the same conditions.
>
> *2nd,* Because it finds profitable employment for our spare steamers, of which there will be three when No. 18 is completed, or 5 if Brunswick steamers are included.
>
> *3rd,* Because it will create a surplus business at a season of the year when Texas Service is in need of North Bound traffic, to which ports (Mobile or Brunswick) we can divert steamers in ballast to load as needs require. Brunswick has been used under these conditions for the past two years.
>
> *4th,* Because lumber shipments will naturally decrease in the next few years, and we must provide employment for the spare ships in advance of this occurring.
>
> Our Railroad connections at Mobile having assured us of their hearty support, which they have given, and of their determination to have a direct steamship service between New York and Mobile, giving Mallory Line the preference over all other applicants, we feel that the line cannot be other than a success.
>
> Statements made based upon ten completed voyages show a good profit, perhaps greater than we had a right to expect for a new venture and under the conditions left behind by our predecessor.

By 1904–1905, the Mobile service was averaging gross receipts of $325,000 per year—about 19 per cent of the $1,705,000 annual gross earned by the Galveston–Key West line. The Brunswick line, which was combined with Mobile in early 1906, averaged $276,000 per annum—16 per cent of the

Galveston–Key West gross.[20] These receipts are only suggestive of the relative volumes of the three Mallory lines in service by 1906. To understand their over-all profitability, more exact data are required.

Despite the new organizational relationships adopted in 1886 and sustained until 1906, the Mallorys continued their long-standing practice of taking profits both as ship operators and as shipowners. The managing partnership's income comprised the commissions it received on gross freight, passage, lighterage, stevedoring, and brokerage; the profits from its real estate and securities; and the interest it earned on bills and notes payable. Against this income, it charged its office payroll and overhead. Income and expense accounts were closed each December 31 to "Profit and Loss." Then, after "Total Losses" were deducted from "Total Profits," the "Net Profits for the Year" were credited to the capital accounts of the partners in proportion to each one's share in the firm. It was then the partner's option to withdraw his profits or allow them to accumulate.[21]

The income of the New York & Texas Steamship Co. comprised receipts from freight, passage, lighterage, and stevedoring and the corporation's net earnings on its notes, bills, balances, and investments. Against these were charged the commissions paid C. H. Mallory & Co.; all other disbursements made on voyage accounts; such recurrent expenses as rentals of wharves, taxes, payrolls, insurance premiums, and repairs; and such nonrecurrent expenses as vessel, cargo, and personal injury claims. After annual "Gross Expenditures" were subtracted from "Gross Receipts," dividends and interest were paid from "Net Earnings," and any remainder was transferred to "Surplus." The surplus account was the reservoir from which capital-equipment purchases, unusual capital expenses, investments, and debt redemptions were made. Net proceeds from the sale of any real estate, capital equipment, or portfolio securities also went directly into the surplus account.

Table 8.1 summarizes the two major sources of the income earned by C. H. Mallory & Co. and the profitability of the partnership over time. The firm did maintain a small investment portfolio in its own name to help smooth its otherwise lumpy income, but interest and dividends were vastly subordinate to commissions in the total profit picture. The portfolio was as much for trade relations as for income, for it was composed mostly of stock of the Galveston Wharf Co. and the New York & Texas Steamship Co. and of bonds of the various railroads with which the Mallory Line was friendly.

The proportional distribution of income and expenses of the New York & Texas Steamship Co. and its profitability are summarized in Tables 8.2, 8.3, and 8.4. The large and constant shares of line earnings and disbursements in gross earnings and expenses underscore the Mallorys' abandonment of such former maritime investments as shipbuilding and berth and tramp sail. Charter earnings reflect the Mallory policy of spot employments for vessels not needed on the lines; income from lighterage, stevedoring, insurance, towing, general average, and salvage were the usual opportunistic amounts which accrue to any shipping line. Regular expenses for insurance, repairs, rentals, and taxes were to be expected and were obviously kept under control.

If one were both a partner in C. H. Mallory & Co. and a stockholder in the New York & Texas Steamship Co., one earned both partnership profits and corporate dividends, but at vastly different rates. Taking the corporate dividend series from Table 8.4 and the partnership net profits series from Table 8.1, the spread is clear: for every $1.00 a stockholder invested in the New York & Texas Steamship Co., he earned 7 cents per year; for every $1.00 a partner invested in C. H. Mallory & Co., he earned $2.12 per year.

The high ratios of net to gross profits and of net profits to equity capital characterized the partnership throughout its lifetime. They were the firm's reason for being, and they reflected the Mallorys' particular adaptation of maritime accounting practices. From at least the late eighteenth century in America, when vessels owned on shares by groups of individuals were operated by separate agents, the agents were compensated not by wages but by a percentage of gross receipts—before *any* voyage expenses were accounted for. After the agent's various commissions were deducted from the gross, all usual and unusual voyage expenses and any capital expenses were charged against the equity. Thus, the agent's costs were never much more than his office payroll and overhead and his own capital expenses.

This system legally assumed that the managing agent and the owning equity were not one and the same, but this seldom was true in reality. As we have seen in the cases of Charles Mallory before the Civil War and of C. H. Mallory & Co. prior to 1886, agents were often part owners, too, and earned income off both the "top" and the "bottom" of voyage accounts. After 1886, C. H. Mallory & Co. and the New York & Texas Steamship Co. so arranged their affairs as to maximize the transactional profits inherent in the agent-owner relationship. In their capacity as executives of the owning company, the partners of the operating agency drew no salaries and received no compensation other than the dividends they earned as majority holders of the company's stock. In their capacity as partners of the operating agency, however, the executives of the owning company earned the sizable profits noted in Table 8.1. And since the corporation was closely held by the partnership, there was small chance of stockholder dissent. Only once, between 1886 and 1906, was any corporate stockholders' vote less than unanimous.

For the first seven years of their corporation's life, the officers of the New York & Texas Steamship Co. obviously gave dividends first call on net earnings. And for the first five years, they used a combination of stock and bond issues and earnings-after-dividends to finance growth. Yet the company's capital structure changed only slightly, and both equity and debt were held primarily by insiders. They voted themselves the power, on April 12, 1887, to issue up to $1,000,000 in 6 per cent, ten-year mortgage bonds for the purposes "of building and purchasing steamships and other property," but only $357,000 worth were ever issued, and they were redeemed five years early. The original capital stock issue of $2,500,000 was increased only twice: by $200,000 on January 1, 1891, and by $300,000 on July 1, 1892, which brought it up to its authorized limit of $3,000,000.

Proceeds from the sale of the bonds to stockholders of record paid for construction at Roach's of the steamship *Nueces,* which joined the line on May 28, 1887. *Leona,* later renamed *Sabine,* was also built at Roach's, but for $370,000 in cash payments during 1888–1889. *Concho,* which was added to the fleet in 1891, was paid for by the sale of *Carondelet* for $39,000, by $177,000 more in cash, and by the proceeds from the January 1, 1891, issue and sale of $200,000 in capital stock. The company also paid cash for half-interest in a set of Key West wharves in 1889 ($3,000); for construction of the barges *Sherwood* and *Martins* in 1890 ($8,000); for *Rio Grande's* new boiler ($30,000) and a new Galveston Wharf shed ($7,000) in 1891. On July 1, 1892, the $357,000 bond issue was redeemed by exchanging it for $57,000 in cash and $300,000 in capital stock; and, thereafter, growth was financed entirely out of reinvested earnings.

From 1892 to 1898, earnings-after-dividends and proceeds from the sale of *State of Texas* ($49,000 in 1898) and *City of San Antonio* ($23,000 in 1898–1899) were either deposited as cash on demand or invested in blue-chip government and railroad bonds. After 1898, idle funds were also put to work in the New York call-loan market through the brokerage of Spencer Trask & Co. These bank deposits and securities and call-loan portfolios, in turn, were the hedges against fluctuations in line and charter earnings and the reservoirs from which large capital expenditures for construction of new vessels, new boilers and wharf improvements were made.[22]

After considering both capital structure and operations, it should be clear that the nineteenth-century turning points in the financial history of the New York & Texas Steamship Co. were 1889, when net earnings hit their first peak and then began an eight-year slide; 1892, when the capital stock was fixed, the bonded debt eliminated, and the investment portfolio begun; 1893, when the quarterly dividend rate was cut from 2 to 1 1/2 per cent under the pressures of depression and a desire to reinvest more of net earnings; and 1897–1899.

The Lone Star Line's competition, which spanned July 1897 through May 1899, and another longshoremen's strike in Galveston during 1898 caused serious problems. Net earnings, which had turned up 6 per cent during 1896, crashed 53 per cent during the following year, and the company ran an annual deficit for the only time in its history. The quarterly dividend rate was cut to 1 per cent during the last six months of 1897, and dividends were passed during the first half of 1898. The rate was returned to 1 per cent during the third quarter of 1898 and finally restored to 1 1/2 per cent during the first quarter of 1899.

The downward trends were short-lived. Net earnings for 1898 ended 286 per cent better than those of the previous year; 1899 topped 1898 by 15 per cent and tallied the company's best nineteenth-century year. The end of the strike and of the Lone Star Line partially explain these shifts, but the Spanish-American War made the big difference.

Given the troop-transport needs of the government, the shallow-draft passenger steamships of the Mallory Line and their proximity to Florida and Cuba were ideal. Over the 229 days between the declaration of war on April 25, 1898 and the signing of the peace treaty on December 10, eight Mallory-flag steamships served a combined total of 934 days under federal charter. Put another way, the New York & Texas Steamship Co. provided 12 per cent of the vessels and 19 per cent of the tonnage chartered by the government during the Spanish-American War. All the Mallory Line vessels served only on Atlantic or Gulf waters, and there represented 19 and 23 per cent of vessels and tonnage, respectively. In addition, between November 29, 1898 and April 28, 1899, *Comal* was rechartered for 81 days by the military for the distribution of supplies to indigent Cubans.

Like the other civilian vessels chartered by the Quartermaster General as transports, the Mallory liners were outfitted with additional sleeping accommodations, stalls for animals, extra water tanks, improved galleys and ventilation and lighting plants. They probably required a minimum of this, as they were designed as combined passenger-freight vessels, but they were improved at government expense. It was well worth it, however, for in the course of their 1,015 days of military service, the eight Mallory steamships transported and/or quartered 8,433 able-bodied troops, 3,703 sick or injured troops, 77 stevedores, and 52 nurses and served 186,843 meals! [23]

Two of the older Mallory vessels also saw service under humanitarian charter to various "Cuban Relief" agencies. *State of Texas* and *City of San Antonio* compiled 159 days of this kind of service, but it was the former's experiences that earned that "snug little ship its place in American history."

State of Texas was chartered by the Central Cuban Relief Committee early in 1898, loaded with 1,400 tons of "food, clothing, medicines, and hospital supplies," and cleared New York on April 23 for Key West under the neutral flag of the American National Red Cross. She was to be boarded in Key West by Miss Clara Barton, the redoubtable founder of the Red Cross, and a relief staff of twenty and then proceed to Cuba to distribute her cargo among the *reconcentrados* under Miss Barton's personal direction. *State of Texas* arrived at Key West on April 28 and was joined by Miss Barton the following day. Unfortunately for her plans, however, war between the United States and Spain had been declared on April 25, and she found herself and her ship restrained from going on to Cuba by order of Rear Admiral William T. Sampson, commander in chief, U.S. Naval Force, North Atlantic Station.

For the next two months, *State of Texas* grew barnacles in Key West—the center of a whirlwind of international publicity as Miss Barton badgered the navy, the Congress, and the President to let her sail. Finally, she was allowed to clear for Cuba on June 20 and six days later anchored off Siboney in consort with the American naval squadron. While at Key West, *State of Texas'* saloon had been converted into an operating room, her purser's office into a dispensary, and some of her staterooms into wards. Thus, she could and did serve as a neutral hospital ship throughout the next month.

With the fall of Santiago, however, *State of Texas* reverted to her original role of relief vessel. On July 17 she was given the singular honor of leading the American Fleet into the captured city's harbor. It was one of the most dramatic incidents of the war, as recalled by Miss Barton in a letter to Henry R. Mallory on March 28, 1900:

> . . . It seems to me now like history, the memory of the time when I boarded and took charge of your *State of Texas* under the command of the almost boy captain, tall, quiet, obliging, and even bashful, but competent always for everything he undertook. It is history also how long we followed the navy, how we went in at Siboney, and how, from over our laden decks the food went out to the famishing

City of San Antonio fitting out as a hospital ship for the use of the American National Red Cross, 1898. Courtesy Mariners Museum.

State of Texas under the flag of the American National Red Cross, 1898. She served as a hospital ship and headquarters for Clara Barton during the Spanish-American War and was given the honor of leading the American fleet into captured Santiago Harbor. Courtesy Mariners Museum.

Leona carrying troops during the Spanish-American War. Eight of Mallory's vessels combined to transport 8,433 able-bodied troops, 3,703 casualties, 77 stevedores, and 52 nurses to and from the Caribbean war zone. Courtesy Mariners Museum.

armies. Among all the craft that lay in that harbor nothing carried the comfort, nothing bestowed the benefits like the little *State of Texas*. She had no white sides, no red and green stripes, nothing to mark her but the Red Cross as we dared to paint it on either side, and the little flag that floated above her; yet every ship in the harbor knew her, and every flag lowered and dipped as it passed her; every band of rowing sailors cheered as they came alongside, and the proudest of our ships on the waters was the little *State of Texas* when she sailed alone into Santiago. . . .

(The navy version of the story was less dramatic but certainly funnier. As Miss Barton was thanking Admiral Sampson for the honor he had accorded her, Admiral Winfield S. Schley was heard to remark: "Don't give him too much credit, Miss Barton. He was not quite sure how clear the channel might be. Remember that was a trial trip.") [24]

Dramatics aside and by any objective standard, the fortuitous coincidence of the government's needs with those of the Mallorys in 1898 was an accident in history. The New York & Texas Steamship Co.'s responsibility for the Spanish-American War was no greater than its $500 contribution to William McKinley's campaign chest in 1896, but McKinley's war proved to be the company's greatest windfall (see Table 8.5). And its impact on Mallory finances was all the more, because it came at the lowest ebb of their line's financial history. After a brief recession in 1900, net earnings went up annually through 1905. [25]

Clara Barton's letter to Henry R. Mallory implies the other great change in the Mallory firms during the 1890's: the succession of the third generation of the family to managerial control of the business. The transition was completed between 1890 and 1893.

Charles Henry Mallory was sixty-eight when he formed the New York & Texas Steamship Co. in 1886, and he had already shown many signs of his eagerness to phase himself into retirement. He had never lost his taste for sailing yachts, and his designing and cruising instincts, which he had held in check through the stormy 1870's, were rekindled in the 1880's. In 1879, he had sold his famous yacht *Fanny* for $5,500, but he immediately commissioned D. O. Richmond to build him another. The schooner *Sylph* was launched on May 13, 1880, and Charles Henry sailed her through the summer season, but sold her on September 17. On May 6, 1881, Richmond launched another Mallory yacht, *Water Witch,* which became her owner's all-time favorite. He sailed her every season until her sale on April 13, 1887, for $10,000.

Henry R. Mallory had also persuaded his father to buy what became the family's summer colony at Clifton, near Port Chester, New York, in 1884. Protesting all the while over such "an expensive plaything," Charles Henry obviously relished the change from Brooklyn and spent longer and longer times at the estate. On August 16, 1888, he launched the steam yacht *Clifton* (built at Roach's yard), and it became the cruising counterpart of his summer home. Nostalgically, he kept up his parents' old home in Mystic, too, but seldom visited his birthplace; it had too many memories. In his family's tradition of mutual aid, however, he allowed his brothers Franklin and Benjamin and his cousin Frances to live there at his expense. [26]

Time was much on his mind, though, as he saw such dear friends as John Roach and Cornelius H. Delamater pass in 1887 and 1889. He carefully arranged his own affairs, totaling his personal estate and writing his will. His assets and their market value (as of April 3, 1888) reflected how far the former cabin boy had come: 5,856 shares of the New York & Texas Steamship Co. ($351,360); 94 bonds of same ($94,000); a two-thirds partnership in C. H. Mallory & Co. ($47,500); other stocks and bonds ($619,730); real estate ($140,000); and cash on demand ($234,000)—a total estate of $1,486,670. The end came on March 21, 1890, six months short of his seventy-second birthday. His testamentary letter, written "To my beloved Wife and Children" thirteen months before, was typical of his life: " 'Live in harmony,' if difficulties arise between you, reconcile or compromise them."

Charles Henry Mallory also advised his family to "consult with Captain Spicer, whom I consider a man of good judgement, and who I think has an interest in your welfare." [27] As well as remaining the adviser and friend of the family, Spicer carried on the management of both the operating partnership and the owning company.

Because it was a copartnership, C. H Mallory & Co. had been automatically dissolved by Charles Henry's death. On March 22, 1890, it was formally reconstituted. Spicer and Charles Henry's three sons agreed "to carry on a general shipping and commission business under the firm name of 'C. H. Mallory & Co.' to have its principal place of business in the City of New York, to continue so long as the majority of us agree, but subject to being terminated at any time at the written request of any two of us on reasonable notice." As to capital, the partners agreed "to contribute what may be needed in the following proportions, viz: Elihu Spicer, three-ninths; Charles Mallory, two-ninths; Henry R. Mallory, two-ninths; and Robert Mallory, two-ninths," and they agreed "to share the profits and losses of the business in the same respective proportions."

On September 13, however, and retroactive to July 1, several modifications were made in the agreement. Henceforth, any partner could withdraw on six months' notice; the capital was fixed at $60,000; and the shares were rearranged to confer equity on a long-time employee: Elihu Spicer, 36 4/9 per cent; Charles Mallory, 20 4/9 per cent; Henry R. Mallory, 20 4/9 per cent; Robert Mallory, 20 4/9 per cent; and William Mason, 2 2/9 per cent. A final portion of the earlier agreement remained unchanged:

> The business shall be conducted on a cash basis, except that the firm may borrow from any of its members. No notes, no endorsements, nor any obligations in the firm name shall be made or given to any outside party whatsoever, unless all of us shall execute a formal agreement to that effect, except, however, that premium notes in the firm name for insurance may be given. No member shall overdraw his individual account. Any member may loan money to the firm whenever the firm needs it and agrees to take it at such rate of interest as may be agreed upon.

The managerial transition within the New York & Texas Steamship Co. was far simpler. Just as William Delamater had succeeded his deceased father as director on February 12, 1889, Henry R. Mallory was elected to his father's seat on the board on April 8, 1890. On September 9, Captain Spicer was elected to the company's vacant presidency, Henry succeeded Spicer as vice president, Robert succeeded Henry as treasurer, and Mason continued as secretary. Charles Rogers Mallory remained a director and liked to refer to himself as "the senior member of the firm," but he had obviously abdicated his hereditary position as eldest son to his younger brother. Charles Henry left each of his five children 1,000 shares in the New York & Texas Steamship Co., and his three sons had equal shares in C. H. Mallory & Co. There was no doubt, however, that Henry was heir apparent. [28]

Henry had come into his own. It was twenty-three years since he had entered the firm and twenty since he had made his first small investments (1/64 in the bark *Brazos* and 1/128 in the steamship *City of Galveston*). He was now forty-two and earning upward of $40,000 a year. He had also outgrown that peculiarly morbid outlook which many had mistaken for rudeness in his youth. He could chuckle and savor the honor when his shipmasters dubbed him "The Admiral" because he had never been to sea. [29]

No little credit for this transformation was due his wife. From the moment she entered the Mallory clan on December 2, 1873, Cora Nellie Pynchon was her husband's social entrepreneur and his family's social arbiter. Through a succession of fashionable musicales, excursions, flower shows, and galas she brought Henry out of his shell and revealed the gentle and courteous man of manners that had been there all along. The sudden death of their first-born son "Harry" (Charles Henry Mallory, II) at two in 1876 only bound them closer together. And, like Mallorys before them, they had made their three surviving children their special joy: Cora Pynchon, who was thirteen by 1890; Clifford Day, who was nine; and Philip Rogers, who had just turned five.

Henry's personal, marital, and familial maturity showed more each day. At the office his charisma was unmistakable. Lyle Bull, Henry's office boy for two years, recalled it thus:

> . . . when Mr. Mallory did not have other visitors, he and I used to have lengthy conversations. On one occasion I remember he remarked that I did not seem to be as awed or afraid of him as it appeared the clerical staff at 80 South Street seemed to be when he

entered the door and walked to his office in the rear, a deep hush fell over the big, unpartitioned room with the eyes of the staff glued to their desks. This bothered him because he did not understand why he affected his employees in this way. I suppose, because of my youth and lack of inhibitions, it never occurred to me to be other than respectful of him. Although not a handsome man (he had a crooked, flattened nose as if it might have been broken at some time), Mr. Mallory had a kindly face with deep, brown eyes which invited trustfulness. . . . [H]e invariably replied with words of sound advice. [30]

Though Henry was destined to follow his father as head of the firm, full credit is due Captain Spicer. His was a skillful, deserving, and firm hand when it took the tiller of the Mallory enterprises in 1890. But Spicer was sixty-four when Charles Henry Mallory died, and he lived for only another three years. On February 15, 1893, his death caused another shuffling of executive responsibilities. C. H. Mallory & Co. was reconstituted on February 20, with each of the three Mallorys assuming a 29 per cent liability and Mason a 13 per cent share. On April 13, Robert Mallory filled Spicer's seat on the board of the New York & Texas Steamship Co. On December 14, Henry R. Mallory moved up to the company's presidency; Charles Mallory replaced him as vice president; and Robert Mallory and William Mason remained treasurer and secretary, respectively.

The relationship between C. H. Mallory & Co. and the New York & Texas Steamship Co. changed little under either Spicer or Henry R. Mallory. The original contract of 1887 between the operating agency and the owning company was unanimously renewed by each in 1892 and 1897. In January 1902, however, questions were raised by minority stockholders in the corporation as to the merits of the arrangement. William Delamater, as proxy for 537 shares owned by his sisters, Mrs. Adah Delamater Vezin and Mrs. Zillah Delamater Moore, registered the only dissenting stockholders' votes in the company's history—against a ten-year, rather than the usual five-year, renewal of the agency contract. Delamater himself abstained from casting his 262 votes, but the motion carried 24,917 to 537. As was to be expected, Delamater resigned his seat on the board in May.

Delamater was replaced by George E. Weed, the late John

Roach's right-hand man and representative of the Roach heirs, who joined the three Mallorys, Hutchings, and George R. Edgcumbe on the board. Edgcumbe was purchasing agent of the Mallory Line and had been added as a sixth director in December 1896 to comply with New Jersey law that one board member must reside in that state; he was in no sense an influence on policy. John Sealy, Jr., replaced Hutchings when the latter died in 1906.

With one exception, these were the only major executive changes in either the partnership or the corporation after 1893. The exception was the rise of Harry Howard Raymond, a Nova Scotian who had joined the Mallory Line as a purser in 1885. "H. H." had soon become the field supervisor for the Brunswick service, and on December 1, 1899, he joined the New York headquarters team in the newly created post of general superintendent. In many ways, Raymond became Henry R. Mallory's Captain Spicer. [31]

The death of Charles Henry Mallory in 1890 and of Elihu Spicer, Jr., in 1893 thus precipitated the third generation of Mallory family management, which remained in full control until 1906. It was Henry R. Mallory and his brothers who met the challenges of the Lone Star Line and the Morgan Line, accommodated the railroads, carried on the resistance to organized labor, and responded to the government's wartime needs. Henry's son Clifford recalled his father's and his uncle's contribution: "The steamship-line, which had been inaugurated principally as a local proposition, had branched out to become the recognized New York Terminal, via Gulf, of the Atchison Ry. System, the Gould Ry. System, the M. K. & T. Ry., the National Rys. of Mexico, & the Mobile & Ohio Ry., and through freight arrangements had been established to Kansas, Colorado, Utah, and California." [32] But, profitably secure in their tradition of conservative family ownership and management, the Mallorys little realized in 1906 the magnitude of the changes the next decade would bring.

Chapter 9

THE ATLANTIC, GULF & WEST INDIES

STEAMSHIP LINES, 1906–1915

"In 1906 I retired from business, and looked forward to a few
years of recreation and pleasure, but in 1907 I was pressed
into service again, and—you know the rest."
—Henry R. Mallory to Galen L. Stone, August 30, 1910

A S he addressed the nineteenth annual meeting of the New
York & Texas Steamship Co. on January 23, 1906, President Henry R. Mallory felt justifiable pride. It was eighty-nine
years since Charles Mallory had begun as a sailmaker on his own
account, and his family now counted eighty-four years of continuous prominence as American-flag shipowners. C. H. Mallory
& Co. had just closed the books on its fourth decade of
profitable operation, and the New York & Texas Steamship
Co.'s condition was excellent: net earnings as a proportion of
gross receipts had hit an all-time high in 1905 (see Table 8.4);
the company had no debts beyond current obligations; and its
fleet served the Atlantic and Gulf coasts as never before (see
Figure 9.1).

Yet the meeting closed with the passage of two curious
resolutions: first, "that any information of a general character
of the Company's business which the Directors or Officers or
the General Managers may see fit to make public be furnished
to all stockholders of the Company alike and that special
information be not given individual stockholders"; second,
"that the stockholders of this Company hereby ratify and
approve the actions of the Directors and also the actions of the
Officers and General Managers, in the conduct and management
of the Company's business generally, down to this time." [1]

Why were these resolutions, which were a sort of vote of confidence in themselves by the Mallorys, necessary in the midst of prosperity? The answer is rooted in both past decisions and future prospects. In essence, the brothers were justifying their past refusals to admit "outsiders" or to encumber themselves with debt—but, at that very moment, they were seriously considering selling out out altogether.

Any corporation as profitable, as debt-free, and as closely held as the New York & Texas Steamship Co. could naturally expect suitors, and the Mallorys had received their share of proposals during the turn-of-the-century merger movement. As one of the largest coastal steamship lines free of railroad ownership, they were always prospects for the planners of new rail-water systems. They had considered overtures by Missouri Pacific in 1901 and 1902; by unknown parties (but probably J. P Morgan & Co.) in 1902–1903; by Southern Pacific and Santa Fe in 1903; and by Rock Island–Frisco in 1903 and 1905. In each case, the Mallorys politely declined. Charles and Robert were usually willing, at least, to talk—"almost anything one had was for sale at a price," Robert told Edgar S. Marston of Blair & Co. on December 19, 1901; but Henry's position always decided—"You know that there are many things that a man has that he will not sell at a price," he told J. D. Lindsay, another broker, on December 30, 1902.[2]

By 1906, however, the Mallorys were confronted by an offer more concrete, more attractive, and more unusual than any in their past experience. Charles W. Morse wanted to purchase their business for cash, and he talked flatteringly of the Mallory Line as the vital link in his plans to monopolize American coastal shipping.

Morse was no crackpot—far from it. He was the current darling of Wall Street. Born in Bath, Maine, in 1856 into a family of Kennebec River towboatmen, he had graduated from Bowdoin College in 1877 and moved to Brooklyn in 1880. By the 1890's he had made a fortune in the ice trade and had begun to pyramid and interlock banks, trust and insurance companies, public utilities, and real-estate corporations. By April 30, 1906, the New York *American* totaled the capitalization of the thirty-one "Morse companies" at $320,782,113.

San Jacinto, second-to-last steamship built for the New York & Texas Steamship Co. prior to its sale to Morse's Consolidated Steamship Lines in 1906. Later a stalwart of AGWI's Clyde-Mallory Lines. Courtesy Mariners Museum.

Dining saloon, *San Jacinto* (while refitting). Courtesy Mariners Museum.

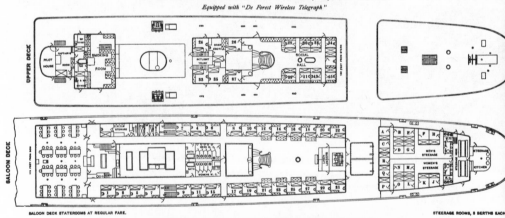

Stateroom plan of *San Jacinto*. Courtesy Mariners Museum.

In 1900, Morse's fancy had turned to shipping, and prior to his proposal to the Mallorys, he had created four large coastal corporations out of several smaller, more closely held companies: the Eastern Steamship Co. of Maine, incorporated October 8, 1901, to consolidate the Kennebec, the Boston & Bangor, the Portland, and the International steamship companies, and to which he added the Rockland & Bluehill and the Portland & Rockland steamboat companies in February 1906; the Hudson Navigation Co. of New Jersey, incorporated November 20, 1902, which absorbed the New Jersey Steam Boat Co. (People's Line to Albany) and the Citizens' Steamboat Co. of Troy in April 1905 and January 1906; the Metropolitan Steamship Co. of Maine, incorporated May 1, 1905, and as successor to a Massachusetts company operating between Boston and New York; and the Clyde Steamship Co. of Maine, incorporated February 7, 1906, as successor to the Clydes' former Delaware corporation.

The Mallorys were, thus, being wooed by a man who was on public record as desiring to purchase "every" American coastal line and a man "credited in shipping circles with having access to sufficient capital to enable him to organize any kind of a shipping combination he desires." What J. Pierpont Morgan's International Mercantile Marine Co. was then trying to accomplish among transatlantic lines, Charles W. Morse now proposed to try among coastal carriers.[3]

Morse's stature and persistence demanded a reply, and the matter was under discussion among the partners of C. H. Mallory & Co. during the first quarter of 1906. Before responding to Morse's proposal, however, and with characteristic conservatism, they tested their freedom to decide. Violating their own resolution of January 23 to keep all stockholders of the New York & Texas Steamship Co. equally informed, they solicited a single, crucial proxy and then clamped a security blanket over the entire deliberation.

The four partners of C. H. Mallory & Co., in their own or in family names, owned 12,827 of the 30,000 shares in the steamship company. They also held ironclad proxies for about 200 shares owned by current employees or the heirs of deceased employees. These votes were theirs when the time came for a decision; but to guarantee a majority, a confidential letter went out from Henry R. Mallory to William J. Spicer (Elihu's nephew and trustee) on May 19: "Can I count on your entire family's holding of S. S. Stock, acting with all of our holdings should we decide in the near future that it was best to sell for cash our stock and at what we thought was a good price?" The answer was back in three days: "[W]hat you decide is best for your own & your family's interest will also be best for us."[4]

With Spicer sworn to secrecy and safely remote in Mystic, and with the 1,938 Spicer family proxies secure, Henry and his brothers became even more their own counsel. The Morse proposal was discussed only among themselves and with their partner William Mason; it was never mentioned in the monthly board meetings of the New York & Texas Steamship Co., and no other officers or stockholders of that corporation were consulted until the brothers had made up their minds.

For once in his life, Henry was indecisive. Three years earlier he had publicly scoffed at just the idea he now confronted. When asked by the Galveston *Daily News* on February 6, 1903, if he thought a Morgan-style shipping cartel was likely in the coastal market, he replied that "a merger of the steamship lines in the coastal trade would simply be impossible. There are but two independent lines doing business in the coast—the Mallory Line and the Clyde Line. All the others are owned by railroad companies, whose interests would not permit a merger of any sort."[5] Yet now, in 1906, he beheld the Clyde Line, a charter member of what seemed such a combination, and its managers, whose judgment he respected, now busily working for Morse.

To collect his own thoughts and to recuperate from a spell of indifferent health, Henry secluded himself at Hot Springs, Virginia. But before he left in early June, he asked brother Robert to study the Morse proposal precedent to discussion upon his return.[6] By August 15, Robert had devoured the reports on Morse's treatment of the Clyde Line and had presented his brothers with seventeen handwritten and closely reasoned pages of discussion and recommendations.

Robert squarely addressed the central issues. "First, If we don't sell, what is Morse likely to do? Second, If we don't sell, what is prospect for continuing indefinitely on present lines?" And then, a Mallory to the core, he jotted down a revealing thought: "Charles & Mr. Mason, no boys, would undoubtedly sell. Henry & Robert, with boys, must look further."

As Robert saw it, his first question was easily answered: "The chances of competitors, consolidations, etc. are no greater today than for several years, but they exist and may come at any time." He obviously thought the second question more important and carefully appraised the Mallory Line's commitments and prospects. Beginning with the basic service, he pointed out:

> While the future of the Galveston line is bright, it is dependent to a large degree upon our ability to satisfy our rail connections, as well as the public, in the matter of service; and, considering the growth of traffic, tri-weekly service in the near future is necessary. . . . If we can satisfy all interests, it is fair to assume that the present conditions will continue indefinitely.

Turning to the Brunswick-Mobile line, he observed that it was "doing better each year; and, while the future is not over bright, I am inclined to believe that the increase will continue; besides, this route furnishes employment for the older ships." The key to satisfying "all interests," however, was ships.

> It may be that, excluding *Comal,* [our] fleet is in better physical condition than in 1903, but the ships are three years older, and getting older every day, not only in age but in effectiveness. For look at it as we may, the fact remains that the modern ship is more effective and more adapted to competitive conditions. At present we are doing fairly well with the older ships, but the pace set by [the] Morgan Line must in turn force us into building fast, expensive ships which cannot show the same percentage of earnings.

Had they been privy to Robert Mallory's memorandum, Galveston's merchants would have wholeheartedly agreed. The Galveston *Daily News* of November 3, 1906, noted:

> For a long time it has been generally recognized that the Galveston-New York freight service justifies more ships. Parties who are in the habit of frequently visiting New York declare that the Mallory wharves at that port are continually congested with freight which can

not be given cargo space for three weeks after it is received at the docks. . . . It has also been generally recognized for a long time that the passenger business between Galveston and New York justifies more ships.

The same pressures were apparent in the Brunswick-Mobile service. "I am convinced," Robert told Henry, "that the building of cheap freighters by Clyde and A. & B. will make it difficult, if not impossible, to operate our older ships at a profit. . . . If we are to remain in the Bwk. business, a complete change of policy is advisable if not necessary."

Robert went on: "Everything points to a continuance of prosperity and I think it safe to say that the increase in the next five years will be as great as in the past ten years"—*but only* if they took action. He recommended two choices: either raise a minimum of $3,000,000 in new capital to improve the older steamships, complete a new one then building, and build two more by 1909; or sell out to Morse.

Even if they did not sell out, Robert rejected equity expansion. If the new capital had to be raised "by issuing stock," he argued, "our hold on the business is weakened for necessarily some of this stock will pass into 'outside' hands who may not be favorable to the present administration." He preferred debt financing. "While so far Mallory Line has incurred no debt, I fear the time has arrived when, if we are to progress and hold the increase of traffic which is certain, we must either by bonds or notes secure capital."

More important than the comparative advantages of equity versus debt financing, however, were his fears that either sort of expansion would cost the family profits and freedom:

> While we now have control, and may be able to continue in control indefinitely, it is useless to disguise the fact that the line could be administered as well, possibly better, for one half what we get . . . nor . . . we can hardly hope for any increased remuneration, as all if not more of the increased commissions must go to expenses—for we must either do our work ourselves or pay, and pay well, for some one to do it for us.

This was the kernel of Robert's position. Why work more and enjoy it less? He concluded:

While of course there is the "other side," the more consideration I give to the subject the more I am convinced of the brightness of the future and, were we all younger and differently constituted, it is a question, speaking for myself, if any offer which could be expected would be accepted. The question, however, must be met and, while not over anxious to sell, I am willing to do so at a figure which will net me between 250 and 300; which will make a price for stock of 200, and from $500,000 upwards for the business of C.H.M. & Co.

Robert had worked up his figures from a comparison of the earning power demonstrated by the Mallory and Clyde lines and from Morse's valuation of Clyde. "If business earning (1905) 19.25% [Clyde] is worth 125% of value of property," he reasoned, "business earning (1905) 23.60 plus 3% if operated on salary basis or say 26% [Mallory] is worth 169%." His two most interesting opinions were that the New York & Texas Steamship Co., if "operated on salary basis" rather than on commission by C. H. Mallory & Co., "would net at least 3% more" and "that *our* business [therefore] is worth something in addition to the *company's* business . . . in additon to $200 for the stock, *we* should receive not less than $500,000." [7]

Charles Mallory made no detailed analysis of the Morse proposal, but his candidly expressed views aligned him in principle with Robert: "It seems to me that they are willing to pay fancy prices to complete the thing." Henry apparently made up his mind in September 1906, and he and his brothers set their terms: $200 per share "or nothing," for "a majority of the stock of N.Y. & T.S.S. Co.," and $500,000 for C. H. Mallory & Co. Although Morse "pressed us to take $80 . . . for the S. S. Co.," there was apparently only perfunctory haggling before he accepted the Mallorys' price early in October.

For $500,000 cash, in Henry's summary of the agreement,

C.H.M. & Co. surrendered its organization perfected by 40 years of Copartnership of hard work and varied experience. *Also* its good will in business, promising loyal support to Mr. Morse's S. S. Co. *Also* its office plant, fixtures, stationery, etc. *It* promised to liquidate its firm's business, and agrees that none of its 4 partners during their lives will engage in or give succor or support to any S.S. Co. that is competitive to Mr. Morse's Lines. [8]

The four partners of C. H. Mallory & Co. then agreed to negotiate the sale of the New York & Texas Steamship Co. For themselves, for those employees whose proxies they held, and as agents for the Spicers, they accepted Morse's offer per share of $150 cash and $50 in the 5 per cent, twenty-five year bonds of a new corporation to be called the "Mallory Steamship Company of Maine"—provided "that at least two of the Mallory Bros. will go on the board of 'Mallory S.S. Co.' and aid Mr. Morse in perfecting its plans, and in the future operations of his Co." [9]

Then and only then, the partners prepared a "confidential" letter from C. H. Mallory & Co. to the remaining stockholders of the steamship company.

> We beg to advise that we have disposed of the majority interest in the Stock of the New York & Texas S.S. Co. at the rate of $200 per share, subject to a brokerage of 1 1/2 per cent thereon ($3.00 per share), payable as follows: 75 per cent in Cash and 25 per cent in 5% Bonds of the new Company at par. All Stockholders have the privilege of participating on the same basis as shown above. The Bonds are secured by lien on all the property now owned by the New York & Texas S.S. Co. We believe the price a good one, and recommend that it be accepted.... Please reply *at once* by return mail.... [10]

The confidential form letter was dated and was to be mailed October 31, 1906; and with it, the Mallorys obviously intended to present a *fait accompli* to their minority stockholders—a handsome *fait accompli* that sold the company at twice the par value of its stock, but a *fait accompli* nevertheless. Morse mortified them, however, by announcing on October 26 that he had purchased "95 per cent" of the Mallory Line! Thus, two-thirds of the directorate (Weed and Sealy), about 49 per cent of the stockholders, and most of the employees of the New York & Texas Steamship Co. learned of its sale in the newspapers. [11] Henry Mallory spent the next week apologizing and explaining to relatives, business associates, and friends, but the size of Morse's tender had a remarkably palliative effect on ruffled feathers. [12]

On October 31, Morse formally incorporated the Mallory

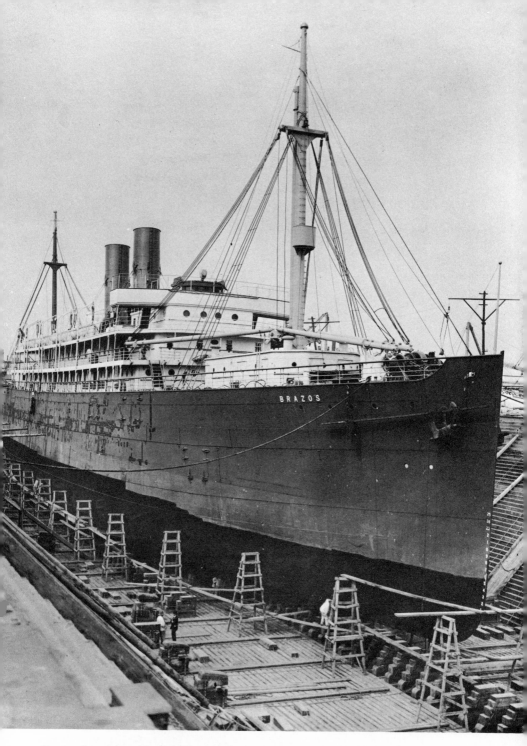

Brazos, last steamship built for the New York & Texas Steamship Co. prior to its sale to Morse's Consolidated Steamship Lines in 1906. Later a stalwart of AGWI's Clyde-Mallory Lines. Courtesy Mariners Museum.

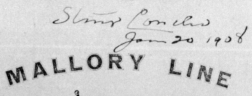

Stmr Concho
Jan 20, 1908

MALLORY LINE

Dinner

JARDINIERE

OLIVES   CELERY   GHERKINS

BOILED HALIBUT, PARSLEY SAUCE

CHICKEN A LA MARENGO
APPLE FRITTERS   FRUIT SAUCE

BOILED VEAL AND OYSTER SAUCE

PRIME RIBS OF BEEF
LEG OF LAMB, MINT SAUCE
LIMA BEANS   BEETS   GREEN PEAS
MASHED POTATOES   BOILED POTATOES

LETTUCE WITH FRENCH DRESSING

BAKED APPLE ROLL, HARD AND BRANDY SAUCE
RHUBARB PIE
ICE CREAM   SMALL PASTRY
ASSORTED FRUIT
CHEESE   CRACKERS
TEA   COFFEE

- - - - -

Menu, *Concho*, January 20, 1908. Courtesy Mystic Seaport.

Steamship Co. of Maine. Its charter authorized a capital stock of $14,000,000 in $50 shares and $6,000,000 in 5 per cent, twenty-five-year first-mortgage bonds. Morse syndicated the entire stock issue at prices between $25 and $30 and used the cash so raised to help purchase the New York & Texas Steamship Co. stock. One-half of the authorized bonds were also issued—$1,500,000 going to stockholders in the old company as part of the exchange and $1,500,000 being sold on the open market. On November 14, the board and stockholders of the New York & Texas Steamship Co. formally ratified the sale, effective December 1, 1906.

Morse's Mallory Steamship Co. received the eleven Mallory Line steamers then in operation (*Rio Grande, Colorado, San Marcos, Lampasas, Alamo, Comal, Nueces, Sabine, Concho, Denver,* and *San Jacinto*), twelve steam lighters (*R. M King, G. W. Sherwood, S. B. Baker, E. Brandon, G. Thompson, S. Walker, O. M. Hitchcock, P. C. Golder, C. E. Goin, O. F. Martin, C. F. Deering,* and *Perry*), and all other assets of C. H. Mallory & Co. and the New York & Texas Steamship Co.—including the then-building steamship *Brazos* and two partially completed lighters (*Mobile* and *Brunswick*); the Mallory Line's Key West terminal; leases of Piers 15 and 16, East River, Pier 32, Brooklyn, and piers and wharves at Brunswick, Mobile, and Galveston plus stevedoring equipment at each port; and $677,848 cash realized from liquidation of deposits, agency accounts, and investment portfolios.[13]

The Mallory Line's headquarters staff, outport agencies, captains, and crews also passed to the new company, but the executive cadre changed. As president of the Mallory Steamship Co., Morse appointed his right-hand man, Calvin Austin, who was already president of Eastern, Metropolitan, and Clyde. N. H. Campbell, then secretary-treasurer of Hudson and Clyde, also assumed that post for Mallory. The board was composed of Morse, Austin, John Englis (on all the Morse boards), James T. Morse (treasurer and director of Eastern and Metropolitan), William H. Hill (a director of Eastern, Metropolitan, and Clyde), Henry R. Mallory, and Robert Mallory. For the first time in their lives, the Mallory brothers had no business of their own.

While their sale of the New York & Texas Steamship Co.

was the most important decision made by the third generation of Mallorys, Charles W. Morse's incorporation of the Mallory Steamship Co. of Maine on October 31, 1906, was only another step toward fulfillment of his grand design—a coastal cartel. Subsequent to the Mallory purchase, he acquired and reorganized what proved to be his final two lines: the New York & Cuba Mail Steamship Co. of Maine, incorporated on March 6, 1907, as successor to the Ward Line; and the New York & Porto Rico Steamship Co. of Maine, incorporated on April 8, 1907, as successor to an earlier New Jersey corporation. These two lines he combined with Eastern, Metropolitan, Clyde, and Mallory to form the Consolidated Steamship Lines of Maine. Because it was a river rather than a coastal service, the Hudson Navigation Co. was kept as a separate Morse enterprise.

The Consolidated Steamship Lines of Maine, with Calvin Austin as president and N. H. Campbell as secretary-treasurer, were incorporated on January 2, 1907, to aquire "substantially the entire share capital" of Morse's six coastal companies. The aggregate capitalization of those "constituent companies" totaled $62,000,000 in common stock and $26,222,000 in 5 per cent, first-mortgage bonds, as follows:

Company	Capital Stock	Bonds Issued
Eastern	$ 3,000,000	$ 2,961,000
Metropolitan	3,000,000	2,600,000
Clyde	14,000,000	4,495,000
Mallory	14,000,000	3,000,000
N. Y. & C. M.	20,000,000	10,666,000
N. Y. & P. R.	8,000,000	2,500,000

Consolidated's $60,000,000 in common stock was exchanged for $59,985,600 of the common stock of the six subsidiaries, share for share: Eastern, 28,563 shares; Metropolitan, 28,975; Clyde, 133,148; Mallory, 137,234; N. Y. & C. M., 193,936; N. Y. & P. R., 78,000. These 599,856 shares in the constituent companies were then pledged to the American Trust Co. of Boston to secure the issuance of $60,000,000 in Consolidated 4 per cent, collateral-trust bonds. Each constituent share-holder received $100 of these bonds per share, and the remainder was publicly tendered. The first-mortgage bonds of the constituents were not affected by the consolidation, as each of these issues was to be retired by its own company at the rate of 4 per cent of the outstanding bonds per year.

As expressed in a broker's circular of July 26, the

> fundamental idea in this consolidation was the benefits to be derived from concentration of control which would result in the working of all lines under one management, the securing of the lowest possible cost of operation, the elimination of idle tonnage, the curtailment of pier room, harmonious arrangements between the various lines, the most favorable price for the purchase of supplies and fuel, the lowest cost of insurance, repairs, legal expenses, etc.

Whatever the "idea," however, the financial world and the public were unquestionably dazzled. Morse's Consolidated had 97 American-flag steamships (aggregating 265,729 gross tons), 65 steam lighters, and 7 tugs under a single management; and, as the *Wall Street Journal* of November 14, 1906, had remarked, he had done it "single handedly . . . not by destruction through sinister or pernicious methods of rivals, but by out and out purchase from first hands or direct owners."

The firm of Hornblower & Weeks, which acted as Morse's prime broker, was especially impressed:

> While the lines of the six steamship companies forming the consolidation occupy a field of operation extending from St. John, N. B., on the Atlantic coast, to Vera Cruz, Mexico, on the Gulf coast, these lines touch many important intervening points, and the ports of Cuba, Porto Rico, Santo Domingo, Turk's Island, and the Bahamas. Working in close conjunction with railroads diverting from the various ports, there is practically no limit to the scope of the companies' possibilities in the movement of through freight and passenger traffic.

The brokers reported that the six companies in 1906 had earned "approximately $3,500,000 net on a gross business of nearly $18,000,000" and predicted a 30 per cent increase in the net for 1907.[14]

As the summer of 1907 progressed, however, the brokers' golden predictions turned to lead. The combined net earnings of Consolidated's four "southern lines"—Clyde, Mallory, N. Y. & C. M., and N. Y. & P. R.—were up, but only about 7 per cent over 1906; Eastern's earnings were down, and Metropolitan was running a deficit. Stiff competition from railroad-controlled coastal steamships was the major cause. Despite what Morse and his brokers claimed, there was a significant number of powerful water carriers *outside* of Consolidated Steamship Lines, and they were in no mood to wish it well (see Table 9.1). Also, payments to shipbuilders on account of the twelve to fourteen new steamships for which Morse had contracted cut net returns. There was little enough left over to meet interest payments on the bonded indebtedness of the constituent companies.

In October, things got worse as Charles W. Morse's bubble burst. On October 16, his Mercantile National Bank applied to the New York Clearing House for assistance in meeting its obligations. On October 23, a $34,000,000 run on his Trust Company of America began. These uncertainties, and a run on the Knickerbocker Trust Company which began on October 21, triggered the Panic of 1907. Morse was soon found particularly at fault. "He had used his stock in one institution as collateral on which to borrow money; the proceeds he had used to buy stock in another bank, repeating the process with each new acquisition." With the Morse banking empire crumbling, and the "Ice King" himself under federal indictment for fraud, Consolidated Steamship Lines' future darkened.[15]

Those officers of the four "southern" lines who had been the proprietors of their companies prior to the Morse consolidation soon had enough of supporting Eastern, Metropolitan and Consolidated. In a swift power play, they ousted Calvin Austin from the presidencies of Mallory, N. Y. & C. M., and N. Y. & P. R. and nullified his influence in Clyde. Leaders of the revolt were Henry R. Mallory, who resumed the presidency of Mallory; H. H. Raymond, who was made vice president and general manager of Clyde in addition to retaining those posts in Mallory; Henry P. Booth, who resumed the presidency of N. Y. & C. M.; Alfred G. Smith, former general manager and current vice president of N. Y. & C. M.; John E. and Edwin J. Berwind, former president and vice president of N. Y. & P. R.; and Franklin D. Mooney, former secretary-treasurer and general manager of N. Y. & P. R., who now became president of that company.

The motives of the steamship men in ousting the bankers were made quite clear to the public. The Boston *News Bureau* of October 26 summarized their position: "Rather than permit a business with which their names had been connected for 50 or 60 years to be under a cloud, they would themselves advance the necessary funds to pay off current obligations and assume the management of the companies pending such time as the entire system could be reorganized, if a reorganization is deemed advisable." Henry P. Booth spoke for all, and the message to Morse was loud and clear: "We shall attend to our business just as if there never had been a consolidation, and the other companies will do the same. We shall pay our expenses and interest on our bonds out of our receipts, and if we are successful enough to make more money than is necessary for these purposes, then we will hand it over to the Consolidated Company for that company to divide among its bondholders as it may see fit."

A financial analysis prepared by the accounting firm of Gunn, Richards & Co., and widely circulated on Wall and State streets during November 1907, supported the actions of the steamship men. The report estimated that Consolidated's net earnings for 1907 (through November 30) would be 32 per cent *below* those of 1906—a far cry from Hornblower & Week's July prediction of a 30 per cent *increase.* Gunn, Richards & Co. again pinpointed Eastern and Metropolitan as the problem children of the combination; and, as early as November 2, the *Commercial and Financial Chronicle* reported that it was "commonly understood" that Consolidated would be unable to pay the January 1, 1908, coupon on its collateral-trust bonds.[16]

The reaction was inevitable. By December 28, 1907, a Bondholders' Protective Committee had been formed, chaired by Alvin W. Krech, president of the Equitable Trust Co. of New York, and including Governor William T. Cobb of Maine, Henry Hornblower of Hornblower & Weeks, William H. Granbery of W. H. Granbery & Co., and Galen L. Stone of Hayden, Stone &

Co. By January, Cobb and Granbery had been replaced by Henry J. Braker, president of the Mexican Sugar Refining Co., Ltd., and William H. Chesebrough, president of Chesebrough Building Co. Three of the steamship men were also added: Edwin J. Berwind (former vice president of N. Y. & P. R. and now a director of Clyde), Henry P. Booth (president of N. Y. & C. M. and a director of Clyde, Mallory, and N. Y. & P. R.), and Henry R. Mallory (president of Mallory and a director of N. Y. & C. M. and Clyde). Alexander R. Nicol, a New York banker, served as nonvoting secretary.

As expected, Consolidated Steamship Lines passed its January 1, 1908, coupon, and on January 30, a bondholders' suit was filed in the U.S. Circuit Court for the District of Maine asking that receivers be appointed for Consolidated, Eastern, and Metropolitan. Receivers were so appointed on February 4; and, on March 4, the American Trust Co. opened proceedings to foreclose Consolidated's collateral-trust indenture. In the meantime, of course, the Bondholders' Protective Committee was hard at work, and on June 30 it published its "Report and Plan of Reorganization."

The plan, which was largely the work of Stone, Mallory, and Nicol, presumed that when the American Trust Co.'s mortgage on Consolidated Steamship Lines was foreclosed, the committee would be able to purchase Consolidated's shares in the six subsidiary companies. This property would then be transferred to a new Maine corporation, the "Atlantic, Gulf & West Indies Steamship Lines" (a name suggested by Mallory). "AGWI," as it was soon nicknamed, would then liquidate Consolidated's bonded debt, replace it as the parent holding company, and fund the floating debts of its constituents. The constituents would remain responsible for their own first mortgages, as they had been under Consolidated.

On October 9, the U.S. Circuit Court for the District of Maine found for the American Trust Co. and ordered the foreclosure sale of Consolidated to be held in Portland on November 25. At that sale, the only bidder was the Sub-Purchasing Committee of the Bondholders' Protective Committee—composed of Krech, Booth, and Mallory—and its offer of $6,500,000 was accepted. AGWI was formally incorporated on the same day, and the 599,856 shares Consolidated had owned in Eastern, Metropolitan, Clyde, Mallory, N. Y. & C. M., and N. Y. & P. R. were transferred to the new holding company. The reorganization plan of June 30 was activated.[17]

Under this reorganization plan, there were no changes in size to either the equity or the bonded debt of Clyde, Mallory, N. Y. & C. M., and N. Y. & P. R. Each of the holders of Consolidated's 4 per cent collateral-trust bonds, however, exchanged them for $200 in AGWI bonds, $250 in AGWI preferred stock, and $125 in AGWI common—a total of $575 in new securities for each $1,000 in old bonds. This exchange achieved one of the prime purposes of the reorganization, "to reduce the fixed interest charges of the new company to a figure well within a reasonable expectation of its annual income." Whereas Consolidated had faced annual fixed-interest charges of $2,400,000 (4 per cent on $60,000,000 in collateral-trust bonds), AGWI reduced this charge to $750,000 per year (5 per cent on $15,000,000 in collateral-trust bonds). No coupons on the AGWI bonds were to mature before July 1, 1909, which gave the new holding company a six months' breathing spell, and dividends on the $20,000,000 of per cent preferred stock were payable only "as shall be determined and declared" by AGWI's board of directors.

Significantly, the reorganization plan left "provision for the financial requirements" of Eastern and Metropolitan "optional" and empowered AGWI "to dispose of or deal with" its shares in those companies however it pleased. On December 15, it sold 22,000 of its 28,563 shares of Eastern, at $50 per share, to a Hayden, Stone & Co. syndicate and deposited the proceeds with Eastern's treasurer. These funds were used to lift Eastern's receivership, and it embarked on its own corporate course outside of the AGWI consolidation. The remaining 6,563 shares in Eastern were sold at $105 per share sometime prior to 1915. The 28,975 shares in Metropolitan, "which had no intrinsic value, as all of the property of the Company was sold under foreclosure of the mortgage, were later disposed of for a nominal consideration in order to effect a settlement of certain claims against the Metropolitan Steamship Company." [18]

As Henry R. Mallory put it, they had "again started out on

a 'clean' basis; and care must be taken to see that no stigma attaches to the 'new' co. either in name or management." Mallory was in the best position to assure his own hopes, for it was he who had headed the executive cadre which organized AGWI and which now assumed the managerial helm of both the parent and the four subsidiary companies. On October 28, 1908, he, Stone, and Berwind had been appointed a subcommittee to choose a president for the new combination. But by early November, and particularly at Stone's urging, the full reorganization committee chose Mallory himself as president of AGWI, Clyde, N. Y. & C. M., N. Y. & P. R., and his beloved Mallory Line—at a combined salary of $50,000 per year.

From the earliest days of the reorganization, the committee had steadfastly determined it "best to place men in charge of affairs whose names are a guaranty of able and conservative management." Henry Mallory certainly fitted that description, but his decision to end his one-year "retirement" and, at sixty, take up a new career in shipping surprised even his family. Brother Charles, from his retirement life at Port Chester, was aghast. "I hope you will say NO, NO, NO," he wrote Henry in November 1908, while the matter was still pending. "They are all anxious for you to hold the bag. . . . There is a limit to human endurance and that limit is not nearly so great at sixty as it was at forty." Robert, who was about to join Spencer Trask & Co., was more understanding and gave his older brother some good advice. "These are days of big things in which details are relegated to subordinates. I think that perhaps we gave too much of our personal time to working out details which others could have just as well worked out for us."

But, as his father had said years before, Henry was a "curious mixture," and so was his decision to resume an active managerial position. Unquestionably, he felt challenged; he wrote Stone in 1910 that "the problems are most interesting and the business fascinating." But there was something else, too; a sense of responsibility, seldom articulated, but glimpsed in a letter to a friend in December 1906, just after the sale to Morse: "Death only will make me pull down the flag of Mallory, and the Admiral will remain 'on deck' even though shorn of the title, which was given him many years ago because he never went to sea." [19]

Galen Stone also had much to do with Henry Mallory's return to business. Stone "was a handsome man," Lyle Bull recalled, "typifying the popular conception of a prosperous banker. . . . He was always courteous and kind but a truly hard-headed Yankee business man." Stone and Mallory "first met around the Committee table of the Consl. S. S. Co.," and the skills of the flamboyant, extroverted Boston banker and the reserved, introspective New York shipman were obviously complementary. "They had never met anyone like each other," recalled Henry's son Philip, and "they hit it off at once." Though they always remained "Mr. Stone" and "Mr. Mallory," they relished their friendship and delighted in exchanging gossip, puns, and *double entendre.* And, concerning Mallory's management of AGWI, Stone spoke for his fellow directors: "I am very anxious that you have all the time away from the office that you want. . . . On the other hand, I have no thought at all of changing the man at the helm, although we will give him all the first, second, and third mates that he may wish." [20]

On these terms, Henry R. Mallory served as president of AGWI (and of all its major subsidiaries) from its incorporation on November 25, 1908, until he chose to retire on May 27, 1915. He was an active managing executive, not a figurehead in any sense, and his tenure was one of consolidation and cautious expansion for the group of corporations over which he presided. Unquestionably, he left AGWI in far better physical and financial condition than he had found it.

Most of Mallory's business problems between 1908 and 1915 were of the same kind that he, his father, and his brothers had handled all their lives: the procurement, deployment, maintenance, and replacement of ships; the improvement of terminal facilities; and the constant reconciliation of schedules, routes, and rates with shippers' demands and the competitive situation. In a great many aspects, the view from the top in line carriage was always the same. What differed in AGWI from anything in Henry Mallory's experience was the scale of the operation, the need to coordinate business policies between a parent and numerous subsidiaries, and the more conscious attention to structure and strategy the large corporate group required.

The structure born of the financial reorganization was the prime master to be served. Sometimes it was compatible with the needs of operating steamships; sometimes it was not. At the subsidiary corporate level, of course, the first goal was to operate as efficiently as possible so as to maximize earnings after operating expenses. The second goal was to use these net earnings to meet maturing coupons on the subsidiaries' bonded debts. But once these coupons were met, next came decisions whether to retain earnings after interest payments, to use them to improve or replace equipment and vessels, or to pay them over to AGWI as dividends on the subsidiaries' common stock. Since AGWI's major source of income was dividends received from its operating subsidiaries, its management participated in these decisions. Within the parent, though, first responsibilities were to its bonds and notes; then, AGWI's managers had to choose whether to pay dividends on its own preferred and common stock or to use its earnings after interest payments in other ways.

Obviously, there were potential incompatibilities built into the AGWI group: between obligations inherited from the past and prospects of the present and future; between financial and physical needs; between parental and subsidiary needs. But the group's founders hoped that their personalities and their organizational structure could anticipate and overcome frictions and stresses in decision-making. The parent and its subsidiaries shared a common president (Mallory) and a common treasurer (Nicol), and Mallory, Nicol, and Stone (who was also vice president of AGWI) formed a nucleus common to all the various boards of directors. Each operating subsidiary was headed by a vice president–general manager, who also served on his own company's directorate and on the boards of the other subsidiaries: H. H. Raymond headed both the Clyde and the Mallory lines; Franklin D. Mooney led the Porto Rico Line; and Alfred G. Smith headed the Ward Line. These men comprised the prime executive teams and since they interlocked the AGWI companies through the three top levels of management, they were expected to formulate strategies agreeable to all.

Mallory's own preferences were quite evident in the strategies AGWI and its constituents pursued during his tenure as their president. He gave first priority to debt servicing; second to improvement of vessels and terminal facilities; third to organizational and operational efficiency; and last to equity earnings.

Neither AGWI nor any of its subsidiaries missed an interest payment during Mallory's presidency. And it was his clear preference that any surplus after debt servicing was to be plowed back into better capital equipment and not to be paid out as dividends. Dividends from the subsidiaries to AGWI, of course, were paid, but were only internal transfers of funds from profit centers to the holding company. AGWI itself paid no dividends whatsoever on its preferred stock until April 10, 1916; none ever on its common.

As for vessels during Mallory's tenure, AGWI chose to maintain forty-seven of the sixty-two steamships, all seven of the tugs, and forty-one of the fifty-seven steam lighters it had taken over from Consolidated. Over the same period, Mallory and his fellow executives added twenty-three steamships, eight tugs, and fifty-three lighters to the AGWI fleet. All but eight of these new vessels were built on the accounts of the subsidiary operating companies: six steamships, two tugs, and eight lighters by and for the Clyde Line; four steamships, two tugs, and sixteen lighters by and for the Mallory Line; one steamship, four tugs, and eighteen lighters by and for the Ward Line; and four steamships by and for the Porto Rico Line.

The new-vessel construction program was planned and coordinated by the AGWI board, but was funded by the subsidiaries. Each decision to build was related to the demand on the route concerned, to the age and condition of vessels already serving that route, to the ability of the relevant subsidiary to finance the ship, and to possible alternative uses for the same funds. Of the other eight steamships added to the fleet, five were acquired on AGWI's own account from the Brunswick Steamship Co. Both transactions were routine absorptions of small competitors.

The Brunswick Steamship Co. had been organized in 1905 as a subsidiary of the Atlantic, Birmingham & Atlantic Railroad Co., and by 1908 it had *Satilla, Assabaw, Ogeechee, Ocmulgee,* and *Altamaha* operating between New York and Georgia. These steamships had been a small nuisance to both the old Clyde and Mallory lines (they were the "A. & B." ships mentioned in Robert Mallory's memorandum prior to the Morse consolidation), but they were never a threat. They were also mortgaged to the Old Colony Trust Co. for $1,250,000 in 5 per cent bonds, leading to their ultimate acquisition by AGWI.

While its railroad parent went into receivership on January 2, 1909, the Brunswick Steamship Co. met its own coupons through July 1, 1910. Thereafter, however, AGWI assumed its mortgage in return for title to its five ships. AGWI then incorporated the Texas City Steamship Co. of Maine, on August 6, as a wholly owned subsidiary, and it time-chartered the five vessels. They were shifted from the Brunswick run to a New York–Texas City weekly freight line, which opened a new port to AGWI service.

The Southern Steamship Co. was another small line dating from pre-Morse days, operating *Algiers, William P. Palmer,* and *Shawmut* from Philadelphia to Jacksonville, Key West, and Tampa. It had pestered the Clyde Line at Jacksonville and the Mallory Line at Key West and (after 1908) at Tampa. Finally, on October 9, 1914, AGWI bought it out and merged it with the Texas City Steamship Co. Thereafter, under the name of the Southern Steamship Co., AGWI used the eight steamships on runs from New York and Philadelphia to Tampa and Texas City.

Second only to his efforts to honor his companies' debts and improve their floating equipment, Mallory worked to secure better terminal facilities for the AGWI lines.

It was not always necessary to purchase such improved facilities. In many of the ports they served, the AGWI subsidiaries could acquire the terminals they required without buying them. While the Clyde Line owned its own wharves in Norfolk and Brunswick, the Mallory Line owned its own Key West terminal, the Ward Line owned the Havana Lighterage Co., and the Porto Rico Line owned Pier 1 in San Juan, more often they and their peers leased what water frontage they needed from municipal or private hands. By 1915, for example: Clyde was leasing Lewis Wharf in Boston, Piers 36, 44, and 45 (North

River) in New York, and Piers 1, 2, and 3 in Philadelphia; Mallory was leasing Piers 37 and 38 (North River) in New York, the Henry & Knight Terminal in Tampa, and Piers 23 to 27 of the Galveston Wharf Co.; Ward was leasing Piers 13 and 14 (East River) and 12, 16, and 17 (Brooklyn) in New York and the Port of Havana Dock Co. wharves; the Porto Rico Line was leasing Piers 34 and 35 (Brooklyn); and the Southern Steamship Co. was subleasing Pier 44 (North River) from Clyde.

In two Caribbean and two southern ports, however, AGWI deemed it advantageous to purchase terminal and lighterage facilities which it then leased or otherwise made available to its subsidiary lines. In each case, the purpose was to secure more exclusive and/or cheaper use of the properties. In San Juan, AGWI bought the stock and bonds of the San Antonio Docking and San Antonio companies when it acquired the Porto Rico Line. On January 4, 1910, it purchased 60 per cent of the equity and debt of the Santiago Terminal Co. to insure the Ward Line's exclusive use of that Cuban facility. In Florida, and for the use of Clyde and Mallory, it acquired the Jacksonville Lighterage Co. and the Tampa Towing & Lighterage Co. during 1909. Also for Clyde's use, AGWI purchased, reorganized, and improved three large water-front facilities in Jacksonville, Charleston, and Wilmington (North Carolina): the Clyde Steamship Terminal Co. (incorporated July 7, 1909), the Carolina Terminal Co. (incorporated December 13, 1911), and the Wilmington Terminal Co. (incorporated July 25, 1913).[21]

In contrast to his intensely personal role in improving the capital structure and equipment of the AGWI group, Henry Mallory chose not to concern himself too much with improving either the deployment or the operational efficiency of the individual lines. This was a tough decision for an old-time steamship man to make; but, for the chief executive of a large holding company, it was a defensible one. His first obligations, he felt, were to increase the quality and value of his companies' assets at least cost, to decrease their debts, and to allocate surpluses wisely. It was primarily the responsibility of the subsidiary vice presidents to improve their lines' operating ratios, schedules, and service.

Because of Henry Mallory's preoccupations and prefer-

ences, then, AGWI's subsidiary companies remained fairly au-
tonomous business entities (see Figure 9.2). Save for parental
control of their new-ship construction and review of their rates,
schedules, and policies, they were virtually on their own. Such
independence was beneficial to the extent that each of the
operating companies had experienced organizations and personnel, knew the tricks of their particular trades, and lived up to
their long-established reputations for quality service and competitive price. Constituent autonomy was costly, however, to
the extent that it complicated decision-making with antiquated
administrative practices, ill-defined and duplicative jobs, and
poorly drawn lines of authority and responsibility; and to the
extent that tradition could cloud visions of new opportunities.

The Clyde and Mallory lines had probably the best management group. Immediately after their acquisition by AGWI, their
administrative organizations and personnel had been merged
under the firm hand of H. H. Raymond. Raymond served as
vice president and general manager of both companies at a
combined salary of $20,000 and headed an excellent cadre of
line managers: J. S. Raymond, his brother and former Mobile
agent of the Mallory Line, served as secretary and assistant
general manager of Clyde at a salary of $7,800; Clifford D.
Mallory, Henry's son and former junior member of C. H. Mallory & Co., was secretary and assistant general manager of
Mallory at $6,000 per year; J. B. Denison, the Mallory Line's
old Galveston agent, now served as traffic manager for both
Clyde and Mallory at $7,500 per year.

Under these men, Clyde and Mallory improved their floating equipment and terminal facilities, but made few changes in
their traditional services (see Tables 9.1 and 9.2). Tampa was
added as a Mallory port of call during 1908–1909 and was later
combined with the Mobile line. Brunswick was dropped as a
Clyde port of call, but no other significant changes were made.

The Ward Line, under Alfred G. Smith (who earned
$20,000 per year as its vice president and general manager),
received less new equipment than did the other subsidiaries, but
it expanded its services to include a large number of Mexican as
well as Cuban ports (see Tables 9.1 and 9.2). The Porto Rico
Line, under Franklin D. Mooney (who earned $16,900 as its

vice president and general manager), expanded its services to include freight lines from Galveston, Port Arthur, and Mobile to all Puerto Rican ports: San Juan, Fajardo, Puerto Mulas, Punta Arenas, Humacao, Arroyo, Santa Isabel, Ponce, Guánica, Mayagüez, Aguadilla, and Arecibo (see Tables 9.1 and 9.2).[22]

The Southern Steamship Co. was managed by George W. DeLanoy (vice president and traffic manager at $6,000 per year) and played a leading role in the birth of a new deepwater port. Ever since Charles Morgan's old line had closed, Houston had been trying to deepen and improve his ship channel to the Gulf. With federal and county assistance, the dream was finally realized and a new channel was formally dedicated on November 10, 1914. Several ocean-going tramp vessels used the new waterway almost immediately, but the port's managers approached the Southern Steamship Co., which was already serving nearby Texas City, to open the first "regular coastwise service" to Houston. They "carried a bond signed by a hundred citizens, promising to pay a thousand dollars each to the line if any losses were incurred in giving Houston the desired service." AGWI's management thought the prospects inviting enough without the guarantee, and on August 22, 1915, *Satilla* inaugurated a Houston–New York freight line. She, her sisters, and her company became part of Houston's maritime history—"the first deep-water vessel to dock at the port after its official opening."[23]

Even though all of AGWI's subsidiaries bettered their equipment, terminals, and services under Henry Mallory's presidencies, they did so at far less than optimum administrative efficiency. Few policies emanated from the parent to simplify or to systematize the hodgepodge of titles and practices the subsidiaries inherited from the past. Although all the lines were in the same business and confronted virtually the same set of administrative problems, no efforts were made to standardize their organizational structures, job descriptions, titles, salaries, or performance criteria. More seriously, however, AGWI ignored some chances to reduce costs and improve services by neglecting to centralize some activities on a corporation-wide basis.

From his middle-management position, Clifford D. Mallory saw these lost opportunities more clearly than his father could or would. The younger Mallory, on his own initiative, intensively studied AGWI's operations and repeatedly recommended corporate centralization of the accounting, engineering, insurance, purchasing, advertising, and legal staffs which each of the subsidiaries independently maintained. He was also critical of the lack of coordination respecting excess capacity. Each of the lines made its own decisions when to add or subtract ships and whether and when to charter or lay up unneeded vessels. There was no shifting about of vessels from one line to another, which sometimes resulted in one line's chartering extra capacity in the general market while another had idle vessels. Clifford Mallory proposed a central department to collect and manage an excess-capacity pool, which could specialize in chartering out extra vessels and, perhaps, even develop new liner trades.[24]

Except for the centralization of corporate-wide accounting under Treasurer Nicol, Clifford Mallory's suggestions were not taken by his father and Stone or by the subsidiary vice presidents Raymond, Smith, and Mooney. The elder Mallory and Stone were reluctant to centralize AGWI any further, because they were already overworked by the financial problems they felt should receive top management's first priority. The vice presidents, to whom much operational authority had been delegated, naturally opposed further centralization as a threat to their hard-won autonomy. Most important in the senior executives' reasoning, however, was the unarguable fact that AGWI's organizational *status quo* was achieving the goals of consolidation and cautious expansion its founders had set. The data in Tables 9.3 and 9.4, which cover the period of Henry R. Mallory's presidency, support their view.

The stability of the operating companies' net earnings during 1909-1914, for example, seconds Mallory's faith that there was a profitable demand for the services these lines offered. Despite strikes among coastal seamen and longshoremen, despite tariffs in 1909 and 1913 which cut sugar imports from Cuba, despite the Mexican Revolution, and despite less than "best" administrative practices, net earnings held up well. Although the lines' operating ratio (net earnings as a percentage of gross receipts) was poorer than the New York & Texas Steamship Co. had once achieved (see Table 8.4), it did not reflect any serious cost-price squeeze or gross inefficiency; and the jump in earnings during 1915 (caused by opportunities to charter vessels at high wartime rates) reflects the lines' capacity and ability to turn windfall profits.

Further evidence of the strength of AGWI's subsidiary lines is found in their ability to fund construction of a large number of new vessels, meet all their interest payments, retire 26 per cent of their first-mortgage debt, and still pay handsome dividends to the parent corporation. In short, the subsidiary companies did all that AGWI's founders expected of them, financially speaking.

At the corporate level, of course, AGWI's founders chose not to do everything they might have done. They did meet all interest payments on AGWI's collateral-trust bonds and notes, and they retired the latter on schedule. They also paid off the Brunswick Steamship Co. mortgage early. But during Mallory's tenure, they chose not to pay dividends on AGWI's preferred or common stock and not to retire any of its collateral-trust bonds. Further, they chose not to venture too far from tried and true routes, technology, and organization.

Henry Mallory's conviction that a strong parent tree could grow only from strong constituent roots thus dedicated him to freeing the subsidiaries from debt and to familiar trades, methods, and equipment. He made his conviction clear, and his priorities were adhered to; they were defensible, given the situation he confronted; they were supported by the men who had chosen him to lead. He had been recalled to active management because of his experience; his actions and preferences quite naturally reflected that experience; and he achieved what he had set out to do. His final annual report to the stockholders concluded, with justifiable pride: "The financial condition of this corporation, also of all subsidiary companies, has never been so favorable as at the present time." [25]

Mallory's fellow directors gave credit where credit was due. Though many of the words they chose for their official resolutions of thanks were rhetorical, they still captured precisely the qualities of Mallory's character and leadership: "technical knowledge, long experience, and remarkable tact"; "unusual kindness and patience"; "his open mind on every proposition";

"wise, safe, and conservative counsel"; "invariable courtesy and gentleness always displayed." [26]

The $47,000,000 corporation which Henry R. Mallory relinquished on May 29, 1915, was his most impressive contribution to his family's history of maritime enterprise. AGWI's seventy steamships, fourteen of which still flew the Mallory house flag, plied the same trades as had Charles Mallory's first coaster, the sloop *Connecticut,* eighty-nine years before. The closely held family firms, of course, were gone. But in Henry's eyes, he and his brothers had sacrificed them in two greater causes: financial security for the oncoming fourth generation of Mallorys, and the creation of the powerful, railroad-free, non-subsidized American-flag shipping line of which he and his father had dreamed. In his elder son Clifford, who now moved up a notch in the Clyde-Mallory management, he felt he had trained his successor, and he had placed him, he thought, at the center of the shipping world.

But the future and men are seldom predictable. Within two years after his retirement, Henry Mallory's world was topsy-turvy: Clifford had left AGWI for government service and was not likely to return to the position and the course his father had charted for him. No Mallory now worked for, much less headed, the Mallory Line! Just as the Civil War had drawn a line between the first and second generations, so the third and fourth were divided by World War I.

Chapter 10

THE ERA OF WORLD WAR I,

1915–1919

"It has been my ambition to be a private ship owner, and it looks as if present conditions [have] made this the opportunity of a lifetime."—Clifford D. Mallory to George D. Barron, February 18, 1915

H ENRY and Cora Mallory raised their three children in the family traditions of honesty, interdependence, and hard work, and they had every reason to be proud of their "fry." But the world of Cora Pynchon, Clifford Day, and Philip Rogers Mallory was far different from those of their parents' and grandparents' youth. The family was more economically successful and socially prominent than ever. For the fourth generation, home was cosmopolitan New York, with summer sailing on Long Island Sound and winter fishing excursions to Florida; for them, youth was fashionable companionship, economic security, social position, and wide vistas of opportunity. But security and position also gave Cora, Clifford, and Philip an independence of mind and a freedom of choice which their parents had, apparently, never experienced or sought. The questioning of some of the family's traditional assumptions and goals was always a part of the fourth generation's makeup, but it took the antitraditional atmosphere of the era of World War I to call it fully forth.

When Clifford and Philip were born, in 1881 and 1885, it was still assumed that they would follow their father in the family business as he and his brothers were then following Charles Henry Mallory. Partnership in C. H. Mallory & Co. and equity and office in the New York & Texas Steamship Co. were their rightful, if still-to-be-earned, due. But to give his boys a broader start on social and economic life than his generation had been able to enjoy, Henry Mallory planned for them to attend college before joining the firm. Clifford was to prep at Lawrenceville School, with an eye toward Cornell and the study of marine architecture; for Philip it was to be the Hill School, followed by Yale.

Clifford entered the famous school immortalized in the stories of Owen Johnson in 1896—the Lawrenceville of the Tennessee Shad, the Varmint, and the Prodigious Hickey. But permissive as Johnson portrayed it, Lawrenceville's discipline was rigid enough to trip up the young Mallory. For an unauthorized jaunt to a Princeton football game in the fall of 1900, Clifford was suspended. The offense was trivial and the punishment severe, but Henry Mallory took the matter hard. He put a choice squarely to his son: either a monastic study program to re-enter school, or a tough clerkship at the bottom of the firm.[1]

Already nineteen—seven years older than the age at which his great-grandfather had become an apprentice sailmaker, four years older than the age at which his grandfather had sailed before the mast, and a year older than the age at which his father had entered C. H. Mallory & Co.—Clifford chose the firm, and that was that. In October 1900, just as he had been apprenticed to Captain Spicer in 1867, Henry Mallory placed his elder son as apprentice clerk to the doubly efficient H. H. Raymond. Clifford took to his work with a vengeance, thoroughly immersing himself in the business and more than fulfilling Raymond's demands and his father's hopes. On his twenty-first birthday, in 1902, Henry rewarded him with a block of shares in the New York & Texas Steamship Co., but, characteristically, reminded him of the obligations which went with equity in the firm:

New York, May 26th, 1902

My dear Son Clifford,

On this your 21st birthday my thoughts go back to the past filled with pleasant memories of your childhood days, coupled with the devotion of your Mother to you.

Today you are a full-fledged man surrounded by a large family circle, every member of which is personally interested in your future, and with willing hands will do all that they can to help you to a successful life.

Charles Mallory	your great Grandfather was born in	1796
Charles Henry Mallory "	" " " "	1818
Henry R. Mallory "	Father " " "	1848
You were born in "		1881

You are the first one of the 4th generation to be identified with "the business" and much is expected of you. Your grandfather established the Mallory Line, and his sons have done what they could with the ability they possessed to perpetuate it, and all are anxious for you to assume the burdens and responsibilities that are ready to be shifted to your shoulders. We are ready to help you, and you must be ready yourself to the cares.

Did you ever know of a young man at 21 with brighter prospects and better backing?

Today you start out on a trail which has been blazed and trodden for 3 generations, covering a period of 106 years and we ask you to keep in it to the end, so that you may be able to say to your son on his 21st birthday: "4 generations have preceded you over a well defined road, and it will be safe for you to follow in their footsteps as I have followed the 3 generations which have preceded me."

Your predecessors have helped to make a fairly good road for you, but they cannot make you walk in it.

It remains with you to select the road over which you will travel, and I pray that God may direct you to the right one, and help you in all things which work for good.

My father was 30 years older than I, while I am 32 years older than you, and based upon experience of these two lives, let me say to you in all earnestness that—

Honesty and straightforward dealings are essential to a permanently successful business career. No business can long stand on any other foundation.

Every one of the "old time merchants" possessing these qualities has left behind him an honored name.

Economical management in business is as necessary, especially in these days of combinations and fierce competition. Any business extravagantly managed will surely fail. Some one must economize and he that does is sure to profit by it.

"Temperate in all things" means extravagant in nothing, but to be cool, calm, seeing in everything, the observance of which will surely work to one's good in morals, health and business.

The person adopting these principles early in life will be the best

fitted to withstand the temptations and trials which come into every
one's life, private as well as business.

Honesty you must possess, Economy you should strive for, otherwise those having these qualities will beat you in the long run.

From this date you are a stockholder in the Mallory Line, and can
vote at its annual meetings. How long shall it be before you become a
director, and an Officer of the Co.?

Your affectionate

Father[2]

No clearer prescription of what was expected of a Mallory
could have been written. And no clearer evidence of Henry
Mallory's continued preoccupation with his son's preparation
exists than his memorandum to himself entitled "About Clifford, May 28, 1903:"

> He should be given another position for now [as there is now] no
> definite work assigned him, & associates not inclined to teach him,
> and no one with authority to require of him compliance with any
> rules or regulations. Many calls now from outsiders, etc.
>
> Placed under Mr. [H. H.] Raymond, he would have specific position
> & work to perform, and have some one who would be interested
> in his future. Mr. R. would be his instructor, and should hold him
> strictly to his work.
>
> Discuss with Mr. R. what duties, etc., then discuss with C. what he
> would have to do under Mr. R.
>
> Time is advancing rapidly, & we must train some one to fill
> important positions. Mr. R. is an excellent man, and C.'s training
> under him would be the very best he could have. Economy in
> business & personal affairs.
>
> Who are we training to take charge of financial affairs?
>
> Must not let business pass out of family.[3]

For the first half-dozen years of the twentieth century,
Clifford and Philip dutifully played the roles cast for them.
Though too junior, still, for partnership in C. H. Mallory & Co.
or executive office in the New York & Texas Steamship Co.,
Clifford became Superintendent Raymond's right-hand man and
trouble shooter. Philip, in the meantime, finished Hill in 1904,
entered Yale, and spent his summers in the offices of the firm.

Then came the sale of the business to Morse in 1906. Suddenly, there was no family partnership, no family corporation. Suddenly, Henry Mallory and his brothers had retired. By all accounts, Clifford and Philip were as surprised as everyone else at their father's decision. But in his own way, Henry was convinced that the sale bettered his sons' prospects: Clifford became secretary and assistant general manager of the new Mallory Steamship Co., and a place was open for Philip, pending his graduation from college. Both boys were assured a good salary, challenging work, meaningful authority and responsibilities, financial security, and bright prospects to succeed to the top of the American maritime world—or so their father believed.

With all due respect to Henry Mallory's genuine love for his sons, he clearly misunderstood their talents and desires. Where he saw Consolidated Steamship Lines and, later, AGWI as mature organizational solutions to the competitive and growth needs of their constituent companies, his sons saw rather ponderous, conservative, and bureaucratic creatures capable of the suppression and stultification of youthful ideas. To their father, life at the top could be "fascinating." At the lower managerial levels, however, things could be pretty routine. Most important, however, the fourth generation had lost a crucial incentive. No Mallory had ever shirked a challenge, and Clifford and Philip were as industrious and purposeful as the best. But no Mallory before them had ever worked for any but a family firm, except by his own choice. No matter how their father rationalized it, he and his sons were still the salaried employees of a public corporation they did not own. They were no longer the sole proprietors of the Mallory Line. For the boys, the difference proved unbearable.[4]

For Philip, the sale to Morse convinced him of his lack of interest in shipping. Upon his graduation, he declined employment in either Consolidated or, later, in AGWI. At his father's "earnest request," he did take two years of law at Columbia University and passed the New York bar examinations in 1910. Law proved as dull to him as shipping, and, again at his father's urging, he tried Wall Street. In 1912, he began as a trainee with Kidder, Peabody & Co., and he soon moved on to the bond department of Hayden, Stone & Co. By 1914, however, his interests had turned "along industrial lines," and he had become general manager and treasurer of the Commercial Research Co., a small, patent-protected manufacturer of platinum and copper-clad wire used in incandescent lamps. There, he met G. F. Yessler, a young industrial engineer whose talents complemented his own, and by April 10, 1916, the two had raised $40,725 and broken away to found P. R. Mallory & Co., Inc.

The financial angels of Philip Mallory's new enterprise, over and above his own assets, were his brother-in-law Frank C. Munson and his great-uncle, J. Barstow Smull. His father took a portion of the stock, too, but with something less than enthusiasm. "I remember well my father's reactions," Philip recalled in 1941. "He was ultraconservative, brought up in the old school, never took a chance, and always had money in the bank to pay for any commitment that he made. He thought I was crazy and frankly told me so, prophesying that I would lose every dollar in the venture—not only my own, but my friends' as well." P. R. Mallory & Co., of course, did not fail, but went on to play a leading role in the development of America's electrical and electronics industries. Its birth, however, was one key watershed between the third and fourth generations of Mallory enterprises.[5]

Clifford was less inclined than Philip to allow the sale of the New York & Texas Steamship Co. to alter his business way of life. With his six years of seniority and experience as Raymond's understudy, he moved into positions of authority and responsibility in the new Mallory Steamship Co. and worked diligently for the cause of both Consolidated Steamship Lines and AGWI. Nevertheless, he was restive. The least of his irritations was that, for eight years, his suggestions for improved organization and possible new business were tabled by his superiors; and, for those same eight years, while his duties increased, his title and his salary were frozen in keeping with his father's preferences for economy and the *status quo*.

At the core of Clifford Mallory's dissatisfaction, however, was that he was not a shipowner as his forebears had been. He had earned his place on the AGWI corporate ladder, and he respected the obligations and rewards of his position. But like his great-grandfather and his grandfather, and like his father at an earlier time, he wanted to work for himself with ships of his own. The coming of war to Europe in July 1914 unexpectedly gave him sufficient incentive and opportunity to try his hand.

The most dramatic and immediate effects of World War I on the American merchant marine occurred in the foreign trades. For almost a decade, the demand for tonnage in American foreign commerce had been fairly inelastic and the market shares of the various maritime powers steady. By the last prewar year (ending July 31, 1914), the bulk of the tonnage that carried America's foreign trade was British (58 per cent), German and Austrian (15 per cent), Norwegian (5 per cent), Italian (3 per cent), French and Dutch (2 per cent each). Only 8 per cent of the net tonnage engaged in American foreign commerce was American. Similarly, there had been no sudden shifts in the value of overseas trade for a half-dozen years. The outbreak of war, however, removed the German and Austrian merchant fleets from the high seas, and the elasticity of demand for American, British, and other-flag vessels increased accordingly. Furthermore, as the most productive neutral nation, the United States was fully expected to increase her share of world trade.

Actually, American exports increased 28 per cent by value during the first year of the war (ending July 31, 1915) over the previous year's total, while imports decreased 14 per cent. More relevant to the maritime history of the Mallorys, however, were the changes that took place in the composition of the fleet that carried these cargoes. In response to the abrupt upward shifts in demand, the number of merchant vessels engaged in American foreign commerce increased a net 23 per cent in one year. The American-flag share of total tonnage grew to 12 per cent, Norway's to 9 per cent, Italy's to 5 per cent, Holland's and France's to 4 per cent each, Denmark's to 3 per cent, Greece's, Japan's, Sweden's, and Spain's to 2 per cent each. Britain's share fell to 54 per cent, and Germany's and Austria's disappeared.

Mirroring these shifts in demand and supply, 45 per cent of the vessels engaged in American foreign trade during the year ending July 31, 1915, had *not* been so engaged in the preceding year. Of these 1,848 ships, 207 were American-flag vessels of which 8 were freshly launched, 14 were transfers from foreign registry, and 185 were transfers from the domestic coasting trades. Of the foreign-flag vessels, 161 were newly built and 1,480 had been diverted from other trades.

Even with the rapid increase in vessels, however, supply could not keep pace with demand. Part of the difficulty lay in the nature of the vessels themselves. While there was a net increase of 23 per cent in their number, their addition in terms of carrying capacity was only 12 per cent. Too many were too small. And despite even the 12 per cent increase in capacity, vessel-ton efficiency declined 14 per cent because of longer periods for loading and discharging in crowded ports, more sailers and slower steamers, longer voyages to avoid war zones, and time lost to boarding inspections by belligerents. In simple terms, more vessels carried fewer ship-tons of cargo on fewer voyages in 1914–1915 than in 1913–1914.[6] The result of the acute undercapacity of supply in relation to demand was an amazing seller's market.[7] Of course, operating costs also escalated. Officers and crews commanded bonuses for hazardous duty, the prices of fuel and supplies and the wages of longshoremen rose, and the costs of war-risk insurance steadily mounted. Even so, the Shipping Board concluded that "all these factors do not justify the progressive multiplication of charter rates, nor the hitherto inconceivable heights to which freight charges have advanced."[8]

Plainly and simply put, there were now profits available to owners and operators of American-flag shipping that were higher than any they had tasted since the Civil War. As one veteran shipman recalled in 1919:

> The man who bought a ship at five times her ante-bellum value, and paid for her in the first voyage or two, became so common in 1915 and 1916 as hardly to cause remark. The schooner that paid for herself in prepaid freight before she lifted her anchor was really quite common. The wreck that was bought for a song, repaired for a symphony, and sold at grand opera price was so numerous as almost to be worthy a special place in the census. . . . Any man who could offer tonnage or room was besieged with applications night and day . . . any freight rate asked was eagerly paid.

But the same commentator also noted "that for the first two years of the war the big money was made by newcomers in the business, who took unthinkable risks and reaped undreamed of profits; while those experienced in the trade stood aside with bristling hair and horror-struck faces." [9] Given the situation, one must concur with his condemnation of both inertia and excess, be they by upstarts or veterans. But his observation confirms the working of a more basic truth. Regardless of how "obvious" ideas or things may seem, men usually perceive problems quite personally and in the light of their previous experience. And most important, they are likely to act upon their respective, personalized "images" of the circumstances and not upon any uniform, absolute "reality." So it was in shipping in the years 1914–1917. Startling new conditions were real enough, but they were not perceived in equal measure or kind by all men; obstacles to some seemed challenges to others. The differences of opinion in the Mallory family are cardinal cases in point.

Initially and predictably, given his seniority, Henry Mallory's analysis of the times prevailed in both family and firm. And for a variety of personal and corporate reasons, he chose not to exercise all the new market options available. Much of the new demand, he felt, was for transoceanic service, while AGWI's expertise and equipment had been carefully tailored to the rather specific needs of the coastal market. Vessels and crews had not even been interchanged among the various AGWI subsidiaries, much less sent off to Europe. More important to President Mallory, however, was the simple fact that AGWI's operating companies were line carriers. They were committed by contract and custom to well-defined trades; for them, regularly scheduled service on established routes was a way of life. All the subsidiaries had, of course, maintained a small competence in the charter markets, but only to add or subtract vessels on their lines and turn an occasional windfall profit. They had never sought and had never confronted such an elastic demand for tramps as materialized in 1914–1917.

As Henry Mallory assessed the rapidly changing market, he saw its new dynamics as a dilemma for AGWI: how to maintain basic liner services while not letting the unusual new opportunities for legitimate and high profits pass? Had he and his fellow AGWI executives been tramp operators, they could have easily redeployed their steamships and tied down the throttle. As line carriers, however, they felt an obligation to serve their historic constituency first. Consequently, each subsidiary company was empowered to make its own choices within certain corporate guidelines: no AGWI vessels were to be offered for charter until all basic line commitments had been satisfied; no tonnage was to be added by construction or purchase solely to capitalize on wartime demands, but only as part of previously approved, long-range line-improvement plans; personal ventures in charters by AGWI executives were authorized, if on the individual's own time and with his own funds; and in both corporate and personal affairs, American neutrality laws were to be scrupulously observed.

Curiously, the initial effect of the war on AGWI was one not anticipated by its officers: "The business of our coastwise lines was greatly affected in that the shipments of cotton, lumber and naval stores were materially curtailed, as were the shipments southbound, owing to the low price of those commodities." Also, the "continued demoralization of affairs in the Republic of Mexico caused a partial suspension of service to its ports, and almost a discontinuance of shipments." [10] The unexpected depression in the coastal market was not necessarily a drawback. To the extent that reduced coastal demand released ships for opportunistic deployment, it could have been an advantage. For the first three months of the war, however, AGWI's experience in the charter market was discouraging.

Things got off to a bad start in August, when *Denver* and *San Marcos* of the Mallory Line were time-chartered to the U.S. Army. The formal declaration of hostilities between Great Britain and Germany on August 4 had panicked the American Quartermaster General into laying on extra transport capacity. Of the seven coastal steamships he chartered, however, only three were actually put into military service. The other four, including *Denver* and *San Marcos,* lay idle for four months at minimal rates while their owners gnashed their teeth at lost opportunities in the booming civilian market. [11]

AGWI's first two ventures in that civilian market were profitable, but quite embarrassing. During the first week of August, the Porto Rico Line voyage-chartered two of its vessels to the Hamburg-Amerika Line at the exceptionally high rate of $15 per deadweight ton. Although Hamburg-Amerika had canceled its own-flag sailings on July 29, it could legitimately charter neutral tonnage and was doing so in abundance—allegedly to carry coal and provisions to its vessels stranded in West Indian and South American ports. Consequently, *Berwind* cleared Newport News for Buenos Aires on August 4, and *Lorenzo* sailed from New York for the same Argentine port the following day.

On September 10, however, *Lorenzo* was stopped and boarded by H.M.S. *Berwick* near Tobago, some 350 miles off the New York–Buenos Aires track. Among the papers of her German supercargo, the British found clear evidence that *Lorenzo's* cargo was intended for German naval cruisers and commerce raiders then operating in the South Atlantic. The neutral ship was to be intercepted by German vessels before reaching South America, escorted to a secret island rendezvous, and her cargo transferred—by force, if necessary. *Lorenzo* was seized by the British as a prize; her cargo was impounded as contraband and later condemned in Kingston, Jamaica. Ultimately, her German charterers in New York were tried and convicted for violation of American neutrality, but no AGWI personnel shared their fate. The captain, the crew, and the owners pleaded ignorance of the German plans and were acquitted.

The other Porto Rico Line vessel chartered to Hamburg-Amerika was also intercepted by a British man-of-war, but in much more compromising circumstances. On September 14, *Berwind* was discovered by H.M.S. *Carmania*, hove-to off the remote island of Trinidada in consort with two Hamburg-Amerika Line colliers and the German commerce raider *Cap Trafalgar*. In the ensuing action, the German raider was sunk, but the colliers escaped. *Berwind* reached Rio de Janeiro on September 18, discharged her cargo, and soon returned home. Her German charterers were tried and convicted in the United States courts, but, again, all the AGWI personnel involved

successfully pleaded innocent. The fact that *Berwind* had sailed
prior to the actual declaration of British-German hostilities
weighed heavily in their defense.[12]

AGWI was fully compensated by Hamburg-Amerika for the
loss of *Lorenzo* and for the inconveniences caused *Berwind,* but
the Porto Rico Line and its parent took a beating in the
American and British press. President Mallory bore the criticism
with dignity, but it made him more cautious than ever. He
permitted no AGWI vessels even to be offered, much less fixed,
in the charter market for a full month following *Lorenzo's*
capture. As the last quarter of 1914 began, however, market
conditions suddenly changed so radically as to end even the
elder Mallory's hesitation.

The causes of change were sharply rising wartime demands
which were outrunning the supply of neutral-flag shipping. How
long this seller's market would continue was uncertain, of
course, but all indications pointed toward its persistence for at
least a year. And, as transatlantic freight and charter rates
escalated steeply (see Table 10.1), even shipowners who had
traditionally specialized in the coastal market began to transfer
vessels to the booming transoceanic trades. The Morgan Line
moved first, but Henry Mallory's AGWI was not far behind.

Creole and *Antilles* of the Morgan Line grabbed the early
headlines and profits by dashing pell-mell across the Atlantic to
evacuate Americans stranded in Liverpool and Genoa. Besides
their drama, however, these voyages had transcending implica-
tions, as noted by *Shipping Illustrated* on October 3: "It was
never contemplated when they were designed that they should
undertake trips across the Atlantic; but the mere fact that they
underwent such a journey without requiring special alterations
speaks volumes for their seaworthiness and staunchness of construction." [13]

Henry Mallory and his associates in AGWI got the message.
They knew that the Morgan Line's vessels were similar to and
no better than their own, and they were already tempted by the
amazing rise in freight and charter rates. Now shown by their
prime competitor that coastal liners *could* make highly profitable transatlantic passages, they ended their self-imposed mora-
torium on nonline business. AGWI vessels once again began to

appear in the charter market: *Mantanzas* of the Ward Line cleared New York on October 7 to load beet sugar, chemicals, and dyestuffs in Rotterdam ($9,000 net for the round voyage); *Massapequa* of the Porto Rico Line cleared on November 3 with 4,000 tons of food for Belgian Relief under charter to the Rockefeller Foundation; between November 14 and December 19, *Mantanzas, Berwind,* and the newly launched *Neches* and *Medina* of the Mallory Line all cleared under round-voyage charters to Rotterdam.[14]

Some opportunistic AGWI managers found that the most lucrative segment of the transatlantic charter market was the carriage of cotton to Germany, and they centered their corporate and personal speculations in that trade. To release the tremendous stocks of cotton which had been accumulating in United States ports since the beginning of the war, American diplomatic pressure had been applied to Great Britain and, by agreement of October 29, cotton was declared *not* to be contraband. American-flag vessels were, thus, just as free to carry it to Germany as to British, Danish, Dutch, French, and Italian ports.

The immediate result of these British concessions was a boom in the transatlantic cotton trade to Liverpool and Bremen. Although the volume of trade to England was greater, the profitability of the German trade was superior. Cotton purchased in the South at depressed American prices could command prices in Bremen high enough to cover war-risk insurance premiums of 6 per cent on hulls and 5 per cent on cargoes and freight rates as much as 200 per cent above those to Liverpool—and still earn excellent profits for both shippers and carriers. For example, when *Pathfinder* of AGWI's Porto Rico Line cleared Galveston for Bremen on Christmas Day, 1914, she carried Texas' first German-bound cotton cargo since the outbreak of war (6,550 bales) and at the highest freight rate ever recorded to that time in Galveston: $3 per 100 pounds! In contrast, the New York–Liverpool rate on the same day was 75 cents (see Table 10.1), and the Galveston–Continental Europe rate one year earlier had been 35 cents.

AGWI vessels accounted for at least ten of the twenty-three known clearances from United States ports for Germany between December 1, 1914, and June 30, 1915 (43 per cent).[15]

Henry Mallory passively acquiesced in this trade with Germany, although he was personally an Anglophile. He was much more concerned with the traditional routes and long-run financial health of his company than with incurring high risks in quest of short-term profits. [16] Clifford Mallory was more aggressive and saw the transatlantic cotton boom as the answer to his long-suppressed "ambition to be a private ship owner . . . it looks as if present conditions [have] made this the opportunity of a lifetime." If America was to remain neutral, he reasoned, there was no reason why American-flag shipowners should not bene-fit. Let President Wilson ponder ideologies. He would stick to economics.

The younger Mallory had been carefully studying the freight and charter markets for some time and was well aware of the undersupply of ships. He also knew that shipbuilding costs, although lagging behind freight and charter rates for the moment, would soon escalate. He was convinced that the Euro-pean war could not end before 1916, at the earliest, and that now was the time "to get some of the cream" available to neutral-flag tonnage. He first "tried to purchase vessels already built," but was "unable to do so, except at exorbitant figures." He then began to investigate the possibility of contracting "for one or more ships." [17]

In January 1915, Clifford took his ideas to Theodore E. Ferris, the marine architect who had designed most of AGWI's vessels and was, most recently, the creator of the "Elwell ships"—seven all-steel, coal-burning, single-screw, 'tween-deck, three-island ocean freighters built in 1911–1912 by the Great Lakes Engineering Works of Detroit for J. W. Elwell of New York. Though destined for a place in the history of American marine architecture as prototypes for several thousand "Lakers," the Elwell ships were then piling up profits in the wartime charter market. Ferris told Mallory that he had learned "from pretty reliable sources that the Elwell ships' average charter per month has been in excess of $7,000 . . . and . . . these ships have paid 7% on the preferred stock, 5% on the common stock, 10% of bonds, 6% interest since they came out and up to the present time." This was, he asserted, the vessels' profitability under "normal conditions." Under the euphoric conditions of war, however, vessels of this type were chartering "anywhere from $20,000 to $40,000 per month."

At Clifford's request, and to his specifications, Ferris obtained a quotation from the Great Lakes Engineering Works for the construction of two hypothetical steamships similar to the Elwell ships: $285,000 each, deliverable in New York on October 1 and November 1, respectively; 75 per cent payment on delivery and 25 per cent within twelve months thereafter. While the Elwell ships were of "full canal dimensions," so as to pass through the Welland Canal locks between Lakes Erie and Ontario, Mallory wanted ships which could be lengthened by fifty feet (once they had passed out of the Great Lakes), yet shallow enough "to enter practically any port":

	Elwell	Mallory
Length, over all	261 feet	311 feet
Length, between perpendiculars	253 feet	300 feet
Beam, molded	43 feet, 6 inches	43 feet, 6 inches
Load draft	24 feet	22 feet
Deadweight at load draft	4,050 tons	5,000 tons

His specifications called for vessels which could be crewed by twenty-eight men, carry 4,500 to 4,600 tons of freight, and accommodate bulk shipments of cotton, sugar, coal, lumber, and ties as well as general cargoes of measurement goods.

Armed with Ferris' quotations and his own extensive estimates of costs and profits, Clifford set out in search of sufficient funds to become an American-flag shipowner in his own right. His plan was to capitalize each vessel at $300,000 (cost plus working capital) and sell 20 to 40 per cent of that amount as stock. The remaining 60 to 80 per cent would be debt-financed through bonds or borrowing. He did not base his "calculations on present high rates or the continuance of the War," but, even "under normal conditions," he predicted handsome profits.

Each ship, he estimated, could command a normal time-charter rate of at least $8,000 per month and yield a net $31,000 per year to equity after "interest, insurance, depreciation, pay of crew, subsistence, supplies, etc." Thus, if 20 per cent of each ship's capitalization was stock, that stock would earn 53 per cent per year. He hoped, however, that no dividends would be paid out until at least 50 per cent, and preferably all, of the ships' indebtedness had been liquidated. "Under war conditions," he was sure that this indebtedness could "be entirely paid off" in "from four to six months," plus "a very nice stock dividend." The "stockholders would then have a proposition that could make a living at any time," one that could "compete with anything afloat."

Clifford was personally willing to "put $20,000 to $30,000 into the venture" and planned to earn that stake from the profits of his "*Ogeechee* venture"—on his own account and risk, he chartered AGWI's steamship *Ogeechee,* loaded her with cotton in Savannah, and cleared her for Bremen on February 22. For the remainder of his proposed ships' cost, he approached his family and friends: "I can put it through with outsiders, but wish to confine it to as few as possible and people of the best standing." He urged them to join him swiftly so that the ships could be delivered "before the close of navigation on the Lakes" and in time "to get some of the cream."

Because his father was vacationing in Florida, Clifford first discussed his plans with his uncle Robert and his brother-in-law Frank C. Munson. He asked them to subscribe $10,000 to $20,000 each per vessel, to assist in placing the remaining equity and debt, and, above all, to help secure Henry Mallory's blessings and financial assistance. Clifford obviously wanted as much support in hand as possible before approaching the elder Mallory for consent and aid. He also wanted his family's pledges before taking his proposition to "outsiders."

Munson's response was ambiguous. He admitted that his brother-in-law's idea was, "under [the] circumstances, [a] very good proposition," but he offered no financial assistance. Robert Mallory pledged $10,000 per vessel, but *only* because he had "more confidence in the man than the proposition." He also exercised his uncle's prerogative to "talk Dutch" to his favorite nephew: "My judgement is that you should not invest one cent *of your money* in ships." Unlike Clifford, Robert Mallory's business philosophy was "count cost, rather than figure profit. . . . Don't deceive yourself by figuring as earning on stock, what is left after paying interest, but consider what the return is on actual investment. I believe you will agree with me that 15% is the minimum one should expect on ship property." Using Clifford's own cost figures, Robert went on to reestimate the venture's probable gross rate of return at not more than 10 to 11 per cent, and concluded:

> Frankly, but sincerely, I doubt the advisability of making the investment. If you were to give all your time to management, and had the experience in this class of steamshipping either Luckenback or Bull has, and could operate a number of ships, it might be different, but as none of these items are yours, I think the risk is out of proportion to any profit you have shown.

Despite his strong reservations, Uncle Robert encouraged Clifford to pursue his ideas further and to broach the proposition to Henry Mallory. Clifford carefully marshaled his arguments and did so, hoping that his father would invest $10,000 to $30,000 in each of the proposed vessels. But it was also clear that he considered his father's blessing of this, his first step toward business independence, most important of all. He met a sore disappointment. Henry assured his elder son that he gave the proposal "careful consideration . . . and tried to look at the subject from your view point." Nevertheless, his assessment of the proposal's prospects disagreed with Clifford's own views on almost every point.

The elder Mallory agreed that the wartime market could only be a short-term phenomenon but that it was the place to *sell* ships, not to build or buy them: "AGWI does not believe it policy to build what it does not have need of, and is willing to sell anything that it cannot operate at a profit—even more when charters are high." Indeed, he was at that moment selling off *Navahoe* and *Carib* of the Clyde Line and *Seguranca* and *Vigilancia* of the Ward Line. As to a minimally acceptable level of profits, he was more conservative than even his brother Robert: "We used to figure that a steamer should earn 20% per annum to cover interest, ins., depreciation, and profit"—and he saw no chance of such income in Clifford's proposal. He went on to display strong prejudices against American-flag ocean tramps in general ("they cannot compete with foreign flagged ships"), or with "lake steamers" in particular ("this type is not desirable"). The "Elwell boats," he contended, "did not make any money before the war." In fact, they "were offered to us cheap. They cannot make any money after the war closes, and like other tramps, are considered pirates."

Clifford could discount these opinions as merely the prejudices of a sixty-seven-year-old, battle-scarred line operator. He could excuse his father's natural propensity to take the long-run rather than the short-run view. But his father's incredulity that he could even *consider* ventures outside of AGWI must have cut him deeply: "Do you think you could own and manage one or more tramp steamers and hold your present position? . . . If you gave up your present position do you think you could earn as much [as] you do now? . . . You are now receiving from the Mallory Co. what is equal to 6% on $100,000 without the investment of one dollar." Why sacrifice security for uncertainty? "There is no business as hazardous as the steamship business except the manufacture of dynamite."

This said, however, Henry still could not refuse his elder son, and he finally agreed to "commit myself to as much as your Uncle Robert has, but must do it in his name or Philip's. I cannot be known in the matter." [18]

Bolstered by these firm, if reluctant and small, pledges of financial aid from the senior members of his family, Clifford next sought to raise the remainder of his needs from his close friends. At no time did he enter the formal capital market or seek the assistance of institutional intermediaries. Rather, he laid his proposition before a group of older, but fellow, yachtsmen with whom he had recently been associated in the underwriting of an America's Cup aspirant: George M. Pynchon, a banker and his mother's brother; George D. Barron, a retired mining engineer and executive who was Philip Mallory's father-in-law; William H. Childs, the president of American Coal Products Co., Barrett Manufacturing Co., Bon-Ami Co., and the U.S. Wood Preserving Co.; and John Monks, Jr., president of John Monks & Sons and the New York & Baltimore Transportation Co.

As the "Tri-City Syndicate" these men and Clifford had

commissioned George Owen to design *Defiance*, a 115-foot sloop delivered by the Bath Iron Works on July 22, 1914. She had cost $75,000, but proved hopelessly unable to defeat the Herreshoff-designed *Resolute* or the Lawley-designed *Vanitie* in the America's Cup Trials. Disappointed, the syndicate sold her for $7,500, and she was scrapped in January 1915. Nevertheless, the syndicate's members were friends of long standing, and it was to that friendship that Clifford Mallory now appealed.

Again, he was disappointed. Men who were willing to collect $75,000 for an America's Cup yacht proved unwilling to subscribe the $520,000 Clifford still needed to build and outfit his two tramp steamers. Monks's and Childs's reactions were typical. Monks considered Clifford's "assumptions and estimate . . . most modest and very reasonable and . . . would only go in on the basis that you were to have absolute control." But, he concluded, "Just now I think I had better stand close by my obligations and not take on any more." Childs was blunter: "It looks to me more of a gamble than I care to take." [19] Their misgivings sprang not from a lack of confidence in Clifford Mallory, but from their inexperience in tramp shipping and from the heating up of the sea war which, unfortunately, coincided with Clifford's search for funds. Between January 28 and February 24, three American-flag vessels bound for Bremen struck mines and sank—the first United States ships lost.

To make matters worse, Germany announced on February 2 that beginning February 18 she would "endeavour to destroy every enemy merchant-ship" found in "all the waters surrounding Great Britain and Ireland, including the entire English Channel." Britain retaliated with an Order in Council of March 11 that instructed the Royal Navy to intercept *all* merchant vessels sailing to or from German ports after March 1 and to escort them to British or Allied ports where their cargoes would be impounded. Goods of enemy origin or destination which were enemy property were to be seized; goods which were the property of neutrals were to be allowed to pass.

Mallory's *Ogeechee* was one of the first neutral vessels to run afoul of this new British policy. She cleared Bremen for New York on April 2, but on April 13 she was intercepted by the Royal Navy and her cargo seized at Stornoway (the vessel was then allowed to proceed home in ballast). Clifford immediately appealed the seizure to the Admiralty prize court, arguing that *Ogeechee* had made her return freight contracts in Bremen prior to March 1 and prior to the actual publication of the British Order in Council on March 15. Seizure of her cargo therefore constituted an ex post facto violation of international contract law. His position was sustained, but it was not until August 2 that Great Britain began to make restitution to him and the more than two hundred other cargo owners involved.[20]

This failure to reap immediate profits from his *Ogeechee* venture and further heating up of the war dashed Clifford Mallory's "ambition to be a private ship owner"—for the present. With insufficient aid from either his family or his friends, and given his reluctance to seek institutional assistance, Clifford was forced to surrender. He released his option on the two hulls and returned to the secure but routine anonymity of a salaried officer of AGWI.

By August, with unrestricted German submarine warfare rampant and cotton on the British Royal Navy's absolute contraband list, the unusual market conditions which had triggered his first bid for business freedom passed. For what became almost two years, he had to accept the galling truth that he could not command the necessary resources to go into shipping for himself on any acceptable scale. His continued servitude was all the more painful, as he saw inexperienced upstarts making killings in the charter market. And within his own familial generation, he was the least free: Cora's husband Frank had just succeeded his father as president of the Munson Steamship Line, and Clifford's younger brother was busily engaged in breaking with family tradition to establish a manufacturing enterprise bearing his own name.

But such disagreements and frustrations over business matters as arose between Henry Mallory and his sons never threatened familial cohesion. There was no such animosity or rancor within or between the third and fourth generations as had once driven Charles Henry Mallory and his brothers apart. Philip's plant was located in Port Chester, and he settled in his wife's home town of Rye—both close to his father's and his Uncle Charley's estates at Byram Shore. Clifford and Uncle Robert lived nearby in Greenwich, and fathers, sons, uncles, and brothers were almost constant luncheon and dinner companions, fellow yachtsmen, automobile excursionists, raconteurs, and vestrymen. The Munsons's home in Brooklyn was the stopover for any Mallory detained by business overnight in the city, but Henry's estate, "Bonnie Cliff," now served the function once performed by Grace Court. It was the family focal point. The others streamed in and out—for afternoons, evenings, week ends, summers; and Henry's greatest pleasure—his most "beautiful time"—was an outing or a dinner with all "the family complete including in-laws and grandchildren."

And it was to this life he chose to retire in May 1915. Henceforth, summers meant gardening and grandchildren at Bonnie Cliff, with a monthly two-day excursion to 11 Broadway to attend executive-committee and board meetings of AGWI and its subsidiaries and a stop at the Mercantile Safe Deposit Company to clip coupons; winters meant fishing, cruising, and sunning in Florida. He was a man content.[21]

For Clifford, however, his father's retirement increased his business frustrations. There was a reshuffling of titles within AGWI and its subsidiaries, but no real redistribution of responsibility, authority, power, or profits. Galen Stone moved into AGWI's presidency and left his previous slot as vice president vacant; his fellow banker, Alex Nicol, remained secretary-treasurer of AGWI and treasurer of all the subsidiaries. In each of the subsidiary companies, the chief executive's title was upgraded from vice president and general manager to president and general manager, but there were no personnel changes: Raymond retained control of Clyde and Mallory; Smith kept his post in Ward; and Mooney kept his job in Porto Rico. Clifford Mallory's titles were also upgraded, but not his salary or scope: he became vice president and a director of the Clyde Line; vice president, secretary, and a director of the Mallory Line. He did not become an officer or a director of AGWI or of any other of its subsidiaries; nor did he become a member of the executive committee of either parent or subsidiaries.

The paradox was ironic, indeed. The day before his father's retirement, Clifford had turned thirty-four. On January 3, 1911, he had married Rebecca Sealy, daughter of Texas' richest family, and was already once a father. In his own right, he was financially and socially secure. His father was helping him build a beautiful home in Greenwich; he was an expert competitive yachtsman, belonged to the best clubs, and moved in the highest of society. But professionally, he still worked for someone else. And, in the last eight years on the job, little had changed except the titles on his letterhead.

Nothing changed during 1916 or 1917. In fact, when Clifford made a major effort to broaden his scope *within* AGWI, he was denied. On March 10, 1916, when AGWI formed the International Shipping Corporation of Maine, its purpose was to assume ownership of some of the parent's vessels then on time charter in overseas markets. Clifford Mallory, however, saw the new subsidiary as a chance to reiterate his suggestions for improved coordination of tramp and charter activities and to press his pleas for a larger role in AGWI's executive constellation. On February 7, 1917, he took the plunge and addressed a letter containing his plans to his father—with copies to Stone and Nicol, but not to "Mr. Raymond and the other presidents [who] are, of course, not in sympathy with this matter." He ticked off, once again, his suggestions concerning centralization of insurance, engineering, accounting, legal, purchasing, and treasury, but concentrated on his proposals to revamp AGWI's chartering and foreign operations:

> The AGWI has built and is building a large number of vessels for seasonable traffic, such as sugar. They must be kept busy during the out of season period to make them profitable. Some of the lines reduce their service during the summer season, and the vessels thus released, make up quite a formidable fleet. It would be my idea to appoint a traffic director, or a director of foreign traffic, who should be a very able steamship man, and broad enough to understand the coastwise situation as well as the foreign trade. He would take over the operation of the International Shipping Corporation, as well as handle his other duties, and any vessels would be turned over to him by the lines whenever available, and he would use them to the best possible advantage. It would be his duty to familiarize himself with the situation of each line by reports or otherwise, and if one line was short of tonnage, he would fill it with any available vessel, and probably would also settle upon the compensation for the service. If vessels could not be used in the allied services, he would charter or

engage freights for foreign trade. By the use of the word foreign, I mean foreign to our regular lines and not necessarily the European or South American trade.

Clifford obviously cast himself in the new office he proposed, and he was certainly well qualified. He also took the longer view for both himself and AGWI:

> As business becomes more normal, a foreign department could undoubtedly open up services to territory as yet uncovered by the AGWI. As a matter of fact, this should be done before the situation becomes normal, so that we might be established before serious competition starts in. Routes are open to us where the heavy movement exists during our dull period, so that there would be no conflict, and our fleet would be kept busy during the entire year.

The crux of the matter, however, was "that the above suggestions mean a material curtailment of the subsidiary lines' general managers' duties." Clifford was taking risks in addressing his suggestions directly to the members of AGWI's executive committee and in recommending the reduction of his superiors' authority. But they were calculated risks, for Henry Mallory, Stone, and Nicol had been discussing possible streamlining of AGWI for some time. And, at its regular monthly meeting of April 6, the AGWI board agreed "that a consolidation or merger of the subsidiary companies into this company is not only most desirable but under all the conditions most necessary." Determination of "the form that such consolidation or merger shall take" was deferred until "after careful consideration of all the various questions involved and under advice of counsel," but Clifford could feel optimistic that his ideas and preferences would be carefully weighed.[22]

As it turned out, Clifford's proposals were never formally considered by the AGWI board. For suddenly, the United States was at war. The declaration came the very day of the AGWI meeting of April 6. Overnight, the company's vessels no longer flew neutral flags; they were now part of the merchant fleet of a belligerent nation; and the immediate needs of the government supplanted corporate or personal plans in the scale of priorities. From the Wilson administration's point of view, the highest priority was to land an American military force on European soil as soon as possible. But the sea-lift capability of the army and navy was pathetic. Captain (later Vice Admiral) Albert Gleaves, who was designated Commander of Convoy Operations in the Atlantic, later recalled the situation he faced in April and May 1917:

> The Navy then had three vessels available for troop transport work, the *Hancock,* the *Henderson,* and the recently seized German converted steamer *Prinz Eitel Friedrich,* renamed the *De Kalb.* The Army had few regular transports, but none were suitable and ready for trans-Atlantic convoy operations. It was necessary to commandeer such ocean-going vessels as could be found and alter them as quickly as possible for carrying troops.[23]

To augment its meager transport force, the government turned to the maritime industry, and between April 17 and 24 five AGWI vessels became the first American-flag vessels impressed for service as military troopships: *Henry R. Mallory* and *San Jacinto* of the Mallory Line, *Lenape* of the Clyde Line, and *Saratoga* and *Havana* of the Ward Line. By May, nine more merchant vessels had joined the AGWI liners under government control: *Antilles, Momus,* and *El Occidente* of the Morgan Line; *Montanan* and *Dakotan* of the American & Hawaiian Steamship Co.; *Tenadores* and *Pastores* of the United Fruit Co.; *Edward Luckenbach* of the Luckenbach Steamship Co.; and *Finland* of the International Mercantile Marine Co. These fourteen merchantmen, two of the navy's three transports, and nineteen men-of-war cleared New York for France on June 14 carrying General John J. Pershing and the vanguard of his American Expeditionary Force. Only sixty-six days had elapsed since the American declaration of war!

The speed and efficiency with which this first American troop convoy was mobilized sprang from tireless and harmonious efforts by the army, navy, and civilian personnel involved. But much of the burden was shouldered by a committee of three industry representatives: Philip A. S. Franklin, then vice president of the International Mercantile Marine Co.; William J. Love, assistant American manager for Furness, Withey & Co.; and Clifford D. Mallory, Jr., vice president of AGWI's Clyde and

Henry R. Mallory, flagship of AGWI's Clyde-Mallory Lines. Built in 1916, she carried more troops to and from Europe during World Wars I and II than any other single vessel. Affectionately known as "Hell-Rolling Mallory" to those who sailed on her. Courtesy Mariners Museum.

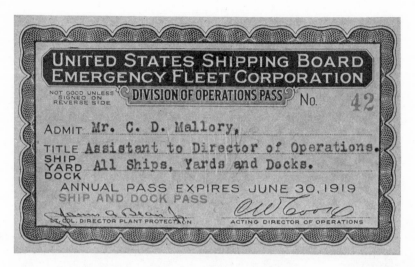

Clifford D. Mallory's government pass, 1918 (obverse). Courtesy Mystic Seaport.

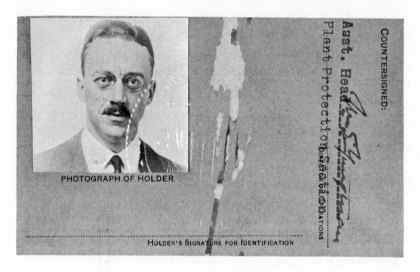

Clifford D. Mallory's government pass, 1918 (reverse). Courtesy Mystic Seaport.

Mallory lines. These men were jointly chosen by their companies and the military as qualified and able to superintend the myriad details involved in converting merchantmen into troopships: gun mounts, lookout stations, and camouflage had to be installed; communications, berthing, messing, and safety facilities had to be enlarged; damage control and abandon-ship bills had to be revised and civilian crews drilled in such unfamiliar evolutions as battle stations and convoy stationkeeping; 500 black stevedores had to be recruited to load the vessels and accompany them to France; soldiers unfamiliar with shipboard accommodations and routine had to be embarked; fuel and water had to be topped off prior to rendezvous and departure. The list seemed endless, but it was completed on schedule.

Franklin, Love, and Mallory brought their extensive shipping experience and managerial talents to bear in the national interest and for the best interests of their companies; but, for Clifford, the bustle of mobilization meant much more: it brought unexpected but exciting demands for his expertise. The dull routine of his life in AGWI was broken as he scurried between the Atlantic ports of embarkation and Washington. More important still, he was moving in higher and broader business and government circles than ever before in his career, and his obvious ability did not go unnoticed. During the first week in September, he was "offered a very important position by the Navy Department." And while he was considering this invitation, he received another. Edward F. Carry, who on September 20 was appointed Director of Operations of the United States Shipping Board, asked Clifford to become his right-hand man.[23]

Carry's acute need for Mallory's knowledge and skills was rooted in his own inexperience in shipping (he was a railroad equipment manufacturer) and in the mission of the organization he had been selected to direct. The United States Shipping Board and the United States Shipping Board Emergency Fleet Corporation had been authorized by the Federal Shipping Act of September 7, 1916, to use federal power and funds to improve the quantity and quality of the American-flag merchant marine and to regulate purely water-borne common carriers in coastal, intercoastal, and transoceanic commerce. The

Shipping Board was a wholly public agency which was to investigate the costs of building and operating vessels, to fix rates and supervise competition, and to endorse carrier practices and recommend legislation that would better the American share of world commerce. The Emergency Fleet Corporation was a $50,000,000 public-private agency whose role was to be the "purchase, construction, equipment, lease, charter, maintenance, and operation of merchant vessels in the commerce of the United States." Its power to build ships was to be "limited only by the measure of the appropriations" made for their construction, but its authority to operate them was to be exercised only if "it should prove impossible to procure private enterprise to purchase or charter them under proper terms and conditions."

The American entrance into World War I, however, changed these peacetime definitions of both the board's and the corporation's goals. By the third quarter of 1917, the board had been instructed "to give chief attention to the requisition, construction, purchase, and charter of [such merchant vessels as are required by the national interest] and to their effective operation for war purposes." Functionally, these tasks were to encompass the general regulation of rates, prices, wages, competition, and working conditions in American-flag shipping and shipbuilding; the acquisition of vessels as required by the national interest; and the operation of such vessels as were acquired.[24]

It was to its Division of Operations that the Shipping Board delegated the crucial and complex tasks of matching the somewhat inelastic supply of ships with the highly elastic demand for their services. The division, when created on September 29, 1917, was intended as the managerial bridge between an effective vessel acquisition program and an efficiently operating merchant fleet. It was to take charge of all vessels already or to be built, seized, commandeered, requisitioned, purchased, or chartered by the Shipping Board and see to it that their builders, owners, and/or operators were justly compensated; it was to assign all vessels acquired by the Shipping Board among the numerous governmental agencies and private parties in need of tonnage; it was to allocate tonnage owned or controlled by the

Shipping Board (once assigned) among cargoes and trade routes as required by the shifting priorities of war; and it was to lay on and lay off non-Shipping Board vessels (via voyage or time charters for same) as required to improve short-run irregularities in supply and/or demand. This was the division headed by Edward F. Carry, and it was this division which Carry invited Clifford D. Mallory, Jr., to join.

Mallory received Carry's offer while bedridden with the chronic stomach ailment that plagued his adult life. But he had no hesitancy in accepting: "I decided that the Shipping Board's operations required commercial shipping knowledge to a far greater extent than did the Navy's operations of transports, direction of which the Navy Department had asked [me] . . . to assume." By November 16, 1917, he had resigned his offices and sold his holdings in the Clyde and Mallory companies and begun work at 1519 F Street in Washington, D.C., as Assistant to the Director of Operations of the United States Shipping Board at an annual salary of $4,800.[25]

Mallory reported directly to Carry and, since the latter had no shipping experience whatsoever, and because (as a colleague noted admiringly in 1918) "Mr. Mallory [always] . . . insisted upon overloading himself," Clifford's responsibilities came to be defined as "general supervision over all operating matters." This assignment ranged from informing the messenger boys of Mr. Carry's displeasure at their scuffling in the halls, through "office organization and . . . office details, such as the employment of clerks, supervision of filing systems, requisitions for supplies, etc.," to the handling of complex problems concerning the acquisition, assignment, and allocation of vessels and the constant and delicate liaison involved in dealing with other governmental agencies. In several key areas, he made truly major contributions to the solution of operational and policy problems.[26]

The first task managed by Mallory was the fixing of just compensation for the builders and owners of two groups of American-flag vessels that had been summarily acquired by the Shipping Board prior to his employment. On August 3, Chairman Edward N. Hurley had "commandeered" title and use of all hulls and materials then in American shipyards and intended

253

for use in constructing steel vessels of 2,500 or more dead-weight tons (431 vessels). And, on October 12, he had "requisitioned" the services of all steel, power-driven, American-flag, cargo vessels of 2,500 or more deadweight tons and all American-flag passenger vessels of 2,500 or more gross register tons (657 vessels). Mallory, F. C. Lockhart, and W. S. Houston, representing the Division of Operations, gradually worked out general compensatory principles and oversaw their implementation in each of the 1,088 cases. Titles to all vessels building for foreign account when commandeered on August 3 were retained by the Shipping Board subject to postwar claims by their builders and former owners. Titles to all vessels building for American account when commandeered on August 3, and use of the American-flag vessels requisitioned on October 12, accrued to the Shipping Board for the duration of the war plus six months. In most cases, the owners of these vessels agreed to operate them for the board, with expenses shared, and at rates calculated as functions of time, capacity, and speed—the so-called "requisition rates." [27]

But compensation problems concerning the 1,088 "commandeered" and "requisitioned" ships paled in proportion to the jobs of "assigning" and "operating" them and the 1,526 other vessels which came to be owned or controlled by the Shipping Board (see Table 10.2). These tasks were the prime responsibility of Carry, Mallory, and their colleagues in the Division of Operations. In effect, the entire deep-sea American-flag merchant marine was being managed by a single government agency. And in the nerve center of that agency, Clifford Mallory was the number two man.

Mallory was especially involved in the development of a rationale for priorities of assignment. As policy in this area was articulated, it gave preference to the operation of Shipping Board vessels by private parties rather than to their operation by government agencies per se. And among private operators, first assignment priority was given "to the steamship owners from whom steamers had been requisitioned for use by the Army and Navy, in such proportion as they had lost tonnage, and ... until each company had under its direction vessels controlled by the Shipping Board to a sufficient amount to replace all of the tonnage which they had lost." Next priority was given to "organizations which had been time charterers and had operated time chartered vessels and those who had acted as leading agents for owners" before the war; next to those who had experience as "owners of sailing vessels, tug boats, and barges." Much of this scheme was Mallory's idea, and it effectively implemented the Shipping Board's general wish to utilize "to the fullest extent the private shipping organizations that were available."

Mallory also worked out much of the policy concerning compensation and supervision of these private operators of Shipping Board tonnage. Tasks were divided functionally between "managing agents" and "operating agents." The former, under contracts with the Shipping Board, were made responsible for "the husbanding of the steamers which means the appointing and employment of crews, purchase of supplies and fuel, attention to repairs, etc."; the latter, also under contract, performed "the loading agents' duties which involve the arranging for cargoes, collection of freights, securing of docks, and any other matters involved in getting and handling freight." Thus for each vessel under Shipping Board control, "two contracts were required . . . as one company might husband the ship and yet not be proficient in the cargo arrangements, and therefore another company would be employed for that purpose. . . . Separate commissions were paid for the management and operation of the steamers. In some cases both were paid to the same agent and in other cases two agents were involved."

The continual and difficult process of allocating the vessels under the control of the Shipping Board among competing cargoes and trade routes was a third area in which Mallory worked long, hard, and productively. Prior to February 2, 1918, these decisions were usually made in the Division of Operations with Clifford a regular participant. After that date, however, the Shipping Board established a blue-ribbon Shipping Control Committee composed of Philip A. S. Franklin (now president of the International Mercantile Marine Co.), H. H. Raymond (still president of the Clyde and Mallory companies of AGWI), and Sir Connop Guthrie (representing the British Ministry of Shipping) to take over these tasks.

Because he had worked so harmoniously with Franklin and W. J. Love (who was now director of the Shipping Control Committee's Division of Allocation and Trades) in fitting out the AEF convoy, and because Raymond was his friend and former tutor and boss, Mallory was chosen to maintain liaison between the New York–based Shipping Control Committee and the Washington-based Division of Operations. In that role, he became one of the government's prime expediters of top-priority cargoes: nitrate from Chile; manganese ore from Brazil and Cuba; chrome ore from New Caledonia; wool from Australia and South America; mahogany from Central America and West Africa; hemp from the Philippines; sugar from Cuba, the Philippines, and Hawaii; coal from Chesapeake Bay ports; lumber and piling from Gulf and South Atlantic ports; and wheat and flour from Atlantic, Gulf, and Pacific ports. Clifford's main assignment was making sure that ships were where they were needed, when they were needed, and in proper capacities. And to supplement Shipping Board tonnage, he and his associates found it necessary to charter vessels from France, Norway, Sweden, Denmark, Holland, Japan, Peru, Uruguay, and Brazil.

Mallory also filled other key interagency roles. He was the Division of Operations's representative in dealing with the Emergency Fleet Corporation's Division of Construction and the Shipping Board's Board of Survey and Consulting Engineers. He was a member of the Emergency Fleet Corporation's Dry-Dock and Repair-Plant Committee and Ship Protection Committee—the latter being responsible for hearing and evaluating the thousand and one proposals made by both professionals and amateurs "relative to the protection of merchant vessels from submarine attack." And he served as liaison man among the Division of Operations, the Shipping Control Committee, and the New York–based Ship Chartering Committee which was established "to exercise a salutary degree of control" over neutral shipping in American foreign trade and over American-flag vessels "not under the direct control of the Shipping Board." The committee had veto power over all charter parties to or from United States ports so as "to induce neutral tonnage to assume its fair share of trans-Atlantic trade" and "to effect a material reduction in the high charter rates prevailing." Mallory was a valued consultant concerning most of the 7,139 charters considered by the committee prior to September 30, 1918.

Thus, Clifford served his country well in many ways during World War I and drew double satisfaction from doing what he did best while serving the national interest. Just as his grandfather had found the 1860's, Clifford found 1917–1918 to be "exciting times," when "a man has ten years experience in one." He thrived on being such a key decision-maker in the operation of 2,614 vessels spread all over the globe (see Table 10.2), and he constantly pressed himself to broaden and deepen his already considerable managerial talents.

But his job also took its toll. The tension and strain often aggravated his stomach condition, and his duties kept him too often away from New York, Connecticut, family, and friends. Director Carry's resignation in August 1918, and his replacement by John H. Rosseter, changed Mallory's role considerably, too. At the time of his appointment, Rosseter was a vice president of both W. R. Grace & Co. and the Pacific Mail Steamship Co. and, as a lifelong shipping man, did not have to depend on Mallory's advice as much as Carry had. Also, as the Armistice was signed, Mallory's commitment to government service at a token salary waned.

On December 5, 1918, he made his choice and tendered his resignation as Assistant to the Director of Operations, effective December 31. With regret, but with their unanimous "appreciation of the services which you have so loyally, unselfishly, and capably rendered the Government during the war emergency," the members of the Shipping Board accepted his resignation on December 12. A formal resolution of thanks was put into the board's minutes, but Chairman Hurley in a personal note said it best: "You did a splendid piece of work." [28]

New Year's Day 1919 thus found Clifford Mallory at another turning point in his personal and professional lives. His old jobs with the Clyde and Mallory lines were his for the asking, and his father, Stone, Nicol, and Raymond were urging him to take up what he had put aside fourteen months before.

Indeed, they talked of bettering his position in the AGWI hierarchy because of his Shipping Board experience and contacts. At the same time, however, he could reflect on how often he had been his own man during the war and how close he had come to his oft-expressed hope of becoming an independent shipowner and operator.

But he chose neither to plunge back into the familiar world of the Clyde-Mallory lines nor to dash off alone. Instead, because of a spell of poor health and because he wished to take stock of his goals, resources, and prospects, he decided to pause during the first quarter of 1919. Sentimentally, he moved into C. H. Mallory & Co.'s old office at 25 Broad Street, which was still tended by his father's secretary as a sort of family storeroom. His first letter from his new address, handwritten to his wife Rebecca, caught the essence of the Mallory tradition and Clifford's mood:

25 Broad St.

Jan. 7th 1919

Dearest Beck.

Here I am in a dirty old office surrounded with pictures and relics of C. H. Mallory & Co.

Sneider is faithful as the day is long but dirty. I don't think the room has been dusted since they moved in years ago.

I am writing at Uncle Charley's desk with a ship model over it, an old barometer that belonged to my grandfather at the left, behind me a series of large photographs of Uncle Charley landing a tarpon on a beach in Florida. I am delighted with the atmosphere and have a feeling that big things are going to develop to my advantage. . . .[29]

Chapter 11

C. D. MALLORY & CO., INC., AGENTS FOR

THE U.S. SHIPPING BOARD,

1919–1925

"We have incorporated the above Company for the purpose of operating vessels and have placed our names ... requesting assignments of Shipping Board vessels for management and operating. It is also our purpose to purchase ships from the Shipping Board, providing we can arrive at a mutually satisfactory arrangement as to contracts."
—Clifford D. Mallory to Barton B. Payne, September 2, 1919

CLIFFORD MALLORY began his self-imposed self-appraisal by considering two proposals from former employers. The first came from his old business tutor H. H. Raymond, who was still president and general manager of AGWI's Clyde and Mallory companies, but it offered no more than a return to Clifford's *status quo ante bellum:* "I have hesitated about perfecting our organization," Raymond wrote, "for the reason that there is, as you know, a place for you in it as Vice President, provided you care to return." Mallory politely declined because, unknown to Raymond, he had received a more interesting offer from AGWI's president and its treasurer, Galen L. Stone and Alexander R. Nicol. They invited Clifford to submit a confidential critique of AGWI's history and present prospects and to include his suggestions for improvement. He did so on January 30, 1919, and they responded by offering him the joint treasurership of AGWI and its numerous subsidiaries.

Stone was planning to move up to the chairmanship of AGWI and to have Nicol succeed him as president. They wanted to keep the Mallory name associated with the companies Henry R. Mallory had helped them create, and they saw Clifford as the

259

logical answer to their needs. He would be an experienced successor to Nicol, and one who would be acceptable to both the "banker" and the "steamship" factions that had polarized in AGWI since the elder Mallory's retirement.

Thus, Stone's and Nicol's offer of the third-ranking post in the second-largest American-flag shipping company was both flattering and genuine. But its substance reflects how poorly they understood Clifford Mallory's talents and ideas. In their bankers' eyes, the health of AGWI's capital structure and flow of funds were supremely important, and the post of intercorporate treasurer almost sacrosanct. Henry R. Mallory agreed. But to offer that post to Clifford entirely missed the point of his critique of AGWI and of his own career plans. In the six-page memorandum that he submitted in answer to Stone's and Nicol's queries, he had taken AGWI's financial health as given and of little current interest to him. Instead, he had made pointed suggestions for "a decided change in policy and organization" *in relation to operations.*

Clifford urged the abandonment of the division of labor that kept AGWI a holding company and cast its subsidiaries in the roles of quarrelsome children jealously competing for their parent's financial favor. He criticized the inability of AGWI's executive committee to make "impartial" decisions amongst the operating alternatives open to the subsidiaries, and he laid the blame for AGWI's ponderous and old-fashioned ways of doing business on the lack of profit-sharing opportunities at any but the top level of management. Shipping was too competitive a business to motivate one's employees by salary alone, he argued.

Mallory proposed a vertical consolidation of AGWI and its subsidiaries into a single "AGWI operating company." In his plan, the old structure and chain of command would be scrapped in favor of a new, leaner organization centralized in a president and two vice presidents. Each vice president would wield corporation-wide authority; one would be a staff officer in charge of administration; the other would be a line executive in charge of operations.

He implored Stone and Nicol to recognize that "investment in brains is undoubtedly the best expenditure of funds that can be recommended," arguing that "a successful working scheme of co-operative compensation or interest in the ventures of the corporation must be arrived at, . . . a scheme involving an assured income, with the prospect of materially increased profits to be derived through co-operative methods." Officers and employees must "also be given an opportunity to participate in either an insurance fund, or pension system, or both . . . [and] they should be given preferential consideration in the matter of the purchase of securities of the corporation."

As the discussions dragged on through the first quarter of 1919, Stone and Nicol constantly reassured Clifford that they knew "of no one who could as well or whom we would rather have fill this position." They cited past glories of the Mallory association with AGWI and frequently invoked the image of his father's long and faithful service to the company. But it became increasingly apparent to Clifford that Stone and Nicol wanted him on their terms and not on his. Just as his prewar ideas had been tabled by his corporate superiors, his postwar suggestions for energizing AGWI were discounted. Instead of being made the profit-sharing vice president in charge of operations which he proposed, he was merely invited to return as a salaried, staff administrator in an organization he believed to be moribund.[1]

Then, suddenly, in the midst of the negotiations, Clifford's most binding tie to AGWI and to the past was severed. On March 4, 1919, Henry Rogers Mallory died at Winter Park, Florida. The elder Mallory had been failing for almost two years, but his passing still came unexpectedly. Words were inadequate to express the family's sense of loss, but Galen L. Stone's thoughts echoed those who had known Clifford's father best: "As I look back upon my associations with Mr. Mallory I cannot help thinking that the title 'Christian gentleman' fits him completely."[2]

Clifford took his father's death hard, and this and a flare-up of his chronic stomach ailment induced him to absent himself from business affairs for almost two months. But as his mourning period abated and his health improved, his sense of family tradition grew. As never before, he became convinced that the future of the Mallory name in shipping lay in his hands. His brother Philip was engrossed in manufacturing, and his father's surviving brother Robert had long since retired. If Clifford's three-year-old son was to become the fifth successive generation of Mallorys in American-flag shipping, he was the only member of the fourth generation who could contribute toward that end. And just as his father's death lessened his sense of obligation to Henry Mallory's former associates, so did it increase Clifford's resolve to reestablish an independent Mallory shipping company in his own name. Thus, on June 4, he politely declined the offer of the AGWI treasurership. He pleaded poor health, which was true enough; but there was far more to it than that. The elder son of the fourth generation of Mallorys, at thirty-eight, was finally on his own.

But what to do and how to do it? What resources could he command and to what purposes? For the third quarter of 1919 the questions ever were how might he blend his experience with the prospects before him into an amalgam of personal and familial success; and, in the process, could he honor his family's traditions or would he find some or all of them untenable?

Clifford's executive abilities were considerable and demonstrated, and his personal financial resources were not meager. He had inherited securities and real estate from his grandfathers, his uncles, his father, and his wife's father and had made investments of his own. By 1919, he could command assets in his own name worth approximately $500,000.

Of greater importance, however, was his intimate and ready access to such powerful financiers as Galen Stone, who wrote him on Hayden, Stone & Co.'s letterhead, "I have the confidence to join you in almost anything which you may decide to be good enough for your own time and money." Mallory's normal, businessman's familiarity with public capital markets was, thus, augmented by friendships springing from his family's social and economic position. His brother-in-law George Sealy headed one of the South's largest banking and commission houses. His brother-in-law Frank C. Munson headed one of America's fastest-growing steamship companies. Men like Alexander Smith, president of Peabody, Houghteling & Co., Inc., and Malcolm G. Chace, president of Chace & Harriman, Inc., were yachting cronies.

He also had superior market information and personal

contacts in shipping gained through his experiences in AGWI and with the Shipping Board. If he didn't know the answer to a maritime question, he certainly knew the first name of the man who did—whether that man was in or out of the government. But to what end were these financial and practical resources to be put? It certainly never occurred to him to abandon either shipping or the American flag, but within these constraints his ideas gradually jelled. First came purpose; next came organization; and then came action.[3]

At every point in his planning, however, Mallory encountered the omnipotence and omnipresence (if not the omniscience) of the government agency he had just left. For between the Armistice of November 11, 1918, and the passage of the Merchant Marine Act of June 5, 1920, America's public policies toward merchant shipping were whatever the United States Shipping Board said they were. Mallory's old boss, Chairman Edward N. Hurley, and John Barton Payne, who succeeded Hurley in August 1919, had the difficult duty of applying the grandiose but vague provisions of the Shipping Act of 1916 to a situation that act never contemplated. An act passed to expand the small, prewar American-flag merchant marine was now the only statutory authority for demobilizing a massive postwar fleet. Beginning in December 1918, a few small or antiquated cargo vessels and tankers were reconveyed to their previous owners or sold foreign; and, after February 1919, most of the smaller requisitioned or chartered vessels were released from government service. Even so, on June 30, 1919, the Shipping Board still had 961 merchant ships afloat and 1,300 more under construction.

Hurley, Payne, and their associates on the board decided against either massive scrapping or indiscriminate sales of these vessels. Instead, they chose to keep them under government control and to spoon-feed American-flag shipping's two protected markets while mounting a major new trade offensive overseas. Decisions to release tonnage to the coastal market were to be made in cognizance of the increasing competition from railroads and motor carriers. Decisions to allocate tonnage to the intercoastal market were to be geared to rising demands generated by the recent opening of the Panama Canal. The bulk of Shipping Board tonnage, however, was reserved for the transoceanic market and seen as the key by which the United States would unlock a larger share of world trade. Chairman Hurley estimated the postwar lack of cargo space at between 14,000,000 and 16,000,000 gross tons and cited ocean freight rates 150 per cent higher than before the war. And under his and his successor's urgings, the Shipping Board decided to continue and expand its war-born system of consigning government tonnage to private operators and managers. Its goal was betterment of what it considered the dismal situation of 1911–1915, when only 9.1 per cent of America's water-borne exports and 12.5 per cent of her water-borne imports had been carried on American-flag vessels.[4]

These directions in government policy were clear to Clifford Mallory by mid-1919, and they played some part in his decision not to return to AGWI. Indeed, the Shipping Board's commitment to operate its vessels on all trade routes considered essential to American economic development offered him three opportunities he had often sought but never before achieved. As an operator and/or manager of Shipping Board tonnage he could fully employ his skills in shipping on a large scale, but with almost a nominal capital investment; he could do so as a profit-sharing, independent businessman; and he could abandon his father's preoccupation with the coastal market and "go offshore" as his grandfather and great-grandfather had so successfully done. If he managed well and if the government kept its word, he could gradually purchase those services and/or ships which seemed most profitable and become an owner as well as an operator of an American-flag (*and* Mallory-flag) fleet.

He sought out two particular kinds of fare from amidst the Shipping Board's vast smorgasbord of services and ships. Fully within his family's tradition, he hoped to secure the agency for one or more of the board's newly established lines; but contrary to what would have been his father's preferences, he eschewed combined passenger and freight services and the coastal and intercoastal markets in favor of all-freight, transoceanic lines. Second (and heresy of heresies), he was interested in the possibilities of employing some of the government's vessels as American-flag, oceanic, dry-cargo tramps. His affinity for tramps was a by-product of his line experience. "Foreign trade is dependent on the maintenance of established lines," he conceded, but "practically all trades have their seasons and therefore a minimum and maximum period of cargo offerings." It was precisely for this reason that successful shipping lines owned only a minimum fleet and counted on chartering tramps during the maximum season to handle the additional cargo. Thus, concluded Mallory, "a tramp owner always has the world's trade before him and can shift his operations to the better paying market." [5]

Of course, Clifford Mallory had no monopoly on such ideas. Indeed, during 1919 alone, several hundred new American shipping companies were formed. Their aggregate authorized capital amounted to $323,613,500—a sum equal to two-thirds of all the private capital invested in American-flag shipping for the preceding five years! And most of these new companies were seeking Shipping Board assistance in one form or another. Mallory's clear advantages over most of the field were his name, his reputation, and his experience, but they were useful only to the extent that they could be mobilized and multiplied through purposeful organization. By late summer, he was ready to take the plunge. On August 16, 1919, he replaced C. H. Mallory & Co.'s nameplate at 8–10 Bridge Street with one of his own: "C. D. Mallory & Co., Inc.—Steamship Operators, Managers, Agents." [6]

Omission of any reference to vessel ownership in the new firm's title was not accidental. It reflected Mallory's reasoned decision to defer that kind of commitment to a hopefully more profitable future date. It also reflected his intense desire for his company to be everything AGWI was not. He wanted to create a lean, knowledgeable, flexible organization finely tuned to present and future opportunities; not one mired in bureaucracy or overly intoxicated by its power and past. His firm's stock in trade would be men and ideas, not dollars and equipment; brains and imagination which could efficiently be brought to bear on challenging maritime problems would be its prime assets. And he wanted to motivate those men and their ideas with assurances and rewards he had felt lacking in AGWI: a common sureness of purpose, authority as well as responsibility, and a share in the prestige and profits of success. If AGWI had become an ungainly ark conned by bankers and manned by bureaucrats, C. D. Mallory & Co. would be a lively and maneuverable cutter whose volunteer crew sailed on shares because they had confidence in the master mariner at the helm.

In choosing his associates, Mallory benefited from both his personal charisma and his numerous friendships in the maritime industry. He had a name and a magnetic quality that attracted men to his causes, but he also had the knowledge and judgment to pick the good ones from amongst the bunch. The two partners he chose are cases in point. C. D. Mallory & Co.'s authorized capital was $300,000, but only $100,000 in equity was initially opened for subscription. As founder and president, Mallory took $50,000. Two vice presidents, William S. Houston and Edward E. Palen, were each credited with $25,000, but it is clear that they were admitted to equity not because they were good for that amount but because of the skills they possessed.

Palen was an experienced and practical shipping man who had risen from office boy to the positions of general agent, secretary-treasurer, auditor, and assistant general manager of the Old Dominion Steamship Line. He had served as assistant director of the Shipping Board's Division of Operations for the South Atlantic District, with headquarters at Norfolk, and he knew the American coastal market, its commodities, its ports, and its railroad connections like the back of his hand. He stayed with Mallory for only two years, but his contributions to personnel recruitment and organization during the early days of the firm were considerable.

It was Houston, however, who was Mallory's prize catch. Where Mallory was gregarious, outgoing, and prone to spin off ideas with infectious enthusiasm, Houston was reserved, self-effacing, task-oriented, and devoted to detail. He had come up through the ranks of John M. Campbell's Sons, one of Glasgow's largest and most successful tramping houses, and had an encyclopedic knowledge of world ports, trades, vessels, rates, and documentation. He had organized and managed the vast Contract Department required by the U.S. Shipping Board's Division of Operations and there, during 1917–1918, had come into daily contact with Mallory (who approved the charter

First known advertisement for C. D. Mallory & Co., *Shipping*, December
31, 1919.

Carenco, shown at Gibraltar flying the colors of the U. S. Shipping Board Emergency Fleet Corporation while under the management of C. D. Mallory & Co. *Carenco* served in Mallory's Baltimore-Oceanic Steamship Line and in Mallory Transport Lines, 1921–1924. Courtesy Mariners Museum.

Eastern Glade, owned by U. S. Shipping Board Emergency Fleet Corporation and managed 1922–1925 by Mallory Transport Lines. In 1922 she inaugurated the first permanent American-flag liner service to South Africa. Courtesy Mariners Museum.

parties and agreements Houston prepared). The skills and personalities of the urbane New Yorker and the dour Scot complemented each other with the powerful attraction of true opposites, and throughout their government service they had shared ideas. Houston was the first man Mallory sought out to join him in business, and he remained Mallory's most trusted lieutenant, friend, and alter ego for a decade. With no criticism of either man intended, their confidential secretary's recollection catches the essence of their relationship: "Mr. Mallory got the business; Mr. Houston kept it." [7]

Mallory, Houston, and Palen pooled their talents to recruit a remarkably able staff, most of whom stayed with the firm for its lifetime and were important sources of its strength. For the key technical posts, which demanded widely experienced mariners and engineers, Mallory raided AGWI: Port Captain I. P. Gavitt was a former captain of Clyde and Mallory vessels; Superintendent Engineer M. Marshall was formerly senior engineer and superintendent of construction for the Clyde and Mallory lines. For financial, traffic, and operations personnel, Mallory and his partners sought out younger men willing to trade the security of niches in government or large shipping lines for the excitement of a smaller, vigorous company. By the end of 1919, the original cadre was on board: James Houston, W. Lyle Bull, F. Willard Bergen, and Frank M. Bynum. Each could point to a solid record of past achievements, but all were eager to accept the new challenges Mallory offered them.

Houston came as his uncle's understudy in the area of ship operations. Bull was an experienced traffic and terminal man hired on the rebound from AGWI. He had begun in 1909, at the age of sixteen, as Henry R. Mallory's office boy, but had moved swiftly upward in the freight traffic and operations departments of the Clyde-Mallory Lines. During the 1915–1916 shipping boom, Bull, as assistant superintendent of terminals in New York, had come into daily contact with Clifford Mallory. A tour with the AEF in Europe had followed during 1917–1919; and when H. H. Raymond "was not too encouraging" about his reemployment at Clyde-Mallory, Bull jumped at Clifford's invitation to join C. D. Mallory & Co. as its secretary. Bergen was an expert on chartering operations, who had served under

Houston as an examiner in the Contract Department of the Shipping Board's Division of Operations and was recruited by his old boss. Bynum had been clerk to one of the Shipping Board's commissioners, followed by a stint as executive secretary to J. H. Rosseter, Edward F. Carry's successor as Director of Operations.

The talents of all the employees of C. D. Mallory & Co. were initially focused on securing as much government tonnage as they could, consistent with the goals of the firm's founder and the capacity of its organization to handle. Mallory and Houston opened negotiations with the Shipping Board on September 2 and, in the course of extensive correspondence and conversation, presented their proposals with logic and conviction. Repeatedly, they assured the board that "our reputation is such that we cannot afford to put our name behind any project that we do not expect to be able to carry through, even after the Government support is withdrawn."

Mallory and Houston had a long shopping list, but its specificity reflected their familiarity with the niches available to American-flag shipping in world markets. They asked for steel vessels suitable for dry-cargo ocean tramping and bulk carriage—preferably in the range of 8,000 to 9,000 d.w.t.—which they felt sure they could profitably employ against foreign-flag competitors in Mediterranean, Adriatic, and Indian waters. They also applied for vessels in the 5,000 d.w.t. range for use to, from, and among American possessions and dependencies in the Pacific and/or the Chilean nitrate trade. As for liners, they "looked over" the field and decided "that of those left for assignment, the opportunities are better out of Baltimore than elsewhere." Consequently, they applied for any or all the Shipping Board's general cargo services from Baltimore to Rotterdam, Le Havre, Bordeaux, Marseilles, Cette, Trieste and/or Fiume.

The Shipping Board responded first and favorably on the tramp proposals and, between September 19, 1919, and January 14, 1920, assigned ten tramp vessels to the Mallory firm: seven "lakers" for one-way delivery to the Philippines, with a promise to replace them with larger vessels better suited to ocean tramping; one "laker" for employment in the nitrate trade; and two 8,800 d.w.t.-class ships for use in Indian and Far Eastern waters. In mid-October 1919, the Shipping Board also awarded Mallory a "Mediterranean Line" from Baltimore to "the Azores and Canary Islands, Portuguese and Spanish Atlantic, Spanish and French Mediterranean, West Coast of Italy, Adriatic ports, and North Africa west of Bizerta."

Mallory's use of government vessels, both as tramps and as liners, was governed by standard managing agency agreements which he signed with the United States Shipping Board Emergency Fleet Corporation. The government corporation retained ownership of the vessels and agreed "to provide and pay for all fuel, fresh water, stevedoring, port charges, pilotages, agencies, commissions, and consular charges, except those pertaining to the master, officers, and crew, and all other expenses which are usually borne by a time charterer of a vessel." Mallory agreed to procure cargoes and operate the vessels in such trades or services as were mutually acceptable to him and the corporation; to collect all freights and other moneys due the corporation; and to provide "a competent shore force" and perform "all of the customary agency duties concerned with loading and discharging cargoes" at all ports included in the vessels' itineraries.

As managing agent, Mallory also agreed to man, equip, victual, and supply the vessels consigned to him and "to provide and pay for all provisions, wages, and consular, shipping, and discharging fees of the master, officers and crew, all cabin, deck, engine room, and other necessary stores, and all other costs and expenses" properly incident to their management. He agreed to maintain the vessels "in a thoroughly efficient state in hull, machinery, tackle, apparel, furniture, and equipment" and to procure "for and on behalf of the corporation the necessary labor and material to effect ordinary running repairs and replacements."

For his managing and operating services, Mallory was guaranteed a husbanding fee payable "from the day of delivery of each vessel to the manager until redelivery or loss": $400 per month for each vessel up to and including the fifth; $350 per month for each vessel in excess of five. He was also authorized commissions and fees as follows: 2-1/2 per cent on the gross ocean freight list of general cargo from United States ports;

1-1/4 per cent on the gross ocean freight list of bulk cargo from United States ports; 5 per cent on all mails, express, and commercial passenger revenues to or from United States ports; and $250 per vessel per cargo-carrying voyage into United States ports from foreign and dependency ports.

Since he had posted $250,000 bond for the proper execution of his duties and since the Shipping Board could terminate his agreements on any or all vessels on twenty-four hours' notice, there were incentives besides Mallory's own enthusiasm for him to perform fast and well. Also, since he had committed himself to transoceanic operations from Baltimore as well as from New York, he had to expand his staff and organization accordingly.

Mallory was firmly and correctly convinced that "the headquarters of an American tramp owner should be in New York which is the center of such business." Therefore, C. D. Mallory & Co.'s primary roles, as originally conceived, were to function as "an executive office and control our tramp business." To manage and operate his Mediterranean Line, however, Mallory organized a new corporation with himself as its president. Chartered in Delaware in late September 1919, the Baltimore-Oceanic Steamship Co. opened its offices in Baltimore's Munsey Building. Its capitalization of $30,000 was in no-par-value stock, and it was actually a wholly owned subsidiary of C. D. Mallory & Co. of New York. Lyle Bull was placed in charge of the new company, with the title of vice president, and he quickly integrated himself and the Mallory line into Baltimore's maritime community. Schedules were prepared, a house flag was designed, stevedores and wharfage were hired, and cargoes were solicited. *Clavarack,* the first Shipping Board vessel assigned to the line, was delivered on November 20; and, by January 20, 1920, she had been joined by four other steamships (see Table 11.2).

The cordial reception accorded the Baltimore-Oceanic Steamship Co. and his initial attempts at ocean tramping prompted Mallory to apply for additional Shipping Board tonnage. During January and February of 1920 he pressed for the allocation of vessels for purposes of opening liner services from Galveston and its adjacent ports (Texas City and Houston) to

Glasgow, with the privilege of loading to Belfast, Dublin, Bristol, or London, as necessary. In presenting his case, Mallory cited his family's historic affinity for Galveston and his own superior knowledge of the trades of the western Gulf of Mexico. He suggested that his brother-in-law George Sealy and a particularly experienced local agent, B. M. Bloomfield, would be "associated with me in Galveston when we are able to establish ourselves there." He cited similar connections in Glasgow based on Houston's long-standing connection with John M. Campbell's Sons. As an afterthought, Mallory also inquired if a Galveston-Japan line appealed to the board.

Neither a Glasgow line nor a Japanese line caught the Shipping Board's fancy. No reason was given Mallory for their refusal to accept his proposals, but the board's members probably felt that both he and they already had their hands quite full enough. Indeed, they did. By June 30, 1920, the board had 202 general-cargo "berths" in operation between American and foreign ports: 100 sailing from the North Atlantic range of ports (including Mallory's tramps and liners); 27 from the South Atlantic range; 54 from the Gulf of Mexico; and 21 from Pacific ports. The board also had 7 general-cargo berths between foreign ports and 2 combination passenger-cargo berths in operation to and from New York. The Shipping Board's 211 berths employed 1,294 American-flag and 208 other-flag vessels. Baltimore-Oceanic Steamship's 7 liners and C. D. Mallory & Co.'s 8 tramps made them the board's forty-eighth and forty-ninth largest operators. In all, Mallory was operating 1.3 per cent of the Shipping Board's total tonnage.[8]

Even had he received the additional Shipping Board vessels that he requested in early 1920, it is doubtful that either Mallory or his young organization could have fulfilled extra responsibilities at that time. The man's health was too poor and his firms' personnel and procedures were not yet shaken down. In mid-March, Mallory was stricken with a severe stomach hemorrhage and was bedridden for almost three months while Houston and Palen ran the business. Even so, Palen had already decided to withdraw from the Mallory organization to pursue his own interests in the Norfolk area. He was always "very much a man of mystery" to his younger associates, and the "arrangement he evidently made with Messrs. Mallory and Houston" was never clear. By mid-1920, however, he had "faded out of the picture." In June, Mallory also lost Lyle Bull's services for a year. At the request of the Shipping Board, Bull was "loaned" to the government and "placed in charge of Mediterranean trades." Since Mallory operated a Mediterranean line for the board, it probably helped him to have Bull in Washington. But Bull's absence left an important gap in both C. D. Mallory & Co. and the Baltimore-Oceanic Steamship Co.

The two Houstons, Frank Bynum, and Willard Bergen shouldered many of the burdens caused by Mallory's illness, Palen's departure, and Bull's leave of absence. But Maitland Smith and J. Ellis Knowles, who joined them during 1920, shared the load and became mainstays of the firm. Smith was recruited by Palen from the Shipping Board's Division of Operations. Actually, Mallory, Houston, and Palen had approached C. P. Stone, head of the division's Actuarial Department, with whom they had worked during the war. Stone declined "the opportunity to join the Mallory organization" because "he was returning to Grace Lines on the West Coast," but recommended his young understudy, Smith, who reported for work at C. D. Mallory & Co. on March 1 as its auditor. Knowles, who was in the fold by December, had been a classmate of Philip Mallory at Yale and was a member of an experienced Florida family of ship operators. His particular expertise concerned insurance, admiralty law, and claims.[9]

Mallory's liner operations and their supporting organization and staff had stabilized on an even keel by the last quarter of 1920. The Baltimore-Oceanic Steamship Co. had moved to new offices in the Continental Bank Building of Baltimore and was being managed, in Bull's absence, by Bynum and Bergen. Relations with the Shipping Board were smooth, and Mallory was playing an active and constructive role in the process. Not only was he concerned with his own firm's health but, as one of twelve founding governors of the United States Ship Operators Association, he was a prime spokesman for all managers and operators of Shipping Board tonnage.[10] One result was a steady allocation of vessels to the Baltimore-Oceanic Steamship Co. which, at its peak during November 1920–January 1921, operated nine ships in its Mediterranean Line (see Table 11.1).

The situation in tramping, however, was markedly different. C. D. Mallory & Co. had opened larger offices (which became permanent) at 11 Broadway early in 1920, still with the firm conviction that its members were "especially well qualified to develop a field in which American ships have heretofore made little progress; i.e., the tramping trade." The Shipping Board had been receptive to these ambitions, although not overwhelmingly so. By July 30, 1920, Mallory's New York organization was operating eight government-owned tramp vessels. Suddenly and steadily things changed for the worse. The Shipping Board began to deemphasize tramping and to recall such vessels without replacing them: in August, Mallory was cut to seven vessels; to five in October; to three in November; and by March 1921, he had only two government-owned tramps left.

Why? The reasons for this abrupt change in Shipping Board policy sprang from ambiguities to be found in the Merchant Marine Act of 1920—the famous and long-awaited Jones Act, which President Wilson signed into law on June 5. That act deemed it

> necessary for the national defense and for the proper growth of its foreign and domestic commerce that the United States shall have a merchant marine of the best equipped and most suitable types of vessels sufficient to carry the greater portion of its commerce and serve as a naval or military auxiliary in time of war or national emergency, ultimately to be owned and operated privately by citizens of the United States.

It was further

> declared to be the policy of the United States to do whatever may be necessary to develop and encourage the maintenance of such a merchant marine, and . . . the United States Shipping Board shall, in the disposition of vessels and shipping property, . . . in the making of rules and regulations, and in the administration of the shipping laws keep always in view this purpose and object as the primary end to the attained.

Among the politicians, the most controversial provisions of

273

the Jones Act were those which permitted lower inland rail rates on goods imported or exported in American ships; which empowered the Shipping Board and the Interstate Commerce Commission to investigate transportation and traffic conditions prevailing in the hinterlands of important American ports and to suggest improvements; which denied entry to American ports to any vessel granting "deferred rebates" and to any line making use of "fighting ships" or which black-listed or otherwise retaliated against shippers; and which authorized repeal of treaties preventing the imposition of discriminating tariff duties on goods imported in American ships.

Among shipowners, however, and particularly among such managers and operators of Shipping Board tonnage as Mallory, other sections of the Jones Act were of far greater and more personal interest. They applauded the act's reaffirmation of American cabotage and the extension of the coastwise laws to insular possessions and territories of the United States; they approved its provision that the United States mails be carried only by American ships whenever practicable; they seconded its designation of the American Bureau of Shipping as the official classification agency for American-flag vessels; and they were encouraged by its desire to create and foster American marine insurance companies, associations, and pools through relaxation of certain portions of the Sherman and Clayton antitrust acts. Of greatest concern to them, however, were the sections of the Jones Act that revised the government's policies toward the tonnage owned and operated by the Shipping Board and toward the financing and construction of new American-flag vessels.

Section 7 of the Jones Act required the Shipping Board to keep itself informed as to

> what steamship lines should be established and put in operation from ports in the United States, or any Territory, District, or possession thereof to such world and domestic markets as in its judgement are desirable for the promotion, development, expansion, and maintenance of the foreign and coastwise trade of the United States, and an adequate postal service ... with a view to furnishing adequate, regular, certain, and permanent service.

To achieve the goal implicit in this requirement, the board

was authorized to sell or charter its vessels to American citizens "who agree to establish and maintain such lines." If no citizens could be found to do this, the board itself would "operate vessels on such line until the business is developed so that such vessels may be sold on satisfactory terms and the service maintained, or unless it shall appear within a reasonable time that such line can not be made self-sustaining."

As for sales, the Shipping Board was given discretionary authority to offer its vessels to competitive bidders. Terms were a minimum of 25 per cent cash and a maximum payment period of fifteen years. Care was to be taken not to disrupt the used-ship market by massive and/or low-priced dumping of government tonnage, and sales to aliens were made quite difficult. Government shipbuilding, except for military needs, was ended, and a five-year revolving fund of $25,000,000 per year was allocated to finance new construction of American-flag ships by United States citizens on terms similar to those for sales. As a further incentive for private rather than public investment in shipping, American steamship companies were exempted from the excess profit tax for ten years if they invested, either in government-owned ships or in new construction in American shipyards, a sum equivalent to the amount of taxes they would otherwise have paid.

Finally, to facilitate debt financing of ships a new standard ship mortgage was designed and guaranteed as at least a "preferred" if not a prior lien. Historically, the so-called "maritime liens" of persons "furnishing repairs, supplies, towage, use of dry dock or marine railway, or other necessaries" had never been subordinate to a first mortgage. The Jones Act did not make them so, but it strengthened the claim of first-mortgage holders in ways designed to encourage previously wary financial institutions to make more loans secured by ship mortgages.

For managers and operators of Shipping Board tonnage such as the Baltimore-Oceanic Steamship Co. and C. D. Mallory & Co., and for aspiring shipowners like Clifford Mallory, the Jones Act seemed made to order. Mallory was pleased by the act's endorsement of the Shipping Board's existing services and by the prospect of an orderly return of the American merchant fleet from public to private hands. He felt that Section 7 of the act provided the means for achieving one of the two goals he had set for his organization in his original application to the Shipping Board: "to operate such lines as we feel would be sufficiently secure in the future for us to put our names behind and to remain in permanently." He also assumed, since it was for the benefit of "any vessel documented under the laws of the United States," that the act would further his second goal: "to operate tramp vessels in the World's trades and to become tramp owners." This latter assumption proved tenuous, at best, and ultimately false.

The Shipping Board, which was empowered to interpret and implement the Jones Act, initially decided that it did not apply to tramp shipping. The act repeatedly expressed the desirability of fostering "steamship lines and regular service," but not once did it use the words "tramps" or "tramp service." The board decided that this was sufficient ground to reduce its commitment to tramps, and this decision was what prompted its recall of six of the eight tramp vessels being managed and operated by C. D. Mallory & Co.

Mallory was livid; and what infuriated him most was evidence that the board's decision was more the product of personalities than of logic. A curious conflict of laws had placed the decision in the hands of one man, Admiral William S. Benson, and that man just did not like tramps.[11]

Benson was able, but the almost dictatorial powers he possessed were the result of a comedy of partisan and administrative errors. The Shipping Act of 1916 had authorized a five-man Shipping Board, but President Wilson had allowed its membership to dwindle, once the war had ended. By April 5, 1920, only two men were incumbent on the board: John A. Donald, one of the original commissioners, whose appointment dated from January 23, 1917, and who was tired of the whole business; and Admiral Benson, who had been appointed chairman on March 13, 1920, and was quite willing to assume command. When the Jones Act became law on June 5, 1920, it authorized the appointment of an entirely new seven-man board, but it required Benson and Donald to remain in office until all members of the enlarged board could be appointed by the President and confirmed by the Senate. On November 10, following his defeat for re-election, President Wilson finally tendered "recess appointments" to Benson, Donald, and five other men who took office on December 1. But none of these appointments was confirmed by the Senate when it reconvened, and they lapsed on March 4, 1921. On March 11, President Harding asked Benson to act until a new board could be appointed and confirmed. On June 9, a new seven-man board, including Benson, was appointed, and all were confirmed by June 15. Albert D. Lasker was designated chairman of the new board and T. V. O'Connor its vice chairman.

While this administrative comedy held center stage, it obscured some more basic facts: for all practical purposes, from March 13, 1920, to June 15, 1921, Benson was the Shipping Board and, as such, the prime interpreter of American maritime policy; and during that period, he did make it quite difficult for Mallory or anyone to employ Shipping Board vessels (or even their own) as tramps.

An example of Benson's tactics was the Charter Filing Regulation, which he issued under the authority of the Jones Act effective October 1, 1920. This regulation made customs clearance for any vessel under charter contingent upon prior filing of two certified copies of its charter party with the Shipping Board's New York office. Where time was crucial, a letter or telegram "giving details pertaining to said charter" was acceptable, to be followed by the certified copies in due course. The announced purpose of the order was to secure better statistical data concerning this segment of American commerce, but "general cargo and passenger vessels, those in ballast, and those carrying cargo for owners' account" were exempt. Tramp operators screamed discrimination and alleged, with considerable truth, that the filing regulation infringed their freedom to make private contracts, reduced the speed with which they could act in their fast-breaking market, and would broadcast proprietary information concerning vessels, cargoes, schedules, and rates to foreign-flag competitors.

Benson compounded the tramp operators' ire by forming a Tramp Steamer and Bulk Cargo Conference. Membership in the conference was open to all "Managing Agents of Shipping Board steamers operating exclusively in Tramp Service (West Indies and Coastwise trade excepted)," but was contingent upon each agent's promise to submit all proposed business to the conference for its approval of the rates and form of charter party involved. Although membership was not mandatory, the implication was strong that members would have first claim on whatever Shipping Board vessels might be allocated to tramping or bulk-cargo carriage. [12] Mallory did not join, and he began to see his tramp fleet dwindle from eight to two ships.

Before taking on Admiral Benson, however, Mallory secured the support of the author of the Merchant Marine Act of 1920, Senator Wesley L. Jones. In a blunt letter of November 26, Mallory noted that he had been assigned no tramp tonnage by the Shipping Board since May 8 and had only three such vessels left. He voiced his conviction that Benson was discriminating against tramp operators and hiding behind the Jones Act's silence on the subject. He then wrote Benson a much more conciliatory letter citing promises made to him by the Admiral's predecessors, the past successes of C. D. Mallory & Co. with tramps, his firm's unique knowledge of tramp and bulk-cargo trades as embodied in the skills of its personnel; and he made a plea for the assignment of additional tonnage. Jones supported Mallory's position and in a sharp letter instructed the Admiral that the act which bore the Senator's name was meant to apply to tramps as well as liners.

Benson responded by assuring Jones that tramp operators were getting a fair shake from the board. The Admiral gave similar assurances to Mallory and solicited the latter's views on the reasons for the apparent inability of American-flag tramps to compete in world markets. Heartened by more encouragement on the subject than he had ever received from Benson before, Mallory responded.

As he saw it, the problems of competing with British-flag tramps, not to mention Scandinavian, Japanese, and Dutch vessels, were three. First, British wages for officers and crews were "materially lower." Second, British carriers demanded payments for freights in American dollars, but paid most of their expenses in sterling. Under current exchange conditions, this gave them an advantage of 25 per cent. Third, American ships were primarily oil burners, but there were few oil bunkering stations around the world. And for coal burners, the competitive outlook was bleaker as British vessels could usually command preferential rebates on their coal purchases which were unavailable to American ships. Yet Mallory was confident that organizations as skilled and efficient as his could still compete if they were allocated quality ships by the board, if the board would allocate some of its funds to the construction of tramp-type vessels able to convert back and forth between oil and coal, and if the United States government would invest in more overseas bunkering facilities for its citizens' use.

Benson was not convinced, and C. D. Mallory & Co. received no additional tonnage for tramping until April 21, 1921 (see Table 11.1). [13] Even so, pickings were slim. Then, the new Shipping Board headed by Lasker and O'Connor took office, and the bottom dropped out completely. On June 30, 1921, the Shipping Board had 300 steamers allocated to tramping, of which Mallory was operating 6. One year later, both totals were zero. In his first annual report as chairman, Lasker explained why:

> It was evident from the beginning that these so-called tramp steamers were losing considerable money, and as no definite results could be attained in the interests of the American merchant marine by keeping these steamers in service they were promptly withdrawn and laid up, the board restricting its operations to the building up of regular trade routes considered essential to the future of the American merchant marine as required by the Merchant Marine Act, 1920.

Because of a lack of surviving accounting data, it is impossible to determine whether all or any of the tramps operated by C. D. Mallory & Co. for the Shipping Board were profitable or not. Mallory certainly thought most of them were or he would not have sought so vigorously and continually to expand his quota. In all, he received twenty-two vessels (including two tankers) which he employed for a total of 5,089 ship-days of tramping (see Table 11.1). This record meant nothing, however, once the board had made up its mind. And under Lasker's chairmanship, which lasted until June 19, 1923, the Shipping Board did not change its decision on tramps and Mallory's periodic requests for such vessels went begging. [14]

The Lasker administration also had to consider some Mallory proposals concerning liners; and here they were much more responsive to his desires than in the case of tramps. The Baltimore-Oceanic Steamship Co. was not living up to early expectations, and Mallory was eager to improve matters. The problem was simple: not enough traffic. Lyle Bull recalled the situation:

> . . . about every place along our coasts with water enough to float a ship, [had] clamored, through their Chambers of Commerce and their Congressional representatives, for the establishment of ocean services to ports abroad. In response to political pressures, many applicants were assigned ships who should not have been and were obviously doomed to failure. Then too, the proliferation of lines resulted in many American companies competing for the same business without a sufficient volume of traffic to utilize all of the shipping space offered.

Mallory and his associates were certainly not among what another experienced shipping man, Robert E. Annin, called "the black horse cavalry." They knew that they were doing and were capable, but they had simply miscalculated the volume of traffic which could be generated on their service between Baltimore and Mediterranean ports. During 1920, they had kept as many as nine and never fewer than seven ships busy. By the second quarter of 1921, however, their service was feeling the effects of world depressions; and, by June 13, 1921, when Lasker succeeded Benson as chairman of the Shipping Board, they could only justify three vessels on the route. This was just too few, as Bull noted: "when a sufficient number of ships was assigned, the per diem fee would usually be enough to support an office and a modest shore-based operating staff, but [even then] the profit margins were not great."

To cut his losses in Baltimore and broaden the base of his line operations, Mallory put a series of proposals before the Shipping Board. His primary goal was to convert his small, unprofitable Baltimore-based line into a larger, more diversified, and hopefully more profitable New York–based line. He also realized the need to take up the slack in his New York operations caused by his loss of Shipping Board tramps.

First, he asked the board's permission to transfer management and operation of the vessels allocated to the Baltimore-Oceanic Steamship Co.'s Mediterranean Line to a new corporation to be based in New York and called Mallory Transport Lines, Inc. New York was where the action was. Baltimore was second among American ports in the amount of cargo tonnage it generated for Shipping Board vessels, but the gap between its share and that of New York was still considerable. During the year ending June 30, 1921, for example, 9 per cent of all imports and 13 per cent of all exports carried by Shipping Board vessels moved through Baltimore. New York, however, accounted for 35 per cent of imports and 20 per cent of exports. New York's greater volume of trade, its more central location amidst the North Atlantic range of ports, and its decided advantage in attracting return cargoes gave it greater appeal. Also, it was Mallory's home and where his organization was strongest; and by changing the name of his Mediterranean Line's proprietor he felt he could more fully capitalize on his and his family's reputation in American and foreign ports.

The Shipping Board approved Mallory's request, and on December 15, the Baltimore-Oceanic Steamship Co.'s vessels were reallocated to Mallory Transport Lines. Mallory announced the changeover on December 27, and the transfer of vessels began on January 16, 1922. Assignment of other vessels directly to Mallory Transport Lines began on February 6, and by March 31, that company was operating six ships on its Mediterranean Line. It was also operating two of the fifteen ships that the Shipping Board had allocated to private firms in mid-January 1922 for the transportation of wheat for famine relief in Russia. *Aledo* and *Duquesne* each made one voyage to Reval with full cargoes of grain, but returned in ballast so as not to compete with regular Shipping Board services to Russia. Both vessels were returned to the board in May (see Table 11.3).

Mallory's plans for rejuvenation of his liner franchise did not end with the transfer of his Mediterranean service from Baltimore to New York. He also had his eye on a North Atlantic–South and East Africa berth authority held by the United States & Australasian Steamship Co. Opened in February 1919, when freight rates on general cargo had stood at $35 a ton, the U. S. & A. line had enjoyed some success before slacking off. By September 1921, with freight rates sliding downward past $25, the Shipping Board had suspended the service "in spite of strenuous efforts to increase the volume of business." Even so, there was much sentiment to reopen the line among exporters of automobiles and parts, lubricating and case oils, agricultural and mining equipment, textiles, and iron and steel, and among importers of chrome, copper, and wool.

Through Houston and John M. Campbell's Sons, Mallory could command considerable experience with the South African trade, and he rapidly accumulated some more. He persuaded his old friend and associate William J. Love (by then vice president for traffic of the Emergency Fleet Corporation) to spend $800 for a study of the trade's prospects to be carried out by a Mallory employee, E. P. Merrell. With Merrell's favorable report and Love's personal endorsement of March 30, 1922 in hand, Mallory applied for the African berth. The Shipping Board consented on April 1 and assigned it to Mallory Transport Lines. By September 16, five vessels were in operation.

Management of these two berths for the Shipping Board was no mean task. The Mediterranean Line offered a variety of schedules from the North Atlantic range: monthly sailings to Portuguese and Spanish Atlantic ports (including the Azores and the Canary Islands) and to North African ports west of Bizerta; semimonthly sailings to Marseilles, Genoa and the west coast of Italy; and sailings every five weeks to Adriatic ports. Its operating area stretched 4,890 miles from New York to Trieste. The South African Line offered monthly sailings from New York to Cape Town (Table Bay), Port Elizabeth (Algoa Bay), East London and Port Natal (Durban) in the Union of South Africa and to Delagoa Bay (Lourenco Marques) and Beira in Mozambique; and return sailings to Gulf and/or Atlantic ports "when cargo offers." This "main line" included "the longest nonstop steamship run in the world," the 6,786 miles between New York and Cape Town, plus 1,604 additional coasting miles between Cape Town and Beira.

Three organizations were primarily responsible for the integration and efficient operation of these lines. In New York, Mallory Transport Lines acted as managing operators for both the Mediterranean and South African lines, but was indistin-

Wytheville, owned by U. S. Shipping Board Emergency Fleet Corporation and managed in the Mediterranean and African liner trades by Mallory Transport Lines, 1922–1924. Courtesy Mariners Museum.

Astmahco IV (later renamed *Glendaruel*). She and her sister, *Ormidale* (ex-*Astmahco III*), were the first tramp vessels owned and managed by C. D. Mallory & Co. (1922–1927) as independent shipping operators. Courtesy Mariners Museum.

Swiftlight, one of the famous seven-ship Swiftsure Fleet of tankers managed by C. D. Mallory & Co., 1921–1941. Courtesy Mariners Museum.

Mevania, one of the seven-tanker Malston Fleet purchased from the U. S. Shipping Board Emergency Fleet Corporation in 1923–1924 for $45 per d.w.t. and operated by C. D. Mallory & Co. until 1941. Courtesy Mariners Museum.

guishable except in name from C. D. Mallory & Co. Houston's old firm, John M. Campbell's Sons of Glasgow, acted as European general agents for Mallory Transport Lines, and the exceptionally experienced firm of John T. Rennie & Sons of Port Natal performed similar functions in Africa.

The Baltimore-Oceanic Steamship Co. became nothing more than Mallory Transport Lines' Baltimore agent, but common personnel interlocked the two firms: Mallory was president and chairman of both; Houston was a director of both and vice president of MTL; Bull was vice president and general manager of Baltimore-Oceanic; Bergen was secretary of both companies; Smith was treasurer of MTL; and Bynum was treasurer of Baltimore-Oceanic and a director of MTL. Effective May 1, 1923, however, Baltimore-Oceanic was sold to Lyle Bull. He had been finding it more and more difficult to get along with the elder Houston, and to solve matters he withdrew from C. D. Mallory & Co. to become president of Baltimore-Oceanic. That firm continued to represent MTL in Baltimore, but as an independent shipping agency. [15]

As for ships, MTL was allocated three more Shipping Board vessels between February 28 and March 23, 1923. These assignments, which were all in operation by May 2, brought MTL to its peak as a managing agent of Shipping Board tonnage: fifteen steamships operating on two transoceanic services totaling 26,560 round-voyage miles (see Table 11.3).

But activity and profit are not synonymous, and there was increasing question whether MTL's berths were sufficiently remunerative for either their managing operator (Mallory) or their owner (the Shipping Board). Like his fellow operators, Mallory was paid flat husbanding fees of $350 to $400 per ship per month, plus earned commissions dependent on the volume of gross receipts generated by his berths. These commissions had been set in 1920 at 5 per cent on outbound and 2-1/2 per cent on inbound freights. He also made additional profits by employing C. D. Mallory & Co. to provide some of the services purchased by MTL for the Shipping Board's vessels, particularly in the procurement of deck and engine room stores, provisions, crews, stevedores, and general upkeep and maintenance. Still, like most of his peers, Mallory was convinced that the fee commission levels should be higher. The Shipping Board, of course, disagreed because any increase in expenses only raised its over-all deficit on operations. The board was committed to supporting "essential trade routes" at government expense, *but only until they became reasonable risks for private investment.* It was *not* committed to deficit financing of the American merchant marine in perpetuity. The question was never whether the board would pick up the operating deficits of its lines, but rather how big a deficit could it support and for how long?

Part of the problem lay in the simple fact that most American-flag liners were not competitive. They were older, smaller, and slower than European and oriental vessels; their operating expenses were greater; and their freedom to engage in price competition was limited. Everywhere, they ran into British, Norwegian, German and Japanese lines whose fuel costs and wages were less and whose freight conferences maintained lower rates and granted deferred rebates of 10 per cent to shippers who confined their shipments to "Conference Lines" for stated periods—usually four or six months. By statute, American-flag vessels could form their own conferences, but could not join those populated by foreign-flags; and all American ships and companies were forbidden to grant rebates of any kind. America's legal position on these questions was more moral and equitable than the world's, but it subverted the competitive position of the United States merchant marine.

Another aspect of the problem lay in the overexpansion of Shipping Board services during 1920–1922. There were four lines besides Mallory's from American to Mediterranean ports: Export Steamship Co., from the North Atlantic range to Malta, Greece, Constantinople, the Levant, Syria, Palestine, and North Africa east of Bizerta; A. H. Bull & Co., from the North Atlantic range to Constantinople and all Black Sea ports; Tampa Interocean Steamship Co., whose service was like MTL's except from Gulf and South Atlantic ports; and Trosdal, Plant & La Fonta, whose service was like Export's but from the Gulf and South Atlantic range. To Africa, Mallory had it a little better. MTL's only competitor was A. H. Bull & Co., who ran from the North Atlantic range to the Canary Islands, Dakar, and other West African ports. The Shipping Board had fostered such "overlapping" to keep its agents and operators on their toes. This proved a stupid policy, given existing levels of American trade and foreign competition.

The government's error was clear by early 1923. On April 28, the Shipping Board announced its intention "to consolidate as many as possible of the services operating between the same general ranges of territory" and proposed eighteen recombinations as a start. One of the eighteen proposals involved MTL's Mediterranean Line. Mallory studied the proposal carefully, but declined to bid for either the whole or any portion of the new and larger "range." In a strongly worded letter to Chairman Lasker of May 23, he defended the viability of MTL's existing Mediterranean service. If forced to withdraw, Mallory concluded, he would "have wasted several years of serious effort in the promotion of American trade on American vessels." The board could find no other takers, and the proposal was shelved when Lasker unexpectedly resigned as chairman of the Shipping Board on June 19. His successor, Edward P. Farley, took office on June 20, but postponed reopening of the matter until he could "study" it.

A Shipping Board resolution of November 30, 1923, opened the matter again. The board announced its intention "to place the operation of its vessels more completely on a basis of economy and efficiency" and specified its policies to come: "the consolidation of routes to avoid overlapping and duplication"; the "elimination and consolidation of managing operators," so as to reduce the thirty-eight in service on July 1 to twenty-five; "revamping of the operating agreement to provide for an adequate fixed fee which shall be the sole compensation of the operator and entirely dependent upon the volume of gross receipts"; the elimination of all fixed allowances for husbanding; and the prohibition of sales of goods and services to managing operators by subsidiary companies.

Clifford Mallory's initial reactions to these pronouncements were in industrial rather than personal terms. As one of the governors of the United States Ship Operators Association and a member of its Standing Committee on Managing Agents Agreements, he played a major role in preparing counterproposals to the Shipping Board's emerging policies. Where the board proposed a new standard operating agreement that abolished "all of the fixed fees for husbanding, deck and engine room stores, and subsistence" and prohibited operators from employing "subsidiary companies to perform stevedoring work or furnish supplies to the government ships," Mallory and his fellow governors and committeemen held out for the retention of these perquisites. Where the board proposed new commissions of 7 1/2 per cent on outbound and 3 per cent on inbound freights, the operators' representatives bargained for 10 and 5, respectively. The debate dragged on and on.

By mid-1924, however, the Shipping Board's proposals had come home to Mallory in very personal terms. Farley resigned on January 28 and was succeeded as chairman by T. V. O'Connor on February 5. O'Connor and Admiral Leigh C. Palmer (who had been appointed president of the Emergency Fleet Corporation on January 7) began to turn the screws. By June 16, they had gotten around to reviewing the Mediterranean trades and had scheduled a hearing for June 24. Mallory Transport Lines, Export Steamship Co., and A. H. Bull & Co. were ordered to show cause why their Mediterranean lines should not be consolidated.

For Mallory, the hearing could not have come at a worse time. On May 19 he had been stricken with another severe stomach hemorrhage and was laid up in bed. Houston, who was never as persuasive as Mallory, had to carry the ball and did not present a strong case. Mallory followed up from his bed on July 8 with a handwritten note to Chairman O'Connor. He expressed his regrets at being unable to attend the hearing of the week before, and urged the chairman to pause. The new trading area proposed by the board was too large for one line to cover. It would be "a grave mistake to try it," he argued. He asked postponement of further action until he had recuperated, which would be at least six weeks. O'Connor's reply was noncommital. Trouble was unquestionably brewing.

At the hearing it was made clear that the Shipping Board hoped "to secure, if possible, an amalgamation of the several operating agencies into one organization, thereby conserving the experience and business-getting connections of all operators." If this could not be brought about, however, the board reserved the right "to select the operator whose past record and whose known ability gave the best assurance of faithful and efficient work." Houston, acting on his partner's advice, had opposed any merger. Both were confident, if worse came to worst, that MTL would be chosen over Export and Bull. During 1919–1922 that assumption would have been a safe one; by mid-1924, it was not.[16]

Mallory's trade association activities in opposition to the proposed revision of the standard operating agreement had begun to irritate the board, particularly Chairman O'Connor. The government had announced its revision on November 30, 1923; but, as late as July 17, 1924, virtually none of the operators had renegotiated their contracts. The Shipping Board and the United States Ship Operators Association had locked in a cold war, and officers of the latter were held increasingly suspect by the former—Mallory doubly so because MTL's own charges to the board seemed high.

The Shipping Board had never expected the cost of operating unprofitable but essential trade routes to be cheap. The first ten voyages of Mallory's South African Line, for example, were all in the red in amounts averaging $38,841. But the board accepted this deficit on the simple rationale "that this was an essential service where American trade might soon lose its newly gained markets if the Government did not underwrite the venture until it should improve enough to make it a reasonable risk for private capital." By mid-1924, however, and under congressional pressure to reduce its over-all deficit, the board had developed several statistical tests of agent and line performance. The key inputs to these tests were data concerning the gross ton-miles per voyage and the government deficit per voyage for each berth operated for the board. The key measurement that emerged was the government deficit per gross ton per 100 miles; this became the yardstick by which the board judged the viability of its lines and the efficiency of its operators. Whether these were valid tests of performance is questionable. The point is, they were the tests that were used, and their results became inputs to government policy.

Mallory did not measure well on the Shipping Board's new scale. MTL's Mediterranean Line was costing the government $0.04988 per gross ton per 100 miles (roughly $25,000 per round voyage). Against the over-all average of eighty-nine cargo lines operated for the Shipping Board ($0.02975), MTL's rate ranked sixteenth highest. Against other Mediterranean services, however, it compared more favorably. It was higher than Export Steamship Co.'s $0.04139, but lower than A. H. Bull & Co.'s $0.05327. MTL's South African Line was costing the government $0.05301 per gross ton per 100 miles (roughly $56,000 per round voyage), which made it the seventh most expensive Shipping Board berth. A. H. Bull & Co.'s comparable rate to West Africa was $0.05141—not much less, but less.[17]

The board recognized that both of Mallory's lines were in highly competitive trades and were not likely to be profitable for some time. What the government officials had begun to question was whether MTL was operating its lines at least cost. Admiral Benson, who was still on the board and the commissioner specifically responsible for its Bureau of Construction, had fired the first salvo. In a formal memorandum to the board dated December 26, 1923, he reported "very unsatisfactory conditions as regards repairs and maintenance" on MTL's vessels—particularly *Eastern Sun* and *Wytheville*. "I strongly recommend," he continued, "that these vessels be taken from this company, and that none be given to replace them, and unless they show good cause as to why these great expenses have been incurred, that all vessels be taken from them and turned over to some more efficient operating concern."

At its regular meeting of January 15, 1924, the Shipping Board had received Benson's memorandum, but turned the matter over to President Palmer of the Emergency Fleet Corporation "for consideration and appropriate action." Palmer, in turn, referred it to R. D. Gatewood, manager of the EFC's Department of Maintenance and Repair. Gatewood rapidly identified the weak links: Mallory's superintendent engineer, M. Marshall, was not doing his job, and his superior in the Mallory organization, Vice President Houston, was either unaware of or indifferent to the situation. Under pressure from Gatewood, Marshall was fired in June and replaced by H. D. Haverfield. But there was little improvement. Haverfield was too often on business for C. D. Mallory & Co. to supervise MTL's government vessels.

On July 26, Gatewood filed his reports. To MTL, he commented: "In my judgment it is even worse than it was in the days of Mr. Marshall. . . . In the four years that I have been in this position I have never seen any case showing an unwillingness to cooperate and a disregard of the desires of this office any more plain than this one." To the EFC, he noted that $140,076.33 had been laid out on repairs to MTL vessels since March 17 and commented that the work of "the Mallory staff . . . in the past has been extremely inefficient and unsatisfactory. . . . In view of the inability of the Mallory Line to properly direct and control the efforts of its port staff insofar as the work of maintenance and repair is concerned," he continued, "it is the strong recommendation of the office that the ships be withdrawn from the Mallory Line and that they be not allowed to handle Government vessels." [18]

Forty-five years later, it is difficult to judge the accuracy of these evaluations. They do not jibe with the usual Mallory reputation for efficiency. True or not, they hurt because these strongly worded reports were filed when Mallory was already skating on thin ice: just when he had aroused the Shipping Board's ire because of his trade association activities; just when the viability of the berths he operated were under review; and just when he was too ill to investigate the charges personally or to rise to his own defense. For one of the few times in his life, Mallory was out of touch with his organization; and, for one of the few times in its history, his organization let him down.

The government tightened the screws another turn on July 17, when the Shipping Board directed the Emergency Fleet Corporation to require all operators to sign the new-type agreements within ten days. "This resolution brought to a close the efforts of certain of the operators [including Mallory] to obtain modifications in the agreement," reported the *Marine News.* The "ship operators were visibly disappointed by the Shipping Board's ultimatum that the operating contract must be immediately signed, [but] it was ascertained that none of the managing operators would break relations with the Board." Mallory signed, only to have the board break relations with him! [19]

When Clifford Mallory picked up his morning newspaper on August 28 he learned with amazement that, at a meeting on the previous day, the Shipping Board had terminated his Mediterranean and South African lines and recalled its vessels. The morning's mail brought confirmation in the form of a brusque letter from President Palmer of the EFC: the board had decided to consolidate its three services between the North Atlantic range and the Mediterranean and had allocated the combined service to the Export Steamship Co.; the board had further decided to consolidate its services to South, East, and West Africa and had allocated the combined service to A. H. Bull & Co. Vessels "now allocated to you will be withdrawn and assigned to the aforementioned companies," Palmer continued. "This will eliminate your Company as managing agent of Shipping Board tonnage and it will, therefore, be unnecessary to complete the new operating agreements which have been signed by you." Mallory Transport Lines was out of business on twenty-four hours' notice!

Mallory was furious and fired off a heated letter to Chairman O'Connor. He argued that MTL had leaned over backward to accommodate the board; that they had submitted reports and briefs and appeared at the hearing of June 24. Also, at President Palmer's request and subsequent to that hearing, they had participated in negotiations to merge the three competing companies, "were perfectly willing to do so," but "the Export Steamship Company refused to agree." He ended by protesting the board's summary treatment of MTL and himself and demanded that he be informed of the board's reasoning and given an opportunity to respond. O'Connor replied, on September 2, that the board's reasoning was simple and consistent with its oft-quoted policy: when competing operators would not agree to consolidate, the board would choose one to the exclusion of the others. Nevertheless, a hearing was set for September 15 to receive Mallory's protest.

At the hearing, Mallory got short shrift. The statistical data and exhibits he brought to substantiate his case were ignored. Testimonial letters from such large-volume MTL customers as International Harvester Co., Federal Motor Truck Co., Ford Motor Co., Hudson Motor Car Co., and the American Trading Co. arrived too late to introduce as evidence. The Benson and Gatewood criticisms of Mallory's operating staffs were exhumed and presented out of context. It was clear from the outset that the matter was closed. At the conclusion of the hearing, the board upheld its decisions of August 27: Export Steamship Co. got the Mediterranean; A. H. Bull & Co. got Africa; and Mallory Transport Lines got nothing. By January 31, 1925, MTL had redelivered its last vessel to the Shipping Board and its 12,215 ship-days of operations came to an end (see Table 11.3).[20]

In all, Mallory had been allocated forty-nine Shipping Board vessels. He had employed them in 21,715 ship-days of transoceanic tramp and liner services. He had predicated his entry into his own business in 1919 on his ability to secure and retain such vessels. He could point to some notable accomplishments: showing the American tramp flag on all seven seas; participation in the Russian Famine Relief Expedition; and the beginning of permanent American-flag service on the South African run. But he had lost his tramps during 1921–1922; now, during 1924–1925, he had lost his liners, too. Why had such an imaginative and experienced shipping man failed to achieve his goals?

One reason was that his goals proved faulty. Mallory was one of the optimists during 1919–1920 who predicted great things for the American merchant marine; the Cassandras of 1919–1920 turned out to be right. Writing in the *Journal of Political Economy* in early 1921, E. S. Gregg had put his finger on the problem—"There is 25 per cent more tonnage than in 1913 to do two-thirds the amount of work"—and had made black predictions that most shipping men rejected: "It seems impossible to escape the conclusion that cargo shipping is facing some of the leanest years ever known. . . . Shipping, which ordinarily yields a small direct return, will barely make expenses during the next few years." The point was, said Gregg, "it costs more to operate vessels under the American flag than under other registries," and under falling or depressed rates, American-flag vessels would always be hurt first and most severely. In a companion article in the *Quarterly Journal of Economics*, Gregg summarized what, in retrospect, was a remarkably accurate prediction: "The conclusion seems inescapable that shipping in general is confronted with a depression of unprecedented intensity and duration. The present depression may be the most trying one that the old established lines have experienced, it will certainly test severely the new companies, and it is likely to prove almost disastrous to our government-owned fleet." [21]

The Shipping Board, of course, was expected to be the buffer between rising costs and falling prices. Through prudent management of its fleet and its program of construction and operating subsidies, the board was supposed to implement the Jones Act and carry the nation's merchant marine and "essential" trade routes through the lean years to ultimate glory. It did not. The board and its programs were not scrapped until 1936, but the trend toward failure was well set by 1924. [22] In a real sense, then, part of Mallory's failure was his government's failure to set realistic goals or to implement them efficiently.

But another fact remained. For whatever reason—poor routes, poor ships or poor management—Mallory just could not operate his Shipping Board tonnage as economically as the board thought he should or as cheaply as his competitors could. This made him vulnerable, and when the inevitable political showdown came, he was forced to bargain from weakness rather than strength.

Most important, however, in explaining Mallory's failure to reach the goals he had set for himself in 1919 was the simple fact that these goals had changed. While he would have loved to have beaten out Export and Bull for the consolidated Mediterranean and African lines (and worked hard to do so), his original fixation with government tonnage had weakened. By 1924–1925, he had so many promising private options open to him that all was not lost when he failed to win the Shipping Board over. As things turned out, it was as an independent shipping operator and not as an agent of the government that Clifford Mallory was to make his most impressive mark.

Chapter 12

C. D. MALLORY & CO., INC., INDEPENDENT

SHIPPING OWNERS AND OPERATORS,

1921–1941

". . . we will have to seek employment for our organization in different directions. . . . I have had considerable time to look around."

—Clifford D. Mallory to H. I. Cone, December 4, 1924

LOSS of his government contracts angered and disappointed Mallory, but it did not discourage or ruin him. He had too many irons in the fire for that. It was true that C. D. Mallory & Co. and its associated companies had concentrated on managing and operating Shipping Board tonnage from their inception in late 1919 through early 1921. But it was also true that Mallory had always planned for his firms to evolve into full-service shipping houses: owning and operating tonnage of their own as well as managing vessels for public and private owners. Every man that Mallory and Houston had recruited to join them had been given this promise; and every man had been assured "that if the operations were successful," he "would get a share in the business." Thus, among the proprietors and executives of C. D. Mallory & Co. there was always the desire to expand their activities into own-flag and nongovernment operations. The beginning of the general depression in American-flag shipping in late 1920 gave them their first opportunities to diversify. Their initial success contributed to the neglect of their less remunerative government business. But their success also gave them a base on which to build when their government business was taken away.

During 1921–1922, C. D. Mallory & Co. began to build a well-deserved reputation as an efficient manager of "distress companies." Many of the shipping companies formed in the euphoria of 1918–1919 had begun to stumble and fail amidst the depressed market of 1920–1921. And as the number of maritime foreclosures and reorganizations mounted, bankers and other creditors found themselves with ships on their hands, but with little knowledge of what to do with them. The solution many of them found was to consign such vessels to experienced shipping firms for employment or liquidation. C. D. Mallory & Co. became one of the busiest firms in this kind of arrangement; its two most frequent clients were Alexander Smith and Malcolm G. Chace.[1]

Smith was president of the investment-banking house of Peabody, Houghteling & Co. (later, Peabody, Smith & Co.) of Chicago and New York. His firm had long specialized in the financing of Great Lakes shipping companies and had helped develop the standard vessel mortgage bond used in that business. During and after World War I, Smith had also begun to invest in coastal and transoceanic tonnage and in the debt securities spawned by the ship-mortgage provisions of the Jones Act. He and Mallory were fellow members of the New York Yacht Club and were first drawn together by mutual enthusiasms for marine architecture and fine pleasure craft. But like many of Mallory's social friendships, their relationship soon blossomed to include business.

Sailing had also brought Chace and Mallory together. Chace had been a top amateur tennis and hockey player at the turn of the century and had then turned to yachts, where it was impossible not to encounter Clifford Mallory. In business, Chace had formed the investment houses of Chace & Harriman (with Henry I. Harriman of Boston) and M. G. Chace Co. From his home town of Providence, Chace specialized in New England textile, transportation, and public utility companies. A description of his style might also have fitted his friend and associate Smith:

> Mr. Chace was seldom in the public eye . . . [but he was] a financier and industrialist of importance in the United States for more than forty years. . . . Frequently Mr. Chace bought large blocks of stock in concerns and exercised considerable control behind the scenes. At times his interest in a company would [only] be made

public when he took part in a fight with other stockholders for control.[2]

The first three bits of business that Smith and Chace threw Mallory's way were connected with disparate but financially troubled American companies: United States Food Products Corp., American Bauxite Co., and Huron Navigation Co. In each case, Mallory's services were satisfactory but minimally profitable.

United States Food Products Corp. was the successor of Distillers Securities Corp., a manufacturer and marketer of whisky which found its traditional product banned by Prohibition in 1919. Smith and other underwriters had reorganized the firm, and it had diversified into sugar, vinegar, molasses, syrups, preserved fruits, compressed yeast, and cattle feeds. Its principal subsidiary was Sugar Products Co., which, as a buyer, seller, and distributor of molasses and sugar, had large receiving tanks and stations in Cuba, Puerto Rico, Santo Domingo, Barbados, Venezuela, the United States, Canada, and Great Britain and owned twenty ships of various sizes and flags to interconnect these facilities. At Alexander Smith's suggestion, C. D. Mallory & Co. was retained for one year commencing March 15, 1921, to manage and operate a portion of Sugar Product Co.'s fleet in the Cuban trade. In all, twelve vessels were involved: the British-flag steamships *Rochelie, Macoris, Manx Isles, J. Oswald Boyd, Delmira,* and *Sagua* and the American-flag steamship *Julius Kessler*—all of which had been extensively modified to carry sugar in bags and molasses in bulk; the American-flag, diesel, molasses tankers *Theodore F. Reynolds, Pinthis,* and *Barge W*; and the British-flag, self-propelled, bulk-carriers *Hopper No. 46* and *Hopper No. 62*. All twelve were returned to Sugar Products Co.'s receivers on March 15, 1922, for liquidation.[3]

The two American Bauxite Co. vessels were the steamships *George B. McKenzie* and *John R. Gibbons,* which were consigned to C. D. Mallory & Co. in November and December 1921 for operation in the coastal market. They were returned to their owner in February and March 1922. The Huron Navigation

Co.'s vessels were nine enormous wooden schooners: *Oakley C. Curtis, Edward J. Lawrence, Cora F. Cressey, Camilla May Page, Singleton Palmer, Ruth E. Merrill, Dorothy Palmer, Jane Palmer,* and *Wyoming.* Maine-built between 1901 and 1909, these white elephants were the largest sailing vessels in the American-flag fleet. They had operated in both the coastal and Great Lakes trades, but were tied up in Mobile when consigned to C. D. Mallory & Co. for sale on December 1, 1921. By March 25, 1922, they had been peddled to various purchasers and never sailed under Clifford Mallory's flag.[4]

Mallory's profits from this motley collection of twenty-three ships were small, but these consignments from Smith and Chace were important milestones in his course toward independence as a shipping operator. He used them to show himself, his employees, and the industry that he could find opportunities outside of the Shipping Board web, and in the process he demonstrated his competence to two influential financiers able to throw other, more profitable, business his way. And they did. In mid-1921, Smith and Chace offered Mallory a plum: exclusive agency of seven tankers commonly known as the Swiftsure Fleet.

Swiftsure, Swiftarrow, Swiftstar, Swifteagle, Swiftscout, Swiftwind, and *Swiftlight* were 464-foot, all-steel, 12,000 d.w.t. tankers built in 1921 by the North West Barge & Iron Co. of Portland, Oregon. Their original owner had been the France and Canada Oil Transport Co. under the subsidiary name of Swiftsure Oil Transport, Inc. They had been financed, however, by a twelve-year "first preferred mortgage" to the United States Shipping Board (under the Jones Act) for $12,600,000 at 5 per cent ($150 per d.w.t.) and by a ten-year second mortgage of $4,200,000 at 8 per cent to Peabody, Houghteling & Co. (51 per cent), M. G. Chace Co. (34 per cent), and Old Colony Trust Co. (15 per cent). Interest payments on these obligations had lapsed almost immediately, and in June 1921 Smith and Chace formed the Tanker Syndicate, Inc., of Maine (representing the second-mortgage bondholders) and took possession of the seven ships.[5]

Even prior to formation of the Tanker Syndicate, Chace had sounded out Clifford Mallory on the latter's interest in managing the Swiftsure Fleet. Mallory had expressed strong interest, but was still surprised when Chace telephoned him on July 26, 1921, and asked him to take the ships over "immediately." What followed is best told in Mallory's own words, as it represents the shipping expertise he and his organization could instantaneously provide to companies in distress:

> Upon investigation we found that four of these tankers had been loaded with grain in bulk and bags at Portland, Oregon, for Europe. Three of them were on that date [July 26] in mid-Atlantic enroute to Europe, and one was at the Panama Canal, held for tonnage dues. Another ship was held up at New Orleans on account of lack of funds, and I think had been libeled, and the seventh ship was still at the yard of the builders in Portland, having never been delivered. There were no funds available and the ships were heavily obligated for a large amount of money. We had no knowledge of the character of the crews on any of the vessels, and as it was an unheard of thing for a tank steamer to carry grain, we were at a loss to know how the steamers so loaded were to be discharged in Europe. We finally delivered all of the grain cargoes; got the vessels back to the United States; released the ships held on account of lack of funds; and started their employment in the oil business. . . .
>
> In taking over the Swiftsure Fleet we [also] found that the insurance premiums were, in our opinion, exceedingly heavy, and we immediately commenced negotiations with Lloyd's for replacing this insurance. As the former brokers took an arbitrary stand in the matter, premiums not having been paid, we got the Shipping Board, who held the first mortgage on the vessels, to carry the insurance until such time as we could place it satisfactorily in London. When the insurance was finally placed, it was at a materially lower rate than before and the underwriters wrote into the policies: "Warranted Mallory Management." [6]

The employment which Mallory found for the Swiftsure Fleet was with the New England Oil Refining Co. That company was the brain child of F. Douglas Cochrane, senior partner in the Boston investment house of Cochrane, Harper & Co., but its history soon became intimately entwined with that of C. D. Mallory & Co.

In March 1920, Cochrane, Harper & Co. had organized three firms which collectively were intended to function as an integrated oil company: New England Oil Corp., Inc., the parent and financial coordinator; New England Oil Corp., Ltd., a production subsidiary with oil leases and concessions in Venezuela; and New England Oil Refining Co., a subsidiary specializing in the transportation of crude oil, refining, and the transportation and marketing of petroleum products. New England Oil Refining Co. commenced the group's active operations by opening a fifty-acre refinery on tidewater at Fall River and a three-acre tidewater terminal at New Bedford. The refinery's capacity was 25,000 barrels of crude per day, and it was designed to produce gasoline, kerosene, lubricants, fuel oil, gas oil, road oil, and asphalt for distribution to customers throughout the northeastern states. Cochrane's plans were to own or control one-half of his group's crude requirements, a three-month crude supply at the refinery, and two-thirds of his companies' transportation needs. These goals proved unrealistic.

New England Oil Corp., Ltd. was never able to go into production on its Venezuelan properties. This forced New England Oil Refining Co. to purchase its entire crude supply from its competitors. To make matters worse, there were no producing fields nearby and no crude-oil pipe-line outlets closer than Bayonne, New Jersey. Finally, maximum crude-storage facilities in Fall River and New Bedford (and within the financial reach of the group) were found to be no more than 330,000 barrels—only 13.2 days leeway for a 25,000 barrel per day refinery! The net result was summarized by New England Oil Refining Co.'s managing director (and later president) Warwick Greene:

> ...the refinery was ENTIRELY DEPENDENT ON OCEAN TRANSPORTATION FOR ITS SUPPLY OF RAW MATERIAL: CRUDE OIL.
>
> Not only was ocean transportation essential to the Fall River Refinery for its supply of crude, but its inadequate crude storage made its operations dependent on regular schedules of deliveries.

For the first nine months of its operation, New England Oil Refining Co. met these very demanding requirements for raw material and transport in the open markets for oil and ships. During 1921, using the services of various brokers, the company negotiated seventy-one tanker charters to Fall River from Mexican oil ports and nine from Gulf ports, and received nine additional shipments C.I.F. or F.O.B. Fall River. It was a precarious existence, as Greene later recalled:

> Owing to the limited storage at the plant . . . any irregularity in deliveries would jeopardize the Company's business. Empty crude tanks meant shutting down the plant and defaulting on large sales commitments. . . . As a round trip to Mexico consumed twenty-one days, and to California nearly fifty days, it will be seen how easily the refinery might have been left without crude in times of heavy demand on the current charter market, had the Company been wholly dependent on charters.[7]

Clifford Mallory was first aware of New England Oil Refining Co.'s transportation problems in the spring of 1921. Cochrane had used him as a broker in chartering several tankers from the Shipping Board, but their acquaintance was only slight. After he received the Swiftsure Fleet's agency from Malcolm Chace in July, however, Mallory's interest in Cochrane warmed:

> . . . I went to Boston to see Mr. Cochrane and suggested to him that it might be advantageous for both interests for him to meet and discuss with Mr. Chace the possibility of the New England employing the Swiftsure fleet of vessels. This suggestion was accepted; Messrs. Chace and Cochrane discussed the matter quite fully, and finally agreed that if the Shipping Board would relieve the New England of the charters of Shipping Board tankers they were obligated to, Mr. Cochrane would employ the Swiftsure vessels. The first charter to the New England was the S.S. *Swiftarrow,* on Aug. 1st, 1921. Through my efforts with the Shipping Board, we were able to assist the New England in getting rid of the Shipping Board charters.[8]

For the remainder of 1921, C. D. Mallory & Co. functioned simultaneously as exclusive owner's broker for the Tanker Syndicate and as one of several chartering agents employed by the New England Oil Refining Co. As owner's broker, Mallory's task was to find employment (charters) for the Swiftsure Fleet at a commission of 1 1/4 per cent on the gross freight or hire earned by the seven tankers. As a chartering agent, his task was to find vessels to transport New England Oil's crude at another 1 1/4 per cent commission on gross freight or hire.

Naturally, Mallory used Swiftsure's supply of tankers to

meet as much of the oil company's demand for transport capacity as was possible. During the last five months of 1921, he negotiated nineteen charters between his two clients: all were for single voyages between Mexican ports and Fall River; 1,419,581 barrels of crude oil were so transported; and C. D. Mallory & Co. collected commissions totaling $15,417 on the transactions. To put these arrangements in even clearer perspective: New England Oil employed 100 per cent of Swiftsure's seaworthy capacity; Swiftsure supplied 48 per cent of the shipments and 57 per cent of the crude delivered to the Fall River refinery; and Mallory profited from both isdes of the marriage he had so perceptively arranged.[9]

But there were ambiguities in his relationship to his clients. His obligation to the Tanker Syndicate was to secure the highest possible rates of freight and hire and, since his compensation was a function of *gross* freight or hire, it was in his own best interest as owner's broker to maximize those rates. In his role of chartering agent, however, the better he served his client, the lower was his reward, for his obligation to New England Oil was to secure the lowest possible rates of freight or hire. To overcome these ambiguities, Mallory proposed a longer-term, contractual relationship which would combine his and his clients' respective strengths in common cause to overcome their respective needs. The Tanker Syndicate had tankers and capital, but no experience in either oil or marine transportation. New England Oil had an operating refinery with a voracious appetite for crude, and an unusual dependence on water carriers, but needed funds to expand its production and marketing functions. Mallory had no ships of his own and, as yet, insufficient capital to acquire any, but he had shipping expertise to burn and an intense desire to diversify the activities of his young firm.

On November 29, 1921 (effective January 1, 1922), the financiers, the oil men, and the shipping men pooled their interests and resources under contract. In return for 100,000 of New England Oil Refining Co.'s 600,000 shares of common stock, the Tanker Syndicate loaned the oil company $1,300,000 for ten years at 8 per cent interest per annum. In return for a twelve-year bareboat charter of the seven Swiftsure tankers and their ownership after that period of time, New

England Oil assumed the two obligations then outstanding on the vessels: the Shipping Board's $12,600,000 ($150 per d.w.t.), 5 per cent, twelve-year "first preferred" mortgage and the Tanker Syndicate's $4,200,000 ($50 per d.w.t.), 8 per cent, ten-year "second" mortgage. Thus, the Tanker Syndicate shifted encumbrances whose principals totaled $200 per d.w.t. from its shoulders to those of New England Oil. In addition, the oil company agreed to pay the Tanker Syndicate a premium of $5 per d.w.t. ($420,000 more) for the seven vessels. The final condition of the contract was that New England Oil must retain C. D. Mallory & Co. as exclusive managing agents for the Swiftsure Fleet.[10]

For assuming complete managerial responsibility for the Swiftsure Fleet to the order and for the account of New England Oil, C. D. Mallory & Co. was to be paid a "husbanding fee" of $13.33 per ship per operating day ($400 per month per ship) and 5 per cent of the fleet's "gross profits" (i.e., gross revenue less all operating expenses but before interest and depreciation). The Mallory firm could also claim brokerage not exceeding 1 1/4 per cent on any charters of Swiftsure tankers New England Oil might choose to make *to* "outside" companies.

Mallory's financial arrangements with the New England Oil Refining Co. respecting management of the Swiftsure Fleet were unique in American maritime practice (see Figure 12.1). He designed his particular compensation formula, he said, "in accordance with the best practice in England, Scotland, and I believe in other countries," but it rapidly became the most important means by which he differentiated C. D. Mallory & Co.'s philosophy, fee structure, and services from those of his competitors. He developed the formula in response to his opportunity to manage the Swiftsure Fleet, but he applied it in all subsequent instances in which his firm undertook the operation of "privately owned vessels."

The purpose of the husbanding fee, Mallory told his clients, was to cover the "approximate cost of our overhead necessary to supervise and maintain each vessel," but it was "not expected to cover executive overhead or profit." (This fee was comparable in purpose and amount to the $350 to $400 per ship per month compensations allowed managing agents by the Shipping Board.) The idea of figuring the manager's commission on gross profits, however, was Mallory's innovation, and he was always quite persuasive in pointing out the uniqueness and competitive advantages of his idea:

> I believe we are the only ship managers who have insisted that their contracts for the management of vessels shall be on the basis of a husbanding fee to cover part of the overhead, plus a percentage of the gross profits. All other contracts that I know of are based on a husbanding fee and a percentage of the gross freights, which is quite different as you can readily understand. In the latter case the ship manager makes a profit so long as there are any freights and when the ship may be losing money, whereas on our basis we do not receive any profit unless the ship is making a profit over and above operating expenses.

> . . . I say it is the best practice. . . . The difference as you will readily note, is that our commission is based on the results after deducting the operating cost from the gross freights, which to our mind is much more satisfactory, as a ship manager is interested in the economy of operation to approximately the same extent as the owner. The trouble with the commission on gross freights is that an unscrupulous manager might continue to run a vessel that is losing money for the stockholders, in order to get his commission, whereas in the method that we are working on, no compensation would accrue if the vessel was losing money.[11]

Although he developed his $400—5 per cent formula initially for the management of the Swiftsure Fleet, Mallory was quick to apply it to two more vessels brought to him by his friends Smith and Chace. The two bankers had forced the Astoria Mahogany Co. (a Long Island firm trading with Nicaragua and Mexico) into receivership early in 1922, and, on February 20, they placed the firm's two ships—the twin-screw, diesel freighters *Astmahco III* and *IV*—with C. D. Mallory & Co. pending liquidation of the mahogany company's affairs. On April 28, Peabody, Houghteling & Co. purchased the 3,500 d.w.t. vessels at a U.S. marshal's sale for $20 per d.w.t., renamed them *Ormidale* and *Glendaruel,* and sold them to two new companies owned by Smith and Chace, effective May 5. C. D. Mallory & Co. continued as managing agents for these ships, operating them in the coasting trades, until mid-1927 when Mallory acted as broker for their sale at original cost— another neat piece of business for himself, Smith, and Chace. [12] Nevertheless, this venture was only a profitable diversion compared to his major responsibilities to New England Oil.

Mallory's dual obligations to New England Oil were to seek full employment for the Swiftsure Fleet and to meet whatever transport requirements for crude oil and petroleum products the Fall River refinery might generate. In theory, these obligations were compatible and complementary; in practice, the demand schedule of the refinery and the supply schedule of the tanker fleet could never be perfectly matched. It was Mallory's prime responsibility, of course, to equate refinery demand and tanker supply insofar as possible. But the difficulties in doing that also made him responsible for meeting excessive demand (by chartering "outside" tonnage when the Swiftsure tankers were taxed to capacity or unavailable) and for handling over-supplies (by chartering Swiftsure tankers to "outside" parties when New England Oil had no cargoes for them).

As things turned out, C. D. Mallory & Co.'s agreement with New England Oil lasted six and three-quarters years rather than the twelve originally planned. Nevertheless, Mallory gave full service, and the arrangement was unquestionably beneficial to both parties. Financial and administrative data for the life of the agreement have not survived, but the record for the first five and one-half years is sufficient to establish the mutual profitability of the relationship.

First, respecting the employment of the Swiftsure Fleet: from January 1, 1922, to June 1, 1927, 81 per cent of its time was devoted to its prime responsibility, that of supplying New England Oil's Fall River refinery with Mexican, Venezuelan, and American crude (see Table 12.1). Another 13 per cent of the fleet's time was divided between deliveries of products from Fall River to various American and Canadian ports and the carriage of crude in the spot-charter market. And all this was accomplished with the loss of only one of the seven tankers— *Swiftstar* (in 1923 through no fault of her owners or managers)—and repair and lay-up down time amounting to only 1 per cent of total fleet ship-days per year: an excellent record by any standard of ship management.

As for providing "outside" tonnage on New England Oil's demand, Mallory never faltered, and he fulfilled this charge in three ways (all for additional compensation beyond the Swift-sure formula): by spot charters in the general market; by one major time charter of government tonnage; and by buying vessels on his own account and time-chartering them to the oil company with a portion of their hire creditable toward purchase.

The spot charters were routine, involved twelve to fifteen ships per year, and grossed Mallory $8,000 to $10,000 broker-age per annum. The government time charter was a more complex negotiation involving nine Shipping Board tankers for ten months of 1923. New England needed the vessels on short notice to tap new California sources of crude, but had been unable to charter them because of the company's shaky financial reputation at that time. Mallory stepped in, acted as negotiator and guarantor for the oil company before the skeptical Shipping Board, obtained and operated the tankers for twenty-three voyages, and grossed brokerage of $48,211 on the deal.[13]

A total of eight vessels were purchased by Mallory and resold to New England Oil on the charter-purchase plan: the single-screw, diesel tanker *Pinthis* and the steam tug *Interstate No. 2* in 1922; the twin-screw, diesel tanker *Bacoi* in 1924; the steam tanker *Mexicano* in 1925; the steam tanker *Colmar* and three tank barges, *NEO Nos. 2, 5,* and *6,* during 1925–1928. These vessels were used by New England Oil for products deliveries, and the pattern of their acquisition was consistent. In each case, upon request of the oil company, C. D. Mallory & Co. formed a wholly owned subsidiary firm to buy the vessel and, once bought, negotiated a resale price with New England Oil (usually incorporating a 30 to 50 per cent markup). The vessel was then time-chartered to the oil company at market rates, but with 30 to 50 per cent of the hire applying toward purchase.[14]

New England Oil's managers were certainly satisfied with Mallory's performance. They gained a modern tanker fleet and ready access to a thoroughly competent ship-management team that guaranteed to have vessels where needed, when needed, as needed. They fully appreciated that

> Mallory & Co. are in the position of being able to give their immediate attention and should . . . trouble occur at more than one place, they have the organization to despatch at once, thereby making a saving in time and expense. . . . [These] services could [not] be covered as efficiently from another source as the personal contact which Mallory & Co.'s men enjoy with the underwriters, surveyors, drydock, and ship repairs and supply people

—and at competitive prices. President Warwick Greene, in a thorough memorandum dated March 31, 1927, summarized New England Oil's conviction that Mallory management had saved *at least* 1.04 per cent to that date of the "cost of moving the same volume of oil between the same ports at current market rates." [15]

Mallory, for his part, found New England Oil a satisfactory, if often exasperating, client. The oil company cut his "managers commission" from 5 per cent to 2 1/2 per cent (effective July 1, 1923), haggled endlessly over the settlement of accounts, and demanded a host of special services for which he received no additional compensation (such as short-term financing of accounts payable "in sums up to $200,000" and shopping trips to inspect for possible purchase "tug boats, barges, steamers, etc. located in various parts of the country"). But Mallory never considered terminating the contract, and he certainly lost no money on it—far from it. Furthermore, he was astute enough to perceive that he derived a variety of qualitative benefits from the relationship that helped him to hone and tune his young firm's organization and personnel, enhance its reputation, and sharpen its purpose and direction. [16]

As but one example: the charter-purchase agreements between C. D. Mallory & Co. and New England Oil were used by Mallory to initiate the profit-sharing plan he had promised his managers. Mallory and Houston (and sometimes Smith and Chace) financed such companies as the Fall River Steamship Co. (created in July 1922 to purchase *Pinthis*) and the Bacoi Steamship Co. (created in June 1924 to purchase *Bacoi*), but they donated a portion of the capital stock of these firms to their five key managers: James Houston, Frank Bynum, Willard Bergen, Maitland Smith, and Ellis Knowles. As earnings on this stock grew and accumulated, the five incorporated themselves as the Lamton Corp. and thenceforth paid into Lamton "half of the profit-sharing compensation earned by them under the arrangement they had with C. D. Mallory & Co., Inc." And, as Lamton's assets grew, the five reinvested them in vessels owned and/or operated by the various Mallory firms.

The most important benefit Mallory derived from his New England Oil contract, however, was the intimate exposure it provided him to and in the American petroleum industry. He knew that here was a market requiring a large supply of marine transportation and that a considerable portion of it involved the coastal and intercoastal carriage of oil and products in American-flag ships. But it was not a market that had attracted his interest when he had founded his firm. Given his family's historic commitment to dry-cargo and passenger vessels and his own and Houston's original fixation with offshore liner and tramp services under the Shipping Board wing, Mallory's neglect of the tanker market in 1919–1920 is understandable, if myopic. By 1921, however, he had seen the light, and much of the credit belongs to Malcolm Chace. As Maitland Smith recalled, "Chace came to our office at least once a week, for meetings with us, and by bringing the Tankers to us originally, he was largely responsible for the success of C. D. Mallory & Co., Inc." By 1922, under Chace's encouragement, Mallory was active as a broker in the spot-charter market for tanker tonnage and had the agency of the Swiftsure Fleet in hand. By 1923, with Chace's financial support, Mallory began to take a major position in tankers on his own account and risk.[17]

The first result of Mallory's new awareness of tankers was Malston Co., Inc., a Delaware corporation capitalized at $850,000 (raised to $1,500,000 two months after formation) and chartered in March 1923. Mallory and Houston, as partners in C. D. Mallory & Co., subscribed 17 per cent of the new company's stock, while Chace and Alexander Smith took the remainder. The company's purpose was to capitalize on a sudden upward shift in the private demand for American-flag tankers and the Shipping Board's consequent decision to meet that demand by dumping some of its excess capacity on the public ship market at bargain prices. [18] To understand the situation and the opportunities it bred for Mallory, however, some backtracking is necessary.

During World War I, the Shipping Board had acquired a fleet of 178 steel tankers by construction, requisition, and purchase. All these vessels remained in federal hands until August 16, 1920, when a modest disposal program was initiated. The program sought to deal equitably with those who had lost tonnage by requisition, to retain sufficient tankers for government needs, and to stabilize prices in the markets for new and used ships. By June 30, 1922, the board had reconveyed the 61 requisitioned tankers to their former owners, transferred its 12 best war-built tankers to the Navy Department, and auctioned off 17 more to the major American oil companies at prices ranging from $160 to $185 per d.w.t. This left a board-controlled tanker fleet of 88 ships: 18 were operated by managing agents primarily to supply government bunker and power stations; 70 were laid up but available for charter to private shippers or carriers like New England Oil or C. D. Mallory & Co.

While the Shipping Board's fleet represented the largest and most available pool of American-flag tankers, there had been only a modest demand for its services among private shippers and carriers during the years 1919 through 1922. The reason was simple. Much of the crude oil moving in the American petroleum market during those years came from Mexico and Venezuela, and foreign-flag vessels (which were cheaper to operate than American-flag tankers) could be used extensively in its carriage. American-flag vessels had to content themselves with the smaller coastal trade to and from Gulf ports and the intercoastal trade to and from California—both protected by cabotage. Then matters changed dramatically.

"Starting late in 1922 and continuing until early summer, 1923, the demand for steel-tanker tonnage was very active," reported the Shipping Board in retrospect. "As a consequence of the diminished supply of crude oil from the Mexican fields and the attendant demands from the southern California territory, the tanker requirements of the oil industry in this country were estimated to have doubled. The Board was enabled to seize this opportunity for the disposal of more than one-half of its tanker fleet." Early in March 1923, the board announced the withdrawal of its idle tank steamers from the charter market and invited bids on any or all of its fleet. By June 30, it had sold forty-four tankers to twenty companies for a total of $18,875,004.90. Thus, 412,420 d.w.t. of shipping were sold in less than four months at an average price of $45.76 per ton— half the previous government price level! And over the next twelve months, the board sold six more tankers (49,215 d.w.t.) to four of these companies for $1,674,637.50 ($34.03 per ton).[19]

Mallory and his associates interpreted the Shipping Board's change in sales policies as a genuine effort to turn over its tanker fleet to private entrepreneurs and to end its domination of the sales and charter markets for American-flag petroleum carriers. Thus Malston Co. was quickly organized, and its officers were in the thick of the bidding.

Between March 26, 1923, and January 2, 1924, Malston Co. bid on nine of the Shipping Board tankers and purchased seven at prices totaling $3,207,507: *Halsey, Durango, Dillwyn, Hugoton, Imlay, Mevania,* and *Hoxbar.* Thus, Mallory and his associates bought 15 per cent of the tanker tonnage dumped by the Shipping Board during its sales orgy of 1923–1924 and accounted for 16 per cent of the total dollar sales involved. All these vessels were acquired on the standard Shipping Board terms: 50 per cent cash and 50 per cent payable over five years at 5 per cent per annum interest on the unpaid balance.

Close scrutiny of these acquisitions reveals distinct preferences which reflect conscious strategy. Bids were made only for oil-powered steamships in the 9,500 to 10,500 d.w.t. range, which were not more than five or six years old and could be operated by crews of thirty to thirty-two men. Bids were made only on vessels with which the Mallory organization had previous personal experience (such as those they had operated on time charter for New England Oil). Mallory also refused to bid more than $46 per ton for vessels under 10,000 d.w.t. or more than $45 per ton for larger vessels, and he timed his bids with movements in the petroleum-freight market: he bid for vessels only when the California rate approached or passed 95 cents per barrel or the Gulf and Mexican rates approached or passed 35 cents per barrel. He arrived at these bidding rules of thumb on the basis of his experience and the best cost-revenue estimates he could make. In retrospect, his choices appear quite perceptive and again demonstrate his always careful and usually profitable attention to detail.[20]

Most important, however, Mallory acted as he did when he did because he had a clear idea of what use the Malston tankers could serve: he had a very particular kind of customer in mind. As correctly stated by B. B. Howard and M. D. Stauffer of Standard Oil (N.J.)'s Marine Department in 1940, all integrated oil companies "having definite [marine] transportation requirements over a long period are compelled to stabilize their cost of transportation by ownership of tankers or by time chartering for long terms or by a combination of both." The question, of course, is how and when to mix, and the dilemma was well put by R. K. Kelly, marine manager of the Tidewater Oil Co. in 1935:

> There are so many unknown variables in the equations for forecasting charter market trends that the problem has consistently defied solution efforts of the best statisticians. It is practically impossible to retain a balanced tonnage position over any extended period of time. With respect to the alternative, there are those whose policy is to own tonnage to the extent of 70 per cent to 80 per cent of the average estimated transportation requirements, and obtain the remainder in the . . . market; and others who establish absolute protection for their requirements by overtonnaging their position, and endeavoring to employ their excess tonnage in the service of others to avoid idle ships.[21]

What Mallory was looking for was major integrated oil companies who had chosen to "undertonnage" themselves in American-flag markets and would consequently welcome his independent fleet as a reserve on which they could depend. He was not looking for one-shot "spot" charters, but for time charters or that hybrid form of charter which covered "a specified number of consecutive voyages or as many consecutive voyages as can be made in a given period of time." And he found what he sought: during 1923–1924, Standard Oil Co. (N.J.) took *Durango, Halsey, Dillwyn, Mevania,* and *Hoxbar* on a series of six-month and twelve-month "consecutive-voyage charters," and the General Petroleum Co. took *Hugoton* and *Imlay* on similar terms. In each case, Malston & Co. earned freight at market rates (see Figure 12.2) and C. D. Mallory & Co. earned brokerage at 1 1/4 per cent of total freight.[22]

What Mallory perceived and understood in businessman's terms in 1923 was the economic situation best described in retrospect by Koopmans in 1939:

> For an oil company the maintenance of a tanker fleet which is sufficiently large to meet any situation that may arise by means of its own ships would involve the cost of maintaining a considerable average of unused tonnage. If no "free" tankers existed, this cost could only be reduced by some practice of reciprocal chartering between oil companies. Such chartering is, indeed, practised even with the existence of an independent fleet, but, rather than rely entirely on the services of their competitors in such a matter, the oil companies naturally choose to preserve a free market where their marginal needs may always be covered at a price which is equal for all competitors.
>
> Thus, the independently owned fleet represents a kind of reserve on which oil companies may draw in order to meet in an efficient way fluctuations in their individual tonnage requirements. This is probably the main reason why the big oil companies have allowed the independent fleet to grow. . . .[23]

Koopmans was describing the world supply and demand of tankers, but his generalizations also held true for the branch market in which Clifford Mallory saw his chance in 1923—and with an interesting twist. Rising costs of building, owning, and operating American-flag ships were encouraging American oil companies to "undertonnage" their position in American-flag tankers. Yet, increasingly large amounts of their crude oil and products *had* to be transported in such vessels; for coastal and intercoastal shipments, recourse to the independent foreign-flag tanker pool was impossible. Thus, there was considerable demand for the formation of an efficient but independent American-flag tanker pool. Clifford Mallory perceived the demand correctly, and he determined to fill it insofar as he could.

Thus, management of the Sugar Products Fleet introduced Clifford Mallory to tankers; responsibility for the Swiftsure Fleet introduced him to the marine transportation of petroleum and its products; and his purchase of what became the Malston Fleet began a broader plan to create and manage the largest independent tanker fleet under the American flag. With constant encouragement and financial support from Malcolm Chace, Mallory began to search out the kinds of vessels and customers he had in mind. And in this quest, he received the full and powerful support of another old friend, Robert L. Hague.

Bob Hague was one year older than Clifford Mallory and came from a vastly different social and economic background. Born in Rhode Island, he had an early career that cut across a wide swath of transportation experience: as a seaman on Gloucester fishing boats and transpacific trading barks; as a machinist, fireman, and locomotive engineer for the New York, New Haven & Hartford Railroad; as an oiler, engineer, and assistant superintendent of construction for the American-Hawaiian Line; and as assistant superintending engineer and marine superintendent for Standard Oil Co. (Calif.). When Mallory first met him in 1918, Hague was serving as chief of the Construction and Repair Division of the Shipping Board, and the two and William Houston formed a close friendship based on common government service and mutual respect. Nothing of a business nature came of the relationship, however, until after Hague went to work for Standard Oil Co. (N.J.) in 1920.

Hague remained with Standard Oil until his death in 1939 and bore various titles, including vice president and president of the Standard Shipping Co. and general manager of Standard's Marine Department. Regardless of his title, Hague was for those nineteen years *the* American expert on the marine transportation of petroleum and its products. He "was a leader in the advancement of new ideas in tank ship construction"; he composed and copyrighted the "Haguecoast" form which became the standard tank steamer voyage charter party used in the Western Hemisphere; he created the *Register of Tank Vessels of the World,* published by his company but copyrighted in his name, which became the broker's bible; and he supervised the operations of Standard's "two hundred odd ships in all quarters of the world." As imperious and autocratic as he was able, Hague made his policies his company's policies. And, as "the head of the largest private fleet of vessels in the world," by his decisions to build, buy, sell, lay up, scrap, or charter tankers he could "make" markets for other shippers and carriers.[24]

When Hague began to throw business their way in 1923, it was both a compliment and a boost for the partners and managers of C. D. Mallory & Co. Much of the decision to purchase the Malston Fleet was predicated on Hague's assurances that Standard Oil would employ five of the tankers on long-term, consecutive voyages; and the pledge was kept. In mid-1924, Hague offered Mallory another deal: first option to buy four of Standard Oil's older but perfectly seaworthy tankers at the bargain price of $25 per d.w.t. Mallory consulted his associates, and his manager of tanker operations, Willard Bergen, suggested they accept the offer if Hague would pledge to charter the vessels back on long-term, consecutive-voyage arrangements at market rates. Hague readily consented, and the sale and charter-back transactions were speedily completed.

Mallory and Houston (as C. D. Mallory & Co.), their six managers (as Lamton Co.), and Chace contributed funds to the creation of four Delaware corporations, each named for the ship it purchased, each capitalized at $300,000. Mallory announced the purchases on October 15, and *Matinicock, Ardmore, Malabar* (formerly *John D. Rockefeller*), and *Muskogee* were all under his flag by November 12.

It should now be evident that when the Shipping Board notified Mallory, on August 28, 1924, of its intention to cancel his Mediterranean and African lines, it was far from the end of the world. His pride was wounded, but he had plenty of other irons in the fire. As of the final termination date of his Shipping Board agreements, on January 31, 1925, Mallory was two years into both the Swiftsure-New England Oil and the Ormidale-Glendaruel contracts; one year into Malston; and two months into the Matinicock-Ardmore-Malabar-Muskogee arrangement. Whether they were a cause or an effect of his loss of the Shipping Board vessels, he was still in control of twenty tankers and two tramp freighters on his own account. And in an interview with the New York *Herald Tribune,* he made his intentions as clear as his displeasure:

> ... Mr. Mallory [said] that the Board's action had convinced him "that it was a waste of time to think of buying any of their services, ..."
>
> Mr. Mallory said that he and his associates had decided to confine their activities to tankers and tramp steamers, unless the government decides to remove itself from the shipping business.
>
> ... Mr. Mallory said that in buying tankers he was fairly sure that he would not meet with government competition. ...[25]

Mallory followed these intentions to the letter during the years 1925 – 1930, with one slight exception. During "the early days of the Florida land and building expansion period," he was approached by Robert T. Hasler, a Virginia-based entrepreneur, with a proposition for a line to carry general cargo between New York and Miami. In early November 1925, Mallory and Hasler bought two five-year old "Lakers" from the Shipping Board for $7 per d.w.t.: *Ripon* (renamed *Malsah*) and *Lake Horesti* (renamed *Osceola*). The two vessels operated as the Mallory-Hasler Line until the capsizing of a sailing vessel in the Miami channel blocked navigation for such a long period that liner service was discontinued. *Malsah* and *Osceola* were redeployed as coastal tramps until their sale in 1928 and 1929.

The Mallory-Hasler Line is more notable in that it brought Mallory the final key executive of his firm, William N. Westerlund. Westerlund joined C. D. Mallory & Co. in March 1926 with fifteen years of solid experience in shipping behind him. He was a specialist in traffic and cargo operations, having carried out important assignments in those areas as a "special expert" for the Shipping Board. More recently he had been associated with Hasler and had managed the Mallory-Hasler Line. When that service was discontinued, he moved over to the Mallory fold. He also bought into Lamton Corp. and soon emerged as a leader among the junior partners.

Except for this brief Florida line, all of Mallory's other dry-cargo vessels were employed in American-flag tramping. *Ormidale* and *Glendaruel* were operated in the coastal trades until their sale in 1927 and, when the ship and the price were right, Mallory picked up additional tramp tonnage. He regularly bid for suitable vessels in both public and private markets, and his preferences were for ten-knot, oil-burning, steel steamships, not over ten years old, and in the 3,500 to 6,500 d.w.t. range. He was successful five times.

On October 29, 1826, Mallory bought the six-year old *Juvigny* for $12 per d.w.t. from the Independent Steamship Co. *Carolinas* (renamed *Maltran*), seven years old, followed for $12 per d.w.t. from the Carolina Steamship Co. On December 12, 1928, after selling *Malsah,* he purchased two eight-year-old Shipping Board vessels for $5 per d.w.t. plus the pledge to spend an additional $20 per d.w.t. in "betterments": *Chickamagua* (renamed *Malchace*) and *Wekika* (renamed *Mallemak*). And on April 24, 1929, after selling *Osceola* and losing *Juvigny* at sea, he bought the nine-year-old *Eastern Leader* (renamed *Malang*) from the Shipping Board at $5 per d.w.t. plus a pledge of $7 per d.w.t. in betterments.

These transactions reveal the (by then) typical pattern in which C. D. Mallory & Co., Lamton Corp., and M. G. Chace Co. interlocked themselves in various proportions. *Malsah, Osceola, Juvigny,* and *Maltran* were each purchased by single-ship, namesake companies organized for that purpose. When *Malsah* was sold in 1928, its namesake company was used to purchase *Malchace* and *Mallemak.* The Osceola and Juvigny companies disappeared in 1929 when *Osceola* was sold and *Juvigny* sank. *Malang* was purchased by the single-ship but nonnamesake Malco Steamship Co. Because it had no purpose following the termination of its Shipping Board operations, Mallory Transport Lines became the operator of this dry-cargo tramp fleet.[26]

Like all tramps, Mallory's specialized in carrying "commodities (1) of sufficiently low value that cheapness in transport outweighs any value of speed or regularity of delivery, (2) of relatively large bulk or heavy weight, (3) that do not require exceptional facilities on the part of the carrier for preserving or handling them, and (4) that are available for shipment in full cargo lots." For his size of American-flag vessel during the years 1925–1930, this meant coal and coke from Philadelphia, Baltimore, Norfolk, and Newport News; mahogany and cedar logs from Central America and Mexico; lumber, pulpwood, woodpulp, and newsprint from Eastern Canada and Gulf ports; potatoes from Maine; china clay and potash from the southeastern states; sulphate, phosphate, and nitrate fertilizers from the Middle Atlantic states; minerals and chemicals for paper manufacture, such as sulphur, sulphuric acid, soda ash, caustic soda, and chlorine; and such fertilizer materials as liquid anhydrous ammonia and Florida land pebble phosphate. [27] Charles S. Haight, Mallory's attorney, captured the flavor of his client's tramp operations in testimony before the House Committee on Merchant Marine and Fisheries:

> . . . these ships . . . go anywhere that cargo is located which wants to be moved, and they discharge the cargo to any place where there is a market for it. . . .
>
> The demand for this kind of tonnage varies enormously from time to time. The vessels must be especially adapted. Out-of-the-way ports must be served. The destination must be changed often by radio while the ship is in transit. You get the cargo aboard. You do not know whether the best market is going to be Philadelphia, New York, or Boston. You start out from the Gulf; you find your market and order the captain. . . . [28]

Shades of Charles Henry Mallory and Elihu Spicer! Haight went on:

> . . . the Mallorys supply . . . a pool of tonnage from which [shippers] . . . can draw, as their necessity arises, ships available to go anywhere, to deliver at any port, able to carry cheaply and able above all other things to quote a rate instantaneously on request—not rates fixed in advance, filed and advertised to the world, but rates bargained over the telephone at a moment's notice. . . .
>
> . . . Many a deal is handled with two telephones going at the same time, one to the buyer of the goods and the other to the supplier of the transportation, and the buyer of the goods will buy the goods [only] if they can be delivered cost, insurance, and freight to him at a price that beats the foreign competitor, and the transportation is a vital thing. You have on one telephone Mallory & Co. and say "Can you give me transportation from here to here at so much?" If they can, they can sell the goods; if not, they cannot sell them.

Mallory's tanker business during these same years 1925–

1930 was hardly as frenetic, principally because Bob Hague provided plenty of work (on consecutive voyage charters) for the Malston, Matinicock, Ardmore, Malabar, and Muskogee ships. Chace and Mallory continued to bid on used tankers when the price-rate formula developed in the Malston bidding seemed right. In February 1925, they also offered to take over management of all remaining Shipping Board tankers on the $400–5 per cent formula developed for Swiftsure, but were turned down. On February 19, however, they did purchase one of the last Shipping Board tankers offered for sale: the six-year-old *Bethelridge* (renamed *Malacca*), for $35 per d.w.t., through the medium of a single-ship, namesake company. She, too, was chartered to Standard Oil (N.J.) on a long-term, consecutive-voyage basis. Maitland Smith, treasurer of C. D. Mallory & Co. and its affiliates, summed up these years and these arrangements clearly enough: "Profits of operation were incredible, and our debts were promptly paid off out of earnings, and the shares continued to pay exceptional dividends. It was a gold mine." [29]

The only real threat to the prosperity of Mallory and his associates during the late 1920's was the increasing financial instability of New England Oil. By 1928, under chaotic management, that company had expanded far beyond its modest initial purpose. Besides its refinery at Fall River, it now operated a marine terminal at New Bedford, a tank farm at Assonet, and bulk depots at Fall River, Bridgeport, Bangor, New Haven, New London, Wellesley, Lowell, Chelsea, Plymouth, Salem, and Braintree; 85 filling stations in Massachusetts and New Hampshire; 500 tank cars; 75 trucks; the Swiftsure Fleet; *Pinthis, Bacoi, Interstate No. 2,* and three barges; and 502,000 acres of leases in Venezuela and Mexico on which not one drop of oil had yet been produced!

Here was a quasi-integrated oil company with a marketing structure and sales commitments that exceeded its refining capacity; one that had to buy every drop of crude it used from its competitors; and one that had to charter ever-increasing amounts of "outside" tonnage to carry its oil and products. Here was an impossibility. By October, New England Oil had declared bankruptcy and was negotiating a sellout to the Shell Oil Group, which was eager to penetrate the New England market and had made preliminary offers as early as the previous January. In December, Shell Union Oil Corp. agreed to terms and, on January 22, 1929, Shell Eastern Petroleum Products, Inc., was organized. On February 4, Shell Eastern purchased New England Oil's marketing properties and, the next day, its refinery.

Had Mallory and Chace been dozing, it would have been easy to get lost in this fast shuffle. They kept their eyes open, however, and actually improved their situation. The first step was to protect the Swiftsure Fleet, which they accomplished by foreclosing New England Oil's mortgage on the vessels on August 2, 1928. From that date until October 31, 1929, Mallory operated the six tankers on the $400—5 per cent formula, but for the account of the Farmers Loan & Trust Co. On November 1, the Swiftsure Fleet was transferred to a new corporation organized by Chace and Mallory, the Boat Owning and Operating Co., and remained under that corporate umbrella until 1941.

The next steps were to protect the Mallory-Chace-Lamton investment in *Pinthis, Bacoi, Colmar, Interstate No. 2, NEO No. 2, NEO No. 5,* and *NEO No. 6* (*Mexicano* had been sold in 1927), which New England Oil had never succeeded in paying for, and to find some new employment for these vessels and those of the Swiftsure Fleet. Happily, the Shell Group's peculiar transportation needs along the Gulf and Atlantic coasts and on the Great Lakes created a demand for their services.

Unlike New England Oil, Shell could supply its refineries in Curaçao, Houston, Norco (La.), Wood River (Ill.), and East Chicago (Ind.) with crude by pipe line. Its problem related to the delivery of gasoline, kerosene, gas oil, fuel oil, road oil, asphalt, and other products from those refineries to its large marine and lake terminals in Tampa, Jacksonville, Wilmington, Sewaren (N.J.), and Fall River, or from there to smaller terminals, bulk stations, or customers. In the absence of products pipe lines, tank cars, and tank trucks of sufficiently low-cost capacity, most of these deliveries were made by water. But, as a Dutch company, Shell could not own American-flag vessels, and only American-flag vessels could engage in such lake, river, and coastal trades.

317

Thus, Shell had worked out several complicated shipping arrangements. Water transportation among its Great Lakes properties was handled by the Lake Tankers Corp., a venture organized, financed, and operated by Frederic W. Allen and Frank C. Wright of Lee, Higginson & Co. in June 1927. Tankers belonging to the Group could deliver Curaçao products to any port on the eastern seaboard or load cargoes for shipment to points outside the United States, because a foreign-flag vessel was permitted under the law to come in to discharge or pick up a cargo. The real rub, however, was that Shell Eastern had to bring its supplies by water. The Shipping Act of 1916 made it impossible for the company to own its own tankers, and Group tankers could not be employed to deliver products from Houston and Norco to Atlantic Coast ports, for this would have constituted coastwise shipping.

Here was the kind of niche Mallory and Chace sought. Since it was impossible for Shell to own and operate ocean tankers between United States ports, the Swiftsure Fleet could not be sold to New England Oil's purchasers. But Mallory and Chace were able to have it specified in the sales contract that Shell Eastern would give the Swiftsure Fleet preference whenever it chartered tankers. As for the other vessels, Mallory and Chace repossessed them, sold *Colmar* and *NEO No. 2* for scrap, and sold *Pinthis, Bacoi, Interstate No. 2, NEO No. 5* (renamed *LTC No. 5*), and *NEO No. 6* (renamed *LTC No. 6*) to Lake Tankers Corp. The transfer date was February 4, 1929, and on that day C. D. Mallory & Co. became managing operators (on the $400—5 per cent formula) for all present and future Lake Tankers Corp. vessels to be exclusively employed by Shell on the Great Lakes and Atlantic Coast.

Obviously, Mallory and Chace had convinced Allen and Wright to consign the operation of the Lake Tankers Corp. vessels to professional ship managers; and C. D. Mallory & Co. kept this agency until 1941. By the end of 1930, however, this fleet was composed of *Bacoi, Interstate No. 2, LTC No. 5, LTC No. 6,* and ten other vessels built or purchased by the corporation: the tankers *Martha E. Allen, Irene W. Allen, Justine C. Allen, LTC Nos. 1, 2, 3* and *4*; and the barges *LTC Nos. 7, 8,* and *9*. Mallory's old friend *Pinthis* was sunk on June 10, 1930, in one of New England's most spectacular maritime disasters. Loaded with 504,000 gallons of high-test gasoline, *Pinthis* was rammed by *Fairfax* of the Merchants & Miners Line in the fog off Scituate, Massachusetts. Forty-seven persons, including the tanker's entire crew, were lost. The fire alone burned for four days. *Pinthis* was entirely blameless, and Lake Tankers Corp. later collected some $350,000 in damages, but her loss was still the worst ever suffered by a ship owned or operated by Clifford Mallory.[30]

Except for the horror of the *Pinthis* tragedy, however, the half-dozen years preceding the Great Depression were Mallory's happiest. His business was prosperous far beyond his expectations, and he had commitments for the future from such powerful men as Malcolm Chace, Bob Hague, Frederic Allen, and Frank Wright. His health was better than ever, except for one serious stomach hemorrhage in August 1926. He had time for Beck and their lovely home on Old Church Road in Greenwich. He had time for his brood: Margaret, who had transferred from Rosemary Hall and was now at Ethel Walker; Cliff, who was headed for Lawrenceville; and Barbara, who was headed for Rosemary Hall. He thought often of his family's heritage, in these years, and began to badger his relatives for anecdotes and memories of his father, grandfather, and great-grandfather. He began to comb attics and warehouses in Mystic, Galveston, and New York for Mallory ship models, logbooks, and memorabilia, and he commissioned his cousin Julius to prepare a history of the shipping activities of the Mallory family. He was a mature man, content. And he had time once again for sailing.

Clifford's yachting experience dated back to the late 1880's, when he was his father's constant day-sailing companion during the family's summers at Bonnie Cliff. By the 1890's, he was jury-rigging every rowboat and dinghy on the place, until his father bought him a 22-foot "cabin cat" in 1893. The twelve-year-old sailor dubbed her *Hornet,* and over the next three years, he later recalled, "I learned more about sailing from my experience with her than any other boat."

His first real racing experience came as a teenager on yachts built for his uncle Charley and his father during 1896–1905: the "half-rater" *Yola,* the "25-foot cabin class" *Skimmaug,* and the "one-rater" *Goldbug,* designed and built by the famous centerboard specialist Thomas Clapham; the "knockabout" *Bonnie,* built by Nat Herreshoff; and the oversize "25-foot cabin-class" *Hanley,* built by C. C. Hanley. From 1906 to 1916, with breaks in 1907-1908 (when he abandoned boats to tour in his first automobile, a 1907 Peerless runabout) and 1913 (because of poor health), Mallory sailed in all the major eastern regattas and established himself as one of America's premier yacht owners and skippers: with *Banzai,* a Herreshoff-New York Yacht Club 30-foot design, he took fourth in class in 1906 and seventh in 1907; with *Cliphora,* a Crowningshield-American Yacht Club One design, he sailed to second in class in 1910 and firsts in 1911 and 1912; with *Margaret,* a Goeller R design, he took first in class 1914 and seconds in 1915 and 1916; and also in 1916, as manager and skipper for an Indian Harbor Yacht Club syndicate, he chartered the Herreshoff P design, *Joyant,* and sailed her to second in class.

World War I and the establishment of C. D. Mallory & Co. had kept Clifford out of competitive sailing during 1917-1922 (except for a few day sails in *Reni* in 1919-1921), but over the years 1923-1932, he reached the top of the yachting world. With *Clytie,* a 6-meter boat he bought from Henry B. Plant, he won first in class in 1923 and was selected as captain of the American racing team sent to Cowes-on-the-Clyde to sail the British-American 6-Meter Match that year. *Clytie* took two fifths, two fourths, one eighth, and one first as the American team lost the six races by a score of 129 to 86. Mallory and his team then sailed in the Clyde Series, but were beaten in singles, pairs, and team. With *Barbara,* an Alden R design built for him in Germany, Mallory took seventh in class in 1925 and ninth in the following year.

Mallory's greatest contributions to competitive yachting—as builder, skipper, organizer, and arbiter—clustered in the years 1925-1932. He was president of the Yacht Racing Association of Long Island Sound (1923-1926), vice commodore (1923-1929) and commodore (1930-1935) of the Indian Harbor Yacht Club, founder (1925) and first president (1925-1935) of the North American Yacht Racing Union, and chairman for yachting for the Olympic Games (1932). In 1927, he founded

Yachting cronies for almost forty years: (l. to r.), Clifford D. Mallory, Robert Monks, and Gifford Beal. Courtesy Mariners Museum.

Clifford D. Mallory's *Tycoon* (left) and W.A.W. Stewart's *Iris. Tycoon*, one of the founders of the 12-meter class, was designed by Burgess & Morgan and built by Abeking & Rasmussen in 1928. Mallory sold her to H. T. von Frankenburg in 1936 after a stellar racing career. Courtesy Mariners Museum.

the 10-meter class, of which fourteen were built. He sailed his own, *Twilight* (designed by Burgess, Riggs & Morgan and built for him in Germany), to the Long Island Sound Championship and second in her class. In 1928, he chartered the 6-meter *Lanai* to sail in the East-West Intersectional 6-Meter Match in Los Angeles. *Lanai* placed sixth in the first series and won the second series, but Mallory's eastern team lost the match 72 to 55-3/4. Also in 1928, he founded the 12-meter class, of which six were built including his own *Tycoon* (designed by Burgess & Morgan and built in Germany). With Mallory at her helm, *Tycoon* won the Long Island Sound Championship in 1928; was first in her class in 1928, 1929, 1930; finished fourth for the Astor Cup in 1930; and remained one of the most beautiful and swiftest of American yachts until Mallory sold her in 1936.[31]

The prosperity of these pre-Depression years, which made Mallory's family, business, and sailing lives so pleasant, also permitted him to indulge an old friend, Graham Brush, who was the inventor of a curious vessel he called a "seatrain." The commercialization of Brush's idea became one of the most interesting chapters in recent American maritime history; and a large ingredient of Brush's success was the encouragement and support he received from Clifford Mallory.

Brush was a natural-born inventor, engineer, Yale '17, and the son-in-law of Henry R. Mallory's old associate in AGWI, Alfred G. Smith of the New York and Cuba Mail Steamship Co. Smith and his freight traffic manager, Joseph Hodgson, had interested Brush in the problems of cargo transshipment and vessel turn-around; and, by 1926 Brush and Hodgson were discussing their ideas with their Greenwich neighbor Clifford Mallory. What they had worked out was a revolutionary new type of ocean-going vessel that could load, unload, and transport fully loaded railroad cars easily, economically, and without breaking bulk or transshipping any of the cargoes involved. Mallory enthusiastically endorsed the idea and placed himself and his organization at their disposal to commercialize it.

Between 1927 and 1932, as an investor, agent, and cheerleader, Mallory helped Brush and Hodgson patent their ideas; acquire terminal properties in Belle Chasse (8.5 miles below

New Orleans), Havana, and Hoboken; finance and build three ships, *Seatrain New Orleans* (1929), *Seatrain New York* (1932), and *Seatrain Havana* (1932); and begin operations under several corporations consolidated in 1931–1932 as Seatrain Lines, Inc. Mallory served as a Seatrain director until his death. As his managers later recalled: "Brush had the invention, but Mallory put it over. Seatrain's offices were in the same building as C. D. Mallory & Co., its calls came to our switchboard, it used some of our space and personnel, we acted as its building and insurance brokers, and we made some of its earliest freight fixtures." Because it was such an unusual and radical idea, because it anticipated so many of today's concepts of containerized freight movement, and because it was an idea that Mallory had so much to do with, a 1933 description of the operation is worthy of note:

> Seatrain vessels are approximately 480 feet long, with 63-foot beams, and have a speed of 16.5 knots, or better. They are ocean-going. . . . While the original vessel has tank space for 2,000 tons of liquid cargo, and the new vessels have tank space for 4,000 tons of liquid cargo, each vessel is designed primarily for transportation of cargo only when loaded in railroad cars. Each vessel has four decks, and each deck has four sets of railroad tracks of standard gage, the aggregate length of tracks on each vessel being approximately 1 mile. The original vessel has a capacity of 95 cars, and each of the new vessels has a capacity of 100 cars. These vessels can handle cargo in railroad cars only between ports at which special loading facilities have been provided . . . namely, Hoboken, New Orleans, and Havana.
>
> The loading facilities consist of a combination elevator and crane, the elevator shaft being erected on the dock, and the stationary arms of the crane extending from the frame of the elevator shaft out over the slip. The floor of the elevator is a movable platform called a cradle on which is laid a single track of standard gage. The cradle, when in place on the dock, forms a section of the railroad track over which cars are moved to and from the cradle. . . .
>
> In loading a Seatrain vessel, a car is moved by locomotive . . . and stopped on the section of track laid on the cradle where it is blocked and secured. The four corners of the cradle are connected to bails which in turn are attached to an overhead crane. The crane through the bails and cradle lifts the car vertically until the car and cradle are higher than the bulwark of the vessel. Car and cradle are then moved

along the arms of the crane to a position over one of the four hatchways of the vessel and lowered through the hatchway, which forms another elevator shaft, to one of the four decks on which the car is to be stowed. The cradle for the time being becomes a part of that particular deck, the tracks of the cradle articulating with the tracks on the deck to form a continuous track over which the car is moved from the cradle by a car puller to the desired position on the deck track, where it is secured and made fast to take care of motion of the ship while at sea. When a deck has been loaded the cradle is left in place and serves as a hatch cover for that deck. Unloading is the reverse of the process of loading. Often cars may be loaded and unloaded at the same time. That is, the cradle instead of being hoisted out empty is loaded with a car. . . .[32]

Obviously, Seatrain went far beyond the roll-on-roll-off, single-deck car ferries with which some ignorant critics compared it, and its concepts and design have certainly been validated by time. In their day, however, Brush, Hodgson, and Mallory received their share of brickbats, and it is to their credit that they persevered—particularly through the depths of the Great Depression.

Like most Americans, Mallory was surprised by the suddenness and scale of the stock market crash and economic downturn. And, as a thoroughgoing Republican who voted for Hoover in 1932, Landon in 1936, and Willkie in 1940, he was eternally skeptical of Roosevelt and the New Deal. Nevertheless, he weathered both the economic and political storms by avoiding the latter and "minding his business." And he had plenty to mind during the years 1930–1936.

First, there was a reorganization of his partnership, triggered by the retirement of the two Houstons in 1930–1931 and his other five managers' desire to get "a bigger piece of the action." The Houston affair, which cost Mallory his closest friend, only partner, and a key manager, was an emotional nightmare. William Houston was already suffering from a nervous disorder when his wife ran off with his married nephew Jim. This shattered the elder Houston beyond repair, and he retired to his native Scotland in 1931. Emotionally spent, Mallory allowed his five remaining managers to dictate the reorganizations that were required by the situation. Lamton Corp. bought

75 per cent of Houston's share in C. D. Mallory & Co.,
which gave it 40 per cent of the total against Mallory's 60 per
cent. Lamton also purchased 75 per cent of Houston's share in
the tanker and tramp companies. Obviously, Bergen, Bynum,
Knowles, Smith, and Westerlund were now to be heard from
more than ever before.[33]

Mallory had little difficulty in keeping his small tankers
and dry-cargo tramps employed during the Depression. The
Lake Tankers Fleet worked steadily for Shell Oil, making products deliveries along the Great Lakes and Atlantic Coast. And a
fortuitous advance in chemistry (that linked the chlor-alkali and
chemical-nitrogen industries for the first time) and several chemical processing plant relocations created new demands for the
Mallory tramps.

During 1930-1934, a new process was discovered to produce synthetic sodium nitrate and its fertilizer derivatives by
treating soda ash with nitric acid made from anhydrous ammonia. The world's largest producer of ammonia and nitric acid
was, of course, the famous Hopewell, Virginia, plant of the
Allied Chemical and Dye Corp. Mallory tramps had been carrying sulphur and phosphate rock into and ammonia and ammonium sulphate and ammonium phosphate fertilizers out of
that plant since it opened in December 1928. By the end of
1935, they were also supplying it with soda ash produced by
three brand-new plants opened in the South during 1934-1935:
Southern Alkali Corp. at Corpus Christi; Mathieson Alkali
Works at Lake Charles; and Solvay Process Co. at Port Allen
across from Baton Rouge.[34]

This gave Mallory a two-way coastal trade of considerable
value, which he kept at throughout the middle 1930's with the
four tramps he had in 1930 and four more: *Eleanor Boling,* a
small, formerly British vessel purchased in consort with Hasler
& Co., Inc., in 1933, renamed *Vamar,* and conveyed to the
newly formed Vamar Steamship Co.; *Baron Glenconner,* a
wrecked British-flag ship, purchased from underwriters by the
reactivated Osceloa Steamship Co. in 1933, redocumented
American, and named *Malton; Missoula,* purchased by the Maltran Steamship Co. from the Hammond Lumber Co. in 1935
and renamed *Malamton*; and *American Cardinal,* purchased by

Ardmore, one of four tankers purchased from Standard Oil (N.J.) in 1924 for $25 per d.w.t. and operated by C. D. Mallory & Co. until 1941. Courtesy Mariners Museum.

Malton, a ten-year-old tramp purchased in 1933 and operated by C. D. Mallory & Co. until 1941. Note Diamond-M stack insignia. Courtesy Mariners Museum.

The skeleton crew employed during the lay up of the Mallory tanker fleet, 1931–1933. Among this group are nine masters, nine mates, ten chief engineers. Each man received $72.50 a month and board. Courtesy Marine Transport Lines, Inc.

Maltran in 1936 from the American Foreign Steamship Co. and renamed *Mallard.* [35]

Thus, Mallory more than held his own with small tankers and dry-cargo tramps through 1935. For the large tankers, however, the story was much more bleak. By early 1930, Mallory knew that Standard Oil (N.J.) would not renew its consecutive-voyage charters of the Malston Fleet or of Mallory's six other similar tankers when the contract expired on January 1, 1931. He had also been given notice that Shell's employment of the six-vessel Swiftsure Fleet would be terminated on January 1, 1932. Furthermore, with Gulf and California rates already fallen to 9 1/2 to 10 cents per barrel, there was no prospect for profitable employment of these eighteen tankers in the general market.

Mallory, the members of Lamton, and Chace caucused continually through the last half of 1930 debating alternative strategies. Finally, as befitted his majority financial interest in the tankers, Malcolm Chace made the decision. "Rather than charter them at break-even rates," Maitland Smith recalled, "Chace decided to carry them through these lean years." As each vessel's charter expired, it was sailed to Mobile, painted with crude-oil preservative, and laid up in fresh water. Seventeen of the eighteen "never turned a wheel" until 1934; one was briefly chartered during that same period. By 1935, however, as Smith recalled, "a boom in the tanker trade brought in handsome profits, and all losses, including lay-up expenses, were made up in very short time, by the phenomenal earnings of the ships." [36]

In Clifford Mallory's mind, however, even the return of prosperity paled in significance before two other profoundly moving events of the middle 1930's: his recapture of his family's most cherished symbol, and his only son's majority.

The symbol was the Mallory house flag, which dated from at least 1843. An entry of that year in Washington Frederick's journal of Charles Mallory's sealing schooner *Emeline* mentions sighting the whaler *Aeronaut* off the entrance to the harbor of Deception Island in the Antarctic flying her owner's private signal: "a red ball or star in a white ground with blue border; at the end of the fly, one blue, another red." The same flag had flown over every Mallory vessel until the sellout to Morse in 1906. Thereafter, it had become the property of the Clyde-Mallory Lines. When he formed C. D. Mallory & Co. in 1919, Clifford Mallory had tried to repurchase his family's flag, but to no avail. He had to be content with a new emblem designed by Lyle Bull, a blue "M" in a white diamond on a field of red.

The traditional symbol meant so much to him, however, that he constantly badgered the executives of AGWI to let him have it, and they finally and courteously agreed. Mallory himself wrote the account of the ceremonies surrounding the flag's return, and the event, on December 22, 1934, became but one more ingredient in the family's maritime tradition:

> ... In the presence of her Father and his entire shore staff, her brother Clifford and sister Margaret, Miss Barbara Sealy Mallory, youngest daughter of Mr. Clifford D. Mallory, lowered the flag that has flown from the mainmasts of probably one hundred vessels operated by her Father's organization since 1919, and in its place unfurled the flag which served the Clippers of her great-great-grandfather. ... [37]

Clifford Jr.'s majority was another ceremonial occasion, prompting a letter that should leave no further doubt as to the role played by tradition in the Mallory family's economic life:

October 13, 1937

My dear Son,

This is your 21st birthday and in this letter I will try to convey to you my sentiments and thoughts on the momentous occasion of your having attained your majority. In the first place, I extend to you every good wish for your continued health and happiness.

I hope that you will find the freedom and the obligations which come with legal age all that you had anticipated, and I trust that you will not be disappointed at finding your expectations of independence too much circumscribed by the burdens which responsibilities, inherited and assumed, are so likely to bring with them.

There are many things that I would like to say to you, but most of them were expressed by my Father on the occasion of my 21st birthday on May 26th, 1902 in such a clear manner and so much better than I could possibly do that I am attaching a copy of his letter to me. I request you to read it carefully and I hope that you will strive to do your utmost in living up to his advice and example.

You are in exactly the same position that I was 35 years ago, except that one more generation has preceded you.

I am very proud that I am in position to say to you as my Father instructed me to do "4 generations have preceded you over a well defined road, and it will be safe for you to follow in their footsteps as I have followed the 3 generations which have preceded me." My wish at the moment is that you may have the very great privilege of repeating like words to your son on his 21st birthday.

I will record the generations as my Father did, adding one more to the list of those who have carried on a family business with some degree of success, and always with the highest respect of the shipping industry and of the business and social world:

Charles Mallory	your great-great-grandfather was born in	1796
Charles Henry Mallory	" great-grandfather was born in	1818
Henry R. Mallory	" grandfather was born in	1848
Clifford D. Mallory	Father was born in	1881
You were born in		1916

Every paragraph of your grandfather's letter to me is full of the soundest possible suggestions and advice and all of it is as true today as when it was written.

Don't be influenced too much by the suggestion that we are in a "new era," which is so frequently spoken of, or that modern development has changed conditions to such an extent that our lives must be materially altered.

Confidence in one's self is essential. Confidence is acquired by a complete knowledge gained from careful study and experience.

Egoism, the doctrine that supreme perfection is self, is generally the result of flattery and superficial knowledge and is to be religiously avoided.

Four generations have followed the policies indicated by him and I have found that where I was influenced to feel that perhaps some of these policies were antiquated and not equal to modern times, experience proved this was not the case and that the same principles do prevail.

Conditions have changed somewhat it is true, as is evidenced by the fact that I am dictating this letter, whereas my Father wrote in long hand. It is also true that the development of communication and transportation systems has brought upon us extra burdens and a heavy drain on our time, but in no way does it alter the principles of moral and business life.

I am happy to be able to say to you, as my Father did to me that "from this date you are a stockholder in the Mallory Line and can vote at its annual meetings. How long shall it be before you become a director, and an Officer of the Company?"

In closing, I wish you the greatest possible happiness and complete satisfaction in your accomplishments.

Your affectionate father,. . .[38]

With his personal business depression over, his familial traditions reaffirmed, and his son begun, Mallory took stock of the major maritime and labor legislation coming out of the Congress almost daily in 1936–1938. Of one thing he was certain: he wanted as little to do with government and unions as possible.

Mallory had seen his fill of government attempts to rejuvenate the American merchant marine during 1919–1925, and he was not about to sign up for that course again. Thus, he steadfastly refused to seek or to be considered for any of the cargo-ship construction subsidies or subsidized essential cargo-liner services created and funded by the Merchant Marine Act of 1936. He carefully restricted his activities to ship and marine insurance brokerage, to the ownership and management of unsubsidized tankers and cargo vessels, to the "transportation of liquids in bulk in tank vessels," and to the "transportation of dry commodities in quantity lots by freight cargo vessels under charter or contract." These activities classified him as a tramp and contract carrier and exempted him from any major responsibility to or regulation by the federal government. Consequently, he lobbied only when tramping or contract carriage was threatened by regulation, and that was seldom. For in February 1938, after extensive hearings and investigations, the Maritime Commission officially ruled "that no effort be made to develop tramp shipping under the American flag at this time."

That was fine with Mallory, for it left him free to tramp as he pleased. Actually, he drew a sort of perverse pleasure out of operating unsubsidized and profitable tramps in the face of such Maritime Commission pronouncements as: "Since American tramp operations are practically impossible without large subsidies it would appear inadvisable for citizens of the United States to participate in tramp service with vessels under United

States registry." On October 26, 1936, he consolidated his seven large tramps into the newly formed C. D. Mallory Corp., but continued to operate them through C. D. Mallory & Co. until 1941. (In 1938, he added one final vessel, *Themoni*, a Greek-flag wreck purchased from underwriters, refitted, and renamed *Malantic.*[39]

As for his tankers, Mallory left Malston Co. as it was, but transferred *Swiftwind* (renamed *Malay*) to a single-ship company in 1935. In 1936, the *Matinicock, Ardmore, Malabar,* and *Muskogee* single-ship companies were consolidated as the Ardmore Steamship Co. and *Malacca* was transferred from its own company to C. D. Mallory Corp. In 1938, *Malay* and *Malabar* were transferred to a new firm called Seminole Steamship Co. These reorganizations left five tankers in the Swiftsure Fleet (owned by the Boat Owning and Operating Co.), seven in the Malston Fleet, three in the Ardmore Fleet, two in the Seminole Fleet, and one in C. D. Mallory Corp. until 1941. All eighteen continued to tramp in the petroleum and petroleum products markets, but Mallory found less and less work offered to them by their traditional employers, Standard and Shell.

Standard, which as late as 1930 had moved 36 per cent of its cargoes in chartered vessels, had undergone a complete turn-around as the result of the availability of construction subsidies from the government. From 1936 on, it embarked on a major shipbuilding program with the objective of "maintaining sufficient American tankers fully to cover its transportation requirements in American waters, the level set being 110 per cent of average needs." Bob Hague's death in March 1939 also curtailed the privileged relationship with Standard that Mallory had always enjoyed. At Shell, from 1934 to 1941, only 30 per cent of "the company's Atlantic Coast tanker requirements" were available to independent carriers like Mallory. The remainder was supplied on fixed-rate contracts of affreightment with Charles Kurz's Pennsylvania Shipping Co. Mallory bid on these contracts when they were let in 1934 and when they were renewed in 1939, but lost out to Kurz's lower proposal. Nevertheless, *Malacca* and the Malston, Ardmore, Seminole, and Swiftsure fleets were never again idle or unprofitable. Lake Tankers Corp. continued to work for Shell with no changes except the sale of *Bacoi* in 1937 and the addition of eight more barges, *LTC Nos. 17* through *24,* in 1938, and the small tankers *Tri Cities* and *Twin Cities* in 1940.[40]

Mallory was less successful in avoiding labor unions than government during the years 1936–1941. He felt that he paid his officers and crews competitive wages and offered them working conditions comparable to those of his competitors. He had not signed the agreements concerning unlicensed seamen that the International Seamen's Union of America (AFL) had negotiated with Atlantic and Gulf common carriers in 1935 and 1936—the first in the industry; and he looked with dismay on the militant strike activities of the National Maritime Union (CIO) during 1936–1937. What made the latter strike home was that Joe Curran, the NMU founder, had begun his seagoing career in 1923 on one of Mallory Transport Lines' Mediterranean steamers—a fact Curran never let Mallory and his managers forget.[41]

It was only a matter of time, however. On June 17, 1937, the ISU requested an investigation of C. D. Mallory & Co. and its affiliates by the National Labor Relations Board. Hearings were held on August 23 and 24 as to whether or not the NLRB should supervise elections among Mallory's unlicensed seamen for the selection of certified union bargaining representatives. On September 19, elections were ordered, and they were held between February 4 and April 1, 1938. Of the 558 eligible employees of Seminole Steamship Co., Boat Owning and Operating Co., Malston Co., and C. D. Mallory Corp., 522 (94 per cent) voted: 473 for NMU; 24 for neither; 17 for ISU; 6 void; 1 challenged; 1 blank. This certified the NMU as the bargaining agent for all "unlicensed seamen, except wireless and radio operators, chief electricians on electrically driven ships, and junior engineers who hold licenses" in Mallory's employ.

Contract negotiations between Mallory and the NMU dragged on until March 5, 1939, when a two-year contract similar to that already signed by the NMU with fifty-five other passenger and freight carriers was signed with C. D. Mallory Corp. It took a two-month strike against C. D. Mallory & Co. (as well as against Standard, Socony-Vacuum, and Tidewater Associated) in 1939 and further negotiations before a tanker contract was signed on January 19, 1940. These agreements included no-strike, no-lockout clauses; time and a half for overtime; nine annual holidays; deck wage rates from $65 per month for ordinaries to $100 per month for boatswains; engine-room rates from $75 per month for wipers to $150 per month for machinists; and steward's department rates from $65 per month for messmen to $140 per month for chief stewards. Also in 1939–1940, Mallory's officers chose to affiliate with the Masters, Mates, and Pilots Assn., the Marine Engineers Beneficial Assn., and the American Radio Telegraphists Assn.—the traditional unions for licensed personnel.[42]

The years 1937–1940 also saw Mallory's last attempt to achieve two things he had always dreamed of: "I have waited 33 years to build a Diesel electric-drive ship and I have also waited 20-1/2 years to build a ship of my own," he wrote Bynum and Westerlund on January 11, 1940. His desire to design a really novel cargo ship actually went back to the proposals made to his father before World War I. His interest in diesel-electric propulsion dated from 1915 when he began to devour every word on the subject.[43]

His interest had flamed again in November 1919, when the Winton Engine Works of Cleveland announced an economical and practical installation adaptable to the type of wooden vessels operated by the Shipping Board. From May 4, 1920, to May 3, 1924, Mallory had made proposal after proposal to the board seeking a suitable hull on which to experiment with his own ideas, but to no avail. In the meantime, he patented a novel set of diesel-electric controls and formed the Mallory Diesel Electric Corp. to market them. In January 1924, Alexander Smith had allowed Mallory to install his controls and a Winton-type engine on board his auxiliary schooner-yacht *Cutty Sark,* and the vessel became a floating advertisement for the system. The dominance of Winton and Westinghouse, however, prompted Mallory to sell and retire from the field by 1925.[44]

His dream did not die, however, and in 1937 he rekindled it. In cooperation with his old friend Theodore E. Ferris and America's leading expert on diesel-electric drive, Eads Johnson, Mallory designed a 7,800 d.w.t. cargo vessel with a number of "novel features," including:

331

1. The use of multiplicity of small electric generating sets for diesel electric drive to furnish electricity for one propelling motor.
2. Placing such generating sets on flat directly above propelling motor in same fore and aft compartment.
3. Use of trunk on deck continuous between forecastle and poop and trunk sides for girders between bulkheads to eliminate pillars in cargo holds.
4. Use of different depths of inner-bottom for ballast and trim to eliminate deep tanks.
5. Use of curved poop front for diverting seas in heavy weather.
6. Use of spiral stairways for economizing space in quarters and engine room.
7. Use of stiff leg supported mast instead of standing rigging.
8. Placing electric windlass on main deck under forecastle deck and capstans on forecastle deck operated by windlass below.
9. Thwartship outside stairways to poop and forecastle decks.
10. Angles at gunwale and corner of trunk sides replaced by radius plates at these junctions.

Mallory was so infatuated with the design that he sought to patent it and suffered severe emotional stress when his managers expressed a preference for a more conventional "steam, geared-turbine job." The issue was settled when the Patent Office rejected Mallory's claims of originality and no shipbuilder would quote a price lower than the totally prohibitive figures of $246 per ton for steam or $226 per ton for diesel-electric— "approximately $100 a ton more than we expected." Sadly, in 1941, he "dropped the matter for the time being. The prices are absolutely impossible." He never picked it up again.[45]

Except for these disappointments, Mallory had accomplished all he had set out to do in 1919. By 1940 he was fifty-eight and controlled the largest independent tanker fleet under the American flag and a profitable fleet of American-flag tramps (see Tables 12.2 through 12.5). He had acquired and was operating this fleet free of government subsidies. His forty-one vessels were fully employed with 74 per cent of their business one-way, 6 per cent part-cargo return, and 20 per cent round-trip cargoes. They were certainly among the most efficiently managed in the United States; from 1923 to 1940, his tankers had averaged only 18-3/4 ship-days lost per annum and his cargo ships only 15-1/2. He had persuaded AGWI to return the Mallory house flag lost in the sellout in 1919, and his great-grandfather's colors now flew at the masthead of all his ships. And best of all, his son Cliff was learning the business in preparation for inheriting it someday.[46]

Chapter 13

AN UNEXPECTED END

"... possibly the reorganization of your Father's business might also be necessary, which is usually the case in a partnership."–George Sealy to Clifford D. Mallory, Jr., May 23, 1941

C LIFFORD DAY MALLORY, JR., was eighteen when he completed his formal education at Phillips Exeter Academy and joined C. D. Mallory & Co. as an apprentice clerk. For the next five years he worked at a variety of assignments in the firm, learning the ropes of ship brokerage and vessel management. And, as his twenty-first birthday letter from his father had reiterated, it was only to be a matter of time before he would become an officer and a director in the family firm. Meanwhile, Cliff "turned to" on the paper work while harboring a yen to escape the office and try his sea legs aboard a Mallory-flag ship. He got his chance in January 1940. As a reward for his careful superintendence of the conversion of *Themoni* into *Malantic,* Cliff received his father's permission to ship out as a fireman on board the vessel when she was time-chartered to the Brodin Line with general cargo to Buenos Aires and Montevideo.[1]

The trip was a toughener for the boss's son, who had to bear the brunt of his crew mates' harassment, but the experience was obviously satisfying to both Cliff and his father:

Upon my return here, I found things moving smoothly. Cliff had returned home from a 2-1/2 months South American voyage which he enjoyed so much that he now says he would be thoroughly satisfied to spend most of his days at sea. There is no doubt but that he gained a great deal by this experience. He made the southbound voyage in the Engine Department, serving his watch in the fire room and engine room, and on the return trip he was on deck, part of the time acting as Bos'n. He also gained much physically, losing weight and developing muscle. It is our plan now for him to enter the Insurance Department and gain some experience in that branch of the business.[2]

But Cliff had other plans because his trip had opened his eyes to world affairs for really the first time in his twenty-three years. While in Montevideo he had seen the still-smoldering wreckage of the recently sunk *Graf Spee* and had boggled at the fatalism with which world war was momentarily predicted. The reality of the Anglo-German conflict shocked him into an intensely personal reaction. In July 1940, shortly after his return to New York, he enlisted in the United States Navy as an ensign and specialist in merchant-ship management and control.

Though reluctant to show it, the elder Mallory was pleased with his son's decision. After all, naval discipline and experience would not hurt an aspiring young shipping executive, and the firm would still be there for Cliff when he returned to civilian life. Thus, Mallory Sr. spent most of 1940 merely tuning his business. No new directions were charted, but several profitable loose ends were tied. Three cases in point were the activities concerning Vamar Steamship Co., Farr Spinning & Operating Co., and Oldwood, Inc.

Vamar was a small operation, but is worth mentioning because it is so ultratypical of Mallory's speculative ventures in used ships. In January 1933, two of his friends, R. T. and A. R. Hasler, had asked him to assist them in purchasing and operating *Eleanor Boling*, a small, thirteen-year-old, British-built freighter. To accommodate the Haslers, Mallory incorporated Vamar Steamship Co., Inc., a $3,000 Delaware corporation whose stock was subscribed as follows (at $1 per share): R. T. Hasler, 1,050 shares; A. R. Hasler, 265 shares; W. N. Westerlund, 791 shares; C. D. Mallory, Sr., 394 shares; 500 shares unissued. The $2,500 in cash raised by the stock subscription plus $7,200 in 6 per cent demand promissory notes of the new corporation were used to purchase the vessel, which was renamed *Vamar*. C. D. Mallory & Co. then operated the vessel at its usual husbanding and commission rates through 1939. So successful was this operation that Vamar's promissory notes were retired in less than a year. Finally, in April 1940, with C. D. Mallory & Co. acting as owners' brokers, *Vamar* was sold to Sociedad Navegaciones Dos Oceanos, S.A., for $42,000. This meant a personal capital gain of $6,200 for Mallory and $1,000 in brokerage for his firm—in addition to the dividends and fees earned over six years of operations.[3]

Farr and Oldwood were the result of a fortuitous change in the federal tax laws. The Revenue Act of 1939 permitted net operating losses of individuals, partnerships, and corporations to be carried forward for two years and used as the basis for a deduction from gross income. This type of deduction had not been allowed since 1933, but it was now permitted on returns for taxable years beginning in 1940 and thereafter. The first taxable years from which a net operating loss could be carried forward were either calendar 1939 or fiscal years ending in 1940. Maitland Smith alerted Mallory and Chace to these changes as a means to "soak up" the recent large earnings of their tanker fleets. The plan was simple and quite legal: purchase (at minimal prices) firms with large net operating losses that could be carried forward; transfer ownership of the tanker fleets to these companies; consolidate their accounts and use the "carry-forwards" to eliminate the income taxes that would otherwise have had to be paid on the tankers' earnings. The modest costs involved in purchasing the firms would also be recovered in the process.

, Malcolm Chace came up with the key ingredients: textile companies with substantial tax credits that could be carried forward. M. G. Chace Co. had been active in New England textiles since 1929, when it had refinanced and reorganized the forty-year-old Berkshire Cotton Manufacturing Co. into Berkshire Fine Spinning Associates, Inc. Chace had then used Berkshire as a holding company through which he had purchased seven other smaller mills. On December 8, 1938, when the stockholders of Farr Alpaca Co. of Holyoke voted to liquidate their sixty-six-year-old firm, Chace's attention had swung toward that company as possibly Berkshire's eighth acquisition. He was, thus, already cognizant of the Farr situation when passage of the Revenue Act of 1939 gave him and Mallory the opportunity to act.

On March 28, 1940, three of Farr's four mills were purchased for $675,000 by Oldwood, Inc., a new Maine corporation formed expressly for that purpose and jointly financed by M. G. Chace Co. and Berkshire Fine Spinning Associates. Oldwood announced that it would hold Farr No. 1 (a worsted plant and weave sheds) for sale as a whole or for sale of machinery only and Farr No. 2 (a woolen mill and finishing plant) for sale as a going concern. Farr No. 3 (a cotton-yarn mill) would be sold to another new firm, Farr Spinning & Operating Co., for operation as a spinning mill.

By the end of 1940, ownership of the Swiftsure Fleet had been transferred to Oldwood and that of the Malston and Ardmore fleets to Farr. For the time being, the Seminole Fleet and the one tanker owned by C. D. Mallory Corp. remained as before.[4]

The benefits of these transactions to Mallory were considerably higher personal income and continued management of all the tankers involved—through C. D. Mallory & Co. at "$600 per month husbanding fee and a commission of 7-1/2 per cent of the net operating profit of each vessel before taxes." But the cost was the surrender of some proportion of his tanker equity. While the exact proportions of ownership in the Swiftsure, Malston, Ardmore, and Seminole fleets are not known, Mallory plus the Lamton partners apparently were close to parity with Chace prior to 1940. But because he arranged the deal and came up with most of the financing involved, Chace claimed considerably higher shares in Oldwood and Farr than either Mallory or Lamton received. The pot was larger, of course, which meant that everyone now had more dollars than before, but Chace also gained a clear voting majority in all but one of the Mallory-flag tankers.

This shift in power was not lost on either the Lamton partners or young Clifford, but the senior Mallory was satisfied. His health was poor, but his doctors were not alarmed. He was preoccupied with fitting out a new Luders-built motor-sailer, *Bonnie Dundee III,* and delighted when several yachting maga-

zines chose her as American "yacht-of-the-year." Then, suddenly, it was over. In April 1941, while vacationing in Florida, he
was stricken with a massive coronary attack. While recuperating
in St. Francis Hospital in Miami Beach, his chronic stomach
ailment flared and triggered a relapse. Two weeks after his
sixtieth birthday, Clifford D. Mallory, Sr., died.[5]

Mallory's death unexpectedly snapped an unbroken chain
of 125 years of family-controlled American maritime enterprise.
The great irony was that actions he had taken while alive and
which he believed would insure continuity actually caused a
major break with the past.

At his death, Mallory's primary investments comprised 60
per cent of C. D. Mallory & Co., Inc., C. D. Mallory Corp.,
Mallory Transport Lines, Inc., and C. D. Mallory Brokerage,
Inc.; 50 per cent of Vamar Steamship Co.; and minority interests represented by common stock in Oldwood, Inc., Farr
Spinning & Operating Co., Seminole Steamship Co., Seatrain
Lines, Inc., and P. R. Mallory & Co., Inc. All of these were
profitable enterprises, but in almost every instance Mallory's
claims against them were against their profits and not against
the capital equipment that generated those profits. It was this
circumstance, apparent only after Mallory's death, that ruled
out any automatic succession by his heirs to management in his
stead. The problem is clearer if the assets of each of these
enterprises are summarized and matched with Mallory's (and
hence his heirs') control over them.

The primary assets of C. D. Mallory & Co., Inc., Mallory
Transport Lines, Inc., and C. D. Mallory Brokerage, Inc., were
good will, some retained earnings, and the various charters and
contracts these firms held to manage the tankers and freighters
that sailed under the Mallory flag. As long as they were in force,
these charters and contracts were valuable assets, indeed; but
they all had time limits and were subject to periodic renegotiation. If they should not be renewed by the owners of the vessels
involved, they would no longer be assets at all.

The key question, of course, was: Who owned the vessels
managed by C. D. Mallory & Co., Inc., Mallory Transport Lines,
Inc., and C. D. Mallory Brokerage, Inc., at the time of Mallory's
death? One of the tankers and all eight freighters were owned

by C. D. Mallory Corp.; five of the tankers by Oldwood, Inc.; ten of the tankers by Farr Spinning & Operating Co.; two of the tankers by Seminole Steamship Co.; and seven by Lake Tankers Corp. Vamar Steamship Co. was only a corporate shell with no physical assets in 1941.

The nub of the problem of managerial succession should now be clear: at his death, Mallory had a *majority* voice in only one of the five shipowning companies on which C. D. Mallory & Co., Inc., Mallory Transport Lines, Inc., and C. D. Mallory Brokerage, Inc., depended for sustenance—that is C. D. Mallory Corp. He and his partners had no equity in the Lake Tankers Fleet. In the other three companies, Chace and the Lamton partners could outvote Mallory. That they had never done so during his lifetime is a tribute to their confidence in his judgment and the charisma of his leadership.

With the elder Mallory gone, however, someone had to take the helm. Unfortunately, the timetable for Cliff's executive development had not yet brought the next Mallory to an equity position or an experience level equal to those of either Chace or the Lamton partners. Also, Cliff's inability to secure a discharge or even an extended leave from his overseas naval assignment made it impossible for him to consider any civilian job for at least the duration of the war. Last, Mallory's executor and trustee—The Hanover National Bank—was pressing the family to liquidate all the assets concerned in preparaton for paying the high estate taxes they anticipated would arise in the settlement of so personal and proprietary a business as Mallory's had been. Cliff, his mother, and his two sisters decided to ask Richard Carley Hunt, a partner in Chadbourne, Hunt, Jaeckel, & Brown, to represent their interests in negotiating a settlement among family, executors, and partners.

"Uncle Dick" Hunt had been a trusted Mallory-family counselor since he had handled the incorporation of P. R. Mallory & Co., Inc., in 1916. As a founding director of that firm and, later, of C. D. Mallory Corp., Hunt had been a frequent and valued adviser to both Clifford and Philip Mallory and for a time was the latter's brother-in-law. It was natural for Clifford's heirs to enlist his aid. He sat down with Chace and the Lamton partners for extended discussions in April and May of 1941.

When he got up from the table, the executors were satisfied and the estate taxes were paid, but the Mallorys were out of the shipping business.[6]

Hunt began by liquidating the Mallory shares in Oldwood, Inc., Farr Spinning & Operating Co., Seminole Steamship Co., and Vamar Steamship Co., Inc., in what was almost a forced sale. These were closely held companies, virtual partnerships, whose stock had never been publicly traded and, hence, had no *known* market value. Also, each company's charter gave the remaining equity holders the right to repurchase at par or better any shares offered for sale. Thus, Hunt was bound to offer the Mallory shares to Chace, the Lamton partners, and their associates and to accept any price above par that they offered him. This he did. What they paid him for the Oldwood, Farr, and Seminole shares is not known. For 1,500 Vamar shares, they paid him $6.72 per share (against a par value of $1.00 per share).[7] These transactions certainly increased the cash position of the Mallory estate, but they surrendered any Mallory voice in the future placement of seventeen of the twenty-five tankers which had been under Mallory's management when he died.

Hunt next turned to the partnerships and companies in which Mallory shared ownership 60–40 with Lamton. Here, Hunt deferred to the wishes of Messrs. Bergen, Bynum, Knowles, Smith, and Westerlund: they opposed liquidation per se; they wanted "to preserve the corpus" of the four firms that bore Mallory's name so that they might remain in the shipping business; they wanted their 40 per cent "in kind" and contractual power to manage or dispose of the Mallory 60 per cent as they saw fit (consonant with the best interests of the family, of course); and they asked for agreement that, upon his return, Clifford Mallory, Jr. would have no "inherited priority" in the management of the firms which bore his family's name.[8] Hunt accepted their terms.

May 19, 1941, was the transfer date: C. D. Mallory & Co., Inc., C. D. Mallory Brokerage, Inc., C. D. Mallory Corp., and Mallory Transport Lines, Inc., were liquidated and their assets distributed in kind between the Mallory heirs and the Lamton partners. The Mallory estate received the tanker *Malacca* and the freighters *Malantic, Malang, Malchace,* and *Maltran.* The Lamton partners received the freighters *Mallard, Malamton, Mallemak,* and *Malton* plus operating rights to the Swiftsure, Malston, Ardmore, Seminole, and Lake Tanker fleets and all good will, house flags, and fixtures of the former Mallory companies.

The Lamton partners promptly incorporated themselves into three new interlocking firms: Marine Operating Co., Inc., Marine Transport Lines, Inc., and Marine Brokerage, Inc.[9] These firms immediately assumed the identities of the four former Mallory companies in almost every visible aspect. The Mallory offices, staff, letterhead, house flag, advertising logos, officers' uniforms, and stack emblems were retained exactly as before except for substitution of the word "Marine" for the name "Mallory" wherever the latter had appeared.

More important still, Marine Transport Lines, Inc. and its affiliates rapidly took over all the functions, charters, and contracts of the departed Mallory firms. Operating agreements (including authority to negotiate sales as owners' brokers) were signed with Oldwood, Inc., Farr Spinning & Operating Co., Inc., Seminole Steamship Co., and Lake Tankers Corp. respecting the twenty-five tankers of the Swiftsure, Malston, Ardmore, Seminole, and Lake Tankers fleets. The four freighters inherited from C. D. Mallory Corp. were put to work in the charter and contract-carriage markets. And a very favorable agreement was made (through Hunt) with the executors of the Mallory estate. Marine Transport Lines, Inc., agreed "to operate the tanker and four cargo vessels owned by the estate for a period of one year subject to right of sale," except that at least two of the cargo vessels could not be sold until after February 1, 1942, so as "to meet open tonnage commitments." MTL's terms were: "$600 per month husbanding fee and a commission of 7 1/2 per cent of the net operating profit of each vessel before taxes," the exclusive right "to place the brokerage business on such ships as a cost of operating such ships," and the estate to advance $50,000 as "an operating fund for its vessels." [10]

The key clause in each of these agreements was the "right of sale." This gave the former Lamton partners full power to sell off any of the vessels involved if and when they pleased, to retain those they saw fit to operate, and to purchase any additional vessels they saw fit to acquire. America's declaration of war in December 1941 intervened, however, and accelerated the dispositon of all former Mallory ships.

Imlay and *Mevania*, of the old Malston Fleet now owned by Farr Spinning & Operating Co., and *Malacca*, the one tanker still owned by the Mallory estate, were the first to go. In July 1941, they were sold to Continental Steamship Co. (a syndicate composed of Hartol Oil Co., Consolidated Oil Co., and Pocahontas Refining Co.). Then came war and a new ball game. The First War Powers Act passed by Congress on December 18, 1941, enabled the President to transfer many of the powers of the United States Maritime Commission to other emergency preparedness agencies. One such agency was the War Shipping Administration, which was empowered to requisition American-flag vessels and assume full responsibility for their employment. Vessels so taken were allocated back to civilian managing agents as under the old Shipping Board system of World War I. For shipping firms like Marine Transport Lines, Inc., this cast up only three choices: relinquish the vessels that the government wanted, sell off those that the government refused, and acquire as much government business as possible.

All these goals were accomplished by June 1942. *Mallard, Malamton, Mallemak, Malantic, Malton, Swiftlight, Swiftscout, Matinicock,* and *Muskogee* were requisitioned by the government. *Malang, Malchace, Maltran, Swiftarrow, Swiftsure, Halsey, Durango, Dillwyn, Hugoton, Hoxbar, Ardmore, Malabar,* and *Malay* were all sold to private parties. By November 2, 1942, Marine Transport Lines, Inc., could honestly state that "the greater portion of the business activities of this corporation is in the operation of Oil Tankers and Dry Cargo Vessels for the United States War Shipping Administration under General Agency and Time Charter Managing agreements." [11]

During and after World War II, Marine Transport Lines, Inc., went on to become one of the largest bulk-cargo fleets in the world, but its later history was entirely divorced from that of the Mallory family. When Clifford D. Mallory, Jr., was mustered out of the navy as a lieutenant commander in 1945,

Westerlund offered him a $3,900 per year job at MTL which he refused.

It was not until the mid-1950's that Cliff was able to re-enter the shipping business. When he did, it was as a ship broker specializing in tankers. He reactivated the name "C. D. Mallory & Co., Inc.," which was his as much as it had been his father's. And to his letterhead he added his great-grandfather's red, white, and blue house flag. The destiny of the sixth generation was finally achieved.

As stated at the outset, this book has explicitly been a case study of two little-documented types of American firm: a family business spanning six generations and a set of specialists in American-flag shipping. Its purpose has been to record and analyze *from the inside out;* that is, to view the industry and the economy from the perspective of a specific set of economic decision-makers. Thus, more impersonal industry studies may be complemented and enhanced by reference to the flesh and bones of entrepreneurial history. In that sense, the Mallorys are here used as proxies for those firms which opted for closely held family control and chose to specialize in American-flag water-borne carriage. Their vicissitudes are representative of those who chose similar parameters, and the adjustments they made may be taken as representative of reasonable and better-than-average solutions to the competitive and social problems they encountered.

But *any* case study suffers from its overspecificity. To grant this problem but to offset it to some degree, it is worth ending with a summary of the Mallorys' point of view and behavioral norms with respect to six general sets of issues: business organization; technology; profits; competition; labor; and government. In this way, they can be more firmly fixed in the general context of American business history.

Reference to Figure 13.1 facilitates a summary of the Mallorys' business organization. Four organizational characteristics are plotted against a time scale: key family members by age; the types of business in which the firm was engaged; the particular branch markets served; and the type of service provided in those markets. For example, in 1822 Charles Mallory was twenty-eight and Charles Henry was four; the firm was engaged in sailmaking for others' ships and investment in others' ships; the only branch market involved was sealing and whaling; and the only services provided were as suppliers of sails and capital. Contrast 1850: Charles was fifty-six, Charles Henry was thirty-two, and Henry Rogers was two; the firm was engaged in sailmaking for both own and others' ships, in investment in others' ships, in ownership and management of own ships, and in building both own and others' ships; the three branch markets involved were sealing and whaling, American-flag coastal, and American-flag intercoastal; and the services provided in those markets were as suppliers of sails, ships, capital, managerial services, tramp carriage, and line carriage.

How do the organizational patterns represented in Figure 13.1 compare with industry norms? This is a difficult question to answer because shipping and its organizational forms are so ancient. In this sense, the Mallorys as sailmakers, investors, ship-managers, whaling agents, and shipbuilders were like all the rest. This is not a drawback, however, because it allows us to use their experience as proxy for all the rest.

They did deviate from some particular organizational norms, however, as far as the American merchant marine is concerned. Their use of the family firm over such a long period of time was certainly exceptional, as was their usually adamant refusal to seek governmental subsidy or to sail under any foreign flags of convenience or necessity. The degree to which they came to specialize in the coastal and intercoastal markets was also unusual. Their approach to ship management was unique, especially as it developed under Clifford D. Mallory, Sr.; that is, to work for a percentage of net operating profits rather than for a percentage of gross revenue. It is also fair to say that in almost every branch market they served, they were a larger-than-average competitor. And, finally, the degree to which Clifford D. Mallory, Sr., specialized in bulk-cargo tramp and contract carriage was extremely unusual for the period between the two world wars.

Technologically, the Mallorys at best were consummate masters of the state of the art; at worst, they were in the first rank of followers. In sailmaking, there is no evidence of any innovative behavior just as there is no evidence of anything but the highest standards of state-of-the-art quality. In shipbuilding, they were laying down new wooden sailing ships well into the 1870's, which is far later than most American shipbuilders. On the other hand, they knew how to get their money out of good sailing ships—be they Mallory-built or picked up on the used-ship market. Their clipper ships were among the finest built in America, but they can in no sense be called the innovators of that design. As for steam, they did not use it until the late 1850's—fully two decades later than such innovators as Charles Morgan or Cornelius Vanderbilt—and they continued to put their steam engines in wooden hulls until almost 1880. Here again, though, one cannot fault them too much, for they certainly knew how to design ships for the branch markets they were in and to operate them profitably.

The Mallorys were similarly slow to move into steel hulls and oil-fired propulsion equipment—not until almost World War I. Clifford D. Mallory, Sr., was really the only member of the clan who could ever be seen near the technological frontier, but most of his ideas for diesel-electric drive, new hull forms, and new methods of cargo handling were stillborn. What can be said, then, technologically? The Mallorys' decision to restrict themselves to American-built vessels initially gave them the benefit of the comparative advantages enjoyed by American ship-builders prior to the Civil War. Thereafter, however, they were increasingly at a disadvantage vis-à-vis the world. Also, through-out, they were not themselves highly innovative in any techno-logical sense. How did they survive? In two ways. First, by restricting themselves to branch markets in which most or all of their competitors were at the same technological disadvantage—that is, coastal and intercoastal. Second, by far better than average ship management that got the very best out of what they built or bought.

With respect to profit, the Mallorys deviate ever so slightly from the imputed American norm of maximization. Their religion and the peer groups they frequented legitimized and encouraged both a work ethic and profit and extolled the virtues of industry, thrift, and efficiency. In this they were no different from most American businesses except as they were more honest than the norm. But in one peculiar sense, the kind of business they were in was more important to them than profit maximization per se. If maximum return on investment (in the pecuniary sense) had been their overriding criterion for economic action, it is doubtful that they would have restricted themselves so doggedly to family control and their specialty of American-flag water transportation. They were well aware that higher profits lay elsewhere, especially by the twentieth century. This point is not to be overstressed, because within their specialty the Mallorys certainly aspired to maximization. But it is important to note in passing their clear and persistent deviation from any classic model of American economic man.

Thus, the basic proposition of the Mallory business strategy may be stated as profit maximization constrained by the ethics of their zealous Protestantism, by their unswerving devotion to family ownership and control, and by their propensity to concentrate their activities in American-flag shipping. Religion and family, in turn, determined the parameters of behavior and organization. Cabotage, in turn, determined their relevant markets, costs, capital, labor, and technology.

From this core, much more specific strategies flowed, which may be summarized as follows:

1. Take a solid position in all major American-flag branch markets as they evolved, but trail early leaders so as to benefit from their experience. The measure of success in any branch market should be profits per vessel operated there rather than degree of market penetration.

2. To be economically justifiable, any vessel should show (after meeting her ordinary running costs) a gross return of not less than 15 per cent per annum on original cost over a working lifetime of at least twenty years. This rate allows 5 per cent per annum depreciation, 3 per cent per annum for inflated costs of replacement, and 7 per cent profit and/or interest on capital invested. Ordinary running costs are: wages, stores, provisions, and insurance plus management overheads; reserves for maintenance and repairs not covered by insurance; reserves for annual and special surveys; and petty expenses.

3. Recognize that earnings sufficient to cover ordinary running costs plus depreciation, inflation, plus profit and/or interest will rarely hold for the entire economic life of a vessel.

Therefore, in boom periods retain a maximum of profits with a view to writing the vessel down to a least scrap value (7 percent of original new cost) in the shortest possible time. Once this has been done, and the need to provide for depreciation no longer exists, profitable trading for the remainder of a ship's life becomes possible at much lower levels of freights.

4. Make build or buy decisions on the basis of a *specific* vessel's ability to carry at the smallest cost per ton-mile as great as possible a variety of the commodities that dominate the branch market of intended service. But shave on technology and age so as to be able to foray across branch market lines when or if possible.

5. Recognize that there are no significant economies of scale in shipping beyond rather small firm sizes, but that what economies there are derive primarily from efficient utilization of available capacity and shoreside facilities and from frequency, regularity, and reliability of service. Thus concentrate on providing the best available service and let prices take care of themselves. Give preference, in other words, to those branch markets which are service-elastic and price-inelastic.

6. Be willing at all times to cooperate rather than compete with other carriers, with owners of shoreside facilities, with connecting land carriers, and with public agencies. In these arrangements, maximize the complementarity of services, but minimize any competitiveness in price.

7. Consider labor a cost of doing business that must be minimized.

8. Consider the letter of the law imperative but the spirit of the law (as embodied in government institutions and policies) as malleable.

The Mallorys certainly never tabulated their basic strategy in these words or in this way, but careful analysis of their operations reveals such underlying consistency along these lines. In kind, this strategy is reasonably representative of the approach of most maritime entrepreneurs of nineteenth-century America, but the Mallorys rate much better than average marks for their perception and execution of what was required. The last two strategic components also bear additional attention.

In their attitude toward their workforce, the Mallorys

mirror their industry's norms: labor had no rights and management knew what was best for them. Yet there was a curious blend of paternalism and exploitation. Charles and Charles Henry, for example, were products of the ancient apprenticeship system, and they carried over the quasi-filial affection of master for journeyman in their relationships with their captains, their engineers, their skilled sailmakers and shipbuilders, and their trusted clerks. Henry Rogers and Clifford Day carried on similar relationships, but, because they were products of the white-collar rather than the blue-collar world, they were more detached and impersonal about it.

Toward their seamen and longshoremen, however, the Mallorys were stern, even harsh—again mirroring the disgraceful record of the American maritime industry as a whole. They acquiesced in the vicious hiring-hall and share systems as long as they endured; and they were among the last to accept unionization and collective bargaining in almost the last industry to do so. Charles Henry summed up the family's philosophy: "I know of no good reason why I should not have the privilege of employing whomever I wish" (and at whatever price I wish, he would well have added). [12] This philosophy died hard, but it died under the external pressures of the labor movement and the government.

Finally, what of the Mallorys' attitudes toward government? To begin with, the very essence of their business depended on continuance of the American policy of cabotage. They recognized this fact and thrived within it. It was cabotage that set the basic ground rules for sailmaking, sealing, fishing, whaling, shipbuilding, and shipowning. Obviously, the Mallorys supported this deviation from a pure laissez-faire ideal and in doing so were representative of their industry as a whole. Similarly, they saw an appropriate role for government as a consumer of shipping services. Indeed, it was the rumor of government contract work on the Great Lakes that induced Charles Mallory to leave New London and set him on the road to Mystic. Mexican War, Civil War, Spanish-American War, and World War I contract and charter work came apace and was welcome. So, too, did they seek mail contracts, usually successfully. Again this was typical for any American ship-operator.

But the Mallorys were atypical in their general lack of interest in or support for construction or operating subsidies. Their first venture into a subsidized line was with John Roach to Brazil (1878–1881), and that was financed with Brazilian, not American, public funds. Otherwise they remained silent during the nineteenth-century debates over the need for a subsidized merchant marine. In the twentieth century, only Clifford D. Mallory, Sr., flirted with the idea of subsidy during his years as a managing agent for the Shipping Board (1919–1925). Thereafter, he became one of the few voices in the industry which opposed the subsidies enacted in 1936, and he ran his own companies entirely free from any form of public aid from 1925 to his death in 1941. He did work for a stronger merchant marine, but in his heart of hearts he probably agreed with Robert Annin's contemporaneous opinion: "The only real advantage of government, as compared with private, operation, is a greater ability to endure punishment. . . . In almost every other respect government management is at a hopeless disadvantage." [13]

The Mallorys, in sum, believed that water-borne commerce was vital to the American economy; they believed that it was in the national interest to protect the coastal and intercoastal markets through cabotage; and they believed that the deep-sea success of American-flag ships depended *not* on administration by politicans, national legislation, or subsidization, but on competition. These beliefs led them to seek their economic chance in the maritime sector, and they did so with notable success. Ironically, the sustenance of family enterprise, which was their basic motivating force, escaped them in the long run. But for a century and a quarter they represented the forefront of the American merchant marine.

NOTES

To conserve space in the footnotes, many primary-source locations have been abbreviated. Full citations to the collections and libraries represented by these abbreviations are included in the Bibliography.

Chapter I. Charles Mallory, Sailmaker, 1816–1853

1. Josephine M. Peck, "Mallory Family Genealogy" (typescript), MFP; undated obituaries of Charles Mallory, Mystic *Press* and New York *Herald,* box 13–1, MFP.

2. Charles Henry Mallory Autobiography, May 1870, box 10–3, MFP (hereafter cited as CHM Autobiog.).

3. D. Hamilton Hurd, "Charles Mallory," *History of New London County, Connecticut* (Philadelphia: J. W. Lewis & Co., 1882), pp. 691–693.

4. R. B. Wall, "Charles Mallory," New London *Evening Day,* August 21, 1923.

5. *Ibid.*

6. CHM Autobiog. For earlier version, see Charles Henry Mallory Diary, December 24, 1865, MFP (hereafter cited as CHM Diary).

7. Carl C. Cutler, "Mallory Shipping and Family History," chap. 2 (typescript), MFP; Virginia B. Anderson, *Maritime Mystic* (Mystic: Marine Historical Association, 1962), *passim.*

8. CHM Autobiog., MFP.

9. Wall, "Charles Mallory." For earlier version, see Hurd, "Charles Mallory."

10. Francis G. Clarke, *The Seaman's Manual* (Portland: Shirley, Hyde & Co., 1830), pp. 52–82; M. V. Brewington, "The Sailmaker's Gear," *American Neptune* IX (October 1949), 278–296. Tools similar to Mallory's are displayed in the Mallory Sail Loft at Mystic Seaport. Mallory's account books and his sail plan book are preserved in the Seaport's Library.

11. Boston Board of Trade, *Third Annual Report* (Boston: George C.

Rand & Avery, 1857), pp. 64–68; Levi R. Trumbull, *A History of Industrial Paterson* (Paterson: C. M. Herrick, 1882), pp. 43, 46, 52.

12. Sales of Cotton Duck & Cotton Twine by Order and on Account of John Colt of New York by Charles Mallory of Mystic Bridge, Connecticut, September 21, 1832–April 13, 1838, CMP; Caroline F. Ware, *The Early New England Cotton Manufacture: A Study in Industrial Beginnings* (Boston: Houghton Mifflin, 1931), pp. 160, 164–165.

13. Charles Mallory Daybook, January 20, 1826–January 13, 1830, CMP; Charles Mallory Daybook, October 8, 1832–August 10, 1835, MFP; Sloop *George Eldredge* & Owners to Chas. Mallory Dr., July 10, 1837–June 29, 1843, EP; Boat *Charles & Edward* & Owners to Mallory & Grant September 17, 1838–April 9, 1839, EP; Ownrs. Sloop *George Eldredge* to Mallory & Grant Dr., October 15, 1840–October 3, 1841, EP. Mallory's first daybook, commencing January 3, 1818, was seen by Carl C. Cutler in the 1930's and quoted in his "Mallory Shipping and Family History," chap. 2. Cutler to Clifford D. Mallory, Sr., July 30, 1931, box 6–13, MFP. Present whereabouts of this daybook is unknown.

14. Hurd, "Charles Mallory."

15. CHM Autobiog., MFP.

16. Analysis based on materials in MFP and CMP and on Pimer Papers, Marine Historical Association., Mystic Conn. John K. Pimer (1807–1884) was a prominent New London sailmaker from 1828 until his death.

17. Stanley Lebergott, *Manpower in Economic Growth: The American Record since 1800* (New York: McGraw-Hill, 1964), p. 119.

18. State of Connecticut, *Report of the Bank Commissioners to the General Assembly* (Hartford: various printers, annually, 1835–1849); William F. Hasse, Jr., *A History of Money and Banking in Connecticut* (New Haven: Whaples-Bullis Co., 1957), chaps. 2–3.

19. Conclusions of this and six preceding paragraphs derived from comparison of account books of Mallory and his associates with generalizations found in Fritz Redlich, *The Molding of American Banking: Men and Ideas* (new ed., 2 parts, New York: Johnson Reprint Corp., 1968), part I, pp. 1–66, and J. Van Fenstermaker, *The Development of American Commercial Banking, 1782–1837* (Kent: Bureau of Economic and Business Research, Kent State University, 1965), pp. 21–53, 113–114, 189–190.

20. Spar Account with Charles Mallory, April 2, 1839–June 19, 1840, Cottrell & Hoxie Ledger A, CHP.

21. E.g., Cottrell & Hoxie Ledgers A and B, April 2, 1839–February 1, 1846, CHP; Charles Mallory, January 1845–January 30, 1849, Conn., vol. 45, p. 46, DB; B. F. Hoxie & Co., March 14, 1842–January 30, 1849, Conn., vol. 45, p. 46, DB; D. D. Mallory & Co., January 1845–January 30, 1849, Conn., vol. 45, p. 47, DB.

22. CHM Autobiog., MFP; Charles Mallory, January 30, 1849, Conn., vol. 45, p. 46, DB; Cottrell & Hoxie in Account with Mallory & Grant, April 28, 1838-April 1, 1845, Cottrell & Hoxie Ledgers A and B, CHP; I. D. Clift Ledger, 1853-1877, CP.

23. CHM Autobiog., MFP.

Chapter 2. Whaling Investors and Agents, 1822-1860

1. Alexander Starbuck, "History of the American Whale Fishery from Its Earliest Inception to the Year 1876," Appendix A to part IV of U.S. Commission of Fish and Fisheries, *Report of the Commissioner for 1875-1876* (Washington: Government Printing Office, 1878), pp. 660-661; Walter S. Tower, *A History of the American Whale Fishery* (Philadelphia: University of Pennsylvania, 1907), pp. 47-79, 121.

2. John G. B. Hutchins, *The American Maritime Industries and Public Policy, 1789-1914: An Economic History* (Cambridge: Harvard University Press, 1941), pp. 228-230.

3. Douglass C. North, *The Economic Growth of the United States, 1790-1860* (Englewood Cliffs: Prentice-Hall, 1961), pp. 185-186, 234, 245, 250, 254.

4. Cutler, "Mallory Shipping and Family History," chap. 2; Anderson, *Maritime Mystic*, pp. 50-55; Thomas F. Godfrey, "The Whaling Industry of New London, Connecticut: A Case Study in American Economic History" (Senior Essay in American Studies, Yale University, 1966), pp. 20-29.

5. RENLS; Starbuck, "History of the American Whale Fishery," pp. 246-247; Cutler, "Mallory Shipping and Family History," chap. 2.

6. Wall, "Charles Mallory." For earlier version, see Hurd, "Charles Mallory."

7. CHM Autobiog.; Peck, "Mallory Family Genealogy."

8. RENLS; Starbuck, "History of the American Whale Fishery," *passim.*

9. This and next six paragraphs based on Elmo P. Hohman, *The American Whaleman* (New York: Longmans, Green, 1928), esp. pp. 222-223, 273, 277-278, 284-288, 324-325, 331-332; David Moment, "The Business of Whaling in America in the 1850's," *Business History Review,* XXXI (Autumn 1957), 261-291.

10. Hohman, *American Whaleman,* pp. 284-288.

11. Investor in: Ship *Acasta,* Schooner *Pacific,* Ship *Charles Adams,* Ship *Meteor,* Schooner *McDonough,* Ship *Atlas,* Schooner *Amazon,* Bark *Friends,* Schooner *Mentor,* Bark-Ship *George,* Brig *Rebecca Groves,* Bark-Ship *Bolton.* Owner of: Ship *Aeronaut,* Ship *Bigham,* Brig *Uxor,* Ship *Blackstone,* Brig *Tampico,* Brig *Leander,* Ship *Romulus,* Bark *Vermont,*

Ship *Atlantic*, Ship *Coriolanus*, Ship *Trescott*, Ship *Robin Hood*, Schooner *Lion*, Schooner *Cornelia*, Schooner *Frank*, Schooner *Wilmington*. RENLS and RENYC.

12. Starbuck, "History of the American Whale Fishery," pp. 212–596, 663–693; Tower, *History of the American Whale Fishery*, pp. 122–124. After tabulating returns for all the 103 voyages performed by Mystic's 28 whalers over the years 1832–1862, Charles R. Schultz concludes: "Charles Mallory, with a total of sixteen vessels was by far the largest operator [i.e., managing agent]. He was followed by Jedediah and William P. Randall who managed six vessels. Other agents were Geo. W. Ashby & Co. and Randall, Smith & Ashby with four each, Jedediah Randall with two and Joseph Avery and Silas Beebe with one each." Of the 319 persons who invested in Mystic's whalers, Schultz says: "The two individuals who owned shares in the most vessels were Charles Mallory and Joseph Cottrell. They each owned portions of sixteen vessels. Elisha Faxon, with shares in twelve vessels, was the second largest owner. William P. Randall and Benjamin F. Stoddard each owned portions of ten vessels. From there, ownership spread rather widely with five people holding shares in nine vessels, three in eight, five in seven, nine in six, nine in five, fifteen in four, nineteen in three, fifty-five in two and 194 in only one vessel." "Whalers out of Mystic," Information Bulletin 69–3, G. W. Blunt White Library, Marine Historical Association, Mystic, Conn., p. 6.

13. For an enlightening discussion of the risk-reducing properties of marine insurance, fractional-share shipowning, and the lay system, see Hohman, *American Whaleman*, pp. 273, 277–278.

14. Daniel Wheeler (Decd.) to Owns & Agt. Ship *Robin Hood* Dr., October 5, 1854–May 23, 1857, 1–2, MFP.

15. Hohman, *American Whaleman*, pp. 222–223.

16. Charles P. Williams, January ?, 1845–December 13, 1861, I. & W. P. Randall, March 19, 1842–April 20, 1855, Randalls Smith & Ashbey, September 15, 1854–June 4, 1861, Conn., vol. 45, pp. 167, 97, 52, DB; Godfrey, "Whaling Industry of New London," p. 39.

17. John G. B. Hutchins, "The Rise and Fall of the Building of Wooden Ships in America, 1607–1914" (Ph.D. dissertation, Harvard University, 1937); Dorothy S. Brady, "Relative Prices in the Nineteenth Century," *Journal of Economic History*, XXIV (June 1964), 145–203; "Whalers out of Mystic," pp. 2–4.

18. For example, Mallory and associates purchased the 366-ton, twelve-year-old *Romulus* in March 1842 for $7,000. When several shares in their 375-ton, forty-year-old *Bingham* changed hands in May 1844, her market price was $6,500. In contrast, the new, 368-ton whaler *Charles W. Morgan*, built in New Bedford during 1840–1841, cost $26,877.78 exclusive of outfit, and Hohman's "cost of a typical whaling vessel . . . of 351

tons at New Bedford in 1841" is set up at $31,224.72. Cottrell & Hoxie Ledger B, p. 231 (October 18, 1842), CHP; Ira H. Clift to Chas. Mallory Dr., May 18, 1844, CP; Charles R. Schultz, "Costs of Constructing and Outfitting the Ship *Charles W. Morgan,* 1840-1841," *Business History Review,* XLI (Summer 1967), 198-216; Hohman, *American Whaleman,* p. 324.

19. Schultz, "Costs of Constructing and Outfitting," *passim;* Cottrell & Hoxie Ledger B, p. 21 (October 9, 1841), p. 231 (October 18, 1842), CHP; Account Book, Owns. Ship *Bingham* to Chas. Mallory Dr., March 26, 1844-December 29, 1852, CMP.

20. Daniel Wheeler (Decd.) to Owns. & Agt. Ship *Robin Hood* Dr., October 5, 1854-May 23, 1857, 1-2, MFP.

21. Cottrell & Hoxie, January ?, 1845-April 14, 1853, Joseph Cottrell, May 3, 1853-September 1, 1860, B. F. Hoxie & Co., March 14, 1842-July 30, 1852, David D. Mallory & Co., January ?, 1845-March 7, 1860, Conn., vol. 45, pp. 46, 47, 53, DB; Cottrell & Hoxie Ledgers A and B, CHP.

22. Account Book, Owns. Ship *Bingham* to Chas. Mallory Dr., March 26, 1844-December 29, 1852, CMP.

23. The full list of lays was as follows: captain, 1/17; first mate, 1/25; second mate and third mate, each 1/30; fourth mate, 1/40; cooper, 1/50; shipkeeper, 1/60; 3 boat steerers, 1/85-1/90; carpenter, 1/125; cook and steward, each 1/135; 7 "seamen," 1/120-1/140; 3 "ordinaries," 1/150-1/160; "boy," 1/200; and 7 "green hands," 1/160-1/225.

24. Daniel Wheeler (Decd.) to Owns. & Agt. Ship *Robin Hood* Dr., October 5, 1854-May 23, 1857, 1-2, MFP; Starbuck, "History of the American Whale Fishery," pp. 420-421, 522-523; Tower, *History of the American Whale Fishery,* p. 128.

25. For further discussion of this procedure by its creator, see Godfrey, "Whaling Industry of New London," p. 39. Landings and durations are from Starbuck; prices are from Tower. In "Whalers out of Mystic," Schultz has performed similar calculations using prices from Starbuck. I prefer to use Tower's prices as they are more representative of industry norms and they permit comparison of Mallory with Godfrey's samples of New London entrepreneurs.

26. Godfrey, "Whaling Industry of New London," pp. 84-98, 106.

27. *Ibid.*

28. Arthur Gordon, "The Great Stone Fleet: Calculated Catastrophe," *U.S. Naval Institute Proceedings,* XCIV (December 1968), 72-82.

Chapter 3. Sailing Tramps and Sailing Packets, 1826–1860

1. Arnljot S. Svendsen, *Sea Transport and Shipping Economics* (Bremen: Institute for Shipping Research, 1958), *passim;* Carleen O'Loughlin, *The Economics of Sea Transport* (London: Pergamon Press, 1967), *passim.*

2. Robert G. Albion, *The Rise of New York Port, 1815–1860* (New York: Scribner, 1939), pp. 213–286.

3. S. G. Sturmey, *On the Pricing of Tramp Ship Service* (Bergen: Institute for Shipping Research, 1965), p. 3. See also Frank M. Fisser, *Tramp Shipping* (Bremen: Carl Schünemann Verlag, 1957), pp. 5–17.

4. S. G. Sturmey, *Some Aspects of Ocean Liner Economics* (Manchester: Manchester Statistical Society, 1964), p. 1.

5. Thomas Thorburn, *Supply and Demand of Water Transport* (Stockholm: Business Research Institute, Stockholm School of Economics, 1960), pp. 8–202; Svendsen, *Sea Transport,* pp. 275–335; Fisser, *Tramp Shipping,* pp. 93–103, 125–159, 183–207; Sturmey, *On the Pricing,* pp. 3–20; Sturmey, *Some Aspects,* pp. 1–22.

6. Thorburn, *Supply and Demand,* p. 71.

7. Hutchins, *American Maritime Industries,* pp. 41–48, 228–230, 270–271; Albion, *Rise of New York Port,* pp. 122–142, 165–193; Robert G. Albion, *Square-Riggers on Schedule: The New York Sailing Packets to England, France, and the Cotton Ports* (Princeton: Princeton University Press, 1938), pp. 49–76.

8. Sloops *Connecticut, Tiger, Mary Ann, Whale, James Monroe, Magellan, Paragon, Relief, Plume, Sidney, Phenix, Mystic, Charles Mallory, Francis Park, George Eldredge, Caution, Alabama, Richard H. Watson, Ann B. Holmes, Emily, Vineyard, Active, J. A. Burr;* Schooners *Orient, Augustine, Sarah, Emeline I, Hero, Mobile, Francis Amy, Comet, Meteor, Dolphin, Swallow, Coasting Trader, Bolina, Empire, Panama, Mechanic, D. D. Mallory;* Brigs *Toison, Tampico, Apalachicola, Francis Ashbey, Ann Eliza, Republic, Metamora, Napoleon:* Barks *Mazeppa, White Oak, Montauk;* Ships *Charles P. Williams, John Minturn.* For dates of equity and physical characteristics see documents in RENLS, REHM, and RENYC.

9. Charles Henry Mallory to John Levey, September 20, 1861, Charles Henry Mallory Letterbooks, March 13, 1858–February 17, 1865, vols. 39 and 40, MFP (hereafter cited as CHM Letterbooks).

10. Charles Henry Mallory to J. W. Holmes, July 16, 1858, CHM Letterbooks, MFP.

11. Henry Ashbey Account Book, October 6, 1837–September 30, 1840, AP.

12. Calculated from ton-days under register (document necessary to

engage in foreign trade) and ton-days under enrollment (document necessary to engage in domestic trade) of the 53 vessels listed in note 8.

13. Charles Henry Mallory to George Griswold, October 21, 1859, CHM Letterbooks, MFP.

14. Powers of Attorney, Charles Mallory, *et al.*, to Elam Eldridge, October 17, 1835, November 13, 1841, EP.

15. Charles Henry Mallory to Gurdon Gates, March 19, June 29, 1858, CHM Letterbooks, MFP.

16. Charles Henry Mallory to William T. Coleman & Co., March 13, 1858, to J. W Holmes, April 3, May 3, 1858, CHM Letterbooks, MFP.

17. Charles Henry Mallory to William Gwynne, March 22, 1858, to J. W. Holmes, July 16, 1858, CHM Letterbooks, MFP.

18. *Disturnell's Guide through the Middle, Northern, and Eastern States* (New York: J. Disturnell, 1847), pp. 6, 16; Carl C. Cutler, *Five Hundred Sailing Records of American Built Ships* (Mystic: Marine Historical Association, 1952), pp. 97-106; Robert L. Thompson, *Wiring A Continent: The History of the Telegraph Industry in the United States, 1832-1866* (Princeton: Princeton University Press, 1947), pp. 37-56, 140-166.

19. Fla. vol. 6, pp. 118-119, 121-123, DB; Jefferson B. Browne, *Key West: The Old and the New* (St. Augustine: The Record Co., 1912), *passim*.

20. Dorothy Dodd, "The Wrecking Business on the Florida-Reef, 1822-1860," *Florida Historical Quarterly*, XXII (April 1944), 172.

21. *Ibid.*, pp. 176-199.

22. James D. Fish, *Memories of Early Business Life and Associates* (New York: Privately printed, 1907), pp. 11-14.

23. Owners of Sloop *George Eldredge* Cr., 1838, EP; Charles Mallory Daybook, January 20, 1826-January 13, 1830 CMP; Charles Mallory Daybook, October 8, 1832-August 10, 1835, MFP.

24. Carl C. Cutler, *Queens of the Western Ocean: The Story of America's Mail and Passenger Sailing Lines* (Annapolis: U.S. Naval Institute, 1961), pp. 92-131, 149-193, 222-274, 306-338, 371-548.

25. Robert G. Albion, "Early Nineteenth-Century Shipowning: A Chapter in Business Enterprise," *Journal of Economic History*, I (May 1941), 1-11; Albion, *Square-Riggers*, pp. 106-139.

26. See, e.g., Charter Party, Charles H. Mallory and Cornelius Comstock, June 11, 1862, and Agreement, Charles H. Mallory and Cornelius Comstock, June 11, 1862, box C-94, COMP.

27. Fish, *Memories, passim*.

28. *Ibid.*, pp.6-8 13.

29. Cutler, *Queens,* pp. 130, 178, 250, 309, 348, 396–397, 399, 484, 486, 505, 513, 529,

30. *Ibid.,* pp. 491, 492, 497, 504, 506, 510, 511, 538.

31. CHM Autobiog., MFP; Charles Henry Mallory Journal, October 1, 1835–May 15, 1836, box 14–1, MFP; Charles Henry Mallory to Franklin Chase, November 22, 1858, CHM Letterbooks, MFP; Reminiscences of Charles M. Williams and Fanny Williams Mason, box 10–4, MFP; Elizabeth T. Mallory to Clifford D. Mallory, June 17, 1930, box 6–4, MFP; Obituaries of Charles Henry Mallory, box 13–2, MFP.

32. Charles H. Mallory, September 15, 1854–January 25, 1865, Conn., vol. 45, p. 50, DB.

33. Sloops *Mary W. Baker, Martha, Appollo;* Schooners *Bay State, California, E. L. Hammond, Emma C. Latham, Minna, Telegraph, Mustang, B. W. Eldredge, R. L. Keeney, S. B. Howes, Elizabeth Seegar, Wilmington, M. L. Rogers, Eliza S. Potter, Ocilla, Mystic Valley, R. Fowler, Sarah L.;* Barks *Fanny, Ann, Frances, Lapwing, Tycoon;* Ships *Henry, Charles Mallory, Caroline Tucker, Eliza Mallory, Alboni, Pampero, Hound, Samuel Willetts, Elizabeth F. Willetts, Mary L. Sutton, Twilight I, Prima Donna, Haze.* For dates of equity and physical characteristics see documents in RENLS, REHM, and RENYC.

34. Agreement between Charles Henry Mallory and James Packer, November 25, 1861, CHM Letterbooks, MFP.

35. Cutler, *Queens,* pp. 388, 398, 464, 492, 497, 517.

36. On the New York–Charleston run the two all-time, one-way sailing passages were 77 hours by the brig *Franklin* (1820) and 67 hours by the ship *Henry Allen* (1833). In 1837, the steamship *Home* made the run in 64 hours; the steamship *Southerner* broke this record in 1846 with a run of 59 hours only to relinquish the honor to her sister ship *Palmetto's* run of 55 hours later the same year. In 1855, the steamship *Nashville* set a record of 45 hours which stood until 1896. From 1846 on, Spofford, Tileston & Co., proprietors of the New York–Charleston steamers, advertised "average passage 60 hours." Among sailing packets, "there were a few 84-hour records, and four-day passages were fairly common, with 14 days even more common, plus an extra week occasionally thrown in for good measure." *Ibid.,* pp. 125–126, 220, 227, 295–296; John H. Morrison, *History of American Steam Navigation* (reprinted, New York: Stephen Day, 1958), pp. 484–514, 545–571.

37. As late as 1861, no railroad system could do better than three to four days from New York to New Orleans, and the usual trip was more likely to consume a week. *Appleton's National Railway and Steam Navigation Guide* (New York: Appleton, 1861), *passim.*

38. Ralph P. Bieber, "California Gold Mania," *Mississippi Valley Historical Review*, XXXV (June 1948), 3–28; Raymond A. Rydell, "The Cape Horn Route to California, 1849," *Pacific Historical Review*, XVII (May 1948), 149–163; John H. Kemble, "The Gold Rush by Panama, 1848–1851," *ibid.*, XVIII (February 1949), 45–56.

39. Carl C. Cutler, *Greyhounds of the Sea: The Story of the American Clipper Ship* (revised ed., Annapolis: U.S. Naval Institute, 1961), pp. 142–162.

40. Charles Henry Mallory to Wells and Emanuel, December 27, 1859, CHM Letterbooks, MFP.

41. CHM Letterbooks, MFP.

42. The discovery of gold in Australia and California and the abolition of Negro slavery in the West Indies and Latin America increased demands in those areas for cheap indentured or contract laborers. Chinese "coolies" supplied much of this demand, and there was a mini-boom in transporting them in the late 1850's. Conditions on the "coolie ships" were so regularly foul, however, that an American act of 1862 prohibited the "coolie trade" by American citizens in American-flag vessels. Mallory shipmasters usually avoided this trade, but *Hound* did make at least one Macao-Havana "coolie voyage" in 1855. Eldon Griffin, *Clippers and Consuls: American Consular and Commercial Relations with Eastern Asia, 1845–1860* (Ann Arbor: Edwards Brothers, Inc., 1938), pp. 98–99, Appendix 4.

43. The Mallorys paid their captains "30 dolls. per month and 5% primage on the amount of freight and passage money earned by the ship. When there is no primage on the freight your 5% comes out of the freight. You are to furnish your own nautical instruments and keep them in order at your own expense." Also, they never employed a captain who was not willing to invest 1/8 to 1/4 in his ship. Charles Henry Mallory to D. Colden Murray, July 26, 1860, to Thomas C. Forsyth, November 5, 1863, January 26, 1864, CHM Letterbooks.

44. Ocean mail between New York and San Francisco via Panama (the quickest sea route) averaged 33 to 35 days before completion of the Panama Railroad in 1855; then, the average one-way time was 23 to 26 days. Overland stage mail was established between San Francisco and St. Louis on September 15, 1858, with a contract time of 25 days; in 1860, as the eastern end of the first transcontinental telegraph reached Fort Kearney and the western end reached Fort Churchill, 15-day stage mail was established between those points. The Pony Express, which inaugurated service between Saint Joseph, Missouri, and San Francisco on April 3, 1860, never broke eight days between Forts Kearney and Churchill until

news of Lincoln's election, in November 1861, was carried fort to fort in six. Not until October 24, 1861, was telegraphic service between New York and San Francisco available. LeRoy R. Hafen, *The Overland Mail 1849-1869* (Cleveland: Arthur A. Clark, 1926), *passim.* In January 1862, one Hong Kong dispatch reached New York in 40 days (39 via the ship *Charger* to San Francisco; 1 via telegraph to New York). The average one-way time for the year, however, was 60 days. *Annual Report of the Chamber of Commerce of the State of New York for the Year 1861-62* (New York: Wheeler & Williams, 1862), p. 188; *ibid., 1862-63,* p. 171.

45. CHM Letterbooks, MFP.

46. As differentiated from the "continuation rate" (that "rate which if his ship can be fully employed year in and year out, will provide the owner with a level of profit such that he will happily stay in the business") and the "lay up rate" (that "rate which will yield a revenue equal to the level of voyage costs minus the costs of lay up and is the absolute rock bottom rate which the owner will ever accept"). Sturmey, *On the Pricing,* p. 5.

47. "The rate of return on railroad stocks traded at Boston for the years 1856-60 was 9.8 per cent, and New York and Boston short-term money rates were 8.1 and 8.5 per cent for the same period." Robert Evans, Jr., " ' Without regard for Cost': The Returns on Clipper Ships," *Journal of Political Economy,* LXXII (February 1964), 42n.

48. These data and those in Table 3.2 compiled from Cutler, *Greyhounds, passim;* Octavius T. Howe and Frederick C. Matthews, *American Clipper Ships, 1833-1858* (2 vols., Salem: Marine Research Society, 1926), *passim;* and clipper ship sailing cards in possession of Baker Library, Harvard Graduate School of Business Administration, Boston, Mass.

49. Sources for Figure 3.1 are Evans, " 'Without Regard for Cost,' " Table 4, and accounts of four voyages by *Samuel Willets* and *Mary L. Sutton* in MFP and ESP.

50. Charles Henry Mallory to Gurden Gates, September 19, 1859, CHM Letterbooks, MFP; Evans, " 'Without Regard for Cost,' " pp. 33-43.

Chapter 4. Shipbuilders and Bankers, 1849-1860

1. Hutchins, *American Maritime Industries,* pp. 272-276.

2. Anderson, *Maritime Mystic,* pp. 28-34.

3. Sloops *Mystic, Caution, Richard H. Watson;* Schooners *Francis Amy, Mechanic, Bay State, Emma C. Latham, R. L Keeney, S. B. Howes;* Ships *Charles P. Williams, Caroline Tucker, Prima Donna,* RENLS; George Greenman & Co., Ledger No. 1, pp. 71, 76, 80, 92, 112, 226, Ledger No.

2, pp. 7, 23, 78, 102, 477 (August 29, 1853–March 16, 1865), GP. for *Prima Donna,* see Cutler, *Greyhounds,* pp. 342, 447, 513.

4. Sloop *Ann B. Holmes;* Schooners *Empire, D. D. Mallory, California;* Bark *Montauk;* Ship *Charles Mallory,* RENLS.

5. Leonard Mallory, June 19, 1862, David D. Mallory & Co., November 21, 1851, April 20, 1855, Conn., vol. 45, pp. 47, 60, DB.

6. Charles H. Mallory, September 15, 1854–January 25, 1865, Conn., vol. 45, p. 50, DB; CHM Letterbooks, MFP.

7. The Schooner *Telegraph* (1852) was built by David D. and George W. Mallory and John A. Forsyth at the new yard for a local group of merchants associated with Issac W. Denison & Co. *Eliza S. Potter* (1857), built at the old yard, was sold to outsiders, with Charles Mallory retaining a passive 1/8 interest until 1876. *Mustang* (1853) was built in the new yard by Charles Henry Mallory as a schooner and altered to a "bark ship" in 1854. The Mallorys had 15/32 in her as late as 1862.

The Bark *Fanny* (1849) was the first Mallory-built vessel, and her construction was supervised by Peter Forsyth at the old yard. The Mallorys held 20/32 in her and Ashbey & Fish of New York most of the rest. *Ann* (1854) and *Frances* (1855) were built at the new yard by Mason Crary Hill. The Mallorys retained all of *Frances* and approximately 1/2 of *Ann* until their sale in the late 1850's to W. H. Hazard.

8. Cutler, *Greyhounds,* pp. 237–239, 415, 420, 485; Howe and Matthews, *American Clipper Ships,* I, 88.

9. Cutler, *Greyhounds,* pp. 237, 273, 284, 419, 430, 473, 486, 492, 494, 497, 500, 512, 518; Howe and Matthews, *American Clipper Ships,* I, 4–6, II, 468–470; Cutler, *Five Hundred Sailing Records,* p. 68.

10. Howard I. Chappelle, *The History of American Sailing Ships* (New York: Norton, 1935), p. 286.

11. Charles Henry Mallory to Thomas C. Forsyth, November 5, 1863, CHM Letterbooks, MFP.

12. See, e.g., cards for *Elizabeth F. Willets, Mary L. Sutton,* and *Haze* in Manuscript Division, Baker Library, Harvard Graduate School of Business Administration, Boston, Mass.

13. I am in complete agreement with Howard I. Chappelle's plea for "dimensionless" analysis and can only marvel at his herculean labors in fairly comparing the speeds of vessels varying widely in size and construction. See, e.g., Chappelle, *The Search for Speed under Sail, 1700–1855* (New York: Norton, 1967). Unfortunately, the absence of plans or reliable half-models prevents a Chappelle-like analysis of the Mallory fleet.

14. Cutler, *Five Hundred Sailing Records,* p. 50.

15. Cutler, *Greyhounds,* pp. 273, 312–313, 318, 346, 354, 428, 435,

453, 498-499, 506, 511, 515, 518; Howe and Matthews, *American Clipper Ships*, I, 157-158.

16. Cutler, *Greyhounds*, pp. 321, 344, 371, 445, 504, 508, 512, 517, 519; Howe and Matthews, *American Clipper Ships*, II, 383-385; Cutler, *Five Hundred Sailing Records*, p. 63.

17. Clipping from New York *Herald*, *ca.* 1868, in MFP.

18. Cutler, *Greyhounds*, pp. 343, 346, 447, 510, 516; Howe and Matthews, *American Clipper Ships*, II, 672-673.

19. The only other antebellum Mallory-built ship *Constitution* (1857), is not comparable, as she was built on contract as a whaler.

20. Charles Henry Mallory to Jas. K. Caskie, May 1, 1860, CHM Letterbooks, MFP.

21. Evans, " 'Without Regard for Cost,' " *passim;* Capt. Elihu Spicer, Jr., In Acct. Current and Interest Acct. to Sept. 8, 1857, with Chas. Mallory, box 1-1, SP; Charles Henry Mallory to A. O. Peck, October 14, 1859, to Jas. K. Caskie, May 1, 1860, to D. Colden Murray, July 26, 1860, to Cap. Wilson, *ca.* February 1862, CHM Letterbooks, MFP.

22. Charles Henry Mallory to Chas. H. Haswell, July 10, 1858, CHM Letterbooks, MFP.

23. Charles Henry Mallory to Geo. Heusted, July 19, 1858, to Henry Butler, November 9, 1858, *ibid.*

24. Charles Henry Mallory to Geo. Heusted, July 19, 1858, to Henry Butler, August 24, 1858, to Chas. H. Haswell, July 1, 1859, June 11, 1860, April 27, 1864, *ibid.*

25. Agreement between Geo. Heusted and Charles Henry Mallory, November 27, 1858, *ibid.* On prices and terms, also see Charles Henry Mallory to Geo. F. Wing, November 22, 1858, to Chas. H. Haswell, November 22, 1858, March 1, 1859, June 11, 1860, to R. L. Muillard, May 10, 1860, to Geo. Talbot Olyphant, August 3, 1861, *ibid.*

26. Charles Henry Mallory to Chas. H. Haswell, May 10, 1859, *ibid.*

27. RENLS; CHM Letterbooks, *passim*, MFP; Charles Mallory Diary, April 19, 1858-March 17, 1859, vol. 19, MFP; Cutler, "Mallory Shipping and Family History," chap. 9.

28. Hutchins, *American Maritime Industries*, p. 275.

29. *Ibid.*, pp. 267-268; Cutler, *Greyhounds*, pp. 411-447.

30. Cutler, *Five Hundred Sailing Records*, pp. 113-114.

31. Mystic River Bank, Stockholders and Directors Minute Book No. 1, August 1, 1851-September 1, 1931, Stockholders Ledger, August 1, 1851-September 1, 1931, MRBP.

32. Hasse, *History of Money and Banking in Connecticut*, pp. 19-46, 123-162.

33. State of Connecticut, *Report of the Bank Commissioners, 1851,* p. 5.

34. *Ibid., 1847,* pp. 47–48, *1848,* pp. 30–31, *1849,* pp. 34–35, *1850,* pp. 44–45, *1851,* pp. 27, 38, *1852,* pp. 47, 53, *1853,* pp. 28, 43.

35. *Ibid., 1844,* p. 6, *1849,* p. 4, 7, *1852,* p. 7, *1853,* p. 5, *1854,* pp. 8–9, *1855,* p. 7, *1857,* p. 7, *1860,* p. 13; "Niebuhr," *A Report Concerning Banks* (n.p., n.d., *ca.* 1854), pp. 2–4 (analyzing the Connecticut *Report of the Bank Commissioners, 1854).*

36. State of Connecticut, *Report of the Bank Commissioners, 1852,* p. 38, *1853,* p. 29, *1854,* p. 45, *1855,* p. 39, *1856,* p. 56; Mystic River Bank, Stockholders and Directors Minute Book No. 1, *passim,* MRBP.

37. Mystic River Bank, Stockholders and Directors Minute Book No. 1, *passim,* MRBP; *Banker's Almanac* (Boston: Phillips, Sampson & Co., annually, 1851–1864), *1851,* pp. xxviii, 7–8, *1852,* pp. xxiv, 7, *1853,* pp. xxiv, 53 *1854,* pp. xxiv–xxv, *1855,* pp. 26, 53, 124, *1856,* p. 36, *1857,* pp. 12–13, 48, 51, *1858,* pp. 12, 119, *1859,* p. 12, *1861,* pp. 88–89, 93, 172–173, 175, *1862,* pp. 73, 90, *1863,* p. 13, *1864* p. 13; Fish, *Memories, passim.*

38. E.g., Mystic River Bank, Stockholders and Directors Minute Book No. 1, August 11, 1851, 1857. On the general practice in Connecticut, see State of Connecticut, *Report of the Bank Commissioners, 1842,* p. 7, *1845,* p. 5, *1846,* p. 14.

39. Redlich, *Molding of American Banking,* part I, p. 11.

40. State of Connecticut, *Report of the Bank Commissioners, 1853,* pp. 61–62, *1854,* p. 5.

Chapter 5. The Era of the Civil War, 1861–1865

1. Charles Mallory, November 21, 1851, March 13, 1852, August 30, 1859, June 7, 1860, Conn., vol. 45, p. 46, DB.

2. Charles Henry Mallory, Assets and Liabilities, January 1, 1857, January 1, 1858, January 1, 1859, January 1, 1861, January 1, 1862, vol. 39, pp. 228–239, MFP; Charles H. Mallory, April 7, September 26, 1860, Conn., vol. 45, p. 50, DB; David D. Mallory & Co., September 28, 1858, February 23, August 30, 1859, March 7, April 7, September 1, 1860, February 19, April 5, 1861, Conn., vol. 45, p. 53, DB.

3. RENLS.

4. U.S. Bureau of the Census, *Historical Statistics of the United States, 1789–1945* (Washington: Government Printing Office, 1949), pp. 207–208.

5. Survey of Federal Archives, *Ship Registers and Enrollments of Providence, Rhode Island* (2 vols., Providence: Survey of Federal Archives,

1941), I, 29, 239, 274, 337, 622, 822, 823, 839, 840, 845, 985, 1104; Charles Henry Mallory to John Baistern (?), September 5, 1861, CHM Letterbook, MFP; Fred E. Dayton, *Steamboat Days,* (New York: Stokes, 1925), pp. 192–194. *Penguin* (launched on November 3, 1859, and first documented on January 6, 1860) and *Falcon* (first documented on November 18, 1861) were similar in appearance: the former was 155 feet in length by 30 feet in beam by 9 feet depth of hold; the latter was 156'6" by 23'3" x 9'4"; each had one deck, three masts, auxiliary sails, and a single engine. *Eagle* (which was contracted for on September 5, 1861, and first documented on November 19, 1861), was a side-wheeler, not a propellor, 100' x 26'4" x 7'6" one deck, and two masts.

6. Mystic Machine Co., December 5, 1857–March 7, 1862, Conn., vol. 45, p. 105, DB; Hogg & Delamater, October 3, 1853–September 8, 1857, Corns. H. Delamater, September 14, 1857–May 2, 1862, N.Y., vol. 316a, pp. 115, 180, 185; "Cornelius H. Delamater," *Transactions of the American Society of Mechanical Engineers,* X (1888–1889), 836–838.

7. Charles Henry Mallory to Gurdon Gates, January 30, 1860, to Gurdon I. Coit, May 9, 1860, to F. S. Mitchell, May 9, 1860, to S. R. Mallory, March 25, 1861, CHM Letterbooks, MFP; RENLS.

8. Charles Henry Mallory to John Levey, February 11, 1861, to J. C. Kuhn, March 9, 1861, CHM Letterbooks, MFP. While *Varuna I* was 217' x 35' x 18'6", *Stars and Stripes* was to be 145' x 34' x 9'. The larger vessel was rated at 14 knots with a 12-foot draft (loaded); the smaller at 11 knots with an 8-foot draft (loaded).

9. Joseph T. Durkin, *Stephen R. Mallory: Confederate Navy Chief* (Chapel Hill: University of North Carolina Press, 1954), *passim*; William N. Still, Jr., *Confederate Shipbuilding* (Athens: University of Georgia Press, 1969), pp. 1–9.

10. Charles Henry Mallory to S. R. Mallory, March 25, 1861, CHM Letterbooks, MFP.

11. Charles Henry Mallory to William A. Buckingham, April 22, 1861, to Gideon Welles, April 22, 1861, *ibid.* For an excellent description of Connecticut's response to Sumter, see John Niven, *Connecticut for the Union: The Role of the State in the Civil War* (New Haven: Yale University Press, 1965), pp. 40-70.

12. RENLS; Gordon, "Great Stone Fleet," p. 78; Testimony of Charles H. Mallory, April 22, 1862, "Government Contracts," 37 Cong., 2 Sess., *House Reports,* No. 2 (2 vols., Serials 1142–1143), II, 1512.

13. Charles Henry Mallory, Assets and Liabilities, January 1, 1861, vol. 39, pp. 230–231, MFP; Charles Henry Mallory to Cap. Rogers, January 1, 28, 1861, to Ellery Nash, December 23, 1861, to G. Frank Dickman, September 14, 1863, to Messrs. Bonner & Brown, October 12,

1863, to A. K. Williams, October 30, 1863, CHM Letterbooks, MFP; Charles Henry Mallory Daybook, May 20, 1862–July 7, 1870, vol. 43, MFP (hereafter cited as CHM Daybook), November 12, 1862, October 13, 1863.

14. Charles Henry Mallory, Assets and Liabilities, January 1, 1861, January 1, 1862, vol. 39, pp. 228–231, MFP; Charles Henry Mallory to J. D. Fish & Co., May 8, 1863, to Messrs. Thayer & Peabody, October 27, 1863, to Thomas C. Forsyth, November 5, 1863, January 26, 1864, to John Ogden, September 22, 1864, CHM Letterbooks, MFP; CHM Daybook, December 5, 1862, March 23, 1863, MFP.

15. Charles Henry Mallory, Assets and Liabilities, January 1, 1861, January 1, 1862, vol. 39, pp. 228–231, MFP; Owns. Ship *Mary L. Sutton* In Acct. with Chas. Mallory, November 1, 1858–February 1, 1862, box 1–2, SP; Charles Henry Mallory to P. E. Rowland, February 9, 1865, CHM Letterbooks, MFP.

16. Charles Henry Mallory, Assets and Liabilities, January 1, 1861, vol. 39, pp. 230–231, MFP; Charles Henry Mallory to J. W. Spencer, August 23, 1864, CHM Letterbooks, MFP; CHM Daybook, September 22, 1862, MFP.

17. Charles Henry Mallory, Assets and Liabilities, January 1, 1861, vol. 39, pp. 230–231, MFP; Charles Henry Mallory to E. Williams, June 10, 1861, CHM Letterbooks, MFP.

18. Charles Henry Mallory to Messrs. Bower, Hamburg & Co., November 7, 22, 1861, to Ellery Nash, November 7, 1861, to A. K. Williams, November 7, 22, December 23, 1861, May 3, 1862, to Geo. C. Henderson, November 7, 1861, CHM Letterbooks, MFP; CHM Daybook, October 6, November 14, 1862, April 6, 1863, MFP.

19. Charles Henry Mallory to A. K. Williams, May 14, October 10, 30, 1863, February 1, 1864, to Messrs. Olyphant & Co., June 6, 1864, CHM Letterbooks, MFP; CHM Daybook, December 5, 14, 1864, MFP.

20. Charles Henry Mallory, Assets and Liabilities, January 1, 1861, January 1, 1862, vol. 39, pp. 228–231, MFP; Charles Henry Mallory to Messrs. Terry & Della Torre, May 13, 1862, to J. L. Prouty, May 13, 1862, CHM Letterbooks, MFP; CHM Daybook, November 24, December 1, 1862, April 23, 1863, MFP.

21. Charles Henry Mallory, Assets and Liabilities, January 1, 1861, January 2, 1862, vol. 39, pp. 228–231, MFP; Charles Henry Mallory to S. R. Greenman, February 18, June 10, 1861; Frank L. Owsley, Jr., *The C.S.S. Florida: Her Building and Operations* (Philadelphia: University of Pennsylvania Press, 1965), pp. 61–63.

22. Charles Henry Mallory, Assets and Liabilities, January 1, 1861, January 2, 1862, vol. 39, pp. 228–231, MFP; Charles Henry Mallory to

John Levey, December 24, 1860, February 11, September 20, 1861, February 10, April 11, 1862, CHM Letterbooks, MFP; CHM Daybook, October 21, 1862, MFP; "Vessels Bought, Sold, and Chartered by the United States, April, 1861-July, 1868," 40 Cong., 2 Sess., *House Exec. Docs.*, No. 337 (Serial 1346), pp. 100-101; Philip Van Doren Stern (ed.), *The Confederate Raider Alabama* (Bloomington: Indiana University Press, 1962), p. 365.

23. Testimony of Cornelius S. Bushnell, October 9, 1861, Testimony of Charles Mallory, April 22, 1862, Testimony of Charles H. Mallory, April 22, 1862, Testimony of Nathaniel L. McReady, April 22, 1862, "Government Contracts," I, 673-683, II, 1509-1516, 1525-1528.

24. Naval History Division, Office of the Chief of Naval Operations, *Civil War Naval Chronology, 1861-1865* (6 parts, Washington: Government Printing Office, 1961-1966), *passim.*

25. "Report on Iron-Clad Vessels, September 16, 1861," in *Annual Report of the Secretary of the Navy* (Washington: Government Printing Office, 1862), pp. 152-157; Testimony of Cornelius S. Bushnell, October 9, 1861, "Government Contracts," I, 673-683; Edward William Sloan, III, *Benjamin Franklin Isherwood, Naval Engineer: The Years as Engineer in Chief, 1861-1869* (Annapolis: U.S. Naval Institute, 1965), pp. 30-31, 49-50.

26. Charles Mallory per Charles Henry Mallory to C. S. Bushnell, June 17, 1861, CHM Letterbooks, MFP; Testimony of Charles Mallory, April 22, 1862, "Government Contracts," II, 1510-1511.

27. *Ibid.;* "Naval Vessels," p. 7.

28. E.g., Charles Henry Mallory to J. J. Comstock, September 20, 1861, CHM Letterbooks, MFP; Testimony of Charles Mallory, April 22, 1862, Testimony of Charles H. Mallory, April 22, 1862, "Government Contracts," II, 1509-1516.

29. RENLS; RENYC; Charles Henry Mallory to "Experiment," February 10, 1862, to Edwin M. Stanton, February 17, 1862, to C. S. Bushnell, April 29, 1862, to Messrs. E. D. Hurlburt & Co., May 2, 1862, to Messrs. Albertson & Douglass, May 6, 1862, to Benjamin E. Mallory, May 15, 1862, to William Morgan, May 15, 1862, to Edward E. Dunbar, May 21, 1862, to C. B. Fessenden, May 14, 1863, CHM Letterbooks, MFP; CHM Daybook, October 10, November 12, December 5, 1862, January 7, 1863, MFP; "Vessels Bought, Sold, and Chartered," pp. 24-25, 46-47, 100-101; "Naval Vessels," pp. 13, 18, 22.

30. RENLS; RENYC; Charles Henry Mallory to J. D. Fish & Co., May 29, 1863, to Proprietors of Mystic Iron Works, December 1, 1863, to T. H. Gregory, December 4, 1863, to Messrs. N. L. McReady & Co., August 22, 1864, to F. W. Cooley, October 17, 1864, to Ed. Whitehurst, October 17, 1864, to C. G. Devins, October 19, 1864, CHM Letterbooks,

MFP; "Vessels Bought, Sold, and Chartered," pp. 104-105, 112-113; "Naval Vessels," p. 16.

31. RENLS; RENYC; Charles Henry Mallory to T. H. Gregory, July 4 (not sent), December 4, 1863, to S. W. Pook, July 6, 1863, to Messrs. Swift & Allen, July 14, 1864, to C. G. Devine, October 19, 1864, to John Ogden, November 9, 1864, CHM Letterbooks, MFP; George W. Mallory Ledger, January 1, 1865, GWMP; "Vessels Bought, Sold, and Chartered," pp. 6-7, 34-35, 58-59, 90-91, 102-103, 145-146.

32. Charles Henry Mallory to C. G. Devine, October 19, 1864, CHM Letterbooks, MFP; James P. Baughman, *Charles Morgan and the Development of Southern Transportation* (Nashville: Vanderbilt University Press, 1968), p. 254.

33. Charles Henry Mallory to "Experiment," February 10, 1862, to J. D. Fish & Co., May 8, 29, 1863, October 25, 1864, February 4, 1865, to Messrs. Potter, Anthony & Denison, January 18, 1864, to Messrs. N. L. McReady & Co., August 22, September 1, 1864, CHM Letterbooks, MFP; Testimony of Charles H. Mallory, April 22, 1862, Testimony of Nathaniel L. McReady, April 22, 1862, "Government Contracts," II, 1513-1516, 1525-1528; Fish, *Memories, passim.*

34. Charles Henry Mallory to Benjamin E. Mallory, May 15, 1862, to William Morgan, May 15, 1862, CHM Letterbooks, MFP.

35. Charles Henry Mallory to William Morgan, May 15, 1862, to Messrs. Wagdell & Co., September 22, 1864, to F. W. Cooley, October 17, 1864, to Ed. Whitehurst, October 17, 1864, to E. Spicer, Jr., July 17, 1865, *ibid.*

36. Charles Henry Mallory to S. R. Mallory, March 25, 1861, September 5, 1861, to Cap. Wilson, *ca.* February 1862, to Dexter H. Follett, September 16, 23, October 27, 1863, to Messrs. N. L. McReady & Co., August 22, 1864, to C. G. Devine, October 19, 1864, to John Ogden, November 9, 1864, to Messrs. Williams & Brewster, December 19, 1864, *ibid.;* George W. Mallory Ledger, January 1, 1865, GWMP.

37. Charles Henry Mallory to "Experiment," February 10, 1862, to Edwin M. Stanton, February 17, 1862, to Messrs. Albertson & Douglass, May 6, 1862, to C. H. Delamater, May 12, 1862, to Edward E. Dunbar, May 21, 1862, to T. H. Gregory, December 4, 1863, CHM Letterbook, MFP; Corns. H. Delamater, February 3, 1860-May 2, 1865, N.Y., vol. 316a, p. 115, DB.

38. Reliance Machine Co., November 6, 1858-June 12, 1865, Conn., vol. 45, p. 183, DB.

39. Mystic Iron Works, February 7, 1863-March 11, 1867, Conn., vol. 45, p. 203, DB; Charles Henry Mallory to Proprietors of Mystic Iron Works, December 1, 1863, to Messrs. Ludlam, Heineken & Co., February

23, 1864, to Messrs. James C. Jewett & Co., October 14, 1864, CHM Letterbooks, MFP; Mystic *Pioneer,* February 21, 1863.

40. Sloop Yacht *Kate,* Schooner Yacht *Josephine,* RENLS; Boat Building Account, May 31, 1862–January 30, 1865, J. & W. Batty Account, October 1, 1863, CHM Daybook, MFP; Mystic *Pioneer* February 21, 1863.

41. Niven, *Connecticut for the Union,* pp. 71–108, 267–348.

42. Mystic *Pioneer,* February 21, 1863; Charles Henry Mallory to C. H. Haswell, May 11, 1863, April 16, 1864, to E. Spicer, Jr., June 20, 1864, to J. N. Clark & Co., July 14, August 3, 9, 12, 15, 1864, CHM Letterbooks, MFP.

43. Charles Henry Mallory to Messrs. N. L. McReady & Co., August 22, 1864, CHM Letterbooks, MFP.

44. Conn., vol. 45, p. 42E, DB.

Chapter 6. C. H. Mallory & Co., 1865–1875

1. CHM Diary, April 14–15, 29, May 1, 1865, MFP.

2. *Ibid.,* May 8, October 13, November 17, December 14, 1865, MFP.

3. *Ibid.,* March 23, December 21, 31, 1865, January 11, February 2, November 11, 1866, February 9, October 8, 28, November 23, 1868, April 4, 15, May 24, 1870, MFP.

4. Contracting and selling for the Mallory yard was usually routine. On August 14, 1865, for example, William H. Lincoln & Co. of Boston placed an order for a $45,000 steamer to be completed in ninety days. *A. J. Ingersoll* was the result, and on March 20, 1866, she was placed with C. H. Mallory & Co. for resale. They ran her briefly in the coastal market until a sale for $105,000 was consummated on December 14 to Forbes & Co. of Boston. To cite another case, in 1875 the firm assisted George W. Mallory (Charles Henry's brother and an employee) and Charles Mallory in designing and marketing three steam fishing vessels: *Aeronaut, Garet Polhemius,* and *Henry F. Sisson.*

5. *Ibid.,* May 21, 1865–December 31, 1875, MFP; Charles Mallory to Cornelius Comstock & Co., November 17, 1868, box C–123, COMP.

6. Sturmey, *On the Pricing,* p. 5.

7. February 12, 1866–December 31, 1875, MFP.

8. CHM Diary, May 5–6, 25, July 25, August 4, September 1, 6, 23, October 18, 21, 28, 30, November 9–11, 24, December 10, 21, 27, 1869, January 8, 1870, MFP; Geo. Greenman & Co., Ledger No. 1 (1865–1883), pp. 179, 414, Daybook (1866–1875), p. 225, GP; New York *Herald,* August 5, 1869.

9. John F. Stover, *The Railroads of the South, 1865-1900: A Study in Finance and Control* (Chapel Hill: University of North Carolina Press, 1955), *passim*; Baughman, *Charles Morgan*, pp. 134-207; Maury Klein and Kozo Yamamura, "The Growth Strategies of Southern Railroads, 1865-1893," *Business History Review*, XLI (Winter 1967). 358-377.

10. *Supply and Demand*, p. 157.

11. New Orleans *Price Current*, September 9, 1864, February 10, October 14, 1865; Morrison, *History of American Steam Navigation*, pp. 457-462.

12. CHM Diary, July 12, 1865-April 12, 1867, MFP.

13. Advertisements and daily lists of entrances and clearances, New Orleans *Price Current*, 1862-1875; advertisements and schedules in box 12-1, MFP; notations and comments on New Orleans Trade in CHM Diary, 1865-1875, MFP.

14. Advertisements and schedules in box 12-1, MFP; notations and comments on Galveston trade in CHM Diary, 1865-1875, MFP; advertisements in *Lloyd's Rail Road Guide* (New York: W. Alvin Lloyd & Co., 1867), p. vii; entries for William Hendly & Co. and T. H. McMahan & Co., Texas, vol. 13, pp. 34, 45, 86, DB; documents of vessels named in RENLS and RENYC.

15. Entries for Ball, Hutchings & Co., Galveston, Houston & Henderson Railroad Co., and Galveston Wharf Co., Texas, vol. 13, pp. 34, 69, 92, 161, DB; "Historical History of the Galveston Wharf Company" (manuscript), GWCP; Houston Direct Navigation Co., Board of Directors Minute Book No. 1 (1866-1896), pp. 1-87, HDNCP.

16. Galveston Wharf Co., Board of Directors and Stockholders Minute Book No. 1, July 12, 1854-December 14, 1877, pp. 145-147, 149-159, 163, 202, 217, GWCP; extracts from minutes of Galveston Wharf Co., June 2-July 2, 1870, box 3-1, MFP; documents of vessels name in RENLS and RENYC.

17. CHM Diary, February 27, 1866-October 7, 1873, MFP; documents for vessels named in RENLS and RENYC; advertisements and schedules in box 12-1, MFP; "The Delamater Iron Works," New York *Nautical Gazette*, January 17, 1874; Leonard A. Swann, Jr., *John Roach, Maritime Entrepreneur* (Annapolis: U.S. Naval Institute, 1965), pp. 76-78; Galveston Wharf Co., Board of Directors and Stockholders Minute Book No. 1, p. 202, GWCP.

18. Chas. H. Mallory & Co., May 2, 1867-December 12, 1873, NYC, vol. 371, p. 833, DB; Charles Mallory, September 18, 1866-December 13, 1873, Conn., vol. 45, p. 42E, DB; Charles Henry Mallory, Assets and Liabilities, July 1, August 1, September 1, October 1, November 1, December 1, 1870, March 1, July 1, August 1, November 1, December 1,

1871, January 1, May 1, August 1, October 1, 1872, February 1, 1873, vol. 28, end papers, MFP.

19. CHM Diary, September 1, 1873–July 31, 1875, MFP; "Mallory Lines," New York *Nautical Gazette,* November 13, 1873; New Orleans *Republican,* September 7, 1875.

20. Baughman, *Charles Morgan, passim.*

21. CHM Diary, August 28–December 31, 1875, MFP.

Chapter 7. C. H. Mallory & Co., 1876–1885

1. Andrew F. Muir, "Railroads Come to Houston, 1857–1861," *Southwestern Historical Quarterly,* LXIV (July 1960), 42–63; Earl W. Fornell, *The Galveston Era: The Texas Crescent on the Eve of Secession* (Austin: University of Texas Press, 1961), pp. 157–192; Marilyn M. Sibley, *The Port of Houston: A History* (Austin: University of Texas Press, 1968), pp. 31–78; James P. Baughman, "The Evolution of Rail-Water Systems of Transportation in the Gulf Southwest, 1836–1890," *Journal of Southern History,* XXXIV (August 1968), 357–372.

2. Baughman, *Charles Morgan,* pp. 191–207; Sibley, *Port of Houston,* pp. 89–105.

3. Galveston Wharf Co., Board of Directors and Stockholders Minute Book No. 1, numerous entries during 1870–1877, GWCP; CHM Diary, numerous entries during 1870–1877; GWCP; Robert E. Caudle, *History of the Missouri Pacific Lines, Gulf Coast Lines and Subsidiaries, International Great Northern* (Mimeographed, Houston: The Author, 1949), *passim.*

4. CHM Diary, February 12, 1876–September 10, 1877, MFP; RENYC; advertisements and schedules in box 12–1, MFP; advertisements and schedules in Texas Directory Co., *Texas Business Directory for 1878–1879* (Galveston: Shaw & Blaylock, 1878), pp. 106–109.

5. CHM Diary, January 13, 1877–June 10, 1878, MFP; Baughman, *Charles Morgan,* p. 216.

6. This and next seven paragraphs based on: Robert Mather, "How the States Make Intrastate Rates," *Annals of the American Academy of Political and Social Sciences,* XXXII (July–December 1908), 102–119; Charles S. Potts, *Railroad Transportation in Texas* (Austin: University of Texas, 1909), pp. 73–85, 175–178, 184–186; U.S. House of Representatives, *Proceedings of the Committee on the Merchant Marine and Fisheries in the Investigation of Shipping Combinations under House Resolution 587* (4 vols., Washington: Government Printing Office, 1913–1914), ll, 930–1027, 1104–1203, IV, 383–402; Theodore A. Fetter, *Southwestern Freight Rates* (Boston: Christopher Publishing House, 1934); S. G. Reed, *A History of the Texas Railroads* (Houston: St. Clair Publishing Co.,

1941), pp. 565–569, 589–591; Baughman, "Evolution of Rail-Water Systems," pp. 377–381.

7. Fetter, *Southwestern Freight Rates,* p. 132.

8. *Ibid,* pp. 39–40, 60.

9. CHM Diary, January 22, 1876–December 31, 1884, MFP; advertisements and schedules in box 12–1, MFP; advertisement in *Appleton's Railway and Steam Navigation Guide* (New York: Appleton, 1877), p. 35.

10. Charles A. Sindall, "The Development of the Traffic between the Southern States and the Northern and Northwestern States," in U.S. Bureau of Statistics, *Report on the Internal Commerce of the United States for 1886* (Washington: Government Printing Office, 1886), pp. 679–738 plus diagrams and map appended.

11. Quotations from: U.S. Bureau of Statistics, *Report on the Internal Commerce of the United States for 1879* (Washington: Government Printing Office, 1879), pp. 171, 172–173. For fuller history of the Southern Railway & Steamship Association and rate-making in the Southeast, see William H. Joubert, *Southern Freight Rates in Transition* (Gainesville: University of Florida Press, 1949), *passim.*

12. CHM Diary, January 1, 1876–December 31, 1889, MFP; advertisements and schedules in box 12–1, MFP: documents for vessels named in RENYC; Galveston Wharf Co., Board of Directors and Stockholders Minute Book No. 2, January 7, 1878–March 17, 1893, GWCP; Hutchins, *American Maritime Industries,* pp. 371–440.

13. For a full account of the United States and Brazil Mail Steamship Line, see Swann, *John Roach,* pp. 95–124. Swann makes extensive use of CHM Diary, MFP.

14. Swann, *John Roach,* p. 102.

15. *Ibid.,* pp. 102–103.

16. *Ibid.,* p. 122.

17. *Ibid.,* p. 119; CHM Diary, May 8, July 2, 1880, May 5, 1881, MFP.

18. In the foreign trade, wage rates had been climbing since 1863 and had been standardized in 1872 at 40 cents per hour for daywork, 80 cents at night, and $1.00 on Sundays. Most coastal lines paid a flat rate of 25 cents an hour for day, night, and Sunday work, but the Mallory, Morgan, and Clyde lines paid 30 cents for daywork, 45 cents for nights, and 60 cents on Sundays. Charles B. Barnes, *The Longshoremen* (New York: Russell Sage Foundation, 1915), pp. 76–81.

19. Maud Russell, *Men Along the Shore* (New York: Brussel & Brussel, Inc., 1966), p. 25; Barnes, *Longshoremen,* pp. 98–102.

20. CHM Diary, February 9, 1879, MFP.

21. CHM Diary, November 4, 1883–April 27, 1886, MFP.

22. CHM Diary, *passim*, MFP; reminiscences of Dr. Charles M. Williams and Fanny Williams Mason regarding Charles Henry Mallory, box 10-4, MFP.

23. Miscellaneous records of Elihu Spicer, Jr., SP; "Elihu Spicer," Henry Hall (ed.), *America's Successful Men of Affairs* (2 vols., New York: New York *Tribune*, 1895), I, 610.

24. Charles Mallory Diary, April 19, 1858-March 17, 1859, May 1-December 30, 1861, January 1, 1862-September 23, 1863, March 12-June 20, 1876, vols. 19-22, MFP (hereafter cited as CM Diary); CHM Diary, September 3, 6, 7, 11, 19, October 3, 24, 1865, MFP.

25. CM Diary and CHM Diary, *passim*, MFP; Charles Henry Mallory to S. French, January 17, 1864, CHM Letterbooks, MFP; Henry Rogers Mallory to Robert Sealey, April 28, 1903, box 2-1, MFP; undated handwritten autobiographical sketch, "Henry Rogers Mallory," box 4-3, MFP.

26. CHM Diary, *passim*, MFP; W. Lyle Bull to author, January 15, 1969.

27. N.Y.C., vol. 371, p. 882a/78, DB.

28. C. H. Mallory & Co., Profit and Loss Statements, 1867, 1868, 1882, 1883, boxes 1-4, 1-5, 1-6, SP; various memoranda concerning Henry Rogers Mallory's income from C. H. Mallory & Co. and from Mallory vessels, 1878-1884, box 1-7, MFP.

29. Conn., vol. 45, pp. 96a, 191-193, vol. 46, pp. 228, 252, 259, 281, 452, DB; CHM Diary, *passim*, MFP.

30. CHM Diary, *passim*, MFP; Ledger, January 1, 1865-January 1, 1880, Letterpress Copybook, December 19, 1873-August 2, 1877, GWMP; advertisement in *Poor's Manual of Railroads for 1883* (New York: H. V. Poor, 1883), p. 120.

31. CHM Diary, August 26, 1882, MFP.

Chapter 8. The New York & Texas Steamship Co., 1886-1906

1. CHM Diary, December 31, 1885, MFP.

2. Documents and correspondence concerning various suits in boxes 1-6, and 1-8, MFP.

3. 60/64 of *City of San Antonio* ($140,625); 59/64 of *Carondelet* ($110,625); 60/64 of *State of Texas* ($168,750); *Rio Grande* ($220,000); *Colorado* ($300,000); *San Marcos* ($325,000); *Lampasas* ($400,000); *Alamo* ($400,000); *Comal* ($400,000); the lighters *C. F. Deering, C. E. Goin, P. C. Golder, S. A. Walker, O. M. Hitchcock, S. B. Baker,* and *E. Brandon* ($17,500).

4. Charles Henry Mallory (5,189 shares), Elihu Spicer, Jr. (3,322), Charles Rogers Mallory (557), Henry Rogers Mallory (557), Robert Mal-

lory (305), William Mason (370), and 1,829 shares in the name of the firm.

5. Cornelius H. Delamater (3,645 shares) and John Roach (1,426).

6. Estate of George Ball (2,255 shares), Estate of John Sealy (1,611), John H. Hutchings (1,611), George Sealy (820), Henry Rosenberg (324), Joseph J. Hendly (95), and the Mallory agent, Captain Jeremiah N. Sawyer (440).

7. Joseph W. Spencer, the New Jersey attorney, held 432 shares, the rest being held by: Hampton Young (63 shares), Thomas Eldredge (47), Jeremiah Mulford (47), George H. Robinson (23), and Fannie Mallory Williams (32). The missing shares of *City of San Antonio, Carondelet,* and *State of Texas* were owned by the Estate of R. J. Holmes and were never changed for corporate stock.

8. New York & Texas Steamship Co., Board of Directors and Stockholders Minute Book No. 1 (1886-1893), pp. 3-45, vol. 52, MFP; *ibid.,* Stock Certificate Book (1886-1906), vol. 56, MFP; Property Account, N. Y. & T. S. S. Co., at Time of Formation of Co., Sept. 1886, loose in vol. 54, MFP; CHM Diary, June 24, September 1, October 6, 1886, MFP.

9. By-Laws of The "New York and Texas Steamship Company," pp. 13-21, vol. 52, MFP; *By-Laws of the New York & Texas Steamship Co.,* (New York: The Company, 1886), copy amended by hand by corporate secretary through December 10, 1896, box 12-1, MFP.

10. Agreements between New York & Texas Steamship Co., and C. H. Mallory & Co., December 30, 1886, December 17, 1891, January 26, 1897, January 18, 1902, and associated minutes, pp. 38-44, 53-59, 197-203, 262-268, vol. 52, pp. 3-6, 71-80, 168-171, 174-183, vol. 53, MFP.

11. Caudle, *History of the Missouri Pacific Lines, passim;* V. V. of Oklahoma Press, 1952), *passim;* Reed, *History of the Texas Railroads, passim.*

12. L. L. Waters, *Steel Trails to Santa Fe* (Lawrence: University of Kansas Press, 1950), *passim;* Reed, *History of the Texas Railroads, passim.*

13. Baughman, *Charles Morgan,* pp. 208-235; Mallory Line advertisements and schedules in box 12-1, MFP; Mallory Line, Morgan Line, and Cromwell Line advertisements in *ABC Pathfinder Shipping & Mailing Guide* (Boston: New England Railway Publishing Co., annually, 1892-1902).

14. New York & Texas Steamship Co., Board of Directors and Stockholders Minute Book No. 1, pp. 141-145, 175-179, *et passim,* vol. 52, MFP; *ibid.,* No. 2 (1893-1902), pp. 137-138, vol. 53, MFP; Morgan's Louisiana & Texas Railroad & Steamship Co., Board of Directors Minute Book No. 1 (1878-1902), *passim,* MLTP; Galveston Wharf Co., Board of

Directors and Stockholders Minute Books No. 2 (1878-1893) and No. 3 (1893-1910), *passim*, GWCP.

15. New York *Maritime Register*, July 14, 28, August 4, 18, September 1, 1897; New York & Texas Steamship Co., Board of Directors and Stockholders Minute Book No. 2, pp. 88, 90, 96, vol. 53, MFP; New York & Texas Steamship Co., Analyses of Annual Reports Nos. 11, 12, and 13, boxes 1-10 and 1-11, MFP; William Schneider to Clifford D. Mallory, February 25, 1932, box 6-14, MFP.

16. *Matter of Alleged Unlawful Discrimination*, 11 I.C.C. Reports 595-597.

17. U.S. House of Representatives, *Proceedings of the Committee on the Merchant Marine and Fisheries in the Investigation of Shipping Combinations*, II, 930-1027, 1104-1203, IV, 383-402; *Southern Pacific Company's Ownership of Atlantic Steamship Lines*, 43, I.C.C. Reports 168-181; John L. Hazard, *Crisis in Coastal Shipping: The Atlantic-Gulf Case* (Austin: Bureau of Business Research, University of Texas, 1955), *passim.*

18. New York & Texas Steamship Co., Board of Directors and Stockholders Minute Book No. 2, pp. 137-138, vol. 53, MFP; *Galveston, Harrisburg and San Antonio Railway Company, et al.*, 36 I.C.C. Valuation Reports 704-705; *Southern Pacific Company's Ownership of Atlantic Steamship Lines*, 43 I.C.C. Reports 168-181; U.S. Bureau of Corporations, *Transportation by Water in the United States* (4 parts, Washington: Government Printing Office, 1909-1913), part II, pp. 10-11, 142-146, part III, pp. 152-156, 267-268, 321-323.

19. New York & Texas Steamship Co., Board of Directors and Stockholders Minute Book No. 1, pp. 47-48, 119, 131-132, vol. 52, MFP; *ibid.*, No. 2, pp. 116-117, 163-164, *et passim*, MFP; U.S. Bureau of Corporations, *Transportation by Water*, part II, pp. 9-10, 86-125, part III, 127-142, 268-269, 310-319; U.S. House of Representatives; *Proceedings of the Committee on the Merchant Marine and Fisheries in the Investigation of Shipping Combinations*, II, 1154-1175, 1177-1203, IV, 369-403; Joubert, *Southern Freight Rates, passim.*

20. New York & Texas Steamship Co., Board of Directors and Stockholders Minute Book No. 2, pp. 199-201, vol. 53, MFP; receipts calculated from various financial statements in boxes 1-11 and 2-13 and in vols. 54 and 55, MFP.

21. The financial analysis contained in this and the next twelve paragraphs is derived from: C. H. Mallory & Co., Profit and Loss Accounts, 1882-1883, box 1-6, SP; C. H. Mallory & Co., Profit and Loss Accounts, 1900-1906, boxes 2-13 and 2-17, MFP; Income and Expenses, H. R. Mallory, 1890-1904, and Financial Condition, H. R. Mallory, 1891-1905, box 1-7, MFP; New York & Texas Steamship Co., Treasurer's Reports

Nos. 1-78 (1886-1906), pp. 1-89, vol. 55, MFP, and Analyses of Annual Reports Nos. 1-19 (1886-1905), boxes 1-6 through 1-14, MFP; Statement, *Net Results* of New York & Texas S. S. Co. from Date of Incorporation, Sept. 1st 1886 to Dec. 31st 1902, Surplus Account, N. Y. & T. S. S. Co., Showing Total Amount Received in Surplus from Date of Incorporation, Sept. 1st 1886 to Dec. 31st 1903, loose in vol. 54, MFP.

22. Construction of new vessels: *Denver,* 1900-1902 ($535,000); *San Jacinto,* 1902-1905 ($795,341); *Thompson* and *King,* 1899 ($12,000); and *Perry,* 1902 ($2,000). New boilers for old steamships: *Lampasas,* 1896 ($50,000); *Alamo,* 1898 ($59,000); *Sabine,* 1900 ($80,000); *San Marcos,* 1901-1902 ($103,000); *Rio Grande* (new bottom), 1901 ($32,000); *Nueces,* 1903-1904 ($49,000); *Concho,* 1904 ($143,000); *Colorado,* 1905 ($94,000). New wharves, piers, etc. or improvements to old: new shed, Pier 20, East River, 1896 ($16,000); rebuilding fire damage, same, 1900 ($18,000); new shed, Pier 20, East River, 1901 ($3,000); rebuilding storm damage at Galveston, 1901-1902 ($58,000); purchase and improvement of Key West wharves, 1901-1904 ($204,000); new shed, Pier 16, East River, 1903 ($36,000).

23. Results of Govt. Charters, 1898, Stewards Dept., 1898, box 1-11, MFP; U.S. Army, *Annual Report of the Quartermaster-General of the Army to the Secretary of War for the Fiscal Year Ended June 30, 1898* (Washington: Government Printing Office, 1898), pp. 12-13, 15, 31, 57-60, 62, 65-67, 70, 74.

24. Clara Barton to Henry R. Mallory, March 28, 1900, box 1-13, MFP; Clara Barton, *The Red Cross* (Washington: American National Red Cross, 1898), pp. 365-396, 549-580; Ishbel Ross, *Angel of the Battlefield: The Life of Clara Barton* (New York: Harper, 1956), pp. 203-226.

25. See note 16, above.

26. CHM Diary, 1879-1890, *passim,* MFP; Port Chester materials in MFP, esp. in boxes 1-6 and 4-9.

27. Charles H. Mallory, Last Will and Testament, September 24, 1889 (recorded April 21, 1890), copy in box 1-6, MFP; Private Letter of C. H. Mallory to My Children, Not to Be Opened Except in Case of My Death, February 23, 1889, box 1-6, MFP; Eunice C. Mallory to My Dear Children, originally undated (updated November 2, 1893, Thanksgiving Day, 1894, and May 3, 1895), box 1-9, MFP; undated obituaries of Charles Henry Mallory, box 13-2, MFP; *Memorial Services on The Death of Capt. Charles Henry Mallory at the Methodist Episcopal Church, Mystic Bridge, Conn., Sunday, March 30, 1890* (New York: Broun, Green & Adams, 1890).

28. Agreement between Elihu Spicer, Charles Mallory, Henry R. Mallory, and Robert Mallory, March 22, 1890, Agreements between Mallory, Mallory, and William Mason, September 13, 1890, February 20, 1893,

February 20, 1903, boxes 1-7 and 1-8, MFP; New York & Texas Steamship Co., Board of Directors and Stockholders Minute Books Nos. 1 and 2, *passim*, vols. 52-53, MFP.

29. Memorandum of H. R. Mallory's Ownership in Vessels, 1870-1885, Income and Expenses, H. R. Mallory, 1878-1883, 1890-1904, H. R. Mallory's Financial Condition, 1891-1905, box 1-7, MFP; Henry R. Mallory to Robert Sealey, April 28, 1903, box 2-1, MFP.

30. W. Lyle Bull to author, January 15, 1969.

31. New York & Texas Steamship Co., Board of Directors and Stockholders Minute Books Nos. 1 and 2, *passim*, vols. 52-53, MFP; Charles Vezin to Henry R. Mallory, January 3, 1902, Mallory to Vezin, January 4, 1902, box 1-15, MFP; H. H. Raymond to Clifford D. Mallory, February 18, 1932, box 6-14, MFP.

32. Suggestions for Inclusion in Biography of Mr. Henry R. Mallory, Oct. 8, 1940, box 9-2, MFP.

Chapter 9. The Atlantic, Gulf & West Indies Steamship Lines, 1906-1915

1. Memoranda in Henry R. Mallory's handwriting: "Read at Annual Meeting S.C., Jany. 24th 1905," and "Read at S.S. Co. Annual Meeting, January 23d. 1905 [6]," boxes 2-9 and 2-14, MFP; New York & Texas Steamship Co., Board of Directors and Stockholders Minute Book No. 2, pp. 239-240, vol. 53, MFP.

2. Robert Mallory to Henry R. Mallory, December 19, 1901, box 1-14, J. B. Denison to Henry R. Mallory, November 24, 1902, box 1-17, Dun & Bradstreet credit report on J. D. Lindsay, November 27, 1901, box 1-14, Memoranda by Henry R. Mallory concerning interviews with J. D. Lindsay, December 30, 1902-May 23, 1903, box 2-1, Lindsay to Mallory, May 11, 1903, and Mallory to Lindsay, May 13, 23, 1903, box 2-1, Memorandum by Henry R. Mallory, February 18, 1903, E. F. Jeffrey to Edgar S. Marston (copy) and Marston to Henry R. Mallory, March 25, 1903, box 2-1, Memoranda by Henry R. Mallory, June 10, 14, 19, 1905, box 2-11, MFP.

3. New York *American*, April 30, New York *Evening Post*, May 1, New York *Press*, November 11, 1906; *Moody's Manual of Corporation Securities* (New York: Moody Manual Co., 1903-1920), *1903*, pp. 1474-1475, *1904*, p. 1381, *1905*, p. 1691, *1906*, pp. 1729, 1761, 1791-1792, 1835, *1907*, pp. 1994-1995, 2063, 2146-2147, *1908*, pp. 2206-2210, 2310-2311, *1909*, pp. 2306-2307, 2403, 2477, 2538, 2624; Harry F. Morse, *One Yankee Family* (New London: H. F. Morse Associates, 1969), pp. 66-88.

4. Mallory to Spicer, May 19, 1906, Spicer to Mallory, May 21, 1906, box 2-14, MFP.

5. Interviews with Henry R. Mallory reported in Galveston *Daily News,* February 5-6, Dallas *Morning News,* Houston *Post,* February 5, 1903; recollections of Mallory Line by Ben C. Stuart, Galveston *Daily News,* March 19, April 30, November 6, 1911.

6. Andrew Fletcher (Morse's agent) to Henry R. Mallory, June 18, 1906, Robert Mallory to Fletcher, June 29, 1906, Fletcher to Robert Mallory, June 30, 1906, box 2-14, MFP.

7. Memoranda in Robert Mallory's handwriting: "*Sale* 7/19/06," "N.Y. Aug. 15th 1906," "Morse paid Clyde . . . ," box 2-15, "In 'making figures' . . . ," box 2-16, MFP.

8. Charles Mallory to Henry R. Mallory, September 17, 1906, box 2-15, MFP.

9. Memorandum in Henry R. Mallory's handwriting: "C. H. M. & Co.," box 2-16, MFP.

10. Printed form letter, "*Confidential,* Office of C. H. Mallory & Co., No. 129 Front Street, New York, October 31st, 1906, To Stockholders," sample copy in box 2-15, MFP.

11. New York *Evening Sun,* October 26, New York *Tribune, Herald, Journal of Commerce, Times, Commercial, World,* Philadelphia *Record,* Richmond *Times-Dispatch,* October 27, Galveston *Daily News,* October 28, November 3, 1906.

12. See, e.g., Albert E. Day to Henry R. Mallory, October 28, 31, 1906, L. Mason Clarke to Mallory, October 29, 1906, J. B. Denison to Mallory, October 31, November 10, 1906, Henry McMurtrie to Mallory, November 8, 1906, box 2-15, MFP. All the stockholders had consented by November 3, 1906, however. "List of Stockholders, N. Y. & Texas S. S. Co., Oct 31/06," a handwritten checkoff list used to tabulate responses to the form letter of October 31, and which was closed out with the notation "Nov. 3. Stock in," box 2-15, MFP.

13. New York & Texas Steamship Co., Board of Directors and Stockholders Minute Book No. 2, pp. 252-267, vol. 53, MFP; New York & Texas Steamship Co., Treasurer's Report No. 78, pp. 88-89, vol. 55, MFP; C. H. Mallory & Co., Gen. Agts. in Account with New York & Texas Steamship Co., December 19, 1906 (final settlement), box 2-16, MFP; *Wall Street Journal,* October 27, Boston *News Bureau,* October 27, November 5, *Commercial and Financial Chronicle,* November 7, 1906.

14. Hornblower & Weeks, "Mallory Steamship Company, December 26, 1906" (broker's circular), box 2-16, MFP; Hornblower & Weeks, "Consolidated Steamship Lines, July 26, 1906" (broker's circular), Consolidated Steamship Lines File, CRD; *Wall Street Journal,* November 14, *Shipping Illustrated,* November 3, 1906.

15. New York *Press,* August 27, New York *Times,* New York *Sun,*

September 30, October 3, New York *World,* October 1, New York *Herald,* October 3, *Wall Street Journal,* September 30, October 1, December 6, 10, 1909, February 10, March 10, 1910.

16. Boston *News Bureau,* October 26, *Commercial and Financial Chronicle,* October 26, November 7, 16, New York *Sun,* December 28, 1907; Abstract of Gunn, Richards & Co. Report on Consolidated Steamship Lines Co. as of Date November 30, 1907 (typescript), Consolidated Steamship Lines File, CRD.

17. AGWI first pledged its newly acquired stock in Clyde, Mallory, N. Y. & C. M., and N. Y. & P. R. to Krech's Equitable Trust Co. of New York, on December 9, to secure issuance of $15,000,000 in fifty-year, 5 per cent collateral-trust bonds. The first-mortgage bonds of the same four constituent companies were then pledged to Equitable, on December 16, to secure issuance of $2,400,000 in 6 per cent collateral-trust notes. Hayden, Stone & Co. purchased these notes for resale to fund the floating debt of the four "southern" companies. The notes were to be redeemed by AGWI in increments: $850,000 on January 1, 1909; $850,000 on January 1, 1910; and $700,000, plus a bonus to their holders of $7,200,000 in AGWI common stock, on January 1, 1911. AGWI's authorized capitalization was $20,000,000 in common stock and $20,000,000 in noncumulative, 5 per cent preferred stock.

The holders of Consolidated's old collateral-trust bonds received $12,000,000 of AGWI's $15,000,000 collateral-trust issue; $400,000 of the new bonds went to Hayden, Stone & Co. in partial payment for that firm's underwriting of AGWI's collateral-trust notes; $600,000 were sold to defray the expenses of the reorganization; and the remaining $2,000,000 were reserved in the corporate treasury. Of the $20,000,000 preferred stock issue, $15,000,000 went to holders of Consolidated's old bonds and $5,000,000 were held in AGWI's treasury. Consolidated's bondholders also received $7,500,000 of AGWI's common stock issue; $7,200,000 went to subscribers to the collateral-trust note issue; $300,000 went to Hayden, Stone & Co. in partial payment for its underwriting of the note issue; and $5,000,000 were retained in the treasury.

18. Consolidated Steamship Lines, *Four Per Cent. Collateral Trust Gold Bonds, Bondholders' Protective Agreement Dated December 28th 1907* (New York: Bondholders' Protective Committee, 1908); *Wall Street Journal,* January 2, New York *Times,* January 7, New York *Journal of Commerce,* January 8, New York *Herald,* January 21, 1908, *Commercial and Financial Chronicle,* December 30, 1907, January 11, 30, February 4, March 4, 1908; Consolidated Steamship Lines, *Report and Plan of Reorganization Dated June 30, 1908* (New York: Bondholders' Protective Committee, 1908); New York *Sun,* November 13, New York *Press,* New

377

York *American,* New York *Tribune,* November 26, Boston *Post,* December 7, 1908; "Atlantic, Gulf and West Indies Steamship Lines," *New York Stock Exchange Listing Statement No. A-4602, June 28, 1916,* CRD.

19. Reorganization Committee Resolution, October 28, 1908 (copy), box 2-17, Henry R. Mallory to E. M. Bulkley, December 7, 1906, box 2-16, to Albert E. Day, April 23, 1910, box 3-1, to Galen L. Stone, August 25, 30, November 19, 1910, boxes 3-1, 4-3, Charles Mallory to Henry R. Mallory, February 5 (no year), November 7, 12, 1908, July 28, 1909, boxes 2-14, 2-17, 2-18, MFP.

20. W. Lyle Bull to author, January 15, 1969; Mallory to Stone, August 25, 30, November 19, 25, December 23, 1910, May 29, September 2, October 27, November 3, 1911, August 22, 1915, Stone to Mallory, August 29, November 22, 23, 1910, May 27, June 21, July 12, October 28, 1911, boxes 3 and 4, MFP.

21. Atlantic, Gulf & West Indies Steamship Lines, *Balance Sheet* (New York: The Company, annually, 1909-1915), *passim*; Atlantic, Gulf & West Indies Steamship Lines, *Annual Report* (New York: The Company, annually beginning in 1915), *passim*; "Atlantic, Gulf and West Indies Steamship Lines," *New York Stock Exchange Listing Statement No. A-4602, June 21, 1916,* CRD; *Moody's Manual of Corporate Securities, 1909,* pp. 2305-2307, *1910,* pp. 2506-2507, 2722, *1911,* pp. 43, 2724, 2726, 3811-3815, *1912,* pp. 3811-3815, *1913,* p. 4637, *1915,* pp. 3694-3698, *1916,* pp. 3940-3944; *Financial America,* October 9, 1914, October 27, 1915, Boston *News Bureau,* September 16, *Wall Street Journal,* November 8, 1915, March 4, 1916, *Commercial and Financial Chronicle,* June 10, 1916.

22. *Ibid.*; letters cited in note 19 above; Memorandum, "Officers, Salary, Duties," *ca.* 1912, box 3-9, MFP; Alfred G. Smith to Henry R. Mallory, H. H. Raymond to same, Theodore E. Ferris to same, May 29, 1911, Alexander R. Nicol to same, November 28, 1911, H. H. Raymond to same, January 17, 1912, boxes 3-4, 3-5, 3-7, 3-10, MFP.

23. Sibley, *Port of Houston,* pp. 148-151.

24. See, e.g., Clifford D. Mallory to Henry R. Mallory, June 23, July 11, 1911, February 7, 1917 (two letters), boxes 3-5, 3-6, 4-8, MFP; Interview with Philip R. Mallory, July 23, 1965.

25. Atlantic, Gulf & West Indies Steamship Lines, *Balance Sheet, 1914-1915,* p. 1.

26. Resolutions, 1915, of the Atlantic, Gulf & West Indies Steamship Lines, Clyde Steamship Co., Mallory Steamship Co., New York & Cuba Mail Steamship Co., and New York & Porto Rico Steamship Co. upon the Retirement of Henry R. Mallory, vol. 62, MFP; Henry R. Mallory to Alexander R. Nicol, August 21, 1915, to Galen L. Stone, August 22, 1915, to H. H. Raymond, August 28, 1915, box 4-2 MFP.

Chapter 10. The Era of World War I, 1915-1919

1. Interview with Philip R. Mallory, July 23, 1965.
2. Henry R. Mallory to Clifford D. Mallory, May 26, 1902, box 1-16, MFP.
3. Box 2-2, MFP.
4. Interview with Philip R. Mallory, July 23, 1965.
5. *Ibid.*; Philip R. Mallory to Henry R. Mallory, May 14, 1914, box 3-16, MFP; Henry R. Mallory Diary, March 29, April 21, December 25, 1916, May 12, 1917, vol. 9, MFP; Philip R. Mallory, *Personal Background* (Privately printed, 1941), pp. 8-22; Philip R. Mallory, *Recollections: Fifty Years with the Company* (Privately printed, 1966), *passim.*
6. U.S. House of Representatives, *Hearings before the Committee on Merchant Marine and Fisheries: Creating a Shipping Board, a Naval Auxiliary, and a Merchant Marine* (Washington: Government Printing Office, 1916), pp. 63-99 *et passim.*
7. Pausing for breath in its first annual report, the United States Shipping Board dramatically recalled the tempo of the times:

"Time charter rates on cargo steamers in the spring of 1914 were at a prevailing rate of about $1 per deadweight ton per month. An average of six time charters of American vessels, ranging from three to six months, made in July to September, 1917, for trades not in the war zone, gave a figure of $13.88 per deadweight ton per month. For steamers on voyages to the war zone, during the summer of 1917, charters were made at rates as high as $21 per ton per month for New York-Genoa trade, and $20 per ton per month for New York-France trade, the charterer bearing war risk. Time charter rates on tankers in 1914 were at approximately $1.70 per deadweight ton per month for long periods and $2.40 for short periods. In the summer of 1917 the prevailing rates were in excess of $12.50.

"Freight rates have shown an even greater advance, largely because freight rates include war risk on vessels, while under a time charter war risk is borne by charterer. Rates on cotton in the spring of 1914 from Savannah to Liverpool were about 35 cents per 100 pounds and to Genoa about 55 cents. From New Orleans the rates ranged about 10 cents higher. Rates in the summer of 1917 were at a level of $6 per 100 pounds to Liverpool and $10 per 100 pounds to Genoa, with New Orleans rates about 25 cents to 35 cents higher. Rates on petroleum from New York to Liverpool in 1914 were about $4 per ton. By 1917 they had reached $50, including war risk on vessels. Rates on grain from New York to the United Kingdom early in 1917 were approximately $5.50 per quarter, as compared with 50 cents per quarter early in 1914.

"... the price of ships, also, has steadily mounted, until ships which before the war would have sold at from $60 to $8 have recently (1917) changed hands at $300 or over, per d.w. ton."

8. U.S. Shipping Board, *Annual Report* (Washington: Government Printing Office, 1917-1933), *1917*, pp. 13-14; U.S. House of Representatives, *Hearings before the Committee on Merchant Marine and Fisheries: Creating a Shipping Board, a Naval Auxiliary, and a Merchant Marine*, pp. 100-122, 772-818.

9. Robert E. Annin, *Ocean Shipping: Elements of Practical Steamship Operation* (New York: Century, 1920), pp. 15-19, 21-26, 40-50.

10. Atlantic, Gulf & West Indies Steamship Lines, *Balance Sheet, 1914-1915*, p. 1.

11. *Shipping Illustrated*, August 29, September 5, December 12, 1914.

12. *Ibid.*, August 15, December 26, 1914, March 6, 1915; C. Ernest Fayle, *Seaborne Trade* (3 vols., New York: Longmans, Green, 1920-1924), I, 112, 223-224.

13. *Shipping Illustrated*, August 22, October 3, November 14, 1914.

14. *Ibid.*, October 10, November 7, 14, 21, December 19, 1914; Atlantic, Gulf & West Indies Steamship Lines, *Balance Sheet, 1914-1915*, p. 1.

15. Edwin J. Clapp, *Economic Aspects of the War* (New Haven: Yale University Press, 1915), pp. 112-139; *Shipping Illustrated*, December 12, 19, 1914, January 2, 16, 23, February 6, 1915; U.S. House of Representatives, *Hearings before the Committee on the Merchant Marine and Fisheries: Creating a Shipping Board, a Naval Auxiliary, and a Merchant Marine*, pp. 75-98.

16. Interview with Philip R. Mallory, July 23, 1965.

17. Clifford D. Mallory to Henry R. Mallory, February 8, 1915, to George D. Barron, February 18, 1915, box 4-1, MFP.

18. Theodore E. Ferris to Antonio C. Pessano, February 2, 4, 1915, Pessano to Ferris, February 3, 4, 1915, Robert Mallory to Clifford D. Mallory, February 8, 20, 1915, Clifford D. Mallory to Henry R. Mallory, February 8, 10, 1915, Henry R. Mallory to Clifford D. Mallory, February 11, 22, 1915, Clifford D. Mallory memoranda to self, February 11 (handwritten), 18 (typed), 1915, box 4-1, MFP; Edward J. Dowling, *The "Lakers" of World War I* (Detroit: University of Detroit Press, 1967), pp. 4-5.

19. Clifford D. Mallory to George D. Barron, February 18, 1915, John Monks, Jr., to Mallory, February 18, 1915, William H. Childs to Mallory, February 24, 1915, box 4-1, MFP; *Shipping Illustrated*, January 9, 1915; Garnett L. Eskew, *Cradle of Ships* (New York: Putnam, 1958), pp. 100-101, 255.

20. New York *Maritime Register,* 1914-1915 (esp. February 24, May 26, 1915; Edward L. DeHart (ed.), *Lloyd's Reports of Prize Cases* (10 vols., London: Lloyd's, 1919), V, 413-420; *Shipping Illustrated,* April 27, 1915, *Shipping,* May 4, 1918; Clapp, *Economic Aspects,* pp. 140-168; Marion C. Siney, *The Allied Blockade of Germany, 1914-1916* (Ann Arbor: University of Michigan Press, 1957), pp. 126-130 *et passim.*

21. Henry R. Mallory Diary, January 1, 1916-December 14, 1917, vol. 9, MFP; Interview with Philip R. Mallory, July 23, 1965.

22. Clifford D. Mallory to Henry R. Mallory, February 7, 1917 (two letters), box 4-8, MFP; Henry R. Mallory Diary, April 6, 1917, vol. 9, MFP; Atlantic, Gulf & West Indies Steamship Lines, *Annual Report, 1916,* p. 7.

23. Albert Gleaves, *A History of the Transport Service* (New York: Doran, 1921), pp. 32-33, 34-41; Clifford D. Mallory to Edward N. Hurley (in reply to Hurley to Mallory, June 8, 1922), undated, box 4-17, MFP.

24. U.S. House of Representatives, *Hearings before the Committee on the Merchant Marine and Fisheries: Creating a Shipping Board, a Naval Auxiliary, and a Merchant Marine, passim;* U.S. House of Representatives, *Hearings before the Committee on the Merchant Marine and Fisheries: Inquiry into the Operations of the United States Shipping Board* (2 vols., Washington: Government Printing Office, 1919), *passim;* J. Russell Smith, *Influence of the Great War upon Shipping* (New York: Oxford University Press, 1919), pp. 185-216; Edward N. Hurley, *The Bridge to France* (Philadelphia: Lippincott, 1927), pp. 19-31.

25. Lester Sisler to Clifford D. Mallory, December 1, 1917, box 4-8, MFP; Clifford D. Mallory to Edward N. Hurley (in reply to Hurley to Mallory, June 8, 1922) undated, box 4-17, MFP; Henry R. Mallory Diary, April 13-26, June 18-23, 1916, September 6, 26-October 13, 1917, vol. 9, MFP; Hurley, *Bridge to France,* pp. 94-100.

26. Present Organization of Division of Operations April 23, 1918, Mallory to Charles R. Page, July 8, 1918, to Edward F. Carry, July 31, 1918, Carry to Mallory, August 1, 15, to Edward N. Hurley, August 3, 1918, Mallory to J. H. Rosseter, October 5, 1918, C. W. Cook to Mr. Campbell, November 19, 1918, Memorandum for Mr. Mallory, undated, Division of Operations General File 21181, USSB.

27. This and next seven paragraphs based on: *ibid.;* Clifford D. Mallory to Edward N. Hurley (in reply to Hurley to Mallory, June 8, 1922), undated, box 4-17, MFP; Robert L. Hague to Frank J. Taylor, May 20, 1938, box 8-3, MFP; Raymond G. Gettell, *Functional Chart of U.S. Shipping Board, and Its Main Subdivisions, July 1st, 1918* (Washington: U.S. Shipping Board, 1918); United States Shipping Board, *Annual Report, 1917,* pp. 5-20, *1918,* pp. 7-71, 91-93, 116-117, *1919,* pp. 9-22, 33-56, 75-76, 101-125, 195; U. S. House of Representatives, *Hearings*

before the Committee on the Merchant Marine and Fisheries: Inquiry into the Operations of the United States Shipping Board, I, 136–415, II, 584–794 (esp. p. 638); Hurley, *Bridge to France,* pp. 31–38, 42–45, 101–109 *et passim.*

28. Clifford D. Mallory to J. H. Rosseter, to John A. Donald, December 5, 1918, Lester Sisler to Mallory, December 13, 1918, Edward N. Hurley to Mallory, July 29, 1919, June 8, 1922, boxes 4–10, 4–12, 4–17, MFP.

29. Clifford D. Mallory to Rebecca Sealy Mallory, January 7, 1919, box 4–11, MFP.

Chapter 11. C. D. Mallory & Co., Inc., Agents for the U.S. Shipping Board, 1919–1925

1. Memorandum by Clifford D. Mallory, "Atlantic Gulf & West Indies Steamship Lines: Present Organization and Suggestion for Re-Organization," January 30, 1919, Raymond to Mallory, March 20, 1919, Nicol to Mallory, June 5, 1919, Stone to Mallory, June 7, 1919, boxes 4–11, 4–12, MFP; Interview with Philip R. Mallory, July 23, 1965.

2. Press releases and clippings concerning Henry R. Mallory's retirement years and death, boxes 13–3, 13–9, MFP; Galen L. Stone to Cora Pynchon Mallory, March 14, 1919, box 4–11, MFP.

3. Philip R. Mallory to Clifford D. Mallory, December 11, 1918, Galen L. Stone to Clifford D. Mallory, June 7, 1919, Albert M. Day to same, September 21, 1919, boxes 4–10, 4–11, 4–12, MFP; Charles H. Mallory and Henry R. Mallory estate records, box 12–8, vols. 44–50, MFP; Sealy estate correspondence, "Sealy File," MFP; New York *Times,* July 20, December 16, 29, *Shipping,* December 25, 1921.

4. Shipping Board, *Annual Report, 1917, 1918, 1919, 1920, passim;* Carroll H. Wooddy, *The Growth of the Federal Government, 1915–1932* (New York: McGraw-Hill, 1934), pp. 228–238; John G. B. Hutchins, "The American Shipping Industry since 1914," *Business History Review,* XXVIII (June 1954), 105–118; Jeffrey J. Safford, "The United States Merchant Marine and American Commercial Expansion, 1860–1920" (Ph.D. dissertation, Rutgers University, 1968), chap. 7.

5. Mallory to John A. Donald, September 12, 1919, General File 582–10, USSB; see also Mallory to Thomas M. Scott, September 2, 8, 1919, to Barton B. Payne, September 2, 1919, to W. F. Taylor, September 12, 1919, to Donald, October 21, 1919, *ibid.*

6. *Marine News,* VI (October 1919), 153, VI (February, 1920), 93, IX (February 1923), 64; *Shipping,* December 31, 1919 (1st known C. D. Mallory & Co. advertisement on p. 85).

7. This and the eleven following paragraphs based on: William S. Houston to Mallory, August 16, 1918, Division of Operations General File 21181, USSB; Houston to Mallory, January 2, 1919, box 4-11, MFP; Houston to Mallory, December 11, 17, 1919, Houston to John A. Donald, March 22, 1920, Mallory to Houston, December 17, 1919, to Thomas M. Scott, September 2, 8, 1919, February 2, 1920, to Barton B. Payne, September 2, 1919, to W. F. Taylor, September 12, 1919, January 31, 1920, to Donald, September 12, October 21, 1919, May 4, 27, 1920, to William S. Benson, December 1, 1920, General File 582-10, USSB; Joseph L. Webber to Arthur M. Boal, June 30, 1923, Contract Dept. to Boal, September 25, 1923, General File 582-40A, USSB; G. R. Snider to Dowling, Hutchinson & Pattison, November 19, 1921, General File 589-2-I, USSB; Maitland Smith to author, June 4, 1965; Interviews with F. Willard Bergen, Frank M. Bynum, J. Ellis Knowles, William N. Westerlund, and George J. Farrell, July 12, 1965; Interview with Philip R. Mallory, July 23, 1965; W. Lyle Bull to author, December 18, 1968, January 17, November 22, 1969; J. Ellis Knowles to Clifford D. Mallory, Jr., January 1, 1968, November 24, 1969 (copies to author); William N. Westerlund to Mallory, Jr., November 26, 1969 (copy to author); Frank M. Bynum to Mallory, Jr., December 18, 1969 (copy to author).

8. Shipping Board, *Annual Report, 1920,* pp. 54-57 *et passim.*

9. See sources cited in note 7 above.

10. Mallory to Thomas Scott, February 6, March 3, 6, 1920, to J. E. Cushing, March 4, 1920, General File 589-2-I, USSB; *Marine News,* VI (December 1919), 99-100, VI (March, 1920), 117; *Shipping,* February 25, 1920.

11. Mallory to John A. Donald, September 12, October 21, 1919, May 4, 1920, to William S. Benson, December 1, 1920, General File 582-10, USSB; Erich W. Zimmermann, *Zimmermann on Ocean Shipping* (New York: Prentice-Hall, 1923), pp. 593-615, 648-679; U.S. Shipping Board, *Annual Report, 1921,* pp. 190-191.

12. U.S. Shipping Board, *Annual Reports, 1919-1921, passim;* Zimmermann, *Ocean Shipping,* pp. 455-459, 537-538, 680-682.

13. Mallory to Jones, November 26, 1920, to Benson, December 1, 16, 1920, Jones to Benson, December 2, 1920, Benson to Jones, December 8, 13, 1920, General File 582-10, USSB.

14. U.S. Shipping Board, *Annual Report, 1922,* pp. 99-100; *Marine News,* IX (February 1923), 60, IX (March 1923), 57-58, IX (May 1923), 58-59, 65, X (June 1923), 58.

15. Memoranda of William J. Love, March 30, 31, April 1, 1922, Mallory to H. S. Kimball, May 10, 1922, Memorandum of Carl P. Kremer, March 30, 1923, General File 582-10, USSB; Contract Dept. to Arthur M.

Boal, September 25, 1923, General File 582-40A, USSB; *Marine News,* VI (December 1919), 128, 149, IX (April 1923), 94, X (June 1923), 73, X (July 1923), 133, X (November 1923), 102, X (April 1924), 85, X (May 1924), 132; New York *Times,* May 28, 1922, March 12, 1924, New York *Tribune,* December 28, 1921; *Fairplay,* February 2, 1922; W. Lyle Bull to author, December 18, 1968, January 17, November 22, 1969.

16. Mallory to Albert D. Lasker, May 23, 1923, to Thomas V. O'Connor, July 8, 1924, L. C. Palmer to Mallory Transport Lines, Inc., Export Steamship Co., and A. H. Bull & Co., June 16, 1924, General File 582-10, USSB; U.S. Shipping Board, *Annual Report, 1923,* pp. 3-10, 182-185, *1924,* pp. 4-7, 45-48, 116-117, 120-123; *Marine News,* XI (August 1924), 67.

17. U.S. Shipping Board, *Annual Report, 1924* p. 49, *1925,* p. 121; U.S. Senate, Committee on Legislation of the United States Shipping Board, *Report on Matters Affecting the Merchant Marine* (Washington: Government Printing Office, 1926), pp. 55-68, 81-90.

18. Memoranda of William S. Benson, December 26, 1923, January 15, 1924, R. D. Gatewood to Mallory Transport Lines, Inc., July 26, 1924, Memoranda of Gatewood, July 26, August 5, 1924, William J. Houston to Gatewood, July 30, 1924, G. K. Nichols to H. I. Cone, August 7, 1924, General File 582-10, USSB.

19. *Marine News,* XI (August 1924), 67.

20. L. C. Palmer to Mallory Transport Lines, Inc., August 28, 1924, Mallory to Thomas V. O'Connor, August 28, September 19, 1924, O'Connor to Mallory September 2, 10, 17, 1924, General File 582-10, USSB; U.S. Shipping Board, *Annual Report, 1925,* pp. 18-22; Robert G. Albion, *Seaports South of Sahara: The Achievements of an American Steamship Service* (New York: Appleton-Century-Crofts, 1959), pp. 86-88.

21. E. S. Gregg, "The Crux of Our Shiping Problem," *Journal of Political Economy,* XXIX (June 1921), 500-508; E. S. Gregg, "Vicissitudes in the Shipping Trade, 1870-1920," *Quarterly Journal of Economics,* XXXV (August 1921), 603-617.

22. Hutchins, "The American Shipping Industry since 1914," pp. 110-115.

Chapter 12. C. D. Mallory & Co., Inc., Independent Shipping Owners and Operators, 1921-1941

1. Maitland Smith to author, June 4, 1965; Interviews with F. Willard Bergen, Frank M. Bynum, J. Ellis Knowles, William N. Westerlund, and George J. Farrell, July 12, 1965.

2. Testimony of Malcolm G. Chace, July 14, 1924, U.S. Circuit Court of Appeals for the First Circuit, October Term, 1925, No. 2070,

Francis R. Hart *et al.*, Appellants, v. Ernest Wiltsee *et al.*, Appellees, *In the Matter of Henry S. Parker v. New England Oil Corporation: Transcript of Record* (12 vols., Boston: Privately printed, ca. 1930), V, 1565–1576 (hereinafter cited as *Parker v. NEOC);* obituary of Malcolm Greene Chace, New York *Times,* July 17, 1955.

3. Imbrie & Co., New York, Statistical Department, "U.S. Food Products Corporation, October 29, 1920" (typescript), U.S. Food Products Corp. file, CRD; *Reorganization of Properties Pledged to Secure Obligations of U.S. Food Products Corporation: Plan and Agreement dated January 31, 1924* (n.p., n.d.), in *ibid.*

4. Interviews with F. Willard Bergen, Frank M. Bynum, J. Ellis Knowles, William N. Westerlund, and George J. Farrell, July 12, 1965.

5. *Parker v. NEOC,* vols. IV–VII, *passim.*

6. Mallory to Warwick Greene, July 3, 1923, NEO.

7. *Parker v. NEOC,* IV, 1200–1203; Memorandum of Warwick Greene, April 28, 1927, NEO; "Copies of Exhibits Covering Financial Data and Swiftsure Fleet Operating Results Put in Evidence for the Most Part through F. C. Martin" (mimeographed), Exhibit 703, pp. 26–27, NEO (hereinafter cited as "Financial Data and Swiftsure Fleet Operating Results").

8. Mallory to Warwick Green, July 3, 1923, NEO.

9. "Financial Data and Swiftsure Fleet Operating Results," Exhibit 703, pp. 26–27, NEO.

10. *Parker v. NEOC,* vols, IV–VIII *passim;* "Brief Summary of Relations and of Instruments in Connection therewith Having to do with Purchase by New England Oil Refining Company of the Seven Swiftsure Tank Steamers, Dictated by Samuel Vaughan, June 21, 1924" (typescript), NEO.

11. William S. Houston to Edward S. Perot, Jr., January 21, 1922, Mallory to Warwick Greene, March 2, July 3, December 12, 13, 1923, J. N. Watson to Greene, September 20, 1923, NEO.

12. *Marine News,* VIII (April 1922), 134, IX (June 1922), 112, IX (October 1922), 99; Maitland Smith to author, June 4, 1965.

13. "Financial Data and Swiftsure Fleet Operating Results," *passim,* Mallory to F. Douglas Cochrane, February 17, 1923, to Warwick Greene, March 2, July 3, December 12, 13, 1923, to Samuel Vaughan, March 3, 1923, "Report on Compensation Paid to C. D. Mallory & Co., Operators of N. E. O. R. Co. Fleet, 1922–1923" (typescript), NEO.

14. Mallory to Warwick Greene, July 3, 1923, October 10, 1924, to Malcolm G. Chace, February 19, 1925, NEO; New England Oil Refining Co., Executive Committee Minutes (typescript), May 2, October 7, 1924, NEO.

15. "Results of Tanker Syndicate Contract, 3/31/27," NEO. See

also: Llewellyn Howland to William S. Houston, March 8, 1923, to
F. Douglas Cochrane, July 16, December 3, 1923, Houston to Howland,
March 10, 12, 1923, Warwick Greene to J. N. Watson, September 14,
1923, Watson to Greene, May 24, September 20, 1923, "Report on
Compensation Paid to C. D. Mallory & Co., Operators of N. E. O. R. Co.
Fleet, 1922-1923" (typescript), "Proposals for Operating Fleet Received
from other Ship Operating Companies" (typescript), "Cost of Establishing
Marine Dept., N. E. O. R. Co." (typescript), NEO.

16. Mallory to F. Douglas Cochrane, February 17, 1923, to Warwick
Greene March 2, July 3, December 12, 13, 1923, to Samuel Vaughan,
March 3, 1923, to Llewellyn Howland, November 14, 1923, F. Willard
Bergen to P. B. Watson, October 8, 1924, NEO.

17. Maitland Smith to author, June 4, 1965, Interviews with
F. Willard Bergen, Frank M. Bynum, J. Ellis Knowles, William N. Westerlund, and George J. Farrell, July 12, 1965.

18. *Ibid.; Marine News,* IX (May 1923), 66; New York *Times,* May
23, 1923.

19. U.S. Shipping Board, *Annual Report, 1920,* pp. 72-73, 149,
1921, pp. 64-67, 201-202, *1922,* pp. 103-104, 188-194, *1923,* pp.
64-65, 110-111, 143-151, *1924,* pp. 74, 85, 93-98; *Marine News,* IX
(April 1923), 60, IX (May 1923), 100; S. D. Schell to Edward F. McClen-
nen, April 18, 1927, General File 605-1-595, USSB.

20. Bids of April 27, June 23, 1923, February 10, 12, 16, 1925,
October 12, November 24, 1926, Sales of March 26, April 20, May 2, 8,
June 8, 13, 1923, January 2, 1924, Mallory to Thomas V. O'Connor, July
6, 1925, General File 580-1035, USSB; Mallory to H. I. Cone, December
4, 1924, General File 582-10, USSB; Sale of Ships, Malston Co., Inc.,
General File 605-1-1089, USSB.

21. B. B. Howard and M. D. Stauffer, "Marine Transportation," in
E. De Golyer (ed.), *Elements of the Petroleum Industry* (New York:
American Institute of Mining and Metallurgical Engineers, 1940), pp.
323-328; T. Koopmans, *Tanker Freight Rates and Tankship Building: An
Analysis of Cyclical Fluctuations* (London: P. S. King & Son, Ltd., 1939),
pp. 141-142.

22. Frank N. Bynum to Warwick Greene, January 27, 1927 (enclos-
ing copies of "Malston Co., Inc. Charter Parties" for 1923-1926), NEO;
Tank Steamer Fixtures #1 (manuscript log of charter market kept by
W. L. Inslee, 1919-1923) and Tank Steamer Fixtures #2 (ditto, 1923-
1926), NEO.

23. Koopmans, *Tanker Freight Rates,* pp. 142-143.

24. *Marine News,* XXV (March 1939), 35-36; George S. Gibb and
Evelyn H. Knowlton, *History of Standard Oil Company (New Jersey): The
Resurgent Years, 1911-1927* (New York: Harper, 1956), pp. 156-165,

475–480; Henrietta M. Larson, Evelyn H. Knowlton, and Charles S. Popple, *History of Standard Oil Company (New Jersey): New Horizons, 1927–1950* (New York: Harper & Row, 1971), chap. 8.

25. New York *Herald Tribune*, October 16, 1924; *Marine News*, XI (November 1924), 57, 72, XI (December 1924), 108; Interviews with F. Willard Bergen, Frank M. Bynum, J. Ellis Knowles, and William N. Westerlund, July 12, 1965.

26. U.S. House of Representatives, Committee on Merchant Marine, Radio, and Fisheries, *Merchant Marine Investigation* (Washington: Government Printing Office, 1932), Data on Individual Ship Sales, April 1, 1924–December 31, 1931 (between pp. 948 and 949); *Marine News*, XII (December 1925), 111, XII (January 1926), 92, 100, XII (February 1926), 84–85, XIII (December 1926), 80, XII (March 1927), 80, 91, XIII (April 1927), 93, 96, XV (May 1929), 113, 126, XVI (June 1929), 115–116; *Fairplay*, February 17, 1927; New York *Times*, December 13, 1928; Maitland Smith to author, June 4, 1965; J. Ellis Knowles to Clifford D. Mallory, Jr., November 24, 1969 (copy to author); Frank M. Bynum to Mallory, Jr., December 18, 1969 (copy to author).

27. U.S. House of Representatives, Committee on Merchant Marine and Fisheries, *Report of United States Maritime Commission on Tramp Shipping Service* (Washington: Government Printing Office, 1938), *passim*.

28. U.S. House of Representatives, Committee on Merchant Marine and Fisheries, *Regulation of Water Carriers* (2 parts, Washington: Government Printing Office, 1937), part II, pp. 442–451.

29. Mallory to H. I. Cone, February 16, 1925, to U. J. Gendron, May 28, 1925, Asa F. Davison to Cone, March 13, 1925, Cone to Mallory, March 20, 1925, General File 582–10, USSB; Gendron to Davison, May 6, 1925, to Mallory, May 18, 23, 1925, Mallory to Thomas V. O'Connor, July 6, August 26, 1925, to L. C. Palmer, July 6, August 7, September 15, 1926, to Elmer E. Crowley, February 9, 1926, General File 580–1035, USSB; Maitland Smith to author, June 4, 1965.

30. *Parker v. NEOC*, vols. I–XII, *passim*; "Financial Data and Swiftsure Fleet Operating Results," *passim*, NEO; Kendall Beaton, *Enterprise in Oil: A History of Shell in the United States* (New York: Appleton-Century-Crofts, 1957), pp. 318–319, 322–326, 330–347, 423–424, 460–462; *Marine News*, XIV (September 1927), 88, XVI (January 1930), 78–79, XVI (February 1930), 61, 64–65, XVII (July 1930), 82, XVII (September 1930), 83, XVII (October 1930), 81, XVII (November 1930), 82, XVII (December 1930), 82, XXIII (January 1937), 76; New York *Times*, June 11–August 29, 1930.

31. Gleaned from yachting memoirs, records, and clippings in boxes 7–20, 9–4, 10–14 to 10–22, 12–11, 13–11, MFP.

32. *Marine News*, XV (September 1928), 48–51; *Marine Engineering*,

XXXIV (January 1929), 30, XXXVII (October 1932), 412, 414, 429; *Investigation of Seatrain Lines, Inc.*, 195 I.C.C. Reports 215-234, 206 I.C.C. Reports 328-346; Interviews with F. Willard Bergen, Frank M. Bynum, J. Ellis Knowles, William N. Westerlund, and George J. Farrell, July 12, 1965; Interview with David M. Brush, May 14, 1969.

33. Mallory to Malcolm G. Chace, October 10, 1930, to Albert M. Day, December 29, 1930, W. H. Campbell to Mallory, July 2, 1931, boxes 6-6, 6-7, 6-12, MFP; Maitland Smith to author, June 4, 1965.

34. Allied Chemical and Dye Corporation, *Annual Report, 1926, 1928, 1934, 1935*, CRD; *Wall Street News*, November 27, 1928; *Wall Street Journal*, December 5, 1928, June 16, 26, 1934; New York *Times*, May 3, 1935; S. D. Kirkpatrick, "Why These New Chemical Industries 'Went South': Six Case Studies in Plant Location," *Chemical & Metallurgical Engineering*, XLI (August 1934), 400-415; R. S. McBride, "What and Where Are the Process Industries of the South," *ibid.*, pp. 416-423; U.S. Tariff Commission, *Chemical Nitrogen* (Washington: Government Printing Office, 1937), *passim*; William Haynes, *American Chemical Industry* (6 vols., New York: American Chemical Society, 1949-1954), IV, 86-87, V, 91-93.

35. *Marine News*, XXII (September 1935), 72, XXII (October 1935), 69, XXIII (October 1936), 85, XXIII (December 1936), 119; *Fairplay*, August 15, 1935, September 17, October 1, 1936; Vamar Steamship Co., Inc., Minute Books No. 1 (1933) and No. 2 (1933-1940), MTL-CWT.

36. Mallory to Malcolm G. Chace, October 10, 23, 1930, box 6-6, MFP; Maitland Smith to author, June 4, 1965; Interviews with F. Willard Bergen, Frank M. Bynum, J. Ellis Knowles, William N. Westerlund, and George J. Farrell, July 12, 1965.

37. "A Voyage on the Sealer *Emeline*, and Excerpts from the Journal of Washington Fosdick," by Arthur C. Watson (reprint from vol. IX of *Zoologica*, 1931), vol. 73, MFP; Mallory to John A. Donald, May 27, 1920, General File 582-10, USSB (first known picture of Bull-designed flag—this flag still used by Marine Transport Lines, Inc.); W. Lyle Bull to author, December 18, 1968; New York *Times*, December 30, New York *Journal of Commerce*, December 28, 1934.

38. Box 7-18, MFP.

39. U.S. House of Representatives, Committee on Merchant Marine and Fisheries, *Regulation of Water Carriers*, part II, pp. 442-451; *ibid.*, Report of United States Maritime Commission on Tramp Shipping Service, *passim*; "Maritime Commission against Tramp Ships," *Marine News*, XXIV (February 1938), 30, 33; U.S. Maritime Commission, *Economic Survey of the American Merchant Marine* (Washington: Government Printing Office, 1937), pp. 17-19.

40. Henrietta M. Larson *et al., op. cit.;* Shell Union Oil Corporation, Registration Statements (S.E.C. Form A-2 with attachments), March 6, 1936, July 14, 1939, CRD.

41. Bernard Raskin, *On a True Course: The Story of the National Maritime Union of America, AFL-CIO* (Washington: National Maritime Union of America, AFL-CIO, 1967), pp. 5-41; Joseph P. Goldberg, *The Maritime Story: A Study in Labor-Management Relations* (Cambridge: Harvard University Press, 1958), pp. 130-178.

42. 3 NLRB 692 (1937); 5 NLRB 599, 707 (1938); 6 NLRB 271, 394, 398 (1938); New York *Times,* March 6, 1939, January 20, 1940; *Wall Street Journal,* June 14, 1939; John J. Collins, *Never Off Pay: The Story of the Independent Tanker Union, 1937-1962* (New York: Fordham University Press, 1964), pp. 28-101.

43. Mallory to Bynum and Westerlund, January 11, 1940, box 8-13, MFP.

44. *Ibid.;* Mallory to John A. Donald, May 4, 1920, to William S. Benson, October 22, 1920, General File 582-10, USSB; *Marine News,* VI (November 1919), 158-159, XI (June 1924), 68-69, XIV (December 1927), 74-75; *American Shipping,* XVIII (January 1924), 7, XVIII (June 1924), 23-28, XVIII (October 1924), 16-21.

45. J. B. Woodward Jr., to Eads Johnson, June 29, 1937, Johnson to Mallory, July 6, 9, 14, 1937, March 4, 1940, to William N. Westerlund, November 7, 1940, Mallory to Johnson, July 19, 1937, November 13, 1940, to Leon Robbin, July 20, 1937, May 5, October 15, 1938, February 15, 21, 1940, to Maitland Smith, December 28, 1939, to William H. Campbell, January 16, April 16, August 7, 1940, to Westerlund, March 21, 1940, to Russel A. Cowles, May 23, 1940, to John R. Campbell, June 6, 1940, to I. P. Gavitt and W. G. Ross, November 18, 1940, D. Arnott to Mallory, July 14, 1937, Robbin to Mallory, February 9, October 12, 1938, January 24, September 5, 1939, February 1, 27, 1940, Smith to Mallory, January 29, 1940, William H. Campbell to Mallory, September 4, 1940, Theodore E. Ferris to V. B. Edwards, October 11, 1940, Ferris to Mallory, February 13, 1941, Bynum to Mallory, October 11, 1940, Mallory Memoranda of May 5, 1938, January 11, 15, February 15 (2), 1940, Memoranda by Westerlund, January 31, February 17, 1940, Memorandum by George J. Farrell, February 17, 1941, boxes 7-16 through 9-6, MFP.

46. Shipping Finance: C. D. Mallory & Co., General File 625-6-129, USSB; Mallory to John R. Campbell, October 25, 1939, January 16, April 16, 1940, to William N. Westerlund, November 7, 1940, Westerlund to Mallory, February 2, 17, 1940, Maitland Smith to Mallory, February 16, 26, 1940, boxes 8-10, 8-13, 8-14, 8-15, and 9-3, MFP.

Chapter 13. An Unexpected End

1. Mallory to John R. Campbell, October 25, 1939, January 16, 1940, boxes 8-10, 8-11, and 8-13, MFP; Interview with Clifford D. Mallory, Jr., November 11, 1969.

2. Mallory to John R. Campbell, April 16, 1940, box 8-15, MFP.

3. Vamar Steamship Co., Inc., Minute Books No. 1 and No. 2, *passim,* MTL-CWT.

4. Maitland Smith to Mallory, March 5, 1940, box 8-15, MFP; Smith to author, June 4, 1965; Interview with Clifford D. Mallory, Jr., December 6, 1969; *Poor's Industrial Manual, 1940,* pp. 2509-2510, *1941,* pp. 3295; *Moody's Manual, Industries, 1941,* pp. 1577-1578, *1942,* pp. 348-353; Robert H. Montgomery, *Federal Tax Handbook, 1940-41* (2 vols., New York: Ronald, 1940), vol. I, chap. 15.

5. New York *Herald Tribune,* April 8, Greenwich *Press,* April 10, 1941; miscellaneous clippings and memorials in box 13-4 and vols. 63-71, MFP.

6. Mallory, *Recollections,* pp. 23, 75, 117-118, 179; Interview with Clifford D. Mallory, Jr., November 11, 1969.

7. Vamar Steamship Co., Inc., Minute Book No. 3, May 19, 1941, MTL-CWT.

8. Maitland Smith to author, June 4, 1965; Interview with F. Willard Bergen, Frank M. Bynum, J. Ellis Knowles, and William N. Westerlund, July 12, 1965; Interview with Clifford D. Mallory, Jr., November 11, 1969.

9. Marine Operating Co., Inc., was created out of the corporate shell of Vamar with Bynum as president and director, Smith as vice president, treasurer, and director, and Bergen, Knowles, and Westerlund as vice presidents and directors. Marine Transport Lines, Inc., had Westerlund as president and director, Smith as vice president, treasurer, and director, and Bergen, Bynum and Knowles as vice presidents and directors. Marine Brokerage, Inc., had Bergen as president and director, Smith as vice president, treasurer, and director, and Bynum, Knowles, and Westerlund as vice presidents and directors. All were Delaware corporations chartered on May 19, 1941, with their five directors as sole stockholders in equal proportions. Vamar Steamship Co., Inc. (Marine Operating Co., Inc.), Minute Book No. 3 and Marine Transport Lines, Inc., Minute Book No. 1, *passim,* MTL-CWT.

10. *Ibid.*

11. *Ibid.* See also Hutchins, "The American Shipping Industry since 1914," p. 118; Frederic C. Lane, *Ships for Victory: A History of Ship-*

building under the U.S. Maritime Commission in World War II (Baltimore: Johns Hopkins Press, 1951), pp. 161-162, 754-787.

   12. CHM Diary, February 9, 1879, MFP.

   13. Annin, *Ocean Shipping*, p. 4.

Table 1.1

PRICES FOR RAW MATERIALS CHARGED BY CHARLES MALLORY, SAILMAKER, 1826–1835

Material	Description	Price
"#2 Cotton Duck"	(41 lbs. per 38yd. x 24in. bolt, double thread)	$.37 to .38 per yd.
"#3 Cotton Duck"	(38 lbs. per 38yd. x 24in. bolt, double thread)	$.35 to .36 per yd.
"#4 Cotton Duck"	(35 lbs. per 38yd. x 24in. bolt, double thread)	$.33 to .34 per yd.
"#5 Cotton Duck"	(32 lbs. per 38yd. x 24in. bolt, double thread)	$.31 to .32 per yd.
"#6 Cotton Duck"	(29 lbs. per 38yd. x 24in. bolt, double thread)	$.31 to .34 per yd.
"#7 Cotton Duck"	(24 lbs. per 38yd. x 24in. bolt, single thread)	$.30 to .31 per yd.
"#8 Cotton Duck"	(21 lbs. per 38yd. x 24in. bolt, single thread)	$.28 to .29 per yd.
"#9 Cotton Duck"	(18 lbs. per 38yd. x 24in. bolt, single thread)	$.27 to .28 per yd.
"#10 Cotton Duck"	(15 lbs. per 38yd. x 24in. bolt, single thread)	$.25 to .27 per yd.
"#11 Cotton Duck"	(12 lbs. per 38yd. x 24in. bolt, single thread)	$.25 per yd.
"Russia Duck"		$.52 to .54 per yd.
"Rover's Duck"		$.25 to .28 per yd.
"Colton Duck"		$.26 to .29 per yd.
"Sheeting"		$.25 per yd.
"Ticklingburg"		$.10 to .11 per yd.
"Ossnaburg"		$.10 per yd.
"Old Canvas"		$.10 per yd.
"Twine, cotton"		$.38 to .40 per ball
"Twine, flax"		$.50 per ball
"Spunyarn & marling"		$.25 to .34 per ball

"Boltrope"	$.14	per lb.
"Bonetline"	$.23 to .25	per lb.
"Manilla"	$.16	per lb.
"White rope"	$.18	per lb.
"Hand rope"	$.05	per lb.
"Chain"	$.07	per lb.
"Leather"	$2.00 to $5.00	per pc.
"Bee's wax"	$.25	per lb.
"Tar"	$.05	per qt.
"Needles"	$.04 to .06	ea.
"Thimbles"	$.08 to .10	ea.
"Lacing thimbles"	$.04 to .05	ea.
"Clew thimbles"	$.17 to .18	ea.
"Clew irons"	$.62 to .75	ea.
"Block pins"	$.03	ea.
"1 pricker lost over board"	$.25	

Source: Same as Table 1.2.

393

Table 1.2

LABOR CHARGES OF CHARLES MALLORY, SAILMAKER, 1826–1835

"Working duck"	$2.50 to $2.75 per bolt of 38 yards
"Lapping duck"	$2.00 per bolt
"Sidestitching"	$1.37 per bolt
"Middlestitching"	$ .75 per bolt
"Repairing" or "Altering" sails	$1.25 per 10-hour day to February 13, 1833
	$1.34 per day thereafter
"Worming"	$ .16 per lb. of rope
"Parsling"	$ .12 per lb. of rope
"Whipping & serving"	$ .04 per lb. of rope
"Reefpoints"	$ .03 per point
"Making mast coat"	$ .25 ea. to February 13, 1833
	$ .50. ea. thereafter
"Making bonet"	$1.00 to $2.00 ea.
"Making bonet to jib"	$ .75 to .87 ea.
"Making pump hose"	$ .25 to .30 ea.
"Pump coats"	$ .20 to .25 ea.
"Making skow sail"	$1.50 ea.
"Making boat sail"	$2.00 to $10.00 ea.
"Making jib"	$2.00 to $3.00 ea.
"Making storm jib"	$1.00 ea.
"Making tarpoling"	$ .42 to .62 ea.
"Making topsail"	$3.00 ea.
"Fitting foot tabling"	$1.00 to $1.50 ea.

"Fenders"	$ .14 ea.
"Dimond Peaces"	$ .05 ea.
"Side leathers"	$2.75 to $4.25 ea.

Source: Daybooks for the periods January 20, 1826–January 18, 1830, and October 8, 1832–August 13, 1835, of Charles Mallory, Sailmaker. Original of earlier book is vol. 42 of MFP. Original of second book in CMP with microfilm copy in MFP.

Note: Prior to 1829, many of these charges were entered per unit in shillings and pence but were totaled in dollars; e.g. "bonetline @ 6/ . . . $1.00." By 1830 only dollars and cents are used to express prices. These piece and job tasks use Mallory's own terminology but are quite recognizable to anyone familiar with the modern terminology of marlinspike seamanship. They represent all the standardized tasks and rates to be found in 2,582 separate jobs. Obviously, each of the 2,582 jobs included most if not all of the standardized tasks. Also, there were hundreds of instances in which Mallory merely recorded his labor charges for miscellaneous work at rates of $1.25 to $1.50 per 10-hour day. These figures were arrived at by using the ancient sailmakers' rules of thumb: 1¼ to 1½ cents per yard for routine "sewing," times ten yards per hour, times ten hours per day, equals 100 yards a day @ $1.25 to $1.50 per day. 100 yards of sewing per day was considered the minimum productivity for a full-time sailmaker; 200 yards per day was quite common among journeymen; 300 yards of straight sewing per day was an outstanding performance and only rarely achieved.

395

TABLE 1.3

"SALES OF COTTON DUCK & TWINE BY ORDER AND ON ACCOUNT OF
JOHN COLT OF NEW YORK BY CHARLES MALLORY OF MYSTIC BRIDGE, CONNECTICUT"

Accounting Period	Duck Sold		Twine Sold		Gross Sales	SM Comm.	SM Perq.	Frgt.	Net Sales	Inventory on Hand with SM
	Bolts	$	Bales	$	$	$	$	$	$	Bolts of Duck
9-21-32/7-4-33	274	4,183	2	72	4,255	502	56	22	3,674	87
7-4-33/10-30-33	175	3,097	1	57	3,154	315	44	14	2,781	113
10-30-33/4-26-34	94	1,712	1	62	1,774	177	8	24	1,566	179
4-26-34/12-6-34	379	7,117	3	95	7,212	749	95	31	6,337	58
12-6-34/12-31-35	304	5,762	4	135	5,897	590	76	25	5,207	19
1-1-36/2-4-37	404	8,021	6	184	8,205	821	97	32	7,257	18
2-4-37/4-13-38	221	4,789	5	111	4,900	490	55	18	4,335	Not shown
Period Totals	1,851	34,681	22	716	35,297	3,644	431	166	31,157	
Adjusted to annual income & rates for period (6 yrs.)	309	5,780	4	119	5,883	607	72	28	5,193	

All numbers rounded to nearest bolt, bale, dollar, or year.
Source: Original accounts in CMP. Microfilm in MFP.

Table 2.1

CONNECTICUT, MYSTIC, AND MALLORY WHALING FLEETS COMPARED

Year	Conn.[a]	Mystic[b]	Mallory-Interest	Mallory-Flag	Mallory-Flag % Conn.	Mallory-Flag % Mystic
1811–1819	0	0	0	0	0	0
1820	4	0	0	0	0	0
1821	10	0	0	0	0	0
1822	9	0	2	0	0	0
1823	4	0	3	0	0	0
1824	4	0	3	0	0	0
1825	4	0	4	0	0	0
1826	3	0	2	0	0	0
1827	10	0	1	0	0	0
1828	8	0	1	0	0	0
1829	11	0	1	0	0	0
1830	16	0	1	1	6	0
1831	16	0	1	1	6	0
1832	25	1	1	1	4	100
1833	22	0	3	1	5	0
1834	26	4	4	3	12	75
1835	26	1	3	4	15	100
1836	30	2	7	4	13	50
1837	28	2	7	4	14	50
1838	28	5	8	5	18	60

Table 2.1 (continued)

CONNECTICUT, MYSTIC, AND MALLORY WHALING FLEETS COMPARED

Year	Conn.[a]	Mystic[b]	Mallory-Interest	Mallory-Flag	Mallory-Flag % Conn.	Mallory-Flag % Mystic
1839	36	6	8	5	14	66
1840	59	5	8	5	22	80
1841	53	3	6	6	23	100
1842	50	6	3	5	16	50
1843	68	4	2	6	12	100
1844	70	7	1	8	13	43
1845	99	10	1	10	11	60
1846	114	2	1	10	10	100
1847	117	5	1	9	9	40
1848	100	4	1	7	8	25
1849	86	3	1	6	8	100
1850	73	1	0	5	7	100
1851	63	6	0	5	8	50
1852	63	2	0	6	10	50
1853	70	5	0	6	9	80
1854	37	0	0	6	9	0
1855	36	1	0	5	7	100
1856	32	3	0	4	7	66
1857	32	1	0	5	8	100
1858	32	5	0	6	10	100

1859	28	0	0	6	11	0
1860	25	2	0	5	11	100
1861	19	0	0	3	9	0
1862	13	0	0	1	6	0
1863	9	0	0	0	0	0

[a]1811–1839, vessel clearances; 1840–1863, vessels registered.
[b]1811–1863, vessel clearances.

Source: Compiled from Alexander Starbuck, *History of the American Whale Fishery* (Washington, 1878).

Table 2.2

PERFORMANCE OF SELECTED MALLORY WHALERS COMPARED TO SELECTED MORGAN WHALERS

Vessel Tonnage Years	Yrs. of Vessel's Life	No. of Voyages	Total Days	Days at Sea	Days in Port	Ratio Sea:Port	Yrs. per Voyage
AERONAUT 265 tons 1832–1853	11–32 (22)	10	7,549	6,631	918	7:1	2
BINGHAM 375 tons 1834–1846	31–43 (13)	6	4,325	3,423	903	4:1	2
BLACKSTONE 265 tons 1835–1845	9–19 (11)	5	3,773	3,307	466	7:1	2
CORIOLANUS 269 tons 1844–1860	18–34 (17)	6	5,755	4,884	871	6:1	3
LEANDER 213 tons 1841–1858	17–35 (19)	8	6,320	5,344	976	5:1	2

ROBIN HOOD 395 tons						
1845–1858	21–35 (15)	5	5,782	4,925	857	6:1	3
ROMULUS 366 tons						
1842–1858	13–30 (18)	5	4,609	3,724	885	4:1	4
CHARLES W. MORGAN 351 tons						
1841–1863	1–23 (24)	6	7,739	6,785	954	7:1	4
EMILY MORGAN 368 tons						
1833–1863	1–31 (32)	7	11,146	10,137	1,009	10:1	4

Source: Computed from Alexander Starbuck, *History of the American Whale Fishery* (Washington, 1878). Additional data on Mallory landings and voyages computed from *New London Gazette & General Advertiser.*

Table 2.3

"BEST," "WORST," AND "AVERAGE" VOYAGES (BY ESTIMATED GROSS VALUE)

OF MALLORY-FLAG WHALERS, 1830–1862

Vessel	No. of Voyages	Best (Year completed)	Worst (Year completed)	Average
AERONAUT	11	$53,964 (1852)	$17,926 (1834)	$25,778
BINGHAM	6	$37,731 (1844)	$21,458 (1839)	$29,518
BLACKSTONE	5	$27,928 (1845)	$21,470 (1841)	$24,453
LEANDER	9	$49,528 (1854)	$12,510 (1856)	$24,743
ROMULUS	6	$63,511 (1857)	$17,581 (1848)	$40,476
VERMONT	1	$27,897 (1846)	$27,897 (1846)	$27,897
ATLANTIC	1	$38,044 (1847)	$38,044 (1847)	$38,044
CORIOLANUS	6	$45,185 (1853)	$14,686 (1847)	$32,891
TRESCOTT	1	$40,748 (1848)	$40,748 (1848)	$40,748
ROBIN HOOD	6	$84,965 (1857)	$25,268 (1861)	$51,346
CORNELIA	2	$20,570 (1858)	$17,419 (1860)	$18,995

This total of 54 voyages represents 89 per cent of the known 61 voyages of Mallory-flag whalers, 1830–1862. Estimated gross value of catch calculated by multiplying catch of sperm oil, whale oil, and bone as recorded in Starbuck by average annual prices for these products in year of return as recorded by Tower. See Bibliography and text for complete citations.

Table 2.4

ESTIMATED GROSS INCOME AND EARNING POWER OF
SELECTED MALLORY WHALERS

Vessel Years	No. of Voyages[a]	Estimated Gross Value of Catch[b]	Estimated Gross Income per month/ton at sea[c]
AERONAUT 1832–1854	11	$283,562	$4.64
BINGHAM 1834–1846	6	177,110	4.23
BLACKSTONE 1835–1845	5	122,266	4.18
LEANDER 1841–1860	9	222,690	5.87
ROMULUS 1842–1860	6	242,858	4.05
VERMONT 1843–1846	1	27,897	3.16
ATLANTIC 1844–1847	1	38,044	3.76

Table 2.4 (continued)

ESTIMATED GROSS INCOME AND EARNING POWER OF SELECTED MALLORY WHALERS

Vessel Years	No. of Voyages[a]	Estimated Gross Value of Catch[b]	Estimated Gross Income per month/ton at sea[c]
CORIOLANUS 1844–1859	6	197,346	4.51
TRESCOTT 1845–1848	1	40,748	3.15
ROBIN HOOD 1845–1861	6	308,176	4.13
CORNELIA 1858–1862	2	37,989	4.08
		Total $1,698,686	Average 4.16

[a]This total of 54 voyages represents 89 per cent of know 61 voyages of own-flag Mallory whalers. It does not include 8 sealing voyages by *Uxor* and *Tampico* for which no price data are available.

[b]Calculated by multiplying catch of sperm oil, whale oil, and bone as recorded in Starbuck by average annual prices for these products in year of return as recorded in Tower (see bibliography and text for citations).

[c]Calculated by dividing estimated gross value of catch by the product of the vessels tonnage and the number of months at sea.

Table 2.5

COMPARISON OF ESTIMATED GROSS INCOME AND EARNING POWER
OF CHARLES MALLORY AND NEW LONDON WHALING AGENTS

Name and Yrs. Operating	Numbers of Voyages and Ships Employed		Estimated Gross Value of Catch[a]	Estimated Gross Income per month/ton at sea[b]
R. H. Chappell 1855–1870	14	36	$1,063,030	$8.50
Benjamin Brown 1827–1859	8	45	$1,054,841	$7.04
Williams & Havens 1846–1872	26	68	$2,675,214	$5.08
N. & W. W. Billings 1821–1851	12	69	$2,075,730	$5.06
Williams & Barnes 1834–1872	18	86	$3,760,325	$4.91
Perkins & Smith 1842–1860	21	60	$1,964,742	$4.66
Havens & Smith 1834–1848	22	49	$1,247,987	$3.89

Table 2.5 (continued)

COMPARISON OF ESTIMATED GROSS INCOME AND EARNING POWER
OF CHARLES MALLORY AND NEW LONDON WHALING AGENTS

Name and Yrs. Operating	Numbers of Voyages and Ships Employed		Estimated Gross Value of Catch[a]	Estimated Gross Income per month/ton at sea[b]
T. W. Williams 1819–1842	12	74	$1,715,861	$3.78
Charles Mallory 1832–1862	11 (73%)	54 (89%)	$1,698,686	$4.16

New London agents are all those managing 30 or more voyages as compiled by Godfrey. See Bibliography and text for complete citation. These are the top 8 from Godfrey's sample of 36.

[a]Calculated by multiplying catch of sperm oil, whale oil, and bone as recorded in Starbuck by average annual prices for these products in year of return as recorded in Tower. See Bibliography and text for complete citations.

[b]Calculated by dividing estimated gross value of catch by the product of the vessel's tonnage and the number of months at sea.

Table 2.6

SELECTED STATISTICS OF WHALING OUT OF MYSTIC, CONNECTICUT,
1832–1862

Number of "Mystic whalers"	28
Number of voyages	103
Number of captains	46
Number of seamen	3,100
Number of managing agents	7
Number of owners	319

Estimated value of catch	$2,675,000
Less crew shares on lays	890,000
Gross to owners	$1,785,000
Less initial costs of vessels	300,000
Less costs of outfits	925,000
Net to owners before interest and depreciation	$ 560,000

Source: "Whalers Out of Mystic," Information Bulletin 69–3, G. W. Blunt White Library, Marine Historical Association, Mystic, Conn.

Table 3.1

SAMPLE MALLORY TRANSFER RATES, 1850's

Trade Route (Dates)	Range of Freight Rates (Cargo)	Approximate Mallory Transfer Rates
New York–Havana and Gulf (1855–1863)	5¢ @ 15 per cu. ft. (measurement goods)	13¢
New York–Liverpool (1855–1865)	2d @ 13 1/2d per bushel (grain)	9d
New York–San Francisco (1851–1861)	22 1/2¢ @ 80¢ per cu. ft. (measurement goods)	30¢
Chincha Islands–Hampton Roads (1853–1861)	$10 @ $25 per long ton (guano)	$15
Hawaii–New England (1855–1863)	5¢ @ 10¢ per gallon (whaleoil)	7¢
China–New York (1855–1863)	$5 @ $25 per 800-lb. ton	$15

Sources: Mallory rates from CHM Letterbooks. Other rates from *Annual Report of the Chamber of Commerce of the State of New York for years 1858–1865, passim,* and Evans, " 'Without Regard for Cost,' " pp. 38–39.

Table 3.2

MALLORY-FLAG BARK AND SHIP ITINERARIES, 1849–1865

Bark FANNY (1849–1860)

1. New York–Mobile–New York shuttle in Hurlbut Line
2. New York–San Francisco–Shanghai–New York
3. New York–New Orleans–New York shuttle in Eagle Line
4. New York–Mobile–New York shuttle in Eagle Line (sold)

Ship CHARLES MALLORY (1851–1853)

1. New York–Mobile–New York shuttle in Hurlbut Line
2. New York–San Francisco–Honolulu–New London (lost on homeward leg)

Ship ELIZA MALLORY (1851–1859)

1. New York–Mobile–New York shuttle in Hurlbut Line
2. New York–San Francisco–Honolulu–New York
3. New York–New Orleans–New York shuttle in Eagle Line
4. New York–Antwerp in S Line
5. Antwerp–Bristol–Havana–Falmouth–Galway–New York
6. New York–New Orleans in Oakley & Keating Line
7. New Orleans–San Blas–Mazatlán–New York (lost en route)

Schooner–Bark MUSTANG (1853–1863)

1. Miscellaneous coasting
2. New York–Matagorda Bay–New York shuttle in Texas & New York Line
3. New York–Galveston–New York shuttle in New Line
4. New York–Mobile–New York shuttle in New Line (sold)

Table 3.2 (continued)

MALLORY-FLAG BARK AND SHIP ITINERARIES, 1849–1865

Ship HOUND (1853–1863)

1. New York–New Orleans–New York shuttle in Eagle Line
2. New York–San Francisco–Manila–Macao–Havana–New York
3. New York–San Francisco–Hong Kong–New York
4. New York–San Francisco–New York
5. New York–San Francisco–Hong Kong–San Francisco–Altata–New York
6. New York–London–Shanghai–Foochow–New York (sold)

Ship ELIZABETH F. WILLETS (1854–1864)

1. New York–San Francisco–Hong Kong–Foochow–New York
2. New York–San Francisco–New York
3. New York–San Francisco–British Columbia–San Francisco–Honolulu–New London–New York
4. New York–San Francisco–Honolulu–New Bedford–New York
5. New York–San Francisco–Shanghai–New York–Philadelphia
6. Philadelphia–Shanghai–Whampoa–San Francisco–Shanghai (sold)

Ship SAMUEL WILLETS (1854–1857)

1. New York–San Francisco–Hong Kong–Anjer–Adelaide–Melbourne–Hong Kong–New York
2. New York–Liverpool–New York shuttle on Tapscott's Line (lost)

Bark ANN (1854–1858)

1. New York–New Orleans–New York shuttle in Eagle Line (sold)

Bark FRANCES (1855–1858)

1. New York–New Orleans–New York shuttle in Eagle Line (sold)

Ship MARY L. SUTTON (1855–1864)

1. New York–San Francisco–New York
2. New York–San Francisco–Honolulu–New Bedford–New York
3. New York–San Francisco–Hong Kong–San Francisco–Rio de Janeiro–New York
4. New York–San Francisco–New York
5. New York–San Francisco–Callao–New York
6. New York–Le Havre–New York
7. New York–San Francisco–New York
8. New York–San Francisco–New York
9. New York–San Francisco–Baker Island (lost)

Ship TWILIGHT (1857–1865)

1. New York–San Francisco–Honolulu–Hong Kong–Anjer–New York
2. New York–San Francisco–Callao–Norfolk–Baltimore–Rotterdam–New York
3. New York–San Francisco–New York
4. New York–San Francisco–New York
5. New York–San Francisco–New York (sold)

Bark LAPWING (1859–1863)

1. New York–Matagorda Bay–New York shuttle in Texas & New York Line
2. New York–Mobile–Le Havre–Cárdenas–Cork–Boston
3. Boston–Batavia (captured en route)

411

Table 3.2 (continued)

MALLORY-FLAG BARK AND SHIP ITINERARIES, 1849–1865

Ship HAZE (1859–1864)

1. New York–San Francisco–Shanghai–Hong Kong–Shanghai–Hong Kong–Whampoa–Macao–New York
2. New York–San Francisco–New York

Bark TYCOON (1860–1864)

1. New York–Galveston–Liverpool–Galveston–Antwerp–Naples–New York
2. New York–Tortuga–Pensacola–Ship Island–New York under federal charter
3. New York–Philadelphia–Key West–Havana–New York
4. New York–San Francisco (captured en route)

Table 3.3

PER ANNUM NET RETURN ON ACTUAL VALUE OF CAPITAL OF THREE MALLORY VESSELS VERSUS CLIPPER SHIP AVERAGES

FANNY	2-year actual average	(1853–1854)	43.0
SAMUEL WILLETS	3-year actual average	(1856–1858)	30.3
MARY L. SUTTON	4-year actual average	(1858–1861)	23.5
Evans	5-year estimated average	(1851–1855)	41.0–54.0
Evans	5-year estimated average	(1856–1860)	11.3–18.3

Sources: Manuscript vessel accounts in MFP and ESP; Robert Evans, Jr., " 'Without Regard for Cost': The Returns on Clipper Ships," *Journal of Political Economy*, LXXII (February 1964), 33–43.

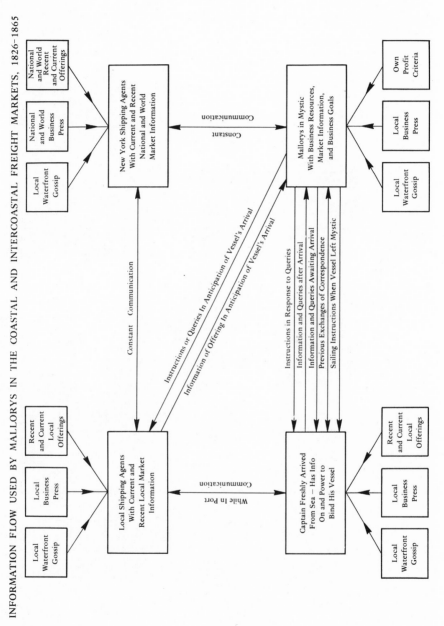

FIGURE 3.1

INFORMATION FLOW USED BY MALLORYS IN THE COASTAL AND INTERCOASTAL FREIGHT MARKETS, 1826–1865

FIGURE 3.2

SHIP INCOME AND EXPENDITURE PER REGISTER TON (PER VOYAGE)

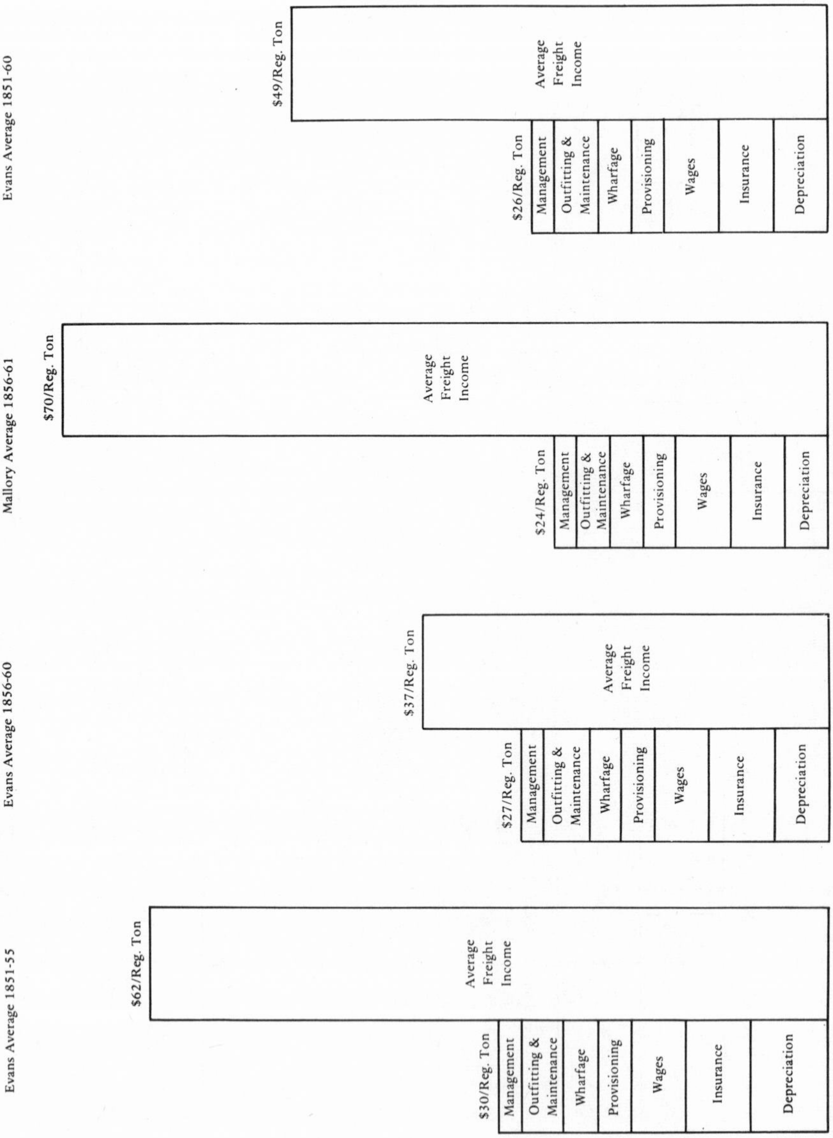

Evans Average 1851-55   Evans Average 1856-60   Mallory Average 1856-61   Evans Average 1851-60

Sources: See Chapter 3, note 49.

Table 4.1

GEOGRAPHIC DISTRIBUTION OF AMERICAN "CLIPPER" LAUNCHINGS, 1850–1859 (INCLUSIVE)

State	Percentage of Total Number[a]	Percentage of Total Tonnage
Massachusetts	47	49
Maine	18	17
New York	14	15
New Hampshire	6	6
Maryland	6	5
Connecticut	5	5
Rhode Island	1	1
Pennsylvania, New Jersey, Virginia, and Florida combined	3	2

Source: Computed from Carl C. Cutler, *Greyhounds of the Sea: The Story of the American Clipper Ship* (Revised ed., Annapolis: U.S. Naval Institute, 1961), Appendix I(c) and MFP.

[a]Total number was 445.

Table 4.2

DISTRIBUTION OF MYSTIC-BUILT "CLIPPERS" BY YARD, 1850–1859 (INCLUSIVE)

Yard	Percentage of Total Number[a]	Percentage of Total Tonnage
Mallory	43	39
Greenman	24	30
Irons & Grinnell	24	23
Maxson, Fish	10	8

Source: Same as Table 4.1. Does not add due to rounding.
[a]Total number was 21.

415

Table 4.3

NATIONAL MARKET SHARES, FIVE LARGEST AMERICAN BUILDERS OF CLIPPERS, 1850–1859 (INCLUSIVE)

Yard	Percentage of Total Number[a]	Percentage of Total Tonnage
Donald McKay, East Boston	5	8
William H. Webb, New York	3	4
Samuel Hall, East Boston	3	3
George Raynes, Portsmouth	2	2
Charles Mallory, Mystic	2	2

Source: Same as Table 4.1

[a]Total number was 445.

Table 5.1

GOVERNMENT CHARTERS ON MALLORY ACCOUNT, 1861–1865

Vessel	Duration	Gross Rate
Bk TYCOON	2-7-62 to completion of voyage	$5,000 for voyage
Bk TYCOON	8-22-63 to 9-11-63	$ 200 per day
Ss HAZE	3-18-62 to 11-1-62	$ 200 per day
Ss HAZE	11-25-62 to 1-14-63	$ 250 per day
Ss THORN	4-16-62 to 1-18-63	$ 255 per day
Ss ELLA	7-1-63 to 8-6-63	$ 125 per day
Ss ELLA	8-8-64 to 8-21-65	$ 150 per day
Ss VARUNA II	2-20-64 to 5-1-65	$ 450 per day
Ss VARUNA II	6-5-65 to 7-24-65	$ 322 per day
Ss VICTOR	4-7-64 to 7-15-65	$ 602 per day
Ss GENERAL SEDGWICK	8-6-64 to 7-27-65	$ 365 per day
Ss ARIADNE	9-27-64 to 5-10-65	$? per day
Ss ATLANTA	11-23-64 to 7-14-65	$ 474 per day
Ss EUTERPE	?-?- 64 to ?-?-65	$? per day
Ss LOYALIST	1-21-65 to 9-11-65	$ 152 per day

Sources: Compiled from "Vessels Bought, Sold, and Chartered by the United States," *House Exec. Docs.*, 40 Cong., 2 Sess., No. 337 (Serial 1346) and from MFP.

Table 5.2

DISTRIBUTION OF MYSTIC-BUILT STEAMSHIPS BY YARD, 1861–1865 (INCLUSIVE)

Yard	Percentage of Total Number[a]
Mallory	39
Greenman	29
Maxson, Fish	30
Other	2

Source: Carl C. Cutler, *Mystic: The Story of a Small New England Seaport* (Mystic: Marine Historical Association 1945), 158.

[a]Total number was 56.

Table 6.1

MALLORY-FLAG TRAMP ITINERARIES, 1865–1875

Ship HAZE (1865–1875)

1. New York–San Francisco–New York
2. New York–San Francisco–New York
3. New York–San Francisco–Liverpool–New York
4. New York–San Francisco–Manila–San Francisco–Hong Kong–New York
5. New York,–Liverpool–New Orleans–Boston–Antwerp–Key West–Brashear City, Louisiana–San Francisco–Liverpool–New York
6. New York–Valparaiso–Falmouth–Hamburg–New York
7. New York–Shanghai–Hong Kong–New York

Bark CALEB HALEY (1866)

1. New York–Galveston–Mexican coast (lost)

Bark GALVESTON (1866–1865)

1. New York–Nassau–Galveston–Liverpool–New York
2. New York–Galveston–Le Havre–Key West–Havana–New York
3. New York–Shanghai–Singapore–Penang–Amoy–Shanghai–Hong Kong–San Francisco–Yokohama–Rangoon–Amoy–Java–Penang–Amsterdam–New York
4. New York–Galveston–Liverpool–Havana–New York
5. New York–Shanghai–San Francisco–New York
6. New York–Galveston–Liverpool–Key West–Havana–Falmouth–Le Havre–New York

Ship TWILIGHT III (1867-1875)

1. New York–San Francisco–New York
2. New York–San Francisco–Liverpool–New York
3. New York–Liverpool–New York
4. New York–Bristol–Liverpool–New Orleans–Liverpool–New York
5. New York–San Francisco–Singapore–Calcutta–New York
6. New York–San Francisco–Liverpool–New York
7. New York–San Francisco–Liverpool–New York
8. New York–San Francisco–Shanghai–China coasting–Havana–New York

Bark SABINE (1868-1875)

1. New York–Galveston–Liverpool–New York
2. New York–Galveston–Liverpool–Galveston–Liverpool–New York
3. New York–Galveston–Liverpool–Galveston–New York
4. New York–Liverpool–Galveston–Boston–Havana–Falmouth–Havana–New York
5. New York–Galveston–Key West–Le Havre–Liverpool–New York
6. New York–Galveston–Liverpool–Galveston–New Haven–New York
7. New York–Galveston–New York
8. New York–Galveston–Liverpool–New York
9. New York–Galveston–Liverpool–Galveston–New York

Ship ANNIE M. SMULL (1868-1875)

1. New York–San Francisco–Queenstown–Dublin–Newport, Wales–New York
2. New York–San Francisco–Hong Kong–San Francisco–Liverpool–Le Havre–Cardiff–New York
3. New York–Portland, Oregon–Dublin–New York
4. New York–Le Havre–Cardiff–Shanghai–Manila–London–New York
5. New York–San Francisco–New York

Table 6.1 (continued)

MALLORY-FLAG TRAMP ITINERARIES, 1865–1873

Bark BRAZOS (1870–1875)

1. New York–Galveston–Liverpool–San Francisco–Liverpool–New York
2. New York–Galveston–Liverpool–Galveston–Liverpool–New York
3. New York–Galveston–Liverpool–New York

Table 6.2

MALLORY-FLAG STEAMSHIP-LINE AND BERTH-SAIL PERFORMANCE, 1866–1875

New York–New Orleans steamships via Havana ("Southern Line")

Date	Voyages Southbound	Gross Freight Receipts	Voyages Northbound	Gross Freight Receipts
1866	3	?	3	?
1867	21	?	21	?
1868	21	$ 55,150	17	$104,165
1869	20	96,630	19	105,880
1870	15	87,610	17	75,550
1871	33	176,770	32	152,550
1872	42	219,445	41	186,950
1873	32	126,217	32	212,350
1874	45	144,175	49	196,970
1875	2	4,025	4	10,400

New York–Galveston steamships via Key West ("Texas Line")

Year				
1866	21	?	21	?
1867	35	?	35	?
1868	21	$109,550	25	$141,900
1869	32	128,190	30	152,342
1870	58	541,090	40	188,011
1871	48	422,580	53	303,350
1872	53	569,039	53	332,215
1873	46	478,020	53	451,830
1874	50	473,144	51	364,550
1875	58	370,613	56	357,579

New York–Morehead City steamships

Year				
1874–1875	15	$ 4,045	15	$ 19,750

New York–Galveston berth sailers often via Key West

Year				
1866	13	?	13	?
1867	19	?	19	?
1868	15	$42,400	3	$14,000
1869	27	78,860	12	34,590
1870	32	88,944	6	11,600
1871	25	74,200	1	3,300
1872	26	79,224	0	—
1873	21	97,323	0	—
1874	20	60,358	5	11,575
1875	13	26,961	0	—

Table 7.1

"COMPARISON OF EARNINGS," MALLORY'S "GALVESTON
STEAMSHIP LINE," 1882–1883

Service[a]	1882	1883
Galveston:		
"Outward Freights"	$510,288.35	$547,706.49
"Outward Passages"	38,807.00	75,196.30
"Homeward Freights"	486,959.56	667,712.24
"Homeward Passages"	33,985.55	40,340.11
Key West:		
"Outward Freights"	52,927.20	60,053.10
"Outward Passages"	8,750.25	11,509.00
"Homeward Freights"	28,521.62	34,747.42
"Homeward Passages"	10,539.90	11,468.50
Totals:	$1,170,779.43	$1,448,733.16

[a]"Outward" was New York–Key West–Galveston; "Homeward" was the reverse.
Source: "Galveston Steamship Line–Year 1883. Comparison of earnings between the Years 1882 and 1883." Elihu Spicer Papers, box 1, folder 6.

Table 7.2

MALLORY-FLAG TRAMP ITINERARIES, 1876–1885

Ship HAZE (1886–1887)

1. New York–Yokohama–Manila–Havana–New York
2. New York–Yokohama–Russian government time charter–Hong Kong–New York
3. New York–Yokohama–Hong Kong–New York
4. New York–Melbourne–Yokohama–New York
5. New York–Singapore–? –New York (laid up)

Bark GALVESTON (1876)

1. New York–Galveston–Liverpool–Key West (lost)

Ship TWILIGHT III (1876–1885)

1. New York–Sydney–Melbourne–Hong Kong–New York (interspersed with China coasting and lay-ups)

Bark SABINE (1876–1879)

1. New York–Liverpool–Galveston–New London–New York
2. New York–Java–St. Helena–Portland–Boston–New York
3. New York–Yokohama–New York

Ship ANNIE M. SMULL (1876–1883)

1. New York–San Francisco–Liverpool–New York
2. New York–San Francisco–London–New York
3. New York–Shanghai–China coasting–New York
4. New York–Java–Baltimore–Manila–New York

Table 7.2 (continued)

MALLORY-FLAG TRAMP ITINERARIES, 1876–1885

Bark BRAZOS (1876–1882)

1. New York–Liverpool–Galveston–Liverpool–Galveston–Liverpool–New York
2. New York–Yokohama–Java–Queenstown–Manila–Boston–New York

Ship PRIMA DONNA (1875–1883)

1. New York–San Franciso–New York
2. New York–San Francisco–London–New York
3. New York–Yokohama–Hong Kong–London–New York
4. New York–Zanzibar–Bombay–New York
5. New York–Yokohama–St. Helena–New York

Table 7.3

"PROFIT AND LOSS ACCOUNT," C. H. MALLORY & CO. 1882–1883

Accounts	1882	1883
Profits		
Commission a/c	$102,905.09	$134,366.22
Merchandise a/c	1,156.31	725.40
Advertising a/c	1,787.98	1,676.48
Printing a/c	2,811.40	2,162.63
Key West Coal a/c	1,542.51	2,051.20
New York Coal a/c	4,156.09	6,592.25
Interest a/c	2,262.10	11,694.90
Galveston Water Tank	1,120.00	1,473.00
Tarpaulin a/c	—	1,471.54
Postage Stamp a/c	—	67.92
TOTAL	$117,741.48	$162,281.54
Loss		
Expense a/c	$ 27,605.82	$ 22,236.10
Postage Stamp a/c	93.39	—
TOTAL	$ 27,699.21	$ 22,236.10
New Profit [on book account]	$ 95,411.99	$134,675.72
C. H. Mallory 2/3	$ 64,951.11	$ 89,783.81
E. Spicer, Jr. 1/3	$ 30,460.88	$ 44,891.91
Analysis of Commission a/c		
Galveston Steamers	$ 44,829.32	$ 53,335.74
Florida, Nassau & Matz. Stmrs.	17,005.03	14,106.08
Returns on sail vessels	919.14	nil
Returns from Agents	16,578.51	19,687.31
Miscellaneous		
Comms. building new stmrs. and returns from J. Roach	10,324.42	26,415.33
Discounts on bills, sundries, etc.	13,248.67	20,821.76
TOTAL	$102,905.09	$134,366.22

Source: "Profit and Loss a/c 1883 [*sic*]," box 1, folder 6, SP.

Table 8.1
SELECTED ANNUAL FINANCIAL DATA, C. H. MALLORY & CO.,
1867–1906

Calendar Year	Commissions as % of Gross Profits	Interest and Dividends as % of Gross Profits	Net Profits ($1,000)	Net Profits as % of Gross Profits	Net Profits as % of Equity Capital
1867	82	3	32	82	53
1868	79	2	45	85	73
1882	87	2	95	81	63
1883	83	9	135	83	144
1894	na	na	101	na	168
1895	na	na	124	na	206
1896	na	na	98	na	164
1897	na	na	79	na	132
1898	na	na	117	na	196
1899	93	3	114	84	190
1900	92	3	109	76	182
1901	94	4	145	84	241
1902	93	4	148	82	247
1903	96	2	146	80	244
1904	97	1	156	76	259
1905	95	3	151	70	252
1906	91	8	169	67	281

Sources: Computed and reconstructed from "Profits 1867," "Profit & Loss 1868," "Profit and Loss a/c 1883," box 1, folders 4–6, SP; Income & Expenses, H. R. Mallory and "Profit and Loss Account," 1900–1906, box 1, folders 7, 13–14, 17, box 2, folders 3, 6, 13, 17, MFP.

Table 8.2

PERCENTAGE SHARES OF INCOME ACCOUNTS IN ANNUAL GROSS RECEIPTS,
NEW YORK & TEXAS STEAMSHIP CO., 1887–1905

Year	Line Earnings	Charter Earnings	Lighterage-Stevedoring	Railroad Payments	Interest & Dividends	Insurance, Towing, General Average, Salvage
1887	96	2	2	0	less than 1	0
1888	94	4	2	0	less than 1	less than 1
1889	98	1	1	0	less than 1	1
1890	97	0	2	0	less than 1	1
1891	96	1	3	0	less than 1	1
1892	95	3	2	0	less than 1	0
1893	93	5	1	1	less than 1	0
1894	95	3	1	0	less than 1	1
1895	98	1	1	0	less than 1	0
1896	97	0	1	1	1	less than 1
1897	95	2	2	1	1	less than 1
1898	72	26	2	0	less than 1	less than 1
1899	90	5	2	2	1	0
1900	95	1	0	2	2	less than 1
1901	96	0	less than 1	2	1	0
1902	96	0	less than 1	2	1	less than 1
1903	97	0	0	2	1	less than 1

Table 8.2 (continued)

PERCENTAGE SHARES OF INCOME ACCOUNTS IN ANNUAL GROSS RECEIPTS, NEW YORK & TEXAS STEAMSHIP CO., 1887–1905

Year	Line Earnings	Charter Earnings	Lighterage-Stevedoring	Railroad Payments	Interest & Dividends	Insurance, Towing, General Average, Salvage
1904	98	0	less than 1	1	less than 1	less than 1
1905	97	0	0	1	less than 1	1
Average	94	3	1	1	less than 1	less than 1

Source: Computed from Treasurer's Reports, Nos. 1–78, and Annual Reports, Nos. 1–19, N. Y. & T. S. S. Co., MFP.
Note: Year 1887 is 9–1–86 to 11–30–87; years 1888–1898 end on 11–30; year 1899 is 12–1–98 to 12–31–99; years 1900–1905 are calendar years.

Table 8.3

PERCENTAGE SHARES OF EXPENSE ACCOUNTS IN ANNUAL GROSS EXPENDITURES, NEW YORK & TEXAS STEAMSHIP CO., 1887–1905

Year	Disbursements on Line & Charter Voyages	Insurance on Hulls	Ordinary Repairs to Vessels	Rentals, Taxes, General Expenses
1887	89	7	4	1
1888	88	4	8	1
1889	90	4	5	1

1890	89	4	6	1
1891	89	4	7	1
1892	87	5	7	2
1893	84	5	8	2
1894	89	4	4	1
1895	88	4	5	3
1896	87	4	6	2
1897	83	4	9	3
1898	86	5	4	4
1899	80	3	3	3
1900	88	4	1	4
1901	87	5	1	4
1902	88	4	3	5
1903	86	4	3	5
1904	87	4	2	5
1905	86	4	3	5
Average	87	4	5	3

Source: Computed from Treasurer's Reports, Nos. 1–78, and Annual Reports, Nos. 1–19, N. Y. & T. S. S. Co., MFP.

Note: Year 1887 is 9–1–86 to 11–30–87; years 1888–1898 end on 11–30; year 1889 is 12–1–98 to 12–31–99; years 1900–1905 are calendar years.

429

Table 8.4

SELECTED ANNUAL FINANCIAL DATA, NEW YORK & TEXAS STEAMSHIP CO., 1887–1905

Year	Net Earnings ($1,000)	Net Earnings as % of Gross Receipts	Net Earnings as % of Equity Capital	Dividends (%)	Surplus Available for Interest and Investment (%)
1887	330	18	13	8	5
1888	374	24	15	8	7
1889	431	24	17	8	9
1890	390	21	16	8	8
1891	324	17	12	8	4
1892	273	16	9	8	1
1893	275	16	9	8	1
1894	256	17	9	6	3
1895	216	12	7	6	1
1896	229	14	8	6	2
1897	108	8	4	6	(2)
1898	417	30	14	2	8
1899	480	24	16	6	10
1900	325	19	11	6	5
1901	496	24	17	6	11
1902	469	22	17	6	11
1903	471	20	16	6	10

1904	541	21	18	6	12
1905	624	24	21	6	15
Average	370	20	13	7	6

Source: Computed from Treasurer's Reports, Nos. 1–78, and Annual Reports, Nos. 1–19, N. Y. & T. S. S. Co., MFP.

Note: Year 1887 is 9–1–86 to 11–30–87; years 1888–1898 end on 11–30; year 1899 is 12–1–98 to 12–31–99; years 1900–1905 are calendar years.

Table 8.5

**NEW YORK & TEXAS STEAMSHIP CO. EARNINGS
FROM SPANISH-AMERICAN WAR,
APRIL 25, 1898, THROUGH APRIL 29, 1899 ($1,000)**

Results of Government Charters			
Charter Money Collected	$604		
Board Money Collected	33		
Repairs & Damages Collected	54		
Total Wharfage Collections	7		
		$698	
Machinists Bills Charged	$ 23		
Marine Insurance	33		
Stores	34		
Other Disbursements	169		
		$259	
Net Return on Government Transactions			$439
Cuban Relief			
Collected for Charters	$29		
Collected for Board	5		
Total Disbursements		$ 34	
		$ 21	
Net Returns on Cuban Relief			$ 13
Combined Net Returns			$452

Sources: Computed from various accounts in box 1, folder 11, MFP.
Note: Names of accounts are those used by the Mallory Line itself.

Table 9.1

SUBSIDIARY COMPANIES OF MORSE'S CONSOLIDATED STEAMSHIP LINES AND MAJOR COMPETITORS, 1907

Morse Lines	Competing Lines
Eastern Steamship Co. 18 vessels, over 7 routes from Boston to Portland, Bangor, Kennebec River ports, New Brunswick, and Nova Scotia.	Maine Steamship Co. 3 vessels, Portland–New York, and controlled by New York, New Haven & Hartford Railroad. Plant Line Boston–Halifax.
Metropolitan Steamship Co. 7 vessels, Boston–New York.	New England Navigation Co. 27 vessels, between New York and southern New England ports via Long Island Sound, and controlled by N. Y., N. H. & H. R. R. Joy Steamship Co. 6 vessels, New York–Fall River and Providence–Bridgeport, and controlled by N. Y., N. H. & H. R. R. Boston and Philadelphia Steamship Co. 7 vessels, Boston–Philadelphia and Fall River–Providence-Philadelphia, and controlled by N. Y., N. H. & H. R. R.
Clyde Steamship Co. 23 vessels, New York–Charleston–Jacksonville; New York–Wilmington–Georgetown; New York to Dominican ports and Turks Island; Boston–Charleston–Brunswick–	Old Dominion Steamship Co. 24 vessels, New York–Norfolk–Richmond and Chesapeake Bay ports, and controlled by Atlantic Coast Line, Chesapeake & Ohio, Norfolk & Western, Southern, and

Table 9.1 (continued)

SUBSIDIARY COMPANIES OF MORSE'S CONSOLIDATED STEAMSHIP LINES AND MAJOR COMPETITORS, 1907

Morse Lines	Competing Lines
Jacksonville; Philadelphia–New York; Philadelphia–Norfolk–Newport News; Jacksonville–Sanford.	Seaboard Air Line railroads.
	Ocean Steamship Co.
	11 vessels, Boston–New York–Savannah, and controlled by Central of Georgia Railway.
	Baltimore & Philadelphia Steamboat Co.
	6 vessels, via Chesapeake & Delaware canal.
	Chesapeake Steamship Co.
	6 vessels, Baltimore–Norfolk–York River ports, and controlled by Southern and Atlantic Coast Line railroads.
	Baltimore Steam Packet Co.
	5 vessels, Baltimore–Norfolk, and controlled by Seaboard Air Line Railroad.
	Merchants & Miners Transportation Co.
	17 vessels, Boston–Baltimore; Providence–Baltimore; Baltimore–Savannah; Philadelphia–Savannah. One-half controlled by N. Y., N. H., & H. R. R.
Mallory Steamship Co.	Southern Pacific Co. Atlantic Steamship Lines
12 vessels, New York–Brunswick–Mobile and New York–Key West–Galveston.	24 vessels, New York–New Orleans, New York–Galveston, New Orleans–Havana.

New York & Cuba Mail Steamship Co.
19 vessels, New York–Havana, New York–Nassau–Santiago, New York–Havana–Mexican ports, New York–Tampico.

New York & Porto Rico Steamship Co.
12 vessels, New York–Porto Rico and New Orleans–Porto Rico.

Brunswick Steamship Co.
5 vessels, New York–Brunswick, and controlled by Atlanta, Birmingham & Atlantic Railroad.

Southern Steamship Co.
Philadelphia–Jacksonville– Key West–Tampa.

Munson Steamship Co.
New York–Cuba and Mobile and Cuba

Peninsular & Occidental Steamship Co.
4 vessels, Tampa–Key West–Havana and Miami–Nassau–Havana, and controlled by Atlantic Coast Line and Florida East Coast railroads.

Red D Line
2 vessels, New York–Porto Rico–Venezuela.

Source: U.S. Bureau of Corporations, *Transportation by Water in the United States* (4 parts, Washington: Government Printing Office, 1909–1913), part I, 164–169, 187–199.

435

Table 9.2

**ATLANTIC, GULF & WEST INDIES STEAMSHIP LINES, VESSELS
AND SERVICES, DECEMBER 31, 1915**

Clyde Steamship Company ("The Clyde Line")

Steamships: ALGONQUIN, APACHE, ARAPAHOE, CHEROKEE, CHIPPEWA, CITY OF JACKSONVILLE, COMANCHE, DELAWARE, GEORGE W. CLYDE, HURON, INCA, IROQUOIS, KATAHDIN, LENAPE, MOHAWK, MOHICAN, NEW YORK, ONONDAGA, OSCEOLA, PAWNEE, YAQUI, YUMA. Plus four tugs and twenty-eight steam-lighters.

Services: New York–Charleston–Jacksonville (freight and passengers), New York–Wilmington–Georgetown (freight and passengers), Jacksonville–Palatka–Astor–De Land–Sanford via St. Johns River (freight and passengers), Boston–Charleston–Jacksonville (freight only), New York–Turks Island–all Dominican ports (freight and passengers), New York–Philadelphia–Norfolk–Newport News (freight only).

Mallory Steamship Company ("The Mallory Line")

Steamships: ALAMO, BRAZOS, COMAL, CONCHO, LAMPASAS, MEDINA, NECHES, NUECES, RIO GRANDE, SABINE, SAN JACINTO, SAN MARCOS, SAN SABA, SANTIAGO. Plus two tugs and twenty-five steam-lighters.

Services: New York–Key West–Galveston (freight and passengers), New York–Key West–Tampa–Mobile (freight and passengers), New York–Brunswick (freight only).

New York & Cuba Mail Steamship Company ("The Ward Line")

Steamships: ANTILLA, BAYAMO, CAMAGUEY, ESPERANZA, GUANTANAMO, HAVANA, MANZANILLO, MATANZAS, MEXICO, MONTEREY, MORRO CASTLE, SANTIAGO, SARATOGA, YUMURI. Plus nine tugs and thirty-nine steam-lighters.

Services: New York–Nassau–Havana–Progreso–Vera Cruz–Tampico (freight and passengers), New York–Guantánamo–Santiago–Manzanillo–Cienfuegos–Havana (freight only), New York–Progreso–Tampico–Vera Cruz (freight and passengers), New Orleans–Progreso (freight and passengers).

New York & Porto Rico Steamship Company ("The Porto Rico Line")

Steamships: BERWIND, CAROLINA, COAMO, COROZAL, ISABELA, MARIANA, MASSAPEQUA, MONTOSO, PATHFINDER, PONCE, SAN JUAN, SANTURCE.

Services: New York–all Puerto Rican ports (freight and passengers), New Orleans–all Puerto Rican ports (freight and passengers), Galveston–Port Arthur–all Puerto Rican ports (freight only), Mobile–all Puerto Rican ports (freight only).

Southern Steamship Company ("The Southern Line")

Steamships: ALTAMAHA, OCMULGEE, OGEECHEE, OSSABAW, SATILLA (all chartered from AGWI); ALGIERS, WILLIAM P. PALMER, SHAWMUT.

Services: Philadelphia–Key West–Tampa–Port Arthur–Texas City (freight only), New York–Houston (freight only).

Source: Atlantic, Gulf & West Indies Steamship Lines, *Annual Report* (New York, 1915).

Table 9.3

SELECTED ANNUAL FINANCIAL DATA, PRINCIPAL SUBSIDIARIES

OF AGWI STEAMSHIP LINES, 1909–1915 ($1,000)

Year	Net Earnings	Net Earnings as % of Gross Receipts	Interest on Bonded Debt, Depreciation, Rentals, etc.	Surplus Available for Dividends to AGWI, Investment, or Debt Retirement
1909	2,486	18	1,467	1,019
1910	2,481	15	1,618	863
1911	2,369	14	1,532	837
1912	2,565	14	1,604	962
1913	3,342	17	1,799	1,543
1914	2,854	16	1,911	943
1915	5,024	24	1,984	3,039

Sources: Atlantic, Gulf & West Indies Steamship Lines, *Annual Reports* (New York, 1909–1915).

Note: This is a consolidated set of accounts for the Clyde, Mallory, New York & Cuba Mail, and New York & Porto Rico steamship companies.

Table 9.4

INCOME ACCOUNT, AGWI STEAMSHIP LINES, YEARS ENDING
DECEMBER 31, 1909–1915 ($1,000)

Year	Total Income	Interest on Bonds and Notes	Sundry Expenses, Taxes, etc.	Marine Insurance	Depreciation on Marine Equipment	Surplus Available for Dividends, Investment, or Debt Retirement
1909	613	395	6	—	—	212
1910	1,298	695	36	18	—	548
1911	1,055	708	209	42	63	33
1912	1,006	705	12	44	63	183
1913	1,194	702	162	43	63	225
1914	1,496	699	39	44	63	650
1915	2,247	667	36	46	63	1,435

Source: *New York Stock Exchange Listing Statement A–4602, June 28, 1916.*

Notes: Does not include undivided surplus earnings of subsidiary companies (see Table 9.3). "Total Income" is comprised of "Dividends from subsidiary and other companies" and "Interest on Investments and Loans, Charters, etc." "Sundry Expenses" for 1911 include $200,000 depreciation on investments; same for 1913 include $155,000 depreciation on investments.

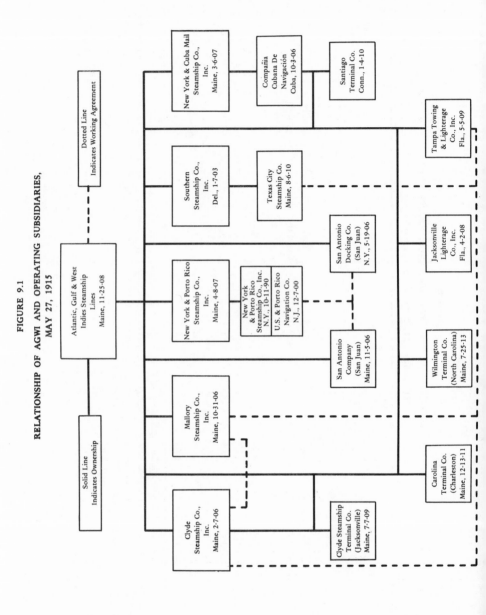

FIGURE 9.1

RELATIONSHIP OF AGWI AND OPERATING SUBSIDIARIES,
MAY 27, 1915

Table 10.1

SELECTED OCEAN FREIGHT RATES FROM NEW YORK TO EUROPEAN PORTS, 1914-1916

Date	Liverpool		Copenhagen		Rotterdam		Le Havre		Genoa	
	(1)	(2)	(1)	(2)	(1)	(2)	(1)	(2)	(1)	(2)
1914										
1–17	28.0¢	$ 4.25	40.0¢	$ 5.17	35.0¢	$ 4.00	30.0¢	$ 5.00	40c	$ 6.08
2–14	25.0	4.25	40.0	5.17	25.0	4.00	25.0	5.00	30.0	6.08
3–14	20.0	4.25	40.0	5.17	25.0	4.00	25.0	5.00	25.0	6.08
4–18	20.0	4.25	40.0	5.17	25.0	4.00	25.0	5.00	25.0	6.08
5–16	20.0	4.25	40.0	5.17	25.0	4.00	21.0	5.00	22.0	6.08
6–13	20.0	4.25	40.0	5.17	25.0	4.00	21.0	5.00	22.0	6.08
7–18	20.0	4.25	40.0	5.17	25.0	4.00	21.0	5.00	22.0	6.08
8–15			No rates quoted on freight of any kind to any European port							
9–12	40.0	4.25	—	5.17	—	4.00	45.0	5.00	75.0	6.08
10–17	35.0	4.86	—	11.25	—	6.00	45.0	6.00	75.0	9.73
11–14	50.0	4.86	—	11.25	—	6.00	60.0	6.00	80.0	9.73
12–12	75.0	7.30	—	14.60	120.0	6.00	100.0	10.00	100.0	12.17
1915										
1–16	100.0	7.30	—	17.03	200.0	8.00	200.0	12.00	125.0	24.33
2–13	100.0	9.73	250.0	17.03	250.0	12.00	200.0	20.00	125.0	24.33
3–13	125.0	9.73	250.0	19.47	225.0	12.00	200.0	20.00	125.0	24.33
4–17	200.0	24.33	250.0	19.47	225.0	12.00	300.0	25.00	150.0	24.33
5–15	200.0	24.33	250.0	19.47	225.0	12.00	300.0	25.00	150.0	19.47

Table 10.1 (continued)

SELECTED OCEAN FREIGHT RATES FROM NEW YORK TO EUROPEAN PORTS, 1914–1916

Date	Liverpool		Copenhagen		Rotterdam		Le Havre		Genoa	
	(1)	(2)	(1)	(2)	(1)	(2)	(1)	(2)	(1)	(2)
6–12	125.0	14.60	200.0	19.47	200.0	16.00	150.0	20.00	125.0	19.47
7–17	100.0	14.60	200.0	19.47	130.0	16.00	125.0	20.00	100.0	19.47
8–14	100.0	14.60	200.0	19.47	130.0	16.00	150.0	20.00	125.0	19.47
9–18	125.0	14.60	200.0	19.47	160.0	16.00	135.0	20.00	135.0	19.47
10–16	125.0	15.20	200.0	20.00	160.0	18.00	150.0	25.00	135.0	20.00
11–12	125.0	18.80	200.0	20.00	160.0	18.00	150.0	25.00	135.0	20.00
12–11	150.0	18.80	225.0	20.00	225.0	18.00	150.0	25.00	135.0	20.00
1916										
1–15	250.0	25.20	275.0	20.00	250.0	18.00	300.0	25.00	135.0	20.00
2–11	250.0	25.20	275.0	25.20	250.0	20.00	300.0	25.00	135.0	30.00
3–11	275.0	25.20	300.0	30.00	300.0	20.00	300.0	35.00	135.0	30.00

(1) Cotton, compressed, per 100 pounds; (2) Measurement goods, per ton or 40 cu. ft.

Source: Derived from U.S. House of Representatives, *Hearings . . . Creating a Shipping Board, a Naval Auxiliary, and a Merchant Marine* (Washington: Government Printing Office, 1916), 783–786.

Table 10.2

VESSELS 500 GROSS TONS AND OVER OWNED OR UNDER SOME FORM OF CONTROL BY
THE U.S. SHIPPING BOARD SEPTEMBER 1, 1918

Assignment or Use	Steamships		Sailers		Tankers	
	Number	1,000 D.W.T.	Number	1,000 D.W.T.	Number	1,000 D.W.T.
Grand totals	1,656	7,220	772	657	186	1,473
Army	299	2,229			3	28
Navy	56	206			12	109
Food Administration	3	15	2	1	1	2
New England coal	132	513				
Transatlantic						
British	26	192	1	1	15	106
French	44	261	1	3	16	130
Italian	48	251			10	76
Spanish	2	7	1	1		
Swiss	14	96				
Belgian relief	25	139				
Russian	1	7				
Mediterranean	2	8	2	3		
Northern neutrals	4	23				
Other	11	41	97	82	1	6
French coastwise	37	82				

Table 10.2 (continued)

VESSELS 500 GROSS TONS AND OVER OWNED OR UNDER SOME FORM OF CONTROL BY THE U.S. SHIPPING BOARD SEPTEMBER 1, 1918

Assignment or Use	Steamships		Sailers		Tankers	
	Number	1,000 D.W.T.	Number	1,000 D.W.T.	Number	1,000 D.W.T.
Transpacific						
East Asian	27	126	21	24	4	43
East Indian	14	51	6	6	1	8
Australian	17	76	170	147		
British Indian	11	76	3	3	3	26
Hawaiian	40	162	10	7	4	31
Hawaii (interisland)	6	6				
Philippines (interisland)	2	2				
South America (west)	137	738	27	33	9	91
South America (east)	80	429	234	200	2	21
West Indies	155	445	35	15	14	99
Caribbean	94	243	11	5	3	27
Gulf	48	163	5	3	71	572
Atlantic coast	86	183	30	23		

Pacific coast, excluding Mexico	107	168	45	43	14	78
Pacific coast, Mexico	1	1			1	10
Pacific-Atlantic, en route	5	13			1	1
Other coastwise	80	71	71	57		
Unknown	2	6				
Unassigned	40	191			1	9

Source: Second Annual Report of the U.S. Shipping Board, December 1, 1918 (Washington, 1918), Tables VI–VIII.

Table 11.1

TRAMPS MANAGED AND OPERATED BY C. D. MALLORY & CO., INC., ON JOINT ACCOUNT
WITH U.S. SHIPPING BOARD EMERGENCY FLEET CORPORATION, 1919–1922

Vessel	D.W.T.[c]	Date Assigned	Date Delivered	Date Ordered Withdrawn	Date Redelivered to U.S.S.B.	Days under Mallory Management & Operation
Proctor[a]	3,630	9-10-19	1-12-19	11-2-20	11-11-20	525
West Chatala	8,438	9-19-19	10-11-19	10-19-20	10-20-20	374
Lake Farrar	4,155	9-25-19	9-27-19	1-22-20	3-19-20	173
Glymount	3,701	10-9-19	11-3-19	12-26-19	2-24-20	113
Irvington	8,822	10-14-19	11-21-19	11-19-19	11-21-19	61
West Cobas	8,544	10-29-19	11-25-19	3-4-20	5-21-20	177
Lake Onawa	4,050	11-5-19	11-15-19	1-22-20	3-9-20	114

Table 11.1 (continued)

TRAMPS MANAGED AND OPERATED BY C. D. MALLORY & CO., INC., ON JOINT ACCOUNT WITH U.S. SHIPPING BOARD EMERGENCY FLEET CORPORATION, 1919–1922

Vessel	D.W.T.[c]	Date Assigned	Date Delivered	Date Ordered Withdrawn	Date Redelivered to U.S.S.B.	Days under Mallory Management & Operation[d]
Ashland County[b]	4,155	12-6-19	12-13-19	9-1-20	9-1-20	262
Lake Fabyan	4,155	12-26-19	12-24-19	10-21-20	11-8-20	319
Lake Filbert	4,040	1-3-20	1-7-20	5-10-20	7-3-20	177
Lake Fillion	4,040	1-7-20	1-12-20	11-24-20	11-29-20	321
Lake Stobi	4,155	1-14-20	1-16-20	(Lost off Japan 5-11-20)		125
West Cape	8,541	2-3-20	2-18-20	4-11-20	4-17-21	423
Egremont	9,500	2-10-20	2-12-20	8-24-21	8-29-21	563
Western City	8,680	3-8-20	4-6-20	10-18-21	10-18-21	560
Brookline	8,550	5-8-20	5-15-20	7-26-20	9-3-20	111
John Adams	12,500	4-7-21	4-15-21	8-15-21	8-25-21	132
Waban	9,428	5-5-21	5-12-21	8-27-21	9-3-21	114
Daniel Webster	12,980	5-16-21	5-19-21	10-25-21	12-5-21	200
Bellepline	9,786	5-16-21	5-20-21	9-13-21	9-21-21	124
Higbo	7,500	10-22-21	10-25-21	12-17-21	1-10-22	57
Zarembo	7,632	10-22-21	11-11-21	12-17-21	1-14-22	64
22	156,992					5,089

a Ex Coolspring.

b Ex Lake Hachita.

c All except two were steel steamships, with engines amidships, built by the U.S. Shipping Board Emergency Fleet Corporation during 1918–1920. *John Adams* and *Daniel Webster* were tankers.

d From delivery to C. D. Mallory & Co. to redelivery to U.S. Shipping Board Emergency Fleet Corporation.

Source: U. J. Gendron (Manager, Contract Dept.) To Mr. Hayes (Admiralty Division), January 28, 1925, U.S. Shipping Board Files (Record Group 32, U.S. National Archives), No. 582-10, part 4.

Table 11.2

LINERS MANAGED AND OPERATED BY BALTIMORE-OCEANIC STEAMSHIP CO., INC., ON JOINT ACCOUNT WITH U.S. SHIPPING BOARD EMERGENCY FLEET CORPORATION, 1919–1922

Vessel	D.W.T.[a]	Date Delivered	Date Redelivered to U.S.S.B.	Days under Mallory Management & Operation[b]
Clavarack	7,825	11–20–19	3–25–21	521
Irvington	8,822	11–21–19	2–9–21	476
Lake Girardeau	3,500	12–20–19	12–9–20	354
City of St. Joseph	7,825	12–31–19	1–6–22[c]	736
Coeur D'Alene	7,825	1–20–20	3–31–21	435
Coldwater	7,825	2–21–20	4–22–21	425
Mebanno	9,400	6–1–20	10–20–20	150
Sabale	7,825	10–11–20	4–10–21	181
Yesoking	8,790	10–14–20	5–2–21	200
West Lashaway	8,578	11–20–20	3–3–22[c]	468
Bird City	7,825	11–27–20	2–18–21	83
Absaroka	8,521	4–16–21	9–4–21	141
Carenco	7,825	10–18–21	1–20–22[c]	94
Sinsinawa	7,825	12–2–21	3–19–22[c]	107
Balsam	7,433	12–15–21	1–14–22	30
15	117,644			4,401

[a]All were steel steamships, with engines amidships, built by the U.S. Shipping Board Emergency Fleet Corporation during 1918–1920.

[b]From delivery to Baltimore-Oceanic Steamship Co. to redelivery to U.S. Shipping Board Emergency Fleet Corporation.

[c]Transferred to Mallory Transport Lines, Inc., rather than redelivered to U.S.S.B. Transfer ordered December 15, 1921.

Source: Contract Department to Arthur M. Boal (Assistant Admiralty Counsel), September 25, 1923, U.S. Shipping Board Files (Record Group 32, U.S. National Archives), No. 582–40A.

Table 11.3

LINES MANAGED AND OPERATED BY MALLORY TRANSPORT LINES, INC. ON JOINT ACCOUNT WITH U.S. SHIPPING BOARD EMERGENCY FLEET CORPORATION, 1921–1925

Vessel	D.W.T.[a]	Date Assigned	Date Delivered	Date Ordered Withdrawn	Date Redelivered to U.S.S.B.	Days under Mallory Management & Operation[b]
City of St. Joseph	7,825	12-15-21	1-16-22	11-3-24	11-15-24	1,031
West Lashaway[c]	8,578	12-15-21	3-3-22	8-22-24	8-29-24	909
Carenco[c]	7,825	12-15-21	1-20-22	9-27-24	10-6-24	989
Sinsinawa[c]	7,825	12-15-21	3-19-22	10-14-24	10-22-24	947
Aledo	7,249	1-17-22	1-20-22	4-4-22	5-24-22	124
Duquesne	9,750	1-30-22	2-8-22	3-25-22	5-4-22	85
City of Eureka	8,640	2-6-22	2-8-22	10-16-24	10-22-24	986
Luxpalile	7,825	3-18-22	3-31-22	11-3-24	11-29-24	973
Eastern Glade	8,560	4-25-22	6-4-22	10-24-24	1-31-25	971
Eastern Crown	8,250	6-6-22	6-30-22	10-5-23	12-31-24	914
Western Glen	8,645	6-25-22	7-26-22	10-24-24	10-31-24	827
Eastern Sun	9,066	6-30-22	8-21-22	10-5-23	11-1-23	437
Eastern Glen	8,521	8-4-22	9-16-22	10-14-24	10-18-24	762
Wytheville	9,788	12-21-22	12-27-22	10-24-24	12-5-24	708
Ambridge	9,774	2-28-23	3-15-23	2-23-24	5-28-24	439
West Cawthon	8,800	3-10-23	3-29-23	11-3-24	11-20-24	601
West Elcasco	8,568	3-23-23	5-2-23	9-22-24	9-26-24	512
17	145,489					12,215

[a]All were steel steamships, with engines amidships, built by the U.S. Shipping Board Emergency Fleet Corporation during 1918–1920.

[b]From delivery to Mallory Transport Lines, Inc., until redelivery to U.S. Shipping Board Emergency Fleet Corporation.

[c]Transferred from Baltimore-Oceanic Steamship Co.   *Source:* Same as Table 11.1.

Figure 12.1

FINANCIAL ARRANGEMENTS BETWEEN C. D. MALLORY & CO. AND NEW ENGLAND OIL REFINING CO. CONCERNING MANAGEMENT OF THE "SWIFTSURE FLEET," 1922–1928

"Gross Revenue"

Comparable to the item "gross freight" payable under a voyage charter or to the item "gross hire" payable under a time charter. Under the bareboat charter of the Swiftsure Fleet to the New England Oil Refining Co., however, this was a fictitious amount "arrived at by applying the going market rate to the cargo lifted" during each accounting period. It was not a sum in any sense "paid" by New England Oil Refining Co., but was merely the basis for computing C. D. Mallory & Co.'s compensation. The "going market rate" was renegotiated quarterly between January 1, 1922, and July 1, 1923, and monthly thereafter.

LESS

"Operating Expenses"

All were payable by New England Oil Refining Co. and included: "Husbanding Fee" of $400 per ship per month payable to C. D. Mallory & Co.; wages of officers and crews; fuel and water; deck stores; engine-room stores; steward's stores; medical stores; provisions; port charges (entrance and clearance charges, agency fees, etc.); towage; wharfage; brokerage on cargo procurement (if any); cargo handling charges (loading, stowing, trimming, and discharging—if any); general upkeep and maintenance of vessels and equipment; insurance (hull, machinery, cargo, protection, and indemnity); claims (if any). Of course, as managers C. D. Mallory & Co. handled all disbursements and business concerned with these expenses and then rebilled them to New England Oil Refining Co.

EQUALED

"Gross Profits"

Also known as "Net Operating Profits." Mallory preferred the former somewhat confusing term; his partner Houston used the latter and more truly descriptive term.

LESS	LESS
"Managers Commission" payable to C. D. Mallory & Co.—5 percent prior to July 1, 1925; 2½ percent thereafter.	"Interest" @ 8 percent of book value and "Depreciation" @ 5 percent of same payable by New England Refining Co.

Table 12.1

EMPLOYMENT OF THE "SWIFTSURE FLEET," 1922–1927

(C. D. MALLORY & CO., MANAGERS FOR ACCOUNT OF NEW ENGLAND OIL REFINING CO.)[a]

Route	Ship-Days	Bbls. Carried	Husbanding Fee	Mgrs. Commission
		1-1-22 to 12-31-26		
Tampico–Fall River	2,599	8,714,644.00	$ 34,644.67	$ 44,384,53
U.S. Gulf–Fall River	962	3,521,577.19	12,823.46	11,177.90
Venezuela–Fall River	953	3,442,358.91	12,703.49	11,403.79
Calif.–Fall River	4,489	7,345,804.85	59,838.37	39,872.37
Miscellaneous	1,450	7,229,489.11	19,328.50	23,725.82
Repairs and lay-ups	589	—	7,851.37	—
Period totals	11,042	30,253,847.06	$147,189.86	$130,564.41
		1-1-27 to 5-31-27		
Tampico–Fall River	0	.00	$ .00	$ .00
U.S. Gulf–Fall River	260	959,482.50	3,465.80	?.
Venezuela–Fall River	175	637,137.10	2,332.75	?.
Calif.–Fall River	257	391,358.96	3,425.81	?.
Miscellaneous	143	552,338.14	1,906.19	?.
Repairs and lay-ups	74	—	986.42	?.
Period totals	909	2,540,316.70	$12,116.97	$?

[a]Does not include several time charters for *Swiftlight* during 1922 for which she earned net hire to $178,186.49 for the year.

Source: Calculated from Exhibits 704, 705, 707, and 714 of "Copies of Exhibits Covering Financial Data and Swiftsure Fleet Operating Results," NEO.

Table 12.2

AMERICAN-FLAG TANKERS OWNED AND/OR CONTROLLED BY

C. D. MALLORY & CO. AND AFFILIATES

AND THEIR SHARE OF TOTAL U.S. TANKER FLEET, 1919–1941

December 31:	U.S. No.	U.S. D.W.T.	Mallory No.	Mallory D.W.T.	Mallory D.W.T. as % U.S. D.W.T.
1919	227	2,071,397	0	0	0.00
1920	314	2,939,758	0	0	0.00
1921	399	3,953,335	5	30,300	0.59
1922	401	3,988,413	8	85,778	2.15
1923	400	3,984,812	13	134,229	3.37
1924	394	3,940,937	19	191,109	4.85
1925	382	3,855,763	22	210,383	5.46
1926	381	3,872,237	22	210,383	5.43
1927	375	3,893,922	20	201,363	5.17
1928	373	3,948,967	20	201,363	5.10
1929	371	3,964,648	20	201,363	5.09
1930	379	4,116,594	25	204,607	4.97
1931	383	4,204,776	26	208,007	4.95
1932	380	4,180,246	26	208,007	4.97
1933	377	4,169,636	26	208,007	4.99
1934	374	4,139,658	26	208,007	5.02
1935	371	4,125,181	26	208,007	5.04
1936	370	4,179,667	25	205,707	4.92

Table 12.2 (continued)

AMERICAN-FLAG TANKERS OWNED AND/OR CONTROLLED BY

C. D. MALLORY & CO. AND AFFILIATES

AND THEIR SHARE OF TOTAL U.S. TANKER FLEET, 1919–1941

December 31:	U.S. No.	U.S. D.W.T.	Mallory No.	Mallory D.W.T.	Mallory D.W.T. as % U.S. D.W.T.
1937	382	4,364,459	25	205,707	4.71
1938	393	4,559,148	25	205,707	4.51
1939	383	4,493,493	25	205,707	4.58
1940	379	4,498,684	25	205,707	4.57
1941	389	4,680,863	25	205,707	4.39

Note: Mallory totals for 1921 *exclude* 6 British-flag tankers totaling 25,581 d.w.t.

Sources: Sun Shipbuilding & Dry Dock Co., *Growth of World Tank Ship Fleets, 1900 to September 1, 1945* (n.p., 1945), Table 3; U.S. Department of Commerce, *Merchant Vessels of the United States* (Washington, 1918–1942); MFP.

Table 12.3

MARKET SHARES BY D.W.T. AND TYPE OF OWNER AND/OR OPERATOR OF
AMERICAN-FLAG TANKER FLEET, 1934 AND 1939

1934

17	Oil companies controlled:	85.01% of total fleet tonnage
8	Industrial independents controlled:	4.39% of total fleet tonnage
8	Nonindustrial independents controlled:	10.60% of total fleet tonnage
	C. D. Mallory & Co. controlled:	5.49% of total fleet tonnage
	C. D. Mallory & Co. controlled:	51.75% of nonindustrial independent tonnage

1939

20	Oil companies controlled	84.22% of total fleet tonnage
9	Industrial independents controlled:	2.73% of total fleet tonnage
18	Nonindustrial independents controlled:	13.05% of total fleet tonnage
	C. D. Mallory & Co. controlled:	4.51% of total fleet tonnage
	C. D. Mallory & Co. controlled:	34.56% of nonindustrial independent tonnage

Note: C. D. Mallory & Co. shares of total fleet tonnage do not agree exactly with those given for 1934 and 1939 in Table 12.2 because of different counters and counting dates.

Sources: Robert L. Hague, Vice President, Standard Shipping Co. to Henry H. Heimann, Director, U.S. Shipping Board Bureau, April 3, 1934. General File 580–1035, Records of the U.S. Shipping Board (R. G. 32, U.S. National Archives); Standard Oil Co. (N.J.), Marine Dept., *Register of Tank Vessels of the World* (Revised ed., New York, 1939—compiled by Robert L. Hague).

Table 12.4

**TOP TEN OWNERS AND/OR OPERATORS OF AMERICAN-FLAG TANKERS,
1934 AND 1939**

Company	Percentage Share of Total U.S. D.W.T.
1934	
1. Standard Shipping Co.	16.66%
2. Standard-Vacuum Transportation Co.	12.34
3. Pan American Foreign Corp.	7.61
4. Gulf Refining Co.	7.55
5. The Texas Co.	6.44
6. C. D. Mallory & Co.	5.49
7. Sun Oil Co.	5.44
8. Standard Oil Co. (Calif.)	4.88
9. Cities Service Refining Co.	4.26
10. Atlantic Refining Co.	4.11
Total controlled by top ten	74.78%
1939	
1. Standard Oil Co. (N.J.)	21.95%
2. Socony-Vacuum Oil Co.	11.07
3. Gulf Oil Corp.	7.45
4. The Texas Co.	6.76
5. Atlantic Refining Co.	5.59
6. Sun Oil Co.	5.32
7. Standard Oil Co. (Calif.)	4.93
8. Tidewater-Associated Oil Co.	4.74
9. C. D. Mallory & Co.	4.51
10. Cities Service Oil Co.	3.62
Total controlled by top ten	75.94%

Note: C. D. Mallory & Co. shares do not agree exactly with those given for 1934 and 1939 in Table 12.2 because of different counters and counting dates.
Sources: Same as for Table 12.3.

Table 12.5

**AMERICAN-FLAG FREIGHTERS OWNED AND/OR CONTROLLED BY
C. D. MALLORY & CO. AND AFFILIATES 1919–1941**

December 31:	Number of Vessels	D.W.T.
1919	0	0
1920	0	0
1921	2	9,400
1922	2	7,000
1923	2	7,000
1924	2	7,000
1925	4	15,500
1926	5	19,000
1927	4	17,600
1928	5	23,350
1929	4	21,848
1930	4	21,848
1931	4	21,848
1932	4	21,848
1933	6	27,572
1934	6	27,572
1935	7	34,857
1936	8	40,943
1937	8	40,943
1938	9	47,082
1939	9	47,082
1940	8	46,113
1941	8	46,113

Notes: Excludes vessels operated for U.S. Shipping Board (see Tables 11.1 through 11.3). Totals for 1921 *exclude* 9 sailing schooners totaling 29,175 d.w.t.

Sources: U.S. Department of Commerce, *Merchant Vessels of the United States* (Washington, 1918–1942); MFP.

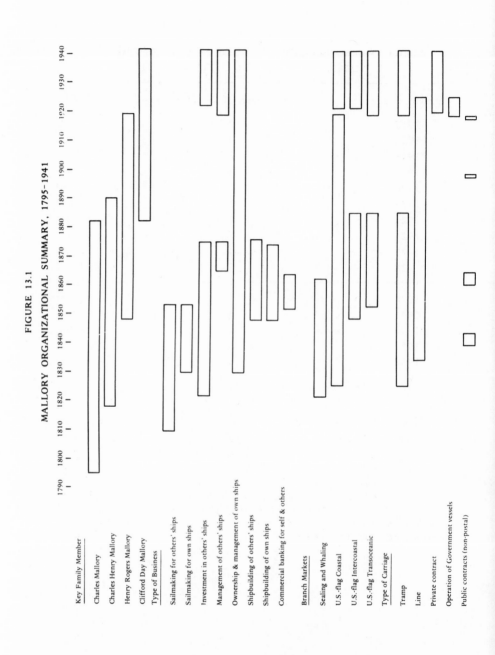

FIGURE 13.1

MALLORY ORGANIZATIONAL SUMMARY, 1795–1941

APPENDIX

AMERICAN-FLAG COMMERCIAL VESSELS
OWNED BY THE MALLORY FAMILY, 1822–1906

Vessel[a]	Tonnage	Acquisition[b]	Disposition[c]	Management[d]
SEALERS AND WHALERS				
Ship HYDASPE	313	P–1822	S–1826	P
Brig HERSILIA II	161	P–1822	S–1826	P
Sloop ONLY SON	47	P–1823	S–1826	P
Brig HUNTRESS	129	P–1825	S–1827	P
Sloop ELIZA ANN	77	P–1825	S–1827	P
Ship ACASTA	330	P–1828	SK–1841	P
Ship AERONAUT	265	P–1830	S–1855	A
Schooner PACIFIC	96	P–1833	S–1834	A
Ship BINGHAM	375	P–1833	S–1848	A
Ship CHARLES ADAMS	268	P–1833	SK–1837	P

[a]Vessels underlined were built in the Mallory shipyards.
[b]P: Purchased; B: Built; C: Time Chartered
[c]S: Sold; SK: Sunk; R: Charter Relinquished
[d]A: Mallorys were active managers as well as investors; P: Mallorys were passive investors.

Vessel[a]	Tonnage	Acquisition[b]	Disposition[c]	Management[d]
Brig UXOR	104	P–1833	SK–1841	A
Ship METEOR	325	P–1834	S–1842	P
Ship BLACKSTONE	258	P–1835	S–1846	A
Schooner MCDONOUGH	124	P–1836	S–1839	P
Ship ATLAS	261	P–1836	SK–1839	P
Schooner AMAZON	71	P–1836	S–1838	P
Bark FRIENDS	403	P–1836	S–1841	P
Ship MENTOR	460	P–1836	S–1841	P
Ship GEORGE	251	P–1838	S–1843	P
Brig TAMPICO	125	P–1838	S–1841	A
Brig REBECCA GROVES	129	P–1839	S–1841	P
Bark WHITE OAK	292	P–1840	S–1841	A
Ship BOLTON	170	P–1840	S–1849	P
Brig LEANDER	213	P–1841	S–1860	A
Ship ROMULUS	366	P–1842	S–1860	A
Bark VERMONT	293	P–1843	SK–1847	A
Ship ATLANTIC	291	P–1844	SK–1847	A
Ship CORIOLANUS	269	P–1844	S–1861	P
Ship ELEANOR	302	P–1845	S–1849	A
Ship TRESCOTT	341	P–1845	S–1849	A
Ship ROBIN HOOD	395	P–1845	S–1861	A
Ship HENRY	333	P–1850	S–1850	P
Schooner LION	83	P–1852	SK–1854	A
Schooner WILMINGTON	136	P–1853	S–1854	A
Ship CONSTITUTION	500	B–1857	S–1857	A
Schooner CORNELIA	197	P–1857	S–1862	A
Schooner FRANK	180	P–1858	SK–1859	A

COASTAL, INTERCOASTAL, AND TRANSOCEANIC SAILERS

Name	Tonnage			
Sloop CONNECTICUT	46	P-1826	S-1828	A
Sloop TIGER	47	P-1827	?	A
Sloop MARY ANN	36	P-1829	?	A
Sloop WHALE	69	P-1830	S-1835	A
Sloop JAMES MONROE	33	P-1831	S-1833	A
Brig TOISON	126	P-1831	?	P
Sloop MAGELLAN	36	B-1831	S-1836	A
Schooner ORIENT	98	B-1831	?	A
Brig TAMPICO	125	P-1831	?	A
Sloop PARAGON	34	P-1832	?	A
Schooner AUGUSTINE	50	B-1832	S-1835	A
Schooner SARAH	84	P-1833	S-1837	A
Sloop RELIEF	35	P-1833	S-1836	A
Brig APALACHICOLA	149	B-1833	S-1840	A
Sloop PLUME	48	P-1833	S-1846	A
Sloop SIDNEY	?	P-1834	?	P
Sloop PHENIX	?	P-1834	?	P
Sloop MYSTIC	60	B-1835	S-1847	A
Ship CHARLES P. WILLIAMS	187	B-1835	?	A
Schooner EMELINE	93	P-1836	S-1846	A
Sloop CHARLES MALLORY	37	B-1836	?	A
Schooner HERO	98	P-1836	?	A
Schooner MOBILE	95	B-1836	?	A

Vessel[a]	Tonnage	Acquisition[b]	Disposition[c]	Management[d]
Sloop FRANCIS PARK	36	B-1837	?	A
Sloop GEORGE ELDREDGE	75	B-1837	?	A
Schooner FRANCES AMY	98	B-1837	?	A
Brig FRANCES ASHBEY	125	B-1837	?	A
Sloop CAUTION	44	B-1838	?	A
Sloop ALABAMA	35	B-1838	?	A
Schooner COMET	99	B-1838	S-1843	A
Schooner METEOR	129	B-1839	?	A
Schooner DOLPHIN	98	P-1839	S-1840	A
Sloop RICHARD H. WATSON	39	B-1839	S-1844	A
Schooner SWALLOW	123	B-1839	S-1842	A
Schooner COASTING TRADER	38	P-1840	S-1842	A
Schooner BOLINA	75	P-1840	S-1842	A
Bark MAZEPPA	235	B-1840	S-1843	A
Brig ANN ELIZA	145	B-1840	S-1850	A
Brig REPUBLIC	139	B-1840	?	A
Brig METAMORA	196	B-1841	?	A
Ship JOHN MINTURN	399	B-1841	S-1846	P

Sloop ANN B. HOLMES	74	B-1843	S-1843	P
Schooner EMPIRE	92	B-1845	S-1846	A
Sloop EMILY	59	P-1846	S-1863	A
Schooner PANAMA	89	B-1846	?	A
Sloop VINEYARD	51	P-1846	?	P
Schooner MECHANIC	89	B-1846	S-1849	A
Brig NAPOLEON	192	P-1847	S-1849	A
Bark MONTAUK	338	B-1847	S-1848	P
Sloop ACTIVE	85	P-1848	S-1856	A
Schooner D. D. MALLORY	75	B-1848	S-1850	A
Sloop J. A. BURR	50	P-1848	?	A
Schooner BAY STATE	83	B-1849	S-1850	A
Bark FANNY	341	B-1849	S-1856	A
Schooner CALIFORNIA	84	P-1849	?	A
Sloop MARY W. BAKER	48	B-1850	?	A
Sloop MARTHA	49	B-1850	S-1851	A
Sloop APOLLO	87	P-1851	?	A
Ship CHARLES MALLORY	698	B-1851	SK-1853	A
Ship CAROLINE TUCKER	897	B-1851	S-1852	P
Ship ELIZA MALLORY	649	B-1851	S-1859	P
Schooner E. L. HAMMOND	88	P-1857	S-1861	A
Schooner MINNA	30	P-1852	S-1853	A
Schooner TELEGRAPH	175	B-1852	?	A
Ship ALBONI	917	B-1852	S-1861	P
Ship PAMPERO	1,375	B-1853	S-1861	P

Vessel[a]	Tonnage	Acquisition[b]	Disposition[c]	Management[d]
Schooner MUSTANG	316	B-1853	?	A
Ship HOUND	713	B-1853	S-1863	A
Schooner B. W. ELDREDGE	58	B-1853	S-1861	P
Schooner R. L. KEENEY	103	B-1853	S-1861	P
Schooner S. B. HOWES	103	B-1853	S-1861	P
Schooner ELIZABETH SEEGAR	122	B-1854	S-1859	P
Schooner WILMINGTON	136	P-1854	S-1855	A
Ship SAMUEL WILLETS	1,386	B-1854	SK-1857	A
Ship ELIZABETH F. WILLETS	825	B-1854	S-1864	A
Bark ANN	642	B-1854	S-1858	A
Bark FRANCES	473	B-1855	S-1858	A
Ship MARY L. SUTTON	1,448	B-1855	SK-1865	A
Schooner FLYING FISH	?	P-1856	S-1862	P
Ship TWILIGHT	1,482	B-1857	S-1865	A
Schooner ELIZA S. POTTER	247	B-1857	S-1876	A
Schooner M. L. ROGERS	93	P-1857	S-1861	P
Schooner OCILLA	82	B-1858	?	A
Ship PRIMA DONNA	1,526	B-1858	S-1858	A
Schooner MYSTIC VALLEY	179	P-1859	?	A
Schooner R. FOWLER	69	P-1859	S-1862	A
Bark LAPWING	590	B-1859	SK-1863	A
Ship HAZE	795	B-1859	SK-1865	A
Schooner SARAH L.	137	P-1860	S-1862	A
Bark TYCOON	717	B-1860	SK-1863	A

Brig FLORENCE	334	B-1865	S-1880	A
Schooner ROBERT PALMER	283	B-1866	S-1875	A
Bark CALEB HALEY	711	P-1866	SK-1866	A
Brig WILLIAM MALLORY, JR.	329	P-1866	S-1876	A
Bark GALVESTON	622	B-1866	SK-1877	A
Ship TWILIGHT	1,263	B-1866	S-1885	A
Schooner ABBIE E. CAMPBELL	333	P-1866	S-1869	A
Brig FRANCES LEVEY	379	P-1866	S-1870	A
Bark SABINE	843	B-1868	S-1879	A
Ship ANNIE M. SMULL	1,054	B-1868	S-1883	A
Schooner RIGHT BOWER	262	P-1869	SK-1870	A
Schooner LOUISA W. BIRDSALL	125	P-1870	S-1871	P
Bark BRAZOS	917	B-1870	S-1882	A
Schooner LOUISE P. MALLORY	300	B-1873	S-1883	A
Schooner ANNIE D. MERRITT	145	B-1874	S-1876	A
Schooner RUTH ROBINSON	427	B-1874	S-1876	P
Schooner JOSEPHINE B. KNOWLES	134	P-1874	S-1876	A
Schooner TELEGRAPH	175	B-1875	S-1875	A
Ship PRIMA DONNA	1,526	P-1875	S-1883	A
Schooner WILLIAM T. ELMER	185	P-1875	SK-1884	A
Schooner MARY E. DOUGLAS	146	P-1882	S-1886	A

Vessel[a]	Tonnage	Acquisition[b]	Disposition[c]	Management[d]
ATLANTIC, CARIBBEAN, AND GULF COASTAL STEAMSHIPS				
Steamship MYSTIC	154	P-1852	S-1854	P
Steamship PENGUIN	389	B-1859	S-1859	A
Steamship FALCON	457	B-1861	S-1861	A
U.S. Steamship OWASCO	507	B-1861	S-1861	A
Steamship STARS AND STRIPES	407	B-1861	S-1861	A
Steamship VARUNA	1,247	B-1861	SK-1862	A
Steamship EAGLE	171	B-1861	S-1873	P
Steamship HAZE	291	B-1861	S-1862	A
Steamship DELAMATER	?	B-1861	?	P
Steamship THORN	403	B-1862	S-1862	A
Steamship CREOLE	1,256	B-1862	S-1862	A
Steamship UNION	1,141	B-1862	S-1863	A
Steamship AUGUSTA DINSMORE	850	B-1862	S-1863	A
Steamship MARY SANDFORD	768	B-1862	S-1863	A
Steamship A. E. BURNSIDE	65	P-1862	S-1863	A
Steamship GOVERNOR BUCKINGHAM	912	B-1863	S-1863	A
Steamship MONTAINES	39	B-1863	S-1863	A
Steamship YAZOO	1,286	B-1863	S-1863	A
Steamship VARUNA II	1,007	B-1863	S-1866	A
Steamship VICTOR	1,327	B-1863	SK-1872	A
Steamship APHRODITE	1,099	B-1864	S-1865	A

Steamship ARIADNE	924	B-1864	SK-1873	A
Steamship ELLA	247	B-1864	S-1872	A
Steamship EUTERPE	824	B-1864	SK-1870	A
Steamship GENERAL SEDGWICK	811	B-1864	S-1873	A
Steamship ATLANTA	1,055	B-1864	SK-1865	A
Steamship LOYALIST	339	B-1864	SK-1869	A
Steamship ULYSSES	239	B-1864	S-1865	A
Steamship CLEOPATRA	1,045	B-1865	S-1865	A
Steamship BALIZE	185	P-1865	S-1867	A
Steamship TWILIGHT	644	B-1865	SK-1865	A
Steamship A. J. INGERSOLL	803	B-1866	S-1866	A
Steamship VIRGINIA	442	P-1866	S-1870	P
Steamship WILMINGTON	737	P-1866	S-1872	P
Steamship LODONA	666	C-1866	R-1871	A
Steamship CHARLES W. LORD	941	C-1866	R-1872	A
Steamship TILLIE	418	C-1867	R-1872	A
Steamship GULF CITY	850	C-1867	R-1869	A
Steamship GULF STREAM	998	C-1867	R-1871	A
Steamship VARUNA III	670	B-1869	SK-1870	A
Steamship BOLIVAR	509	B-1869	S-1872	A
Steamship WEYBOSSET	810	C-1869	R-1872	A
Steamship CITY OF GALVESTON	1,253	B-1870	SK-1876	A
Steamship CLYDE	1,182	P-1870	S-1876	P
Steamship CITY OF AUSTIN	1,295	B-1871	SK-1881	A
Steamship CITY OF HOUSTON	1,220	B-1871	SK-1878	A

Vessel[a]	Tonnage	Acquisition[b]	Disposition[c]	Management[d]
Steamship CITY OF SAN ANTONIO	1,605	B–1872	S–1899	A
Steamship CITY OF DALLAS	1,253	P–1872	S–1881	A
Steamship GEORGE W. CLYDE	1,032	P–1872	S–1876	P
Steamship CITY OF WACO	1,486	B–1873	SK–1875	A
Steamship CARONDELET	1,508	B–1873	S–1889	A
Steamship STATE OF TEXAS	1,548	B–1873	S–1898	A
Steamship AURORA	869	B–1874	S–1878	A
Steamship GARET POLHEMIUS	75	B–1875	S–1879	P
Steamship HENRY T. SISSON	84	B–1875	S–1879	P
Steamship RIO GRANDE	2,556	B–1876	S–1906	A
Steamship WESTERN TEXAS	1,211	B–1877	S–1884	A
Steamship CITY OF RIO DE JANEIRO	3,532	B–1877	S–1881	A
Steamship CITY OF PARA	3,532	B–1878	S–1881	A
Steamship COLORADO	2,765	B–1879	S–1906	A
Steamship GUADELOUPE	2,839	B–1881	SK–1884	A
Steamship SAN MARCOS	2,839	B–1881	S–1906	A
Steamship LAMPASAS	2,943	B–1883	S–1906	A
Steamship ALAMO	2,943	B–1883	S–1906	A
Steamship COMAL	2,252	B–1885	S–1906	A
Steamship NUECES	3,367	B–1887	S–1906	A
Steamship LEONA/SABINE	3,329	B–1889	S–1906	A

Steamship CONCHO	3,724	B–1891	S–1906	A
Steamship DENVER	4,549	B–1901	S–1906	A
Steamship SAN JACINTO	6,069	B–1903	S–1906	A
Steamship BRAZOS	6,399	B–1906	S–1906	A

BIBLIOGRAPHY

MANUSCRIPT SOURCES

Ashbey Papers. G. W. Blunt White Library, Marine Historical Association, Inc., Mystic, Connectcut (AP).

Charles Mallory Papers. In possession of Mrs. Elizabeth Kingsley, Mystic, Connecticut (CMP).

Clift Papers. G. W. Blunt White Library, Marine Historical Association, Inc., Mystic, Connecticut (CP).

Comstock Papers. Baker Library, Harvard University Graduate School of Business Administration, Boston, Massachusetts (COMP).

Corporation Records Division. Baker Library, Harvard University Graduate School of Business Administration, Boston, Massachusetts (CRD).

Cottrell & Hoxie Papers. In possession of Mr. William Dodge, Mystic, Connecticut (CHP).

Dun & Bradstreet Credit Ledgers. Baker Library, Harvard University Graduate School of Business Administration, Boston, Massachusetts (DB).

Eldredge Papers. G. W. Blunt White Library, Marine Historical Association, Inc., Mystic, Connecticut (EP).

Galveston Wharf Co. Records. The Galveston Wharves, Inc., Galveston, Texas (GWCP).

George W. Mallory Papers. In possession of Mrs. Elizabeth Kingsley, Mystic, Connecticut (GWCP).

Greenman Papers. G. W. Blunt White Library, Marine Historical Association, Inc., Mystic, Connecticut (GP).

Houston Direct Navigation Co. Records. Southern Pacific Co. (Texas and Louisiana Lines), Houston, Texas (HDNCP).

Mallory Family Papers. G. W. Blunt White Library, Marine Historical Association, Inc., Mystic, Connecticut (MFP).

Marine Transport Lines, Inc., Records. In custody of Cadwalader, Wickersham & Taft, New York, New York (MTL-CWT).

Morgan's Louisiana & Texas Railroad & Steamship Co. Records. Southern Pacific Co. (Texas and Louisiana Lines), Houston, Texas (MLTP).

Mystic River Bank Papers. In possession of Mr. William Dodge, Mystic, Connecticut (MRBP)).

New England Oil Corp. Records. Baker Library, Harvard University Graduate School of Business Administration, Boston, Massachusetts (NEO).

Pimer Papers. G. W. Blunt White Library, Marine Historical Association, Inc., Mystic, Connecticut (PP).

Ship Registers and Enrollments, New Haven and Hartford (WPA transcripts). G. W. Blunt White Library, Marine Historical Association, Inc., Mystic, Connecticut (REHM).

Ship Registers and Enrollments, New London and Stonington (WPA transcripts). G. W. Blunt White Library, Marine Historical Association, Inc., Mystic, Connecticut (RENLS).

Ship Registers and Enrollments, New York City. Record Group 41, National Archives, Washington, D.C. (RENYC).

Spicer Papers. G. W. Blunt White Library, Marine Historical Association, Inc., Mystic, Connecticut (SP).

United States Shipping Board Records. Record Group 32, National Archives, Washington, D.C. (USSB).

PERIODICALS

American Shipping.
Boston *New Bureau.*
Boston *Post.*
Commercial and Financial Chronicle.
Dallas *Morning News.*
Fairplay.
Financial America.
Galveston *Daily News.*
Greenwich *Press.*
Houston *Post.*
Marine Engineering.
Marine News.
Maritime Reporter.
Mystic *Pioneer.*
Mystic *Press.*
New Bedford *Mercury.*
New London *Chronicle.*
New London *Evening Day.*
New London *Gazette and General Advertiser.*
New Orleans *Price Current.*
New Orleans *Republican.*
New York *American.*
New York *Commercial.*

New York *Evening Post.*
New York *Evening Sun.*
New York *Herald.*
New York *Herald-Tribune.*
New York *Journal of Commerce.*
New York *Maritime Register.*
New York *Nautical Gazette.*
New York *Press.*
New York *Sun.*
New York *Times.*
New York *Tribune.*
New York *World.*
Philadelphia *Record.*
Richmond *Times-Dispatch.*
Shipping.
Shipping Illustrated.
Wall Street Journal.
Wall Street News.

BOOKS AND ARTICLES

ABC Pathfinder Shipping & Mailing Guide. Boston: New England Railway Publishing Co., annually 1892–1902.

Albion, Robert G. "Early Nineteenth-Century Shipowning: A Chapter in Business Enterprise," *Journal of Economic History,* I (May 1941), 1–11.

———*The Rise of New York Port, 1815–1860,* New York: Scribner, 1939.

——— *Seaports South of Sahara: The Achievements of An American Steamship Service.* New York: Appleton-Century-Crofts, 1959.

———*Square-Riggers on Schedule: The New York Sailing Packets to England, France, and the Cotton Ports.* Princeton: Princeton University Press, 1938.

Anderson, Virginia B. *Maritime Mystic.* Mystic: Marine Historical Association, Inc. 1962.

Annin, Robert E. *Ocean Shipping; Elements of Practical Steamship Operation.* New York: Century, 1920.

Appleton's National Railway and Steam Navigation Guide. New York: Appleton, 1861.

Appleton's Railway and Steam Navigation Guide. New York: Appleton, 1877.

Atlantic, Gulf & West Indies Steamship Lines. *Annual Report.* New York: The Company, annually beginning in 1915.

———— *Balance Sheet.* New York: The Company, annually 1909–1915.

Banker's Almanac. Boston: Phillips, Sampson & Co., annually 1851–1864.

Bankers Trust Company. *America's Merchant Marine.* New York: The Company, 1920.

Barber, John E. "Marine Securities," *Proceedings of the Seventh National Foreign Trade Convention.* New York: National Foreign Trade Council, 1920, pp. 588–595.

Barnes, Charles B. *The Longshoremen.* New York: Russell Sage Foundation, 1915.

Barton, Clara. *The Red Cross.* Washington: American National Red Cross, 1898.

Baughman, James P. *Charles Morgan and the Development of Southern Transportation.* Nashville: Vanderbilt University Press, 1968.

————"The Evolution of Rail-Water Systems of Transportation in the Gulf Southwest, 1836–1890," *Journal of Southern History,* XXXIV (August 1968), 357–372.

Beaton, Kendall. *Enterprise in Oil: A History of Shell in the United States.* New York: Appleton-Century-Crofts, 1957.

Berglund, Abraham. *Ocean Transportation.* New York: Longmans, Green, 1931.

Bieber, Ralph P. "California Gold Mania," *Mississippi Valley Historical Review,* XXXV (June 1948), 3–28.

Boczek, Boleshaw A. *Flags of Convenience: An International Legal Study.* Cambridge: Harvard University Press, 1962.

Boston Board of Trade. *Third Annual Report.* Boston: George C. Rand & Avery, 1857.

Brady, Dorothy S. "Relative Prices in the Nineteenth Century," *Journal of Economic History,* XXIV (June 1964), 145–203.

Brewington, M. V. "The Sailmaker's Gear," *American Neptune,* IX (October 1949), 278–296.

A Brief History of the Galveston Wharf Company, Established 1854. Galveston: The Company, 1927.

Browne, Jefferson B. *Key West: The Old and the New.* St. Augustine: The Record Co., 1912.

By-Laws of the New York & Texas Steamship Co. New York: Broun, Green & Adams, 1886.

Calvin, H. C., and E. G. Stuart. *The Merchant Shipping Industry.* New York: Wiley, 1925.

Caudle, Robert E. *History of the Missouri Pacific Lines, Gulf Coast Lines and Subsidiaries, International Great Northern.* Mimeographed. Houston: The Author, 1949.

Chamber of Commerce of the State of New York. *Annual Report.* New York: Wheeler & Williams, 1858-1866.

Chappelle, Howard I. *The History of American Sailing Ships.* New York: Norton, 1935.

_____*The Search for Speed under Sail, 1700-1855.* New York: Norton, 1967.

Clapp, Edwin J. *Economic Aspects of the War.* New Haven: Yale University Press, 1915.

Clarke, Francis G. *The Seaman's Manual.* Portland: Shirley, Hyde & Co., 1830.

Collins, John J. *Never Off Pay: The Story of the Independent Tanker Union, 1937-1962.* New York: Fordham University Press, 1964.

Consolidated Steamship Lines. *Four Per Cent. Collateral Trust Gold Bonds, Bondholders' Protective Agreement Dated December 28th 1907.* New York: Bondholders' Protective Committee, 1908.

_____*Report and Plan of Reorganization Dated June 30, 1908.* New York: Bondholders' Protective Committee, 1908.

"Cornelius H. Delamater," *Transactions of the American Society of Mechanical Engineers,* X (1888-1889), 836-838.

Cufley, C. F. H. *Ocean Freights and Chartering.* London: Staples, 1962.

Cutler, Carl C. *Five Hundred Sailing Records of American Built Ships.* Mystic: Marine Historical Association, 1952.

_____*Greyhounds of the Sea: The Story of the American Clipper Ship.* Revised ed. Annapolis: U.S. Naval Institute, 1961.

_____*Mystic: The Story of a Small New England Seaport.* Mystic: Marine Historical Association, 1945.

_____*Queens of the Western Ocean: The Story of America's Mail and Passenger Sailing Lines.* Annapolis: U.S. Naval Institute, 1961.

Dayton, Fred E. *Steamboat Days.* New York: Stokes, 1925.

Decisions and Orders of the National Labor Relations Board. Washington: Government Printing Office, 1937, 1938.

DeHart, Edward L., ed. *Lloyd's Reports of Prize Cases.* 10 vols. London: Lloyd's, 1919.

"The Delamater Iron Works," New York *Nautical Gazette,* January 17, 1874.

Disturnell's Guide through the Middle, Northern, and Eastern States. New York: J. Disturnell, 1847.

Dodd, Dorothy. "The Wrecking Business on the Florida-Reef, 1822-1860," *Florida Historical Quarterly,* XXII (April 1944), 172-199.

Dowling, Edward J. *The "Lakers" of World War I.* Detroit: University of Detroit Press, 1967.

Durkin, Joseph T. *Stephen R. Mallory: Confederate Navy Chief.* Chapel Hill: University of North Carolina Press, 1954.

Eskew, Garnett L. *Cradle of Ships.* New York: Putnam, 1958.

Evans, Robert, Jr. " 'Without Regard for Cost': The Returns on Clipper Ships," *Journal of Political Economy,* LXXII (February 1964), 33–43.

Fayle, C. Ernest. *Seaborne Trade.* 3 vols. New York: Longmans, Green, 1920–1924.

Fenstermaker, J. Van. *The Development of American Commercial Banking, 1782–1837.* Kent: Bureau of Economic and Business Research, Kent State University, 1965.

Ferguson, Allen R., and others. *The Economic Value of the United States Merchant Marine.* Evanston: Transportation Center at Northwestern University, 1961.

Fetter, Theodore A. *Southwestern Freight Rates.* Boston: Christopher Publishing House, 1934.

Fish, James D. *Memories of Early Business Life and Associates.* New York: Privately printed, 1907.

Fisser, Frank M. *Tramp Shipping: Development, Significance, Market Elements.* Bremen: Carl Schünemann Verlag, 1957.

Fornell, Earl W. *The Galveston Era: The Texas Crescent on the Eve of Secession.* Austin: University of Texas Press, 1961.

Galveston, Harrisburg and San Antonio Railway Company, et al. 36 I.C.C. *Valuation Reports* 704–705.

Gettell, Raymond G. *Functional Chart of U.S. Shipping Board and Its Main Subdivisions, July 1st, 1918.* Washington: U.S. Shipping Board, 1918.

Gibb, George S., and Evelyn H. Knowlton. *History of Standard Oil Company (New Jersey): The Resurgent Years, 1911–1927.* New York: Harper, 1956.

Gleaves, Albert. *A History of the Transport Service.* New York: Doran, 1921.

Godfrey, Thomas F. "The Whaling Industry of New London, Connecticut: A Case Study in American Economic History." Senior Essay in American Studies, Yale University, 1966.

Goldberg, Joseph P. *The Maritime Story: A Study in Labor-Management Relations.* Cambridge: Harvard University Press, 1958.

Gordon, Arthur. "The Great Stone Fleet: Calculated Catastrophe," *U.S. Naval Institute Proceedings,* XCIV (December 1968), 72–82.

473

Goss, R. O. *Studies in Maritime Economics.* Cambridge: Cambridge University Press, 1968.

"Government Contracts." 37 Cong., 2 Sess., *House Reports,* No. 2, 2 vols. (Serials 1142-1143).

Gregg, E. S. "The Crux of Our Shipping Problem," *Journal of Political Economy,* XXIX (June 1921), 500-508.

———"Vicissitudes in the Shipping Trade, 1870-1920," *Quarterly Journal of Economics,* XXXV (August 1921), 603-617.

Griffin, Eldon. *Clippers and Consuls: American Consular and Commercial Relations with Eastern Asia, 1845-1860.* Ann Arbor: Edwards Brothers, Inc., 1938.

Grossman, William L. *Ocean Freight Rates.* Cambridge: Cornell Maritime Press, 1956.

Hafen, LeRoy R. *The Overland Mail 1849-1869.* Cleveland: Arthur A. Clark, 1926.

Hall, Henry, ed. *America's Successful Men of Affairs.* 2 vols. New York: New York *Tribune,* 1895.

Hardy, Alfred, C. *Bulk Cargoes.* New York: Van Nostrand, 1926.

Hasse, William F., Jr. *A History of Money and Banking in Connecticut.* New Haven: Whaples-Bullis Co., 1957.

Haynes, William. *American Chemical Industry,* 6 vols. New York: American Chemical Society, 1949-1954.

Hazard, John L. *Crisis in Coastal Shipping: The Atlantic-Gulf Case.* Austin: Bureau of Business Research, University of Texas, 1955.

Hohman, Elmo P. *The American Whaleman.* New York: Longmans, Green, 1928.

Holdcamper, Forrest R. *Preliminary Inventory of the Records of the United States Shipping Board (Record Group 32).* Washington: National Archives, 1956.

Hough, B. Olney. *Ocean Traffic and Trade.* Chicago: La Salle Extension University, 1914.

Howard, B. B., and M. D. Stauffer, "Marine Transportation," in E. De Golyer (ed.), *Elements of the Petroleum Industry.* New York: American Institute of Mining and Metallurgical Engineers, 1940.

Howe, Octavius T., and Frederick C. Matthews. *American Clipper Ships, 1833-1858.* 2 vols. Salem: Marine Research Society, 1926.

Hurd, D. Hamilton. "Charles Mallory," *History of New London County, Connecticut.* Philadelphia: J. W. Lewis & Co., 1882, pp. 691-693.

Hurley, Edward N. *The Bridge to France.* Philadelphia: Lippincott, 1927.

———*The New Merchant Marine.* New York: Century, 1920.

Hutchins, John G. B. *The American Maritime Industries and Public Policy, 1789-1914: An Economic History.* Cambridge: Harvard University Press, 1941.

_____"The American Shipping Industry since 1914," *Business History Review,* XXVIII (June 1954), 105-118.

_____"The Rise and Fall of the Building of Wooden Ships in America, 1607-1914," Ph.D. dissertation, Harvard University, 1937.

Investigation of Seatrain Lines, Inc. 195 *I.C.C. Reports* 215-234 (1933).

_____206 *I.C.C. Reports* 328-346 (1935).

Joubert, William H. *Southern Freight Rates in Transition.* Gainesville: University of Florida Press, 1949.

Kemble, John H. "The Gold Rush by Panama, 1848-1851," *Pacific Historical Review,* XVIII (February 1949), 45-56.

Kimball, Carol W. "The Spanish Gunboats," *Log of Mystic Seaport,* XXII (Summer 1970), 51-57.

Kirkpatrick, S. D. "Why These New Chemical Industries 'Went South': Six Case Studies in Plant Location," *Chemical & Metallurgical Engineering,* XLI (August 1934), 400-415.

Klein, Maury, and Kozo Yamamura. "The Growth Strategies of Southern Railroads, 1865-1893," *Business History Review,* XLI (Winter 1967), 358-377.

Koop, Eugene J. *History of Spencer Trask & Co.* New York: The Company, 1941.

Koopmans, T. *Tanker Freight Rates and Tankship Building: An Analysis of Cyclical Fluctuations.* London: P. S. King & Son, Ltd., 1939.

Lane, Frederic C. *Ships for Victory: A History of Shipbuilding under the U.S. Maritime Commission in World War II.* Baltimore: Johns Hopkins Press, 1951.

Larson, Henrietta M., Evelyn H. Knowlton, and Charles S. Popple. *History of Standard Oil Company (New Jersey): New Horizons, 1927-1950.* New York: Harper & Row, 1971.

Lawrence, Samuel A. *United States Merchant Shipping Policies and Politics.* Washington: Brookings Institution, 1966.

Lebergott, Stanley. *Manpower in Economic Growth: The American Record since 1800.* New York: McGraw-Hill, 1964.

Lloyd's Rail Road Guide. New York: W. Alvin Lloyd & Co., 1867.

Lovett, Robert W., and Eleanor C. Bishop. *List of Business Manuscripts in Baker Library, Third Edition.* Boston: Baker Library, Harvard University, 1969.

McBride, R. S. "What and Where Are the Process Industries of the South," *Chemical & Metallurgical Engineering*, XLI (August 1934), 416–423.

McDowell, Carl E., and Helen M. Gibbs. *Ocean Transportation*. New York: McGraw-Hill, 1954.

"Mallory Lines," New York *Nautical Gazette*, November 13, 1873.

Mallory, Philip R. *Personal Background*. Privately printed, 1941.

———— *Recollections: Fifty Years with the Company*. Privately printed, 1966.

Masterson, V. V. *The Katy Railroad and the Last Frontier*. Norman: University of Oklahoma Press, 1952.

Mather, Robert. "How the States Make Intrastate Rates," *Annals of the American Academy of Political and Social Sciences*, XXXII (July–December 1908), 102–119.

Matter of Alleged Unlawful Discrimination. 11 *I.C.C. Reports* 595–597.

Memorial Services on The Death of Capt. Charles Henry Mallory at the Methodist Episcopal Church, Mystic Bridge, Conn., Sunday, March 30, 1890. New York: Broun, Green & Adams, 1890.

Moment, David. "The Business of Whaling in America in the 1850's," *Business History Review*, XXXI (Autumn 1957), 261–291.

Montgomery, Robert H. *Federal Tax Handbook, 1940–41*. 2 vols. New York: Ronald, 1940.

Moody's Manual of Corporation Securities. New York: Moody Manual Co., 1903–1920.

Morrison, John H. *History of American Steam Navigation*. Reprint edition. New York: Stephen Day, 1958.

Morse, Harry F. *One Yankee Family*. New London: H. F. Morse Associates, 1969.

Muir, Andrew F. "Railroads Come to Houston, 1857–1861," *Southwestern Historical Quarterly*, LXIV (July 1960), 42–63.

Mystic River National Bank. *Eighty Years of Banking in Mystic, 1851–1931*. Mystic: Riverside Press, 1932.

Naval History Division, Chief of Naval Operations. *Civil War Naval Chronology, 1861–1865*. 6 parts. Washington: Government Printing Office, 1961–1966.

"Niebuhr," *A Report Concerning Banks*, n.p n.d *ca.* 1854.

Niven, John. *Connecticut for the Union: The Role of the State in the Civil War*. New Haven: Yale University Press, 1965.

North, Douglass C. *The Economic Growth of the United States, 1790–1860*. Englewood Cliffs: Prentice-Hall, 1961.

N. Y. & T. S. S. Co., Mallory Lines. Rules and Regulations for Guidance of Employees. C. H. Mallory & Co., General Agents, Pier No. 20, E.R.N.Y. New York: Broun-Green Co., n.d.

O'Loughlin, Carleen. *The Economics of Sea Transport.* London: Pergamon Press, 1967.

Owsley, Frank L., Jr. *The C.S.S. Florida: Her Building and Operations.* Philadelphia: University of Pennsylvania Press, 1965.

Pennington, Robert. *A Treatise on Delaware Corporation Law.* New York: Clark Boardman Co., Ltd., 1925.

Perry, Hobart S. *Ship Management and Operation.* New York: Simmons-Boardman Publishing Co., 1931.

Poor's Manual of Railroads for 1883. New York: H. V. Poor, 1883.

Potts, Charles S. *Railroad Transportation in Texas.* Austin: University of Texas, 1909.

Raskin, Bernard. *On a True Course: The Story of the National Maritime Union of America, AFL-CIO.* Washington: National Maritime Union of America, AFL-CIO, 1967.

Redlich, Fritz. *The Molding of American Banking: Men and Ideas.* New edition, 2 parts. New York: Johnson Reprint Corp., 1968.

Reed, S. G. *A History of the Texas Railroads.* Houston: St. Clair Publishing Co., 1941.

"Report on Iron-Clad Vessels, September 16, 1861," *Annual Report of the Secretary of the Navy.* Washington: Government Printing Office, 1862.

Ross, Ishbel. *Angel of the Battlefield: The Life of Clara Barton.* New York: Harper, 1956.

Russell, Maud. *Men Along the Shore.* New York: Brussel & Brussel, Inc., 1966.

Rydell, Raymond A. "The Cape Horn Route to California, 1849," *Pacific Historical Review,* XVII (May 1948), 149–163.

Safford, Jeffrey J. "The United States Merchant Marine and American Commercial Expansion, 1860–1920." Ph.D. dissertation, Rutgers University, 1968.

Schultz, Charles R. "Costs of Constructing and Outfitting the Ship *Charles W. Morgan,* 1840–1841," *Business History Review,* XLI (Summer 1967), 198–216.

———— *Inventory of the Mallory Family Papers, 1808–1958.* Mystic: Marine Historical Association, Inc., 1964.

Sibley, Marilyn M. *The Port of Houston: A History.* Austin: University of Texas Press, 1968.

Sindall, Charles A. "The Development of the Traffic between the Southern States and the Northern and Northwestern States," in U.S. Bureau of Statistics, *Report on the Internal Commerce of the United States for 1886.* Washington: Government Printing Office, 1886.

Siney, Marion C. *The Allied Blockade of Germany, 1914–1916.* Ann Arbor: University of Michigan Press, 1957.

Sloan, Edward William, III. *Benjamin Franklin Isherwood, Naval Engineer: The Years as Engineer in Chief, 1861-1869.* Annapolis: U.S. Naval Institute, 1965.

Smith, J. Russell. *Influence of the Great War upon Shipping.* New York: Oxford University Press, 1919.

Southern Pacific Company's Ownership of Atlantic Steamship Lines. 43 *I.C.C. Reports 168-181.*

Standard Oil Company of New Jersey. Marine Department. *Register of Tank Vessels of the World, Revised Edition, 1939.* New York: The Company, 1939.

Starbuck, Alexander. "History of the American Whale Fishery from Its Earliest Inception to the Year 1876," Appendix A to part IV of United States Commission of Fish and Fisheries, *Report of the Commissioner for 1875-1876.* Washington: Government Printing Office, 1878.

State of Connecticut. *Report of the Bank Commissioners to the General Assembly.* Hartford: various printers, annually, 1835-1849.

Stern, Philip Van Doren, ed. *The Confederate Raider Alabama.* Bloomington: Indiana University Press, 1962.

Still, William N., Jr. *Confederate Shipbuilding.* Athens: University of Georgia Press, 1969.

Stover, John F. *The Railroads of the South, 1865-1900: A Study in Finance and Control.* Chapel Hill: University of North Carolina Press, 1955.

Stretch, George W. *Chartering of Ships.* 2 vols. New Orleans: Bierne Associates, Inc., 1953.

Sturmey, S. G. *On the Pricing of Tramp Ship Service.* Bergen: Institute for Shipping Research, 1965.

———*Some Aspects of Ocean Liner Economics.* Manchester: Manchester Statistical Society, 1964.

Sun Shipbuilding & Dry Dock Co. *Growth of World Tank Ship Fleets: 1900 to September 1, 1945.* Philadelphia: The Company, 1945.

Survey of Federal Archives. *Ship Registers and Enrollments of Providence, Rhode Island.* 2 vols. Providence: Survey of Federal Archives, 1941.

Svendsen, Arnljot S. *Sea Transport and Shipping Economics.* Bremen: Institute for Shipping Research, 1958.

Swann, Leonard A., Jr. *John Roach, Maritime Entrepreneur.* Annapolis: U.S. Naval Institute, 1965.

Texas Directory Co. *Texas Business Directory for 1878-1879.* Galveston: Shaw & Blaylock, 1878.

Thompson, Robert L. *Wiring a Continent: The History of the Telegraph Industry in the United States, 1832-1866.* Princeton: Princeton University Press, 1947.

Thorburn, Thomas. *Supply and Demand of Water Transport.* Stockholm: Business Research Institute, Stockholm School of Economics, 1960.

Tower, Walter S. *A History of the American Whale Fishery.* Philadelphia: University of Pennsylvania, 1907.

Trumball, Levi R. *A History of Industrial Paterson.* Paterson: C. M. Herrick, 1882.

U.S. Army. *Annual Report of the Quartermaster-General of the Army to the Secretary of War for the Fiscal Year Ended June 30, 1898.* Washington: Government Printing Office, 1898.

U.S. Army Corps of Engineers. *Transportation Lines on the Atlantic, Gulf and Pacific Coasts, 1940.* Washington: Government Printing Office, 1940.

U.S. Bureau of Corporations. *Transportation by Water in the United States.* 4 parts. Washington: Government Printing Office, 1909-1913.

U.S. Bureau of Statistics. *Report on the Internal Commerce of the United States for 1879.* Washington: Government Printing Office, 1879.

U.S. Bureau of the Census. *Historical Statistics of the United States, 1789-1945.* Washington: Government Printing Office, 1949.

U.S. Circuit Court of Appeals for the First Circuit, October Term, 1925, No. 2070, Francis R. Hart *et al.,* Appellants, v. Ernest Wiltsee *et al.,* Appellees. *In the Matter of Henry S. Parker v. New England Oil Corporation: Transport of Record.* 12 vols. Boston: Privately printed, ca. 1930.

U.S. House of Representatives, Committee on Merchant Marine, Radio, and Fisheries. *Merchant Marine Investigation.* Washington: Government Printing Office, 1932.

U.S. House of Representatives, Committee on Merchant Marine and Fisheries. *Report of United States Maritime Commission on Tramp Shipping Service.* Washington: Government Printing Office, 1938.

_____*Regulation of Water Carriers.* 2 parts. Washington: Government Printing Office, 1937.

U.S. House of Representatives. *Hearings before the Committee on Merchant Marine and Fisheries: Creating a Shipping Board, Naval Auxiliary, and a Merchant Marine.* Washington: Government Printing Office, 1916.

_____*Hearings before the Committee on the Merchant Marine and Fisheries: Inquiry into the Operations of the United States Shipping Board.* 2 vols. Washington: Government Printing Office, 1919.

_____*Proceedings of the Committee on the Merchant Marine and Fisheries in the Investigation of Shipping Combinations under House Resolution 587.* 4 vols. Washington: Government Printing Office, 1913-1914.

U.S. Senate, Committee on Legislation of the United States Shipping

Board. *Report on Matters Affecting the Merchant Marine.* Washington: Government Printing Office, 1926.

U.S. Shipping Board. *Annual Report.* Washington: Government Printing Office, 1917–1933.

U.S. Tariff Commission. *Chemical Nitrogen.* Washington: Government Printing Office, 1937.

"Vessels Bought, Sold, and Chartered by the United States, April, 1861–July, 1868," 40 Cong., 2 Sess., *House Exec. Docs.,* No. 337 (Serial 1346).

Wall, R. B. "Charles Mallory," New London *Evening Day,* August 21, 1923.

Ware, Caroline F. *The Early New England Cotton Manufacture: A Study in Industrial Beginnings.* Boston: Houghton Mifflin, 1931.

Waters, L. L. *Steel Trails to Santa Fe.* Lawrence: University of Kansas Press, 1950.

"Whalers Out of Mystic," *Information Bulletin 69-3.* Mystic: G. W. Blunt White Library, Marine Historical Association, Inc., 1969.

Wooddy, Carroll H. *The Growth of the Federal Government, 1915–1932.* New York: McGraw-Hill, 1934.

Zannetos, Zenon S. *The Theory of Oil Tankship Rates: An Economic Analysis of Tankship Operations.* Cambridge: M.I.T. Press, 1966.

Zimmermann, Erich W. *Zimmermann on Ocean Shipping.* New York: Prentice-Hall, 1923.

481

485

This fourth volume in the American Maritime Library

THE MALLORYS OF MYSTIC

has been composed in Journal Roman Medium by
The Type House, Inc. and printed by offset
lithography by Halliday Lithograph Corporation.
The binding is by the Chas. H. Bohn Company.

Published for The Marine Historical Association,
Incorporated, by Wesleyan University Press.